Contents

Haynes mechanic, author and photographer with a 2003 Explorer

Ford
Explorer &
Mercury
Mountaineer
Automotive
Repair
Manual

by Robert Maddox
and John H Haynes
Member of the Guild of Motoring Writers

Models covered:

Ford Explorer and Mercury Mountaineer
2002 and 2003

(9H2 - 36025)

ABCDE
FGHIJ
KLMNO
PQR

Haynes Publishing Group
Sparkford Nr Yeovil
Somerset BA22 7JJ England

Haynes North America, Inc
861 Lawrence Drive
Newbury Park
California 91320 USA

Acknowledgements

Wiring diagrams originated exclusively for Haynes North America, Inc. by Valley Forge Technical Information Services. Technical writers who contributed to this project include Mike Stubblefield, John Wegmann and Larry Warren.

A book in the Haynes Automotive Repair Manual Series

Printed in the U.S.A.

ISBN 1 56392 526 5

Library of Congress Control Number 2003113987

About this manual

Its purpose

The purpose of this manual is to help you get the best value from your vehicle. It can do so in several ways. It can help you decide what work must be done, even if you choose to have it done by a dealer service department or a repair shop; it provides information and procedures for routine maintenance and servicing; and it offers diagnostic and repair procedures to follow when trouble occurs.

We hope you use the manual to tackle the work yourself. For many simpler jobs, doing it yourself may be quicker than arranging an appointment to get the vehicle into a shop and making the trips to leave it and pick it up. More importantly, a lot of money can be saved by avoiding the expense the shop must pass on to you to cover its labor and overhead costs. An added benefit is the sense of satisfaction and accomplishment that you feel after doing the job yourself.

Using the manual

The manual is divided into Chapters. Each Chapter is divided into numbered Sections, which are headed in bold type between horizontal lines. Each Section consists of consecutively numbered paragraphs.

At the beginning of each numbered Section you will be referred to any illustrations which apply to the procedures in that Section. The reference numbers used in illustration captions pinpoint the pertinent Section and the Step within that Section. That is, illustration 3.2 means the illustration refers to Section 3 and Step (or paragraph) 2 within that Section.

Procedures, once described in the text, are not normally repeated. When it's necessary to refer to another Chapter, the reference will be given as Chapter and Section number. Cross references given without use of the word "Chapter" apply to Sections and/or paragraphs in the same Chapter. For example, "see Section 8" means in the same Chapter.

References to the left or right side of the vehicle assume you are sitting in the driver's seat, facing forward.

Even though we have prepared this manual with extreme care, neither the publisher nor the author can accept responsibility for any errors in, or omissions from, the information given.

NOTE

A **Note** provides information necessary to properly complete a procedure or information which will make the procedure easier to understand.

CAUTION

A **Caution** provides a special procedure or special steps which must be taken while completing the procedure where the Caution is found. Not heeding a Caution can result in damage to the assembly being worked on.

WARNING

A **Warning** provides a special procedure or special steps which must be taken while completing the procedure where the Warning is found. Not heeding a Warning can result in personal injury.

Introduction

This manual covers the Explorer and Mountaineer. The available engines are the 4.0L V6 engine and the 4.6L V8 engine.

The chassis layout is conventional with a front-mounted engine transmitting power to the rear wheels through an automatic or manual transmission, via a driveshaft, rear differential, then through independent driveaxles.

On 4WD models, in addition to power being delivered to the rear axle and wheels, a transfer case transmits power via a driveshaft, front differential then to the wheels through independent driveaxles.

These models feature independent front and rear suspension with coil spring/shock absorber units.

The power-assisted steering is rack-and-pinion. The steering unit is mounted to the frame aft of the front wheels. All models have a power assisted disc-type front and rear brake system with Anti-lock Brake System (ABS) standard.

Vehicle identification numbers

Modifications are a continuing and unpublicized process in vehicle manufacturing. Since spare parts manuals and lists are compiled on a numerical basis, the individual vehicle numbers are essential to correctly identify the component required.

Vehicle Identification Number (VIN)

This very important identification number is stamped on a plate attached to the dashboard inside the windshield on the driver's side of the vehicle (see illustration). The VIN also appears on the Vehicle Certificate of Title and Registration. It contains information such as where and when the vehicle was manufactured, the model year and the body style.

Manufacturer's Certification Regulation label

The Manufacturer's Certification Regulation label is attached to the driver's side door end or post (see illustration). The label contains the name of the manufacturer, the month and year of production, the Gross Vehicle Weight Rating (GVWR), the Gross Axle Weight Rating (GAWR) and the certification statement.

VIN engine and model year codes

Counting from the left, the engine code is the 8th character and the model year code letter designation is the 10th character.

On all models covered by this manual the engine codes are:

E	4.0L SOHC V6
K	4.0L SOHC V6, flex fuel
W	4.6L SOHC V8

On all models covered by this manual the model year codes are:

2	2002
3	2003

Engine number

The engine identification number is stamped into a machined pad on the engine block, and also on a label affixed to the valve cover.

The Vehicle Identification Number (VIN) is visible through the driver's side of the windshield

Location of the Manufacturer's Certification Regulation label

Buying parts

Replacement parts are available from many sources, which generally fall into one of two categories - authorized dealer parts departments and independent retail auto parts stores. Our advice concerning these parts is as follows:

Retail auto parts stores: Good auto parts stores will stock frequently needed components which wear out relatively fast, such as clutch components, exhaust systems, brake parts, tune-up parts, etc. These stores often supply new or reconditioned parts on an exchange basis, which can save a considerable amount of money. Discount auto parts stores are often very good places to buy materials and parts needed for general vehicle maintenance such as oil, grease, filters, spark plugs, belts, touch-up paint, bulbs, etc. They also usually sell tools and general accessories, have convenient hours, charge lower prices and can often be found not far from home.

Authorized dealer parts department: This is the best source for parts which are unique to the vehicle and not generally available elsewhere (such as major engine parts, transmission parts, trim pieces, etc.).

Warranty information: If the vehicle is still covered under warranty, be sure that any replacement parts purchased - regardless of the source - do not invalidate the warranty!

To be sure of obtaining the correct parts, have engine and chassis numbers available and, if possible, take the old parts along for positive identification.

Maintenance techniques, tools and working facilities

Maintenance techniques

There are a number of techniques involved in maintenance and repair that will be referred to throughout this manual. Application of these techniques will enable the home mechanic to be more efficient, better organized and capable of performing the various tasks properly, which will ensure that the repair job is thorough and complete.

Fasteners

Fasteners are nuts, bolts, studs and screws used to hold two or more parts together. There are a few things to keep in mind when working with fasteners. Almost all of them use a locking device of some type, either a lockwasher, locknut, locking tab or thread adhesive. All threaded fasteners should be clean and straight, with undamaged threads and undamaged corners on the hex head where the wrench fits. Develop the habit of replacing all damaged nuts and bolts with new ones. Special locknuts with nylon or fiber inserts can only be used once. If they are removed, they lose their locking ability and must be replaced with new ones.

Rusted nuts and bolts should be treated with a penetrating fluid to ease removal and prevent breakage. Some mechanics use turpentine in a spout-type oil can, which works quite well. After applying the rust penetrant, let it work for a few minutes before trying to loosen the nut or bolt. Badly rusted fasteners may have to be chiseled or sawed off or removed with a special nut breaker, available at tool stores.

If a bolt or stud breaks off in an assembly, it can be drilled and removed with a special tool commonly available for this purpose.

Most automotive machine shops can perform this task, as well as other repair procedures, such as the repair of threaded holes that have been stripped out.

Flat washers and lockwashers, when removed from an assembly, should always be replaced exactly as removed. Replace any damaged washers with new ones. Never use a lockwasher on any soft metal surface (such as aluminum), thin sheet metal or plastic.

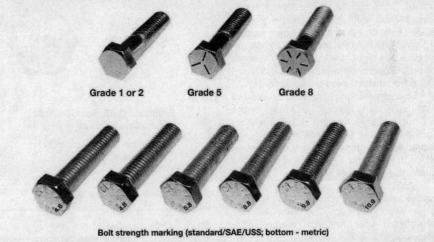

Grade 1 or 2   Grade 5   Grade 8

Bolt strength marking (standard/SAE/USS; bottom - metric)

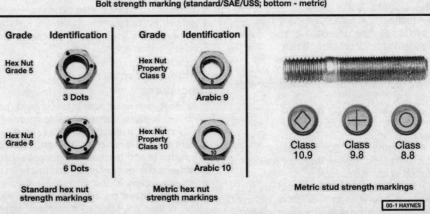

Grade	Identification	Grade	Identification
Hex Nut Grade 5	3 Dots	Hex Nut Property Class 9	Arabic 9
Hex Nut Grade 8	6 Dots	Hex Nut Property Class 10	Arabic 10

Standard hex nut strength markings

Metric hex nut strength markings

Class 10.9   Class 9.8   Class 8.8

Metric stud strength markings

00-1 HAYNES

Fastener sizes

For a number of reasons, automobile manufacturers are making wider and wider use of metric fasteners. Therefore, it is important to be able to tell the difference between standard (sometimes called U.S. or SAE) and metric hardware, since they cannot be interchanged.

All bolts, whether standard or metric, are sized according to diameter, thread pitch and length. For example, a standard 1/2 - 13 x 1 bolt is 1/2 inch in diameter, has 13 threads per inch and is 1 inch long. An M12 - 1.75 x 25 metric bolt is 12 mm in diameter, has a thread pitch of 1.75 mm (the distance between threads) and is 25 mm long. The two bolts are nearly identical, and easily confused, but they are not interchangeable.

In addition to the differences in diameter, thread pitch and length, metric and standard bolts can also be distinguished by examining the bolt heads. To begin with, the distance across the flats on a standard bolt head is measured in inches, while the same dimension on a metric bolt is sized in millimeters (the same is true for nuts). As a result, a standard wrench should not be used on a metric bolt and a metric wrench should not be used on a standard bolt. Also, most standard bolts have slashes radiating out from the center of the head to denote the grade or strength of the bolt, which is an indication of the amount of torque that can be applied to it. The greater the number of slashes, the greater the strength of the bolt. Grades 0 through 5 are commonly used on automobiles. Metric bolts have a property class (grade) number, rather than a slash, molded into their heads to indicate bolt strength. In this case, the higher the number, the stronger the bolt. Property class numbers 8.8, 9.8 and 10.9 are commonly used on automobiles.

Strength markings can also be used to distinguish standard hex nuts from metric hex nuts. Many standard nuts have dots stamped into one side, while metric nuts are marked with a number. The greater the number of dots, or the higher the number, the greater the strength of the nut.

Metric studs are also marked on their ends according to property class (grade). Larger studs are numbered (the same as metric bolts), while smaller studs carry a geometric code to denote grade.

It should be noted that many fasteners, especially Grades 0 through 2, have no distinguishing marks on them. When such is the case, the only way to determine whether it is standard or metric is to measure the thread pitch or compare it to a known fastener of the same size.

Standard fasteners are often referred to as SAE, as opposed to metric. However, it should be noted that SAE technically refers to a non-metric fine thread fastener only. Coarse thread non-metric fasteners are referred to as USS sizes.

Since fasteners of the same size (both standard and metric) may have different strength ratings, be sure to reinstall any bolts, studs or nuts removed from your vehicle in their original locations. Also, when replacing a fastener with a new one, make sure that the new one has a strength rating equal to or greater than the original.

Tightening sequences and procedures

Most threaded fasteners should be tightened to a specific torque value (torque is the twisting force applied to a threaded component such as a nut or bolt). Overtightening the fastener can weaken it and cause it to break, while undertightening can cause it to eventually come loose. Bolts, screws and studs, depending on the material they are made of and their thread diameters, have specific torque values, many of which are noted in the Specifications at the beginning of each Chapter. Be sure to follow the torque recommendations closely. For fasteners not assigned a specific torque, a general torque value chart is presented here as a guide. These torque values are for dry (unlubricated) fasteners threaded into steel or cast iron (not aluminum). As was previously mentioned, the size and grade of a fastener determine the amount of torque that can safely be applied to it. The figures listed here are approximate for Grade 2 and Grade 3 fasteners. Higher grades can tolerate higher torque values.

Fasteners laid out in a pattern, such as cylinder head bolts, oil pan bolts, differential cover bolts, etc., must be loosened or tightened in sequence to avoid warping the com-

Metric thread sizes	Ft-lbs	Nm
M-6	6 to 9	9 to 12
M-8	14 to 21	19 to 28
M-10	28 to 40	38 to 54
M-12	50 to 71	68 to 96
M-14	80 to 140	109 to 154

Pipe thread sizes		
1/8	5 to 8	7 to 10
1/4	12 to 18	17 to 24
3/8	22 to 33	30 to 44
1/2	25 to 35	34 to 47

U.S. thread sizes		
1/4 - 20	6 to 9	9 to 12
5/16 - 18	12 to 18	17 to 24
5/16 - 24	14 to 20	19 to 27
3/8 - 16	22 to 32	30 to 43
3/8 - 24	27 to 38	37 to 51
7/16 - 14	40 to 55	55 to 74
7/16 - 20	40 to 60	55 to 81
1/2 - 13	55 to 80	75 to 108

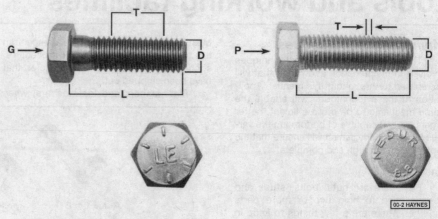

Standard (SAE and USS) bolt dimensions/grade marks

- G   Grade marks (bolt strength)
- L   Length (in inches)
- T   Thread pitch (number of threads per inch)
- D   Nominal diameter (in inches)

Metric bolt dimensions/grade marks

- P   Property class (bolt strength)
- L   Length (in millimeters)
- T   Thread pitch (distance between threads in millimeters)
- D   Diameter

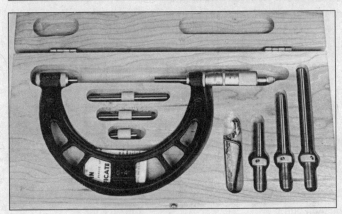

Micrometer set

Dial indicator set

ponent. This sequence will normally be shown in the appropriate Chapter. If a specific pattern is not given, the following procedures can be used to prevent warping.

Initially, the bolts or nuts should be assembled finger-tight only. Next, they should be tightened one full turn each, in a criss-cross or diagonal pattern. After each one has been tightened one full turn, return to the first one and tighten them all one-half turn, following the same pattern. Finally, tighten each of them one-quarter turn at a time until each fastener has been tightened to the proper torque. To loosen and remove the fasteners, the procedure would be reversed.

Component disassembly

Component disassembly should be done with care and purpose to help ensure that the parts go back together properly. Always keep track of the sequence in which parts are removed. Make note of special characteristics or marks on parts that can be installed more than one way, such as a grooved thrust washer on a shaft. It is a good idea to lay the disassembled parts out on a clean surface in the order that they were removed. It may also be helpful to make sketches or take instant photos of components before removal.

When removing fasteners from a component, keep track of their locations. Sometimes threading a bolt back in a part, or putting the washers and nut back on a stud, can prevent mix-ups later. If nuts and bolts cannot be returned to their original locations, they should be kept in a compartmented box or a series of small boxes. A cupcake or muffin tin is ideal for this purpose, since each cavity can hold the bolts and nuts from a particular area (i.e. oil pan bolts, valve cover bolts, engine mount bolts, etc.). A pan of this type is especially helpful when working on assemblies with very small parts, such as the carburetor, alternator, valve train or interior dash and trim pieces. The cavities can be marked with paint or tape to identify the contents.

Whenever wiring looms, harnesses or connectors are separated, it is a good idea to identify the two halves with numbered pieces of masking tape so they can be easily reconnected.

Gasket sealing surfaces

Throughout any vehicle, gaskets are used to seal the mating surfaces between two parts and keep lubricants, fluids, vacuum or pressure contained in an assembly.

Many times these gaskets are coated with a liquid or paste-type gasket sealing compound before assembly. Age, heat and pressure can sometimes cause the two parts to stick together so tightly that they are very difficult to separate. Often, the assembly can be loosened by striking it with a soft-face hammer near the mating surfaces. A regular hammer can be used if a block of wood is placed between the hammer and the part. Do not hammer on cast parts or parts that could be easily damaged. With any particularly stubborn part, always recheck to make sure that every fastener has been removed.

Avoid using a screwdriver or bar to pry apart an assembly, as they can easily mar the gasket sealing surfaces of the parts, which must remain smooth. If prying is absolutely necessary, use an old broom handle, but keep in mind that extra clean up will be necessary if the wood splinters.

After the parts are separated, the old gasket must be carefully removed and the gasket surfaces cleaned. If you're working on cast iron or aluminum parts, stubborn gasket material can be soaked with rust penetrant or treated with a special chemical to soften it so it can be easily scraped off. **Caution:** *Never use gasket removal solutions or caustic chemicals on plastic or other composite components.* A scraper can be fashioned from a piece of copper tubing by flattening and sharpening one end. Copper is recommended because it is usually softer than the surfaces to be scraped, which reduces the chance of gouging the part. Some gaskets can be removed with a wire brush, but regardless of the method used, the mating surfaces must be left clean and smooth. If for some reason the gasket surface is gouged, then a gasket sealer thick enough to fill scratches will have to be used during reassembly of the components. For most applications, a non-drying (or semi-drying) gasket sealer should be used.

Hose removal tips

Warning: *If the vehicle is equipped with air conditioning, do not disconnect any of the A/C hoses without first having the system depressurized by a dealer service department or a service station.*

Hose removal precautions closely parallel gasket removal precautions. Avoid scratching or gouging the surface that the hose mates against or the connection may leak. This is especially true for radiator hoses. Because of various chemical reactions, the rubber in hoses can bond itself to the metal spigot that the hose fits over. To remove a hose, first loosen the hose clamps that secure it to the spigot. Then, with slip-joint pliers, grab the hose at the clamp and rotate it around the spigot. Work it back and forth until it is completely free, then pull it off. Silicone or other lubricants will ease removal if they can be applied between the hose and the outside of the spigot. Apply the same lubricant to the inside of the hose and the outside of the spigot to simplify installation.

As a last resort (and if the hose is to be replaced with a new one anyway), the rubber can be slit with a knife and the hose peeled from the spigot. If this must be done, be careful that the metal connection is not damaged.

If a hose clamp is broken or damaged, do not reuse it. Wire-type clamps usually weaken with age, so it is a good idea to replace them with screw-type clamps whenever a hose is removed.

Tools

A selection of good tools is a basic requirement for anyone who plans to maintain and repair his or her own vehicle. For the owner who has few tools, the initial investment might seem high, but when compared to the spiraling costs of professional auto maintenance and repair, it is a wise one.

To help the owner decide which tools are needed to perform the tasks detailed in this manual, the following tool lists are offered: *Maintenance and minor repair, Repair/overhaul* and *Special.*

The newcomer to practical mechanics should start off with the *maintenance and*

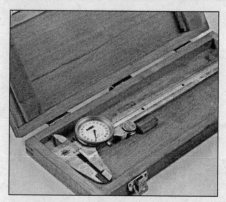

Dial caliper

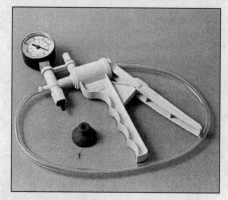

Hand-operated vacuum pump

Timing light

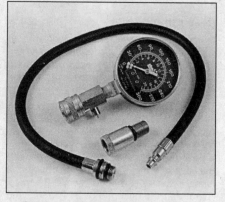

Compression gauge with spark plug hole adapter

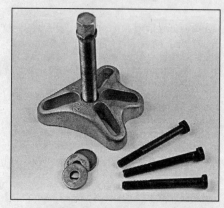

Damper/steering wheel puller

General purpose puller

Hydraulic lifter removal tool

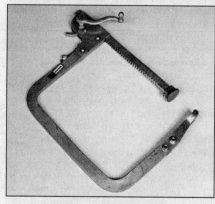

Valve spring compressor

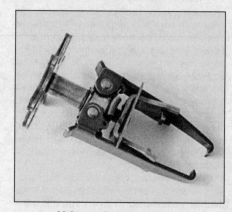

Valve spring compressor

Ridge reamer

Piston ring groove cleaning tool

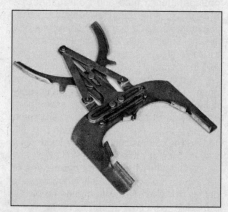

Ring removal/installation tool

Ring compressor

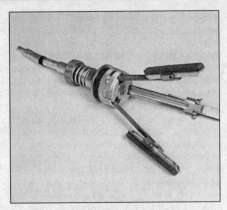

Cylinder hone

Brake hold-down spring tool

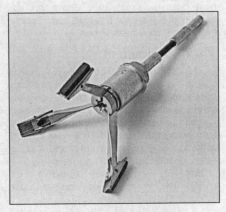

Brake cylinder hone

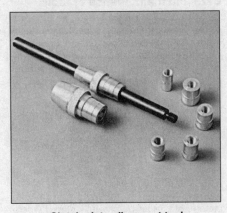

Clutch plate alignment tool

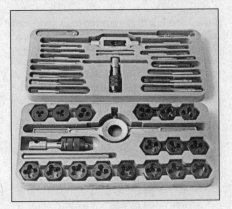

Tap and die set

minor repair tool kit, which is adequate for the simpler jobs performed on a vehicle. Then, as confidence and experience grow, the owner can tackle more difficult tasks, buying additional tools as they are needed. Eventually the basic kit will be expanded into the repair and overhaul tool set. Over a period of time, the experienced do-it-yourselfer will assemble a tool set complete enough for most repair and overhaul procedures and will add tools from the special category when it is felt that the expense is justified by the frequency of use.

Maintenance and minor repair tool kit

The tools in this list should be considered the minimum required for performance of routine maintenance, servicing and minor repair work. We recommend the purchase of combination wrenches (box-end and open-end combined in one wrench). While more expensive than open end wrenches, they offer the advantages of both types of wrench.

Combination wrench set (1/4-inch to
    1 inch or 6 mm to 19 mm)
Adjustable wrench, 8 inch
Spark plug wrench with rubber insert
Spark plug gap adjusting tool
Feeler gauge set
Brake bleeder wrench
Standard screwdriver (5/16-inch x
    6 inch)

Phillips screwdriver (No. 2 x 6 inch)
Combination pliers - 6 inch
Hacksaw and assortment of blades
Tire pressure gauge
Grease gun
Oil can
Fine emery cloth
Wire brush
Battery post and cable cleaning tool
Oil filter wrench
Funnel (medium size)
Safety goggles
Jackstands (2)
Drain pan

Note: If basic tune-ups are going to be part of routine maintenance, it will be necessary to purchase a good quality stroboscopic timing light and combination tachometer/dwell meter. Although they are included in the list of special tools, it is mentioned here because they are absolutely necessary for tuning most vehicles properly.

Repair and overhaul tool set

These tools are essential for anyone who plans to perform major repairs and are in addition to those in the maintenance and minor repair tool kit. Included is a comprehensive set of sockets which, though expensive, are invaluable because of their versatility, especially when various extensions and drives are available. We recommend the 1/2-inch drive over the 3/8-inch drive. Although the larger drive is bulky and more expensive, it has the capacity of accepting a very wide range of large sockets. Ideally, however, the mechanic should have a 3/8-inch drive set and a 1/2-inch drive set.

Socket set(s)
Reversible ratchet
Extension - 10 inch
Universal joint
Torque wrench (same size drive as
    sockets)
Ball peen hammer - 8 ounce
Soft-face hammer (plastic/rubber)
Standard screwdriver (1/4-inch x 6 inch)
Standard screwdriver (stubby -
    5/16-inch)
Phillips screwdriver (No. 3 x 8 inch)
Phillips screwdriver (stubby - No. 2)
Pliers - vise grip
Pliers - lineman's
Pliers - needle nose
Pliers - snap-ring (internal and external)
Cold chisel - 1/2-inch
Scribe
Scraper (made from flattened copper
    tubing)
Centerpunch
Pin punches (1/16, 1/8, 3/16-inch)
Steel rule/straightedge - 12 inch
Allen wrench set (1/8 to 3/8-inch or
    4 mm to 10 mm)
A selection of files
Wire brush (large)
Jackstands (second set)
Jack (scissor or hydraulic type)

Note: *Another tool which is often useful is an electric drill with a chuck capacity of 3/8-inch and a set of good quality drill bits.*

Special tools

The tools in this list include those which are not used regularly, are expensive to buy, or which need to be used in accordance with their manufacturer's instructions. Unless these tools will be used frequently, it is not very economical to purchase many of them. A consideration would be to split the cost and use between yourself and a friend or friends. In addition, most of these tools can be obtained from a tool rental shop on a temporary basis.

This list primarily contains only those tools and instruments widely available to the public, and not those special tools produced by the vehicle manufacturer for distribution to dealer service departments. Occasionally, references to the manufacturer's special tools are included in the text of this manual. Generally, an alternative method of doing the job without the special tool is offered. However, sometimes there is no alternative to their use. Where this is the case, and the tool cannot be purchased or borrowed, the work should be turned over to the dealer service department or an automotive repair shop.

> *Valve spring compressor*
> *Piston ring groove cleaning tool*
> *Piston ring compressor*
> *Piston ring installation tool*
> *Cylinder compression gauge*
> *Cylinder ridge reamer*
> *Cylinder surfacing hone*
> *Cylinder bore gauge*
> *Micrometers and/or dial calipers*
> *Hydraulic lifter removal tool*
> *Balljoint separator*
> *Universal-type puller*
> *Impact screwdriver*
> *Dial indicator set*
> *Stroboscopic timing light (inductive pick-up)*
> *Hand operated vacuum/pressure pump*
> *Tachometer/dwell meter*
> *Universal electrical multimeter*
> *Cable hoist*
> *Brake spring removal and installation tools*
> *Floor jack*

Buying tools

For the do-it-yourselfer who is just starting to get involved in vehicle maintenance and repair, there are a number of options available when purchasing tools. If maintenance and minor repair is the extent of the work to be done, the purchase of individual tools is satisfactory. If, on the other hand, extensive work is planned, it would be a good idea to purchase a modest tool set from one of the large retail chain stores. A set can usually be bought at a substantial savings over the individual tool prices, and they often

come with a tool box. As additional tools are needed, add-on sets, individual tools and a larger tool box can be purchased to expand the tool selection. Building a tool set gradually allows the cost of the tools to be spread over a longer period of time and gives the mechanic the freedom to choose only those tools that will actually be used.

Tool stores will often be the only source of some of the special tools that are needed, but regardless of where tools are bought, try to avoid cheap ones, especially when buying screwdrivers and sockets, because they won't last very long. The expense involved in replacing cheap tools will eventually be greater than the initial cost of quality tools.

Care and maintenance of tools

Good tools are expensive, so it makes sense to treat them with respect. Keep them clean and in usable condition and store them properly when not in use. Always wipe off any dirt, grease or metal chips before putting them away. Never leave tools lying around in the work area. Upon completion of a job, always check closely under the hood for tools that may have been left there so they won't get lost during a test drive.

Some tools, such as screwdrivers, pliers, wrenches and sockets, can be hung on a panel mounted on the garage or workshop wall, while others should be kept in a tool box or tray. Measuring instruments, gauges, meters, etc. must be carefully stored where they cannot be damaged by weather or impact from other tools.

When tools are used with care and stored properly, they will last a very long time. Even with the best of care, though, tools will wear out if used frequently. When a tool is damaged or worn out, replace it. Subsequent jobs will be safer and more enjoyable if you do.

How to repair damaged threads

Sometimes, the internal threads of a nut or bolt hole can become stripped, usually from overtightening. Stripping threads is an all-too-common occurrence, especially when working with aluminum parts, because aluminum is so soft that it easily strips out.

Usually, external or internal threads are only partially stripped. After they've been cleaned up with a tap or die, they'll still work. Sometimes, however, threads are badly damaged. When this happens, you've got three choices:

1) *Drill and tap the hole to the next suitable oversize and install a larger diameter bolt, screw or stud.*

2) *Drill and tap the hole to accept a threaded plug, then drill and tap the plug to the original screw size. You can also buy a plug already threaded to the original size. Then you simply drill a hole to the specified size, then run the threaded*

plug into the hole with a bolt and jam nut. Once the plug is fully seated, remove the jam nut and bolt.

3) *The third method uses a patented thread repair kit like Heli-Coil or Slimsert. These easy-to-use kits are designed to repair damaged threads in straight-through holes and blind holes. Both are available as kits which can handle a variety of sizes and thread patterns. Drill the hole, then tap it with the special included tap. Install the Heli-Coil and the hole is back to its original diameter and thread pitch.*

Regardless of which method you use, be sure to proceed calmly and carefully. A little impatience or carelessness during one of these relatively simple procedures can ruin your whole day's work and cost you a bundle if you wreck an expensive part.

Working facilities

Not to be overlooked when discussing tools is the workshop. If anything more than routine maintenance is to be carried out, some sort of suitable work area is essential.

It is understood, and appreciated, that many home mechanics do not have a good workshop or garage available, and end up removing an engine or doing major repairs outside. It is recommended, however, that the overhaul or repair be completed under the cover of a roof.

A clean, flat workbench or table of comfortable working height is an absolute necessity. The workbench should be equipped with a vise that has a jaw opening of at least four inches.

As mentioned previously, some clean, dry storage space is also required for tools, as well as the lubricants, fluids, cleaning solvents, etc. which soon become necessary.

Sometimes waste oil and fluids, drained from the engine or cooling system during normal maintenance or repairs, present a disposal problem. To avoid pouring them on the ground or into a sewage system, pour the used fluids into large containers, seal them with caps and take them to an authorized disposal site or recycling center. Plastic jugs, such as old antifreeze containers, are ideal for this purpose.

Always keep a supply of old newspapers and clean rags available. Old towels are excellent for mopping up spills. Many mechanics use rolls of paper towels for most work because they are readily available and disposable. To help keep the area under the vehicle clean, a large cardboard box can be cut open and flattened to protect the garage or shop floor.

Whenever working over a painted surface, such as when leaning over a fender to service something under the hood, always cover it with an old blanket or bedspread to protect the finish. Vinyl covered pads, made especially for this purpose, are available at auto parts stores.

Jacking and towing

Jacking

Warning: *The jack supplied with the vehicle should only be used for changing a tire or placing jackstands under the frame. Never work under the vehicle or start the engine while this jack is being used as the only means of support.*

The vehicle should be on level ground. Place the shift lever in Park, if you have an automatic, or Reverse if you have a manual transaxle. Block the wheel diagonally opposite the wheel being changed. Set the parking brake.

Remove the spare tire and jack from stowage. Remove the wheel cover and trim ring (if so equipped) with the tapered end of the lug nut wrench by inserting and twisting the handle and then prying against the back of the wheel cover. Loosen, but do not remove,

the lug nuts (one-half turn is sufficient).

Place the scissors-type jack under the vehicle and adjust the jack height until it engages with the proper jacking point. There is a front and rear jacking point on each side of the vehicle **(see illustrations)**.

Turn the jack handle clockwise until the tire clears the ground. Remove the lug nuts and pull the wheel off. Replace it with the spare.

Install the lug nuts with the beveled edges facing in. Tighten them snugly. Don't attempt to tighten them completely until the vehicle is lowered or it could slip off the jack. Turn the jack handle counterclockwise to lower the vehicle. Remove the jack and tighten the lug nuts in a diagonal pattern.

Install the cover (and trim ring, if used) and be sure it's snapped into place all the way around.

Stow the tire, jack and wrench. Unblock the wheels.

Towing

Two-wheel drive models can be towed from the rear with the front wheels on the ground, using a wheel lift type tow truck. Four-wheel drive models must be towed with all four wheels off the ground. A sling-type tow truck cannot be used, as body damage will result. The best way to tow the vehicle is with a flat-bed car carrier.

In an emergency the vehicle can be towed a short distance with a cable or chain attached to one of the towing eyelets located under the front or rear bumpers. The driver must remain in the vehicle to operate the steering and brakes (remember that power steering and power brakes will not work with the engine off).

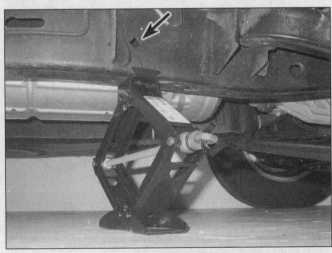

Front jacking location (place the jack head under the diamond-shaped cutout on the frame)

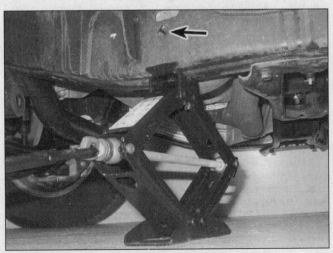

Rear jacking location (place the jack head under the diamond-shaped cutout on the frame)

Booster battery (jump) starting

Observe these precautions when using a booster battery to start a vehicle:

a) *Before connecting the booster battery, make sure the ignition switch is in the Off position.*

b) *Turn off the lights, heater and other electrical loads.*

c) *Your eyes should be shielded. Safety goggles are a good idea.*

d) *Make sure the booster battery is the same voltage as the dead one in the vehicle.*

e) *The two vehicles MUST NOT TOUCH each other!*

f) *Make sure the transaxle is in Neutral (manual) or Park (automatic).*

g) *If the booster battery is not a maintenance-free type, remove the vent caps and lay a cloth over the vent holes.*

Connect the red jumper cable to the positive (+) terminals of each battery **(see illustration)**.

Connect one end of the black jumper cable to the negative (-) terminal of the booster battery. The other end of this cable should be connected to a good ground on the vehicle to be started, such as a bolt or bracket on the body.

Start the engine using the booster battery, then, with the engine running at idle speed, disconnect the jumper cables in the reverse order of connection.

Note: *If the battery has been run down or disconnected, the Powertrain Control Module (PCM) must relearn its idle and fuel mixture trim strategy for optimum drivability and performance (see Chapter 5, Section 1 for this procedure).*

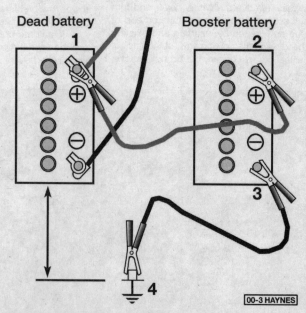

Make the booster battery cable connections in the numerical order shown (note that the negative cable of the booster battery is NOT attached to the negative terminal of the dead battery)

DECIMALS to MILLIMETERS

Decimal	mm	Decimal	mm
0.001	0.0254	0.500	12.7000
0.002	0.0508	0.510	12.9540
0.003	0.0762	0.520	13.2080
0.004	0.1016	0.530	13.4620
0.005	0.1270	0.540	13.7160
0.006	0.1524	0.550	13.9700
0.007	0.1778	0.560	14.2240
0.008	0.2032	0.570	14.4780
0.009	0.2286	0.580	14.7320
		0.590	14.9860
0.010	0.2540		
0.020	0.5080		
0.030	0.7620		
0.040	1.0160	0.600	15.2400
0.050	1.2700	0.610	15.4940
0.060	1.5240	0.620	15.7480
0.070	1.7780	0.630	16.0020
0.080	2.0320	0.640	16.2560
0.090	2.2860	0.650	16.5100
		0.660	16.7640
0.100	2.5400	0.670	17.0180
0.110	2.7940	0.680	17.2720
0.120	3.0480	0.690	17.5260
0.130	3.3020		
0.140	3.5560		
0.150	3.8100	0.700	17.7800
0.160	4.0640	0.710	18.0340
0.170	4.3180	0.720	18.2880
0.180	4.5720	0.730	18.5420
0.190	4.8260	0.740	18.7960
0.200	5.0800	0.750	19.0500
0.210	5.3340	0.760	19.3040
0.220	5.5880	0.770	19.5580
0.230	5.8420	0.780	19.8120
0.240	6.0960	0.790	20.0660
0.250	6.3500		
0.260	6.6040		
0.270	6.8580	0.800	20.3200
0.280	7.1120	0.810	20.5740
0.290	7.3660	0.820	21.8280
		0.830	21.0820
0.300	7.6200	0.840	21.3360
0.310	7.8740	0.850	21.5900
0.320	8.1280	0.860	21.8440
0.330	8.3820	0.870	22.0980
0.340	8.6360	0.880	22.3520
0.350	8.8900	0.890	22.6060
0.360	9.1440		
0.370	9.3980		
0.380	9.6520		
0.390	9.9060	0.900	22.8600
0.400	10.1600	0.910	23.1140
0.410	10.4140	0.920	23.3680
0.420	10.6680	0.930	23.6220
0.430	10.9220	0.940	23.8760
0.440	11.1760	0.950	24.1300
0.450	11.4300	0.960	24.3840
0.460	11.6840	0.970	24.6380
0.470	11.9380	0.980	24.8920
0.480	12.1920	0.990	25.1460
0.490	12.4460	1.000	25.4000

FRACTIONS to DECIMALS to MILLIMETERS

Fraction	Decimal	mm	Fraction	Decimal	mm
1/64	0.0156	0.3969	33/64	0.5156	13.0969
1/32	0.0312	0.7938	17/32	0.5312	13.4938
3/64	0.0469	1.1906	35/64	0.5469	13.8906
1/16	0.0625	1.5875	9/16	0.5625	14.2875
5/64	0.0781	1.9844	37/64	0.5781	14.6844
3/32	0.0938	2.3812	19/32	0.5938	15.0812
7/64	0.1094	2.7781	39/64	0.6094	15.4781
1/8	0.1250	3.1750	5/8	0.6250	15.8750
9/64	0.1406	3.5719	41/64	0.6406	16.2719
5/32	0.1562	3.9688	21/32	0.6562	16.6688
11/64	0.1719	4.3656	43/64	0.6719	17.0656
3/16	0.1875	4.7625	11/16	0.6875	17.4625
13/64	0.2031	5.1594	45/64	0.7031	17.8594
7/32	0.2188	5.5562	23/32	0.7188	18.2562
15/64	0.2344	5.9531	47/64	0.7344	18.6531
1/4	0.2500	6.3500	3/4	0.7500	19.0500
17/64	0.2656	6.7469	49/64	0.7656	19.4469
9/32	0.2812	7.1438	25/32	0.7812	19.8438
19/64	0.2969	7.5406	51/64	0.7969	20.2406
5/16	0.3125	7.9375	13/16	0.8125	20.6375
21/64	0.3281	8.3344	53/64	0.8281	21.0344
11/32	0.3438	8.7312	27/32	0.8438	21.4312
23/64	0.3594	9.1281	55/64	0.8594	21.8281
3/8	0.3750	9.5250	7/8	0.8750	22.2250
25/64	0.3906	9.9219	57/64	0.8906	22.6219
13/32	0.4062	10.3188	29/32	0.9062	23.0188
27/64	0.4219	10.7156	59/64	0.9219	23.4156
7/16	0.4375	11.1125	15/16	0.9375	23.8125
29/64	0.4531	11.5094	61/64	0.9531	24.2094
15/32	0.4688	11.9062	31/32	0.9688	24.6062
31/64	0.4844	12.3031	63/64	0.9844	25.0031
1/2	0.5000	12.7000	1	1.0000	25.4000

Conversion factors

Length (distance)

Inches (in)	X	25.4	= Millimeters (mm)	X	0.0394	= Inches (in)
Feet (ft)	X	0.305	= Meters (m)	X	3.281	= Feet (ft)
Miles	X	1.609	= Kilometers (km)	X	0.621	= Miles

Volume (capacity)

Cubic inches (cu in; in^3)	X	16.387	= Cubic centimeters (cc; cm^3)	X	0.061	= Cubic inches (cu in; in^3)
Imperial pints (Imp pt)	X	0.568	= Liters (l)	X	1.76	= Imperial pints (Imp pt)
Imperial quarts (Imp qt)	X	1.137	= Liters (l)	X	0.88	= Imperial quarts (Imp qt)
Imperial quarts (Imp qt)	X	1.201	= US quarts (US qt)	X	0.833	= Imperial quarts (Imp qt)
US quarts (US qt)	X	0.946	= Liters (l)	X	1.057	= US quarts (US qt)
Imperial gallons (Imp gal)	X	4.546	= Liters (l)	X	0.22	= Imperial gallons (Imp gal)
Imperial gallons (Imp gal)	X	1.201	= US gallons (US gal)	X	0.833	= Imperial gallons (Imp gal)
US gallons (US gal)	X	3.785	= Liters (l)	X	0.264	= US gallons (US gal)

Mass (weight)

Ounces (oz)	X	28.35	= Grams (g)	X	0.035	= Ounces (oz)
Pounds (lb)	X	0.454	= Kilograms (kg)	X	2.205	= Pounds (lb)

Force

Ounces-force (ozf; oz)	X	0.278	= Newtons (N)	X	3.6	= Ounces-force (ozf; oz)
Pounds-force (lbf; lb)	X	4.448	= Newtons (N)	X	0.225	= Pounds-force (lbf; lb)
Newtons (N)	X	0.1	= Kilograms-force (kgf; kg)	X	9.81	= Newtons (N)

Pressure

Pounds-force per square inch (psi; lbf/in^2; lb/in^2)	X	0.070	= Kilograms-force per square centimeter (kgf/cm^2; kg/cm^2)	X	14.223	= Pounds-force per square inch (psi; lbf/in^2; lb/in^2)
Pounds-force per square inch (psi; lbf/in^2; lb/in^2)	X	0.068	= Atmospheres (atm)	X	14.696	= Pounds-force per square inch (psi; lbf/in^2; lb/in^2)
Pounds-force per square inch (psi; lbf/in^2; lb/in^2)	X	0.069	= Bars	X	14.5	= Pounds-force per square inch (psi; lbf/in^2; lb/in^2)
Pounds-force per square inch (psi; lbf/in^2; lb/in^2)	X	6.895	= Kilopascals (kPa)	X	0.145	= Pounds-force per square inch (psi; lbf/in^2; lb/in^2)
Kilopascals (kPa)	X	0.01	= Kilograms-force per square centimeter (kgf/cm^2; kg/cm^2)	X	98.1	= Kilopascals (kPa)

Torque (moment of force)

Pounds-force inches (lbf in; lb in)	X	1.152	= Kilograms-force centimeter (kgf cm; kg cm)	X	0.868	= Pounds-force inches (lbf in; lb in)
Pounds-force inches (lbf in; lb in)	X	0.113	= Newton meters (Nm)	X	8.85	= Pounds-force inches (lbf in; lb in)
Pounds-force inches (lbf in; lb in)	X	0.083	= Pounds-force feet (lbf ft; lb ft)	X	12	= Pounds-force inches (lbf in; lb in)
Pounds-force feet (lbf ft; lb ft)	X	0.138	= Kilograms-force meters (kgf m; kg m)	X	7.233	= Pounds-force feet (lbf ft; lb ft)
Pounds-force feet (lbf ft; lb ft)	X	1.356	= Newton meters (Nm)	X	0.738	= Pounds-force feet (lbf ft; lb ft)
Newton meters (Nm)	X	0.102	= Kilograms-force meters (kgf m; kg m)	X	9.804	= Newton meters (Nm)

Vacuum

Inches mercury (in. Hg)	X	3.377	= Kilopascals (kPa)	X	0.2961	= Inches mercury
Inches mercury (in. Hg)	X	25.4	= Millimeters mercury (mm Hg)	X	0.0394	= Inches mercury

Power

Horsepower (hp)	X	745.7	= Watts (W)	X	0.0013	= Horsepower (hp)

Velocity (speed)

Miles per hour (miles/hr; mph)	X	1.609	= Kilometers per hour (km/hr; kph)	X	0.621	= Miles per hour (miles/hr; mph)

Fuel consumption*

Miles per gallon, Imperial (mpg)	X	0.354	= Kilometers per liter (km/l)	X	2.825	= Miles per gallon, Imperial (mpg)
Miles per gallon, US (mpg)	X	0.425	= Kilometers per liter (km/l)	X	2.352	= Miles per gallon, US (mpg)

Temperature

Degrees Fahrenheit = (°C x 1.8) + 32

Degrees Celsius (Degrees Centigrade; °C) = (°F - 32) x 0.56

*It is common practice to convert from miles per gallon (mpg) to liters/100 kilometers (l/100km), where mpg (Imperial) x l/100 km = 282 and mpg (US) x l/100 km = 235

Safety first!

Regardless of how enthusiastic you may be about getting on with the job at hand, take the time to ensure that your safety is not jeopardized. A moment's lack of attention can result in an accident, as can failure to observe certain simple safety precautions. The possibility of an accident will always exist, and the following points should not be considered a comprehensive list of all dangers. Rather, they are intended to make you aware of the risks and to encourage a safety conscious approach to all work you carry out on your vehicle.

Essential DOs and DON'Ts

DON'T rely on a jack when working under the vehicle. Always use approved jackstands to support the weight of the vehicle and place them under the recommended lift or support points.

DON'T attempt to loosen extremely tight fasteners (i.e. wheel lug nuts) while the vehicle is on a jack - it may fall.

DON'T start the engine without first making sure that the transmission is in Neutral (or Park where applicable) and the parking brake is set.

DON'T remove the radiator cap from a hot cooling system - let it cool or cover it with a cloth and release the pressure gradually.

DON'T attempt to drain the engine oil until you are sure it has cooled to the point that it will not burn you.

DON'T touch any part of the engine or exhaust system until it has cooled sufficiently to avoid burns.

DON'T siphon toxic liquids such as gasoline, antifreeze and brake fluid by mouth, or allow them to remain on your skin.

DON'T inhale brake lining dust - it is potentially hazardous (see *Asbestos* below).

DON'T allow spilled oil or grease to remain on the floor - wipe it up before someone slips on it.

DON'T use loose fitting wrenches or other tools which may slip and cause injury.

DON'T push on wrenches when loosening or tightening nuts or bolts. Always try to pull the wrench toward you. If the situation calls for pushing the wrench away, push with an open hand to avoid scraped knuckles if the wrench should slip.

DON'T attempt to lift a heavy component alone - get someone to help you.

DON'T rush or take unsafe shortcuts to finish a job.

DON'T allow children or animals in or around the vehicle while you are working on it.

DO wear eye protection when using power tools such as a drill, sander, bench grinder, etc. and when working under a vehicle.

DO keep loose clothing and long hair well out of the way of moving parts.

DO make sure that any hoist used has a safe working load rating adequate for the job.

DO get someone to check on you periodically when working alone on a vehicle.

DO carry out work in a logical sequence and make sure that everything is correctly assembled and tightened.

DO keep chemicals and fluids tightly capped and out of the reach of children and pets.

DO remember that your vehicle's safety affects that of yourself and others. If in doubt on any point, get professional advice.

Asbestos

Certain friction, insulating, sealing, and other products - such as brake linings, brake bands, clutch linings, torque converters, gaskets, etc. - may contain asbestos. Extreme care must be taken to avoid inhalation of dust from such products, since it is hazardous to health. If in doubt, assume that they do contain asbestos.

Fire

Remember at all times that gasoline is highly flammable. Never smoke or have any kind of open flame around when working on a vehicle. But the risk does not end there. A spark caused by an electrical short circuit, by two metal surfaces contacting each other, or even by static electricity built up in your body under certain conditions, can ignite gasoline vapors, which in a confined space are highly explosive. Do not, under any circumstances, use gasoline for cleaning parts. Use an approved safety solvent.

Always disconnect the battery ground (-) cable at the battery before working on any part of the fuel system or electrical system. Never risk spilling fuel on a hot engine or exhaust component. It is strongly recommended that a fire extinguisher suitable for use on fuel and electrical fires be kept handy in the garage or workshop at all times. Never try to extinguish a fuel or electrical fire with water.

Fumes

Certain fumes are highly toxic and can quickly cause unconsciousness and even death if inhaled to any extent. Gasoline vapor falls into this category, as do the vapors from some cleaning solvents. Any draining or pouring of such volatile fluids should be done in a well ventilated area.

When using cleaning fluids and solvents, read the instructions on the container carefully. Never use materials from unmarked containers.

Never run the engine in an enclosed space, such as a garage. Exhaust fumes contain carbon monoxide, which is extremely poisonous. If you need to run the engine, always do so in the open air, or at least have the rear of the vehicle outside the work area.

If you are fortunate enough to have the use of an inspection pit, never drain or pour gasoline and never run the engine while the vehicle is over the pit. The fumes, being heavier than air, will concentrate in the pit with possibly lethal results.

The battery

Never create a spark or allow a bare light bulb near a battery. They normally give off a certain amount of hydrogen gas, which is highly explosive.

Always disconnect the battery ground (-) cable at the battery before working on the fuel or electrical systems.

If possible, loosen the filler caps or cover when charging the battery from an external source (this does not apply to sealed or maintenance-free batteries). Do not charge at an excessive rate or the battery may burst.

Take care when adding water to a non maintenance-free battery and when carrying a battery. The electrolyte, even when diluted, is very corrosive and should not be allowed to contact clothing or skin.

Always wear eye protection when cleaning the battery to prevent the caustic deposits from entering your eyes.

Household current

When using an electric power tool, inspection light, etc., which operates on household current, always make sure that the tool is correctly connected to its plug and that, where necessary, it is properly grounded. Do not use such items in damp conditions and, again, do not create a spark or apply excessive heat in the vicinity of fuel or fuel vapor.

Secondary ignition system voltage

A severe electric shock can result from touching certain parts of the ignition system (such as the spark plug wires) when the engine is running or being cranked, particularly if components are damp or the insulation is defective. In the case of an electronic ignition system, the secondary system voltage is much higher and could prove fatal.

Automotive chemicals and lubricants

A number of automotive chemicals and lubricants are available for use during vehicle maintenance and repair. They include a wide variety of products ranging from cleaning solvents and degreasers to lubricants and protective sprays for rubber, plastic and vinyl.

Cleaners

Carburetor cleaner and choke cleaner is a strong solvent for gum, varnish and carbon. Most carburetor cleaners leave a dry-type lubricant film which will not harden or gum up. Because of this film it is not recommended for use on electrical components.

Brake system cleaner is used to remove brake dust, grease and brake fluid from the brake system, where clean surfaces are absolutely necessary. It leaves no residue and often eliminates brake squeal caused by contaminants.

Electrical cleaner removes oxidation, corrosion and carbon deposits from electrical contacts, restoring full current flow. It can also be used to clean spark plugs, carburetor jets, voltage regulators and other parts where an oil-free surface is desired.

Demoisturants remove water and moisture from electrical components such as alternators, voltage regulators, electrical connectors and fuse blocks. They are non-conductive and non-corrosive.

Degreasers are heavy-duty solvents used to remove grease from the outside of the engine and from chassis components. They can be sprayed or brushed on and, depending on the type, are rinsed off either with water or solvent.

Lubricants

Motor oil is the lubricant formulated for use in engines. It normally contains a wide variety of additives to prevent corrosion and reduce foaming and wear. Motor oil comes in various weights (viscosity ratings) from 0 to 50. The recommended weight of the oil depends on the season, temperature and the demands on the engine. Light oil is used in cold climates and under light load conditions. Heavy oil is used in hot climates and where high loads are encountered. Multi-viscosity oils are designed to have characteristics of both light and heavy oils and are available in a number of weights from 5W-20 to 20W-50.

Gear oil is designed to be used in differentials, manual transmissions and other areas where high-temperature lubrication is required.

Chassis and wheel bearing grease is a heavy grease used where increased loads and friction are encountered, such as for wheel bearings, balljoints, tie-rod ends and universal joints.

High-temperature wheel bearing grease is designed to withstand the extreme temperatures encountered by wheel bearings in disc brake equipped vehicles. It usually contains molybdenum disulfide (moly), which is a dry-type lubricant.

White grease is a heavy grease for metal-to-metal applications where water is a problem. White grease stays soft under both low and high temperatures (usually from -100 to +190-degrees F), and will not wash off or dilute in the presence of water.

Assembly lube is a special extreme pressure lubricant, usually containing moly, used to lubricate high-load parts (such as main and rod bearings and cam lobes) for initial start-up of a new engine. The assembly lube lubricates the parts without being squeezed out or washed away until the engine oiling system begins to function.

Silicone lubricants are used to protect rubber, plastic, vinyl and nylon parts.

Graphite lubricants are used where oils cannot be used due to contamination problems, such as in locks. The dry graphite will lubricate metal parts while remaining uncontaminated by dirt, water, oil or acids. It is electrically conductive and will not foul electrical contacts in locks such as the ignition switch.

Moly penetrants loosen and lubricate frozen, rusted and corroded fasteners and prevent future rusting or freezing.

Heat-sink grease is a special electrically non-conductive grease that is used for mounting electronic ignition modules where it is essential that heat is transferred away from the module.

Sealants

RTV sealant is one of the most widely used gasket compounds. Made from silicone, RTV is air curing, it seals, bonds, waterproofs, fills surface irregularities, remains flexible, doesn't shrink, is relatively easy to remove, and is used as a supplementary sealer with almost all low and medium temperature gaskets.

Anaerobic sealant is much like RTV in that it can be used either to seal gaskets or to form gaskets by itself. It remains flexible, is solvent resistant and fills surface imperfections. The difference between an anaerobic sealant and an RTV-type sealant is in the curing. RTV cures when exposed to air, while an anaerobic sealant cures only in the absence of air. This means that an anaerobic sealant cures only after the assembly of parts, sealing them together.

Thread and pipe sealant is used for sealing hydraulic and pneumatic fittings and vacuum lines. It is usually made from a Teflon compound, and comes in a spray, a paint-on liquid and as a wrap-around tape.

Chemicals

Anti-seize compound prevents seizing, galling, cold welding, rust and corrosion in fasteners. High-temperature ant-seize, usually made with copper and graphite lubricants, is used for exhaust system and exhaust manifold bolts.

Anaerobic locking compounds are used to keep fasteners from vibrating or working loose and cure only after installation, in the absence of air. Medium strength locking compound is used for small nuts, bolts and screws that may be removed later. High-strength locking compound is for large nuts, bolts and studs which aren't removed on a regular basis.

Oil additives range from viscosity index improvers to chemical treatments that claim to reduce internal engine friction. It should be noted that most oil manufacturers caution against using additives with their oils.

Gas additives perform several functions, depending on their chemical makeup. They usually contain solvents that help dissolve gum and varnish that build up on carburetor, fuel injection and intake parts. They also serve to break down carbon deposits that form on the inside surfaces of the combustion chambers. Some additives contain upper cylinder lubricants for valves and piston rings, and others contain chemicals to remove condensation from the gas tank.

Miscellaneous

Brake fluid is specially formulated hydraulic fluid that can withstand the heat and pressure encountered in brake systems. Care must be taken so this fluid does not come in contact with painted surfaces or plastics. An opened container should always be resealed to prevent contamination by water or dirt.

Weatherstrip adhesive is used to bond weatherstripping around doors, windows and trunk lids. It is sometimes used to attach trim pieces.

Undercoating is a petroleum-based, tar-like substance that is designed to protect metal surfaces on the underside of the vehicle from corrosion. It also acts as a sound-deadening agent by insulating the bottom of the vehicle.

Waxes and polishes are used to help protect painted and plated surfaces from the weather. Different types of paint may require the use of different types of wax and polish. Some polishes utilize a chemical or abrasive cleaner to help remove the top layer of oxidized (dull) paint on older vehicles. In recent years many non-wax polishes that contain a wide variety of chemicals such as polymers and silicones have been introduced. These non-wax polishes are usually easier to apply and last longer than conventional waxes and polishes.

Troubleshooting

Contents

Engine

1 Engine will not rotate when attempting to start

1 Battery terminal connections loose or corroded. Check the cable terminals at the battery; tighten cable clamp and/or clean off corrosion as necessary (see Chapter 1).
2 Battery discharged or faulty. If the cable ends are clean and tight on the battery posts, turn the key to the On position and switch on the headlights or windshield wipers. If they won't run, the battery is discharged.
3 Automatic transmission not engaged in park (P) or Neutral (N).
4 Broken, loose or disconnected wires in the starting circuit. Inspect all wires and connectors at the battery, starter solenoid and ignition switch (on steering column).
5 Starter motor pinion jammed in driveplate ring gear. Remove starter (Chapter 5) and inspect pinion and driveplate (Chapter 2).
6 Starter solenoid faulty (Chapter 5).
7 Starter motor faulty (Chapter 5).
8 Clutch pedal neutral start switch faulty.
9 Ignition switch faulty (Chapter 12).
10 Engine seized. Try to turn the crankshaft with a large socket and breaker bar on the pulley bolt.
11 Starter relay faulty (Chapter 5).

2 Engine rotates but will not start

1 Fuel tank empty.
2 Battery discharged (engine rotates slowly).
3 Battery terminal connections loose or corroded.
4 Fuel not reaching fuel injectors. Check for clogged fuel filter or lines and defective fuel pump. Also make sure the tank vent lines aren't clogged (Chapter 4).
5 Low cylinder compression. Check as described in Chapter 2C.
6 Water in fuel. Drain tank and fill with new fuel.
7 Defective ignition coil(s) (Chapter 5).
8 Dirty or clogged fuel injector(s) (Chapter 4).
9 Wet or damaged ignition components (Chapters 1 and 5).
10 Worn, faulty or incorrectly gapped spark plugs (Chapter 1).
11 Broken, loose or disconnected wires in the starting circuit (see previous Section).
12 Broken, loose or disconnected wires at the ignition coil or faulty coil (Chapter 5). ·
13 Timing chain failure or wear affecting valve timing (Chapter 2).
14 Fuel injection or engine control systems failure (Chapters 4 and 6).
15 Defective MAF sensor (Chapter 6)

3 Starter motor operates without turning engine

1 Starter pinion sticking. Remove the starter (Chapter 5) and inspect.
2 Starter pinion or driveplate teeth worn or broken. Remove the inspection cover and inspect.

4 Engine hard to start when cold

1 Battery discharged or low. Check as described in Chapter 1.
2 Fuel not reaching the fuel injectors. Check the fuel filter, lines and fuel pump (Chapters 1 and 4).
3 Defective spark plugs (Chapter 1).
4 Defective engine coolant temperature sensor (Chapter 6).
5 Fuel injection or engine control systems malfunction (Chapters 4 and 6).

5 Engine hard to start when hot

1 Air filter dirty (Chapter 1).
2 Bad engine ground connection.
3 Fuel injection or engine control systems malfunction (Chapters 4 and 6).

6 Starter motor noisy or engages roughly

1 Pinion or driveplate teeth worn or broken. Remove the inspection cover on the left side of the engine and inspect.
2 Starter motor mounting bolts loose or missing.

7 Engine starts but stops immediately

1 Loose or damaged wire harness connections at distributor, coil or alternator.
2 Intake manifold vacuum leaks. Make sure all mounting bolts/nuts are tight and all vacuum hoses connected to the manifold are attached properly and in good condition.
3 Insufficient fuel pressure (see Chapter 4).
4 Fuel injection or engine control systems malfunction (Chapters 4 and 6).

8 Engine 'lopes' while idling or idles erratically

1 Vacuum leaks. Check mounting bolts at the intake manifold for tightness. Make sure that all vacuum hoses are connected and in good condition. Use a stethoscope or a length of fuel hose held against your ear to listen for vacuum leaks while the engine is running. A hissing sound will be heard. A soapy water solution will also detect leaks. Check the intake manifold gasket surfaces.
2 Leaking EGR valve or plugged PCV valve (see Chapters 1 and 6).
3 Air filter clogged (Chapter 1).
4 Fuel pump not delivering sufficient fuel (Chapter 4).
5 Leaking head gasket. Perform a cylinder compression check (Chapter 2).
6 Timing chain(s) worn (Chapter 2).
7 Camshaft lobes worn (Chapter 2).
8 Valves burned or otherwise leaking (Chapter 2).
9 Ignition system not operating properly (Chapters 1 and 5).
10 Fuel injection or engine control systems malfunction (Chapters 4 and 6).

9 Engine misses at idle speed

1 Spark plugs faulty or not gapped properly (Chapter 1).
2 Faulty spark plug wires (Chapter 1).
3 Wet or damaged ignition components (Chapter 5).
4 Short circuits in ignition, coil or spark plug wires.
5 Sticking or faulty emissions systems (see Chapter 6).
6 Clogged fuel filter and/or foreign matter in fuel. Remove the fuel filter (Chapter 1) and inspect.
7 Vacuum leaks at intake manifold or hose connections. Check as described in Section
8 Low or uneven cylinder compression. Check as described in Chapter 2.
9 Fuel injection or engine control systems malfunction (Chapters 4 and 6).

10 Excessively high idle speed

1 Sticking throttle linkage (Chapter 4).
2 Vacuum leaks at intake manifold or hose connections. Check as described in Section 8.
3 Fuel injection or engine control systems malfunction (Chapters 4 and 6).

11 Battery will not hold a charge

1 Alternator drivebelt defective or not adjusted properly (Chapter 1).
2 Battery cables loose or corroded (Chapter 1).
3 Alternator not charging properly (Chapter 5).
4 Loose, broken or faulty wires in the charging circuit (Chapter 5).
5 Short circuit causing a continuous drain on the battery.
6 Battery defective internally.

12 Alternator light stays on

1   Fault in alternator or charging circuit (Chapter 5).
2   Alternator drivebelt defective or not properly adjusted (Chapter 1).

13 Alternator light fails to come on when key is turned on

1   Faulty bulb (Chapter 12).
2   Defective alternator (Chapter 5).
3   Fault in the printed circuit, dash wiring or bulb holder (Chapter 12).

14 Engine misses throughout driving speed range

1   Fuel filter clogged and/or impurities in the fuel system. Check fuel filter (Chapter 1) or clean system (Chapter 4).
2   Faulty or incorrectly gapped spark plugs (Chapter 1).
3   Defective spark plug wires (Chapter 1).
4   Emissions system components faulty (Chapter 6).
5   Low or uneven cylinder compression pressures. Check as described in Chapter 2.
6   Weak or faulty ignition coil(s) (Chapter 5).
7   Weak or faulty ignition system (Chapter 5).
8   Vacuum leaks at intake manifold or vacuum hoses (see Section 8).
9   Dirty or clogged fuel injector(s) (Chapter 4).
10   Leaky EGR valve (Chapter 6).
11   Fuel injection or engine control systems malfunction (Chapters 4 and 6).

15 Hesitation or stumble during acceleration

1   Ignition system not operating properly (Chapter 5).
2   Dirty or clogged fuel injector(s) (Chapter 4).
3   Low fuel pressure. Check for proper operation of the fuel pump and for restrictions in the fuel filter and lines (Chapter 4).
4   Fuel injection or engine control systems malfunction (Chapters 4 and 6).

16 Engine stalls

1   Idle speed incorrect (Chapter 4).
2   Fuel filter clogged and/or water and impurities in the fuel system (Chapter 1).
3   Damaged or wet distributor cap and wires.
4   Emissions system components faulty (Chapter 6).
5   Faulty or incorrectly gapped spark plugs

(Chapter 1). Also check the spark plug wires (Chapter 1).
6   Vacuum leak at the intake manifold or vacuum hoses. Check as described in Section 8.
7   Fuel injection or engine control systems malfunction (Chapters 4 and 6).

17 Engine lacks power

1   Faulty or incorrectly gapped spark plugs (Chapter 1).
2   Air filter dirty (Chapter 1).
3   Faulty ignition coil(s) (Chapter 5).
4   Brakes binding (Chapters 1 and 9).
5   Automatic transmission fluid level incorrect, causing slippage (Chapter 1).
6   Fuel filter clogged and/or impurities in the fuel system (Chapters 1 and 4).
7   EGR system not functioning properly (Chapter 6).
8   Use of sub-standard fuel. Fill tank with proper octane fuel.
9   Low or uneven cylinder compression pressures. Check as described in Chapter 2.
10   Vacuum leak at intake manifold or vacuum hoses (check as described in Section 8).
11   Dirty or clogged fuel injector(s) (Chapters 1 and 4).
12   Fuel injection or engine control systems malfunction (Chapters 4 and 6).
13   Restricted exhaust system (Chapter 4).

18 Engine backfires

1   EGR system not functioning properly (Chapter 6).
2   Damaged valve springs or sticking valves (Chapter 2).
3   Vacuum leak at the intake manifold or vacuum hoses (see Section 8).

19 Engine surges while holding accelerator steady

1   Vacuum leak at the intake manifold or vacuum hoses (see Section 8).
2   Restricted air filter (Chapter 1).
3   Fuel pump or pressure regulator defective (Chapter 4).
4   Fuel injection or engine control systems malfunction (Chapters 4 and 6).

20 Pinging or knocking engine sounds when engine is under load

1   Incorrect grade of fuel. Fill tank with fuel of the proper octane rating.
2   Carbon build-up in combustion chambers. Remove cylinder head(s) and clean combustion chambers (Chapter 2).
3   Incorrect spark plugs (Chapter 1).
4   Fuel injection or engine control systems

malfunction (Chapters 4 and 6).
5   Restricted exhaust system (Chapter 4).

21 Engine diesels (continues to run) after being turned off

1   Idle speed too high (Chapter 4).
2   Incorrect spark plug heat range (Chapter 1).
3   Vacuum leak at the intake manifold or vacuum hoses (see Section 8).
4   Carbon build-up in combustion chambers. Remove the cylinder head(s) and clean the combustion chambers (Chapter 2).
5   Valves sticking (Chapter 2).
6   EGR system not operating properly (Chapter 6).
7   Fuel injection or engine control systems malfunction (Chapters 4 and 6).
8   Check for causes of overheating (Section 27).

22 Low oil pressure

1   Improper grade of oil.
2   Oil pump worn or damaged (Chapter 2).
3   Engine overheating (refer to Section 27).
4   Clogged oil filter (Chapter 1).
5   Clogged oil strainer (Chapter 2).
6   Oil pressure gauge not working properly (Chapter 2).

23 Excessive oil consumption

1   Loose oil drain plug.
2   Loose bolts or damaged oil pan gasket (Chapter 2).
3   Loose bolts or damaged front cover gasket (Chapter 2).
4   Front or rear crankshaft oil seal leaking (Chapter 2).
5   Loose bolts or damaged valve cover gasket (Chapter 2).
6   Loose oil filter (Chapter 1).
7   Loose or damaged oil pressure switch (Chapter 2).
8   Pistons and cylinders excessively worn (Chapter 2).
9   Piston rings not installed correctly on pistons (Chapter 2).
10   Worn or damaged piston rings (Chapter 2).
11   Intake and/or exhaust valve oil seals worn or damaged (Chapter 2).
12   Worn or damaged valves/guides (Chapter 2).
13   Faulty or incorrect PCV valve allowing too much crankcase airflow.

24 Excessive fuel consumption

1   Dirty or clogged air filter element (Chapter 1).
2   Incorrect idle speed (Chapter 4).

3   Low tire pressure or incorrect tire size (Chapter 10).
4   Inspect for binding brakes (see Chapter 9).
5   Fuel leakage. Check all connections, lines and components in the fuel system (Chapter 4).
6   Dirty or clogged fuel injectors (Chapter 4).
7   Fuel injection or engine control systems malfunction (Chapters 4 and 6).
8   Thermostat stuck open or not installed.
9   Improperly operating transmission.

25   Fuel odor

1   Fuel leakage. Check all connections, lines and components in the fuel system (Chapter 4).
2   Fuel tank overfilled. Fill only to automatic shut-off.
3   Charcoal canister filter in Evaporative Emissions Control system clogged (Chapter 1).
4   Vapor leaks from Evaporative Emissions Control system lines (Chapter 6).

26   Miscellaneous engine noises

1   A strong dull noise that becomes more rapid as the engine accelerates indicates worn or damaged crankshaft bearings or an unevenly worn crankshaft. To pinpoint the trouble spot, remove the spark plug wire from one plug at a time and crank the engine over. If the noise stops, the cylinder with the removed plug wire indicates the problem area. Replace the bearing and/or service or replace the crankshaft (Chapter 2).
2   A similar (yet slightly higher pitched) noise to the crankshaft knocking described in the previous paragraph, that becomes more rapid as the engine accelerates, indicates worn or damaged connecting rod bearings (Chapter 2). The procedure for locating the problem cylinder is the same as described in Paragraph 1.
3   An overlapping metallic noise that increases in intensity as the engine speed increases, yet diminishes as the engine warms up indicates abnormal piston and cylinder wear (Chapter 2). To locate the problem cylinder, use the procedure described in Paragraph 1.
4   A rapid clicking noise that becomes faster as the engine accelerates indicates a worn piston pin or piston pin hole. This sound will happen each time the piston hits the highest and lowest points in the stroke (Chapter 2). The procedure for locating the problem piston is described in Paragraph 1.
5   A metallic clicking noise coming from the water pump indicates worn or damaged water pump bearings or pump. Replace the water pump with a new one (Chapter 3).
6   A rapid tapping sound or clicking sound that becomes faster as the engine speed

increases indicates "valve tapping." This can be identified by holding one end of a section of hose to your ear and placing the other end at different spots along the valve cover. The point where the sound is loudest indicates the problem valve. Changing the engine oil and adding a high viscosity oil treatment will sometimes cure a stuck lash adjuster. If the problem persists, the lash adjusters and rocker arms must be removed for inspection (see Chapter 2).
7   A steady metallic rattling or rapping sound coming from the area of the timing chain cover indicates a worn, damaged or out-of-adjustment timing chain. Service or replace the chain and related components (Chapter 2).

Cooling system

27   Overheating

1   Insufficient coolant in system (Chapter 1).
2   Drivebelt defective or not adjusted properly (Chapter 1).
3   Radiator core blocked or radiator grille dirty and restricted (Chapter 3).
4   Thermostat faulty (Chapter 3).
5   Cooling fan not functioning properly (Chapter 3).
6   Expansion tank cap not maintaining proper pressure. Have cap pressure tested by a gas station or repair shop.
7   Defective water pump (Chapter 3).
8   Improper grade of engine oil.
9   Inaccurate temperature gauge (Chapters 3 and 6).
10   Blown cylinder head gasket (Chapter 2).

28   Overcooling

1   Thermostat faulty (Chapter 3).
2   Inaccurate temperature gauge (Chapters 3 and 6).

29   External coolant leakage

1   Deteriorated or damaged hoses. Loose clamps at hose connections (Chapter 1).
2   Water pump seals defective. If this is the case, water will drip from the weep hole in the water pump body (Chapter 3).
3   Leakage from radiator core or header tank. This will require the radiator to be professionally repaired (see Chapter 3 for removal procedures).
4   Leakage from the coolant reservoir or degas bottle.
5   Engine drain plugs or water jacket freeze plugs leaking (see Chapters 1 and 2).
6   Leak from coolant temperature switch (Chapter 3).
7   Leak from damaged gaskets or small cracks (Chapter 2).

30   Internal coolant leakage

Note: *Internal coolant leaks can usually be detected by examining the oil. Check the dipstick and inside the rocker arm cover for water deposits and an oil consistency like that of a milkshake.*
1   Leaking cylinder head gasket. Have the system pressure tested or remove the cylinder head (Chapter 2) and inspect.
2   Cracked cylinder bore or cylinder head. Dismantle engine and inspect (Chapter 2).
3   Loose cylinder head bolts (tighten as described in Chapter 2).

31   Abnormal coolant loss

1   Overfilling system (Chapter 1).
2   Coolant boiling away due to overheating (see causes in Section 27).
3   Internal or external leakage (see Sections 29 and 30).
4   Faulty expansion tank cap. Have the cap pressure tested.
5   Cooling system being pressurized by engine compression. This could be due to a cracked head or block or leaking head gasket(s). Have the system tested for the presence of combustion gas in the coolant at a shop.

32   Poor coolant circulation

1   Inoperative water pump. A quick test is to pinch the top radiator hose closed with your hand while the engine is idling, then release it. You may be able to feel a surge of coolant if the pump is working properly (Chapter 3).
2   Restriction in cooling system. Drain, flush and refill the system (Chapter 1). If necessary, remove the radiator (Chapter 3) and have it reverse flushed or professionally cleaned.
3   Loose water pump drivebelt (Chapter 1).
4   Thermostat sticking (Chapter 3).
5   Insufficient coolant (Chapter 1).

33   Corrosion

1   Excessive impurities in the water. Soft, clean water is recommended. Distilled or rainwater is satisfactory.
2   Insufficient antifreeze solution (refer to Chapter 1 for the proper ratio of water to antifreeze).
3   Infrequent flushing and draining of system. Regular flushing of the cooling system should be carried out at the specified intervals as described in Chapter 1.

Clutch

34 Fails to release (pedal pressed to the floor - shift lever does not move freely in and out of Reverse)

1 Leak in the clutch hydraulic system. Check the master cylinder, release cylinder and lines (Chapter 8).
2 Clutch plate warped or damaged (Chapter 8).

35 Clutch slips (engine speed increases with no increase in vehicle speed)

1 Clutch plate oil soaked or lining worn. Remove clutch (Chapter 8) and inspect.
2 Clutch plate not seated. It may take 30 or 40 normal starts for a new one to seat.
3 Pressure plate worn (Chapter 8).

36 Grabbing (chattering) as clutch is engaged

1 Oil on clutch plate lining. Remove (Chapter 8) and inspect. Correct any leakage source.
2 Worn or loose engine or transmission mounts. These units move slightly when the clutch is released. Inspect the mounts and bolts (Chapter 2).
3 Worn splines on clutch plate hub. Remove the clutch components (Chapter 8) and inspect.
4 Warped pressure plate or flywheel. Remove the clutch components and inspect.

37 Squeal or rumble with clutch fully engaged (pedal released)

1 Release bearing binding on transmission bearing retainer. Remove clutch components (Chapter 8) and check bearing. Remove any burrs or nicks; clean and relubricate bearing retainer before installing.

38 Squeal or rumble with clutch fully disengaged (pedal depressed)

1 Worn, defective or broken release bearing (Chapter 8).
2 Worn or broken pressure plate springs (or diaphragm fingers) (Chapter 8).

39 Clutch pedal stays on floor when disengaged

1 Linkage or release bearing binding. Inspect the linkage or remove the clutch components as necessary.

2 Make sure proper pedal stop (bumper) is installed.

Manual transmission

Note: *All the following references are in Chapter 7A, unless noted.*

40 Noisy in Neutral with engine running

1 Input shaft bearing worn.
2 Damaged main drive gear bearing.
3 Worn countershaft bearings.
4 Worn or damaged countershaft endplay shims.

41 Noisy in all gears

1 Any of the above causes, and/or:
2 Insufficient lubricant (see the checking procedures in Chapter 1).

42 Noisy in one particular gear

1 Worn, damaged or chipped gear teeth for that particular gear.
2 Worn or damaged synchronizer for that particular gear.

43 Slips out of high gear

1 Transmission loose on clutch housing.
2 Dirt between the transmission case and engine or misalignment of the transmission.

44 Difficulty in engaging gears

1 Clutch not releasing completely (see clutch adjustment in Chapter 1).
2 Loose, damaged or out-of-adjustment shift linkage. Make a thorough inspection, replacing parts as necessary.

45 Oil leakage

1 Excessive amount of lubricant in the transmission (see Chapter 1 for correct checking procedures). Drain lubricant as required.
2 Transmission oil seal or vehicle speed sensor O-ring in need of replacement.

Automatic transmission

Note: *Due to the complexity of the automatic transmission, it's difficult for the home mechanic to properly diagnose and service this component. For problems other than the following, the vehicle should be taken to a dealer service department or a transmission shop.*

46 General shift mechanism problems

1 Common problems which may be attributed to a misadjusted shift cable are:
a) *Engine starting in gears other than Park or Neutral.*
b) *Indicator on shifter pointing to a gear other than the one actually being selected.*
c) *Vehicle moves when in Park.*
2 Refer to Chapter 6 to check the transmission range (TR) sensor adjustment.

47 Transmission will not downshift with accelerator pedal pressed to the floor

Since these transmissions are electronically controlled, your dealer or a professional shop with the proper equipment will have to diagnose the probable cause.

48 Transmission slips, shifts rough, is noisy or has no drive in forward or reverse gears

1 There are many probable causes for the above problems, but the home mechanic should be concerned with only one possibility - fluid level (see Chapter 1).
2 Before taking the vehicle to a repair shop, check the level and condition of the fluid as described in Chapter 1. Correct fluid level as necessary or change the fluid and filter if needed. If the problem persists, have a professional diagnose the problem.

49 Fluid leakage

1 Automatic transmission fluid is a deep red color. Fluid leaks should not be confused with engine oil, which can easily be blown by airflow to the transmission.
2 To pinpoint a leak, first remove all built-up dirt and grime from around the transmission. Degreasing agents and/or steam cleaning will achieve this. With the underside clean, drive the vehicle at low speeds so air flow will not blow the leak far from its source. Raise the vehicle and determine where the leak is coming from. Common areas of leakage are:
a) *Pan: Tighten the mounting bolts and/or replace the pan gasket as necessary (see Chapter 7).*
b) *Transmission oil lines: Tighten the connectors where the lines enter the transmission case and/or replace the lines.*
c) *Speedometer connector: Replace the O-ring where the output shaft speed sensor enters the transmission case (Chapter 6).*

Transfer case

50 Transfer case is difficult to shift into the desired range

1 Speed may be too great to permit engagement. Stop the vehicle and shift into the desired range.
2 Shift linkage loose, bent or binding on a manual shift transfer case. Check the linkage for damage or wear and replace or lubricate as necessary (Chapter 7).
3 Defective circuit and or range switch on electric shift transfer case (Chapter 7).
4 If the vehicle has been driven on a paved surface for some time, the driveline torque can make shifting difficult. Stop and shift into two-wheel drive on paved or hard surfaces.
5 Insufficient or incorrect grade of lubricant. Drain and refill the transfer case with the specified lubricant. (Chapter 1).
6 Worn or damaged internal components. Disassembly and overhaul of the transfer case may be necessary (Chapter 7).

51 Transfer case noisy in all gears

Insufficient or incorrect grade of lubricant. Drain and refill (Chapter 1).

52 Noisy or jumps out of four-wheel drive Low range

1 Transfer case not fully engaged. Stop the vehicle, shift into Neutral and then engage 4L.
2 Shift linkage loose, worn or binding. Tighten, repair or lubricate linkage as necessary.
3 Shift fork cracked, inserts worn or fork binding on the rail. See your dealer for a new or rebuilt unit.

53 Lubricant leaks from the vent or output shaft seals

1 Transfer case is overfilled. Drain to the proper level (Chapter 1).
2 Vent is clogged or jammed closed. Clear or replace the vent.
3 Output shaft seal incorrectly installed or damaged. Replace the seal and check contact surfaces for nicks and scoring.

Driveshaft

54 Oil leak at seal end of driveshaft

Defective transmission or transfer case

oil seal. See Chapter 7 for replacement procedures. While this is done, check the splined yoke for burrs or a rough condition which may be damaging the seal. Burrs can be removed with crocus cloth or a fine whetstone.

55 Knock or clunk when the transmission is under initial load (just after transmission is put into gear)

1 Loose or disconnected rear suspension components. Check all mounting bolts, nuts and bushings (see Chapter 10).
2 Loose driveshaft bolts. Inspect all bolts and nuts and tighten them to the specified torque.
3 Worn or damaged universal joint bearings. Check for wear (see Chapter 8).

56 Metallic grinding sound consistent with vehicle speed.

Pronounced wear in the universal joint bearings. Check as described in Chapter 8.

57 Vibration

Note: *Before assuming that the driveshaft is at fault, make sure the tires are perfectly balanced and perform the following test.*
1 Install a tachometer inside the vehicle to monitor engine speed as the vehicle is driven. Drive the vehicle and note the engine speed at which the vibration (roughness) is most pronounced. Now shift the transmission to a different gear and bring the engine speed to the same point.
2 If the vibration occurs at the same engine speed (rpm) regardless of which gear the transmission is in, the driveshaft is NOT at fault since the driveshaft speed varies.
3 If the vibration decreases or is eliminated when the transmission is in a different gear at the same engine speed, refer to the following probable causes.
4 Bent or dented driveshaft. Inspect and replace as necessary (see Chapter 8).
5 Undercoating or built-up dirt, etc. on the driveshaft. Clean the shaft thoroughly and recheck.
6 Worn universal joint bearings. Remove and inspect (see Chapter 8).
7 Driveshaft and/or companion flange out of balance. Check for missing weights on the shaft. Remove the driveshaft (see Chapter 8) and reinstall 180-degrees from original position, then retest. Have the driveshaft professionally balanced if the problem persists.

Axles

58 Noise

1 Road noise. No corrective procedures available.
2 Tire noise. Inspect tires and check tire pressures (Chapter 1).
3 Rear wheel bearings loose, worn or damaged (Chapter 8).

59 Vibration

See probable causes under *Driveshaft*. Proceed under the guidelines listed for the driveshaft. If the problem persists, check the rear wheel bearings by raising the rear of the vehicle and spinning the rear wheels by hand. Listen for evidence of rough (noisy) bearings. Remove and inspect (see Chapter 8).

60 Oil leakage

1 Pinion seal damaged (see Chapter 8).
2 Differential oil seals damaged (see Chapter 8).
3 Differential inspection cover leaking. Tighten the bolts or replace the gasket as required (see Chapters 1 and 8).

Brakes

Note: *Before assuming that a brake problem exists, make sure that the tires are in good condition and inflated properly (see Chapter 1), that the front end alignment is correct and that the vehicle is not loaded with weight in an unequal manner.*

61 Vehicle pulls to one side during braking

1 Defective, damaged or oil-contaminated disc brake pads on one side. Inspect as described in Chapter 9.
2 Excessive wear of brake pad material or disc on one side. Inspect and correct as necessary.
3 Loose or disconnected front suspension components. Inspect and tighten all bolts to the specified torque (Chapter 10).
4 Defective brake caliper assembly. (Chapter 9).

62 Noise (high-pitched squeal with the brakes applied)

1 Disc brake pads worn out. The noise comes from the wear sensor rubbing against the disc (does not apply to all vehicles) or the

actual pad backing plate itself if the material is completely worn away. Replace the pads with new ones immediately (Chapter 9). If the pad material has worn completely away, the brake discs should be inspected for damage as described in Chapter 9.
2   Linings contaminated with dirt or grease. Replace pads or shoes.
3   Incorrect linings. Replace with correct linings.

63   Excessive brake pedal travel

1   Partial brake system failure. Inspect the entire system (Chapter 9) and correct as required.
2   Insufficient fluid in the master cylinder. Check (Chapter 1), add fluid and bleed the system if necessary (Chapter 9).
3   Problem with the anti-lock brake system (Chapter 9).

64   Brake pedal feels spongy when depressed

1   Air in the hydraulic lines. Bleed the brake system (Chapter 9).
2   Faulty flexible hoses. Inspect all system hoses and lines. Replace parts as necessary.
3   Master cylinder mounting bolts/nuts loose.
4   Master cylinder defective (Chapter 9).
5   Problem with the anti-lock brake system (Chapter 9).

65   Excessive effort required to stop vehicle

1   Power brake booster not operating properly (Chapter 9).
2   Excessively worn pads. Inspect and replace if necessary (Chapter 9).
3   One or more caliper pistons seized or sticking (Chapter 9).
4   Brake pads contaminated with oil or grease. Inspect and replace as required (Chapter 9).
5   New pads installed and not yet seated. It will take a while for the new material to seat against the disc.
6   Problem with the anti-lock brake system (Chapter 9).

66   Pedal travels to the floor with little resistance

1   Little or no fluid in the master cylinder reservoir caused by leaking caliper piston(s), loose, damaged or disconnected brake lines.

Inspect the entire system and correct as necessary.
2   Worn master cylinder seals (Chapter 9).
3   Problem with the anti-lock brake system (Chapter 9).

67   Brake pedal pulsates during brake application

1   Caliper improperly installed. Remove and inspect (Chapter 9).
2   Disc defective. Remove (Chapter 9) and check for excessive lateral runout and parallelism. Have the disc resurfaced or replace it with a new one.

Suspension and steering systems

68   Vehicle pulls to one side

1   Tire pressures uneven (Chapter 1).
2   Defective tire (Chapter 1).
3   Excessive wear in suspension or steering components (Chapter 10).
4   Front end in need of alignment.
5   Front brakes dragging. Inspect the brakes as described in Chapters 1 and 9.

69   Shimmy, shake or vibration

1   Tire or wheel out-of-balance or out-of-round. Have professionally balanced.
2   Loose, worn or out-of-adjustment front wheel bearings (Chapter 1).
3   Shock absorbers and/or suspension components worn or damaged (Chapter 10).

70   Excessive pitching and/or rolling around corners or during braking

1   Defective shock absorbers. Replace as a set (Chapter 10).
2   Broken or weak springs and/or suspension components. Inspect as described in Chapter 10.

71   Excessively stiff steering

1   Lack of fluid in power steering fluid reservoir (Chapter 1).
2   Incorrect tire pressures (Chapter 1).
3   Lack of lubrication at steering joints (see Chapter 1).
4   Front end out of alignment.
5   Lack of power assistance (see Section 73).

72   Excessive play in steering

1   Loose front wheel bearings (Chapter 1).
2   Excessive wear in suspension or steering components (Chapter 10).
3   Steering gear damaged or out of adjustment (Chapter 10).

73   Lack of power assistance

1   Steering pump drivebelt faulty or not adjusted properly (Chapter 1).
2   Fluid level low (Chapter 1).
3   Hoses or lines restricted. Inspect and replace parts as necessary.
4   Air in power steering system. Bleed the system (Chapter 10).

74   Excessive tire wear (not specific to one area)

1   Incorrect tire pressures (Chapter 1).
2   Tires out-of-balance. Have professionally balanced.
3   Wheels damaged. Inspect and replace as necessary.
4   Suspension or steering components excessively worn (Chapter 10).

75   Excessive tire wear on outside edge

1   Inflation pressures incorrect (Chapter 1).
2   Excessive speed in turns.
3   Front end alignment incorrect. Have professionally aligned.
4   Suspension arm bent or twisted (Chapter 10).

76   Excessive tire wear on inside edge

1   Inflation pressures incorrect (Chapter 1).
2   Front end alignment incorrect (toe-out). Have professionally aligned.
3   Loose or damaged steering components (Chapter 10).

77   Tire tread worn in one place

1   Tires out-of-balance.
2   Damaged or buckled wheel. Inspect and replace if necessary.
3   Defective tire (Chapter 1).

Notes

Chapter 1
Tune-up and routine maintenance

Contents

Specifications

Recommended lubricants and fluids

Note: *Listed here are manufacturer recommendations at the time this manual was written. Manufacturers occasionally upgrade their fluid and lubricant specifications, so check with your local auto parts store for current recommendations.*

Engine oil
    Type .... API "certified for gasoline engines"
    Viscosity
        V6 engines .... SAE 5W-30
        V8 engines .... SAE 5W-20
Fuel .... Unleaded gasoline, 87 octane
Automatic transmission fluid* .... MERCON® V automatic transmission fluid
Manual transmission lubricant* .... MERCON® Multi-Purpose automatic transmission fluid
Transfer case (4WD)* .... MERCON® Multi-Purpose automatic transmission fluid
Rear differential lubricant** .... SAE 75W-140 Motorcraft High Performance Synthetic Rear Axle Lubricant or equivalent.
Front axle lubricant (4WD) .... SAE 80W-90 rear axle lubricant
Brake fluid .... DOT 3 brake fluid
Clutch fluid .... DOT 3 brake fluid
Engine coolant *** .... Motorcraft Premium Engine Coolant (green colored) or Motorcraft Premium Gold Engine Coolant (yellow colored)
Power steering system .... MERCON® Multi-Purpose automatic transmission fluid

***Caution:** *Be sure to use the correct type of transmission fluid. Do not mix MERCON® and MERCON® V.*
****Traction-Lock (limited slip) differentials add 4oz. of friction modifier XL-3 or equivalent when lubricant is changed.*
****** Caution:** *Do not mix coolants of different colors. Doing so might damage the cooling system and/or the engine. The manufacturer specifies either a green colored coolant or a yellow colored coolant to be used in these systems.*

Capacities*

Engine oil (including filter)
V6 engine.. 5.0 quarts (4.7 liters)
V8 engine.. 6.0 quarts (5.7 liters)
Cooling system
V6 engine
without auxiliary climate control .... 16.3 quarts (15.4 liters)
with auxiliary climate control.................................... 18.2 quarts (17.2 liters)
V8 engine
without auxiliary climate control .... 18.6 quarts (17.6 liters)
with auxiliary climate control.................................... 20.1 quarts (19.0 liters)
Automatic transmission (dry fill)... Up to 12.7 quarts (12.0 liters)

Note: *Since this is a dry-fill specification, the amount required during a routine fluid change will be substantially less. The best way to determine the amount of fluid to add during a routine fluid change is to measure the amount drained. Begin the refill procedure by initially adding 1/3rd of the amount drained. Then, with the engine running, add 1/2-pint at a time (cycling the shifter through each gear position between additions) until the level is correct. The correct fluid level should be checked at this time (see Section 27). It is important to not overfill the transmission.*

Manual Transmission... Up to 2-1/2 quarts (2.4 liters)
Transfer case (4WD models).. Up to 1.5 quarts (1.4 liters)
Rear differential
Conventional .... Up to 1.75 quarts (1.7 liters)
Traction-Lock (limited slip) .... Up to 1.59 quarts (1.5 liters)

All capacities approximate. Add as necessary to bring up to appropriate level.

Ignition system

Spark plug type and gap
Type
V6 engine .... AGSF-22PP or equivalent
V8 engine .... AWSF-32P or equivalent
Gap
V6 engine .... 0.052 to 0.056 inch (1.3 to 1.4 mm)
V8 engine .... 0.052 to 0.056 inch (1.3 to 1.4 mm)
Engine firing order
V6 engine.. 1-4-2-5-3-6
V8 engine.. 1-3-7-2-6-5-4-8

Cooling system

Thermostat rating
Starts to open... 194-degrees F (90-degrees C)
Fully open.. 210-degrees F (105-degrees C)

Brakes

Disc brake pad lining thickness (minimum) .... 1/16 inch (1.5 mm)
Parking brake shoe lining thickness (minimum) .... 1/32 inch (0.8 mm)

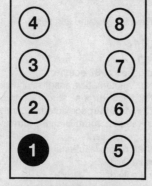

4.6L V8 Engine
1-3-7-2-6-5-4-8

36025-specs.a HAYNES

Cylinder location diagrams -
V8 engine

4.0L
V6 Engine
1-4-2-5-3-6

36025-specs.b HAYNES

Cylinder locations and coil terminal
identification - V6 engine

Torque specifications

	Ft-lbs (unless otherwise indicated)	Nm
Engine oil drain plug		
V6 engine...	19	26
V8 engine...	120 in-lbs	14
Automatic transmission check/fill plug....................	89 in-lbs	10
Automatic transmission		
Drain plug..	19	26
Fluid pan bolts..	96 in-lbs	11
Fluid filter screws	89 in-lbs	10
Manual transmission drain plug................................	36	49
Transfer case (4WD)		
Fill plug...	132 in-lbs	15
Drain plug..	132 in-lbs	15
Rear differential		
Cover bolts	24	32
Check/fill plug	25	34
Spark plugs		
V6 engine..	156 in-lbs	18
V8 engine..	156 in-lbs	18
Drivebelt tensioner mounting bolt(s)		
V6 engine..	35	47
V8 engine..	18	25
Drivebelt idler pulley		
V6 engine..	35	47
V8 engine..	18	25
Wheel lug nuts	100	135

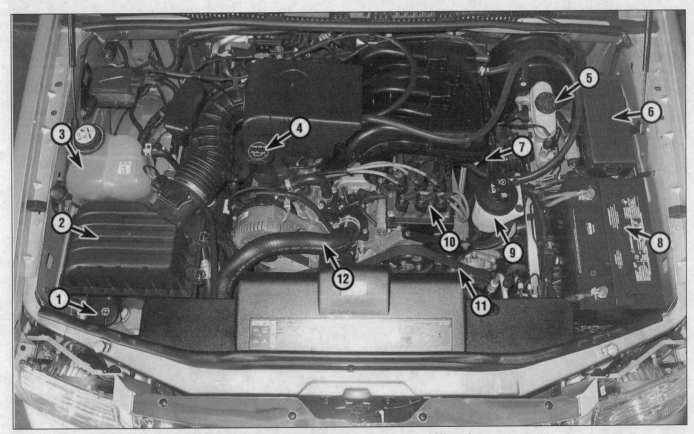

Typical engine compartment components - V6 engine

1	Windshield washer fluid reservoir	5	Brake fluid reservoir	9	Power steering fluid reservoir
2	Air filter housing	6	Fuse/relay block	10	Ignition coil pack
3	Coolant reservoir	7	Engine oil dipstick	11	Drivebelt
4	Engine oil filler cap	8	Battery	12	Radiator hose

Typical engine compartment components - V8 engine

1	Windshield washer fluid reservoir	5	Brake fluid reservoir	8	Battery
2	Air filter housing	6	Fuse/relay block	9	Power steering fluid reservoir
3	Coolant reservoir	7	Engine oil dipstick	10	Radiator hose
4	Engine oil filler cap			11	Drivebelt

Typical engine underside components (2WD) - V6 engine

1	Lower control arm	4	Starter motor
2	Engine oil filter	5	Automatic transmission check/fill/drain plug
3	Engine oil drain plug	6	Lower balljoint

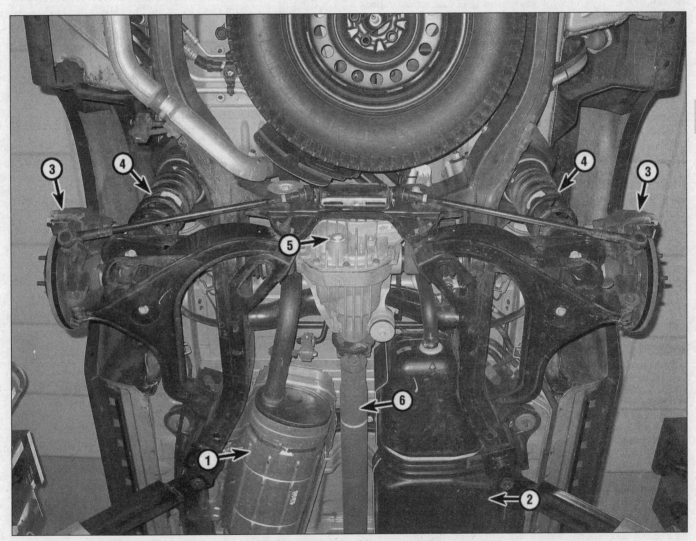

Typical rear underside components

1	Muffler	3	Rear disc brake caliper	5	Differential drain plug
2	Fuel tank	4	Coil spring/shock absorber assembly	6	Driveshaft

1 Maintenance schedule

The maintenance intervals in this manual are provided with the assumption that you, not the dealer, will be doing the work. These are the minimum maintenance intervals recommended by the factory for vehicles that are driven daily. If you wish to keep your vehicle in peak condition at all times, you may wish to perform some of these procedures even more often. Because frequent maintenance enhances the efficiency, performance and resale value of your car, we encourage you to do so. If you drive in dusty areas, tow a trailer, idle or drive at low speeds for extended periods or drive for short distances (less than four miles) in below freezing temperatures, shorter intervals are also recommended.

When your vehicle is new, it should be serviced by a factory authorized dealer service department to protect the factory warranty. In many cases, the initial maintenance check is done at no cost to the owner.

Every 250 miles or weekly, whichever comes first

Check the engine oil level (Section 4)
Check the engine coolant level (Section 4)
Check the brake and clutch fluid level (Section 4)
Check the windshield washer fluid level (Section 4)
Check the power steering fluid level (Section 4)
Check the tires and tire pressures (Section 5)

Every 3000 miles or 3 months, whichever comes first

All items listed above plus:
Change the engine oil and oil filter (Section 6)
Rotate the tires (Section 7)

Every 7500 miles or 6 months, whichever comes first

All items listed above plus:
Inspect and replace, if necessary, the windshield wiper blades (Section 8)
Check and service the battery (Section 9)
Check the cooling system (Section 10)
Check the seat belts (Section 11)

Every 15,000 miles or 12 months, whichever comes first

All items listed above plus:
Inspect and replace, if necessary, all underhood hoses (Section 12)
Inspect the brake system (Section 13)*
Inspect the suspension and steering components (Section 14)

Fuel system check (Section 15)
Inspect and replace, if necessary, air filter (Section 16)*
Check the manual transmission lubricant level (Section 17)
Check the transfer case lubricant level (4WD models) (Section 18)
Check the driveaxle boots (Section 19)
Check the differential lubricant level (Section 26)

Every 30,000 miles or 24 months, whichever comes first

All items listed above plus:
Replace the air filter (Section 16)*
Check the exhaust system (Section 20)
Replace the fuel filter (Section 21)
Service the cooling system (drain, flush and refill) (Section 22)
Change the brake fluid (Section 23)
Check the engine drivebelt (Section 24)

Every 60,000 miles or 48 months, whichever comes first

All items listed above plus:
Replace manual transmission lubricant (Section 25)*
Replace the differential lubricant (Section 26)*
Check the automatic transmission fluid (Section 27)**
Check and replace, if necessary, the Positive Crankcase Ventilation (PCV) valve (Section 28)
Check and replace, if necessary, the spark plugs (conventional, non-platinum or iridium type) (Section 29)
Check the ignition coil (Section 30)
Inspect and replace, if necessary, the spark plug wires (V6 engines) (Section 31)

Every 100,000 miles

Replace the spark plugs (platinum or iridium-tipped type) (Section 29)
Positive Crankcase Ventilation (PCV) replacement (Section 28)

*This item is affected by "severe" operating conditions as described below. If your vehicle is operated under "severe" conditions, perform all maintenance indicated with an asterisk (*) at 3000 mile/3 month intervals. Severe conditions are indicated if you mainly operate your vehicle under one or more of the following conditions:

Operating in dusty areas
Towing a trailer
Idling for extended periods and/or low speed operation
Operating when outside temperatures remain below freezing and when most trips are less than 4 miles

2 Introduction

This Chapter is designed to help the home mechanic maintain the Explorer and Mountaineer with the goals of maximum performance, economy, safety and reliability in mind.

Included is a master maintenance schedule, followed by procedures dealing specifically with each item on the schedule. Visual checks, adjustments, component replacement and other helpful items are included. Refer to the **accompanying illustrations** of the engine compartment and the underside of the vehicle for the locations of various components.

Servicing the vehicle, in accordance with the mileage/time maintenance schedule and the step-by-step procedures will result in a planned maintenance program that should produce a long and reliable service life. Keep in mind that it is a comprehensive plan, so maintaining some items but not others at the specified intervals will not produce the same results.

As you service the vehicle, you will discover that many of the procedures can - and should - be grouped together because of the nature of the particular procedure you're performing or because of the close proximity of two otherwise unrelated components to one another.

For example, if the vehicle is raised for chassis lubrication, you should inspect the exhaust, suspension, steering and fuel systems while you're under the vehicle. When you're rotating the tires, it makes good sense to check the brakes since the wheels are already removed. Finally, let's suppose you have to borrow or rent a torque wrench. Even if you only need it to tighten the spark plugs, you might as well check the torque of as many critical fasteners as time allows.

The first step in this maintenance program is to prepare yourself before the actual work begins. Read through all the procedures you're planning to do, then gather up all the parts and tools needed. If it looks like you might run into problems during a particular job, seek advice from a mechanic or an experienced do-it-yourselfer.

Owner's Manual and VECI label information

Your vehicle owner's manual was written for your year and model and contains very specific information on component locations, specifications, fuse ratings, part numbers, etc. The Owner's Manual is an important resource for the do-it-yourselfer to have; if one was not supplied with your vehicle, it can generally be ordered from a dealer parts department.

Among other important information, the Vehicle Emissions Control Information (VECI) label contains specifications and procedures for applicable tune-up adjustments and, in some instances, spark plugs (see Chapter 6

4.2a Oil dipstick location - V6 engine

for more information on the VECI label). The information on this label is the exact maintenance data recommended by the manufacturer. This data often varies by intended operating altitude, local emissions regulations, month of manufacture, etc.

This Chapter contains procedural details, safety information and more ambitious maintenance intervals than you might find in manufacturer's literature. However, you may also find procedures or specifications in your Owner's Manual or VECI label that differ with what's printed here. In these cases, the Owner's Manual or VECI label can be considered correct, since it is specific to your particular vehicle.

3 Tune-up general information

The term tune-up is used in this manual to represent a combination of individual operations rather than one specific procedure.

If, from the time the vehicle is new, the routine maintenance schedule is followed closely and frequent checks are made of fluid levels and high wear items, as suggested throughout this manual, the engine will be kept in relatively good running condition and the need for additional work will be minimized.

More likely than not, however, there will be times when the engine is running poorly due to lack of regular maintenance. This is even more likely if a used vehicle, which has not received regular and frequent maintenance checks, is purchased. In such cases, an engine tune-up will be needed outside of the regular routine maintenance intervals.

The first step in any tune-up or diagnostic procedure to help correct a poor running engine is a cylinder compression check. A compression check (see Chapter 2) will help determine the condition of internal engine components and should be used as a guide for tune-up and repair procedures. If, for instance, a compression check indicates serious internal engine wear, a conventional

4.2b Oil dipstick location - V8 engines

tune-up will not improve the performance of the engine and would be a waste of time and money. Because of its importance, the compression check should be done by someone with the right equipment and the knowledge to use it properly.

The following procedures are those most often needed to bring a generally poor running engine back into a proper state of tune.

4 Fluid level checks (every 250 miles or weekly)

1   Fluids are an essential part of the lubrication, cooling, brake and windshield washer systems. Because the fluids gradually become depleted and/or contaminated during normal operation of the vehicle, they must be periodically replenished. See *Recommended lubricants and fluids* at the beginning of this Chapter before adding fluid to any of the following components. **Note:** *The vehicle must be on level ground when fluid levels are checked.*

Engine oil

Refer to illustrations 4.2a, 4.2b, 4.4 and 4.6

2   The oil level is checked with a dipstick, which is attached to the engine block **(see illustrations)**. The dipstick extends through a metal tube down into the oil pan.

3   The oil level should be checked before the vehicle has been driven, or about 5 minutes after the engine has been shut off. If the oil is checked immediately after driving the vehicle, some of the oil will remain in the upper part of the engine, resulting in an inaccurate reading on the dipstick.

4   Pull the dipstick out of the tube and wipe all the oil from the end with a clean rag or paper towel. Insert the clean dipstick all the way back into the tube and pull it out again. Note the oil at the end of the dipstick. At its highest point, the level should be between the MIN and MAX marks on the dip-

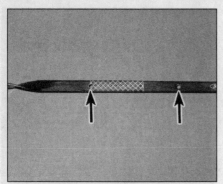

4.4 The oil level should be in the safe range - if it's below the MIN or ADD mark, add enough oil to bring it up to or near the MAX or FULL mark

4.6 The oil filler cap is located on the valve cover - always make sure the area around the opening is clean before unscrewing the cap to prevent dirt from contaminating the engine (V6 engine shown)

4.8 The cooling system expansion tank is located at the right side of the engine compartment

stick **(see illustration)**.

5   It takes one quart of oil to raise the level from the MIN mark to the MAX mark on the dipstick. Do not allow the level to drop below the MIN mark or oil starvation may cause engine damage. Conversely, overfilling the engine (adding oil above the MAX mark) may cause oil fouled spark plugs, oil leaks or oil seal failures. Maintaining the oil level above the OPERATING RANGE mark can cause excessive oil consumption.

6   To add oil, remove the filler cap from the valve cover **(see illustration)**. After adding oil, wait a few minutes to allow the level to stabilize, then pull out the dipstick and check the level again. Add more oil if required. Install the filler cap and tighten it by hand only.

7   Checking the oil level is an important preventive maintenance step. A consistently low oil level indicates oil leakage through damaged seals, defective gaskets or past worn rings or valve guides. If the oil looks milky in color or has water droplets in it, the cylinder head gasket(s) may be blown or the head(s) or block may be cracked. The engine should be checked immediately. The condition of the oil should also be checked. Whenever you check the oil level, slide your thumb and index finger up the dipstick before wiping off the oil. If you see small dirt or metal particles clinging to the dipstick, the oil should be changed (see Section 9).

Engine coolant

Refer to illustrations 4.8 and 4.9

Warning: *Do not allow antifreeze to come in contact with your skin or painted surfaces of the vehicle. Flush contaminated areas immediately with plenty of water. Don't store new coolant or leave old coolant lying around where it's accessible to children or pets - they're attracted by its sweet smell. Ingestion of even a small amount of coolant can be fatal! Wipe up garage floor and drip pan spills immediately. Keep antifreeze containers covered and repair cooling system leaks as soon as they're noticed.*

8   All vehicles covered by this manual are equipped with a pressurized coolant recovery

system. A plastic expansion tank located at the side of the engine compartment is connected by a hose to the radiator **(see illustration)**. As the engine heats up during operation, the expanding coolant fills the tank.

9   The coolant level in the tank should be checked regularly. **Warning:** *Do not remove the expansion tank cap to check the coolant level when the engine is warm!* The level in the tank varies with the temperature of the engine. When the engine is cold, the coolant level should be in the COLD FILL RANGE on the expansion tank **(see illustration)**. If it isn't, remove the cap from the tank and add a 50/50 mixture of ethylene glycol based antifreeze and water.

10   Drive the vehicle, let the engine cool completely then recheck the coolant level. Don't use rust inhibitors or additives. If only a small amount of coolant is required to bring the system up to the proper level, water can be used. However, repeated additions of water will dilute the antifreeze and water solution. In order to maintain the proper ratio of antifreeze and water, always top up the

coolant level with the correct mixture. An empty plastic milk jug or bleach bottle makes an excellent container for mixing coolant.

11   If the coolant level drops consistently, there may be a leak in the system. Inspect the radiator, hoses, filler cap, drain plugs and water pump (see Section 9). If no leaks are noted, have the expansion tank cap pressure tested by a service station.

12   If you have to remove the expansion tank cap wait until the engine has cooled completely, then wrap a thick cloth around the cap and unscrew it slowly, stopping if you hear a hissing noise. If coolant or steam escapes, let the engine cool down longer, then remove the cap.

13   Check the condition of the coolant as well. It should be relatively clear. If it's brown or rust colored, the system should be drained, flushed and refilled. Even if the coolant appears to be normal, the corrosion inhibitors wear out, so it must be replaced at the specified intervals.

Brake and clutch fluid

Refer to illustrations 4.14 and 4.15

14   The brake master cylinder is mounted on the front of the power booster unit in the

4.9 When the engine is cold, the engine coolant level should be between the COLD FILL range marks

4.14 The brake master cylinder is mounted on the front of the power booster unit

4.15 The brake fluid level should be kept at the MAX line

4.22 The windshield/rear window washer fluid reservoir is located in the right front corner of the engine compartment

4.25 The power steering fluid reservoir is located at the left side of the engine compartment (V6 engine shown)

engine compartment **(see illustration)**. The hydraulic clutch master cylinder used on manual transmission vehicles is located next to the brake master cylinder.

15   The brake master cylinder and the clutch master cylinder share a common reservoir. To check the fluid level of either system, simply look at the MAX mark on the brake fluid reservoir **(see illustration)**. The level should be at the MAX line.

16   If the level is low, wipe the top of the reservoir cover with a clean rag to prevent contamination of the brake system before lifting the cover.

17   Add only the specified brake fluid to the reservoir (refer to *Recommended lubricants and fluids* at the front of this Chapter or to your owner's manual). Mixing different types of brake fluid can damage the system. Fill the brake master cylinder reservoir only to the MAX line. **Warning:** *Use caution when filling the reservoir - brake fluid can harm your eyes and damage painted surfaces. Do not use brake fluid that is more than one year old or has been left open. Brake fluid absorbs moisture from the air. Excess moisture can cause a dangerous loss of braking.*

18   While the reservoir cap is removed, inspect the master cylinder reservoir for contamination. If deposits, dirt particles or water droplets are present, the system should be drained and refilled.

19   After filling the reservoir to the proper level, make sure the lid is properly seated to prevent fluid leakage and/or system pressure loss.

20   The fluid in the brake master cylinder will drop slightly as the brake pads at each wheel wear down during normal operation. If the master cylinder requires repeated replenishing to keep it at the proper level, this is an indication of leakage in the brake or clutch system, which should be corrected immediately. If the brake system shows an indication of leakage check all brake lines and connections, along with the calipers and booster (see Section 13 for more information). If the hydraulic clutch system shows an indication of leakage check all clutch lines and connec-

tions, along with the clutch release cylinder (see Chapter 8 for more information).

21   If, upon checking the brake or clutch master cylinder fluid level, you discover the reservoir empty or nearly empty, the systems should be bled (see Chapters 8 and 9).

Windshield washer fluid

Refer to illustration 4.22

22   Fluid for the windshield washer system is stored in a plastic reservoir located at the right front of the engine compartment **(see illustration)**.

23   In milder climates, plain water can be used in the reservoir, but it should be kept no more than 2/3 full to allow for expansion if the water freezes. In colder climates, use windshield washer system antifreeze, available at any auto parts store, to lower the freezing point of the fluid. Mix the antifreeze with water in accordance with the manufacturer's directions on the container. **Caution:** *Do not use cooling system antifreeze - it will damage the vehicle's paint.*

Power steering fluid

Refer to illustrations 4.25 and 4.28

24   Check the power steering fluid level periodically to avoid steering system problems, such as damage to the pump. **Caution:** *DO NOT hold* the steering *wheel against either stop (extreme left or right turn) for more than five seconds. If you do, the power steering pump could be damaged.*

25   The power steering reservoir, located at the right side of the engine compartment **(see illustration)**, has MIN and MAX fluid level marks on the side. The fluid level can be seen without removing the reservoir cap.

26   Park the vehicle on level ground and apply the parking brake.

27   Run the engine until it has reached normal operating temperature. With the engine at idle, turn the steering wheel back and forth about 10 times to get any air out of the steering system. Shut the engine off with the wheels in the straight-ahead position.

28   Note the fluid level on the side of the

4.28 At normal operating temperature, the power steering fluid level should be between the MAX and MIN marks

reservoir. It should be between the two marks **(see illustration)**.

29   Add small amounts of fluid until the level is correct. **Caution:** *Do not overfill the reservoir. If too much fluid is added, remove the excess with a clean syringe or suction pump.*

30   Check the power steering hoses and connections for leaks and wear.

---

5   Tire and tire pressure checks (every 250 miles or weekly)

Refer to illustrations 5.2, 5.3, 5.4a, 5.4b and 5.8

1   Periodic inspection of the tires may spare you the inconvenience of being stranded with a flat tire. It can also provide you with vital information regarding possible problems in the steering and suspension systems before major damage occurs.

2   The original tires on this vehicle are equipped with 1/2-inch wide bands that will appear when tread depth reaches 1/16-inch, at which point they can be considered worn

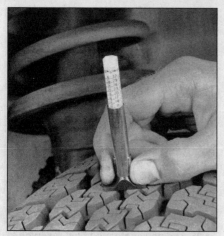

5.2 A tire tread depth indicator should be used to monitor tire wear - they are available at auto parts stores and service stations and cost very little

UNDERINFLATION

OVERINFLATION

CUPPING

Cupping may be caused by:
- **Underinflation and/or mechanical irregularities such as out-of-balance condition of wheel and/or tire, and bent or damaged wheel.**
- **Loose or worn steering tie-rod or steering idler arm.**
- **Loose, damaged or worn front suspension parts.**

INCORRECT TOE-IN
OR EXTREME CAMBER

FEATHERING DUE
TO MISALIGNMENT

5.3 This chart will help you determine the condition of your tires, the probable cause(s) of abnormal wear and the corrective action necessary

out. Tread wear can be monitored with a simple, inexpensive device known as a tread depth indicator **(see illustration)**.

3   Note any abnormal tread wear **(see illustration)**. Tread pattern irregularities such as cupping, flat spots and more wear on one side than the other are indications of front end alignment and/or balance problems. If any of these conditions are noted, take the vehicle to a tire shop or service station to correct the problem.

4   Look closely for cuts, punctures and embedded nails or tacks. Sometimes a tire will hold air pressure for a short time or leak down very slowly after a nail has embedded itself in the tread. If a slow leak persists, check the valve stem core to make sure it is tight **(see illustration)**. Examine the tread for an object that may have embedded itself in the tire or for a "plug" that may have begun to leak (radial tire punctures are repaired with a plug that is installed in a puncture). If a puncture is suspected, it can be easily verified by

spraying a solution of soapy water onto the puncture area **(see illustration)**. The soapy solution will bubble if there is a leak. Unless the puncture is unusually large, a tire shop or service station can usually repair the tire.

5   Carefully inspect the inner sidewall of each tire for evidence of brake fluid leakage. If you see any, inspect the brakes immediately.

6   Correct air pressure adds miles to the life span of the tires, improves mileage and enhances overall ride quality. Tire pressure cannot be accurately estimated by looking at a tire, especially if it's a radial. A tire pressure

gauge is essential. Keep an accurate gauge in the glove compartment. The pressure gauges attached to the nozzles of air hoses at gas stations are often inaccurate.

7   Always check tire pressure when the tires are cold. Cold, in this case, means the vehicle has not been driven over a mile in the three hours preceding a tire pressure check. A pressure rise of four to eight pounds is not uncommon once the tires are warm.

8   Unscrew the valve cap protruding from the wheel or hubcap and push the gauge firmly onto the valve stem **(see illustration)**. Note the reading on the gauge and compare

5.4a If a tire loses air on a steady basis, check the valve core first to make sure it's snug (special inexpensive wrenches are commonly available at auto parts stores)

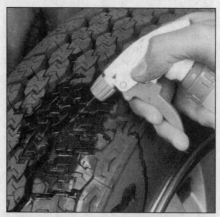

5.4b If the valve core is tight, raise the corner of the vehicle with the low tire and spray a soapy water solution onto the tread as the tire is turned slowly - slow leaks will cause small bubbles to appear

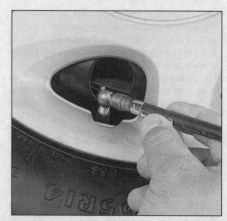

5.8 To extend the life of your tires, check the air pressure at least once a week with an accurate gauge (don't forget the spare!)

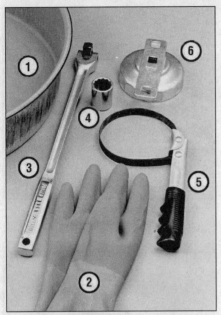

6.2 These tools are required when changing the engine oil and filter

1 **Drain pan** - *It should be fairly shallow in depth, but wide in order to prevent spills*

2 **Rubber gloves** - *When removing the drain plug and filter, it is inevitable that you will get oil on your hands (the gloves will prevent burns)*

3 **Breaker bar** - *Sometimes the oil drain plug is pretty tight and a long breaker bar is needed to loosen it*

4 **Socket** - *To be used with the breaker bar or a ratchet (must be the correct size to fit the drain plug)*

5 **Filter wrench** - *This is a metal band-type wrench, which requires clearance around the filter to be effective*

6 **Filter wrench** - *This type fits on the bottom of the filter and can be turned with a ratchet or beaker bar (different size wrenches are available for different types of filters)*

the figure to the recommended tire pressure shown on the tire placard on the driver's side door. Be sure to reinstall the valve cap to keep dirt and moisture out of the valve stem mechanism. Check all four tires and, if necessary, add enough air to bring them up to the recommended pressure.

9   Don't forget to keep the spare tire inflated to the specified pressure (refer to the pressure molded into the tire sidewall).

6   Engine oil and filter change (every 3000 miles or 3 months)

Refer to illustrations 6.2, 6.7, 6.12 and 6.15

1   Frequent oil changes are the most important preventive maintenance procedures that can be done by the home mechanic. As engine oil ages, it becomes

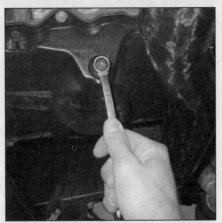

6.7 Use a proper size box-end wrench or socket to remove the oil drain plug and avoid rounding it off

diluted and contaminated, which leads to premature engine wear.

2   Make sure that you have all the necessary tools before you begin this procedure **(see illustration)**. You should also have plenty of rags or newspapers handy for mopping up oil spills.

3   Access to the oil drain plug and filter will be improved if the vehicle can be lifted on a hoist, driven onto ramps or supported by jackstands. **Warning:** *Do not work under a vehicle supported only by a jack - always use jackstands!*

4   If you haven't changed the oil on this vehicle before, get under it and locate the oil drain plug and the oil filter. The exhaust components will be warm as you work, so note how they are routed to avoid touching them when you are under the vehicle.

5   Start the engine and allow it to reach normal operating temperature - oil and sludge will flow out more easily when warm. If new oil, a filter or tools are needed, use the vehicle to go get them and warm up the engine/oil at the same time. Park on a level surface and shut off the engine when it's warmed up. Remove the oil filler cap from the valve cover.

6   Raise the vehicle and support it on jackstands. Make sure it is safely supported!

7   Being careful not to touch the hot exhaust components, position a drain pan under the plug in the bottom of the engine, then remove the plug **(see illustration)**. It's a good idea to wear a rubber glove while unscrewing the plug the final few turns to avoid being scalded by hot oil.

8   It may be necessary to move the drain pan slightly as oil flow slows to a trickle. Inspect the old oil for the presence of metal particles.

9   After all the oil has drained, wipe off the drain plug with a clean rag. Any small metal particles clinging to the plug would immediately contaminate the new oil.

10   Clean the area around the drain plug opening, reinstall the plug and tighten it securely, but don't strip the threads.

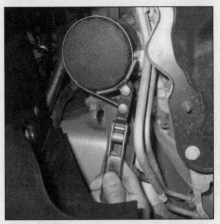

6.12 Use an oil filter wrench to remove the filter (V6 engine shown)

11   Move the drain pan into position under the oil filter.

12   Loosen the oil filter by turning it counterclockwise with a filter wrench **(see illustration)**. Any standard filter wrench will work.

13   Once the filter is loose, use your hands to unscrew it from the block. Just as the filter is detached from the block, immediately tilt the open end up to prevent the oil inside the filter from spilling out.

14   Using a clean rag, wipe off the mounting surface on the block. Also, make sure that none of the old gasket remains stuck to the mounting surface. It can be removed with a scraper if necessary.

15   Compare the old filter with the new one to make sure they are the same type. Smear some engine oil on the rubber gasket of the new filter and screw it into place **(see illustration)**. Overtightening the filter will damage the gasket, so don't use a filter wrench. Most filter manufacturers recommend tightening the filter by hand only. Normally they should be tightened 3/4-turn after the gasket contacts the block, but be sure to follow the directions on the filter or container.

16   Remove all tools and materials from under the vehicle, being careful not to spill

6.15 Lubricate the oil filter gasket with clean engine oil before installing the filter on the engine

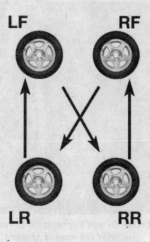

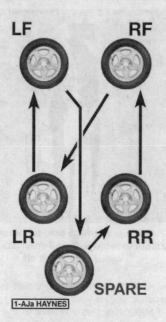

7.2a Four-tire rotation pattern

7.2b Five tire rotation pattern

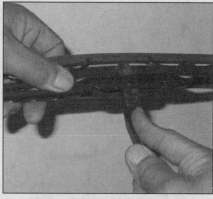

8.4a To release the blade holder, push the release pin . . .

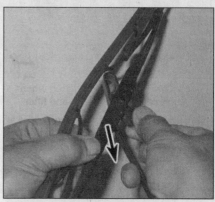

8.4b . . . and pull the wiper blade in the direction of the arrow to separate it from the arm

the oil in the drain pan, then lower the vehicle.

17   Add new oil to the engine through the oil filler cap. Use a funnel to prevent oil from spilling onto the top of the engine. Pour four quarts of fresh oil into the engine. Wait a few minutes to allow the oil to drain into the pan, then check the level on the dipstick (see Section 4 if necessary). If the oil level is in the OK range, install the filler cap.

18   Start the engine and run it for about a minute. While the engine is running, look under the vehicle and check for leaks at the oil pan drain plug and around the oil filter. If either one is leaking, stop the engine and tighten the plug or filter slightly.

19   Wait a few minutes, then recheck the level on the dipstick. Add oil as necessary to bring the level into the OK range.

20   During the first few trips after an oil change, make it a point to check frequently for leaks and proper oil level.

21   The old oil drained from the engine cannot be reused in its present state and should be disposed of. Check with your local auto parts store, disposal facility or environmental agency to see if they will accept the oil for recycling. After the oil has cooled it can be drained into a container (capped plastic jugs, topped bottles, milk cartons, etc.) for transport to one of these disposal sites. Don't dispose of the oil by pouring it on the ground or down a drain!

7   Tire rotation (every 3000 miles or 3 months)

Refer to illustrations 7.2a and 7.2b

1   The tires should be rotated at the specified intervals and whenever uneven wear is noticed. Since the vehicle will be raised and the tires removed anyway, check the brakes also (see Section 13).

2   Radial tires must be rotated in a specific pattern **(see illustrations)**. If your vehicle has a compact spare tire, don't include it in the rotation pattern.

3   Refer to the information in *Jacking and towing* at the front of this manual for the proper procedure to follow when raising the vehicle and changing a tire. If the brakes must be checked, don't apply the parking brake as stated.

4   The vehicle must be raised on a hoist or supported on jackstands to get all four wheels off the ground. Make sure the vehicle is safely supported!

5   After the rotation procedure is finished, check and adjust the tire pressures as necessary and be sure to check the lug nut tightness.

8   Windshield wiper blade inspection and replacement (every 7500 miles or 6 months)

Refer to illustrations 8.4a and 8.4b

1   The windshield wiper and blade assembly should be inspected periodically for damage, loose components and cracked or worn blade elements.

2   Road film can build up on the wiper blades and affect their efficiency, so they should be washed regularly with a mild detergent solution.

3   If the wiper blade elements are cracked, worn or warped, or no longer clean adequately, they should be replaced with new ones.

4   Lift the arm assembly away from the glass for clearance, press on the release lever, then slide the wiper blade assembly out of the hook in the end of the arm **(see illustrations)**.

5   Attach the new wiper to the arm. Connection can be confirmed by an audible click.

9   Battery check, maintenance and charging (every 7500 miles or 6 months)

Refer to illustrations 9.1, 9.6a, 9.6b, 9.7a and 9.7b

Warning: *Certain precautions must be followed when checking and servicing the battery. Hydrogen gas, which is highly flammable, is always present in the battery cells, so keep lighted tobacco and all other open flames and sparks away from the battery. The electrolyte inside the battery is actually diluted sulfuric acid, which will cause injury if splashed on your skin or in your eyes. It will also ruin clothes and painted surfaces. When removing the battery cables, always detach the negative cable first and hook it up last!*

1   A routine preventive maintenance program for the battery in your vehicle is the only way to ensure quick and reliable starts. But before performing any battery maintenance, make sure that you have the proper equipment necessary to work safely around the battery **(see illustration)**.

2   There are also several precautions that should be taken whenever battery maintenance is performed. Before servicing the battery, always turn the engine and all accessories off and disconnect the cables from the

9.1 Tools and materials required for battery maintenance

1   **Face shield/safety goggles** - *When removing corrosion with a brush, the acidic particles can easily fly up into your eyes*
2   **Baking soda** - *A solution of baking soda and water can be used to neutralize corrosion*
3   **Petroleum jelly** - *A layer of this on the battery posts will help prevent corrosion*
4   **Battery post/cable cleaner** - *This wire brush cleaning tool will remove all traces of corrosion from the battery posts and cable clamps*
5   **Treated felt washers** - *Placing one of these on each post, directly under the cable clamps, will help prevent corrosion*
6   **Puller** - *Sometimes the cable clamps are very difficult to pull off the posts, even after the nut/bolt has been completely loosened. This tool pulls the clamp straight up and off the post without damage*
7   **Battery post/cable cleaner** - *Here is another cleaning tool which is a slightly different version of number 4 above, but it does the same thing*
8   **Rubber gloves** - *Another safety item to consider when servicing the battery; remember that's acid inside the battery*

negative terminal of the battery (see Chapter 5).
3   The battery produces hydrogen gas, which is both flammable and explosive. Never create a spark, smoke or light a match around the battery. Always charge the battery in a ventilated area.
4   Electrolyte contains poisonous and corrosive sulfuric acid. Do not allow it to get in your eyes, on your skin, or on your clothes. Never ingest it. Wear protective safety

9.6a Battery terminal corrosion usually appears as light, fluffy powder

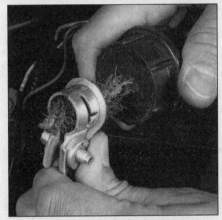

9.7a When cleaning the cable clamps, all corrosion must be removed (the inside of the clamp is tapered to match the taper on the post, so don't remove too much material)

glasses when working near the battery. Keep children away from the battery.
5   Note the external condition of the battery. If the positive terminal and cable clamp on your vehicle's battery is equipped with a rubber protector, make sure that it's not torn or damaged. It should completely cover the terminal. Look for any corroded or loose connections, cracks in the case or cover or loose hold-down clamps. Also check the entire length of each cable for cracks and frayed conductors.
6   If corrosion, which looks like white, fluffy deposits **(see illustration)** is evident, particularly around the terminals, the battery should be removed for cleaning. Loosen the cable clamp bolts with a wrench, being careful to remove the ground cable first, and slide them off the terminals **(see illustration)**. Then disconnect the hold-down clamp bolt and nut, remove the clamp and lift the battery from the engine compartment.
7   Clean the cable clamps thoroughly with a battery brush or a terminal cleaner and a solution of warm water and baking soda **(see illustration)**. Wash the terminals and the top of the battery case with the same solution but

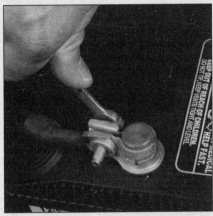

9.6b Removing a cable from the battery post with a wrench - sometimes a pair of special battery pliers are required for this procedure if corrosion has caused deterioration of the nut hex (always remove the ground (-) cable first and hook it up last!)

9.7b Regardless of the type of tool used to clean the battery posts, a clean, shiny surface should be the result

make sure that the solution doesn't get into the battery. When cleaning the cables, terminals and battery top, wear safety goggles and rubber gloves to prevent any solution from coming in contact with your eyes or hands. Wear old clothes too - even diluted, sulfuric acid splashed onto clothes will burn holes in them. If the terminals have been extensively corroded, clean them up with a terminal cleaner **(see illustration)**. Thoroughly wash all cleaned areas with plain water.
8   Make sure that the battery tray is in good condition and the hold-down clamp fasteners are tight. If the battery is removed from the tray, make sure no parts remain in the bottom of the tray when the battery is reinstalled. When reinstalling the hold-down clamp bolts, do not overtighten them.
9   Information on removing and installing the battery can be found in Chapter 5. Information on jump starting can be found at the front of this manual. For more detailed battery checking procedures, refer to the *Haynes Automotive Electrical Manual*.

1

Cleaning

10   Corrosion on the hold-down components, battery case and surrounding areas can be removed with a solution of water and baking soda. Thoroughly rinse all cleaned areas with plain water.

11   Any metal parts of the vehicle damaged by corrosion should be covered with a zinc-based primer, then painted.

Charging

Warning: *When batteries are being charged, hydrogen gas, which is very explosive and flammable, is produced. Do not smoke or allow open flames near a charging or a recently charged battery. Wear eye protection when near the battery during charging. Also, make sure the charger is unplugged before connecting or disconnecting the battery from the charger.*

12   Slow-rate charging is the best way to restore a battery that's discharged to the point where it will not start the engine. It's also a good way to maintain the battery charge in a vehicle that's only driven a few miles between starts. Maintaining the battery charge is particularly important in the winter when the battery must work harder to start the engine and electrical accessories that drain the battery are in greater use.

13   It's best to use a one or two-amp battery charger (sometimes called a "trickle" charger). They are the safest and put the least strain on the battery. They are also the least expensive. For a faster charge, you can use a higher amperage charger, but don't use one rated more than 1/10th the amp/hour rating of the battery. Rapid boost charges that claim to restore the power of the battery in one to two hours are hardest on the battery and can damage batteries not in good condition. This type of charging should only be used in emergency situations.

14   The average time necessary to charge a battery should be listed in the instructions that come with the charger. As a general rule, a trickle charger will charge a battery in 12 to 16 hours.

10   Cooling system check (every 7,500 miles or 6 months)

Refer to illustration 10.4

1   Many major engine failures can be caused by a faulty cooling system.

2   The engine must be cold for the cooling system check, so perform the following procedure before the vehicle is driven for the day or after it has been shut off for at least three hours.

3   Remove the pressure-relief cap from the expansion tank at the right side of the engine compartment. Clean the cap thoroughly, inside and out, with clean water. The presence of rust or corrosion in the expansion tank means the coolant should be changed (see Section 22). The coolant inside the expansion tank should be relatively clean and transparent. If it's rust colored, drain the system and refill it with new coolant.

4   Carefully check the radiator hoses and the smaller diameter heater hoses. Inspect each coolant hose along its entire length, replacing any hose which is cracked, swollen or deteriorated **(see illustration)**. Cracks will show up better if the hose is squeezed. Pay close attention to hose clamps that secure the hoses to cooling system components. Hose clamps can pinch and puncture hoses, resulting in coolant leaks.

5   Make sure that all hose connections are tight. A leak in the cooling system will usually show up as white or rust colored deposits on the area adjoining the leak. If wire-type clamps are used on the hoses, it may be a good idea to replace them with screw-type clamps.

6   Clean the front of the radiator and air conditioning condenser with compressed air, if available, or a soft brush. Remove all bugs, leaves, etc. embedded in the radiator fins. Be extremely careful not to damage the cooling fins or cut your fingers on them.

7   If the coolant level has been dropping consistently and no leaks are detectable, have the expansion tank cap and cooling system pressure checked at a service station.

11   Seat belt check (every 7,500 miles or 6 months)

1   Check seat belts, buckles, latch plates and guide loops for obvious damage and signs of wear.

2   See if the seat belt reminder light comes on when the key is turned to the Run or Start position. A chime should also sound.

3   The seat belts are designed to lock up during a sudden stop or impact, yet allow free movement during normal driving. Make sure the retractors return the belt against your chest while driving and rewind the belt fully when the buckle is unlatched.

4   If any of the above checks reveal problems with the seat belt system, replace parts as necessary.

12   Underhood hose check and replacement (every 15,000 miles or 12 months)

Warning: *Replacement of air conditioning hoses must be left to a dealer service department or air conditioning shop that has the equipment to depressurize the system safely. Never remove air conditioning components or hoses until the system has been depressurized.*

General

1   High temperatures under the hood can cause deterioration of the rubber and plastic

Check for a chafed area that could fail prematurely.

Check for a soft area indicating the hose has deteriorated inside.

Overtightening the clamp on a hardened hose will damage the hose and cause a leak.

Check each hose for swelling and oil-soaked ends. Cracks and breaks can be located by squeezing the hose.

10.4 Hoses, like drivebelts, have a habit of failing at the worst possible time - to prevent the inconvenience of a blown radiator or heater hose, inspect them carefully as shown here

hoses used for engine, accessory and emission systems operation. Periodic inspection should be made for cracks, loose clamps, material hardening and leaks.

2   Information specific to the cooling system hoses can be found in Section 10.

3   Most (but not all) hoses are secured to the fittings with clamps. Where clamps are used, check to be sure they haven't lost their tension, allowing the hose to leak. If clamps aren't used, make sure the hose has not expanded and/or hardened where it slips over the fitting, allowing it to leak.

PCV system hose

4   To reduce hydrocarbon emissions, crankcase blow-by gas is vented through the

PCV valve in the rocker arm cover to the intake manifold via a rubber hose on most models. The blow-by gases mix with incoming air in the intake manifold before being burned in the combustion chambers.

5   Check the PCV hose for cracks, leaks and other damage. Disconnect it from the valve cover and the intake manifold and check the inside for obstructions. If it's clogged, clean it out with solvent.

Vacuum hoses

6   It's quite common for vacuum hoses, especially those in the emissions system, to be color coded or identified by colored stripes molded into them. Various systems require hoses with different wall thickness, collapse resistance and temperature resistance. When replacing hoses, be sure the new ones are made of the same material.

7   Often the only effective way to check a hose is to remove it completely from the vehicle. If more than one hose is removed, be sure to label the hoses and fittings to ensure correct installation.

8   When checking vacuum hoses, be sure to include any plastic T-fittings in the check. Inspect the fittings for cracks and the hose where it fits over each fitting for distortion, which could cause leakage.

9   A small piece of vacuum hose (1/4-inch inside diameter) can be used as a stethoscope to detect vacuum leaks. Hold one end of the hose to your ear and probe around vacuum hoses and fittings, listening for the "hissing" sound characteristic of a vacuum leak. **Warning:** *When probing with the vacuum hose stethoscope, be careful not to come into contact with moving engine components such as drivebelts, the cooling fan, etc.*

Fuel hose

Warning: *Gasoline is flammable, so take extra precautions when you work on any part of the fuel system. Don't smoke or allow open flames or bare light bulbs near the work area, and don't work in a garage where a gas-type appliance (such as a water heater or clothes dryer) is present. Since fuel is carcinogenic, wear latex gloves when there's a possibility of being exposed to fuel, and, if you spill any fuel on your skin, rinse it off immediately with soap and water. Mop up any spills immediately and do not store fuel-soaked rags where they could ignite. The fuel system is under constant pressure, so, if any fuel lines are to be disconnected, the fuel pressure in the system must be relieved first (see Chapter 4 for more information). When you perform any kind of work on the fuel system, wear safety glasses and have a Class B type fire extinguisher on hand.*

10   The fuel lines are usually under pressure, so if any fuel lines are to be disconnected be prepared to catch spilled fuel. **Warning:** *Your vehicle is equipped with fuel injection and you must relieve the fuel system pressure before servicing the fuel lines. Refer*

to Chapter 4 for the fuel system pressure relief procedure.

11   Check all flexible fuel lines for deterioration and chafing. Check especially for cracks in areas where the hose bends and just before fittings, such as where a hose attaches to the fuel pump, fuel filter and fuel injection unit.

12   When replacing a hose, use only hose that is specifically designed for your fuel injection system.

13   Spring-type clamps are sometimes used on fuel return or vapor lines. These clamps often lose their tension over a period of time, and can be "sprung" during removal. Replace all spring-type clamps with screw clamps whenever a hose is replaced. Some fuel lines use spring-lock type couplings, which require a special tool to disconnect. See Chapter 4 for more information on this type of coupling.

Metal lines

14   Sections of metal line are often used for fuel line between the fuel pump and the fuel injection unit. Check carefully to make sure the line isn't bent, crimped or cracked.

15   If a section of metal fuel line must be replaced, use seamless steel tubing only, since copper and aluminum tubing do not have the strength necessary to withstand vibration caused by the engine.

16   Check the metal brake lines where they enter the master cylinder and brake proportioning unit (if used) for cracks in the lines and loose fittings. Any sign of brake fluid leakage calls for an immediate thorough inspection of the brake system.

---

13   Brake check (every 15,000 miles or 12 months)

Warning: *The dust created by the brake system is harmful to your health. Never blow it out with compressed air and don't inhale any of it. An approved filtering mask should be worn when working on the brakes. Do not, under any circumstances, use petroleum-based solvents to clean brake parts. Use brake system cleaner only! Try to use non-asbestos replacement parts whenever possible.*

Note: *For detailed photographs of the brake system, refer to Chapter 9.*

1   In addition to the specified intervals, the brakes should be inspected every time the wheels are removed or whenever a defect is suspected.

2   Any of the following symptoms could indicate a potential brake system defect: The vehicle pulls to one side when the brake pedal is depressed; the brakes make squealing or dragging noises when applied; brake pedal travel is excessive; the pedal pulsates; or brake fluid leaks, usually onto the inside of the tire or wheel.

3   Loosen the wheel lug nuts.

4   Raise the vehicle and place it securely on jackstands.

5   Remove the wheels (see *Jacking and towing* at the front of this book, or your owner's manual, if necessary).

Disc brakes

Refer to illustrations 13.7 and 13.11

6   There are two pads (an outer and an inner) in each caliper. The pads are visible with the wheels removed. The vehicles covered by this manual have disc brakes front and rear, with a mechanical, drum-type parking brake mechanism inside the rear discs.

7   Check the pad thickness by looking at each end of the caliper and through the inspection window in the caliper body **(see illustration)**. If the lining material is less than the thickness listed in this Chapter's Specifications, replace the pads. **Note:** *Keep in mind that the lining material is riveted or bonded to a metal backing plate and the metal portion is not included in this measurement.*

8   If it is difficult to determine the exact thickness of the remaining pad material by the above method, or if you are at all concerned about the condition of the pads, remove the caliper(s), then remove the pads from the calipers for further inspection (refer to Chapter 9).

9   Once the pads are removed from the calipers, clean them with brake cleaner and re-measure them with a ruler or a vernier caliper.

10   Measure the disc thickness with a micrometer to make sure that it still has service life remaining. If any disc is thinner than the specified minimum thickness, replace it (refer to Chapter 9). Even if the disc has service life remaining, check its condition. Look for scoring, gouging and burned spots. If these conditions exist, remove the disc and have it resurfaced (see Chapter 9).

11   Before installing the wheels, check all brake lines and hoses for damage, wear, deformation, cracks, corrosion, leakage, bends and twists, particularly in the vicinity of the rubber hoses at the calipers **(see illustra-**

13.7 You will find an inspection hole like this in each caliper through which you can view the thickness of remaining friction material for the inner pad

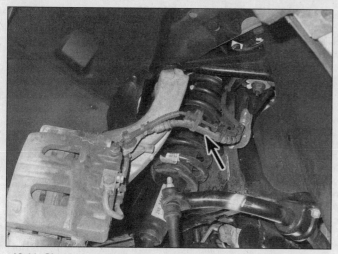

13.11 Check the fitting at the caliper, look along the brake hose for signs of cracking or fluid leakage, and check where the flexible hose meets the steel line on the chassis

14.10 To check a balljoint for wear, try to pry the control arm up and down to make sure there is no play in the balljoint (if there is, replace it)

tion). Check the clamps for tightness and the connections for leakage. Make sure that all hoses and lines are clear of sharp edges, moving parts and the exhaust system. If any of the above conditions are noted, repair, reroute or replace the lines and/or fittings as necessary (see Chapter 9).

Brake booster check

12   Sit in the driver's seat and perform the following sequence of tests.
13   With the brake fully depressed, start the engine - the pedal should move down a little when the engine starts.
14   With the engine running, depress the brake pedal several times - the travel distance should not change.
15   Depress the brake, stop the engine and hold the pedal in for about 30 seconds - the pedal should neither sink nor rise.
16   Restart the engine, run it for about a minute and turn it off. Then firmly depress the brake several times - the pedal travel should decrease with each application.
17   If your brakes do not operate as described, the brake booster has failed. Refer to Chapter 9 for the replacement procedure.

Parking brake

18   One method of checking the parking brake is to park the vehicle on a steep hill with the parking brake set and the transmission in Neutral (be sure to stay in the vehicle for this check). If the parking brake cannot prevent the vehicle from rolling, it's in need of attention (see Chapter 9).

---

14   Steering and suspension check (every 15,000 miles or 12 months)

Refer to illustrations 14.10 and 14.11
Note: *For detailed illustrations of the steering and suspension components, refer to Chapter 10.*

With the wheels on the ground

1   With the vehicle stopped and the front wheels pointed straight ahead, rock the steering wheel gently back and forth. If freeplay is excessive, a front wheel bearing, steering shaft universal joint or lower arm balljoint is worn or the steering gear is out of adjustment or broken. Refer to Chapter 10 for the appropriate repair procedure.
2   Other symptoms, such as excessive vehicle body movement over rough roads, swaying (leaning) around corners and binding as the steering wheel is turned, may indicate faulty steering and/or suspension components.
3   Check the shock absorbers by pushing down and releasing the vehicle several times at each corner. If the vehicle does not come back to a level position within one or two bounces, the shocks/struts are worn and must be replaced. When bouncing the vehicle up and down, listen for squeaks and noises from the suspension components.
4   Check the shock absorbers for evidence of fluid leakage. A light film of fluid is no cause for concern. Make sure that any fluid noted is from the shocks and not from some other source. If leakage is noted, replace the shocks as a set.
5   Check the shocks to be sure they are securely mounted and undamaged. Check the upper mounts for damage and wear. If damage or wear is noted, replace the shocks as a set (front and rear).
6   If the shocks must be replaced, refer to Chapter 10 for the procedure.

Under the vehicle

7   Raise the vehicle with a floor jack and support it securely on jackstands. See *Jacking and towing* at the front of this book for the proper jacking points.
8   Check the tires for irregular wear patterns and proper inflation. See Section 5 in this Chapter for information regarding tire wear and Chapter 10 for information on

14.11 Check the balljoint boot for damage also

wheel bearing replacement.
9   Inspect the universal joint between the steering shaft and the steering gear housing. Check the steering gear housing for lubricant leakage. Make sure that the dust seals and boots are not damaged and that the boot clamps are not loose. Check the steering linkage for looseness or damage. Check the tie-rod ends for excessive play. Look for loose bolts, broken or disconnected parts and deteriorated rubber bushings on all suspension and steering components. While an assistant turns the steering wheel from side to side, check the steering components for free movement, chafing and binding. If the steering components do not seem to be reacting with the movement of the steering wheel, try to determine where the slack is located.
10   Check the balljoints for wear by trying to move each control arm up and down with a pry bar **(see illustration)** to ensure that its balljoint has no play. If any balljoint does have play, replace it. See Chapter 10 for the balljoint replacement procedure.
11   Inspect the balljoint boots for damage and leaking grease **(see illustration)**.

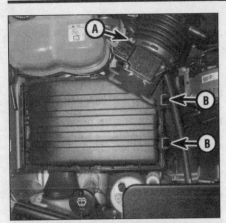

16.1a Loosen the intake hose clamp (A), then unlatch these clips (B) . . .

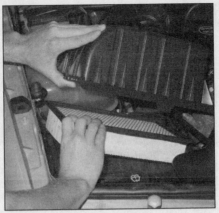

16.1b . . . pull the cover out of the way and lift the element out

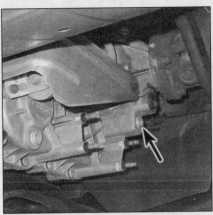

18.2 Remove the transfer case check/fill plug

Replace the balljoints with new ones if they are damaged (see Chapter 10).

12   At the rear of the vehicle, inspect the suspension arm bushings for deterioration. Additional information on suspension components can be found in Chapter 10.

15 Fuel system check (every 15,000 miles or 12 months)

Warning: *Gasoline is flammable, so take extra precautions when you work on any part of the fuel system. Don't smoke or allow open flames or bare light bulbs near the work area, and don't work in a garage where a gas-type appliance (such as a water heater or clothes dryer) is present. Since fuel is carcinogenic, wear latex gloves when there's a possibility of being exposed to fuel, and, if you spill any fuel on your skin, rinse it off immediately with soap and water. Mop up any spills immediately and do not store fuel-soaked rags where they could ignite. When you perform any kind of work on the fuel system, wear safety glasses and have a Class B type fire extinguisher on hand. The fuel system is under constant pressure, so, before any lines are disconnected, the fuel system pressure must be relieved (see Chapter 4).*

1   If you smell gasoline while driving or after the vehicle has been sitting in the sun, inspect the fuel system immediately.

2   Remove the fuel filler cap and inspect it for damage and corrosion. The gasket should have an unbroken sealing imprint. If the gasket is damaged or corroded, install a new cap.

3   Inspect the fuel feed line for cracks. Make sure that the connections between the fuel lines and the fuel injection system and between the fuel lines and the in-line fuel filter are tight. **Warning:** *Your vehicle is fuel injected, so you must relieve the fuel system pressure before servicing fuel system components. The fuel system pressure relief procedure is outlined in Chapter 4.*

4   Since some components of the fuel system - the fuel tank and part of the fuel feed line, for example - are underneath the vehicle, they can be inspected more easily with the

vehicle raised on a hoist. If that's not possible, raise the vehicle and support it on jackstands.

5   With the vehicle raised and safely supported, inspect the gas tank and filler neck for punctures, cracks and other damage. The connection between the filler neck and the tank is particularly critical. Sometimes a rubber filler neck will leak because of loose clamps or deteriorated rubber. Inspect all fuel tank mounting brackets and straps to be sure that the tank is securely attached to the vehicle. **Warning:** *Do not, under any circumstances, try to repair a fuel tank (except rubber components). A welding torch or any open flame can easily cause fuel vapors inside the tank to explode.*

6   Carefully check all rubber hoses and metal lines leading away from the fuel tank. Check for loose connections, deteriorated hoses, crimped lines and other damage. Repair or replace damaged sections as necessary (see Chapter 4).

16 Air filter check and replacement (every 15,000 miles or 12 months)

Refer to illustrations 16.1a and 16.1b

1   The air filter is located inside a housing at the right (passenger's) side of the engine compartment. To remove the air filter, loosen the clamp securing the inlet tube to the air filter cover, release the clamps that secure the two halves of the air cleaner housing together, then separate the cover halves and remove the air filter element **(see illustrations).**

2   Inspect the outer surface of the filter element. If it is dirty, replace it. If it is only moderately dusty, it can be reused by blowing it clean from the back to the front surface with compressed air. Because it is a pleated paper type filter, it cannot be washed or oiled. If it cannot be cleaned satisfactorily with compressed air, discard and replace it. While the cover is off, be careful not to drop anything down into the housing. **Caution:** *Never drive the vehicle with the air cleaner removed. Excessive engine wear could result*

and backfiring could even cause a fire under the hood.

3   Wipe out the inside of the air cleaner housing.

4   Place the new filter into the air cleaner housing, making sure it seats properly.

5   Installation of the housing is the reverse of removal.

17 Manual transmission lubricant level check (every 15,000 miles or 12 months)

1   The manual transmission does not have a dipstick. To check the fluid level, raise the vehicle and support it securely on jackstands. On the side of the transmission housing you will see a plug. Remove it. If the lubricant level is correct, it should be up to the lower edge of the hole.

2   If the transmission needs more lubricant (if the level is not up to the hole), use a syringe or a gear oil pump to add more. Stop filling the transmission when the lubricant begins to run out the hole.

3   Install the plug and tighten it securely. Drive the vehicle a short distance, then check for leaks.

18 Transfer case lubricant level check (every 15,000 miles or 12 months)

Refer to illustration 18.2

1   Raise the vehicle and support it securely on jackstands.

2   Using a ratchet or breaker bar, unscrew the check/fill plug from the transfer case **(see illustration).**

3   Use your little finger to reach inside the housing to feel the lubricant level. The level should be at or near the bottom of the plug hole. If it isn't, add the recommended lubricant through the plug hole with a syringe or squeeze bottle.

4   Install and tighten the plug. Check for leaks after the first few miles of driving.

19   Driveaxle boot check (every 15,000 miles or 12 months)

Refer to illustration 19.2
1   The driveaxle boots are very important because they prevent dirt, water and foreign material from entering and damaging the constant velocity (CV) joints. Oil and grease can cause the boot material to deteriorate prematurely, so it's a good idea to wash the boots with soap and water. Because it constantly pivots back and forth following the steering action of the front hub, the outer CV boot wears out sooner and should be inspected regularly.
2   Inspect the boots for tears and cracks as well as loose clamps **(see illustration)**. If there is any evidence of cracks or leaking lubricant, they must be replaced as described in Chapter 8.

20   Exhaust system check (every 30,000 miles or 24 months)

Refer to illustration 20.2
1   With the engine cold (at least three hours after the vehicle has been driven), check the complete exhaust system from the engine to the end of the tailpipe. Ideally, the inspection should be done with the vehicle on a hoist to permit unrestricted access. If a hoist isn't available, raise the vehicle and support it securely on jackstands.
2   Check the exhaust pipes and connections for evidence of leaks, severe corrosion and damage. Make sure that all brackets and hangers are in good condition and tight **(see illustration).**
3   At the same time, inspect the underside of the body for holes, corrosion, open seams, etc. which may allow exhaust gases to enter the passenger compartment. Seal all body openings with silicone or body putty.
4   Rattles and other noises can often be traced to the exhaust system, especially the mounts and hangers. Try to move the pipes, muffler and catalytic converter. If the compo-

19.2 Flex the driveaxle boots by hand to check for cracks and/or leaking grease

nents can come in contact with the body or suspension parts, secure the exhaust system with new mounts.
5   Check the running condition of the engine by inspecting inside the end of the tailpipe. The exhaust deposits here are an indication of engine state-of-tune. If the pipe is black and sooty or coated with white deposits, the engine may need a tune-up, including a thorough fuel system inspection and adjustment.

21   Fuel filter replacement (every 30,000 miles or 24 months)

Refer to illustration 21.3
Warning: *Gasoline is extremely flammable, so take extra precautions when you work on any part of the fuel system. Don't smoke or allow open flames or bare light bulbs near the work area, and don't work in a garage where a gas-type appliance (such as a water heater or clothes dryer) is present. Since fuel is carcinogenic, wear latex gloves when there's a possibility of being exposed to fuel, and, if you spill any fuel on your skin, rinse it off immediately with soap and water. Mop up any spills immediately and do not store fuel-*

soaked rags where they could ignite. When you perform any kind of work on the fuel system, wear safety glasses and have a Class B type fire extinguisher on hand.
1   The fuel filter is mounted under the vehicle on the right side, in front of the gas tank.
2   Relieve the fuel system pressure (see Chapter 4), then disconnect the cable from the negative terminal of the battery.
3   If necessary, raise the vehicle and support it securely on jackstands. Remove the filter heat and rock shield **(see illustration).**
4   Inspect the fittings at both ends of the filter to see if they're clean. If more than a light coating of dust is present, clean the fittings before proceeding.
5   Release the clips holding the fuel lines to the filter (see Chapter 4).
6   Detach the fuel hoses, one at a time, from the filter. Be prepared for fuel spillage.
7   After the lines are detached, check the fittings for damage and distortion. If they were damaged in any way during removal, new ones must be used when the lines are reattached to the new filter (if new clips are packaged with the filter, be sure to use them in place of the originals).
8   Remove the fuel filter from the mounting bracket, while noting the direction the fuel filter is installed.
9   Install the new filter in the same direction. Carefully push each hose onto the filter until it's seated against the collar on the fitting, then install the clips (see Chapter 4). Make sure the clips are securely attached to the hose fittings - if they come off, the hoses could back off the filter and a fire could result!
10   Start the engine and check for fuel leaks.

22   Cooling system servicing (draining, flushing and refilling) (every 30,000 miles or 24 months)

Refer to illustrations 22.4
Warning: *Do not allow antifreeze to come in contact with your skin or painted surfaces of the vehicle. Rinse off spills immediately with*

20.2 Be sure to check each exhaust system rubber hanger for damage

21.3 Remove the bolts securing the heat shield

22.4 The radiator drain fitting is located at the bottom of the radiator - before opening the valve, push a short length of rubber hose onto the plastic fitting to prevent the coolant from splashing

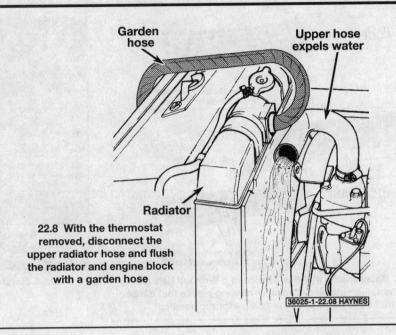

22.8 With the thermostat removed, disconnect the upper radiator hose and flush the radiator and engine block with a garden hose

plenty of water. Antifreeze is highly toxic if ingested. Never leave antifreeze lying around in an open container or in puddles on the floor; children and pets are attracted by its sweet smell and may drink it. Check with local authorities about disposing of used antifreeze. Many communities have collection centers which will see that antifreeze is disposed of safely. Never dump used antifreeze on the ground or pour it into drains.

Caution: *Do not mix coolants of different colors. Doing so might damage the cooling system and/or the engine. The manufacturer specifies either a green colored coolant or a yellow colored coolant to be used in these systems. Read the warning label in the engine compartment for additional information.*

Note: *Non-toxic antifreeze is now manufactured and available at local auto parts stores, but even this type must be disposed of properly.*

1   Periodically, the cooling system should be drained, flushed and refilled to replenish the antifreeze mixture and prevent formation of rust and corrosion, which can impair the performance of the cooling system and cause engine damage. When the cooling system is serviced, all hoses and the expansion tank cap should be checked and replaced if necessary.

Draining

2   Apply the parking brake and block the wheels. If the vehicle has just been driven, wait several hours to allow the engine to cool down before beginning this procedure.

3   Once the engine is completely cool, remove the expansion tank cap.

4   Move a large container under the radiator drain to catch the coolant. Attach a length of hose to the drain fitting to direct the coolant into the container, then open the drain fitting (a pair of pliers may be required to turn it) **(see illustration)**.

5   While the coolant is draining, check the condition of the radiator hoses, heater hoses and clamps (refer to Section 9 if necessary). Replace any damaged clamps or hoses.

Flushing

6   Once the system has completely drained, remove the thermostat housing from the engine (see Chapter 3), then reinstall the housing without the thermostat. This will allow the system to be thoroughly flushed.

7   Disconnect the upper hose from the radiator.

8   Place a garden hose in the upper radiator inlet and flush the system until the water runs clear at the upper radiator hose **(see illustration)**.

9   Severe cases of radiator contamination or clogging will require removing the radiator (see Chapter 3) and reverse flushing it. This involves inserting the hose in the bottom radiator outlet to allow the clean water to run against the normal flow, draining out through the top. A radiator repair shop should be consulted if further cleaning or repair is necessary.

10   When the coolant is regularly drained and the system refilled with the correct coolant mixture there should be no need to employ chemical cleaners or descalers.

Refilling

11   Close and tighten the radiator drain.

12   Place the heater temperature control in the maximum heat position.

13   Slowly add new coolant (a 50/50 mixture of water and antifreeze) to the expansion tank until the level is at the COLD FILL RANGE mark on the expansion tank.

14   Leave the expansion tank cap off and run the engine in a well-ventilated area until the thermostat opens (coolant will begin flowing through the radiator and the upper radiator hose will become hot).

15   Turn the engine off and let it cool. Add more coolant mixture to bring the coolant level between the COLD FILL RANGE mark on the expansion tank.

16   Squeeze the upper radiator hose to expel air, then add more coolant mixture if necessary. Replace the expansion tank cap.

17   Start the engine, allow it to reach normal operating temperature and check for leaks. Also, set the heater and blower controls to the maximum setting and check to see that the heater output from the air ducts is warm. This is a good indication that all air has been purged from the cooling system.

23 Brake fluid change (every 30,000 miles or 24 months)

Warning: *Brake fluid can harm your eyes and damage painted surfaces, so use extreme caution when handling or pouring it. Do not use brake fluid that has been standing open or is more than one year old. Brake fluid absorbs moisture from the air. Excess moisture can cause a dangerous loss of braking effectiveness.*

1   At the specified intervals, the brake fluid should be drained and replaced. Since the brake fluid may drip or splash when pouring it, place plenty of rags around the master cylinder to protect any surrounding painted surfaces.

2   Before beginning work, purchase the specified brake fluid (see *Recommended lubricants and fluids* at the beginning of this Chapter).

3   Remove the cap from the master cylinder reservoir.

4   Using a hand suction pump or similar device, withdraw the fluid from the master cylinder reservoir.

5   Add new fluid to the master cylinder until it rises to the base of the filler neck.

6   Bleed the brake system as described in Chapter 9 at all four brakes until new and uncontaminated fluid is expelled from the bleeder screw. Be sure to maintain the fluid level in the master cylinder as you perform the bleeding process. If you allow the master

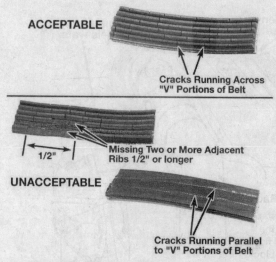

ACCEPTABLE

Cracks Running Across
"V" Portions of Belt

1/2"   Missing Two or More Adjacent
Ribs 1/2" or longer

UNACCEPTABLE

Cracks Running Parallel
to "V" Portions of Belt

24.4 Small cracks in the underside of a V-ribbed belt are acceptable - lengthwise cracks, or missing pieces that cause the belt to make noise, are cause for replacement

24.6 Rotate the tensioner arm to relieve belt tension

cylinder to run dry, air will enter the system.
7   Refill the master cylinder with fluid and check the operation of the brakes. The pedal should feel solid when depressed, with no sponginess. **Warning:** *Do not operate the vehicle if you are in doubt about the effectiveness of the brake system.*

24   Drivebelt check and replacement (every 30,000 miles or 24 months)

Refer to illustrations 24.4, 24.6 and 24.8
1   A single serpentine drivebelt is located at the front of the engine and plays an important role in the overall operation of the engine and its components. Due to its function and material make up, the belt is prone to wear and should be periodically inspected. Although the belt should be inspected at the recommended intervals, replacement may not be necessary for more than 100,000 miles.
2   The vehicles covered by this manual are equipped with a single self-adjusting serpentine drivebelt, which is used to drive all of the accessory components such as the alternator, power steering pump, water pump and air conditioning compressor.

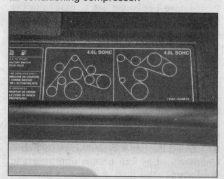

24.8 The routing schematic for the serpentine belt is usually found on the fan shroud

Check

3   With the engine off, open the hood and locate the drivebelt at the front of the engine. Using your fingers (and a flashlight, if necessary), move along the belts checking for cracks and separation of the belt plies. Also check for fraying and glazing, which gives the belt a shiny appearance. Both sides of each belt should be inspected, which means you will have to twist the belt to check the underside.
4   Check the ribs on the underside of the belt. They should all be the same depth, with none of the surface uneven **(see illustration)**.
5   The tension of the belt is automatically adjusted by the belt tensioner and does not require any adjustments. Drivebelt wear can be checked visually by inspecting the wear indicator marks located on the side of the tensioner body. Locate the belt tensioner at the front of the engine on the right (passenger) side, adjacent to the lower crankshaft pulley, then find the tensioner operating marks. If the indicator mark is outside the operating range, the belt should be replaced.

Replacement

6   To replace the belt, rotate the tensioner to relieve the tension on the belt **(see illustration)**. There is a square hole in the tensioner arm that will accept a 3/8-inch drive breaker bar.
7   Remove the belt from the auxiliary components and carefully release the tensioner.
8   Route the new belt over the various pulleys, again rotating the tensioner to allow the belt to be installed, then release the belt tensioner. Make sure the belt fits properly into the pulley grooves - it must be completely en-gaged. **Note:** *Most models have a drivebelt routing decal on the upper radiator panel to help during drivebelt installation* **(see illustration)**.

Tensioner replacement

9   Remove the drivebelt as described previously.
10   On V6 models, remove the bolt in the center of the tensioner, then detach the tensioner from the engine.
11   On V8 models, remove the three bolts securing the tensioner to the engine block.
12   Installation is the reverse of removal. Be sure to tighten the tensioners bolt(s) to the torque listed in this Chapter's Specifications.

25   Manual transmission lubricant change (every 60,000 miles or 48 months)

1   Raise the vehicle and support it securely on jackstands.
2   Move a drain pan, rags, newspapers and wrenches under the transmission.
3   Remove the transmission fill plug on the side of the case and the drain plug at the bottom of the case, then allow the lubricant to drain into the pan.
4   After the lubricant has drained completely, reinstall the drain plug and tighten it securely.
5   Using a hand pump, syringe or funnel, fill the transmission with the specified lubricant until it is level with the lower edge of the filler hole. Reinstall the fill plug and tighten it securely.
6   Lower the vehicle.
7   Drive the vehicle for a short distance, then check the drain and fill plugs for leakage.

26   Differential lubricant check (every 15,000 miles or 12 months) and change (every 60,000 miles or 48 months)

Note: *The differential lubricant level and quality should not deteriorate under normal driv-*

26.1 Differential check/fill plug (rear differential shown)

26.8 Remove the differential drain plug

1

ing conditions. However, it's recommended that you check the level occasionally. The most convenient time would be when the vehicle is raised for another reason, such as an engine oil change.

Level check

Refer to illustration 26.1

1   The differential has a check/fill plug which must be removed to check the lubricant level **(see illustration)**. If the vehicle is raised to gain access to the plug, be sure to support it safely on jackstands - DO NOT crawl under a vehicle which is supported only by a jack!

2   Remove the lubricant check/fill plug from the differential.

3   Use your little finger as a dipstick to make sure the lubricant level is even with the bottom of the plug hole. If the level is low, use a hand pump or large syringe to add the specified lubricant until it is level with the hole.

4   Install the plug and tighten it securely.

Lubricant change

5   This procedure should be performed after the vehicle has been driven so the lubricant will be warm and therefore flow out of the differential more easily.

6   Raise the vehicle and support it securely on jackstands.

Rear

Refer to illustration 26.8

7   Remove the lubricant check/fill plug from the differential.

8   Remove the differential drain plug and allow the differential lubricant to drain completely. After the lubricant has drained, install the plug and tighten it securely **(see illustration)**.

9   Use a hand pump, syringe or funnel to fill the differential housing with the specified lubricant until it's level with the bottom of the filler plug hole.

10   Install the plug and tighten it securely.

Front (4WD)

11   The easiest way to drain the differential is to remove the lubricant through the filler plug hole with a suction pump. If the differential cover gasket is leaking, it will be necessary to remove the cover to drain the lubricant (which will also allow you to inspect the differential).

Changing the lubricant with a suction pump

12   Remove the filler plug from the differential.

13   Insert the flexible hose.

14   Work the hose down to the bottom of the differential housing and pump the lubricant out.

15   Use a hand pump, syringe or funnel to fill the differential housing with the specified lubricant until it's level with the bottom of the filler plug hole.

16   Install the fill plug and tighten it securely.

Changing the lubricant by removing the cover

17   Move a drain pan, rags, newspapers and wrenches under the vehicle.

18   Remove the bolts on the lower half of the cover. Loosen the bolts on the upper half and use them to loosely retain the cover. Allow the oil to drain into the pan, then completely remove the cover.

19   Using a lint-free rag, clean the inside of the cover and the accessible areas of the differential housing. As this is done, check for chipped gears and metal particles in the lubricant, indicating that the differential should be more thoroughly inspected and/or repaired.

20   Thoroughly clean the gasket mating surfaces of the differential housing and the cover plate. Use a gasket scraper or putty knife to remove all traces of the old gasket.

21   Apply a thin bead of RTV sealant to the cover flange. Make sure the bolt holes align properly then install the cover and tighten the fasteners to the torque listed in this Chapter's Specifications. Let the RTV sealant "set up" (harden slightly) but do not wait over 15 minutes or the procedure will have to be repeated.

22   Use a hand pump, syringe or funnel to fill the differential housing with the specified lubricant until it's level with the bottom of the filler plug hole.

23   Install the fill plug and tighten it securely.

27   Automatic transmission fluid check (every 60,000 miles or 48 months)

Warning: *This procedure is potentially dangerous and is best left to a professional shop with a safe lifting apparatus. The vehicle must be kept level while being safely raised high enough for access to the check/fill plug on the transmission.*
Note 1: *When the work is done at a dealership, the factory scan tool is used to read the transmission fluid temperature. To perform the job at home, you will need a special tool to measure the temperature of the oil pan/transmission fluid using infra-red technology or temperature probes with digital readout displays.*
Note 2: *The engine must be running when checking the fluid level and when adding fluid.*

Checking the fluid level

Refer to illustration 27.3a and 27.3b

1   Correct automatic transmission fluid level is extremely important for proper transmission operation. Low fluid level can lead to slipping or loss of drive, while overfilling can cause foaming and loss of fluid. **Note:** *Checking the fluid on these vehicles isn't easy. The transmission is considered by the manufacturer to be a "sealed" unit, to which fluid doesn't need to be added unless a leak is evident. There is no conventional dipstick in the engine compartment, but rather a level-inspection plug accessible only from below the transaxle. Make sure you have a new seal for the plug before you begin. If fluid does have to be added, a special pump will be required.*

2   Transmission fluid expands as it warms up, and the fluid check should only be performed at the specified temperature range of

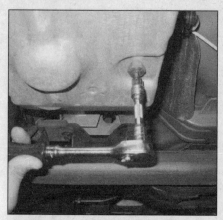

27.3a Use a special tool to remove the check/fill plug - Caution: *Do not remove the drain plug (large plug) to check the fluid level*

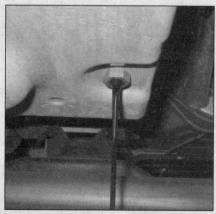

27.3b If fluid drips down in large amounts, the transmission is overfilled

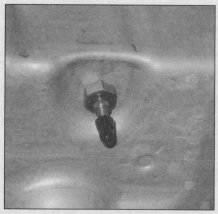

27.4a Install the fitting into the threads occupied by the check/fill plug

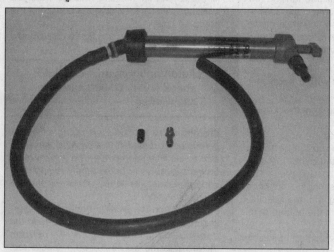

27.4b You will need a special hand pump and fitting to check the level of the transmission fluid

27.5a Carefully pump the transmission fluid into the oil pan

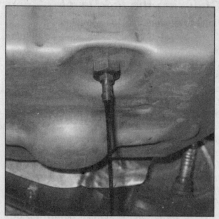

27.5b Remove the pump and observe the fluid drip from the check/fill plug - wait for the excess fluid to drip out then install the plug

80 to 120-degrees F (27 to 49-degrees C). **Note:** *The manufacturer states that a scan tool must be used to monitor the temperature of the transmission fluid. While this is certainly* the best way, you can get a fairly accurate reading after driving the vehicle a short distance (starting with the drivetrain cold) - approximately one trip around the block or so. The transmission pan should feel warm to the touch, but not hot enough to cause pain.

3   Raise the vehicle; if you don't have access to a vehicle hoist, support the vehicle securely on four jackstands (the fluid level must be checked with the vehicle level). Start the engine, then move the shift lever through all the gear ranges, ending in Park. When the transmission temperature reaches 80 to 120-degrees F (27 to 49-degrees C), remove the check/fill plug **(see illustrations)**. If fluid just comes out of the hole as drips, the fluid level is OK. If more fluid comes out, the transmission may have been overfilled. If no fluid comes out, fluid will have to be added.

Adding fluid

Refer to illustrations 27.4a, 27.4b, 27.5a and 27.5b

4   On these transmissions, the fluid is added through the check/fill plug. Two special tools are available for this purpose; a fit-

ting and a pressure pump **(see illustration)**. A hand pump equipped with a rubber hose can be used to pump the fluid up into the pan. The pump and rubber hose is attached to the fitting and fluid is pumped up into the transmission pan **(see illustration)**.

5   Slowly add fluid **(see illustration)**. Periodically check the level by removing the pump and rubber hose from the fitting and observing for any excess fluid dripping down **(see illustration)**. Until transmission fluid begins to drip from the check/fill plug, the transmission fluid level continues to be low. Once fluid flows, then the transmission fluid level has reached the top of the measured tube positioned inside the oil pan. Wait until the excess fluid has dripped out of the pan. Install a new seal on the check/fill plug. Install the check/fill plug and tighten it to the torque listed in this Chapter's Specifications.

Checking fluid condition

6   The condition of the fluid should also be checked along with the level. If the fluid is a dark reddish-brown color, or if it smells burned, it should be changed. If you are in

28.1a On V6 models, the PCV valve is located on the backside of the left valve cover, below the upper intake manifold, to remove the valve turn the PCV valve counterclockwise (the valve isn't visible here, but the arrow points to its general vicinity)

28.1b V8 models have a PCV valve located in the side of the left valve cover

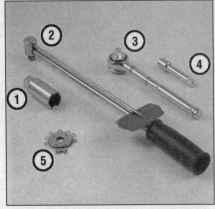

29.2 Tools required for changing spark plugs

doubt about the condition of the fluid, purchase some new fluid and compare the two for color and smell.

28   Positive Crankcase Ventilation (PCV) valve check and replacement (every 60,000 miles or 48 months)

Refer to illustrations 28.1a and 28.1b

1   On V6 models, the PCV valve is located on the back side of the left valve cover **(see illustration)**. On V8 models, the PCV valve is located on the top of the left valve cover **(see illustration)**.

2   Start the engine and allow it to idle, then disconnect the PCV valve from the valve cover and feel for vacuum at the end of the valve. If vacuum is felt, the PCV valve/system is working properly (see Chapter 6 for additional PCV system information).

3   If no vacuum is felt, remove the valve and

check for vacuum at the hose. If vacuum is present at the hose but not at the valve, replace the valve. If no vacuum is felt at the hose, check for a plugged or cracked hose between the PCV valve and the intake plenum.

4   Check the rubber grommet in the valve cover for cracks and distortion. If it's damaged, replace it.

5   If the valve is clogged, the hose might also be plugged. Remove the hose between the valve and the intake manifold and clean it with solvent.

6   After cleaning the hose, inspect it for damage, wear and deterioration. Make sure it fits snugly on the fittings.

7   If necessary, install a new PCV valve.

29   Spark plug check and replacement (see the *Maintenance schedule* for service intervals)

Refer to illustrations 29.2, 29.5a, 29.5b, 29.7a, 29.7b, 29.9, 29.11a and 29.11b

1   The spark plugs are located in the cylinder heads.

1   *Spark plug socket* - This will have special padding inside to protect the spark plug porcelain insulator

2   *Torque wrench* - Although not mandatory, use of this tool is the best way to ensure that the plugs are tightened properly

3   *Ratchet* - Standard hand tool to fit the plug socket

4   *Extension* - Depending on model and accessories, you may need special extensions and universal joints to reach one or more of the plugs

5   *Spark plug gap gauge* - This gauge for checking the gap comes in a variety of styles. Make sure the gap for your engine is included

2   In most cases, the tools necessary for spark plug replacement include a spark plug socket which fits onto a ratchet (spark plug sockets are padded inside to prevent damage to the porcelain insulators on the new plugs), various extensions and a gap gauge to check and adjust the gaps on the new plugs **(see illustration)**. A torque wrench should be used to tighten the new plugs.

3   The best approach when replacing the spark plugs is to purchase the new ones in advance, adjust them to the proper gap and replace the plugs one at a time. When buying the new spark plugs, be sure to obtain the correct plug type for your particular engine. This information can be found in the Specifications Section at the beginning of this Chapter or in your owner's manual.

4   Allow the engine to cool completely before attempting to remove any of the plugs. These engines are equipped with aluminum cylinder heads, which can be damaged if the spark plugs are removed when the engine is hot. While you are waiting for the engine to cool, check the new plugs for defects and adjust the gaps.

5   The gap is checked by inserting the proper-thickness gauge between the electrodes at the tip of the plug **(see illustration)**. The gap between the electrodes should be the same as the one specified on the *Vehicle Emissions Control Information* label or in this Chapter's Specifications. The gauge should

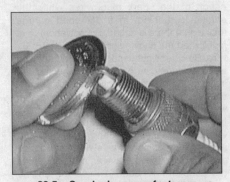

29.5a Spark plug manufacturers recommend using a tapered thickness gauge when checking the gap - slide the thin side into the gap and turn it until the gauge just fills the gap, then read the thickness on the gauge - do not force the tool into the gap or use the tapered portion to widen a gap

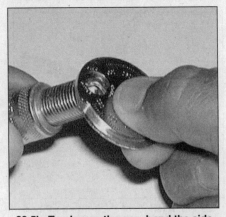

29.5b To change the gap, bend the side electrode only, using the adjuster hole in the tool, and be very careful not to crack or chip the porcelain insulator surrounding the center electrode

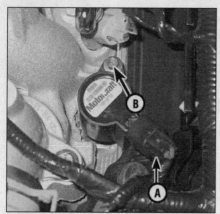

29.7a On V8 engines, the ignition coils must be removed to access the spark plugs - disconnect the electrical connector (A) and remove the coil retaining screw (B) - pull straight up and out to remove the coil

29.7b When removing the spark plug wires, pull only on the boot

29.9 Use a ratchet and extension to remove the spark plugs

just slide between the electrodes with a slight amount of drag. If the gap is incorrect, use the adjuster on the gauge body to bend the curved side electrode slightly until the proper gap is obtained **(see illustration)**. If the side electrode is not exactly over the center electrode, bend it with the adjuster until it is. Check for cracks in the porcelain insulator (if any are found, the plug should not be used). **Note:** *We recommend using a tapered thickness gauge when checking platinum- or iridium-type spark plugs. Other types of gauges may scrape the thin coating from the electrodes, thus dramatically shortening the life of the plugs. However, if dual-electrode spark plugs are used, a wire-type gauge will have to be used.*

6   On V8 engines, remove the engine cover.

7   V8 engines are equipped with individual ignition coils which must be removed first to access the spark plugs **(see illustration)**. On V6 engines, remove the spark plug wire from one spark plug. Pull only on the boot at the end of the wire - do not pull on the wire. A

plug wire removal tool should be used if available **(see illustration)**.

8   If compressed air is available, use it to blow any dirt or foreign material away from the spark plug hole. The idea here is to eliminate the possibility of debris falling into the cylinder as the spark plug is removed.

9   Place the spark plug socket over the plug and remove it from the engine by turning it in a counterclockwise direction **(see illustration)**.

10   Compare the spark plug to those shown in the photos located on the inside back cover to get an indication of the general running condition of the engine.

11   Apply a small amount of anti-seize compound to the spark plug threads **(see illustration)**. Install one of the new plugs into the hole until you can no longer turn it with your fingers, then tighten it with a torque wrench (if available) or the ratchet. It is a good idea to slip a short length of rubber hose over the end of the plug to use as a tool to thread it into place **(see illustration)**. The hose will grip the plug well enough to turn it, but will start to slip if the plug begins to cross-thread in the hole - this will prevent damaged threads and the accompanying repair costs.

12   On V8 engines, before pushing the igni-

tion coil onto the end of the plug, inspect the ignition coil following the procedures outlined in Section 30. On V6 engines, inspect the plug wire following the procedures outlined in Section 31.

13   Repeat the procedure for the remaining spark plugs.

30   Ignition coil check (V8 engines) (every 60,000 miles or 48 months)

1   Remove the ignition coils **(see illustration 29.7a)**. Clean the coil(s) with a dampened cloth and dry them thoroughly.

2   Inspect each coil, for cracks, damage and carbon tracking. If damage exists, replace the coil.

31   Spark plug wire check and replacement (V6 engines) (every 60,000 miles or 48 months)

1   The spark plug wires should be checked at the recommended intervals or whenever new spark plugs are installed.

2   Begin this procedure by making a visual check of the spark plug wires while the engine is running. In a darkened garage (make sure there is adequate ventilation) or at night, start the engine and observe each plug wire. Be careful not to come into contact with any moving engine parts. If possible, use an insulated or non-conductive object to wiggle each wire. If there is a break in the wire, you will see arcing or a small blue spark coming from the damaged area. Secondary ignition voltage increases with engine speed and sometimes a damaged wire will not produce an arc at idle speed. Have an assistant press the accelerator pedal to raise the engine speed to approximately 2000 rpm. Check the spark plug wires for arcing as stated previously. If arcing is noticed, replace all spark plug wires.

29.11a Apply a thin coat of anti-seize compound to the spark plug threads

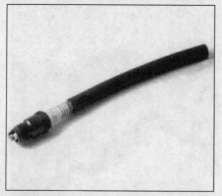

29.11b A length of snug-fitting rubber hose will save time and prevent damaged threads when installing the spark plugs

Chapter 2 Part A
V6 engine

Contents

2A

Specifications

General

Displacement	4.0 liters (244 cubic inches)
Bore and stroke	3.953 x 3.310 inches (100.4 x 80.4 mm)
Cylinder numbers (front-to-rear)	
Left (driver's) side	4-5-6
Right side	1-2-3
Firing order	1-4-2-5-3-6

Camshafts

Lobe lift (intake and exhaust)	0.259 inch (6.584 mm)
Allowable lobe lift loss	0.005 inch (0.127 mm)
Endplay	0.0003 to 0.007 inch (0.075 to 0.185 mm)
Journal diameter (all)	1.099 to 1.101 inches (27.935 to 27.960 mm)
Bearing inside diameter (all)	1.102 to 1.104 inches (28.00 to 28.03 mm)
Journal-to-bearing (oil) clearance	
Standard	0.002 to 0.004 inch (0.040 to 0.095 mm)
Service limit	0.006 inch (0.152 mm)

Cylinder locations and coil terminal identification

4.0L V6 Engine 1-4-2-5-3-6

Torque specifications

	Ft-lbs (unless otherwise indicated)	Nm
Accessory bracket bolts	31	42
Camshaft sprocket bolt*	63	85
Camshaft bearing cap bolts		
Step 1	53 in-lbs	6
Step 2	144 in-lbs	16
Crankshaft pulley bolt**		
Step 1	33	45
Step 2	Tighten an additional 85 degrees	

Torque specifications (continued)

	Ft-lbs (unless otherwise indicated)	Nm
Cylinder head bolts**		
8 mm bolts	24	32
12 mm bolts		
Step 1	25	35
Step 2	Tighten an additional 90 degrees	
Step 3	Tighten an additional 90 degrees	
Drivebelt tensioner bolt	35	47
Flywheel/driveplate bolts		
Step 1	120 in-lbs	13
Step 2	52	71
The right camshaft uses a left-hand threaded bolt		
** Bolt(s) must be replaced.*		
Exhaust manifold nuts	16	22
Exhaust pipe-to-manifold nuts	30	40
Engine front cover bolts	168 in-lbs	19
Intake manifold bolts	89 in-lbs	10
Jackshaft sprocket bolts		
Front		
Step 1	33	45
Step 2	Tighten an additional 90 degrees	
Rear		
Step 1	15	20
Step 2	Tighten an additional 90 degrees	
Jackshaft chain tensioner bolts	80 in-lbs	9
Jackshaft chain guide bolts	168 in-lbs	19
Jackshaft thrust plate bolts	96 in-lbs	11
Oil pump screen cover and tube bolt	89 in-lbs	10
Oil pump-to-block bolts	168 in-lbs	14
Oil pan (sheet metal)-to-crankcase reinforcement section bolts	80 in-lbs	9
Crankcase reinforcement section-to-block		
Perimeter bolts/nuts	89 in-lbs	10
Threaded inserts	27 in-lbs	3
Rear lower block cradle-to-transmission bolts	32	43
Rear lower block cradle-to-engine block (rear main oil seal)	71 in-lbs	8
Lower block cradle bolts		
Step 1	132 in-lbs	15
Step 2	25	34
Timing chain tensioner	32	44
Timing chain cassette bolts		
Right side		
Upper bolt	89 lbs	10
Left side		
Upper bolt	108 in-lbs	12
Lower bolt	168 in-lbs	19
Valve cover bolts	89 in-lbs	10

** Bolt(s) must be replaced.*

1   General information

This Part of Chapter 2 is devoted to in-vehicle repair procedures for the 4.0L SOHC (Singe Overhead Camshaft) V6 engine as well as procedures such as timing chain(s) and sprocket(s) and oil pan (crankcase reinforcement section) removal which require removal of the engine from the vehicle. All information concerning engine removal and installation and engine block and cylinder head overhaul can be found in Part C of this Chapter.

This engine uses a jackshaft, in place of a camshaft on a conventional pushrod engine, to drive the camshaft timing chains and the oil pump. The left cylinder bank camshaft is driven by a chain at the front of the engine and the right cylinder bank camshaft is driven by a chain from the rear of the jackshaft. On four-wheel drive models, the balance shaft assembly is driven by a chain from the crankshaft sprocket.

The Specifications included in this Part of Chapter 2 apply only to the procedures contained in this Part.

2   Repair operations possible with the engine in the vehicle

Many major repair operations can be accomplished without removing the engine from the vehicle.

Clean the engine compartment and the exterior of the engine with some type of degreaser before any work is done. It will make the job easier and help keep dirt out of the internal areas of the engine.

Depending on the components involved, it may be helpful to remove the hood to improve access to the engine as repairs are performed (refer to Chapter 11 if necessary). Cover the fenders to prevent damage to the paint. Special pads are available, but an old bedspread or blanket will also work.

If vacuum, exhaust, oil or coolant leaks develop, indicating a need for gasket or seal replacement, the repairs can generally be made with the engine in the vehicle. The intake and exhaust manifold gaskets and cylinder head gaskets are all accessible with the engine in place.

Exterior engine components, such as the intake and exhaust manifolds, the water pump, the starter motor, the alternator and the fuel system components can be removed for repair with the engine in place.

The cylinder head(s) and the timing chain(s) removal procedures should be performed with the engine removed from the vehicle and bolted to an engine stand. Camshaft removal is also recommended with the engine out. Although professional mechanics perform these procedures in-vehicle, they are equipped with all the special tools and dealer tech information to make this possible. It is recommended for the home mechanic to remove the engine before attempting these repair procedures.

3   Top Dead Center (TDC) for number one piston - locating

Refer to illustration 3.5
Note: *These engines are not equipped with a distributor. Piston position must be determined by feeling for compression at the number one spark plug hole, then aligning the ignition timing marks as described in Step 5.*

1   Top Dead Center (TDC) is the highest point in the cylinder that each piston reaches as it travels up-and-down during crankshaft rotation. Each piston reaches TDC on the compression stroke and again on the exhaust stroke, but TDC generally refers to piston position on the compression stroke.
2   Positioning the piston(s) at TDC is an essential part of many other repair procedures discussed in this manual.
3   Before beginning this procedure, be sure to place the transmission in Neutral and apply the parking brake or block the rear wheels. Remove the spark plugs (see Chapter 1). Disable the ignition system by disconnecting the wiring harness connector from the ignition coil pack (V6 models) or from each coil-on-plug assembly (V8 models) (see Chapter 5).
4   In order to bring any piston to TDC, the crankshaft must be turned using one of the methods outlined below. When looking at the front of the engine, normal crankshaft rotation is clockwise.

a) The preferred method is to turn the crankshaft with a socket and ratchet attached to the bolt threaded into the front of the crankshaft.
b) A remote starter switch, which may save some time, can also be used. Follow the instructions included with the switch. Once the piston is close to TDC, use a socket and ratchet as described in the previous paragraph.
c) If an assistant is available to turn the ignition switch to the Start position in short bursts, you can get the piston close to TDC without a remote starter switch. Make sure your assistant is out of the vehicle, away from the ignition switch, then use a socket and ratchet as described in Paragraph a) to complete the procedure.

5   Turn the crankshaft (see Paragraph 4 above) until you feel compression at the number one spark plug hole, then turn it slowly until the TDC notch is aligned with the pointer on the crankshaft position sensor **(see illustration)**. **Note:** *There are marks for TDC and for 10-degrees BTDC. Make sure you are on the TDC mark.*
6   After the number one piston has been positioned at TDC on the compression stroke, TDC for any of the remaining pistons can be located by turning the crankshaft and following the firing order. On V6 engines, divide the crankshaft pulley into three equal sections with chalk marks at each point, each indicating 120-degrees of crankshaft rotation. On V8 engines divide the crankshaft pulley into fourths, with the marks 90-degrees apart. Rotating the engine clockwise to the next mark will bring the next piston in the firing order sequence to TDC.

4   Valve covers - removal and installation

Removal

1   Disconnect the cable from the negative battery terminal (see Chapter 5).

3.5 Timing marks - align the pointer on the crankshaft position sensor (A) with the mark in the crankshaft pulley (B)

2   Remove the upper intake manifold (see Section 6). **Warning:** *On all models, relieve the fuel system pressure as described in Chapter 4 before disconnecting any fuel lines.*

Right valve cover
Refer to illustrations 4.3 and 4.10
3   Drain the cooling system (see Chapter 1), then disconnect the coolant hose brackets from the cylinder head and position the coolant hoses away from the valve cover **(see illustration)**.
4   Disconnect the ignition wires from the valve cover (see Chapter 5).
5   Disconnect the DPF EGR electrical connector (see Chapter 6).
6   Remove the EGR pipe from the EGR valve and the exhaust manifold (see Chapter 6).
7   Disconnect the fuel line spring coupling (see Chapter 4).
8   Remove the fuel line bracket bolt and separate the fuel supply line from the fuel rail (see Chapter 4).
9   Disconnect the fuel injector connectors (see Chapter 4).
10   Remove the valve cover bolts **(see illustration)**. Lift the valve cover off. Tap gently with a soft-face hammer if necessary to break the gasket seal.

4.3 On the right side of the engine compartment, disconnect the coolant hose brackets from the cylinder head

4.10 Location of the right valve cover mounting bolts

2A

4.17 Location of the left valve cover mounting bolts

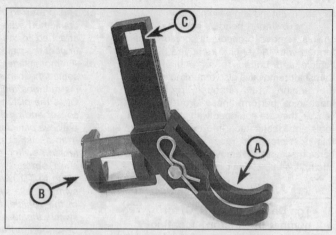

5.2a The special valve spring compressor hooks under the camshaft at (A), pushes on the valve spring retainer at (B), and is operated by a ratchet or breaker bar placed at (C)

Left valve cover

Refer to illustration 4.17

11   Disconnect the electrical connector at the camshaft position sensor (see Chapter 6).

12   Disconnect the electrical connector from the ignition coil pack (See Chapter 5).

13   Remove the cover from the main electrical connector at the valve cover, then push in the clip to detach the other side of the connector from the valve cover.

14   Disconnect the fuel injector electrical connectors (see Chapter 4).

15   Disconnect the accelerator cable (see Chapter 4).

16   Disconnect the ignition wires from the valve cover (see Chapter 5).

17   Remove the valve cover bolts **(see illustration)** and lift the valve cover off. Tap it gently with a soft-face hammer if necessary to break the gasket seal.

Installation

18   Clean the gasket surfaces on the intake manifold, cylinder head and valve cover. Use a shop rag, lacquer thinner or acetone to wipe of all residue and gasket material from the sealing surfaces.

19   Most valve cover gaskets are equipped with self-sticking sealant on the valve cover side. Pull the plastic film off the gasket and stick the gasket to the valve cover.

20   The remainder of installation is the reverse of the removal Steps. Tighten the valve cover bolts evenly, starting with the center bolts and working out, to the torque listed in this Chapter's Specifications.

5   Rocker arms and lash adjusters-removal, inspection and installation

Note: There are two methods of removing the rocker arms and lash adjusters on this model engine. The method recommended by the manufacturer accomplishes the removal of the rocker arms without the removal of the camshaft(s), using a special valve spring compressor made specifically for the SOHC engine. The valve spring compressor uses the camshaft as a pivot point and, with a ratchet or breaker bar attached, pushes down on the valve spring to release tension on the rocker arm. The alternative method requires the removal of the camshaft (see Section 12). Either method will achieve the same results, but it is much easier using the manufacturers special tool, if it can be located.

Removal

Refer to illustrations 5.2a, 5.2b and 5.3

1   Remove the valve cover(s) (see Section 4).

2   Install the special valve spring compressor and compress the spring just enough to remove the rocker arm **(see illustrations)**. **Caution:** *Camshaft rocker arms and hydraulic lash adjusters MUST be reinstalled in the same location they were removed from. Label and store all components to avoid confusion during reassembly.*

3   Remove the hydraulic lash adjuster **(see illustration)**. If there are many miles on the vehicle, the adjusters may have become varnished and difficult to remove. Apply a little penetrating oil around the lash adjuster to help loosen the varnish.

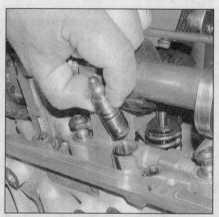

5.3 Remove the lash adjuster and store it and the rocker arm in organized manner so the components will be returned to their original locations

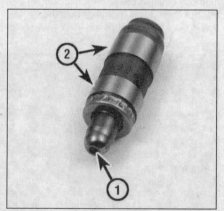

5.4 Inspect the lash adjuster for signs of excessive wear or damage, such as pitting, scoring or signs of overheating (bluing or discoloration) - the areas of wear are the rocker arm pivot point (1) and the side surfaces where the lifter body contacts the cylinder head bore (2)

5.2b Compress the valve spring just enough to allow the rocker arm to be removed

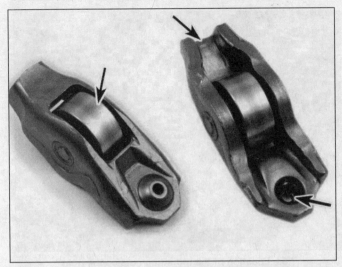

5.6 Check the rocker arm roller, the valve stem contact point and lash adjuster contact point (arrows)

6.4 Disconnect the vacuum hoses from the intake manifold

Inspection

Refer to illustrations 5.4 and 5.6

4   Inspect each adjuster carefully for signs of wear or damage **(see illustration)**. Since the lash adjusters can become clogged as mileage accumulates, we recommend replacing them if you're concerned about their condition or if the engine is exhibiting valve noise.

5   A thin wire or paper clip can be placed in the oil hole to move the plunger and make sure it's not stuck. **Note:** *The lash adjuster must have no more than 1.5 mm of total plunger travel.* It's recommended that if replacement of any of the adjusters is necessary, that the entire set be replaced. This will avoid the need to repeat the repair procedure as the others require replacement in the future.

6   Inspect the rocker arms for signs of wear or damage **(see illustration)**.

Installation

7   Before installing the lash adjusters, bleed them of air. Stand the adjusters upright in a container of oil. Use a thin wire or paper clip to work the plunger up and down. This "primes" the adjuster and removes the air. Leave the adjusters in the oil until ready to install.

8   Lubricate the valve stem tip, rocker arm, and lash adjuster bore with clean engine oil.

9   Install the lash adjusters and, with the valve spring depressed as in Step 2, install each rocker arm.

10   The remainder of installation is the reverse of the removal procedure.

11   When starting the engine after replacing the adjusters, there will normally be some noise until all the air is bled from the lash adjusters. After the engine is warmed-up, raise the speed from idle to 3,000 rpm for one minute. Stop the engine and let it cool down. All of the noise should be gone when it is restarted.

6   Intake manifold - removal and installation

Removal

Refer to illustrations 6.4 and 6.9

1   Disconnect the cable from the negative battery terminal (see Chapter 5).

2   Remove the intake air duct from the air filter housing (see Chapter 4).

3   Disconnect the accelerator cable and the cruise control cable from the throttle valve (see Chapter 4). Remove the harness clips and position the cables off to the side.

4   Disconnect the vacuum hoses from the upper intake manifold **(see illustration)**. Mark each hose with tape to insure correct reassembly.

5   Disconnect the IAC valve, the TPS and any other electrical connectors that may interfere with manifold removal.

6   Disconnect the EGR valve vacuum hose and the EVAP canister purge solenoid vac-

uum hose (see Chapter 6).

7   Disconnect the EGR pipe from the intake manifold and the exhaust manifold (see Chapter 6).

8   Remove the ignition wires from the coil pack and the spark plugs (see Chapter 5).

9   Remove the intake manifold mounting bolts **(see illustration)**.

10   Lift the intake manifold from the engine compartment.

Installation

Refer to illustration 6.12

11   Clean away all traces of old gasket material. Remove oil and dirt with a cloth and solvent, such as lacquer thinner.

12   Install new O-ring gaskets around each of the six intake runners **(see illustration)**. **Note:** *No sealant is required.*

13   Install the manifold to the cylinder heads, making sure the bolt holes are aligned. Install the bolts and tighten them finger-tight. **Note:** *Do not move the manifold*

6.9 Location of the intake manifold mounting bolts (two bolts hidden from view - 8 bolts total)

6.12 When replacing the intake manifold, install new O-ring gaskets around each runner

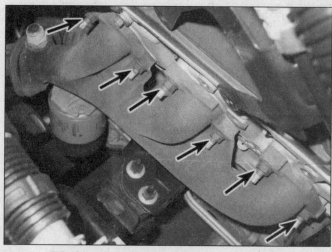

7.5a Location of the mounting nuts on the right side exhaust manifold

back and forth, or the O-ring seals could move out of position, causing vacuum leaks.

14   Tighten the bolts to the torque listed in this Chapter's Specifications, starting with the center bolts and working towards the ends.

15   The remainder of installation is the reverse of the removal steps.

16   Run the engine and check for oil, coolant and vacuum leaks.

tions). **Note:** *On the left side manifold, remove the nut holding the engine oil dipstick tube* (see illustration).

Installation

Refer to illustration 7.7

6   Using a scraper, thoroughly clean the mating surfaces on the cylinder head, manifold and exhaust pipe. Remove residue with a solvent such as acetone or lacquer thinner.

7   Check that the mating surfaces are perfectly flat and not damaged in any way. Warped or damaged manifolds may require machining. Install the new gasket to the cylinder head studs and place the manifold on the cylinder head (see illustration). Tighten the bolts evenly to the torque listed in this Chapter's Specifications.

8   Connect the exhaust pipe to the manifold and tighten the nuts evenly to the torque

7   Exhaust manifolds - removal and installation

Removal

Refer to illustrations 7.5a, 7.5b and 7.5c

1   Disconnect the cable from the negative battery terminal (see Chapter 5).

2   Disconnect the EGR pipe from the right manifold and the EGR valve (see Chapter 6).

3   Raise the vehicle and support it on jackstands.

4   Detach the exhaust pipe from the manifold(s).

5   Unbolt the exhaust manifold(s) from the cylinder head and take it off (see illustra-

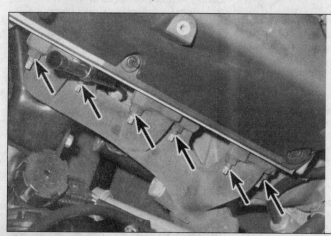

7.5b Location of the mounting nuts on the left side exhaust manifold

7.5c Remove the bolt and the engine oil dipstick tube

7.7 Place the new gasket over the studs on the cylinder head

listed in this Chapter's Specifications.

9   The remainder of installation is the reverse of the removal steps.

10   Run the engine and check for exhaust leaks.

8   Cylinder heads - removal and installation

Caution: *The engine must be completely cool when the heads are removed. Failure to allow the engine to cool off could result in head warpage.*

Note 1: *This is a difficult procedure and it is recommended the engine be removed from the vehicle and placed on an engine stand. It is possible to remove the cylinder heads in-vehicle but this method will require all the necessary special tools and an expert skill level in automotive repairs.*

Note 2: *The rocker arms and valve lash adjusters must be removed before any repair procedures on the cylinder heads, timing chains and jackshaft chains. Refer to Section 5 and remove all the rocker arms and valve lash adjusters.*

Removal

Refer to illustration 8.7

1   Disconnect the cable from the negative battery terminal (see Chapter 5).

2   Drain the cooling system (see Chapter 1).

3   Remove the engine from the vehicle and mount it on an engine stand (see Chapter 2C).

4   Remove the intake manifold (see Section 6).

5   Label and disconnect the electrical connectors from the fuel injectors (see Chapter 4).

6   Remove the exhaust manifolds (see Section 7).

7   Remove the drivebelt (see Chapter 1) and the drivebelt tensioner **(see illustration)**.

8   Remove the rocker arms and valve lash adjusters (see Section 5).

Right cylinder head

Refer to illustration 8.12

9   Remove the alternator and the lower alternator mounting bracket (see Chapter 5).

10   Remove the upper radiator hose and the coolant bypass hose (see Chapter 3).

11   Disconnect the engine coolant temperature (ECT) sensor (see Chapter 6).

12   Remove the accessory bracket **(see illustration)**.

13   Remove the thermostat housing (see Chapter 3).

14   Remove the bolts that retain the engine wiring harness to the engine brackets.

Left cylinder head

Refer to illustrations 8.17, 8.18, 8.19 and 8.20

15   Disconnect the radio capacitor from the side of the ignition coil pack.

16   Remove the ignition coil assembly (see

8.7 Remove the drivebelt tensioner mounting bolt

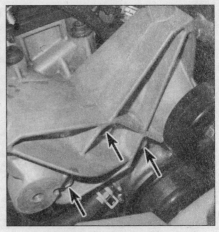

8.12 Remove the bolts from the accessory bracket and set it aside

Chapter 5).

17   Remove the accessory bracket mounting bolts and position it off to the side **(see illustration)**. **Note:** *The accessory bracket must be removed and positioned off to the side with the power steering pump lines and air conditioning compressor lines attached. It will be necessary to remove the coil bracket bolts and carefully move the entire accessory*

bracket assembly toward the front of the vehicle.

18   Remove the hydraulic chain tensioner **(see illustration)**.

19   Remove the bolt from the camshaft sprocket, then remove the Torx bolt below it in the head, which secures the camshaft chain "cassette" to the head **(see illustration)**.

8.17 Location of the accessory bracket mounting bolts

8.18 Remove the hydraulic chain tensioner - left side shown, right side is located at the rear of the cylinder head near the timing chain

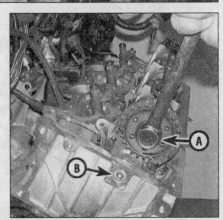

8.19 The chain will hold the camshaft and sprocket in position while you remove the sprocket bolt (A) - then remove the upper cassette bolt (B)

8.20 Slip a heavy-duty rubber band (A) over the chain, just below the sprocket, then remove the cassette bolt (B) - slip the sprocket out of the chain and the rubber band will prevent the slack from falling

20   Remove the bolt holding the chain cassette to the head and pull up on the chain while slipping the sprocket out. Keep the slack out of the chain (to prevent dropping it below) and tie it to the cassette with a large rubber band **(see illustration)**.

Both cylinder heads

21   Repeat Steps 17 through 20 for the right-hand cylinder head. If you are working in-vehicle, the sprocket is at the rear of the right cylinder head, and a special, offset tool is used to remove the sprocket bolt, but it is possible (though difficult) to remove it with a conventional wrench in-vehicle. Tie the chain for the rear sprocket up with a rubber band as in Step 20. **Caution:** *The sprocket bolt for the right cylinder head is a left-hand thread.*

22   Remove the cylinder head bolts, following the reverse of the tightening sequence **(see illustration 8.31)**. Loosen the bolts in sequence 1/4-turn at a time. **Note:** *There are two 8 mm external Torx bolts (one on each side of the chain opening in the head) and*

eight 12 mm internal Torx bolts. If the head is to be completely overhauled, refer to Section 11 for removal of the camshafts.

23   Use a pry bar at the corners of the head-to-block the mating surface to break the gasket seal. Do not pry between the cylinder head and engine block in the gasket sealing area.

24   Lift the cylinder head(s) off the engine. If resistance is felt, place a wood block against the end and strike the wood block with a hammer.

25   Store the cylinder heads on wood blocks to prevent damage to the gasket sealing surfaces.

26   Remove the old cylinder head gasket(s). Before removing, note which gasket goes on which side, they are different and cannot be interchanged.

Installation

Refer to illustrations 8.30, 8.31, 8.35, 8.36 and 8.38

27   The mating surfaces of the cylinder heads and block must be perfectly clean when the heads are installed. Use a gasket scraper to remove all traces of carbon and old gasket material, then clean the mating surfaces with lacquer thinner or acetone. If there's oil on the mating surfaces when the cylinder heads are installed, the gaskets may not seal correctly and leaks may develop. When working on the engine block, cover the open areas of the engine with shop rags to keep debris out during repair and reassembly. Use a vacuum cleaner to remove any debris that falls into the cylinders.

28   Check the engine block and cylinder head mating surfaces for nicks, deep scratches and other damage.

29   Use a tap of the correct size to chase the threads in the cylinder head bolt holes. Dirt, corrosion, sealant and damaged threads will affect torque readings.

30   Make sure the new gaskets are on the correct cylinder banks, and located on the dowels in the block. They are not interchangeable **(see illustration)**.

31   Carefully position the cylinder heads on the engine block without disturbing the gaskets. Install new cylinder head bolts and following the recommended sequence **(see illustration)**, tighten the bolts to the torque listed in this Chapter's Specifications. All bolts are tightened in the first Step, then only the eight 12 mm bolts are tightened in Steps 2 and 3. Mark a stripe on each of the 12 mm head bolts to help keep track of the bolts that have been tightened the additional 90-degrees. **Note:** *The method used for the head bolt tightening procedure is referred to as "torque-angle" or "torque-to-yield" method. A special torque angle gauge (available at most auto parts stores) is available to attach to a breaker bar and socket for better accuracy during the tightening procedure.*

32   Pull up the slack chain and insert the camshaft sprocket, align it with the camshaft and install the sprocket bolt. **Caution:** *Do not tighten the sprocket bolt at this time; the sprocket must rotate freely on the camshaft!* Do this on both cylinder heads and install the bolts that hold the chain cassettes to the heads.

33   Install the camshaft chain tensioning tool into the chain tensioner location on the left cylinder head.

34   Make sure the engine is located at the correct position for cylinder number 1 at TDC (see Section 3). Rotate the engine clockwise to obtain number 1 TDC if necessary.

35   Clamp the special crankshaft holding tool over the crankshaft damper (flush with the rear edge of the damper) and with the straight end against the bottom of the block **(see illustration)**. Tighten the bolt on the holding tool.

36   Install the camshaft holding tool on the rear of the left camshaft **(see illustration 8.38)**. Rotate the camshaft with a wrench to align the off-center slot on the rear of the camshaft with the tool. The slot is positioned down when aligned with the tool. Tighten the tool bolts securely. Install the camshaft sprocket holding tool on the left camshaft sprocket **(see illustration)**. Tighten the hold-

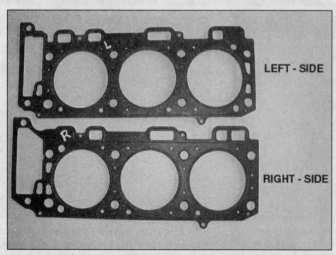

8.30 Make sure the cylinder head gaskets are installed in the correct location - they are not interchangeable

LEFT - SIDE

RIGHT - SIDE

8.31 Cylinder head bolt tightening sequence - bolts (A) are 8 mm bolts, the rest are 12 mm bolts

Chapter 2 Part A V6 engine

8.35 Clamp the special crankshaft holding tool around the damper as shown, then tighten the bolt - this locks the crankshaft at TDC

8.36 Install the camshaft sprocket holding tool to the cylinder head inserting the pins on the aligning tool (A) into the holes in the sprocket - tighten the holder bolts (B), then tighten the sprocket bolt (C)

8.38 Camshaft positioning tool at the front of the right camshaft - align the tool's projection with the slot in the end of the camshaft

2A

ing tool bolts to hold the camshaft sprocket stationary, then tighten the camshaft sprocket bolt to the torque listed in this Chapter's Specifications.

37 Remove the tensioning tool from the left cylinder head and install the hydraulic tensioner. Install the tensioning tool into the right cylinder head tensioner location. Remove the camshaft and camshaft sprocket holding tools and the crankshaft holding tool.

38 Install the camshaft holding tool onto the front of the right camshaft (see illustration). Rotate the camshaft to align the slots in the end of the camshaft with the tool. Tighten the holding tool bolts securely. Install the camshaft sprocket holding tool onto the rear of the camshaft and tighten the sprocket bolt to the torque listed in this Chapter's Specifications. **Caution:** *The right camshaft sprocket bolt is left-hand thread.*

39 Remove the chain tensioning tool and install the hydraulic tensioner. Remove the camshaft and crankshaft holding tools.

40 Install the rocker arms and hydraulic valve lash adjusters (see Section 5).

41 The remaining installation steps are the reverse of removal.

42 Change the engine oil and filter (Chapter 1), then start the engine and check carefully for oil and coolant leaks.

9 Crankshaft pulley and front oil seal - removal and installation

Removal

Refer to illustrations 9.7, 9.8 and 9.9

1 Disconnect the cable from the negative battery terminal (see Chapter 5).

2 Remove the drivebelt (see Chapter 1).

3 Remove the engine cooling fan/shroud assembly (see Chapter 3).

4 Raise the vehicle and secure it on jackstands.

5 Remove the power steering fluid cooler mounting bolts and position the assembly to the side without disconnecting the fluid lines.

6 Remove the crankshaft pulley bolt.

7 Use a breaker bar and socket to remove the crankshaft pulley center bolt (see illustration). Discard the bolt and obtain a new one for installation. **Note:** *It will be necessary to lock the pulley in position using a strap or chain wrench. Be sure to wrap a shop rag around the pulley before installing the special tool.*

8 Using a bolt-type puller, pull the pulley from the crankshaft (see illustration). **Note:** *Because the pulley is recessed, an adapter may be needed between the puller bolt and the crankshaft.*

9 Use a seal puller to remove the crankshaft front oil seal (see illustration). A screwdriver may be used instead, if the tip is wrapped with tape to avoid scratching the crankshaft.

10 Clean the seal bore and check it for nicks or gouges. Also examine the area of the hub that rides in the seal for signs of abnormal wear or scoring. For many popular engines, a repair sleeve is available to restore a smooth finish to the sealing surface. Check with your auto parts store.

9.7 To remove the crankshaft pulley, remove the center bolt

9.8 Remove the pulley with a puller that bolts to the pulley hub; an adapter may be needed between the puller bolt and the crankshaft snout to prevent damaging the threads in the end of the crankshaft

9.9 Use a seal puller to remove the old crankshaft seal, taking care not to damage the crankshaft or the seal bore in the cover

9.11 Drive the new seal in with a large socket or short section of appropriate-size pipe

10.4 Remove the engine front cover bolts - the water pump may remain attached to the cover, if desired

Installation

Refer to illustration 9.11

11   Coat the lip of the new seal with clean engine oil and drive it into the bore with a socket or section of pipe slightly smaller in diameter than the seal **(see illustration)**. The open side of the seal faces into the engine.

12   Using clean engine oil, lubricate the sealing surface of the hub. Install the crankshaft pulley/damper with a special installation tool, available at most auto parts stores. Do not use a hammer to install the pulley/damper. Install a new center bolt and tighten it to the torque listed in this Chapter's Specifications. **Note:** *You must use a **new** pulley bolt.*

13   The remainder of the installation is the reverse of the removal procedure.

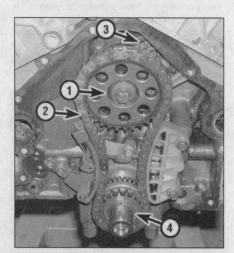

10.5 Timing chain components - 2WD model show (4WD models are equipped with a balance shaft chain attached to the crankshaft sprocket)

1   *Jackshaft sprocket*
2   *Jackshaft chain*
3   *Chain/cassette for left camshaft*
4   *Crankshaft sprocket*

10   Timing chain and sprockets - inspection, removal and installation

Note: *This is a difficult procedure, involving special tools and the removal of the engine from the vehicle. Read through the entire Section and obtain the necessary tools before beginning the procedure.*
Note: *The rocker arms and valve lash adjusters must be removed before any repair procedures on the cylinder heads, timing chains and jackshaft chains. Refer to Section 5 and remove all the rocker arms and valve lash adjusters.*

Removal

Refer to illustrations 10.4, 10.5, 10.6, 10.7, 10.8, 10.9, 10.10a and 10.10b

1   Refer to Chapter 2 Part C and remove the engine from the vehicle. The balance of this procedure is written assuming you have the engine out and mounted on an engine stand.

2   Remove the rocker arms and the valve lash adjusters (see Section 5).

3   Refer to Section 12 and remove the lower oil pan cover, oil pump pickup tube and the crankcase reinforcement section.

4   Remove the bolts/nuts and the front cover from the engine block **(see illustration)**.

5   This engine uses a jackshaft (in place of a camshaft on a conventional pushrod engine) to drive the camshaft timing chains and the oil pump **(see illustration)**. The left cylinder bank camshaft is driven by a chain at the front of the engine and the right cylinder bank camshaft is driven by a chain from the rear of the jackshaft. On four-wheel drive models, the balance shaft assembly is driven by a chain from the crankshaft sprocket.

6   Remove the bolts retaining the jackshaft chain tensioner and the jackshaft chain guide **(see illustration)**.

7   Remove the bolt in the center of the jackshaft sprocket, then remove the sprocket with the jackshaft chain **(see illustration)**.

8   If not previously removed, remove the top cassette bolt **(see illustration 8.19)**, the camshaft sprocket **(see Section 9)**, and remove the lower cassette-to-block bolt. Then remove the cassette, chain and jackshaft sprocket **(see illustration)**.

10.6 Remove the bolts retaining the jackshaft chain tensioner (A) and the chain guide (B)

10.7 Remove the jackshaft sprocket bolt, then remove the sprocket and chain

10.8 Remove the bolt and remove the left camshaft chain cassette and chain

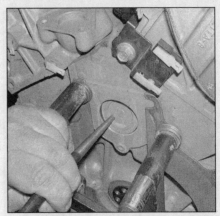

10.9 Remove the rear jackshaft plug by tapping it sideways, then use pliers to extract it

9   To remove the right camshaft chain, remove the large plug covering the rear of the jackshaft **(see illustration)**. Note: *Obtain a new plug for reassembly, the plug is not reusable.*
10   Remove the Torx bolt and spacer through the opening, then remove the cassette bolt and the chain and cassette **(see illustrations)**.

Installation

Refer to illustration 10.16

11   If the crankshaft has been rotated during this procedure, make sure the number one piston is at the top of its stroke (TDC) (see Section 3). The crankshaft keyway should point straight up.
12   Install the right camshaft timing chain cassette to the block. Secure the excess chain at the top of the cassette with a rubber band **(see illustration 8.20)**. Install the rear jackshaft sprocket bolt and tighten it to the torque listed in this Chapter's Specifications. Install the rear jackshaft plug.
13   Install the left camshaft chain and cassette and tighten the lower bolt to the torque listed in this Chapter's Specifications.
14   Drape the jackshaft chain over the jackshaft sprocket and engage the chain onto the crankshaft sprocket. Install the jackshaft

sprocket onto the jackshaft and tighten the jackshaft sprocket bolt to the torque listed in this Chapter's Specifications.
15   Install the jackshaft chain guide and tensioner **(see illustration 10.6)**. Tighten the bolts to the torque listed in this Chapter's Specifications.
16   Clean the front surface of the engine block and front cover with lacquer thinner and install a new gasket **(see illustration)**. Install the front cover, tightening the bolts to the torque listed in this Chapter's Specifications.
17   The remainder of installation is the reverse of the removal Steps. The timing procedure for each individual camshaft, using the special tools is described in Section 9.
18   Run the engine and check for oil or coolant leaks.

11 Camshafts - removal, inspection and installation

Removal

1   Remove the valve covers (see Section 4).
2   Follow the procedure in Section 5 for removing the rocker arms and valve lash

adjusters and see Section 8 for the procedure to disconnect the camshaft sprockets and timing chains from the camshafts.
3   Mount a dial indicator to the front of the cylinder head and measure the camshaft endplay of each camshaft. If the clearance is greater than the value listed in this Chapter's Specifications, replace the camshaft and/or the cylinder head.
4   Loosen the bearing cap bolts in 1/4-turn increments, following the reverse sequence of the tightening procedure **(see illustration 11.13)**, until they can be removed by hand.
5   Remove the bearing caps and lift the camshaft off the cylinder head. Don't mix up the camshafts or any of the components. They must all go back to their original locations, and on the same cylinder head they were removed from.
6   Repeat this procedure for removal of the other camshaft.

Inspection

Refer to illustrations 11.7a, 11.7b, 11.9a and 11.9b

7   Visually examine the cam lobes and bearing journals for score marks, pitting, galling and evidence of overheating (blue, discolored areas). Look for flaking of the

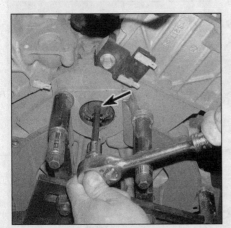

10.10a Remove this bolt and spacer ...

10.10b ... then remove this bolt and the chain and cassette

10.16 Install the new front cover gasket

11.7a Areas to look for excessive wear or damage on the camshafts are the bearing surfaces and camshaft lobes

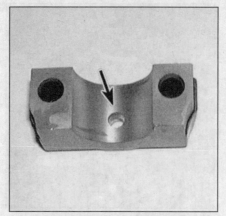

11.7b Also inspect the bearing surface of each camshaft cap

11.9a Lay a strip of Plastigage on each camshaft journal

hardened surface of each lobe **(see illustrations)**.

8 Using a micrometer, measure the diameter of each camshaft journal and the lift of each camshaft lobe **(see Chapter 2, Part C)**. Compare your measurements with the Specifications listed at the front of this Chapter, and if the diameter of any one of these is less than specified, replace the camshaft.

11.9b Compare the width of the crushed Plastigage to the scale on the envelope to determine the oil clearance

9 Check the oil clearance for each camshaft bearing as follows:

a) *Clean the bearing surfaces and the camshaft journals with lacquer thinner or acetone.*

b) *Carefully lay the camshaft(s) in place in the cylinder head. Don't install the rocker arms or lash adjusters and don't use any lubrication.*

c) *Lay a strip of Plastigage on each journal* **(see illustration)**.

d) *Install the camshaft caps.*

e) *Tighten the caps, a little at a time, to the torque listed in this Chapter's Specifications.* **Note:** *Don't turn the camshaft while the Plastigage is in place.*

f) *Remove the bolts and detach the caps.*

g) *Compare the width of the crushed Plastigage (at its widest point) to the scale on the Plastigage envelope* **(see illustration)**.

h) *If the clearance is greater than specified, and the diameter of any journal is less than specified, replace the camshaft. If the journal diameters are within specifications but the oil clearance is too great, the cylinder head is worn and must be replaced.*

10 Scrape off the Plastigage with your fin-

gernail or the edge of a credit card - don't scratch or nick the journals or bearing surfaces.

Installation

Refer to illustration 11.13

11 If the lash adjusters and/or rocker arms have been removed, install them in their original locations (see Section 5).

12 Apply moly-based engine assembly lubricant to the camshaft lobes and bearing journals, then install the camshaft(s).

13 Install the camshaft caps in the correct locations, and following the correct bolt tightening sequence **(see illustration)**, tighten the bolts to the torque listed in this Chapter's Specifications.

14 Refer to Section 10 for the timing procedure for each camshaft, using the special tools.

15 The remainder of installation is the reverse of the removal procedure.

12 Oil pan - removal and installation

Note: *The complete oil pan assembly is comprised of two sections. The lower section is a sheet metal oil pan, while the upper section is*

11.13 Camshaft bearing cap tightening sequence

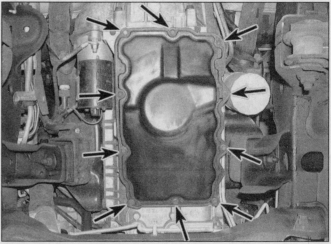

12.2 Lower oil pan bolts

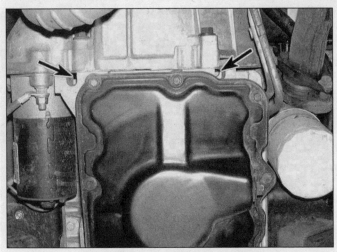

12.5 Remove the two rearmost bolts

12.8 Turn the threaded reinforcement section inserts out (counterclockwise) several turns each with an Allen wrench to ensure they do not contact the main cap bolt head when the section is initially installed

a large aluminum casting that serves as a structural reinforcement for the lower part of the crankcase. The lower oil pan and the oil pump pick-up/screen may be removed with the engine in-vehicle, but the engine must be removed from the vehicle to remove the reinforcement section for access to the oil pump and crankshaft.

Removal

Refer to illustrations 12.2 and 12.5

1   Remove the engine from the vehicle (see Part C of this Chapter).
2   Remove the lower oil pan fasteners **(see illustration)** and remove the sheet metal oil pan.
3   Remove the two bolts and the oil pump screen cover and tube.
4   To remove the reinforcement section, begin by removing the eight bolts in the center of the section **(see illustration 12.16)**.
5   Remove the two rear reinforcement section-to-block bolts **(see illustration)**, then the outside bolts on each side.

6   Carefully remove the reinforcement section from the block. **Caution:** *Do not pry between the reinforcement section and the block on any gasket sealing surface.*

Installation

Refer to illustrations 12.8, 12.9a, 12.9b and 12.16

Caution: *Since two of the oil pan bolts are attached to the transmission, spacers are used between the oil pan and transmission. Failure to check the clearance and select the shims correctly can cause oil pan damage or oil leaks when the pan is installed. The engine must be removed from the engine stand for this check.*

7   Using a gasket scraper, thoroughly clean all old gasket material from the engine block, reinforcement section and oil pan. Remove residue and oil film with a solvent such as acetone or lacquer thinner.
8   The eight center bolts of the reinforcement section are threaded into the main cap bolt heads. Threaded inserts are installed in

the reinforcement section to create support for the bolts without stressing the reinforcement section. Use an Allen wrench to back the inserts out until they are in the "index" position before installing the reinforcement section to the engine block **(see illustration)**.
9   Apply RTV sealant to the rear main cap and the bottom of the front cover **(see illustrations)**. On the front cover, there are four spots to seal, where the cover meets the block, and on either side of the front crankshaft seal, where the rubber end gasket will meet the side gaskets.
10   Position the new gaskets on the engine block. Install the two side gaskets, then the rubber end seals, making sure that the ends of the side gaskets fit into the notches on the rubber end seals. Add a small amount of RTV sealant over the joints between the side gaskets and end seals. Install the reinforcement section.
11   Install, but do not tighten, the reinforcement section side rail bolts, including the two rear bolts.

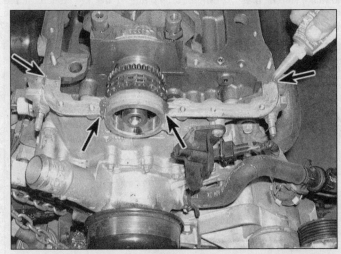

12.9a Apply RTV sealant to the four places indicated on the front cover . . .

12.9b . . . and the two places indicated on the rear main cap

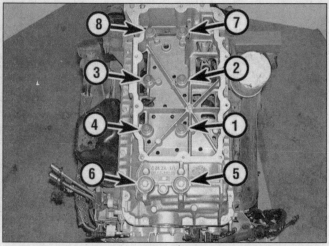

12.16 Crankcase reinforcement section bolt tightening sequence

13.2 Remove the two oil pump bolts

12   Place a straightedge across the transmission mounting surface on the cylinder block and one of the mounting pads for the reinforcement section-to-transmission bolts. Measure the clearance between the mounting pad and straightedge with a feeler gauge.
13   Move the straightedge to the other mounting pad and measure the clearance. The clearance should not exceed 0.010-inch (0.25 mm). If the reinforcement section protrudes over the rear edge of the engine block, tap it toward the front of the engine with a soft-faced hammer until it's flush (it may protrude a maximum of 0.002-inch [0.05 mm]). If the clearance is excessive, tap it to the rear of the engine.
14   Tighten the perimeter bolts/nuts, including the two rear lower block cradle-to-transmission bolts and the two rear lower block cradle-to-engine block bolts, to the torque listed in this Chapter's Specifications.
15   Tighten the reinforcement section threaded inserts to the torque listed in this Chapter's Specifications.
16   Install the interior reinforcement section bolts (lower cradle block bolts), using new seals on the two front bolts (the front two bolts are distinguished by their silver color). Tighten them in sequence to the torque listed in this Chapter's Specifications **(see illustration)**.
17   Repeat the reinforcement section-to-engine block clearance check (see Step 13).
18   Install the oil pump pickup tube, place a new oil pan gasket in position and install the oil pan and bolts. Tighten the bolts to the torque listed in this Chapter's Specifications.

---

13   Oil pump - removal and installation

Removal

Refer to illustration 13.2

1   Remove the lower and upper oil pan sections (see Section 12). **Note:** *This involves removing the engine from the vehicle (see*

Part C of this Chapter).
2   Remove the oil pump bolts and take the pump off the engine **(see illustration)**.
3   Pull the oil pump intermediate driveshaft out of the engine.

Installation

Refer to illustrations 13.5

4   Fill one of the pump ports with clean engine oil and rotate the pump by hand to prime it.
5   Insert the intermediate drive shaft into the engine, pointed end first, until it engages the oil pump drive **(see illustration)**. Make sure the travel limit clip is in place, and closer to the camshaft position sensor end. It fits tightly on a non-machined section of the driveshaft.
6   Install the oil pump on the block, using a new gasket. Make sure the pump engages the driveshaft. Install the oil pump bolts and tighten to the torque listed in this Chapter's Specifications.
7   The remainder of installation is the reverse of removal.
8   Run the engine and make sure oil pressure comes up to normal quickly. If it doesn't, stop the engine and find out the cause.

Severe engine damage can result from running an engine with insufficient oil pressure!

---

14   Flywheel/driveplate - removal and installation

Removal

1   Raise the vehicle and support it securely on jackstands, then refer to Chapter 7 and remove the transmission. If it's leaking, now would be a very good time to replace the front pump seal/O-ring (automatic transmission only).
2   Remove the pressure plate and clutch disc (Chapter 8) (manual transmission equipped vehicles). Now is a good time to check/replace the clutch components and pilot bearing.
3   Use a center punch or paint to make alignment marks on the flywheel/driveplate and crankshaft to ensure correct alignment during reinstallation.
4   Remove the bolts that secure the flywheel/driveplate to the crankshaft. If the crankshaft turns, wedge a screwdriver in the ring gear teeth to jam the flywheel.

13.5 Insert the oil pump driveshaft into the pump, then guide the driveshaft into the engine, making sure the travel limit clip is in place

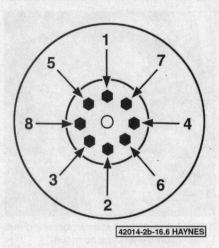

14.9 Flywheel bolt tightening sequence

5   Remove the flywheel/driveplate from the crankshaft. Since the flywheel is fairly heavy, be sure to support it while removing the last bolt. Automatic transmission equipped vehicles have a spacer between the crankshaft and the driveplate.

Installation

Refer to illustration 14.9

6   Clean the flywheel to remove grease and oil. Inspect the surface for cracks, rivet grooves, burned areas and score marks. Light scoring can be removed with emery cloth. Check for cracked and broken ring gear teeth. Lay the flywheel on a flat surface and use a straightedge to check for warpage.

7   Clean and inspect the mating surfaces of the flywheel/driveplate and the crankshaft. If the crankshaft rear seal is leaking, replace it before reinstalling the flywheel/driveplate.

8   Position the flywheel/driveplate against the crankshaft. Be sure to align the marks made during removal. Note that some engines have an alignment dowel or stag-gered bolt holes to ensure correct installation. Before installing the bolts, apply thread locking compound to the threads.

9   Wedge a screwdriver in the ring gear teeth to keep the flywheel/driveplate from turning and tighten the bolts to the torque listed in this Chapter's Specifications. Follow the correct torque sequence **(see illustration)** and work up to the final torque in three or four steps.

10   The remainder of installation is the reverse of the removal procedure.

15 Rear main oil seal - replacement

1   The one-piece rear main oil seal is pressed into engine block and the crankcase reinforcement section. Remove the transmission (see Chapter 7), the clutch components, if equipped (see Chapter 8) and the flywheel (see Section 16).

2   Pry out the old seal with a special seal removal tool or a flat blade screwdriver. **Caution:** *To prevent an oil leak after the new seal is installed, be very careful not to scratch or otherwise damage the crankshaft sealing surface or the bore in the engine block.*

3   Clean the crankshaft and seal bore in the block thoroughly and de-grease these areas by wiping them with a rag soaked in lacquer thinner or acetone. Lubricate the lip of the new seal and the outer diameter of the crankshaft with engine oil. Make sure the edges of the new oil seal are not rolled over.

4   Position the new seal onto the crankshaft. **Note:** *When installing the new seal, if so marked, the words THIS SIDE OUT on the seal must face out, toward the rear of the engine.* Use a special rear main oil seal installation tool or a socket with the exact diameter of the seal to drive the seal in place. Make sure the seal is not off-set; it must be flush along the entire circumference of the seal carrier.

5   The remainder of installation is the reverse of removal.

16 Engine mounts - check and replacement

Check

1   Engine mounts seldom require attention, but broken or deteriorated mounts should be replaced immediately or the added strain placed on the driveline components may cause damage or wear.

2   During the check, the engine must be raised slightly to remove the weight from the mounts.

3   Raise the vehicle and support it securely on jackstands, then position a jack under the engine oil pan. Place a large block of wood between the jack head and the oil pan, then carefully raise the engine just enough to take the weight off the mounts. **Warning:** *DO NOT place any part of your body under the engine when it's supported only by a jack!*

4   Check the mounts to see if the rubber is cracked, hardened or separated from the metal plates. Sometimes the rubber will split right down the center.

5   Check for relative movement between the mount plates and the engine or frame (use a large screwdriver or pry bar to attempt to move the mounts). If movement is noted, lower the engine and tighten the mount fasteners.

6   Rubber preservative should be applied to the mounts to slow deterioration.

Replacement

Refer to illustration 16.9a, 16.9b, 16.9c and 16.9d

7   Disconnect the negative battery cable from the battery (see Chapter 5), then raise the vehicle and support it securely on jackstands.

8   Remove the engine cooling fan/shroud assembly (see Chapter 3).

9   Remove the fasteners holding the mount to the engine bracket and the chassis **(see illustrations)**.

16.9a Location of the right engine mount upper mounting nuts

16.9b Location of the right engine mount lower mounting nut

10   Raise the engine slightly with a jack or hoist. Detach the mount from the chassis bracket.

11   Installation is the reverse of removal. Use thread-locking compound on the mount fasteners and be sure to tighten them securely.

16.9c Location of the through-bolt on the left engine mount

16.9d Location of the lower mounting nut on the left engine mount

Chapter 2 Part B
V8 engine

Contents

Specifications

General

Displacement	4.6 liters (281 cubic inches)
Bore and stroke	3.554 X 3.546 inches (90.2 X 90.0 mm)
Cylinder numbers (front to rear)	
Right side	1-2-3-4
Left (driver's) side	5-6-7-8
Firing order	1-3-7-2-6-5-4-8

Camshaft

Lobe lift	
Exhaust	0.2951 inch (7.497 mm)
Intake	0.2799 inch (7.110 mm)
Allowable lobe lift loss	0.000 inch (0.000 mm)
Endplay	0.0035 to 0.0075 inch (0.09 to 0.19 mm)
Journal diameter (all)	1.060 to 1.061 inches (26.936 to 26.962 mm)
Bearing inside diameter (all)	1.062 to 1.063 inches (26.987 to 27.012 mm)
Journal-to-bearing (oil) clearance	
Standard	0.001 to 0.003 inch
Service limit	0.002 inch maximum (0.05 mm)

**4.6L V8 Engine
1-3-7-2-6-5-4-8**

36025-specs.a HAYNES

**Cylinder location and
firing order**

Torque specifications

	Ft-lbs (unless otherwise indicated)	Nm
Accessory drivebelt pulley (top)	18	25
Accessory drivebelt pulley (bottom)	18	25
Alternator bracket bolts	89 in-lbs	10
Camshaft sprocket		
Step 1	30	40
Step 2	Tighten an additional 90-degrees	
Camshaft caps to cylinder head	89 in-lbs	10
Drive belt tensioner bolts	18	25
Cylinder head bolts		
Step 1	30	40
Step 2	Tighten an additional 90-degrees	
Step 3	Back out (reverse) 360-degrees	
Step 4	30	40
Step 5	Tighten an additional 90-degrees	
Step 6	Tighten an additional 90-degrees	
Crankshaft pulley-to-crankshaft bolt		
Step 1	66	90
Step 2	Loosen one full turn	
Step 3	37	50
Step 4	Tighten an additional 90-degrees	
Driveplate bolts	59	80
Exhaust manifold-to-cylinder head nuts	15	20
Exhaust pipe-to-exhaust manifold nuts	30	40
Intake manifold-to-cylinder head bolts	18	25
Oil pan-to-engine block bolts		
Step 1	18 in-lbs	2
Step 2	15	20
Step 3	Tighten an additional 60-degrees	
Oil filter adapter bolts	18	25
Oil pump-to-engine block mounting bolts	89 in-lbs	10
Oil pick-up screen-to-engine block bolt	18	25
Oil pick-up tube-to-oil pump bolts	89 in-lbs	10
Timing chain cover bolts	18	25
Timing chain guide bolts	89 in-lbs	10
Timing chain tensioner bolts	18	25
Valve cover bolts	89 in-lbs	10

1   General information

This Part of Chapter 2 is devoted to in-vehicle repair procedures for the 4.6L Single Overhead Cam (SOHC) engines. This engine has aluminum cylinder heads, an iron block and two valves per cylinder. All information concerning engine removal and installation can be found in Part C of this Chapter.

These engines are an interference design. In the event the timing chain breaks, the pistons will interfere with the valves and cause damage. The timing chains, tensioners and cylinder heads can be removed with the engine in the vehicle, however it will be necessary to remove the rocker arms and hydraulic valve adjusters first. This will prevent any piston, connecting rod and valve damage. It will be necessary to obtain certain special tools to repair this engine.

The Specifications included in this Part of Chapter 2 apply only to the procedures contained in this Part. Part C of Chapter 2 contains the Specifications necessary for engine block rebuilding.

2   Repair operations possible with the engine in the vehicle

Many major repair operations can be accomplished without removing the engine from the vehicle.

If possible, clean the engine compartment and the exterior of the engine with some type of pressure washer before any work is started. It will make the job easier and help keep dirt out of the internal areas of the engine.

It may help to remove the hood to improve access to the engine as repairs are performed (refer to Chapter 11 if necessary).

If vacuum, exhaust, oil or coolant leaks develop, indicating a need for gasket or seal replacement, the repairs can generally be made with the engine in the vehicle. The intake and exhaust manifold gaskets, timing cover gasket, oil pan gasket, crankshaft oil seals and cylinder head gaskets are all accessible with the engine in place.

Exterior engine components, such as the intake and exhaust manifolds, the oil pan, the water pump, the starter motor, the alternator and the fuel system components can be removed for repair with the engine in place.

Since the cylinder heads can be removed without pulling the engine, valve component servicing can also be accomplished with the engine in the vehicle. Replacement of the timing chain and sprockets and oil pump is also possible with the engine in the vehicle.

In extreme cases caused by a lack of necessary equipment, repair or replacement of piston rings, pistons, connecting rods and rod bearings is also possible with the engine in the vehicle. However, this practice is not recommended because of the cleaning and preparation work that must be done to the components involved.

3 Top Dead Center (TDC) for number one piston - locating

Refer to illustration 3.1

Refer to Chapter 2, Part A for the TDC locating procedure, but use the illustration provided with this Section for the appropriate reference marks and the following exceptions:

a) *Disable the ignition system by disconnecting the primary electrical connectors at the ignition coils (see Chapter 5).*

b) *Remove the spark plugs and install a compression gauge in the number one cylinder. Turn the crankshaft clockwise with a socket and breaker bar as described in Chapter 2.*

c) *When the piston approaches TDC, compression will be noted on the compression gauge. Continue turning the crankshaft until the notch in the crankshaft pulley is aligned with the TDC mark on the front cover (see illustration). At this point number one cylinder is at TDC on the compression stroke.*

4 Valve covers - removal and installation

Removal

Refer to illustration 4.5

1   Disconnect the cable from the negative battery terminal (see Chapter 5).
2   Remove the engine access cover.
3   Disconnect the PCV hose from the valve cover(s) (see Chapter 6).
4   Remove the ignition coils from the valve covers (see Chapter 5).
5   Disconnect the fuel injector harness from the injectors **(see illustration)** and position the harness off to the side (see Chapter 4).

Right side valve cover

Refer to illustration 4.10

6   Remove the air filter housing (see Chapter 4).

3.1 When placing the engine at Top Dead Center (TDC), align the notch in the crankshaft pulley with the TDC indicator on the timing chain cover

7   Remove the heater control valve bracket bolt and vacuum line. Position the heater control valve assembly off to the side.
8   Disconnect the vacuum hoses from the throttle body and the fuel pressure regulator (see Chapter 4). Position the vacuum harness off to the side.
9   Disconnect the MAF sensor connector (see Chapter 6).
10 Loosen the valve cover bolts and remove the valve cover **(see illustration)**. If it's stuck, tap it with a hammer and block of wood. **Note:** *It's a good idea to label the locations of the bolts so they can be reinstalled in their original locations.*

Left side valve cover

11 Disconnect the EVAP canister purge solenoid connector (see Chapter 6).
12 Remove the EVAP canister purge solenoid bracket and assembly (see Chapter 6).
13 Remove the oil dipstick mounting bolt from the side of the cylinder head.
14 Loosen the valve cover bolts and

4.5 Detach the wiring harness from the valve cover studs

remove the cover **(see illustration 4.10)**. If it's stuck tap it with a hammer and block of wood. **Note:** *It's a good idea to label the locations of the bolts so they can be reinstalled in their original locations.*

Installation

Refer to illustration 4.17

15 The mating surfaces of each cylinder head and valve cover must be perfectly clean when the valve covers are installed. Remove all traces of sealant, and clean the mating surfaces with lacquer thinner or acetone. If there's old sealant or oil on the mating surfaces when the valve cover is installed, oil leaks may develop.
16 The valve cover gaskets should be mated to the valve covers with gasket adhesive before the valve covers are installed. Make sure the gasket is pushed all the way into the groove in the valve cover.
17 At the mating joint (two spots per cylinder head) between the timing chain cover and cylinder head, apply a dab of RTV sealant before installing the valve cover **(see illustration)**.

2B

4.10 Valve cover bolt locations - when tightening, tighten the valve cover bolts starting with the upper row (rear to front) then the lower row (rear to front) in two steps

4.17 Apply a dab of RTV sealant to the mating joints between the timing chain cover and the cylinder head before installing the valve cover

18   Carefully position the valve cover on the cylinder head and install the nuts and bolts. **Note:** *Install the covers within five minutes of applying the RTV sealant.*

19   Tighten the fasteners in two steps to the torque listed in this Chapter's Specifications. Wait two minutes between the first and the second round of tightening. Tighten the upper row of bolts first, then the lower row, from rear to front. **Caution:** *Be careful with the plastic valve covers, don't over tighten the bolts!*

20   The remaining installation steps are the reverse of removal.

21   Start the engine and check for oil leaks as the engine warms up.

5   Intake manifold - removal and installation

Removal

1   Disconnect the cable from the negative battery terminal (see Chapter 5).

2   Remove the engine cover.

3   Relieve the fuel system pressure (see Chapter 4).

4   Drain the cooling system (see Chapter 3).

5   Remove the drivebelt (see Chapter 1).

6   Remove the ignition coils from the spark plugs (see Chapter 5).

7   Disconnect the radiator hose from the thermostat housing and the heater hose from the engine (see Chapter 3).

8   Remove the thermostat housing (see Chapter 3).

9   Remove the air filter housing (see Chapter 4).

10   Label and disconnect all vacuum lines connected to the intake manifold.

11   Remove the PCV and canister purge hoses from the valve covers (see Chapter 6).

12   Disconnect the accelerator cable, cruise control linkage (if so equipped), electrical connector at the throttle body, fuel injectors, fuel rails, and disconnect and plug the fuel supply and return lines (see Chapter 4).

13   Disconnect the idle air control valve, the EVAP canister purge solenoid, the EGR valve vacuum hose and the EGR pipe (see Chapter 6).

14   Remove the differential pressure feedback EGR solenoid (see Chapter 6).

15   Remove the alternator bracket from the top of the alternator and the valve cover.

16   Disconnect the brake booster vacuum tube, remove the mounting bolt and position the vacuum tube off to the side.

17   Disconnect the alternator electrical connectors and remove the alternator (see Chapter 5).

18   Remove the bolts retaining the alternator bracket to the intake manifold.

19   Loosen the intake manifold bolts and nuts in 1/4-turn increments, following the reverse order of the tightening sequence **(see illustration 5.29)**, until they can be removed by hand.

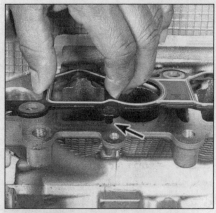

5.27 Install the new intake manifold gaskets and be sure to position the locating tabs in the correct locations in the cylinder head casting

20   Slightly lift the intake manifold from the cylinder heads, disconnect the knock sensor connectors and position the harness off to the side.

21   Lift the intake manifold from the cylinder heads. The manifold may be stuck to the cylinder heads and force may be required to break the gasket seal. A prybar can be used to pry up the manifold, but make sure all bolts and nuts have been removed first! **Caution:** *Don't pry between the manifold and the cylinder heads, or damage to the gasket sealing surface may occur, leading to vacuum leaks. Pry only at a manifold protrusion.*

22   Remove the intake manifold gaskets and clean all traces of gasket or sealant material from the sealing surfaces of the cylinder heads and intake manifold.

Installation

Refer to illustrations 5.27 and 5.29

Caution: *The mating surfaces of the cylinder heads, engine block and intake manifold must be perfectly clean. Gasket removal solvents in aerosol cans are available at most auto parts stores and may be helpful when removing old gasket material that's stuck to the cylinder heads and intake manifold. Since the cylinder heads are aluminum and the intake manifold is aluminum or plastic, aggressive scraping can cause damage! Be sure to follow directions printed on the container, and use only a plastic-tipped scraper, not a metal one.*

23   If the intake manifold was disassembled, reassemble it or if you are replacing it, transfer all components to the new intake manifold. Use electrically conductive sealant on the temperature sending unit threads. Use a new EGR valve gasket.

24   Remove the old gaskets, then clean the mating surfaces with lacquer thinner or acetone. If there's old sealant or oil on the mating surfaces when the intake manifold is installed, oil or vacuum leaks may develop.

25   When working on the cylinder heads and engine block, cover the open engine areas with shop rags to keep debris out of the engine. Use a vacuum cleaner to remove

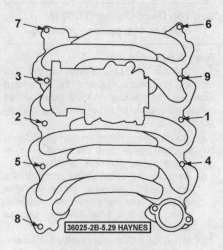

5.29 Intake manifold bolt tightening sequence

any gasket material that falls into the intake ports in the cylinder heads.

26   Use a tap of the correct size to chase the threads in the bolt holes, then use compressed air (if available) to remove the debris from the holes. **Warning:** *Wear safety glasses or a face shield to protect your eyes when using compressed air!* Remove excessive carbon deposits and corrosion from the exhaust and coolant passages in the cylinder heads and intake manifold.

27   Install the gaskets on the cylinder heads **(see illustration)**. Make sure all alignment tabs, intake port openings, coolant passage holes and bolt holes are aligned correctly. The gasket that goes on the cylinder head will have projecting plastic pins to align it with holes in the cylinder head.

28   Carefully set the intake manifold in place. Don't disturb the gaskets and don't move the manifold fore-and-aft after it contacts the gaskets on the engine block.

29   Install the intake manifold bolts and, following the recommended tightening sequence **(see illustration)**, tighten them to the torque listed in this Chapter's Specifications.

30   Replace the O-ring seal on the thermostat housing. Install the thermostat housing and tighten the bolts to the torque listed in Chapter 3 Specifications.

31   The remaining installation steps are the reverse of removal. Start the engine and check carefully for oil and coolant leaks.

6   Exhaust manifolds - removal and installation

Removal

1   Disconnect the cable from the negative battery terminal (see Chapter 5).

2   Raise the vehicle and support it securely on jackstands.

3   Remove the inner splash shield from the fenderwell.

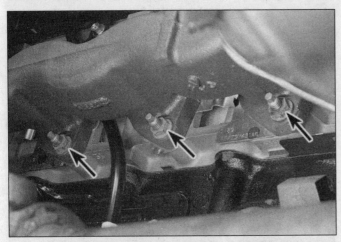

6.9 Locations of the lower exhaust manifold nuts

7.6 Remove the crankshaft pulley with a puller that bolts to the crankshaft pulley hub

4   Working under the vehicle, apply penetrating oil to the exhaust pipe-to-manifold studs and nuts (they're usually corroded or rusty). Also apply some to the EGR pipe fitting on the right exhaust manifold.

Left side exhaust manifold

Refer to illustration 6.9

5   Remove the intermediate shaft from the power steering gear (see Chapter 10).
6   Remove the exhaust manifold heat shield.
7   Remove the dipstick tube bracket bolt and lift the assembly from the engine block.
8   Remove the nuts retaining the exhaust pipe to the manifold.
9   Remove the eight mounting nuts from the exhaust manifold **(see illustration)**.

Right side exhaust manifold

10   Remove the heater control valve bracket from the cylinder head and position the heater control valve assembly off to the side.
11   Remove the exhaust manifold heat shield.
12   Disconnect the EGR pipe from the exhaust manifold (see Chapter 6).
13   Remove the nuts retaining the exhaust pipe to the manifold.
14   Remove the eight mounting nuts from the exhaust manifold.

Installation

15   Check the exhaust manifolds for cracks. Make sure the bolt threads are clean and undamaged. The exhaust manifold and cylinder head mating surfaces must be clean before the exhaust manifolds are reinstalled - use a gasket scraper to remove all carbon deposits.
16   Position a new gasket in place and slip the exhaust manifold over the studs on the cylinder head. Install the mounting nuts.
17   When tightening the mounting nuts, work from the rear to the front, alternating between top and bottom rows. Tighten the bolts in three equal steps to the torque listed in this Chapter's Specifications.
18   The remaining installation steps are the

7.7 Use a special oil seal removal tool - be careful to not damage the crankshaft while using the special tool

reverse of removal. When reconnecting the EGR tube to the left manifold, use a slight amount of anti-seize compound on the threads.
19   Start the engine and check for exhaust leaks.

---

7   Crankshaft pulley and front oil seal - removal and installation

Removal

Refer to illustrations 7.6 and 7.7

1   Disconnect the cable from the negative battery terminal (see Chapter 5).
2   Remove the drivebelt (see Chapter 1).
3   Remove the engine cooling fan and shroud assembly (see Chapter 3).
4   Raise the vehicle and secure it on jackstands.
5   Use a breaker bar and socket to remove the crankshaft pulley center bolt. **Note:** *It will be necessary to lock the pulley in position using a strap or chain wrench. Be sure to wrap a shop rag or a piece of drivebelt material around the pulley before installing the special tool.*

7.9 There is a special tool for installing the front oil seal into the timing chain cover - if the tool is not available, a large socket or section of tubing (the same diameter of the seal) can be used to drive the seal into place

6   Using a bolt-type puller, pull the pulley from the crankshaft **(see illustration)**. **Note:** *Because the pulley is recessed, an adapter may be needed between the puller bolt and the crankshaft.*
7   Use a seal puller to remove the crankshaft front oil seal **(see illustration)**. A screwdriver may be used instead, if the tip is wrapped with tape to avoid scratching the crankshaft.
8   Clean the seal bore and check it for nicks or gouges. Also examine the area of the hub that rides in the seal for signs of abnormal wear or scoring. For many popular engines, a repair sleeve is available to restore a smooth finish to the sealing surface. Check with your auto parts store.

Installation

Refer to illustrations 7.9 and 7.10

9   Coat the lip of the new seal with clean engine oil and drive it into the bore with a socket **(see illustration)** or section of pipe slightly smaller in diameter than the seal. The open side of the seal faces into the engine.

2B

7.10 Inspect the crankshaft pulley for signs of damage or excessive wear

| 1 Oil seal surface | 2 Woodruff keyway |

8.18 Separate the timing chain cover from the engine, using a soft-faced hammer if necessary to break the gasket seal

10   Lubricate the oil seal contact surface of the crankshaft pulley hub **(see illustration)** with moly-base grease or clean engine oil. Apply a dab of RTV sealant to the front end of the keyway in the crankshaft pulley before installation.

11   Install the crankshaft pulley with a special installation tool, available at most auto parts stores. Do not use a hammer to install the pulley. Install the center bolt and tighten it to the torque listed in this Chapter's Specifications.

12   The remainder of the installation is the reverse of the removal procedure.

8   Timing chain cover - removal and installation

Warning: *Wait until the engine is completely cool before beginning this procedure.*

Removal

Refer to illustration 8.18

1   Disconnect the cable from the negative battery terminal (see Chapter 5).

2   Drain the engine oil and remove the oil filter (see Chapter 1).

3   Remove the drivebelt and the water pump pulley.

4   Remove the crankshaft pulley and oil seal (see Section 7).

5   Remove both valve covers (see Section 4).

6   Drain the cooling system (see Chapter 1).

7   Remove the radiator, the upper radiator hose bracket and water pump (see Chapter 3).

8   Remove the transmission fluid cooler line bracket from the lower section of the timing chain cover.

9   Disconnect the electrical connector to the crankshaft sensor (see Chapter 6).

10   Remove the camshaft position sensor (see Chapter 6).

11   Remove the EGR vacuum regulator solenoid (see Chapter 6).

12   Remove the four front oil pan bolts (see Section 13).

13   Drain the power steering fluid from the reservoir and remove the power steering fluid reservoir and bracket (see Chapter 10).

14   Use a special puller and remove the power steering pump pulley (see Chapter 10).

15   Remove the bolts securing the power steering pump to the engine (see Chapter 10). **Note:** *The front lower bolt on the power steering pump will not come all the way out.* Position the pump aside and secure it out of the way.

16   Unbolt and remove the drivebelt idler pulleys from the timing chain cover.

17   Remove the timing chain cover-to-engine block bolts. Including the oil pan bolts, there are 19 bolts to be removed from the timing chain cover. Note the locations of studs and different length bolts so they can be reinstalled in their original locations.

18   Separate the timing chain cover from the engine block **(see illustration)**. If it's stuck, tap it gently with a soft-face hammer to break the gasket bond. **Caution:** *DO NOT use excessive force or you may crack the cover. If the cover is difficult to remove, make sure all of the bolts have been removed.*

Installation

Refer to illustrations 8.20, 8.21 and 8.23

19   Clean the mating surfaces of the timing chain cover, engine block and cylinder heads to remove all traces of old gasket material, oil

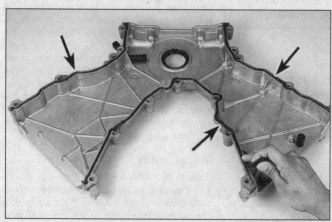

8.20 Install three new gaskets into the grooves in the back of the timing chain cover

8.21 Apply a small bead of RTV sealant to the mating junctions of the oil pan-to-engine block and cylinder head-to-engine block

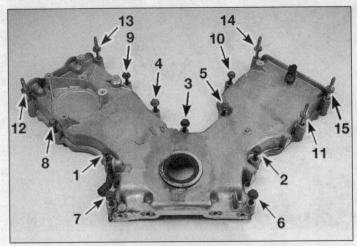

8.23 Timing chain cover bolt tightening sequence

9.3 The V8 engine has two long primary timing chains with two main tensioners

and dirt. Final cleaning should be with lacquer thinner or acetone. **Warning:** *Be careful when cleaning any of the aluminum components. Use of a metal scraper could cause scratches or gouges that could lead to an oil leak later.*

20 Adhere the three new gaskets to the backside of the timing chain cover **(see illustration).**

21 Apply a 1/8-inch bead of RTV sealant to the junctions of the oil pan-to-engine block and the cylinder head-to-engine block **(see illustration).** Apply a small dab of RTV where the timing chain cover and engine block meet at the valve cover surface.

22 Lubricate the timing chains and the lip of the crankshaft front oil seal with clean engine oil.

23 Install the timing chain cover on the engine, within five minutes of applying the RTV sealant. Position the bottom/front edge of the timing chain cover flush with the front edge of the oil pan and "tilt" the top of the cover into place against the engine. Do not press the cover straight in against the engine or the sealant may be scraped off the front of the oil pan and cause a leak. Tighten the tim-

ing chain cover-to-engine block bolts in the recommended sequence **(see illustration),** to the torque and sequence listed in this Chapter's Specifications. Tighten the timing chain cover-to-oil pan bolts.

24 Install the remaining parts in the reverse order of removal.

25 Add the proper type and quantity of engine oil and coolant (see Chapter 1). Run the engine and check for leaks.

9 Timing chains, tensioners and sprockets - removal, inspection and installation

Note: *Because this is an "interference" engine design, if the chain has broken, there will be damage to the valves (and possibly the pistons) and will require removal of the cylinder heads for inspection.*

Removal

Refer to illustrations 9.3, 9.4, 9.6a, 9.6b and 9.8

1 Disconnect the cable from the negative

battery terminal (see Chapter 5).

2 Position the number one cylinder on TDC (see Section 3), and remove the spark plugs (see Chapter 1). **Caution:** *The camshaft(s) MUST be retained exactly at TDC. If the valve timing is off when the timing chain(s) are reinstalled, severe engine damage could result.*

3 Remove the valve covers (see Section 4) and the timing chain cover (see Section 8). Two long timing chains connect the crankshaft to the camshafts **(see illustration).**

4 Remove the crankshaft position sensor toothed-wheel **(see illustration)** by sliding it off the end of the crankshaft nose. Note the stamped word "rear" on the wheel to be sure it's reinstalled in the correct direction.

5 Remove the rocker arms and valve lash adjusters (see Section 10).

6 Remove the right side timing chain tensioner **(see illustrations).**

7 Remove the right timing chain from the crankshaft and camshaft sprockets, by slipping the chain off the camshaft sprocket and pulling the crankshaft sprocket off with the chain.

9.4 The crankshaft sensor tooth wheel has a specific direction to be installed, look for the word "rear" stamped in it

9.6a To remove the timing chain tensioner from the engine block, remove the two bolts from the tensioner . . .

9.6b . . . and detach the guide assembly from the dowel at the opposite end

8   Remove the stationary guide (see illus-tration).

9   Remove the left side timing chain ten-sioner. Lift the chain off the camshaft sprocket and remove the chain along with the crankshaft sprocket.

10   Remove the left side stationary guide.

11   If the camshaft sprockets are to be replaced, remove the camshaft bolts to remove the camshaft sprockets (see Section 11). **Note:** *Note the location and direction of any spacers on the crankshaft or camshafts, but do not remove the spacers unless necessary.*

Inspection

Refer to illustrations 9.13a and 9.13b

12   Inspect the individual sprocket teeth and keyways for wear and damage. Check the chain for cracked plates, pitted or worn rollers. Check the wear surface of the chain guides for wear and damage. Replace any excessively worn or defective parts with new ones. **Caution:** *If excessive plastic material is missing from the chain guides, the oil pan should be removed and cleaned of all debris (see Section 13). Check the oil pick-up tube and screen. Replace the assembly if it is clogged.*

13   Check the primary tensioners for proper operation:

a) *Release the plunger lock* (see illustra-tion) *and make sure the piston moves freely.*

b) *Submerge the tensioner in a can of oil or solvent, remove from the fluid and depress the plunger to make sure the oil feed oil is not plugged* (see illustration). **Note:** *Also inspect the oil feed hole in the engine block to be certain it's not plugged.*

Installation

Refer to illustration 9.15, 9.18a, 9.18b and 9.20

14   Install the stationary chain guides, for both sides, and tighten the bolts to the torque listed in this Chapter's Specifications.

15   Using the special tool (see illustration), position the crankshaft.

16   Install the crankshaft sprocket on the crankshaft with the timing marks facing for-ward.

17   The two timing chains should each have

9.8 The stationary chain guide is removed by removing the bolts at the mount plate

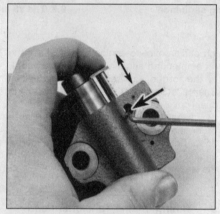

9.13a To fully retract the primary tensioner, release the plunger lock and push the plunger into the tensioner body

9.13b Check the tensioner oil feed hole to be sure it's not plugged by debris

two bright or colored links and 58 links on each chain. The links separate the chain in two equal halves. If no colored links are pre-sent, lay the chain down, make a paint mark on a link, then count links and make another paint mark halfway around the chain.

18   Install the left (inner) timing chain, align-ing the bright link with the dimple on the camshaft sprocket (see illustration). Loop the timing chain under the crankshaft sprocket and align the bright link with the alignment mark on the crankshaft sprocket. The timing marks on the crankshaft sprocket should be in the 6 o'clock position (see illus-tration). **Note:** *The slack side of the chain*

(towards the water pump) must be below the dowel pin on the block.

19   Install the right (outer) chain, but its slack side (the bottom run of the chain) should be above the dowel on the block.

20   The steps for installing the timing chain tensioners/guides are the same for both sides, either side can be done first. Before assembling the tensioner with the chain

9.15 Use this crankshaft positioning tool - the side hole fits over the dowel on the right side of the engine

9.18a When installing the timing chain, align one of the bright links in the timing chain with the dimple on the camshaft sprocket - the sprocket should also align with the keyway in the camshaft

9.18b Align the bright link at the lower end of the chain with the timing mark on the crankshaft sprocket (it should be at 6 o'clock) then bolt the primary camshaft sprocket to the camshaft - both chains are aligned here

9.20 Lock the primary timing chain tensioner in the fully retracted position by placing a paper clip into the hole in the tensioner body

guide, compress the tensioner and lock it in this position with a straightened paper clip, Allen wrench or drill bit (see illustration). **Note:** *The left side tensioner guide has an identification bump next to the dowel hole.*
21   Remove the slack from the chain(s) by hand, and install the moveable guide assembly to the engine block and install the ten-

sioner in the retracted position. Tighten the bolts to the torque listed in this Chapter's Specifications. Repeat for the other chain.
22   Remove the paper clip(s) and apply pressure against the tensioner chain guide so the tensioner fully extends against the chain guide and all slack is removed from the chain.
23   Recheck all the timing marks to make sure they are still in alignment **(see illustration 9.18b).**
24   Install the rocker arms and the valve lash adjusters (see Section 10).
25   Slowly rotate the crankshaft in the normal direction of rotation (clockwise) at least two revolutions and again bring the engine to TDC. If you feel any resistance, stop and find out why. Check all alignment marks to verify that everything is properly assembled.
26   The remainder of installation is the reverse of removal.

10   Rocker arms and valve lash adjusters - removal, inspection and installation

Note: *There are two methods of removing the rocker arms and lash adjusters on these engines. The method recommended by the*

manufacturer accomplishes the removal of the camshaft roller followers without the removal of the camshaft(s) by using two special tools: a valve spring spacer and a valve spring compressor, which are made specifically for the overhead cam V8 engine and are available at auto parts stores that carry special tools. The valve spring compressor uses the camshaft as a pivot point and, with a ratchet or breaker bar attached, pushes down on the spring to release tension on the cam follower. The spring spacer keeps the spring from collapsing too far and hitting the valve stem seal. The alternative method requires the removal of the camshaft (see Section 11) in order to remove the cam followers. Either method will achieve the same results, but it is much easier using the special tools, if they can be located.

Removal

Refer to illustrations 10.3a, 10.3b and 10.4
1   Remove the valve cover(s) (see Section 4).
2   Because of the interference design of these engines, the pistons must be positioned off TDC before compressing the valve springs to remove the rockers arms or lash adjusters. For whatever cylinder you are removing the rockers arms from, remove the spark plug and insert a plastic pen (hold onto it) to see how far the piston is from the top of its travel. If necessary, turn the crankshaft until the pen indicates the piston is down at least an inch or two from TDC.
3   Install the valve spring compressor and compress the spring enough to remove the rocker arm **(see illustrations).** Camshaft rocker arms and hydraulic lash adjusters MUST be reinstalled with the same camshaft lobe that they were removed from. Label and store all components to avoid confusion during reassembly. **Caution:** *A valve spring spacer should be inserted into the coils of the spring before compressing it. If the spacer isn't in place between one of the valve spring coils, the spring can be compressed too far and the valve seal may be damaged.*

2B

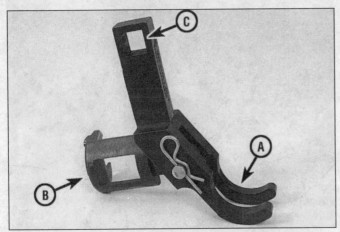

10.3a The special valve spring compressor hooks under the camshaft at (A), pushes on the valve spring retainer at (B), and is operated by a ratchet or breaker bar placed at (C)

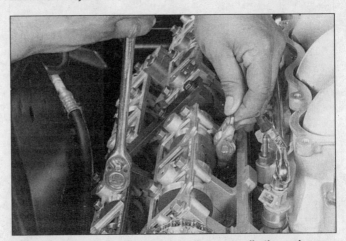

10.3b Compress the valve spring until you can slip the rocker arm out - keep the rocker arms and lash adjusters matched to their original location

4   Remove the hydraulic lash adjuster **(see illustration)**. If there are many miles on the vehicle, the adjusters may have become varnished and difficult to remove. Apply a little penetrating oil around the lash adjuster to help loosen the varnish. **Note:** *Keep the rocker arm and lash adjuster for each valve together in a marked plastic sandwich bag.*

Inspection

Refer to illustrations 10.5 and 10.7

5   Inspect each adjuster carefully for signs of wear or damage. The areas of possible wear are the ball tip that contacts the cam follower and the sides of the adjuster that contact the bore in the cylinder head **(see illustration)**. Since the lash adjusters frequently become clogged as mileage increases, we recommend replacing them if you're concerned about their condition or if the engine is exhibiting valve "tapping" noises.

6   A thin wire or paper clip can be placed in the oil hole to move the plunger and make sure it's not stuck. **Note:** *The lash adjuster must have no more than 1/16-inch of total plunger travel.* It's recommended that if replacement of any of the adjusters is necessary, that the entire set be replaced. This will avoid the need to repeat the repair procedure as the others require replacement in the future.

7   Inspect the rocker arms for signs of wear or damage. The areas of wear are the ball socket that contacts the lash adjuster and the roller where the follower contacts the camshaft **(see illustration)**.

Installation

8   Before installing the lash adjusters, bleed as much air as possible out of them. Stand the adjusters upright in a container of oil. Use a thin wire or paper clip to work the plunger up and down. This "primes" the adjuster and removes most of the air. Leave the adjusters in the oil until ready to install.

9   Lubricate the valve stem tip, rocker arm,

10.4 Pull the lash adjuster straight up and out of the cylinder head

and lash adjuster bore with clean engine oil.

10   Install the lash adjusters and, with the valve spring depressed as in Step 3, install each rocker arm.

11   The remainder of installation is the reverse of the removal procedure.

12   When re-starting the engine after replacing the adjusters, the adjusters will normally make some "tapping" noises, until all the air is bled from them. After the engine is warmed-up, raise the speed from idle to 3,000 rpm for one minute. Stop the engine and let it cool down. All of the noise should be gone when it is restarted.

---

11   Camshaft(s) - removal, inspection and installation

Removal

Refer to illustrations 11.3 and 11.4

1   Remove the valve covers (see Section 4), and the timing chain cover (see Section 8).

2   Remove the timing chains, camshaft sprockets and spacers (see Section 7). **Cau-**

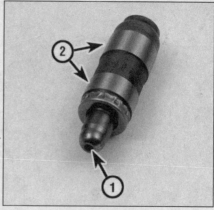

10.5 Inspect the lash adjuster for signs of excessive wear or damage, such as pitting, scoring or signs of overheating (bluing or discoloration), where the tip contacts the camshaft follower (1) and the side surfaces that contact the lifter bore in the cylinder head (2)

tion: *Don't mix up the sprockets, they are marked, as RB (right bank) and LB (left bank), and must go back on the appropriate camshaft.*

3   Measure the thrust clearance (endplay) of the camshaft(s) with a dial indicator **(see illustration)**. If the clearance is greater than the value listed in this Chapter's Specifications, replace the camshaft and/or the cylinder head.

4   These engines have two "camshaft cap clusters" for each camshaft. The configuration of the two cap clusters are different and must be placed in their original locations. Mark the camshaft cap clusters with a front and rear indication, for both the left and right cylinder heads. **Note:** *Make sure all the bolts used on one of the camshaft cap clusters* **(see illustration)** *go back in the same locations on reassembly.*

5   Refer to Section 8 for removal of the front cover and Section 9 for removal of the timing chains. **Note:** *While the timing chains*

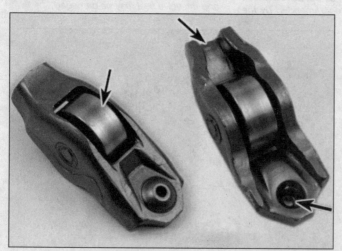

10.7 Check the roller surface of the rocker arms and the areas where the valve stem and lash adjuster contact the rocker

11.3 Camshaft endplay can be checked by setting up a dial indicator off the front of the camshaft and prying the camshaft gently forward and back

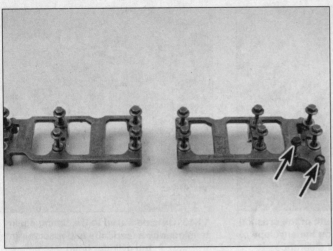

11.4 These engines are equipped with camshaft cap clusters rather than individual bearing caps that hold the camshaft in place on the cylinder head. Note the position of the two different cap clusters

11.9a Areas to look for excessive wear or damage on the camshafts are the bearing surfaces and the camshaft lobes

2B

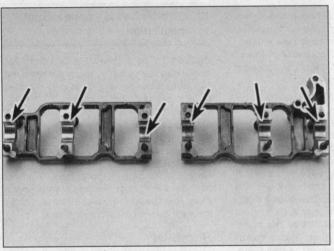

11.9b Inspect the bearing surfaces of the camshaft bearing caps for signs of excessive wear, damage or overheating

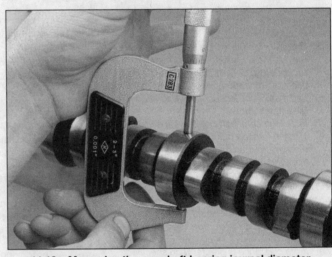

11.10a Measuring the camshaft bearing journal diameter

are off, the crankshaft must not be turned or valve-to-piston interference could result.

6   It's IMPORTANT to loosen the bearing cap bolts only 1/4-turn at a time, following the reverse of the tightening sequence **(see illustrations 11.16)**, until they can be removed by hand.

7   Remove the caps and lift the camshaft off the cylinder head. You may have to tap lightly under the camshaft caps to jar them loose. Don't mix up the camshafts or any of the components. They must all go back on the same positions, and on the same cylinder head they were removed from.

8   Repeat this procedure for removal of the remaining camshaft.

Inspection

Refer to illustrations 11.9a, 11.9b, 11.10a, 11.10b, 11.10c, 11.11a, 11.11b and 11.13

9   Visually examine the cam lobes and bearing journals for score marks, pitting, galling and evidence of overheating (blue, discolored areas). Look for flaking of the hardened surface of each lobe **(see illustrations)**.

10   Using a micrometer, measure the diameter of each camshaft journal and the lift of each camshaft lobe **(see illustrations)**. Compare your measurements with the Specifications listed at the front of this Chapter, and if the diameter of any one of these is less than specified, replace the camshaft.

11.10b Measure the camshaft lobe at its greatest dimension . . .

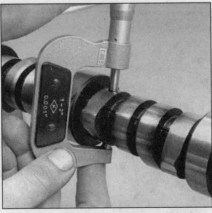

11.10c . . . then subtract the camshaft lobe diameter at its smallest dimension to obtain the lobe lift specification

11.11a Lay a strip of Plastigage on each of the camshaft journals

11.11b Compare the width of the crushed Plastigage to the scale on the envelope to determine the oil clearance

11.13 Oil is delivered to the timing chain tensioner by a feed tube and reservoir in the cylinder head

1   Tensioner oil feed tube
2   Reservoir

11   Check the oil clearance for each camshaft journal as follows:

a) Clean the bearing surfaces and the camshaft journals with lacquer thinner or acetone.

b) Carefully lay the camshaft(s) in place in the cylinder head. Don't install the rocker arms or lash adjusters and don't use any lubrication.

c) Lay a strip of Plastigage on each journal (see illustration).

d) Install the camshaft bearing caps.

e) Tighten the cap bolts, a little at a time, to the torque listed in this Chapter's Specifications. **Note:** Don't turn the camshaft while the Plastigage is in place.

f) Remove the bolts and detach the caps.

g) Compare the width of the crushed Plastigage (at its widest point) to the scale on the Plastigage envelope (see illustration).

h) If the clearance is greater than specified, and the diameter of any journal is less than specified, replace the camshaft. If the journal diameters are within specifications but the oil clearance is too great, the cylinder head is worn and must be replaced.

12   Scrape off the Plastigage with your fingernail or the edge of a credit card - don't

scratch or nick the journals or bearing surfaces.

13   Finally, be sure to check the timing chain tensioner oil feed tube and reservoir before installing the cam caps (see illustration). It must be absolutely clean and free of all obstructions or it will affect the operation of the timing chain tensioner.

Installation

Refer to illustration 11.16

14   If the lash adjusters and/or camshaft followers have been removed, install them in their original locations (see Section 10).

15   Apply moly-base grease or camshaft installation lube to the camshaft lobes and bearing journals, then install the camshaft(s).

16   Install the camshaft caps in the correct locations, and loosely install all the bolts. Refer to Section 9 to align the camshaft sprockets before tightening the cap bolts. Following the correct bolt-tightening sequence (see illustration), tighten the bolts in 1/4-turn increments to the torque listed in this Chapter's Specifications.

17   Install the timing chain(s), tensioners and timing chain cover (see Section 9).

18   The remainder of installation is the reverse of the removal procedure.

12   Cylinder heads - removal and installation

Caution 1: The engine must be completely cool when the cylinder heads are removed. Failure to allow the engine to cool off could result in cylinder head warpage.
Caution 2: The manufacturer does not allow the cylinder head to be milled or machined in the event of warping. If the cylinder head flatness exceeds 0.001 inch (0.0254 mm) replace the cylinder head.
Note: Cylinder head removal is a difficult and time-consuming job requiring several special tools. Read through the procedure and obtain the necessary tools before beginning.

Removal

1   Disconnect the cable from the negative battery terminal (see Chapter 5).

2   Drain the cooling system (see Chapter 1).

3   Remove the valve covers (see Section 4).

4   Remove the intake manifold (see Section 5).

5   Remove the exhaust manifolds (see Section 6).

6   Remove the timing chain cover (see Section 8).

7   Remove the timing chain, tensioners and sprockets (see Section 9).

8   If the cylinder head is to be completely overhauled, refer to Section 11 for removal of the camshafts.

9   Following the reverse of the tightening sequence (see illustration 12.18a), use a breaker bar to remove the cylinder head bolts. Loosen the bolts in sequence 1/4-turn at a time.

10   Use a pry bar at the corners of the cylinder head-to-engine block mating surface to break the cylinder head gasket seal. Do not pry between the cylinder head and engine block in the gasket sealing area.

11   Lift the cylinder head(s) off the engine. If

11.16 The camshaft cap cluster bolt tightening sequence - notice that each cap cluster (two total) is tightened separately and has its own sequence

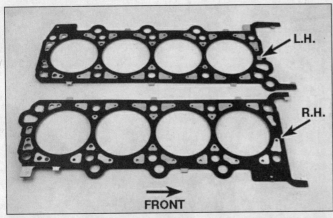

12.16 Identify the left and right cylinder head gaskets, the shapes are different and cannot be interchanged

12.17 Position the gaskets on the correct cylinder banks, then push them down over the alignment dowels

resistance is felt, place a wood block against the end and strike the wood block with a hammer. **Caution:** *The cylinder heads are aluminum, store them on wood blocks to prevent damage to the gasket sealing surfaces.*

12   Remove the cylinder head gasket(s). Before removing, note which gasket goes on which side (they are different and cannot be interchanged).

Installation

Refer to illustrations 12.16, 12.17, 12.18a and 12.18b

Caution: *New cylinder head bolts must be used for reassembly. Failure to use new bolts may result in cylinder head gasket leakage and engine damage.*

13   The mating surfaces of the cylinder heads and engine block must be perfectly clean when the cylinder heads are installed. Use a gasket scraper to remove all traces of carbon and old gasket material, then clean the mating surfaces with lacquer thinner or acetone. If there's oil on the mating surfaces when the cylinder heads are installed, the gaskets may not seal correctly and leaks may develop. When working on the engine block, cover the open areas of the engine with shop rags to keep debris out during repair and reassembly. Use a vacuum cleaner to remove any debris that falls into the cylinders. **Caution:** *Do not use abrasive wheels or sharp metal scrapers on the heads or block surface, use a plastic scraper and chemical gasket remover, or the head gasket surfaces could have future leaks.*

14   Check the engine block and cylinder head mating surfaces for nicks, deep scratches and other damage.

15   Use a tap of the correct size to chase the threads in the cylinder head bolt holes. Dirt, corrosion, sealant and damaged threads will affect torque readings.

16   Make sure the new gaskets are installed on the correct cylinder banks **(see illustration)**. They are not interchangeable.

17   Position the new gasket(s) over the alignment dowels **(see illustration)** in the engine block.

18   Carefully position the cylinder heads on

the engine block without disturbing the gaskets. Install the NEW cylinder head bolts (the cylinder head bolts are torque-to-yield design and they cannot be reused). Following the recommended sequence **(see illustration)**, tighten the cylinder head bolts, in five steps, to the torque listed in this Chapter's Specifications. **Note:** *The method used for the cylinder head bolt tightening procedure is referred to as "torque-angle" or "torque-to-yield" method. Follow the procedure exactly. Tighten the bolts in the first and third steps using a torque wrench, then use a breaker bar and a special torque-angle adapter (available at most auto parts stores) to tighten the bolts the required angle. If the adapter is not available, mark each bolt with a paint stripe*

to aid in the torque angle process **(see illustration)**.

19   The remaining installation steps are the reverse of removal.

20   Change the engine oil and filter (Chapter 1), then start the engine and check carefully for oil and coolant leaks.

13   Oil pan - removal and installation

Removal

Refer to illustration 13.7

1   Disconnect the negative battery cable from the battery (see Chapter 5).

2   Refer to Chapter 1 and drain the engine

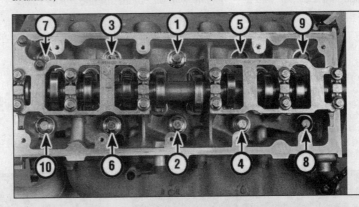

12.18a Cylinder head bolt-tightening sequence

12.18b Mark each cylinder head bolt with a paint stripe and using a breaker bar and socket, tighten the bolts in sequence to the correct torque angle

2B

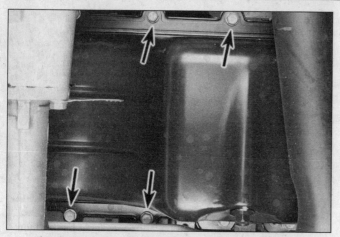

13.7 Remove the bolts from around the perimeter of the oil pan (arrows indicate four) and lower the pan to the frame crossmember

13.11 Apply a bead of RTV sealant at the junctions of the front cover-to-engine block and the rear-seal retainer-to-engine block before installing the oil pan

oil and remove the oil filter.

3   On 2WD models, remove the front stabilizer bar (see Chapter 10).

4   On 4WD models, remove the front axle assembly (see Chapter 8).

5   Raise the vehicle and support it securely on jackstands.

6   Remove the oil level dipstick.

7   Remove the oil pan mounting bolts **(see illustration)**.

8   Carefully separate the oil pan from the engine block. Don't pry between the engine block and oil pan or damage to the sealing surfaces may result and oil leaks could develop. Instead, dislodge the oil pan with a large rubber mallet or a wood block and a hammer.

Installation

Refer to illustration 13.11

9   Use a gasket scraper or putty knife to remove all traces of old gasket material and sealant from the pan and engine block. **Caution:** *Be careful not to gouge the oil pan or block, or oil leaks could develop later.*

10   Clean the mating surfaces with lacquer thinner or acetone. Make sure the bolt holes

in the engine block are clean.

11   Apply a bead of RTV sealant to the four corner seams where the rear seal retainer meets the engine block, and the front cover meets the engine block **(see illustration)**.

12   Carefully position the oil pan against the engine block and install the bolts finger tight. Make sure the gaskets haven't shifted, then tighten the bolts to the torque listed in this Chapter's Specifications. Start at the center of the oil pan and work out toward the ends in a spiral pattern.

13   The remaining steps are the reverse of removal. **Caution:** *Don't forget to refill the engine with oil before starting it (see Chapter 1).*

14   Start the engine and check carefully for oil leaks at the oil pan. Drive the vehicle and check again.

14   Oil pump - removal and installation

Refer to illustrations 14.3, 14.5 and 14.6
Note: *The oil pump is available as a complete replacement unit only. No service parts or*

repair specifications are available from the manufacturer.

Removal

1   Raise the vehicle and support it securely on jackstands.

2   Drain the engine oil (see Chapter 1).

3   Remove the oil pan (see Section 13). Remove the two bolts that attach the oil pump pick-up tube to the oil pump **(see illustration)**.

4   Remove the timing chain cover, timing chains, chain guides and crankshaft sprocket (see Sections 8 and 9).

5   Remove the oil pump mounting bolts **(see illustration)** and separate the pump from the engine block.

Installation

6   Inspect the O-ring gasket on the pick-up tube **(see illustration)**. If it's damaged, replace it.

7   Install the oil pump to the engine and tighten the bolts to the torque listed in this Chapter's Specifications. **Note:** *Prime the oil pump prior to installation. Pour clean oil into the pick-up port and turn the pump by hand.*

14.3 Remove the two bolts retaining the pickup tube to the oil pump

14.5 Remove the oil pump mounting bolts and oil pump from the engine block

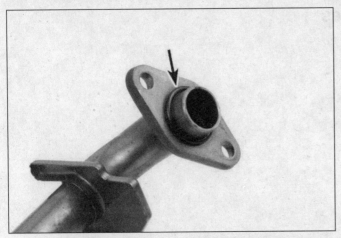

14.6 Before bolting the pickup tube back into the oil pump, inspect the O-ring and replace it if necessary

16.7 Inspect the seal contact surface on the crankshaft for signs of excessive wear or grooves

8   The remainder of installation is the reverse of removal procedure.
9   Fill the engine with the correct type and quantity of oil. Start the engine and check for leaks.

15 Driveplate - removal and installation

This procedure is essentially the same as for the V6 engine. Refer to part A and follow the procedure outlined there. However, use the bolt torque listed in this Chapter's Specifications.

16 Rear main oil seal - replacement

Refer to illustration 16.7
Note: *Rear main oil seal replacement is a time-consuming job requiring several special tools, read through the procedure and obtain the necessary tools before beginning.*

1   Disconnect the cable from the negative battery terminal (see Chapter 5).
2   Raise the vehicle and support it securely on jackstands.
3   Remove the transmission (see Chapter 7).
4   Remove the driveplate from the engine (Section 15).
5   Remove the crankshaft rear oil slinger.
6   Remove the rear main oil seal from the retainer. **Caution:** *To prevent an oil leak after the new seal is installed, be very careful not to scratch or otherwise damage the crankshaft sealing surface or the bore in the engine block.*
7   Clean the crankshaft and seal bore in the block thoroughly and de-grease these areas by wiping them with a rag soaked in lacquer thinner or acetone. Check the seal contact surface on the crankshaft very carefully for scratches or nicks that could damage the new seal lip and cause oil leaks **(see illustration)**. Lubricate the lip of the new seal and the outer diameter of the crankshaft with engine oil. Make sure the edges of the new oil

seal are not rolled over.
8   Position the new seal onto the crankshaft. **Note:** *When installing the new seal, if so marked, the words THIS SIDE OUT on the seal must face out, toward the rear of the engine.* Use a special rear main oil seal installation tool or a socket with the exact diameter of the seal to drive the seal in place. Make sure the seal is not off-set; it must be flush along the entire circumference of the seal carrier.
9   Install the crankshaft rear oil slinger.
10   The remainder of installation is the reverse of removal.

17 Engine mounts - check and replacement

Refer to illustrations 17.1a, 17.1b and 17.1c
This procedure is essentially the same as for the V6 engine. Refer to part A and follow the procedure outlined there but refer to the illustrations for this section.

17.1a Inspect the engine mount components for cracked rubber insulators, missing bolts or cracked metal brackets

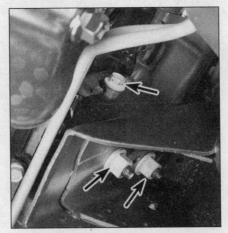

17.1b With the engine raised slightly, remove the mount through-bolt (upper arrow) - lower arrows indicate nuts to remove if the lower bracket is to be replaced

17.1c There are three bolts holding the mount to the block (arrows indicate two; there is one more at the other end of the mount)

2B

Notes

Chapter 2 Part C
General engine overhaul procedures

Contents

2C

Specifications

General

Displacement	
V6 models	4.0 liters (244 cubic inches)
V8 models	4.6 liters (281 cubic inches)
Bore and Stroke	
V6 models	3.950 X 3.310 inches (100.4 x 80.4 mm)
V8 models	3.554 X 3.546 inches (90.2 x 90.0 mm)
Cylinder compression	Lowest cylinder must be within 75 percent of highest cylinder
Oil pressure (engine at operating temperature)	
V6 models	15 psi (103 kPa) @ 2,000 rpm
V8 models	20 to 45 psi (138 to 310 kPa) @ 1,500 rpm

Torque specifications

	Ft-lbs (unless otherwise indicated)	Nm
Flywheel mounting bolts	See Chapter 2A	
Torque converter bolts (V8 models)	28	38
Torque converter nuts (V6 models)	35	47
Connecting rod bearing cap bolts		
V6 models		
Step 1	15	20
Step 2	Tighten an additional 90-degrees	
V8 models **(see illustration 10.45)**		
Step 1	17	23
Step 2	32	43
Step 3	Tighten an additional 90 to 120-degrees	
Main bearing caps		
V6 models	72	97
V8 models **(see illustration 11.19a and 11.19b)**		
Step 1 Bolts 1 through 20	71 to 106 in-lbs	8 to 12
Step 2 Bolts 1 through 10	17 to 20	22 to 28
Step 3 Bolts 11 through 20	28 to 31	37 to 43
Step 4 Bolts 1 through 20	Tighten an additional 90-degrees	
Step 5 Side bolts		
Step 1	30	40
Step 2	Tighten an additional 90-degrees	
Jackshaft thrust plate bolts	96 in-lbs	11
Balance shaft assembly bolts	20	27
Balance shaft chain guide bolts	89 in-lbs	10
Balance shaft tensioner bolts	21	29

1   General information - engine overhaul

Refer to illustrations 1.1, 1.2, 1.3, 1.4, 1.5 and 1.6

Included in this portion of Chapter 2 are general information and diagnostic testing procedures for determining the overall mechanical condition of your engine.

The information ranges from advice concerning preparation for an overhaul and the purchase of replacement parts and/or components to detailed, step-by-step procedures covering removal and installation.

The following Sections have been written to help you determine whether your engine needs to be overhauled and how to remove and install it once you've determined it needs to be rebuilt. For information concerning in-vehicle engine repair, see Chapter 2A or 2B.

The Specifications included in this Part are general in nature and include only those necessary for testing the oil pressure and checking the engine compression. Refer to Chapter 2A or 2B for additional engine Specifications.

It's not always easy to determine when, or if, an engine should be completely overhauled, because a number of factors must be considered.

High mileage is not necessarily an indication that an overhaul is needed, while low mileage doesn't preclude the need for an overhaul. Frequency of servicing is probably the most important consideration. An engine that's had regular and frequent oil and filter changes, as well as other required maintenance, will most likely give many thousands of miles of reliable service. Conversely, a neglected engine may require an overhaul very early in its service life.

Excessive oil consumption is an indication that piston rings, valve seals and/or valve guides are in need of attention. Make sure that oil leaks aren't responsible before deciding that the rings and/or guides are bad. Perform a cylinder compression check to determine the extent of the work required (see Section 3). Also check the vacuum readings under various conditions (see Section 4).

Check the oil pressure with a gauge installed in place of the oil pressure sending unit and compare it to this Chapter's Specifications (see Section 2). If it's extremely low, the bearings and/or oil pump are probably worn out.

Loss of power, rough running, knocking or metallic engine noises, excessive valve train noise and high fuel consumption rates may also point to the need for an overhaul, especially if they're all present at the same time. If a complete tune-up doesn't remedy the situation, major mechanical work is the only solution.

An engine overhaul involves restoring the internal parts to the specifications of a new engine. During an overhaul, the piston rings are replaced and the cylinder walls are reconditioned (rebored and/or honed) **(see illustrations 1.1 and 1.2)**. If a rebore is done by an automotive machine shop, new oversize pistons will also be installed. The main bearings, connecting rod bearings and camshaft bearings are generally replaced with new ones and, if necessary, the crankshaft may be reground to restore the journals **(see illustration 1.3)**. Generally, the valves are serviced as well, since they're usually in less-than-perfect condition at this point. While the engine is being overhauled, other components, such as the distributor, starter and alternator, can be rebuilt as well. The end result should be similar to a new engine that will give many trouble free miles. **Note:** *Critical cooling system components such as the hoses, drivebelts, thermostat and water pump should be replaced with new parts when an engine is overhauled. The radiator should be checked carefully to ensure that it isn't clogged or leaking (see Chapter 3). If you purchase a rebuilt engine or short block, some rebuilders will not warranty their engines unless the radiator has been professionally flushed. Also, we don't recommend overhauling the oil pump - always install a new one when an engine is rebuilt.*

Overhauling the internal components on today's engines is a difficult and time-consuming task which requires a significant amount of specialty tools and is best left to a

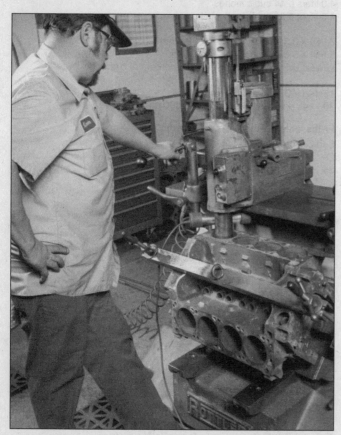

1.1 An engine block being bored. An engine rebuilder will use special machinery to recondition the cylinder bores

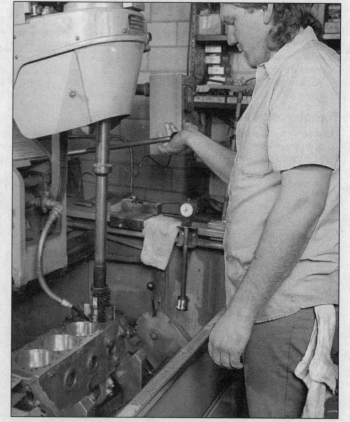

1.2 If the cylinders are bored, the machine shop will normally hone the engine on a machine like this

1.3 A crankshaft having a main bearing journal ground

1.4 A machinist checks for a bent connecting rod, using specialized equipment

1.5 A bore gauge being used to check the main bearing bore

1.6 Uneven piston wear like this indicates a bent connecting rod

2C

professional engine rebuilder **(see illustrations 1.4, 1.5 and 1.6)**. A competent engine rebuilder will handle the inspection of your old parts and offer advice concerning the reconditioning or replacement of the original engine, never purchase parts or have machine work done on other components until the block has been thoroughly inspected by a professional machine shop. As a general rule, time is the primary cost of an overhaul, especially since the vehicle may be tied up for a minimum of two weeks or more. Be aware that some engine builders only have the capability to rebuild the engine you bring them while other rebuilders have a large inventory of rebuilt exchange engines in stock. Also be aware that many machine shops could take as much as two weeks time to completely rebuild your engine depending on shop workload. Sometimes it makes more sense to simply exchange your engine for another engine that's already rebuilt to save time.

2 Oil pressure check

Refer to illustrations 2.2a and 2.2b

1   Low engine oil pressure can be a sign of an engine in need of rebuilding. A "low oil pressure" indicator (often called an "idiot light") is not a test of the oiling system. Such indicators only come on when the oil pressure is dangerously low. Even a factory oil pressure gauge in the instrument panel is only a relative indication, although much better for driver information than a warning light. A better test is with a mechanical (not electrical) oil pressure gauge.

2   Locate the oil pressure sending unit on the engine block:

a)   *On V6 engines, the oil pressure sending unit is located on the front, left side of the engine block near the front cover* **(see illustration)**.

b)   *On V8 engines, the oil pressure sending unit is located near the lower, left side of the engine block near the oil filter housing* **(see illustration)**.

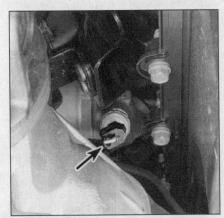

2.2a On V6 engines, the oil pressure sending unit is located on the left side of the engine block near the front cover

2.2b On V8 engines, the oil pressure sending unit is located on the side of the engine block near the oil filter

3.6 Use a compression gauge with a threaded fitting for the spark plug hole, not the type that requires hand pressure to maintain the seal

4.4 A simple vacuum gauge can be handy in diagnosing engine condition and performance

3   Unscrew and remove the oil pressure sending unit and screw in the hose for your oil pressure gauge. If necessary, install an adapter fitting. Use Teflon tape or thread sealant on the threads of the adapter and/or the fitting on the end of your gauge's hose.

4   Connect an accurate tachometer to the engine, according to the tachometer manufacturer's instructions.

5   Check the oil pressure with the engine running (normal operating temperature) at the specified engine speed, and compare it to this Chapter's Specifications. If it's extremely low, the bearings and/or oil pump are probably worn out.

3   Cylinder compression check

Refer to illustration 3.6

1   A compression check will tell you what mechanical condition the upper end of your engine (pistons, rings, valves, head gaskets) is in. Specifically, it can tell you if the compression is down due to leakage caused by worn piston rings, defective valves and seats or a blown head gasket. **Note:** *The engine must be at normal operating temperature and the battery must be fully charged for this check.*

2   Begin by cleaning the area around the spark plugs before you remove them (compressed air should be used, if available). The idea is to prevent dirt from getting into the cylinders as the compression check is being done.

3   Remove all of the spark plugs from the engine (see Chapter 1).

4   Block the throttle wide open.

5   Disconnect the primary (low voltage) wires from the coil pack (V6 models) or the connectors at the ignition coils (V8 models) (see Chapter 5). Remove the fuel pump relay (see Chapter 4). The relays are located in the power distribution center in the engine compartment (see Chapter 12).

6   Install a compression gauge in the spark plug hole **(see illustration)**.

7   Crank the engine over at least seven compression strokes and watch the gauge. The compression should build up quickly in a healthy engine. Low compression on the first stroke, followed by gradually increasing pressure on successive strokes, indicates worn piston rings. A low compression reading on the first stroke, which doesn't build up during successive strokes, indicates leaking valves or a blown head gasket (a cracked head could also be the cause). Deposits on the undersides of the valve heads can also cause low compression. Record the highest gauge reading obtained.

8   Repeat the procedure for the remaining cylinders and compare the results to this Chapter's Specifications.

9   Add some engine oil (about three squirts from a plunger-type oil can) to each cylinder, through the spark plug hole, and repeat the test.

10   If the compression increases after the oil is added, the piston rings are definitely worn. If the compression doesn't increase significantly, the leakage is occurring at the valves or head gasket. Leakage past the valves may be caused by burned valve seats and/or faces or warped, cracked or bent valves.

11   If two adjacent cylinders have equally low compression, there's a strong possibility that the head gasket between them is blown. The appearance of coolant in the combustion chambers or the crankcase would verify this condition.

12   If one cylinder is slightly lower than the others, and the engine has a slightly rough idle, a worn lobe on the camshaft could be the cause.

13   If the compression is unusually high, the combustion chambers are probably coated with carbon deposits. If that's the case, the cylinder head(s) should be removed and decarbonized.

14   If compression is way down or varies greatly between cylinders, it would be a good idea to have a leak-down test performed by an automotive repair shop. This test will pinpoint exactly where the leakage is occurring and how severe it is.

4   Vacuum gauge diagnostic checks

Refer to illustrations 4.4 and 4.6

A vacuum gauge provides inexpensive but valuable information about what is going on in the engine. You can check for worn rings or cylinder walls, leaking head or intake manifold gaskets, incorrect carburetor adjustments, restricted exhaust, stuck or burned valves, weak valve springs, improper ignition or valve timing and ignition problems.

Unfortunately, vacuum gauge readings are easy to misinterpret, so they should be used in conjunction with other tests to confirm the diagnosis.

Both the absolute readings and the rate of needle movement are important for accurate interpretation. Most gauges measure vacuum in inches of mercury (in-Hg). The following references to vacuum assume the diagnosis is being performed at sea level. As elevation increases (or atmospheric pressure decreases), the reading will decrease. For every 1,000 foot increase in elevation above approximately 2,000 feet, the gauge readings will decrease about one inch of mercury.

Connect the vacuum gauge directly to the intake manifold vacuum, not to ported (throttle body) vacuum **(see illustration)**. Be sure no hoses are left disconnected during the test or false readings will result.

Before you begin the test, allow the engine to warm up completely. Block the wheels and set the parking brake. With the transmission in Park, start the engine and allow it to run at normal idle speed. **Warning:** *Keep your hands and the vacuum gauge clear of the fans.*

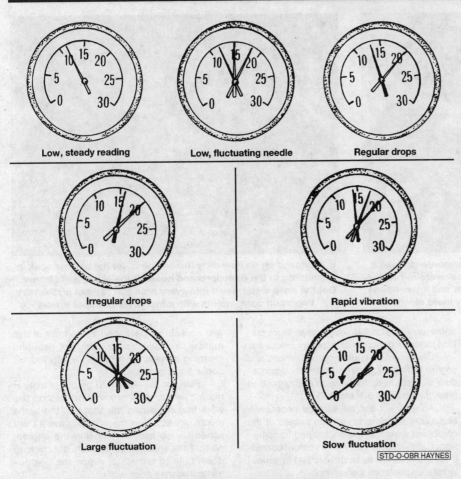

Low, steady reading	Low, fluctuating needle	Regular drops
Irregular drops	Rapid vibration	
Large fluctuation	Slow fluctuation	

STD-O-OBR HAYNES

4.6 Typical vacuum gauge readings

Read the vacuum gauge; an average, healthy engine should normally produce about 17 to 22 in-Hg with a fairly steady needle **(see illustration)**. Refer to the following vacuum gauge readings and what they indicate about the engine's condition:

1   A low steady reading usually indicates a leaking gasket between the intake manifold and cylinder head(s) or throttle body, a leaky vacuum hose, late ignition timing or incorrect camshaft timing. Check ignition timing with a timing light and eliminate all other possible causes, utilizing the tests provided in this Chapter before you remove the timing chain cover to check the timing marks.

2   If the reading is three to eight inches below normal and it fluctuates at that low reading, suspect an intake manifold gasket leak at an intake port or a faulty fuel injector.

3   If the needle has regular drops of about two-to-four inches at a steady rate, the valves are probably leaking. Perform a compression check or leak-down test to confirm this.

4   An irregular drop or down-flick of the needle can be caused by a sticking valve or an ignition misfire. Perform a compression check or leak-down test and read the spark plugs.

5   A rapid vibration of about four in-Hg vibration at idle combined with exhaust smoke indicates worn valve guides. Perform

a leak-down test to confirm this. If the rapid vibration occurs with an increase in engine speed, check for a leaking intake manifold gasket or head gasket, weak valve springs, burned valves or ignition misfire.

6   A slight fluctuation, say one inch up and down, may mean ignition problems. Check all the usual tune-up items and, if necessary, run the engine on an ignition analyzer.

7   If there is a large fluctuation, perform a compression or leak-down test to look for a weak or dead cylinder or a blown head gasket.

8   If the needle moves slowly through a wide range, check for a clogged PCV system, incorrect idle fuel mixture, throttle body or intake manifold gasket leaks.

9   Check for a slow return after revving the engine by quickly snapping the throttle open until the engine reaches about 2,500 rpm and let it shut. Normally the reading should drop to near zero, rise above normal idle reading (about 5 in-Hg over) and return to the previous idle reading. If the vacuum returns slowly and doesn't peak when the throttle is snapped shut, the rings may be worn. If there is a long delay, look for a restricted exhaust system (often the muffler or catalytic converter). An easy way to check this is to temporarily disconnect the exhaust ahead of the suspected part and redo the test.

5   Engine rebuilding alternatives

The do-it-yourselfer is faced with a number of options when purchasing a rebuilt engine. The major considerations are cost, warranty, parts availability and the time required for the rebuilder to complete the project. The decision to replace the engine block, piston/connecting rod assemblies and crankshaft depends on the final inspection results of your engine. Only then can you make a cost effective decision whether to have your engine overhauled or simply purchase an exchange engine for your vehicle.

Some of the rebuilding alternatives include:

Individual parts - If the inspection procedures reveal that the engine block and most engine components are in reusable condition, purchasing individual parts and having a rebuilder rebuild your engine may be the most economical alternative. The block, crankshaft and piston/connecting rod assemblies should all be inspected carefully by a machine shop first.

Short block - A short block consists of an engine block with a crankshaft and piston/connecting rod assemblies already installed. All new bearings are incorporated and all clearances will be correct. The existing camshafts, valve train components, cylinder head and external parts can be bolted to the short block with little or no machine shop work necessary.

Long block - A long block consists of a short block plus an oil pump, oil pan, cylinder head, valve cover, camshaft and valve train components, timing sprockets and chain or gears and timing cover. All components are installed with new bearings, seals and gaskets incorporated throughout. The installation of manifolds and external parts is all that's necessary.

Low mileage used engines - Some companies now offer low mileage used engines which is a very cost effective way to get your vehicle up and running again. These engines often come from vehicles which have been in totaled in accidents or come from other countries which have a higher vehicle turn over rate. A low mileage used engine also usually has a similar warranty like the newly remanufactured engines.

Give careful thought to which alternative is best for you and discuss the situation with local automotive machine shops, auto parts dealers and experienced rebuilders before ordering or purchasing replacement parts.

6   Engine removal - methods and precautions

Refer to illustrations 6.1, 6.2, 6.3 and 6.4

If you've decided that an engine must be removed for overhaul or major repair work, several preliminary steps should be taken. Read all removal and installation pro-

2C

6.1 After tightly wrapping water-vulnerable components, use a spray cleaner on everything, with particular concentration on the greasiest areas, usually around the valve cover and lower edges of the block. If one section dries out, apply more cleaner

6.2 Depending on how dirty the engine is, let the cleaner soak in according to the directions and hose off the grime and cleaner. Get the rinse water down into every area you can get at, then dry important components with a hair dryer or paper towels

cedures carefully prior to committing to this job.

Locating a suitable place to work is extremely important. Adequate work space, along with storage space for the vehicle, will be needed. If a shop or garage isn't available,

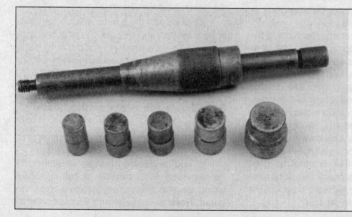

6.3 Get an engine stand sturdy enough to firmly support the engine while you're working on it. Stay away from three-wheeled models; they have a tendency to tip over more easily, so get a four-wheeled unit.

at the very least a flat, level, clean work surface made of concrete or asphalt is required.

Cleaning the engine compartment and engine before beginning the removal procedure will help keep tools clean and organized **(see illustrations 6.1 and 6.2).**

An engine hoist will also be necessary. Make sure the hoist is rated in excess of the combined weight of the engine and transmission. Safety is of primary importance, considering the potential hazards involved in removing the engine from the vehicle.

If you're a novice at engine removal, get at least one helper. One person cannot easily do all the things you need to do to remove a big heavy engine and transmission assembly from the engine compartment. Also helpful is to seek advice and assistance from someone who's experienced in engine removal.

Plan the operation ahead of time. Arrange for or obtain all of the tools and equipment you'll need prior to beginning the job **(see illustrations 6.3 and 6.4).** Some of the equipment necessary to perform engine removal and installation safely and with relative ease are (in addition to a vehicle hoist and an engine hoist) a heavy duty floor jack (preferably fitted with a transmission jack head adapter), complete sets of wrenches

and sockets as described in the front of this manual, wooden blocks, plenty of rags and cleaning solvent for mopping up spilled oil, coolant and gasoline.

Plan for the vehicle to be out of use for quite a while. A machine shop can do the work that is beyond the scope of the home mechanic. Machine shops often have a busy schedule, so before removing the engine, consult the shop for an estimate of how long it will take to rebuild or repair the components that may need work.

---

7   Engine - removal and installation

Refer to illustrations 7.8, 7.10, 7.38a and 7.38b

Warning 1: *Gasoline is extremely flammable, so take extra precautions when you work on any part of the fuel system. Don't smoke or allow open flames or bare light bulbs near the work area, and don't work in a garage where a gas-type appliance (such as a water heater or clothes dryer) is present. Since gasoline is carcinogenic, wear fuel-resistant gloves when there's a possibility of being exposed to fuel, and, if you spill any fuel on your skin, rinse it off immediately with soap and water. Mop up any spills immediately and do not store fuel-soaked rags where they could ignite. The fuel system is under constant pressure, so, if any fuel lines are to be disconnected, the fuel pressure in the system must be relieved first (see Chapter 4 for more information). When you perform any kind of work on the fuel system, wear safety glasses and have a Class B type fire extinguisher on hand.*

Warning 2: *The air conditioning system is under high pressure. DO NOT loosen any fittings or remove any components until after the system has been discharged. Air conditioning refrigerant should be properly discharged into an EPA-approved container at a dealer service department or an automotive*

6.4 A clutch alignment tool is necessary if you plan to install a rebuilt engine mated to a manual transmission

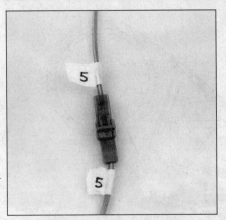

7.8 Label both ends of each wire and hose before disconnecting it

7.10 Remove the engine ground strap mounting bolt from the cylinder head

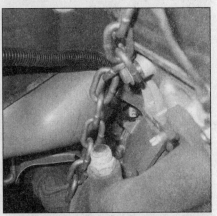

7.38a Attach the chain to the cylinder head using a long mounting bolt - it may be necessary to tap the cylinder head casting to accommodate the lifting chain bolt

7.38b Raise the engine using the engine hoist

air conditioning repair facility. Always wear eye protection when disconnecting air conditioning system fittings.

Warning 3: *The engine must be completely cool before beginning this procedure.*

Removal

1   Disconnect the cable from the negative battery terminal (see Chapter 5).

2   Have the air conditioning system discharged by an automotive air conditioning technician.

3   Relieve the fuel system pressure (see Chapter 4).

4   Remove the fender splash shields, the engine cover and the hood (see Chapter 11). Cover the fenders and cowl using special pads. An old bedspread or blanket will also work.

5   Remove the intake ducts and the air filter housing (see Chapter 4).

6   Disconnect the accelerator cable, the cruise control cable, if equipped, and bracket from the engine and position them aside (see Chapter 4).

7   Remove the battery and the battery tray (see Chapter 5).

8   Clearly label and disconnect all vacuum lines, emissions hoses, wiring harness connectors, ground straps and fuel lines. Masking tape and/or a touch up paint applicator work well for marking items **(see illustration)**. Take instant photos or sketch the locations of components and brackets.

9   Disconnect the electrical connectors from the PCM (see Chapter 6).

10   Detach the positive cables and the electrical connectors from the engine compartment fuse/relay box and the ground cable from the vehicle **(see illustration)**.

11   Detach the electrical connectors from the battery tray support. Also detach any other electrical connectors between the engine and the vehicle.

12   Remove the accessory drivebelt (see Chapter 1).

13   Disconnect the power steering pump return line and hose from the power steering pump (see Chapter 10).

14   Disconnect the fuel lines from the fuel

rail (see Chapter 4).

15   Remove the radiator protector cover (see Chapter 3).

16   Remove the air conditioning lines from the condenser (see Chapter 3).

17   Remove the cruise control actuator assembly mounting bolts and position it off to the side of the engine compartment without disconnecting the accelerator connection.

18   Loosen the front wheel lug nuts, then raise the vehicle and secure it on jackstands. Remove the front wheels and tires.

19   Drain the cooling system (see Chapter 1).

20   Drain the engine oil (see Chapter 1).

21   Detach the lower radiator hose from the engine (see Chapter 3).

22   Lower the vehicle and detach the heater hoses at the firewall (see Chapter 3).

23   Remove the upper radiator hose (see Chapter 3).

24   Remove the cooling fan(s) and shroud(s) (see Chapter 3).

25   Remove the radiator (see Chapter 3).

Note: *On V8 models, detach the air conditioning lines from the top of the radiator and position them off to the side.*

26   On V6 models, remove the EGR pipe (see Chapter 6).

27   Disconnect the shift cable(s) from the transmission (see Chapter 7A or 7B). Also disconnect any wiring harness connectors from the transmission and cable brackets from the engine.

28   Remove the clutch release cylinder and hydraulic line on manual transmissions (see Chapter 8).

29   Disconnect the air conditioning lines at the compressor. Remove the air conditioning compressor (see Chapter 3).

30   Raise the vehicle and secure it on jackstands. Remove the front wheels.

31   Remove the front driveaxles (4WD models) and the driveshaft (see Chapter 8).

32   Remove the transfer case on 4WD models (see Chapter 7C). Disconnect the shift motor electrical connectors.

33   Unplug the oxygen sensor electrical connector(s).

34   Detach the heat shields, exhaust brack-

ets and the exhaust pipes from the exhaust manifolds (see Chapter 4).

35   Remove the inspection cover from the bellhousing on the transmission.

36   If equipped with an automatic transmission, remove the torque converter bolts.

37   Remove the starter motor (see Chapter 5).

38   Roll the engine hoist into position and attach it to the lifting brackets with a couple pieces of heavy-duty chain **(see illustrations)**. Take up the slack in the sling or chain, but don't lift the engine. **Warning:** *DO NOT place any part of your body under the engine when it's supported only by a hoist or other lifting device.*

39   Remove the forward and rear transmission mounts (see Chapter 7).

40   Remove the transmission (see Chapter 7A or 7B).

41   Remove the engine mount fasteners (see the "Engine mount" section in Chapter 2A or 2B).

42   Remove the crossmember.

43   Recheck to be sure nothing is still connecting the engine or vehicle. Disconnect anything still remaining.

9.3 Remove the oil pump drive assembly retaining bolt and clamp (A) and pull the drive assembly (B) straight up and out of the engine block

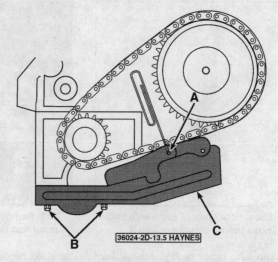

36024-2D-13.5 HAYNES

9.5 Press the balance shaft tensioner in and insert a pin (A) - remove the balance shaft tensioner bolts (B) and remove the tensioner assembly (C)

44 Raise the engine slightly and inspect it thoroughly once more to make sure that *nothing* is still attached, then slowly raise the engine out of the engine compartment. Check carefully to make sure nothing is hanging up.

45 Remove the flywheel/driveplate (see Chapter 2A or 2B) and mount the engine on an engine stand **(see illustration 6.3)**.

46 Inspect the engine and transmission mounts (see the "Engine mount" section in Chapter 2A or 2B). If they're worn or damaged, replace them.

Installation

47 Install the flywheel/driveplate (see Chapter 2A or 2B).

48 If you're working on a vehicle with manual transmission, install the clutch and pressure plate (see Chapter 8). Now is a good time to install a new clutch.

49 Carefully lower the engine into the engine compartment and reattach it to the engine mounts (see the "Engine mounts" section in Chapter 2A or 2B).

50 Install the transmission (see Chapter 7). If you're working on a manual transmission equipped vehicle, apply a dab of high-temperature grease to the input shaft and guide it into the crankshaft pilot bearing until the bell-housing is flush with the engine block. If you're working on a vehicle with an automatic transmission, guide the torque converter into the crankshaft following the procedure outlined in Chapter 7B. Install the transmission-to-engine bolts and tighten them securely. **Caution:** *DO NOT use the bolts to force the transmission and engine together!*

51 Reinstall the remaining components in the reverse order of removal.

52 Add coolant, oil and transmission fluid as needed.

53 Run the engine and check for leaks and proper operation of all accessories, then install the hood and test drive the vehicle.

54 Have the air conditioning system recharged and leak tested, if it was discharged.

55 Reconnect the battery. After you're done, the Powertrain Control Module (PCM) must relearn its idle and fuel trim strategy for optimum driveability and performance (see Chapter 6).

8 Engine overhaul - disassembly sequence

1 It's much easier to remove the external components if it's mounted on a portable engine stand. A stand can often be rented quite cheaply from an equipment rental yard. Before the engine is mounted on a stand, the flywheel/driveplate should be removed from the engine.

2 If a stand isn't available, it's possible to remove the external engine components with it blocked up on the floor. Be extra careful not to tip or drop the engine when working without a stand.

3 If you're going to obtain a rebuilt engine, all external components must come off first, to be transferred to the replacement engine. These components include:

> Clutch and flywheel (models with manual transmission)
> Driveplate (models with automatic transmission)
> Ignition system components
> Emissions-related components
> Engine mounts and mount brackets
> Engine rear cover (spacer plate between flywheel/driveplate and engine block)
> Intake/exhaust manifolds
> Fuel injection components
> Oil filter
> Spark plug wires (V6 engine) and spark plugs
> Thermostat and housing assembly
> Water pump

Note: *When removing the external components from the engine, pay close attention to details that may be helpful or important during installation. Note the installed position of gaskets, seals, spacers, pins, brackets, washers, bolts and other small items.*

4 If you're going to obtain a short block (assembled engine block, crankshaft, pistons and connecting rods), then remove the timing belt, cylinder head, oil pan, oil pump pick-up tube, oil pump and water pump from your engine so that you can turn in your old short block to the rebuilder as a core. See *Engine rebuilding alternatives* for additional information regarding the different possibilities to be considered.

9 Jackshaft and balance shaft (V6 models) - removal, inspection and installation

Note: *All V6 engines are equipped with a jackshaft. 4WD models with the V6 engine are equipped with a jackshaft and a balance shaft.*

Removal

Refer to illustrations 9.3 and 9.5

1 Disconnect the cable from the negative battery terminal (see Chapter 5).

2 The camshafts, timing chains and sprockets and the jackshaft chain and sprocket must be removed before extracting the jackshaft (see Part A of this Chapter).

3 From above, at the top-rear of the block, remove the bolt holding the oil pump drive and pull out the drive assembly **(see illustration)**.

4 Remove the two jackshaft thrust plate bolts, and any spacer that may be in place. Installing a long bolt in the front of the jackshaft to use as a handle, guide the jackshaft gently out of the block, without nicking the

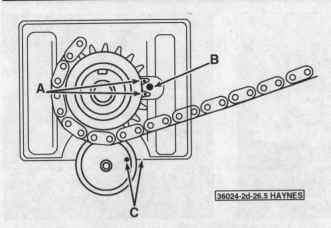

9.14 To align the balance shaft for chain installation, turn the sprocket until the marks on the sprocket (A) align with the hole in the assembly (B) and the lower shaft mark (C) aligns with the mating line of the assembly and engine block

10.1 Before you try to remove the pistons, use a ridge reamer to remove the raised material (ridge) from the top of the cylinders

2C

journals on the jackshaft bearings in the block.

5   Compress the balance shaft tensioner by hand and insert a drill bit or pin to hold it in place, then remove the tensioner bolts and the tensioner **(see illustration)**.

6   Slide the balance shaft chain and crankshaft sprocket from the crankshaft and balance shaft sprocket. **Note:** *Do not remove the bolt from the balance shaft sprocket.*

7   Rotate the engine on the engine stand so that the bottom of the block is up. Remove the two rear bolts and the balance shaft assembly. **Note:** *Two of the balance shaft assembly mounting bolts are the ones removed to take off the tensioner.*

Inspection

8   The jackshaft rides in a bearing at the front of the block and a bushing at the rear. Check the jackshaft bearings in the block for wear and damage. Look for galling, pitting and discolored areas.

9   Jackshaft bearing replacement requires special tools and expertise that place it outside the scope of the home mechanic. Take the block to an automotive machine shop to ensure the job is done correctly.

Installation

Jackshaft

10   Lubricate the jackshaft bearing journals with engine assembly lubricant.

11   Slide the jackshaft into the engine, using a long bolt screwed into the front of the jackshaft as a handle. Support the shaft near the block and be careful not to scrape or nick the bearings. Install the jackshaft thrust plate and tighten the bolts to the torque listed in this Chapter's Specifications.

Balance shaft

Refer to illustration 9.14

12   Lubricate the front bearing and rear journal of the balance shaft with engine oil and insert the balance shaft assembly care-

fully onto the block. The block should be turned bottom-end up on the engine stand, and the crankshaft should be positioned with cylinder number 1 at TDC.

13   Install and tighten the balance shaft bolts to the torque listed in this Chapter's Specifications.

14   Turn the balance shaft sprocket until the two dots on the sprocket align over the hole in the front of the assembly, and the timing mark on the front of the lower shaft aligns with the balance shaft-to-block mating line **(see illustration)**. Install a 4 mm pin or drill bit into the hole to hold it in this position. **Note:** *It make take quite a few turns of the balance shaft sprocket to get the shaft and sprocket timing marks sets to align, because of the reduction gearing in the assembly.*

15   Install the balance shaft chain and the crankshaft sprocket. Install the balance shaft chain guide and tensioner (with the tensioner pinned) **(see illustration 9.5)**. Tighten the chain guide and tensioner bolts to the torque listed in this Chapter's Specifications. Remove the pin from the tensioner and remove the alignment pin from the balance shaft sprocket.

16   Refer to Chapter 2A and install the camshaft timing chain cassettes, jackshaft chain and jackshaft sprocket.

---

10   Pistons and connecting rods - removal and installation

Removal

Refer to illustrations 10.1, 10.3 and 10.4

Note: *Prior to removing the piston/connecting rod assemblies, remove the cylinder head and oil pan (see Chapter 2A).*

1   Use your fingernail to feel if a ridge has formed at the upper limit of ring travel (about 1/4-inch down from the top of each cylinder). If carbon deposits or cylinder wear have produced ridges, they must be completely removed with a special tool **(see illustration)**.

Follow the manufacturer's instructions provided with the tool. Failure to remove the ridges before attempting to remove the piston/connecting rod assemblies may result in piston breakage.

2   After the cylinder ridges have been removed, turn the engine so the crankshaft is facing up.

3   Before the main bearing cap assembly and connecting rods are removed, check the connecting rod endplay with feeler gauges. Slide them between the first connecting rod and the crankshaft throw until the play is removed **(see illustration)**. Repeat this procedure for each connecting rod. The endplay is equal to the thickness of the feeler gauge(s). Check with an automotive machine shop for the endplay service limit (a typical endplay limit should measure between 0.005 to 0.015 inch [0.127 to 0.369 mm]). If the play exceeds the service limit, new connecting rods will be required. If new rods (or a new crankshaft) are installed, the endplay may fall under the minimum allowable. If it does, the rods will have to be machined to restore it. If necessary, consult an automotive machine shop for advice.

4   Check the connecting rods and caps for

10.3 Checking the connecting rod endplay (side clearance) (typical)

identification marks. If they aren't plainly marked, use paint or marker to clearly identify each rod and cap (1, 2, 3, etc., depending on the cylinder they're associated with) **(see illustration)**.

5   Remove the connecting rod cap nuts. **Note:** *New connecting rod cap nuts and bolts must be used when reassembling the engine.*

a) *On V6 models, on cylinders 1, 2 and 3, remove the connecting rod nut at the oil split hole side, first. On cylinders 4, 5 and 6, remove the opposite nut first. Loosen the first nut until it protrudes 0.8 mm above the bolt. Tap on the nut to release the bolt from the connecting rod. Tap the bolts out of the connecting rods and discard the connecting rod bolts and install new ones. Install new connecting rod bolts and make sure that they sit parallel to the side edges of the connecting rod.*

b) *On V8 models, remove the connecting rod nuts evenly until they reach the top of the bolt. Tap the bolts out of the connecting rods and discard the connecting rod bolts and install new ones.*

6   Remove the number one connecting rod cap and bearing insert. Don't drop the bearing insert out of the cap.

7   Remove the bearing insert and push the connecting rod/piston assembly out through the top of the engine. Use a wooden or plastic hammer handle to push on the upper bearing surface in the connecting rod. If resistance is felt, double-check to make sure that all of the ridge was removed from the cylinder.

8   Repeat the procedure for the remaining cylinders.

9   After removal, reassemble the connecting rod caps and bearing inserts in their respective connecting rods and install the cap bolts finger tight. Leaving the old bearing inserts in place until reassembly will help prevent the connecting rod bearing surfaces from being accidentally nicked or gouged.

10   The pistons and connecting rods are

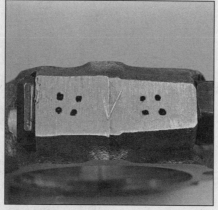

10.4 If the connecting rods and caps are not marked, use permanent ink or paint to mark the caps to the rods by cylinder number (for example, this would be the No. 4 connecting rod)

now ready for inspection and overhaul at an automotive machine shop.

Piston ring installation

Refer to illustrations 10.13, 10.14, 10.15, 10.19a, 10.19b and 10.22

11   Before installing the new piston rings, the ring end gaps must be checked. It's assumed that the piston ring side clearance has been checked and verified correct.

12   Lay out the piston/connecting rod assemblies and the new ring sets so the ring sets will be matched with the same piston and cylinder during the end gap measurement and engine assembly.

13   Insert the top (number one) ring into the first cylinder and square it up with the cylinder walls by pushing it in with the top of the piston **(see illustration)**. The ring should be near the bottom of the cylinder, at the lower limit of ring travel.

14   To measure the end gap, slip feeler gauges between the ends of the ring until a gauge equal to the gap width is found **(see illustration)**. The feeler gauge should slide

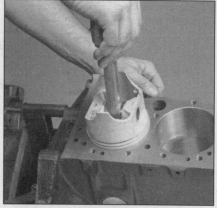

10.13 Install the piston ring into the cylinder then push it down into position using a piston so the ring will be square in the cylinder

between the ring ends with a slight amount of drag. A typical ring gap should fall between 0.010 and 0.020 inch [0.25 to 0.50 mm] for compression rings and up to 0.030 inch [0.76 mm] for the oil ring steel rails. If the gap is larger or smaller than specified, double-check to make sure you have the correct rings before proceeding.

15   If the gap is too small, it must be enlarged or the ring ends may come in contact with each other during engine operation, which can cause serious damage to the engine. If necessary, increase the end gaps by filing the ring ends very carefully with a fine file. Mount the file in a vise equipped with soft jaws, slip the ring over the file with the ends contacting the file face and slowly move the ring to remove material from the ends. When performing this operation, file only by pushing the ring from the outside end of the file towards the vise **(see illustration)**.

16   Excess end gap isn't critical unless it's greater than 0.040 inch (1.01 mm). Again, double-check to make sure you have the correct ring type.

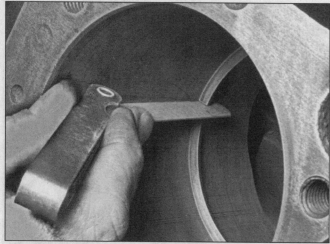

10.14 With the ring square in the cylinder, measure the ring end gap with a feeler gauge

10.15 If the ring end gap is too small, clamp a file in a vise as shown and file the piston ring ends - be sure to remove all raised material

10.19a Installing the spacer/expander in the oil ring groove

10.19b DO NOT use a piston ring installation tool when installing the oil control side rails

17 Repeat the procedure for each ring that will be installed in the first cylinder and for each ring in the remaining cylinders. Remember to keep rings, pistons and cylinders matched up.

18 Once the ring end gaps have been checked/corrected, the rings can be installed on the pistons.

19 The oil control ring (lowest one on the piston) is usually installed first. It's composed of three separate components. Slip the spacer/expander into the groove **(see illustration)**. If an anti-rotation tang is used, make sure it's inserted into the drilled hole in the ring groove. Next, install the upper side rail in the same manner **(see illustration)**. Don't use a piston ring installation tool on the oil ring side rails, as they may be damaged. Instead, place one end of the side rail into the groove between the spacer/expander and the ring land, hold it firmly in place and slide a finger around the piston while pushing the rail into the groove. Finally, install the lower side rail.

20 After the three oil ring components have been installed, check to make sure that both

the upper and lower side rails can be rotated smoothly inside the ring grooves.

21 The number two (middle) ring is installed next. It's usually stamped with a mark which must face up, toward the top of the piston. Do not mix up the top and middle rings, as they have different cross-sections. **Note:** *Always follow the instructions printed on the ring package or box - different manufacturers may require different approaches.*

22 Use a piston ring installation tool and make sure the identification mark is facing the top of the piston, then slip the ring into the middle groove on the piston **(see illustration)**. Don't expand the ring any more than necessary to slide it over the piston.

23 Install the number one (top) ring in the same manner. Make sure the mark is facing up. Be careful not to confuse the number one and number two rings.

24 Repeat the procedure for the remaining pistons and rings.

Installation

25 Before installing the piston/connecting

rod assemblies, the cylinder walls must be perfectly clean, the top edge of each cylinder bore must be chamfered, and the crankshaft must be in place.

26 Remove the cap from the end of the number one connecting rod (refer to the marks made during removal). Remove the original bearing inserts and wipe the bearing surfaces of the connecting rod and cap with a clean, lint-free cloth. They must be kept spotlessly clean.

Connecting rod bearing oil clearance check

Refer to illustrations 10.30, 10.35, 10.37 and 10.41

27 Clean the back side of the new upper bearing insert, then lay it in place in the connecting rod.

28 Make sure the tab on the bearing fits into the recess in the rod. Don't hammer the bearing insert into place and be very careful not to nick or gouge the bearing face. Don't lubricate the bearing at this time.

29 Clean the back side of the other bearing insert and install it in the rod cap. Again, make sure the tab on the bearing fits into the recess in the cap, and don't apply any lubricant. It's critically important that the mating surfaces of the bearing and connecting rod are perfectly clean and oil free when they're assembled.

30 Position the piston ring gaps at 90-degree intervals around the piston as shown **(see illustration)**.

31 Lubricate the piston and rings with clean engine oil and attach a piston ring compressor to the piston. Leave the skirt protruding about 1/4-inch to guide the piston into the cylinder. The rings must be compressed until they're flush with the piston.

32 Rotate the crankshaft until the number one connecting rod journal is at BDC (bottom dead center) and apply a liberal coat of engine oil to the cylinder walls.

2C

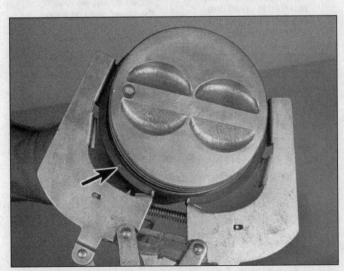

10.22 Use a piston ring installation tool to install the number 2 and the number 1 (top) rings - be sure the directional mark on the piston ring(s) is facing toward the top of the piston

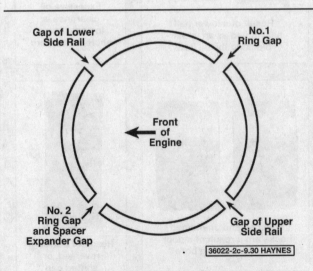

Gap of Lower Side Rail

No.1 Ring Gap

Front of Engine

No. 2 Ring Gap and Spacer Expander Gap

Gap of Upper Side Rail

36022-2c-9.30 HAYNES

10.30 Position the piston ring end gaps as shown

ENGINE BEARING ANALYSIS

Debris

Babbitt bearing embedded with debris from machinings

Microscopic detail of debris

Microscopic detail of gouges

Overplated copper alloy bearing gouged by cast iron debris

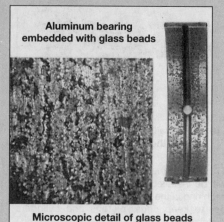

Aluminum bearing embedded with glass beads

Microscopic detail of glass beads

Damaged lining caused by dirt left on the bearing back

Misassembly

Result of a lower half assembled as an upper - blocking the oil flow

Excessive oil clearance is indicated by a short contact arc

Polished and oil-stained backs are a result of a poor fit in the housing bore

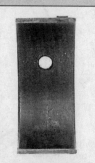

Result of a wrong, reversed, or shifted cap

Overloading

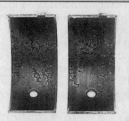

Damage from excessive idling which resulted in an oil film unable to support the load imposed

Damaged upper connecting rod bearings caused by engine lugging; the lower main bearings (not shown) were similarly affected

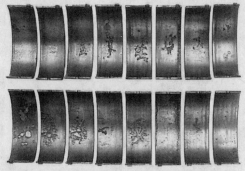

The damage shown in these upper and lower connecting rod bearings was caused by engine operation at a higher-than-rated speed under load

Misalignment

A poorly finished crankshaft caused the equally spaced scoring shown

A tapered housing bore caused the damage along one edge of this pair

A warped crankshaft caused this pattern of severe wear in the center, diminishing toward the ends

A bent connecting rod led to the damage in the "V" pattern

Lubrication

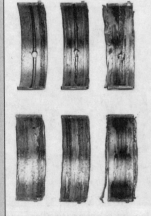

Result of dry start: The bearings on the left, farthest from the oil pump, show more damage

Result of a low oil supply or oil starvation

Severe wear as a result of inadequate oil clearance

Corrosion

Microscopic detail of corrosion

Corrosion is an acid attack on the bearing lining generally caused by inadequate maintenance, extremely hot or cold operation, or interior oils or fuels

Microscopic detail of cavitation

Example of cavitation - a surface erosion caused by pressure changes in the oil film

Damage from excessive thrust or insufficient axial clearance

Bearing affected by oil dilution caused by excessive blow-by or a rich mixture

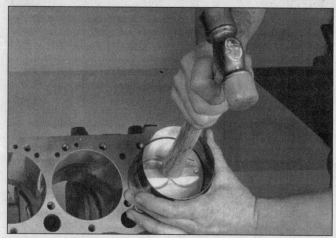

10.35 Use a plastic or wooden hammer handle to push the piston into the cylinder

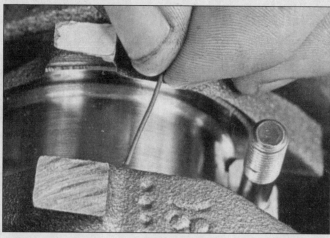

10.37 Place Plastigage on each connecting rod bearing journal parallel to the crankshaft centerline

33   With the weight designation mark on top of the piston facing the front of the engine, gently insert the piston/connecting rod assembly into the number one cylinder bore and rest the bottom edge of the ring compressor on the engine block. Install the pistons with the cavity mark(s) facing toward the timing belt.

34   Tap the top edge of the ring compressor to make sure it's contacting the block around its entire circumference.

35   Gently tap on the top of the piston with the end of a wooden or plastic hammer handle **(see illustration)** while guiding the end of the connecting rod into place on the crankshaft journal. The piston rings may try to pop out of the ring compressor just before entering the cylinder bore, so keep some downward pressure on the ring compressor. Work slowly, and if any resistance is felt as the piston enters the cylinder, stop immediately. Find out what's hanging up and fix it before proceeding. Do not, for any reason, force the piston into the cylinder - you might break a ring and/or the piston.

36   Once the piston/connecting rod assembly is installed, the connecting rod bearing oil clearance must be checked before the rod cap is permanently installed.

37   Cut a piece of the appropriate size Plastigage slightly shorter than the width of the connecting rod bearing and lay it in place on the number one connecting rod journal, parallel with the journal axis **(see illustration)**.

38   Clean the connecting rod cap bearing face and install the rod cap. Make sure the mating mark on the cap is on the same side as the mark on the connecting rod **(see illustration 10.4)**.

39   Install the old rod bolts, at this time, and tighten them to the torque listed in this Chapter's Specifications. **Note:** *Use a thin-wall socket to avoid erroneous torque readings that can result if the socket is wedged between the rod cap and the bolt or nut. If the socket tends to wedge itself between the fastener and the cap, lift up on it slightly until it no longer contacts the cap. DO NOT rotate*

the crankshaft at any time during this operation.

40   Remove the fasteners and detach the rod cap, being very careful not to disturb the Plastigage. Discard the cap bolts at this time as they cannot be reused. **Note:** *You MUST use new connecting rod bolts.*

41   Compare the width of the crushed Plastigage to the scale printed on the Plastigage envelope to obtain the oil clearance **(see illustration)**. The connecting rod oil clearance is usually about 0.001 to 0.002 inch. Consult an automotive machine shop for the clearance specified for the rod bearings on your engine.

42   If the clearance is not as specified, the bearing inserts may be the wrong size (which means different ones will be required). Before deciding that different inserts are needed, make sure that no dirt or oil was between the bearing inserts and the connecting rod or cap when the clearance was measured. Also, recheck the journal diameter. If the Plastigage was wider at one end than the other, the journal may be tapered. If the clearance still exceeds the limit specified, the bearing will have to be replaced with an undersize bearing. **Caution:** *When installing a new crankshaft always use a standard size bearing.*

Final installation

43   Carefully scrape all traces of the Plastigage material off the rod journal and/or bearing face. Be very careful not to scratch the bearing - use your fingernail or the edge of a plastic card.

44   Make sure the bearing faces are perfectly clean, then apply a uniform layer of clean moly-base grease or engine assembly lube to both of them. You'll have to push the piston into the cylinder to expose the face of the bearing insert in the connecting rod.

45   **Caution:** *Install new connecting rod cap bolts. Do NOT reuse old bolts - they have stretched and cannot be reused (see Step 5).* Slide the connecting rod back into place on the journal, install the rod cap, install the nuts or new bolts and tighten them to the torque

listed in this Chapter's Specifications.

46   Repeat the entire procedure for the remaining pistons/connecting rods.

47   The important points to remember are:

a) *Keep the back sides of the bearing inserts and the insides of the connecting rods and caps perfectly clean when assembling them.*

b) *Make sure you have the correct piston/rod assembly for each cylinder.*

c) *The mark on the piston must face the front (timing chain/water pump end) of the engine.*

d) *Lubricate the cylinder walls liberally with clean oil.*

e) *Lubricate the bearing faces when installing the rod caps after the oil clearance has been checked.*

48   After all the piston/connecting rod assemblies have been correctly installed, rotate the crankshaft a number of times by hand to check for any obvious binding.

49   As a final step, check the connecting rod endplay, as described in Step 3. If it was correct before disassembly and the original

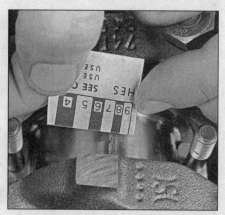

10.41 Use the scale on the Plastigage package to determine the bearing oil clearance - be sure to measure the widest part of the Plastigage and use the correct scale; it comes with both standard and metric scales

11.1 Checking crankshaft endplay with a dial indicator

11.3 Checking the crankshaft endplay with feeler gauges at the thrust bearing journal

11.17 Place the Plastigage onto the crankshaft bearing journal as shown

2C

crankshaft and rods were reinstalled, it should still be correct. If new rods or a new crankshaft were installed, the endplay may be inadequate. If so, the rods will have to be removed and taken to an automotive machine shop for resizing.

11   Crankshaft - removal and installation

Removal

Refer to illustrations 11.1 and 11.3
Note: *The crankshaft can be removed only after the engine has been removed from the vehicle. It's assumed that the flywheel or driveplate, crankshaft pulley, timing belt, oil pan, oil pump body, oil filter and piston/connecting rod assemblies have already been removed. The rear main oil seal retainer must be unbolted and separated from the block before proceeding with crankshaft removal.*

1   Before the crankshaft is removed, measure the endplay. Mount a dial indicator with the indicator in line with the crankshaft and just touching the end of the crankshaft as shown **(see illustration)**.

2   Pry the crankshaft all the way to the rear and zero the dial indicator. Next, pry the crankshaft to the front as far as possible and check the reading on the dial indicator. The distance traveled is the endplay. A typical crankshaft endplay will fall between 0.003 to 0.010 inch (0.076 to 0.254 mm). If it is greater than that, check the crankshaft thrust surfaces for wear after it's removed. If no wear is evident, new main bearings should correct the endplay.

3   If a dial indicator isn't available, feeler gauges can be used. Gently pry the crankshaft all the way to the front of the engine. Slip feeler gauges between the crankshaft and the front face of the thrust bearing or washer to determine the clearance **(see illustration)**.

4   Loosen the main bearing cap bolts 1/4-turn at a time each, until they can be removed by hand. On V8 models, follow the reverse of

the tightening sequence **(see illustrations 11.19a and 11.19b)**. **Note:** *On V6 engines, the cradle block assembly has already been removed to expose the main bearing caps (see Chapter 2A).*

5   Remove the main bearing caps. Gently tap the main bearing cap with a soft-face hammer. Pull the main bearing cap straight up and off the cylinder block. Try not to drop the bearing inserts if they come out with the assembly.

6   Carefully lift the crankshaft out of the engine. It may be a good idea to have an assistant available, since the crankshaft is quite heavy and awkward to handle. With the bearing inserts in place inside the engine block and main bearing caps, reinstall the main bearing cap assembly onto the engine block and tighten the bolts finger tight. Make sure the caps are in the exact order they were removed with the arrow pointing toward the front (timing chain and front cover) of the engine.

Installation

7   Crankshaft installation is the first step in engine reassembly. It's assumed at this point that the engine block and crankshaft have been cleaned, inspected and repaired or reconditioned.

8   Position the engine block with the bottom facing up.

9   Remove the mounting bolts and lift off the main bearing caps.

10   If they're still in place, remove the original bearing inserts from the block and from the main bearing cap assembly. Wipe the bearing surfaces of the block and main bearing cap assembly with a clean, lint-free cloth. They must be kept spotlessly clean. This is critical for determining the correct bearing oil clearance.

Main bearing oil clearance check

Refer to illustrations 11.17, 11.19a, 11.19b and 11.21

11   Without mixing them up, clean the back

sides of the new upper main bearing inserts (with grooves and oil holes) and lay one in each main bearing saddle in the engine block. Each upper bearing (engine block) has an oil groove and oil hole in it. **Caution:** *The oil holes in the block must line up with the oil holes in the engine block inserts.* The thrust washer or thrust bearing insert must be installed in the correct location. **Note:** *The thrust bearing on the V6 is located on the engine block number 3 journal. The thrust washer on the V8 engines is located on the 5th journal (upper) on the engine block. The V8 engine also is equipped with a thrust bearing on the 5th journal main bearing cap. Be sure to install the thrust washer (V8 engine) with the oil groove facing the rear of the engine.* Clean the back sides of the lower main bearing inserts and lay them in the corresponding location in the main bearing cap assembly. Make sure the tab on the bearing insert fits into the recess in the block or main bearing cap assembly. **Caution:** *Do not hammer the bearing insert into place and don't nick or gouge the bearing faces. DO NOT apply any lubrication at this time.*

12   Clean the faces of the bearing inserts in the block and the crankshaft main bearing journals with a clean, lint-free cloth.

13   Check or clean the oil holes in the crankshaft, as any dirt here can go only one way - straight through the new bearings.

14   Once you're certain the crankshaft is clean, carefully lay it in position in the cylinder block.

15   Before the crankshaft can be permanently installed, the main bearing oil clearance must be checked.

16   Cut several strips of the appropriate size of Plastigage. They must be slightly shorter than the width of the main bearing journal.

17   Place one piece on each crankshaft main bearing journal, parallel with the journal axis as shown **(see illustration)**.

18   Clean the faces of the bearing inserts in the main bearing cap assembly. Hold the bearing inserts in place and install the assembly onto the crankshaft and cylinder block. DO NOT disturb the Plastigage.

COMMON ENGINE OVERHAUL TERMS

B

Backlash - The amount of play between two parts. Usually refers to how much one gear can be moved back and forth without moving gear with which it's meshed.

Bearing Caps - The caps held in place by nuts or bolts which, in turn, hold the bearing surface. This space is for lubricating oil to enter.

Bearing clearance - The amount of space left between shaft and bearing surface. This space is for lubricating oil to enter.

Bearing crush - The additional height which is purposely manufactured into each bearing half to ensure complete contact of the bearing back with the housing bore when the engine is assembled.

Bearing knock - The noise created by movement of a part in a loose or worn bearing.

Blueprinting - Dismantling an engine and reassembling it to EXACT specifications.

Bore - An engine cylinder, or any cylindrical hole; also used to describe the process of enlarging or accurately refinishing a hole with a cutting tool, as to bore an engine cylinder. The bore size is the diameter of the hole.

Boring - Renewing the cylinders by cutting them out to a specified size. A boring bar is used to make the cut.

Bottom end - A term which refers collectively to the engine block, crankshaft, main bearings and the big ends of the connecting rods.

Break-in - The period of operation between installation of new or rebuilt parts and time in which parts are worn to the correct fit. Driving at reduced and varying speed for a specified mileage to permit parts to wear to the correct fit.

Bushing - A one-piece sleeve placed in a bore to serve as a bearing surface for shaft, piston pin, etc. Usually replaceable.

C

Camshaft - The shaft in the engine, on which a series of lobes are located for operating the valve mechanisms. The camshaft is driven by gears or sprockets and a timing chain. Usually referred to simply as the cam.

Carbon - Hard, or soft, black deposits found in combustion chamber, on plugs, under rings, on and under valve heads.

Cast iron - An alloy of iron and more than two percent carbon, used for engine blocks and heads because it's relatively inexpensive and easy to mold into complex shapes.

Chamfer - To bevel across (or a bevel on) the sharp edge of an object.

Chase - To repair damaged threads with a tap or die.

Combustion chamber - The space between the piston and the cylinder head, with the piston at top dead center, in which air-fuel mixture is burned.

Compression ratio - The relationship between cylinder volume (clearance volume) when the piston is at top dead center and cylinder volume when the piston is at bottom dead center.

Connecting rod - The rod that connects the crank on the crankshaft with the piston. Sometimes called a con rod.

Connecting rod cap - The part of the connecting rod assembly that attaches the rod to the crankpin.

Core plug - Soft metal plug used to plug the casting holes for the coolant passages in the block.

Crankcase - The lower part of the engine in which the crankshaft rotates; includes the lower section of the cylinder block and the oil pan.

Crank kit - A reground or reconditioned crankshaft and new main and connecting rod bearings.

Crankpin - The part of a crankshaft to which a connecting rod is attached.

Crankshaft - The main rotating member, or shaft, running the length of the crankcase, with offset throws to which the connecting rods are attached; changes the reciprocating motion of the pistons into rotating motion.

Cylinder sleeve - A replaceable sleeve, or liner, pressed into the cylinder block to form the cylinder bore.

D

Deburring - Removing the burrs (rough edges or areas) from a bearing.

Deglazer - A tool, rotated by an electric motor, used to remove glaze from cylinder walls so a new set of rings will seat.

E

Endplay - The amount of lengthwise movement between two parts. As applied to a crankshaft, the distance that the crankshaft can move forward and back in the cylinder block.

F

Face - A machinist's term that refers to removing metal from the end of a shaft or the face of a larger part, such as a flywheel.

Fatigue - A breakdown of material through a large number of loading and unloading cycles. The first signs are cracks followed shortly by breaks.

Feeler gauge - A thin strip of hardened steel, ground to an exact thickness, used to check clearances between parts.

Free height - The unloaded length or height of a spring.

Freeplay - The looseness in a linkage, or an assembly of parts, between the initial application of force and actual movement. Usually perceived as slop or slight delay.

Freeze plug - See Core plug.

G

Gallery - A large passage in the block that forms a reservoir for engine oil pressure.

Glaze - The very smooth, glassy finish that develops on cylinder walls while an engine is in service.

H

Heli-Coil - A rethreading device used when threads are worn or damaged. The device is installed in a retapped hole to reduce the thread size to the original size.

I

Installed height - The spring's measured length or height, as installed on the cylinder head. Installed height is measured from the spring seat to the underside of the spring retainer.

J

Journal - The surface of a rotating shaft which turns in a bearing.

K

Keeper - The split lock that holds the valve spring retainer in position on the valve stem.

Key - A small piece of metal inserted into matching grooves machined into two parts fitted together - such as a gear pressed onto a shaft - which prevents slippage between the two parts.

Knock - The heavy metallic engine sound, produced in the combustion chamber as a result of abnormal combustion - usually detonation. Knock is usually caused by a loose or worn bearing. Also referred to as detonation, pinging and spark knock. Connecting rod or main bearing knocks are created by too much oil clearance or insufficient lubrication.

L

Lands - The portions of metal between the piston ring grooves.

Lapping the valves - Grinding a valve face and its seat together with lapping compound.

Lash - The amount of free motion in a gear train, between gears, or in a mechanical assembly, that occurs before movement can begin. Usually refers to the lash in a valve train.

Lifter - The part that rides against the cam to transfer motion to the rest of the valve train.

M

Machining - The process of using a machine to remove metal from a metal part.

Main bearings - The plain, or babbit, bearings that support the crankshaft.

Main bearing caps - The cast iron caps, bolted to the bottom of the block, that support the main bearings.

O

O.D. - Outside diameter.

Oil gallery - A pipe or drilled passageway in the engine used to carry engine oil from one area to another.

Oil ring - The lower ring, or rings, of a piston; designed to prevent excessive amounts of oil from working up the cylinder walls and into the combustion chamber. Also called an oil-control ring.

Oil seal - A seal which keeps oil from leaking out of a compartment. Usually refers to a dynamic seal around a rotating shaft or other moving part.

O-ring - A type of sealing ring made of a special rubberlike material; in use, the O-ring is compressed into a groove to provide the sealing action.

Overhaul - To completely disassemble a unit, clean and inspect all parts, reassemble it with the original or new parts and make all adjustments necessary for proper operation.

P

Pilot bearing - A small bearing installed in the center of the flywheel (or the rear end of the crankshaft) to support the front end of the input shaft of the transmission.

Pip mark - A little dot or indentation which indicates the top side of a compression ring.

Piston - The cylindrical part, attached to the connecting rod, that moves up and down in the cylinder as the crankshaft rotates. When the fuel charge is fired, the piston transfers the force of the explosion to the connecting rod, then to the crankshaft.

Piston pin (or wrist pin) - The cylindrical and usually hollow steel pin that passes through the piston. The piston pin fastens the piston to the upper end of the connecting rod.

Piston ring - The split ring fitted to the groove in a piston. The ring contacts the sides of the ring groove and also rubs against the cylinder wall, thus sealing space between piston and wall. There are two types of rings: Compression rings seal the compression pressure in the combustion chamber; oil rings scrape excessive oil off the cylinder wall.

Piston ring groove - The slots or grooves cut in piston heads to hold piston rings in position.

Piston skirt - The portion of the piston below the rings and the piston pin hole.

Plastigage - A thin strip of plastic thread, available in different sizes, used for measuring clearances. For example, a strip of plastigage is laid across a bearing journal and mashed as parts are assembled. Then parts are disassembled and the width of the strip is measured to determine clearance between journal and bearing. Commonly used to measure crankshaft main-bearing and connecting rod bearing clearances.

Press-fit - A tight fit between two parts that requires pressure to force the parts together. Also referred to as drive, or force, fit.

Prussian blue - A blue pigment; in solution, useful in determining the area of contact between two surfaces. Prussian blue is commonly used to determine the width and location of the contact area between the valve face and the valve seat.

R

Race (bearing) - The inner or outer ring that provides a contact surface for balls or rollers in bearing.

Ream - To size, enlarge or smooth a hole by using a round cutting tool with fluted edges.

Ring job - The process of reconditioning the cylinders and installing new rings.

Runout - Wobble. The amount a shaft rotates out-of-true.

S

Saddle - The upper main bearing seat.

Scored - Scratched or grooved, as a cylinder wall may be scored by abrasive particles moved up and down by the piston rings.

Scuffing - A type of wear in which there's a transfer of material between parts moving against each other; shows up as pits or grooves in the mating surfaces.

Seat - The surface upon which another part rests or seats. For example, the valve seat is the matched surface upon which the valve face rests. Also used to refer to wearing into a good fit; for example, piston rings seat after a few miles of driving.

Short block - An engine block complete with crankshaft and piston and, usually, camshaft assemblies.

Static balance - The balance of an object while it's stationary.

Step - The wear on the lower portion of a ring land caused by excessive side and back-clearance. The height of the step indicates the ring's extra side clearance and the length of the step projecting from the back wall of the groove represents the ring's back clearance.

Stroke - The distance the piston moves when traveling from top dead center to bottom dead center, or from bottom dead center to top dead center.

Stud - A metal rod with threads on both ends.

T

Tang - A lip on the end of a plain bearing used to align the bearing during assembly.

Tap - To cut threads in a hole. Also refers to the fluted tool used to cut threads.

Taper - A gradual reduction in the width of a shaft or hole; in an engine cylinder, taper usually takes the form of uneven wear, more pronounced at the top than at the bottom.

Throws - The offset portions of the crankshaft to which the connecting rods are affixed.

Thrust bearing - The main bearing that has thrust faces to prevent excessive endplay, or forward and backward movement of the crankshaft.

Thrust washer - A bronze or hardened steel washer placed between two moving parts. The washer prevents longitudinal movement and provides a bearing surface for thrust surfaces of parts.

Tolerance - The amount of variation permitted from an exact size of measurement. Actual amount from smallest acceptable dimension to largest acceptable dimension.

U

Umbrella - An oil deflector placed near the valve tip to throw oil from the valve stem area.

Undercut - A machined groove below the normal surface.

Undersize bearings - Smaller diameter bearings used with re-ground crankshaft journals.

V

Valve grinding - Refacing a valve in a valve-refacing machine.

Valve train - The valve-operating mechanism of an engine; includes all components from the camshaft to the valve.

Vibration damper - A cylindrical weight attached to the front of the crankshaft to minimize torsional vibration (the twist-untwist actions of the crankshaft caused by the cylinder firing impulses). Also called a harmonic balancer.

W

Water jacket - The spaces around the cylinders, between the inner and outer shells of the cylinder block or head, through which coolant circulates.

Web - A supporting structure across a cavity.

Woodruff key - A key with a radiused backside (viewed from the side).

19   Apply clean engine oil to all bolt threads prior to installation, then install all bolts finger-tight. On V6 engines, tighten the main bearing caps starting with the center cap and working out. On V8 engines, tighten the bearing cap assembly bolts in the sequence shown **(see illustrations)** progressing in steps, to the torque listed in this Chapter's Specifications. DO NOT rotate the crankshaft at any time during this operation. **Note:** *The V8 engines are equipped with side bolts that support the main bearings.*

20   Remove the bolts in the *reverse* order of the tightening sequence and carefully lift the main bearing cap assembly straight up and off the block. Do not disturb the Plastigage or rotate the crankshaft. If the main bearing cap assembly is difficult to remove, tap it gently from side-to-side with a soft-face hammer to loosen it.

21   Compare the width of the crushed Plastigage on each journal to the scale printed on the Plastigage envelope to determine the main bearing oil clearance **(see illustration)**. Check with an automotive machine shop for the oil clearance for your engine.

22   If the clearance is not as specified, the bearing inserts may be the wrong size (which means different ones will be required). Before deciding if different inserts are needed, make sure that no dirt or oil was between the bearing inserts and the cap assembly or block when the clearance was measured. If the Plastigage was wider at one end than the other, the crankshaft journal may be tapered. If the clearance still exceeds the limit specified, the bearing insert(s) will have to be replaced with an undersize bearing insert(s). **Caution:** *When installing a new crankshaft always install a standard bearing insert set.*

23   Carefully scrape all traces of the Plastigage material off the main bearing journals and/or the bearing insert faces. Be sure to remove all residue from the oil holes. Use your fingernail or the edge of a plastic card - don't nick or scratch the bearing faces.

Final installation

24   Carefully lift the crankshaft out of the cylinder block.

25   Clean the bearing insert faces in the cylinder block, then apply a thin, uniform layer of moly-base grease or engine assembly lube to each of the bearing surfaces. Be sure to coat the thrust faces as well as the journal face of the thrust bearing.

26   Make sure the crankshaft journals are clean, then lay the crankshaft back in place in the cylinder block.

27   Clean the bearing insert faces and apply the same lubricant to them. Clean the engine block and the bearing caps/bedplate thoroughly. The surfaces must be free of oil residue.

28   On V6 engines, apply a bead of RTV to the engine block on the rear main bearing cap parting line. Be sure the main bearing cap is installed within four minutes after the RTV is applied.

29   Prior to installation, apply clean engine oil to all bolt threads wiping off any excess, then install all bolts finger-tight.

30   Tighten the main bearing caps. On V6 engines, start with the center bearing cap bolts and work out. On V8 models, follow the correct torque sequence **(see illustrations 11.19a and 11.19b)**. Torque the bolts to the Specifications listed in this Chapter.

31   Recheck the crankshaft endplay with a feeler gauge or a dial indicator. The endplay should be correct if the crankshaft thrust faces aren't worn or damaged and if new bearings have been installed.

32   Rotate the crankshaft a number of times by hand to check for any obvious binding. It should rotate with a running torque of 50 in-lbs or less. If the running torque is too high, correct the problem at this time.

33   Install the new rear main oil seal (see Chapter 2A).

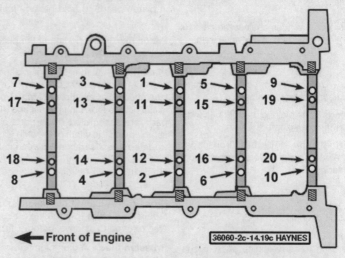

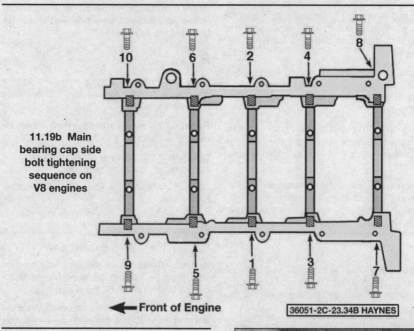

11.19a Main bearing cap bolts tightening sequence on V8 engines

11.19b Main bearing cap side bolt tightening sequence on V8 engines

11.21 Use the scale on the Plastigage package to determine the bearing oil clearance - be sure to measure the widest part of the Plastigage and use the correct scale; it comes with both standard and metric scales

12 Engine overhaul - reassembly sequence

1   Before beginning engine reassembly, make sure you have all the necessary new parts, gaskets and seals as well as the following items on hand:

Common hand tools
A 1/2-inch drive torque wrench
New engine oil
Gasket sealant
Thread locking compound

2   If you obtained a short block it will be necessary to install the cylinder head, the oil pump and pick-up tube, the oil pan, the water pump, the timing chains and timing chain cover, and the valve cover (see Chapter 2A or 2B). In order to save time and avoid problems, the external components must be installed in the following general order:

Thermostat and housing cover
Water pump
Intake and exhaust manifolds
Fuel injection components
Emission control components
Spark plug wires and spark plugs
Ignition coils or coil packs
Oil filter
Engine mounts and mount brackets
Clutch and flywheel (manual transmission)
Driveplate (automatic transmission)

13 Initial start-up and break-in after overhaul

Warning: *Have a fire extinguisher handy when starting the engine for the first time.*

1   Once the engine has been installed in the vehicle, double-check the engine oil and coolant levels.

2   With the spark plugs out of the engine and the ignition system and fuel pump disabled, crank the engine until oil pressure registers on the gauge or the light goes out.

3   Install the spark plugs, hook up the plug wires and restore the ignition system and fuel pump functions.

4   Start the engine. It may take a few moments for the fuel system to build up pressure, but the engine should start without a great deal of effort.

5   After the engine starts, it should be allowed to warm up to normal operating temperature. While the engine is warming up, make a thorough check for fuel, oil and coolant leaks.

6   Shut the engine off and recheck the engine oil and coolant levels.

7   Drive the vehicle to an area with minimum traffic, accelerate from 30 to 50 mph, then allow the vehicle to slow to 30 mph with the throttle closed. Repeat the procedure 10 or 12 times. This will load the piston rings and cause them to seat properly against the cylinder walls. Check again for oil and coolant leaks.

8   Drive the vehicle gently for the first 500 miles (no sustained high speeds) and keep a constant check on the oil level. It is not unusual for an engine to use oil during the break-in period.

9   At approximately 500 to 600 miles, change the oil and filter.

10   For the next few hundred miles, drive the vehicle normally. Do not pamper it or abuse it.

11   After 2,000 miles, change the oil and filter again and consider the engine broken in.

2C

Notes

Chapter 3
Cooling, heating and air conditioning systems

Contents

Specifications

General

Expansion tank cap pressure rating	13 to 18 psi (89 to 124 kPa)
Thermostat rating (opening to fully open temperature range)	194 to 210 degrees F (90 to 105 degrees C)
Cooling system capacity	See Chapter 1
Refrigerant type	R-134a
Refrigerant capacity	Refer to HVAC specification tag

Torque specifications

	Ft-lbs (unless otherwise indicated)	Nm
Accumulator inlet and outlet line mounting nuts	71 in-lbs	8
Condenser inlet and outlet line mounting nuts	71 in-lbs	8
Condenser bracket support bolts	89 in-lbs	10
Radiator bracket support bolts	108 in-lbs	12
Thermostat housing cover bolts		
V6 engine	89 in-lbs	10
V8 engine	18	25
Water pump bolts		
V6 engine	89 in-lbs	10
V8 engine	18	25
Water pump pulley bolts	18	25

1   General information

Engine cooling system

The cooling system consists of a radiator, an expansion tank, a pressure cap (located on the expansion tank), a thermostat, a cooling fan and clutch, and a belt-driven water pump.

The radiator cooling fan is mounted on the front of the water pump. The fan incorporates a fluid drive fan clutch, which saves horsepower and reduces noise. When the engine is cold, the fluid in the clutch offers little resistance and allows the fan to freewheel. As the engine heats up and reaches a predetermined temperature, the fluid in the clutch thickens and drives the fan.

The expansion tank, referred to by the manufacturer as a "degas bottle," functions somewhat differently than a conventional recovery tank. Designed to separate any trapped air in the coolant, it is pressurized by the radiator and has a pressure cap on top. The radiator on these models does not have a pressure cap. When the thermostat is closed, no coolant flows in the expansion tank, but when the engine is fully warmed up, coolant flows from the top of the radiator through a small hose that enters the top of the expansion tank, where the air separates and the coolant falls into a coolant reservoir in the bottom of the tank, which is fed to the cooling system through a larger hose connected to the lower radiator hose. **Warning:** *Unlike a conventional coolant recovery tank, the pressure cap on the expansion tank should never be opened after the engine has warmed up, because of the danger of severe burns caused by steam or scalding coolant.*

Coolant in the left side of the radiator circulates through the lower radiator hose to the water pump, where it is forced through coolant passages in the cylinder block. The coolant then travels up into the cylinder head, circulates around the combustion chambers and valve seats, travels out of the cylinder head past the open thermostat into the upper radiator hose and back into the radiator.

When the engine is cold, the thermostat restricts the circulation of coolant to the engine. When the minimum operating temperature is reached, the thermostat begins to open, allowing coolant to return to the radiator.

Transaxle cooling systems

Vehicles with an automatic transaxle are equipped with a transaxle cooler, located between the radiator and the condenser, which cools the transaxle fluid. The transaxle is connected to the cooler by a pair of hoses: one delivers hot transaxle fluid to the radiator and the other brings the cooled fluid back to the transaxle.

For more information on transaxle oil coolers, refer to Chapter 7.

Heating system

The heating system consists of the heater controls, the heater core, the heater blower assembly (which houses the blower motor and the blower motor resistor), and the hoses connecting the heater core to the engine cooling system. Hot engine coolant is circulated through the heater core. When the heater mode is activated, a flap door opens to expose the heater box to the passenger compartment. A fan switch on the heater controls activates the blower motor, which forces air through the core, heating the air.

These models are equipped with separate front and rear heater controls, heater cores and heater blower assemblies. Also, the heater controls are located in the dash center cluster, the overhead console and the rear console. This allows the rear heating system to be controlled by the front passenger/driver or the rear seating passengers.

Air conditioning system

The air conditioning system consists of the condenser, which is mounted in front of the radiator and transaxle fluid cooler, the evaporator case assembly under the dash, a compressor mounted on the engine, and the plumbing connecting all of the above components.

A blower fan forces the warmer air of the passenger compartment through the evaporator core (sort of a radiator-in-reverse), transferring the heat from the air to the refrigerant. The liquid refrigerant boils off into low pressure vapor, taking the heat with it when it leaves the evaporator.

These models are equipped with separate front and rear air conditioning controls, evaporators and blower assemblies. Also, the air conditioning controls are located in the dash center cluster, the overhead console and the rear console. This allows the rear air conditioning system to be controlled by the front passenger/driver or the rear seating passengers.

2   Antifreeze - general information

Refer to illustration 2.5

Warning: *Do not allow antifreeze to come in contact with your skin or painted surfaces of the vehicle. Rinse off spills immediately with plenty of water. Antifreeze is highly toxic if ingested. Never leave antifreeze lying around in an open container or in puddles on the floor; children and pets are attracted by its sweet smell and may drink it. Check with local authorities about disposing of used antifreeze. Many communities have collection centers which will see that antifreeze is disposed of safely. Never dump used antifreeze on the ground or pour it into drains.*
Caution: *Do not mix coolants of different colors. Doing so might damage the cooling system and/or the engine. The manufacturer specifies either a green colored coolant or a yellow colored coolant to be used in these*

2.5 Use a hydrometer (available at auto parts stores) to test the condition of your coolant

systems. Read the warning label in the engine compartment for additional information.
Note: *Non-toxic antifreeze is now manufactured and available at local auto parts stores, but even this type must be disposed of properly.*

The cooling system should be filled with a water/ethylene glycol based antifreeze solution, which will prevent freezing down to at least -20-degrees F (even lower in cold climates). It also provides protection against corrosion and increases the coolant boiling point. The manufacturer recommends that the correct type of coolant be used and strongly urges that coolant types not be mixed (see Chapter 1).

Drain, flush and refill the cooling system at least every other year (see Chapter 1). The use of antifreeze solutions for periods of longer than two years is likely to cause damage and encourage the formation of rust and scale in the system.

Before adding antifreeze to the system, inspect all hose connections. Antifreeze can leak through very minute openings.

The exact mixture of antifreeze to water, which you should use, depends on the relative weather conditions. The mixture should contain at least 50-percent antifreeze, but should never contain more than 70-percent anti-freeze. Consult the mixture ratio chart on the container before adding coolant.

Hydrometers are available at most auto parts stores to test the coolant **(see illustration)**. **Warning:** *Do not remove the expansion tank cap, drain the coolant or perform any service procedures on the cooling system until the engine has cooled completely.*

3   Thermostat - check and replacement

Check

1   Before assuming the thermostat is to blame for a cooling system problem, check the coolant level, drivebelt tension (see

3.12 Remove the thermostat housing mounting bolts (V6 models shown)

3.13a Remove the O-ring from the thermostat housing . . .

3.13b . . . and lift the thermostat from the housing

Chapter 1) and temperature gauge operation.

2   If the engine seems to be taking a long time to warm up, based on heater output or temperature gauge operation, the thermostat is probably stuck open. Replace the thermostat with a new one.

3   If the engine runs hot, use your hand to check the temperature of the upper radiator hose. If the hose isn't hot, but the engine is, the thermostat is probably stuck closed, preventing the coolant inside the engine from escaping to the radiator. Replace the thermostat. **Caution:** *Don't drive the vehicle without a thermostat. The computer may stay in open loop and emissions and fuel economy will suffer.*

4   If the upper radiator hose is hot, it means that the coolant is flowing and the thermostat is open. Consult the Troubleshooting Section at the front of this manual for cooling system diagnosis.

Replacement

Warning: *Wait until the engine is completely cool before beginning this procedure.*

5   Disconnect the cable from the negative battery terminal (see Chapter 5).

6   Drain the cooling system (see Chap-

ter 1). If the coolant is relatively new and still in good condition, save it and reuse it.

7   On V6 models, disconnect the alternator harness bracket and position it off to the side.

8   On V8 models, remove the engine cover.

9   Follow the upper radiator hose to the engine to locate the thermostat housing.

10   Loosen the hose clamp by squeezing the ends together. Hose clamp pliers work best, but regular pliers will work also. If the radiator hose is stuck, grasp it near the end with a pair of adjustable pliers and twist it to break the seal, then pull it off. If the hose is old or if it has deteriorated, cut it off and install a new one.

11   If the outer surface of the thermostat housing cover, which mates with the hose, is already corroded, pitted, or otherwise deteriorated, it might be damaged even more by hose removal. If it is, replace the thermostat housing cover.

V6 models

Refer to illustrations 3.12, 13.13a and 3.13b

12   Remove the fasteners and detach the thermostat cover **(see illustration)**. If the

cover is stuck, tap it with a soft-face hammer to jar it loose. Be prepared for some coolant to spill as the gasket seal is broken.

13   Note how it's installed (which end is facing up, or out) and remove the thermostat **(see illustrations)**.

V8 models

Refer to illustrations 3.14 and 3.15

14   Remove the fasteners and detach the thermostat housing cover **(see illustration)**. If the cover is stuck, tap it with a soft-face hammer to jar it loose. Be prepared for some coolant to spill as the gasket seal is broken.

15   Note how it's installed (which end is facing up, or out) and remove the thermostat **(see illustration)**.

All models

16   Remove all traces of old gasket material and sealant from the housing and cover with a gasket scraper.

17   Install a new rubber gasket on the thermostat **(see illustrations 3.13a and 3.15)** and install the thermostat in the housing (V6) or housing cover (V8).

18   Install the thermostat housing cover and tighten the bolts to the torque listed in this

3

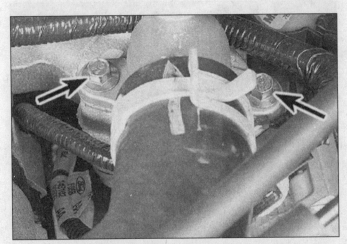

3.14 Location of the thermostat housing mounting bolts on the V8 engine

3.15 Install a new rubber seal around the perimeter of the thermostat

4.8a Remove the radiator protector cover by lifting the ends and releasing the pressure clips and . . .

4.8b . . . the upper air deflector from the radiator

Chapter's Specifications.

19   Reattach the radiator hose to the thermostat housing cover. Make sure that the hose clamp is still tight. If it isn't, replace it.

20   Refill the cooling system (see Chapter 1).

21   Start the engine and allow it to reach normal operating temperature, then check for leaks and proper thermostat operation (as described in Steps 2 through 4).

4   Engine cooling fan - check and replacement

Check

Warning 1: *While checking the fan, make sure that the engine is NOT started. If it is, you could be severely injured.*

Warning 2: *Before the fan clutch operation can be checked in Step 5, the engine must be warmed up to its normal operating temperature and then turned off. Even though the engine won't be running during this check, it's HOT! Make sure that you don't touch the*

engine itself during this check, or you could be burned.

Warning 3: *Keep hands, tools and clothing away from the fan when the engine is running. To avoid injury or damage DO NOT operate the engine with a damaged fan. Do not attempt to repair fan blades - replace a damaged fan with a new one.*

1   Symptoms of fan clutch failure are continuous noisy operation, looseness, vibration and/or silicone fluid leaking from the clutch.

Cold engine checks

2   Rock the fan back and forth by hand to check for excessive bearing play.

3   With the engine cold, turn the blades by hand. The fan should turn freely.

4   Visually inspect for substantial fluid leakage from the fan clutch assembly, a deformed bi-metal spring or grease leakage from the cooling fan bearing. If any of these conditions exist, replace the fan clutch.

Hot engine check

5   Start the engine and allow it to warm up to its normal operating temperature. When the engine is fully warmed up, turn off the

ignition switch. Turn the fan by hand. Some resistance should be felt. If the fan turns easily, replace the fan clutch.

Removal and installation

Refer to illustrations 4.8a, 4.8b, 4.10, 4.11a, 4.11b, 4.12a, 4.12b and 4.14

6   Disconnect the battery cable at the negative battery terminal (see Chapter 5).

7   Drain the cooling system (see Chapter 1).

8   Remove the radiator protector cover **(see illustration)** and the upper air deflector **(see illustration)**.

9   On V8 models, disconnect the air conditioning line retainers at the top of the radiator and position the assembly off to the side.

10   Remove the upper radiator hose **(see illustration)**. Loosen the hose clamp by squeezing the ends together. Hose clamp pliers work best, but regular pliers will work also. If the radiator hose is stuck, grasp it near the end with a pair of adjustable pliers and twist it to break the seal, then pull it off. If the hose is old or if it has deteriorated, cut it off and install a new one.

4.10 Remove the spring clamps and disconnect the radiator hose from the thermostat housing cover and the radiator

4.11a Remove the upper fan shroud mounting bolt from the left side of the radiator . . .

4.11b . . . the shroud mounting bolt from the right side of the radiator

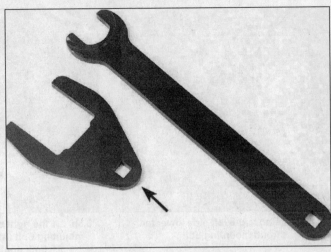

4.12a Typical fan wrench set - the large wrench spans the four pulley mounting bolts

4.12b If you don't have the special wrenches, use a chain wrench to lock the water pump pulley in position and loosen the fan clutch nut with the correct size wrench

11   Remove the upper fan shroud mounting bolts **(see illustrations)** and remove the fan shroud from the radiator. **Note:** *Some models are equipped with additional mounting screws that attach the upper shroud to the lower fan shroud.*

12   Special fan wrenches **(see illustration)** or a chain wrench, available at most auto parts stores, are needed to remove the cooling fan assembly. The fan clutch is attached to the drive hub with a large nut. Hold the water pump pulley with the chain wrench while loosening the clutch nut with the right size fan wrench and, if necessary, an extension **(see illustration)**. Turn the drive hub nut counterclockwise to loosen.

13   Lift the fan assembly up and out of the engine compartment.

14   If you're going to replace the fan or the clutch, unbolt the two components **(see illustration)**. **Caution:** *To prevent silicone fluid from draining from the clutch assembly into the fan drive bearing and ruining the lubricant, place the drive unit so the shaft points UP.*

15   Installation is the reverse of removal. When installing the fan and fan shroud assembly, make sure that the edge of the upper shroud locks into the lower shroud.

5   Coolant expansion tank - removal and installation

Refer to illustrations 5.2 and 5.3
Warning: *Wait until the engine is completely cool before beginning this procedure.*

1   Drain the cooling system (see Chapter 1).

2   Disconnect the expansion tank hoses **(see illustration)**. Plug the hose to prevent leakage.

3   Remove the expansion tank mounting bolts **(see illustration)**. Lift the tank out of the engine compartment.

4   Clean out the tank with soapy water and a brush to remove any deposits inside. Inspect the reservoir carefully for cracks. If you find a crack, replace the reservoir.

5   Installation is the reverse of removal.

3

4.14 Remove the four mounting bolts and separate the fan clutch from the fan

5.2 Remove the spring clamps from the expansion tank hoses and carefully twist the coolant hoses off the expansion tank

5.3 Location of the expansion tank mounting bolt (lower left bolt hidden from view)

6.5a Remove the left side lower fan shroud mounting bolt . . .

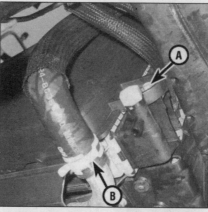

6.5b . . . the right side lower fan shroud mounting bolt (A) and the expansion tank coolant hose (B)

6.6 Remove the lower radiator hose

6.7a Remove the mounting screws from the lower radiator air deflector . . .

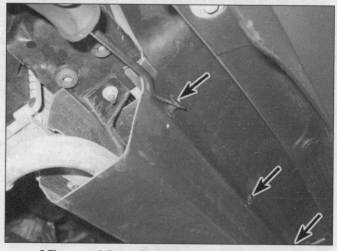

6.7b . . . and the push-pins from the front side of the lower radiator air deflector

6   Radiator - removal and installation

Warning: *Wait until the engine is completely cool before beginning this procedure.*

Removal

Refer to illustration 6.5a, 6.5b, 6.6, 6.7a, 6.7b, 6.9a, 6.9b, 6.11a, 6.11b, 6.12 and 6.18

1   Disconnect the cable from the negative battery terminal (see Chapter 5).
2   Raise the front of the vehicle and place it securely on jackstands.
3   Drain the cooling system (see Chapter 1). If the coolant is relatively new and in good condition, save it and reuse it.
4   Remove the upper radiator hose and the cooling fan (see Section 4).
5   Remove the lower fan shroud mounting bolts **(see illustrations)**. Remove the lower shroud from the radiator.
6   Remove the expansion tank hose and the lower hose from the radiator **(see illustration)**. Loosen the hose clamp by squeezing the ends together. Hose clamp pliers

work best, but regular pliers will work also. If the radiator hose is stuck, grasp it near the end with a pair of adjustable pliers and twist it to break the seal, then pull it off. If the hose is old or if it has deteriorated, cut it off and install a new one.
7   Remove the lower radiator air deflector mounting screws **(see illustrations)**. Sepa-

rate the air deflector from the radiator.
8   Remove the jackstands and lower the vehicle. Be sure to block the tires.
9   Remove the radiator support brackets from the radiator support beam and the radiator **(see illustrations)**.
10   Remove the condenser support brackets (see Section 16).

6.9a Remove the radiator support bracket bolts from the right side . . .

6.9b . . . and the left side bracket

6.11a Remove the side air deflector from the left . . .

6.11b . . . and the right side of the condenser and radiator

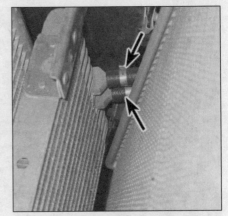

6.12 Use cutting pliers to cut the transmission cooler line clamps

11   Remove the side air deflectors **(see illustrations)**.

12   On automatic transaxle models, disconnect the transaxle oil cooler lines **(see illustration)** from the radiator.

13   Lift the radiator slightly and set it on the frame of the vehicle.

14   Use mechanics wire to support the condenser while the radiator is out. **Note:** *It is not necessary to discharge the refrigerant for radiator removal. Make sure the condenser is supported securely and the air conditioning lines are not bent or damaged.*

15   Lift the radiator from the engine compartment while simultaneously moving the condenser toward the front of the vehicle and onto the frame. **Note:** *It will be necessary to remove the transmission oil cooler and the radiator as a single unit.*

16   Remove the bolts from the transmission oil cooler and separate the cooler from the radiator.

17   Remove the splash shield, the hose and bracket from the radiator assembly.

18   Don't spill coolant on the vehicle or scratch the paint. Make sure the rubber radiator seals or insulators **(see illustration)** that fit on the bottom of the radiator and into the sockets in the body remain in place in the body for proper reinstallation of the radiator.

19   Remove bugs and dirt from the radiator with compressed air and a soft brush. Don't bend the cooling fins. Inspect the radiator for leaks and damage. If it needs repair, have a radiator shop or a dealer service department do the work.

Installation

20   Inspect the rubber insulators in the lower frame bracket for cracks and deterioration. Make sure that they're free of dirt and gravel. When installing the radiator, make sure that it's correctly seated on the insulators before fastening the top brackets.

21   Installation is otherwise the reverse of the removal procedure. After installation, fill the cooling system with the correct mixture of antifreeze and water (see Chapter 1).

22   Start the engine and check for leaks. Allow the engine to reach normal operating temperature, indicated by the upper radiator hose becoming hot. Recheck the coolant level and add more if required.

23   If you're working on an automatic transmission equipped vehicle, check and add fluid as needed.

7   Water pump - check

Refer to illustration 7.3

1   A failure in the water pump can cause serious engine damage due to overheating.

2   If a failure occurs in the pump seal, coolant will leak from the front cover (V6 models) or the water pump housing (V8 models). **Note:** *The water pump on V6 engines is mounted in the front cover and on V8 engines in a water pump housing in the engine block.*

3   Water pumps are equipped with weep or vent holes. It is possible to check the water pump weep hole using a flashlight **(see illustration)**. If a failure occurs in the pump seal, coolant will leak from the hole. Use the flashlight to find the vent hole on the water pump and check for leaks. **Note:** *Some small black staining around the weep hole is normal. If the stain is heavy brown or actual coolant is evident, replace the pump.*

4   If the water pump shaft bearings fail, there may be a howling sound near the water pump while it's running. With the engine off, shaft wear can be felt if the water pump pulley is rocked up-and-down. Don't mistake drivebelt slippage, which causes a squealing sound, for water pump bearing failure.

5   A quick water pump performance check is to put the heater on. If the pump is failing, it won't be able to efficiently circulate hot water all the way to the heater core as it should.

8   Water pump - replacement

Refer to illustration 8.5

1   Disconnect the cable from the negative battery terminal (see Chapter 5).

2   Drain the cooling system (see Chapter 1).

3   Remove the drivebelt (see Chapter 1).

4   Remove the engine cooling fan (see Section 4).

5   Remove the water pump pulley **(see illustration)**. When loosening the bolts, hold the pulley with a strap or chain wrench to prevent it from turning.

6.18 Be sure to check the rubber grommets before installing the radiator

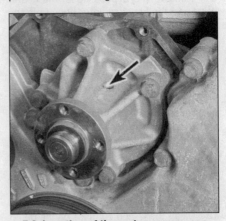

7.3 Location of the water pump weep hole on the V8 engine - the fan shroud, drivebelt and pulley will make it difficult to see the weep hole and it will be necessary to use a flashlight to inspect the water pump

3

8.5 Be sure to install a rubber liner or old drivebelt material under the chain wrench to prevent scoring or burring the water pump pulley

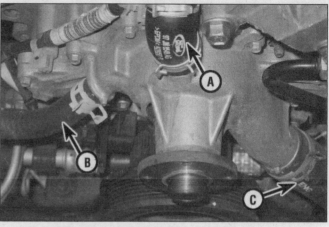

8.6 Water pump details on the V6 engine

A   Bypass hose   *C   Lower radiator hose*
B   Heater hose

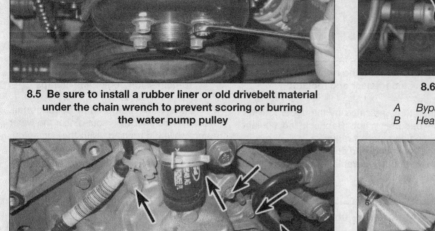

8.7 Location of the water pump mounting bolts on the V6 engine (bolts A hidden from view)

8.9 Location of the water pump mounting bolts on the V8 engine

V6 models

Refer to illustration 8.6 and 8.7

6   Remove the bypass hose, the heater hose and the lower radiator hose from the water pump **(see illustration)**.

7   Remove the bolts attaching the water pump to the engine block and remove the pump from the engine **(see illustration)**. If the water pump is stuck, gently tap it with a soft-faced hammer to break the seal.

8   Clean the bolt threads and the threaded holes in the engine and remove the corrosion and sealant. Remove all traces of old gasket material from the sealing surfaces.

V8 models

Refer to illustrations 8.9, 8.10 and 8.11

9   Remove the water pump mounting bolts **(see illustration)**.

10   Clean the O-ring surfaces on the pump and the housing **(see illustration)**.

11   If you're installing the old pump, install a new O-ring **(see illustration)**.

12   Clean the bolt threads and the threaded holes in the engine and remove the corrosion and debris.

All models

13   Compare the new pump to the old one to make sure that they're identical.

14   On V6 models, apply a thin film of RTV sealant to hold the new gasket in place dur-

8.10 Inspect the sealing surface inside the water pump housing for signs of pitting, scoring or other damage

ing installation. **Caution:** *Make sure that the gasket is correctly positioned on the water pump and the engine block surface is clean and free of old gasket material.*

15   Carefully mate the pump to the water pump housing.

8.11 Install a new O-ring onto the water pump

10.2 Disconnect the blower motor resistor electrical connector

10.5 Use a panel removal tool and pry the quarter trim panel from the rear quarter panel

10.6 Disconnect the rear blower motor resistor connector

16   Install the water pump bolts and tighten them to the torque listed in this Chapter's Specifications. Don't overtighten the water pump bolts; doing so will damage the pump.
17   The remainder of installation is the reverse of removal. Refill the cooling system (see Chapter 1) when you're done.
18   Operate the engine to check for leaks.

9   Coolant temperature sending unit - check and replacement

Warning: *Wait until the engine is completely cool before beginning this procedure.*

Check

1   The coolant temperature indicator system consists of a warning light or a temperature gauge on the dash and a coolant temperature sending unit mounted on the engine. On the models covered by this manual, the Cylinder Head Temperature (CHT) sensor (V8 models) or Engine Coolant Temperature (ECT) sensor (V6 models), which is an information sensor for the Powertrain Control Module (PCM), also functions as the coolant temperature sending unit (see Chapter 6).
2   If an overheating indication occurs, check the coolant level in the system and make sure all connectors in the wiring harness between the sending unit and the indicator light or gauge are tight.
3   When the ignition switch is turned to START and the starter motor is turning, the indicator light (if equipped) should come on. This doesn't mean the engine is overheated; it just means that the bulb is good.
4   If the light doesn't come on when the ignition key is turned to START, the bulb might be burned out, the ignition switch might be faulty or the circuit might be open.
5   As soon as the engine starts, the indicator light should go out and remain off, unless the engine overheats. If the light doesn't go out, the wire between the sending unit and the light could be grounded, the sending unit might be defective, or the ignition switch might be faulty (see Chapter 12). Check the

coolant to make sure it's correctly mixed; plain water, with no antifreeze, or coolant that's mainly water, might have too low a boiling point to activate the sending unit (see Chapter 1).

Replacement

6   See Chapter 6.

10   Blower motor resistor and blower motor - replacement

Warning: *The models covered by this manual are equipped with Supplemental Restraint systems (SRS), more commonly known as airbags. Always disable the airbag system before working in the vicinity of any airbag system component to avoid the possibility of accidental deployment of the airbag, which could cause personal injury (see Chapter 12).*

Blower motor resistor

Front blower motor resistor

Refer to illustration 10.2
1   Remove the lower trim panel from below the glovebox (see Chapter 11).
2   Disconnect the electrical connector from the blower motor resistor **(see illustration)**.
3   Remove the blower motor resistor

mounting screws and remove the resistor from the evaporator housing.
4   Installation is the reverse of removal.

Rear blower motor resistor

Refer to illustrations 10.5 and 10.6
5   Remove the rear, quarter trim panel from the left side of the vehicle **(see illustration)**.
6   Disconnect the electrical connector from the blower motor resistor **(see illustration)**.
7   Remove the rear blower motor resistor mounting screws and remove the resistor from the air conditioning/heater control unit.
8   Installation is the reverse of removal.

Blower motor

Front blower motor

Refer to illustrations 10.11 and 10.12
9   Remove the lower trim panel from below the glovebox (see Chapter 11).
10   Remove the vacuum tank mounting screw and separate the vacuum tank from the heater control unit.
11   Disconnect the blower motor electrical connector **(see illustration)**.
12   Remove the blower motor mounting screws **(see illustration)** and remove the blower motor.
13   Installation is the reverse of removal.

10.11 Location of the front blower motor electrical connector

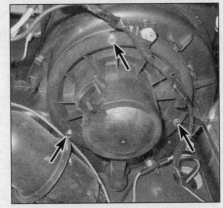

10.12 Location of the front blower motor mounting screws

3

10.16 Disconnect the rear blower motor electrical connector

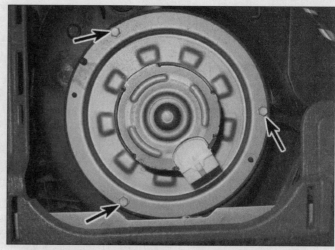

10.17 Location of the rear blower motor mounting screws

11.3 Disconnect the electrical connectors and the vacuum harness from the control assembly

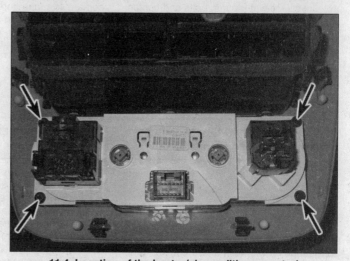

11.4 Location of the heater/air conditioner control assembly mounting screws

Rear blower motor

Refer to illustrations 10.16 and 10.17

14   Remove the rear quarter trim panel from the left side of the vehicle **(see illustration 10.5)**.

15   Disconnect the circulation hose from the blower motor assembly.

16   Disconnect the blower motor electrical connector **(see illustration)**.

17   Remove the blower motor mounting screws **(see illustration)** and remove the blower motor.

18   Installation is the reverse of removal.

---

11   Heater/air conditioner control assembly - removal and installation

Warning: *The models covered by this manual are equipped with Supplemental Restraint systems (SRS), more commonly known as airbags. Always disable the airbag system before working in the vicinity of any airbag* *system component to avoid the possibility of accidental deployment of the airbag, which could cause personal injury* (see Chapter 12).

1   Disconnect the cable from the negative battery terminal (see Chapter 5).

Front heater/air conditioner control assembly

Refer to illustrations 11.3 and 11.4

2   Remove the dashboard center bezel (see Chapter 11).

3   Disconnect the temperature blend door vacuum harness, the blower motor switch and temperature control switch connectors **(see illustration)**.

4   Remove the heater/air conditioner control assembly retaining screws **(see illustration)**.

5   Installation is the reverse of removal.

Rear heater/air conditioner control assembly

Overhead console

6   Lower the overhead console to access the retaining screw. Remove the console screw.

7   Disengage the retaining clips from the rear edges of the console.

11.11 Disengage the pressure clips on the edges of the rear console control assembly

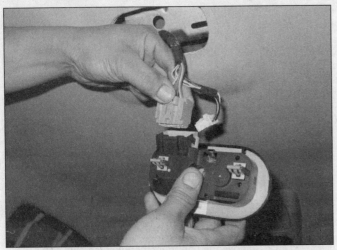

11.12 Disconnect the blower switch and temperature control switch connectors

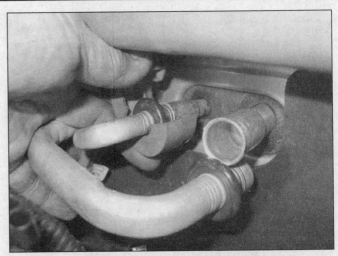

12.6 To disconnect the air conditioning lines from the evaporator, a spring-lock coupling tool (available at most auto parts stores) will be required

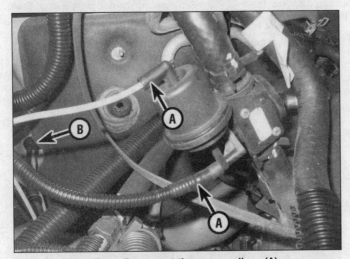

12.9a First, disconnect the vacuum lines (A) . . .

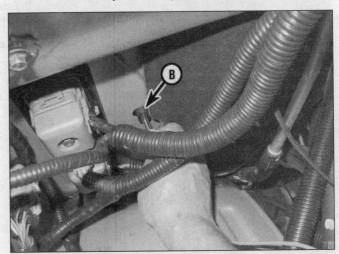

12.9b . . . then push the vacuum lines through the opening in the firewall (B)

8   Lower the overhead console slightly to access the electrical connectors. Disconnect the connectors.

9   Remove the console and remove the rear heater/air conditioner control assembly screws. Separate the assembly from the console.

10   Installation is the reverse of the removal.

Rear console

Refer to illustrations 11.11 and 11.12

11   Disengage the retaining clips **(see illustration)** and lower the console slightly to access the electrical connectors.

12   Disconnect the electrical connectors **(see illustration)** and separate the assembly from the console.

13   Installation is the reverse of removal.

---

12   Heater core - replacement

Warning 1: *The models covered by this manual are equipped with Supplemental Restraint*

systems (SRS), more commonly known as airbags. Always disable the airbag system before working in the vicinity of any airbag system component to avoid the possibility of accidental deployment of the airbag, which could cause personal injury (see Chapter 12).

Warning 2: *The air conditioning system is under high pressure. DO NOT loosen any fittings or remove any components until after the system has been discharged. Air conditioning refrigerant must be properly discharged into an EPA-approved container at a dealer service department or an automotive air conditioning repair facility. Always wear eye protection when disconnecting air conditioning system fittings.*

1   Have the air conditioning system discharged by a dealer service department or an automotive air conditioning shop before proceeding (see **Warning** above).

2   Disconnect the cable from the negative battery terminal (see Chapter 5).

3   Drain the cooling system (see Chapter 1).

Front heater core

Refer to illustrations 12.6, 12.9a, 12.9b, 12.10, 12.12, 12.13, 12.14a, 12.14b, 12.15 and 12.16

4   Remove the engine cover.

5   Disconnect the heater hoses from the heater core inlet and outlet pipes at the firewall **(see illustration 12.10)**.

6   Disconnect the evaporator inlet and outlet lines **(see illustration)**.

7   Remove the instrument panel (see Chapter 11).

8   On 4WD models, disconnect the 4WD module (see Chapter 7C).

9   Disconnect the vacuum lines at the engine compartment firewall **(see illustrations)**. Remove the rubber seal and push the vacuum lines into the passenger compartment.

10   Remove the evaporator/heater core housing mounting bolts **(see illustration)**. Lift the housing from the passenger compartment.

3

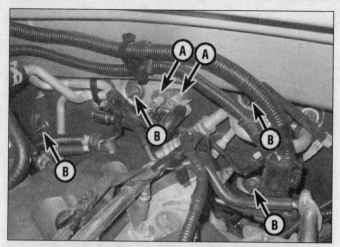

12.10 Location of the heater core hoses (A) and the evaporator/heater core housing mounting bolts (B)

12.12 Remove the floor duct mounting screws and lift the duct from the housing

11　Remove the insulating panel seal from around the heater core inlet and outlet tubes.

12　Remove the floor duct mounting screws **(see illustration)**. Remove the floor duct from the housing.

13　Remove the extension bracket **(see illustration)**. Separate the extension bracket from the housing.

14　Remove the heater core tube cover **(see illustrations)**.

15　Remove the heater core cover **(see illustration)**.

16　Pull the heater core from the housing by carefully gripping the edges to release it from the interior seal **(see illustration)**.

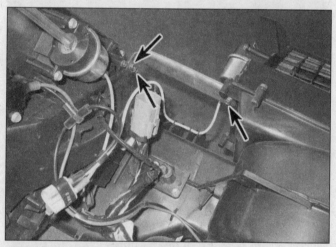

12.13 Remove the extension bracket mounting bolts and lift the bracket from the housing

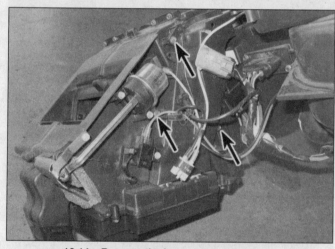

12.14a Remove the heater core tube cover mounting bolts . . .

12.14b . . . and lift the cover from the housing

12.15 Remove the heater core cover mounting screws

12.16 Grip the edges of the heater core and carefully work it away from the interior seal and out of the housing

12.19a Release the upper trim panel from the body using a panel tool to lever the locking tab out of the recess

12.19b Carefully pry the locking tabs using a panel removal tool to separate the rear pillar trim panel from the body

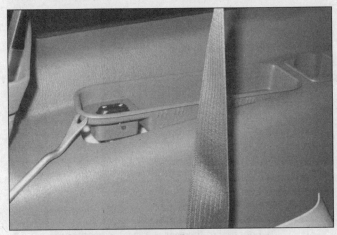

12.20 Using a panel removal tool, pry the tray from the quarter panel

3

17   Installation is the reverse of removal. Don't forget to reconnect the heater core inlet and outlet hoses at the firewall.

18   Refill the cooling system (see Chapter 1). Have the air conditioning system recharged and leak-tested by the shop that discharged it.

Rear heater core

Refer to illustrations 12.19a, 12.19b, 12.20, 12.21, 12.23, 12.24, 12.25, 12.26, 12.28, 12.30, 12.31, 12.32, 12.33, 12.34 and 12.35

19   Remove the rear upper trim panel **(see illustration)** and the pillar trim panel **(see illustration)**.

20   Remove the quarter panel tray **(see illustration)** and disconnect the switch connector.

21   Remove the rear hatch/bumper guard **(see illustration)**.

22   Remove the rear seat (see Chapter 11).

23   Remove the rear quarter panel **(see illustration)** from the left side of the interior.

12.21 Use a trim panel tool to release the pressure clips and lift the hatch/bumper guard out of the rear seal and carpet

12.23 Use a trim panel tool to separate the locking tabs on the quarter panel from the body

12.24 Disconnect the blower motor, resistor and other electrical connectors located on the housing

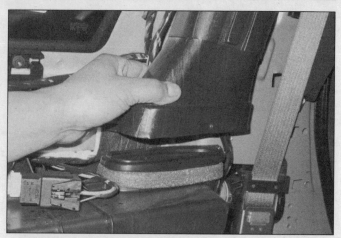

12.25 The vertical air duct can be lifted off the main duct

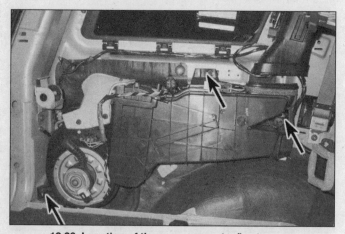

12.26 Location of the rear evaporator/heater core housing mounting bolts and nut

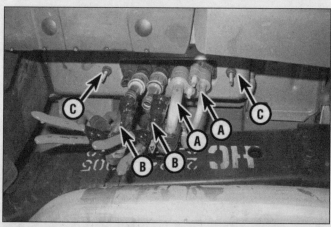

12.28 Remove the refrigerant lines (A), the heater core hoses (B) and the housing mounting nuts (C) - be sure to clamp the coolant hoses to avoid spilling coolant

24   Disconnect the evaporator/heater core housing electrical connectors **(see illustration)**.

25   Disconnect the vertical air duct from above the housing **(see illustration)**.

26   Remove the evaporator/heater core housing mounting bolts and nuts **(see illustration)**.

27   Raise the rear of the vehicle and support it on jackstands.

28   Disconnect the heater hoses **(see illustration)** and the air conditioning lines from below the vehicle.

29   Remove the jackstands and lower the vehicle.

30   Remove the evaporator/heater core housing from the rear of the vehicle **(see illustration)**.

12.30 Remove the evaporator/heater core housing from the rear of the vehicle

12.31 Location of the temperature blend door actuator mounting bolts

12.32 Location of the air distribution blend door actuator mounting bolts

12.33 Disconnect the coolant hoses from the heater core

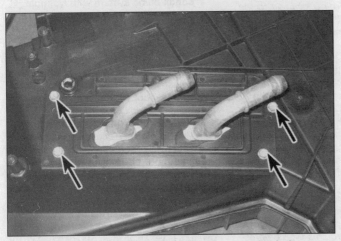

12.34 Remove the heater core cover mounting bolts

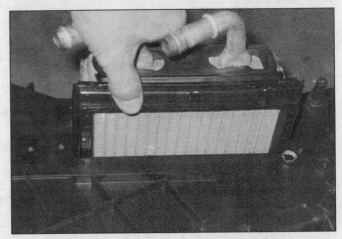

12.35 Lift the heater core from the housing

31 Remove the temperature blend door actuator from the housing **(see illustration)**.

32 Remove the air distribution blend door actuator from the housing **(see illustration)**.

33 Disconnect the hoses from the heater core **(see illustration)**.

34 Remove the heater core cover **(see illustration)**.

35 Remove the heater core from the housing **(see illustration)**.

36 Installation is the reverse of removal. Don't forget to reconnect the heater core inlet and outlet hoses at the firewall.

37 Refill the cooling system (see Chapter 1) when you're done. Have the air conditioning system re-charged and leak tested by the shop that discharged it.

13 Air conditioning and heating system - check and maintenance

Refer to illustration 13.1

Warning: *The air conditioning system is under high pressure. Do not loosen any hose fittings or remove any components until after the system has been discharged by a dealer service department or service station. Always wear eye protection when disconnecting air conditioning system fittings.*

1 The following maintenance checks should be performed on a regular basis to ensure the air conditioner continues to operate at peak efficiency.

a) *Check the compressor drivebelt. If it's worn or deteriorated, replace it (see Chapter 1).*

b) *Check the drivebelt tension and, if necessary, adjust it (see Chapter 1).*

c) *Check the system hoses. Look for cracks, bubbles, hard spots and deterioration. Inspect the hoses and all fittings for oil bubbles and seepage. If there's any evidence of wear, damage or leaks, replace the hose(s).*

d) *Inspect the condenser fins for leaves, bugs and other debris. Use a "fin comb" or compressed air to clean the condenser.*

e) *Make sure the system has the correct refrigerant charge.*

f) *Check the evaporator housing drain tube* **(see illustration)** *for blockage.*

2 It's a good idea to operate the system for about 10 minutes at least once a month, particularly during the winter. Long term non-

13.1 Look for the evaporator drain hose on the floorpan, directly above the transmission; to remove it for cleaning or for removing the evaporator, simply pull it off

use can cause hardening, and subsequent failure, of the seals.

3 Because of the complexity of the air conditioning system and the special equipment necessary to service it, in-depth troubleshooting and repairs are not included in this manual (refer to the *Haynes Automotive*

Heating and Air Conditioning Repair Manual). However, simple checks and component replacement procedures are provided in this Chapter.

4 The most common cause of poor cooling is simply a low system refrigerant charge. If a noticeable drop in cool air output occurs, the following quick check will help you determine if the refrigerant level is low.

Checking the refrigerant charge

5 Warm the engine up to normal operating temperature.

6 Place the air conditioning temperature selector at the coldest setting and the blower at the highest setting. Open the vehicle doors (to make sure the air conditioning system doesn't cycle off as soon as it cools the passenger compartment).

7 With the compressor engaged - the clutch will make an audible click and the center of the clutch will rotate. If the compressor discharge line (the small-diameter pipe) feels warm and the compressor inlet pipe (the large-diameter pipe) feels cool, the system is properly charged.

8 Place a thermometer in the dashboard vent nearest the evaporator and operate the system until the indicated temperature is around 40 to 45 degrees F. If the ambient (outside) air temperature is very high, say 110 degrees F, the duct air temperature may be as high as 60 degrees F, but generally the air conditioning is 30-50 degrees F cooler than the ambient air. **Note:** *Humidity of the ambient air also affects the cooling capacity of the system. Higher ambient humidity lowers the effectiveness of the air conditioning system.*

Adding refrigerant

Refer to illustrations 13.12 and 13.15

9 Buy an automotive charging kit at an auto parts store. A charging kit includes a 12- or 14-ounce can of refrigerant, a tap valve and a short section of hose that can be attached between the tap valve and the system low side service valve. Because one can of refrigerant may not be sufficient to bring the system charge up to the proper level, it's a good idea to buy an additional can. Make sure that one of the cans contains red refrigerant dye. If the system is leaking, the red dye will leak out with the refrigerant and help you pinpoint the location of the leak. **Caution:** *There are two types of refrigerant used in automotive systems; R-12 - which has been widely used on earlier models and the more environmentally-friendly R-134a used in all models covered by this manual. These two refrigerants (and their appropriate refrigerant oils) are not compatible and must never be mixed or components will be damaged. Use only R-134a refrigerant in the models covered by this manual.*

10 Hook up the charging kit by following the manufacturer's instructions. **Warning:** *DO NOT hook the charging kit hose to the system high side! The fittings on the charging kit are designed to fit **only** on the low side of the system.*

11 Back off the valve handle on the charging kit and screw the kit onto the refrigerant can, making sure first that the O-ring or rubber seal inside the threaded portion of the kit is in place. **Warning:** *Wear protective eyewear when dealing with pressurized refrigerant cans.*

12 Remove the dust cap from the low-side charging connection and attach the quick-connect fitting on the kit hose **(see illustration)**.

13 Warm up the engine and turn on the air conditioner. Keep the charging kit hose away from the fan and other moving parts. **Note:** *The charging process requires the compressor to be running. Your compressor may cycle off if the pressure is low due to a low charge. If the clutch cycles off, you can pull the low-pressure cycling switch plug and attach a jumper wire. This will keep the compressor ON.*

14 Turn the valve handle on the kit until the stem pierces the can, then back the handle out to release the refrigerant. You should be

13.12 Cans of R-134A refrigerant (available at auto parts stores) can be added to the low side of the air conditioning system with a simple recharging kit (V6 engine shown)

able to hear the rush of gas. Add refrigerant until the compressor discharge line (the small-diameter pipe) feels warm and the compressor inlet pipe (the large-diameter pipe) feels cool. Allow stabilization time between each addition.

15 If you have an accurate thermometer, place it in the center air conditioning vent **(see illustration)** and note the temperature of the air coming out of the vent. A fully-charged system which is working correctly should cool down to about 40 degrees F. Generally, an air conditioning system will put out air that is 30 to 40 degrees F cooler than the ambient air. For example, if the ambient (outside) air temperature is very high (over 100 degrees F), the temperature of air coming out of the registers should be 60 to 70 degrees F.

16 When the can is empty, turn the valve handle to the closed position and release the connection from the low-side port. Replace the dust cap. **Warning:** *Never add more than two (models with front air conditioning only) or three (models with front and rear air conditioning) cans of refrigerant to the system.*

13.15 Insert a thermometer in the center vent, turn on the air conditioning system and wait for it to cool down; depending on the humidity, the output air should be 30 to 40 degrees cooler than the ambient air temperature

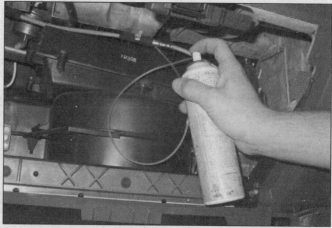

13.23 Remove the glove box (see Chapter 11) and insert the nozzle of the disinfectant can into the evaporator housing by shoving it through the air recirculation door

14.3 Location of the upper mounting nut and stud (A) and the inlet and outlet manifold (B)

14.7 Disconnect the air conditioning line bracket (A) and the harness clip for the compressor clutch field coil (B)

17   Remove the charging kit from the can and store the kit for future use with the piercing valve in the UP position, to prevent inadvertently piercing the can on the next use.

Heating systems

18   If the carpet under the heater core is damp, or if antifreeze vapor or steam is coming through the vents, the heater core is leaking. Remove it (see Section 12) and install a new unit (most radiator shops will not repair a leaking heater core).

19   If the air coming out of the heater vents isn't hot, the problem could stem from any of the following causes:

a) *The thermostat is stuck open, preventing the engine coolant from warming up enough to carry heat to the heater core. Replace the thermostat (see Section 3).*

b) *There is a blockage in the system, preventing the flow of coolant through the heater core. Feel both heater hoses at the firewall. They should be hot. If one of them is cold, there is an obstruction in one of the hoses or in the heater core, or the heater control valve is shut. Detach the hoses and back flush the heater core with a water hose. If the heater core is clear but circulation is impeded, remove the two hoses and flush them out with a water hose.*

c) *If flushing fails to remove the blockage from the heater core, the core must be replaced (see Section 12).*

Eliminating air conditioning odors

Refer to illustration 13.23

20   Unpleasant odors that often develop in air conditioning systems are caused by the growth of a fungus, usually on the surface of the evaporator core. The warm, humid environment there is a perfect breeding ground for mildew to develop.

21   The evaporator core on most vehicles is difficult to access, and dealership service departments have a lengthy, expensive process for eliminating the fungus by opening up the evaporator case and using a powerful disinfectant and rinse on the core until the fungus is gone. You can service your own system at home, but it takes something much stronger than basic household germ-killers or deodorizers.

22   Aerosol disinfectants for automotive air conditioning systems are available in most auto parts stores, but remember when shopping for them that the most effective treatments are also the most expensive. The basic procedure for using these sprays is to start by running the system in the RECIRC mode for ten minutes with the blower on its highest speed. Use the highest heat mode to dry out the system and keep the compressor from engaging by disconnecting the wiring connector at the compressor (see Section 14).

23   Make sure that the disinfectant can comes with a long spray hose. Point the nozzle through the air recirculation door so that it protrudes inside the evaporator housing **(see illustration)**, and spray according to the manufacturer's recommendations. Try to cover the whole surface of the evaporator core, by aiming the spray up, down and sideways. Follow the manufacturer's recommendations for the length of spray and waiting time between applications.

24   Once the evaporator has been cleaned, the best way to prevent the mildew from coming back again is to make sure your evaporator housing drain tube is clear **(see illustration 13.1)**.

14 Air conditioning compressor - removal and installation

Warning: *The air conditioning system is under high pressure. DO NOT loosen any fittings or remove any components until after the system has been discharged. Air conditioning refrigerant should be properly discharged into an EPA-approved container at a dealer service department or an automotive air conditioning repair facility. Always wear eye protection when disconnecting air conditioning system fittings.*

Note: *If you are replacing the compressor, you must also replace the accumulator (see Section 15) and the evaporator orifice tube (see Section 16).*

Removal

1   Have the air conditioning system discharged by a dealer service department or by an automotive air conditioning shop before proceeding (see **Warning** above).

2   Remove the drivebelt (see Chapter 1).

V6 models

Refer to illustrations 14.3 and 14.7

3   Loosen the upper mounting nut and remove the stud **(see illustration)**. **Note:** *The air conditioning compressor cannot clear the mounting stud. The mounting stud must be removed with the air conditioning compressor.*

4   Disconnect the electrical connector from the compressor clutch field coil **(see illustration 14.7)**.

5   Disconnect the compressor inlet and outlet line manifold from the compressor **(see illustration 14.3)**. Remove and discard the old O-rings.

6   Raise the vehicle and secure it on jackstands.

7   Working below the engine compartment, remove the bracket nuts and separate the wiring harness and the air conditioning compressor line from the compressor **(see illustration)**.

8   Loosen the lower compressor mounting nuts and remove the studs. Remove the compressor. **Note:** *The air conditioning compressor cannot clear the mounting studs. The mounting studs must be removed with the air conditioning compressor.*

V8 models

9   Raise the vehicle and secure it on jackstands.

10   Remove the right front wheel and inner fender splash shield.

11   Disconnect the electrical connector from the compressor clutch field coil.

12   Disconnect the crankshaft position sen-

3

15.4 Remove the nuts and separate the condenser line and the evaporator line from the accumulator

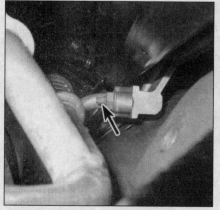

16.5a The refrigerant outlet line is located on the right side of the condenser

16.5b The refrigerant inlet line is located on the left side of the condenser

16.9a Location of the right side condenser core bracket bolt . . .

sor (CKP) connector and position it off to the side (see Chapter 6).

13   Remove the compressor clutch wiring harness bracket nut and set the wiring harness off to the side.

14   Disconnect the compressor inlet and outlet line manifold from the compressor. Remove and discard the old O-rings.

15   Loosen the compressor mounting nuts and studs and remove the compressor. **Note:** *The air conditioning compressor cannot clear the mounting studs. The mounting studs must be removed with the air conditioning compressor.*

Installation

16   If a new compressor is being installed, follow the directions with the compressor regarding the draining of excess oil prior to installation.

17   The clutch may have to be transferred from the original to the new compressor.

18   Before reconnecting the inlet and outlet lines to the compressor, replace all manifold O-rings and lubricate them with refrigerant oil.

19   Installation is otherwise the reverse of removal.

20   Replace the orifice tube (see Section 18).

21   Have the system evacuated, recharged and leak tested by the shop that discharged it.

15   Air conditioning accumulator - removal and installation

Refer to illustration 15.4

Warning: *The air conditioning system is under high pressure. DO NOT loosen any fittings or remove any components until after the system has been discharged. Air conditioning refrigerant should be properly discharged into an EPA-approved container at a dealer service department or an automotive air conditioning repair facility. Always wear eye protection when disconnecting air conditioning system fittings.*

1   Have the air conditioning system discharged by a dealer service department or by an automotive air conditioning shop before proceeding (see **Warning** above).

2   Remove the air filter housing (see Chapter 4).

3   Remove the front grille (see Chapter 11).

4   Disconnect the condenser line **(see illustration)** and the evaporator line from the top of the accumulator. Remove and discard the old O-rings.

5   Push the radiator air deflector forward to access the accumulator mounting nut on the backside of the radiator support panel.

6   Remove the accumulator mounting bolts and remove the accumulator. **Note:** *The lower mounting bolt must be accessed from behind the radiator support panel while the upper bolt can be accessed from inside the engine compartment.*

7   Replace all old O-rings. Before installing the new O-rings, coat them with refrigerant oil.

8   Tighten the inlet and outlet air conditioning line mounting nuts to the torque listed in this Chapter's Specifications.

9   Installation is otherwise the reverse of removal.

10   Take the vehicle to the shop that discharged it and have the system evacuated and recharged.

16   Air conditioning condenser - removal and installation

Refer to illustrations 16.5a, 16.5b, 16.9a and 16.9b

Warning: *The air conditioning system is under high pressure. DO NOT loosen any fittings or remove any components until after the system has been discharged. Air conditioning refrigerant should be properly discharged into an EPA-approved container at a dealer service department or an automotive air conditioning repair facility. Always wear eye protection when disconnecting air conditioning system fittings.*

1   Have the air conditioning system dis-

charged by a dealer service department or by an automotive air conditioning shop before proceeding (see **Warning** above).

2   Remove the air filter housing (see Chapter 4).

3   Remove the radiator protector cover **(see illustration 4.8a)** and the upper air deflector **(see illustration 4.8b)**.

4   Push the inner air deflector forward for additional clearance.

5   Disconnect the refrigerant inlet and outlet lines from the condenser **(see illustrations)**.

6   On vehicles equipped with rear air conditioning, disconnect the spring-lock coupling on the rear air conditioning outlet line.

7   Remove the accumulator bracket bolts and position the accumulator with the air conditioning lines to the side (see Section 15).

8   Remove the left and right radiator brackets **(see illustrations 6.11a and 6.11b)**.

9   Remove the left and right condenser core brackets **(see illustrations)**.

10   Carefully move the radiator forward and remove the condenser. If you're going to reinstall the same condenser, store it with the line fittings facing up to prevent oil from draining out.

11   Remove the side air deflectors from the condenser.

16.9b . . . and the left side bracket bolt

17.1 Disconnect the air conditioning pressure cycling switch connector

12   If you're going to install a new condenser, pour one ounce of refrigerant oil of the correct type into it prior to installation.

13   Before reconnecting the refrigerant lines to the condenser, be sure to coat a pair of new O-rings with refrigerant oil, install them in the refrigerant line fittings and tighten the condenser inlet and outlet nuts to the torque listed in this Chapter's Specifications.

14   Installation is otherwise the reverse of removal.

15   Have the system evacuated, recharged and leak tested by the shop that discharged it.

17   Air conditioning pressure cycling switch and high-pressure cutoff switch - replacement

Refer to illustrations 17.1 and 17.2

Warning: *The air conditioning system is under high pressure. DO NOT loosen any fittings or remove any components until after the system has been discharged. Air conditioning refrigerant should be properly discharged into an EPA-approved container at a dealer service department or an automotive air conditioning repair facility. Always wear eye protection when disconnecting air condi-*

tioning system fittings.

Note: *The pressure cycling switch detects low refrigerant line pressure at 21 to 27 psi, switches the A/C compressor off, then back on again at 42 psi. If the pressure increases over 455 to 495 psi, the high pressure cut-off switch, located in the high pressure line near the compressor, will switch the A/C compressor off.*

1   Unplug the electrical connector from the switch **(see illustration)**.

2   Unscrew the switch from the Schrader valve **(see illustration)**. **Note:** *Since both switches are threaded onto Schrader valves, it isn't necessary to discharge the air conditioning system.*

3   Lubricate the switch O-ring with clean refrigerant oil of the correct type.

4   Screw the new switch onto the threads until hand tight, then tighten it securely.

5   Reconnect the electrical connector.

18   Air conditioning orifice tube - removal and installation

Refer to illustrations 18.2 and 18.3

Warning: *The air conditioning system is under high pressure. DO NOT loosen any hose fittings or remove any components until the system has been discharged. Air condi-*

tioning refrigerant should be properly discharged into an EPA-approved recovery/ recycling unit by a dealer service department or an automotive air conditioning repair facility. Always wear eye protection when disconnecting air conditioning system fittings.

Note: *The orifice tube is located in the condenser to evaporator line. The orifice tube changes the high pressure liquid refrigerant into a low pressure liquid.*

1   Have the air conditioning system discharged by a dealer service department or by an automotive air conditioning shop before proceeding (see **Warning** above).

2   Disconnect the refrigerant line from the condenser to the evaporator **(see illustration)**. Use an open-end wrench on the stationary fitting and a flare nut wrench to avoid rounding off the tube nut.

3   Remove the orifice tube from the line with a pair of needle-nose pliers. If it's really stuck (or breaks off), special extractor tools are available at most auto parts stores **(see illustration)**.

4   Installation is the reverse of removal. Be sure to remove and discard the old O-rings.

5   Take the vehicle back to the shop that discharged it. Have the system evacuated, recharged and leak tested.

3

17.2 Use an open-end wrench to remove the air conditioning pressure cycling switch

18.2 Location of the air conditioning line access to the orifice tube

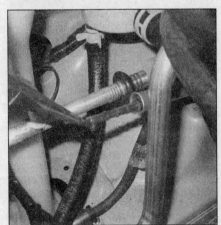

18.3 Remove the orifice tube using needle-nose pliers

Notes

Chapter 4
Fuel and exhaust systems

Contents

Specifications

Fuel pressure

Fuel system pressure

2002
V6 models	30 to 65 psi
V8 models	39 to 65 psi
2003 (all engines)	50 to 65 psi

Injector resistance (approximate)
V6 models	11 to 18 ohms
V8 models	11.4 to 12.6 ohms

Torque specifications

	Ft-lbs (unless otherwise indicated)	Nm
Fuel rail mounting bolts		
V6 models	17	23
V8 models	89 in-lbs	10
Fuel pressure relief valve bolts (V6 models)	53 in-lbs	6
Fuel pressure relief valve (V8 models)	71 in-lbs	8
Fuel pulsation damper bolts (V6 models)	53 in-lbs	6
Fuel tank retaining strap bolts	41	55
Throttle body mounting bolts		
V6 models	80 in-lbs	9
V8 models		
Step 1	90 in-lbs	9
Step 2	Additional 90-degrees (1/4-turn)	

1   General information

Multiport Fuel Injection (MFI) system

All models are equipped with a Multiport Fuel Injection (MFI) system. The MFI system consists of the fuel tank, the electric fuel pump (located inside the fuel tank), the fuel pump relay, the fuel rail and fuel injectors and the pulsation damper (which is mounted on the fuel rail). The removal and installation procedures for all of these components are included in this Chapter. If you're looking for the replacement procedures for emissions-related components, refer to Chapter 6.

The MFI system uses timed impulses to inject fuel directly into the intake port of each cylinder in the same sequence as the firing order. The injectors are controlled by the Powertrain Control Module (PCM). The PCM monitors engine operating conditions, calculates the precise air/fuel mixture needed for those conditions, then delivers the correct amount of fuel through the fuel injectors.

Air induction system

The air induction system consists of the air filter housing, the air intake duct, the throttle body and the intake manifold. The air filter housing provides the engine with a reliable supply of (relatively) cool filtered air, which travels from the filter housing The throttle body controls the amount of air entering the engine. The removal and installation procedures for the filter housing, air intake duct and throttle body are in this Chapter. The removal and installation procedures for the intake manifold are in Chapter 2. The replacement procedures for emissions-related components installed on air induction system components - Mass Air Flow (MAF) sensor, Intake Air Temperature (IAT) sensor, Throttle Position (TP) sensor, etc. - are contained in Chapter 6.

Fuel pump and lines

An electric fuel pump/fuel level sending unit module is located inside the fuel tank. Fuel is pumped from the fuel tank to the fuel injection system through a series of metal and plastic lines running along the underside of the vehicle. The fuel pressure regulator is located on the fuel pump/fuel level sending unit in the fuel tank. When the system fuel pressure exceeds its normal operating pressure, the regulator simply relieves the excess pressure right at the pump, eliminating the need for a return line between the fuel rail and the fuel tank.

The PCM-controlled fuel pump relay controls battery voltage to the electric in-tank fuel pump. When the ignition switch is turned to ON, the PCM grounds the relay for a second or two so that the pump can pressurize the system. The PCM also grounds the fuel pump relay when the ignition switch is turned to START and when the engine is running.

2.3 The fuel pump relay is located in the engine compartment fuse and relay box

When the ignition switch is turned to OFF, the relay is turned off and the fuel pump circuit is deactivated.

Exhaust system

The exhaust system includes the exhaust manifolds, the exhaust pipes, the catalytic converters, the muffler and the tailpipe. There are three catalytic converters: one upstream converter immediately below each exhaust manifold, and a third converter below the first two. Catalytic converters are emission control devices that reduce the three principal exhaust pollutants (hydrocarbons, carbon monoxide and oxides of nitrogen). General exhaust system servicing procedures are included in this Chapter. Refer to Chapter 6 for more information regarding the catalytic converters and the removal and installation procedure for the converter assembly.

2   Fuel pressure relief procedure

Refer to illustration 2.3

Warning: *Gasoline is extremely flammable, so take extra precautions when you work on any part of the fuel system. Don't smoke or allow open flames or bare light bulbs near the work area, and don't work in a garage where a gas-type appliance (such as a water heater or a clothes dryer) is present. Since gasoline is carcinogenic, wear latex gloves when there's a possibility of being exposed to fuel, and, if you spill any fuel on your skin, rinse it off immediately with soap and water. Mop up any spills immediately and do not store fuel-soaked rags where they could ignite. The fuel system is under constant pressure, so, if any fuel lines are to be disconnected, the fuel pressure in the system must be relieved first. When you perform any kind of work on the fuel system, wear safety glasses and have a Class B type fire extinguisher on hand.*
Note: *After the fuel pressure has been relieved, it's a good idea to lay a shop towel over any fuel connection to be disassembled,*

to absorb the residual fuel that may leak out when servicing the fuel system.

1   The fuel system includes the fuel tank, the fuel pump, the fuel pressure regulator (an integral part of the fuel pump), the fuel filter, the fuel rail and fuel injector assembly, and the metal lines and flexible hoses that connect all of these components together. All these contain fuel, which will be under pressure while the engine is running and/or while the ignition is switched on.

2   Even after the ignition has been switched off, the pressure inside the fuel system remains high for some time, so it *must* be relieved before any fuel lines are disconnected prior to servicing fuel system components.

3   To relieve fuel system pressure, start the engine and then remove the fuel pump relay **(see illustration)**. The engine will run briefly, then stall. Turn the engine over once or twice to verify that all fuel system pressure has been released, then switch off the ignition. **Warning:** *This procedure simply relieves the pressure that the engine needs to operate. But fuel is still present in the system components, so don't assume that there is no longer any danger. Be sure to observe all* **Cautions** *and* **Warnings** *when servicing fuel system components. Before working on any part of the fuel system, disconnect the cable from the negative terminal of the battery (see Chapter 5).*

4   Don't forget to install the relay when your work is completed. Note that, once the fuel system has been depressurized and drained (even partially), it will take significantly longer to restart the engine - perhaps several seconds of cranking - before the system is refilled and pressure restored.

3   Fuel pump/fuel pressure - check

Warning: *Gasoline is extremely flammable, so take extra precautions when you work on any part of the fuel system. See the* **Warning** *in Section 2.*

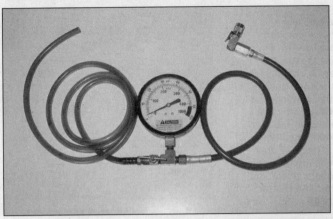

3.4 A typical fuel pressure gauge setup, with an adapter for connecting to the Schrader valve test port

3.6a The fuel system test port is a Schrader valve located on the fuel rail; unscrew the test port cap . . .

Note: *After the fuel pressure has been relieved, it's a good idea to lay a shop towel over any fuel connection to be disassembled, to absorb the residual fuel that may leak out when servicing the fuel system.*

General checks

1   If you suspect insufficient fuel delivery, check the following items first:

   a) *Check the battery and make sure that it's fully charged* (see Chapter 5).

   b) *Check the fuel pump fuse.*

   c) *Check the fuel filter for restriction.*

   d) *Inspect all fuel lines to ensure that the problem is not simply a leak in a line.*

2   Verify that the fuel pump actually runs. Place the transmission in PARK (automatic transmission) or NEUTRAL (manual transmission) and apply the parking brake. Have an assistant turn the ignition switch to ON - you should hear a brief whirring noise as the pump comes on and pressurizes the system. **Note:** *You can easily hear the fuel pump through the fuel tank filler neck.* If the fuel pump makes no sound, check the fuel pump electrical circuit. If the fuel pump runs, but a fuel system problem is suspected, continue with the fuel pump pressure check.

3   If the pump does not turn on (makes no sound) with the ignition switch in the ON position, check the fuel pump fuse and the fuel pump relay, both of which are located in the engine compartment fuse and relay box (see Chapter 12 for information about testing relays). If the fuse and relay are okay, check the wiring back to the fuel pump (see Section 7 for information on how to access the fuel pump electrical connector). If the fuse, relay and wiring are okay, the fuel pump is probably defective. If the pump runs *continuously* with the ignition key in its ON position, the Powertrain Control Module (PCM) is probably defective. Have the PCM checked by a dealer service department or other qualified repair shop.

Pressure check

Refer to illustrations 3.4, 3.6a, 3.6b and 3.6c

4   To check the fuel pressure, you'll need a

3.6b . . . screw on the adapter . . .

fuel pressure gauge with an adapter that fits the Schrader valve on the fuel rail **(see illustration)**.

5   Relieve the fuel system pressure (see Section 2).

6   Remove the cap from the fuel pressure test port **(see illustration)** and, using an adapter, connect the fuel pressure gauge **(see illustrations)**. If you're using a pressure gauge with a bleeder valve, make sure that the valve is closed.

7   Turn off all accessories and turn the ignition key to ON (engine not running). The fuel pump should run for about one or two seconds. Note the reading on the gauge.

   a) *If the fuel pressure is lower than the operating pressure listed in this Chapter's Specifications, look for a leak in the fuel lines and fittings between the fuel pump and the fuel rail. If there's no obvious leak in the lines or fittings, try replacing the fuel filter (see Chapter 1). It might be plugged or restricted. If the filter is okay, remove the fuel pump/fuel level sending unit module (see Section 7) and inspect the inlet strainer at the bottom of the pump. It might be dirty or plugged up. If it is, try cleaning it. If you cannot clean the strainer, replace the fuel*

3.6c . . . and hook up the fuel pressure gauge

pump/fuel level sending unit module. If there is no apparent leak in the system, the fuel filter is unobstructed and the fuel pump inlet strainer is clean, replace the fuel pump/fuel level sending unit module (see Section 7).

   b) *If the fuel pressure is higher than the operating pressure listed in this Chapter's Specifications, the fuel pressure regulator is probably defective. The regulator is an integral component of the fuel pump/fuel level sending unit module, so you'll have to replace the module (see Section 7).*

10   Start the engine and allow it to settle into its normal idle. Note the gauge reading as soon as the pressure stabilizes, and compare it with the pressure listed in this Chapter's Specifications.

   a) *If the pressure is lower than specified, check the fuel lines and hoses for kinks, blockages and leaks. Remove the fuel pump/fuel level sending unit module (see Section 7) and check the fuel strainer for restrictions. If all these components are okay, the fuel filter could be clogged or the fuel pump module could be defective.*

4

4.3a Locking R-clip/quick connect fittings are used on the inlet side of the fuel filter (one of them is actually for the fuel return line back to the tank); these fittings are secured by a removable (and replaceable) clip that wraps around the fitting and clips to itself; to open one of these fittings, pry open the longer side of the clip (A) from the shorter side (B) . . .

4.3b . . . with a small screwdriver

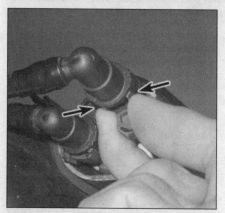

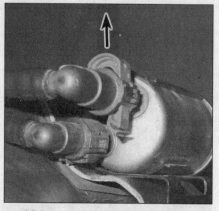

4.3c Then, using your thumb and index finger, squeeze the two legs of the opened clip together and push the clip up . . .

4.3d . . . until it protrudes from the fitting body

4.3e Once the locking clip is released, simply grasp the fitting and pull it straight off

b)   If the fuel pressure is higher than specified, the fuel pressure regulator is defective. Replace the fuel pump/fuel level sending unit module (the fuel pressure regulator, which is part of the pump, is not available separately).

11   Turn off the engine. Verify that the fuel pressure stays at the specified level for about five minutes after the engine is turned off.
12   Relieve the fuel pressure (see Section 2), then disconnect the fuel pressure gauge. Be sure to cover the the fitting with a rag before loosening it. Mop up any spilled gasoline.
13   Start the engine and verify that there are no fuel leaks.

4   Fuel lines and fittings - general information

Warning 1: *Gasoline is extremely flammable, so take extra precautions when you work on any part of the fuel system. See the* **Warning** *in Section 2.*
Warning 2: *Before disconnecting any fuel line couplings, relieve the residual pressure in the fuel system* (see Section 2) *and equalize tank pressure by removing the fuel filler cap. This procedure will merely relieve the increased pressure necessary for the engine to run -*

remember that fuel will still be present in the system components, so you should be ready to mop up fuel spills when disconnecting fuel line couplings.
1   The manufacturer uses three kinds of fuel line "couplings" (connector fittings):

Locking "R-clip" or quick-connect fitting
Push-connect fitting
Spring-lock couplings

The procedure for releasing each type of coupling or connector fitting is different. But a few rules of thumb apply to all of them. First, always disconnect all fuel line couplings from a fuel system component *before* loosening the component for removal. Second, when you disconnect a locking R-clip or push-connect fitting, always inspect the condition of the clip and the coupling *before reconnecting the coupling.* And when you disconnect a spring-lock coupling, always inspect the O-rings and the garter spring before reconnecting the coupling. Most of these couplings are under the same pressure as the rest of the fuel system, so to avoid leaks (and fires!) make very sure that the clip and coupling are in good condition. At one time, the clips for these couplings were generally available, at least at dealerships (for example, factory fuel filter kits included new clips for the couplings connecting the fuel lines to the inlet and outlet sides of the filter). Now that is no longer the case. Even if a clip is the only part of the coupling that's dam-

aged, you might not be able to obtain a new clip without buying a new coupling. And in most cases, the coupling itself is a non-removable part of the fuel line, so you might have to replace an entire fuel line just to get that new clip!

All couplings

2   Relieve the fuel system pressure (see Section 2). Inspect the visible internal parts of the coupling for dirt. If more than a light coating of dust is present, clean off the coupling before disassembling it. The seals in the coupling will stick to the fuel line as they age. Twist the coupling on the line, then push and pull the coupling until it moves freely.

Locking R-clip/quick-connect fittings

Refer to illustrations 4.3a through 4.3e
3   You'll find a pair of these fittings on the inlet side of the fuel filter **(see illustration)**. To open one, pry open the longer side of the clip with a small screwdriver **(see illustration)**. Then, using your thumb and index finger, squeeze the two legs of the opened clip together and push the clip up until it protrudes from the fitting body **(see illustrations)**. (Do not use any tools for this part of the procedure.) Finally, grasp the fitting and pull it straight off **(see illustration)**.

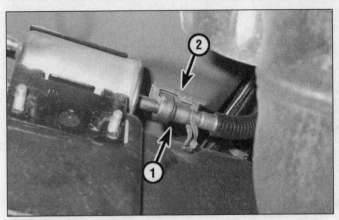

4.7a You'll find a push-connect fitting (1) at the outlet side of the fuel filter; before disconnecting this type of fitting, be sure to remove the safety clip (2) . . .

4.7b . . . by pushing it straight up until it pops loose . . .

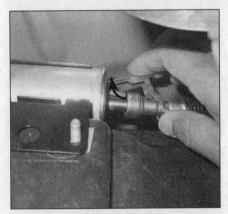

4.7c . . . then unhook the other end of the safety clip from the female side of the fitting

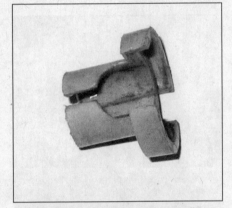

4.7d You'll need a special disconnect tool like this one to disconnect a push-connect fitting; it's available from specialty tool manufacturers and from some automotive parts retailers

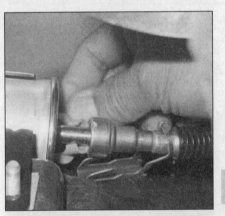

4.7e Install the special disconnect tool on the male side of the quick-disconnect fitting with the narrow end of the tool facing toward the female part of the fitting . . .

4 Inspect the condition of the locking clip. If it's damaged, replace it.

5 Before reinstalling the fitting, wipe off the end of the fuel filter pipe with a clean cloth. Inspect the inside of the fitting and make sure that it's clean.

6 To reconnect the fitting, align it with the fuel filter pipe and push the fitting onto the pipe. When the fitting engages, you will hear

an audible click. Pull on the fitting to verify that it's completely engaged. When installing the locking clip, carefully guide the legs into their respective holes, then push the longer and shorter ends of the clip together until the legs snap into place. The fitting is now locked into place.

Push-connect fittings

Refer to illustrations 4.7a through 4.7h, 4.8a, 4.8b, 4.9a, 4.9b and 4.10

7 This type of fitting is used on the outlet side of the fuel filter **(see illustration)**. Before disconnecting a push-connect fitting, disengage the safety clip by pushing it straight up

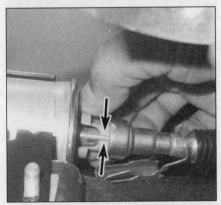

4.7f . . . pinch the tool tightly around the male side . . .

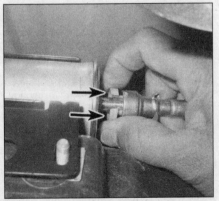

4.7g . . . then grasp the female side of the fitting and firmly push the tool into the female side until it stops

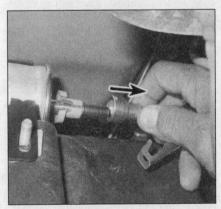

4.7h To disconnect a push-connect fitting, simply off the female side of the fitting

4.8a Be sure to inspect the O-ring inside the female side of the fitting; make sure that the O-ring is in good condition and that the female side is clean and dirt-free

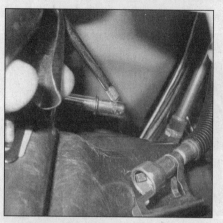

4.8b Lubricate the male side of the fitting with a few drops of clean engine oil before reconnecting the fitting

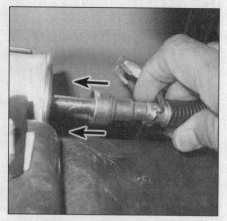

4.9a To reconnect the fitting, push the female half of the fitting onto the male half until you hear/feel an audible click . . .

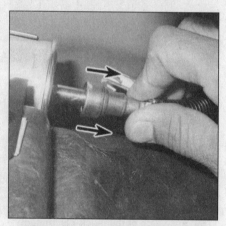

4.9b . . . then verify that the fitting is reconnected by trying to pull the female side off again; if it's fully connected, you won't be able to pull it off

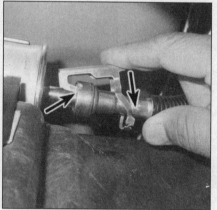

4.10 To install the safety clip, hook one end under the flange on the female side, then push the other end down until it clicks into place

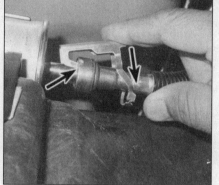

4.13 Remove the safety clamp from the spring lock coupling

until it pops loose from the fitting, then unhook the other end of the clip from the female side of the fitting **(see illustrations)**. To disconnect a push-connect fitting, you'll need a special push-connect fitting disconnect tool **(see illustration)**. Install the special disconnect tool onto the male side of the fitting **(see illustrations)**, then push it into the female side until it stops **(see illustration)**. The spring inside the female half of the fitting is now released. To disconnect the two halves of the fitting, simply pull off the female half off the fitting **(see illustration)**.

8   Inspect the inside of the female side of the fitting **(see illustration)** and make sure that it's free of dirt and that the O-ring is in good shape. Before reconnecting the fitting wipe off the end of the male side with a clean cloth and lubricate it with a few drops of clean engine oil **(see illustration)**.

9   To reconnect the fitting, push the female half of the fitting onto the male half until you hear/feel an audible click **(see illustration)**. Pull on the fitting to verify that it's fully engaged **(see illustration)**.

10   After you've verified that the fitting is fully reconnected, install the safety clip by

hooking one end under the flange on the female side and then push the other end down until it clicks into place **(see illustration)**.

Spring-lock couplings

Refer to illustrations 4.13, 4.14a, 4.14b, 4.15a, 4.15b, 4.15c, 4.15d, 4.15e, 4.16, 4.17a, 4.17b and 4.18

11   The fuel supply line is connected to the fuel rail by a spring-lock coupling. The male side of the spring-lock coupling, which is sealed by two O-rings, is inserted into the flared female side. The coupling is secured by a garter spring that prevents disengagement by gripping the flared end of the female fitting. A safety clamp clips onto the coupling to provide additional security. To disconnect a spring-lock coupling, you will need to obtain a spring-lock coupling tool, available at most auto parts sales stores. Be aware that 3/8-inch and 1/2-inch couplings (and other sizes) require different tools. These tools are inexpensive, and are usually sold in sets anyway.

12   Relieve system fuel pressure (see Sec-

tion 2), then disconnect the cable from the negative battery terminal (see Chapter 5).
13   Remove the safety clamp **(see illustration)**.

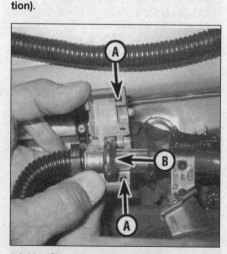

4.14a Open the spring-loaded halves of the spring-lock coupling tool and place it in position around the coupling with the lip (A) of the tool flush against the garter spring housing (B) . . .

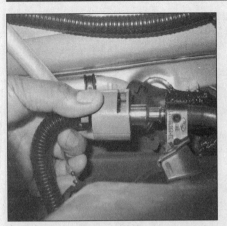

4.14b . . . then close the tool around the coupling

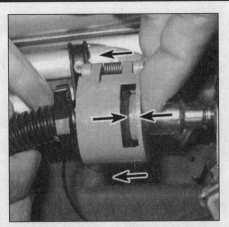

4.15a Push the spring-lock coupling tool toward the garter housing until this gap . . .

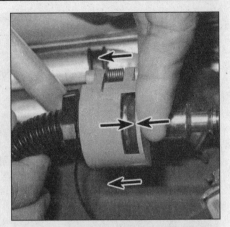

4.15b . . . is closed; the garter spring is now disengaged from the flared end of the female fitting

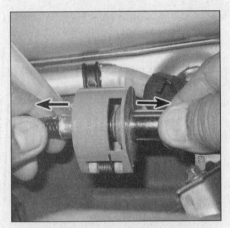

4.15c Pull the two fuel lines apart to disengage the tool from the garter spring . . .

4.15d . . . open and remove the tool . . .

4.15e . . . and disconnect the lines

14   Install the spring-lock coupling tool **(see illustrations)**.

15   Push the coupling tool firmly toward the garter spring housing to disengage the garter spring from the flared end of the female side of the connection **(see illustrations)**. Then

pull the two fuel lines apart to disengage the tool from the garter spring, open and remove the tool and disconnect the lines **(see illustrations)**.

16   Before reconnecting the coupling, wipe off the ends of both fuel lines with a clean cloth. Inspect the condition of the O-rings

and the garter spring. If either O-ring or the garter spring is damaged or worn, replace it. Then lubricate the O-rings with some clean engine oil **(see illustration)**.

17   To reconnect a spring-lock coupling, press the two sides of the connection together **(see illustration)** until the flared end

4.16 Before reconnecting the spring-lock coupling, lubricate the O-rings with a drop or two of clean engine oil

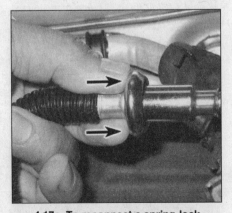

4.17a To reconnect a spring-lock coupling, push the two sides of the connection together until you hear/feel an audible click; the flared end of the male side of the fitting should now be locked into place by the garter spring

4.17b To verify that the spring-lock coupling is fully reconnected, try to pull the two halves of the fitting apart; if it's truly reconnected, you won't be able to disconnect it

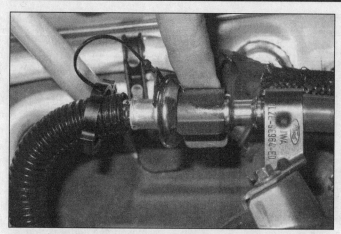

4.18 When you have verified that the spring-lock coupling is reconnected, install the safety clamp

5.6a To remove the fuel filler neck hose, loosen this hose clamp down at the fuel tank . . .

of the male side of the fitting is locked into place by the garter spring. Pull on the coupling to verify that it's fully engaged **(see illustration)**.

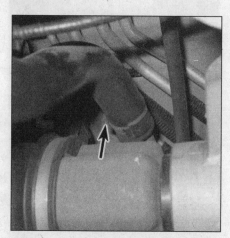

5.6b . . . then loosen this clamp up at the fuel filler neck, and remove the hose (then, if you're going to siphon any fuel from the tank, siphon it from the fuel filler neck hose pipe at the tank)

18   When you have verified that the coupling is reconnected, install the safety clamp **(see illustration)**.
19   Reconnect the cable to the negative battery terminal (see Chapter 5).
20   Turn the ignition key to ON (*not* START) and repressurize the fuel system (see Section 2), which will take a moment, then check for fuel leakage around the coupling. If there are no signs of leaks, start the engine and check again.

5   Fuel tank - removal and installation

Refer to illustrations 5.6a, 5.6b, 5.7, 5.8a, 5.8b, 5.9, 5.10, 5.11, 5.12a, 5.12b, 5.12c, 5.12d, 5.13, 5.14, 5.15 and 5.16
Warning: *Gasoline is extremely flammable, so take extra precautions when you work on any part of the fuel system. See the* **Warning** *in Section 2.*
Note: *Don't begin this procedure until the gauge indicates that the tank is empty or nearly empty. If the tank must be removed when it's full (if the fuel pump malfunctions,*

etc.), siphon as much fuel from the tank as possible before removing the tank.
1   Relieve the fuel system pressure (see Section 2).
2   Disconnect the cable from the negative battery terminal (see Chapter 5).
3   Raise the vehicle and support it securely on jackstands.
4   If the tank is full or nearly full, siphon the fuel into an approved container using a siphoning kit (available at most auto parts stores). The manufacturer recommends disconnecting the fuel filler neck hose (see Step 6), then siphoning it from there. **Warning:** *DO NOT start the siphoning action by mouth! Use a siphoning kit.*
5   Disconnect the fuel inlet and return line connectors on the inlet side of the fuel filter and the connector on the outlet side of the fuel filter (see Section 4), then remove the fuel filter (see Chapter 1).
6   Disconnect the fuel filler neck hose **(see illustrations)**. (If you're going to siphon any residual fuel from the tank, do it now.)
7   Disconnect the vapor hose that connects the canister vent solenoid to the EVAP canisters **(see illustration)**.
8   Detach the heat shields from the trans-

5.7 Disconnect this vapor hose from the canister vent solenoid (which is located right behind the fuel tank)

5.8a To detach the heat shields from the transmission crossmember, remove this bolt . . .

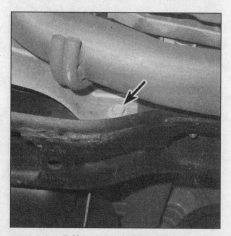

5.8b . . . and this bolt

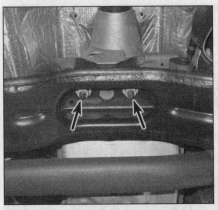

5.9 Loosen these two nuts that attach
the rear transmission mount to
the crossmember

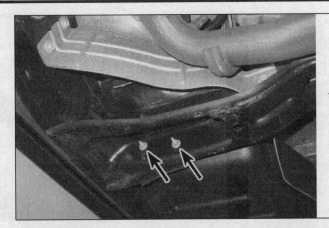

5.10 To detach the
front fuel tank shield
from the transmission
crossmember, remove
these two nuts

5.11 Place a jack under the right end of
the transmission crossmember

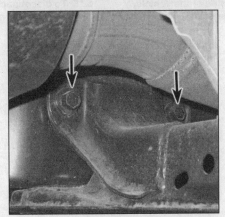

5.12a Loosen these two upper
mounting bolts . . .

5.12b . . . and these two lower mounting
bolts at the left end of the
transmission crossmember

4

mission crossmember **(see illustrations)**.
9   Loosen the two nuts that attach the rear
transmission mount to the transmission
crossmember **(see illustration)**.
10   Remove the two nuts that attach the
front fuel tank shield to the transmission
crossmember **(see illustration)** and remove
the shield.
11   Place a jack near the right end of the

transmission crossmember **(see illustration)**,
but don't place it directly under the crossmember mounting bolts at the right end of
the crossmember. Raise the jack until it's
supporting the crossmember.
12   There are two upper bolts and two lower
mounting bolts at each end of the transmission crossmember. *Loosen* the four left
crossmember mounting bolts **(see illustrations)** and *remove* the four right upper and
lower crossmember bolts **(see illustration)**,

then carefully lower the right end of the
crossmember about four to six inches **(see
illustration)**.
13   Support the fuel tank with a jack **(see
illustration)**. If you're going to use a floor
jack, be sure to insert a large square of sturdy
plywood between the jack head and the fuel
tank to protect the tank.

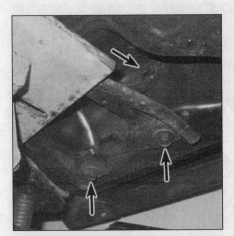

5.12c . . . then remove these four bolts
(other upper bolt not visible) at the right
end of the crossmember . . .

5.12d . . . then lower the right end of the
transmission crossmember about four to
six inches

5.13 Before unbolting the fuel tank straps,
support the fuel tank with a jack; if you're
going to use a floor jack, be sure to insert
a sturdy piece of plywood between the jack
head and the fuel tank to protect the tank

5.14 To detach the fuel tank from the underside of the vehicle, remove the front strap nut and the rear strap bolt

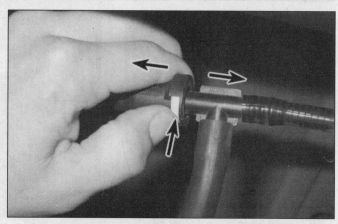

5.15 To disconnect the fuel filler neck vapor hose, depress this release button and pull the connector and the T-fitting apart

14   Remove the front tank retaining strap nut and the rear strap bolt **(see illustration)** and carefully lower the tank just far enough to access the fuel filler neck vapor hose and electrical connector on top of the tank.

15   Disconnect the fuel filler neck vapor hose **(see illustration)**, which is located at the upper rear end of the fuel tank.

16   Disconnect the electrical connector for the fuel pump/fuel level sending unit module **(see illustration)**.

17   Slowly lower the jack while an assistant steadies the tank until it's low enough for both of you to lift it onto the floor.

18   If the inside of the fuel tank is dirty, refer to Section 6.

19   To remove and install the fuel pump/fuel level sending unit module, refer to Section 7. To remove and install Evaporative Emissions Control (EVAP) system components from the tank, refer to Chapter 6.

20   Installation is the reverse of removal.

6   Fuel tank - cleaning and repair

Warning: *When the fuel tank is removed from the vehicle, it should not be placed in an area where sparks or open flames could ignite the fumes coming out of the tank. Be especially careful inside garages where a gas-type appliance is located, because the appliance could cause an explosion.*

1   Plastic fuel tanks cannot be repaired. No reliable repair procedures are available to correct leaks or damage. Fuel tank replacement is the only approved service.

2   To remove sediment from the bottom of the tank, have the fuel tank steam-cleaned. Remove the fuel tank sending unit/fuel pump (see Section 7) and all EVAP system components (see Chapter 6) prior to cleaning. Allow plenty of time for the tank to air dry before returning it to service.

7   Fuel pump/fuel level sending unit module - removal and installation

Refer to illustrations 7.5, 7.6, 7.7, 7.8 and 7.12

Warning: *Gasoline is extremely flammable, so take extra precautions when you work on any part of the fuel system. See the* **Warning** *in Section 2.*

Note: *The fuel pump, fuel level sending unit and fuel pressure regulator are not serviceable separately. If one of these components is defective, you must replace the entire fuel pump/fuel level sending unit module as a single assembly.*

1   Relieve the system fuel pressure (see Section 2).

2   Disconnect the cable from the negative battery terminal (see Chapter 5).

3   Raise the vehicle and support it securely on jackstands.

4   Remove the fuel tank (see Section 5).

5   Disconnect the electrical connector from the fuel tank pressure sensor **(see illustration)**.

6   Note the two arrows on top of the fuel pump/fuel level sending unit module **(see illustration)**. These arrows indicate the position of the locator bosses underneath that must be aligned with their corresponding slots in the edge of the mounting hole in the fuel tank for the module **(see illustration 7.13)**. Using these arrows as stationary index marks, make your own marks with a laundry marker on the retaining ring, adjacent to the two arrows, to ensure that the ring is retightened correctly.

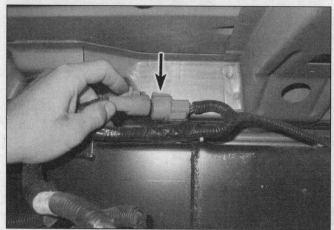

5.16 Disconnect the electrical connector for the fuel pump/fuel level sending unit (the half of the connector indicated by the arrow is attached to the frame)

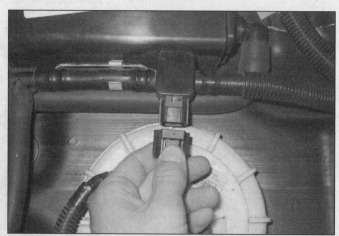

7.5 Unplug the electrical connector from the fuel tank pressure sensor and set the harness aside

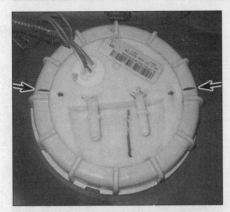

7.7 Using a brass punch and hammer, loosen the locking ring by carefully tapping the ridges on the ring (you can also use large groove-joint pliers to remove the retaining ring)

7.6 The two arrows on top of the fuel pump/fuel level sending unit module indicate the position of the two locator bosses (underneath the edge of the module mounting flange), which must be aligned with their corresponding slots in the fuel tank when installing the pump; using these arrows as the stationary index marks, make a couple more marks next to them on the locking ring to ensure that the ring is retightened sufficiently when installing the pump

7   Using a brass punch and a hammer **(see illustration)**, turn the retaining ring counter-clockwise until it's loose, then unscrew it by hand. If you don't have a hammer and punch, you can also use a very large pair of groove-joint pliers. **Note:** *A special fuel pump lock ring removal and installation tool is also available at automotive tool suppliers and some auto parts retailers.*

8   *Carefully* remove the fuel pump/fuel level sending unit module from the fuel tank

(see illustration). If you're planning to reuse the same unit, be extremely careful not to damage the arm and float for the fuel level sending unit.

9   Remove the old fuel pump gasket and discard it.

10   Clean the fuel pump mounting flange and the mounting surface for the fuel pump gasket.

11   Install a new gasket. Apply a thin coat of heavy grease to the new gasket to hold it in place during assembly.

12   When installing the fuel pump/fuel level sending unit module, make sure that the fuel pump locator bosses are aligned with their corresponding slots in the edge of the mounting hole **(see illustration)**.

13   Installation is otherwise the reverse of removal.

7.8 When removing the fuel pump/fuel level sending unit module, make sure that you don't damage the fuel level sending unit arm and float (they're not replaceable separately, so if you damage anything, you will have to replace the entire fuel pump/fuel level sending unit module as an assembly)

8   Air intake duct and filter housing - removal and installation

Air intake duct

Refer to illustrations 8.1, 8.2, 8.3, 8.4 and 8.6

1   On V6 models, detach the cruise control cable from the air intake duct **(see illustration)**.

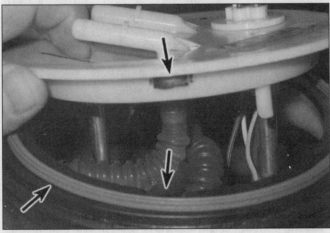

7.12 When installing the fuel pump/fuel level sending unit module, make sure that the gasket is correctly seated and that the locator bosses on the underside of module mounting flange are aligned with their corresponding slots in the edge of the fuel tank

8.1 On V6 models, detach the cruise control cable from the air intake duct

8.2 To disconnect the crankcase fresh air inlet hose from the air intake duct, grasp it firmly and pull it out (V6 model shown)

8.3 To detach the air intake duct from the air filter housing, loosen this hose clamp (V6 model shown)

8.4 To detach the air intake duct from the throttle body, loosen this hose clamp (V6 model shown)

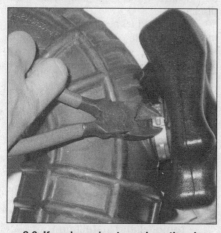

8.6 If you're going to replace the air intake duct or the resonator, cut off this clamp and remove the resonator; you'll need to a new clamp to reattach the resonator (V6 model shown, V8 models similar, except that the air intake duct has two resonators)

8.10 Disconnect the electrical connector from the MAF sensor

2   Disconnect the crankcase fresh air inlet hose (part of the PCV system) from the air intake duct **(see illustration)**.
3   Loosen the air intake duct hose clamp at the air filter housing **(see illustration)**.
4   Loosen the air intake duct hose clamp at the throttle body **(see illustration)**.
5   Remove the air intake duct.
6   If you're replacing the air intake duct or the resonator, separate the resonator from the air intake duct **(see illustration)**.
7   Installation is the reverse of removal.

Air filter housing

Refer to illustration 8.10, 8.12a and 8.12b

8   Disconnect the cable from the negative battery terminal (see Chapter 5).
9   Remove the air intake duct (see Steps 1 through 5).
10   Disconnect the electrical connector from the Mass Air Flow (MAF) sensor **(see illustration)**.
11   Remove the air filter element (see Chapter 1).
12   To disengage the four air filter housing locator pins from their rubber grommets, lift up first to disengage the two lower locator pins, then firmly pull the housing sideways,

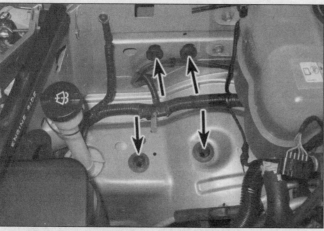

8.12a There are four locator pins on the air filter housing (two underneath and two on the right side); they're secured by these four grommets (air filter housing removed for clarity)

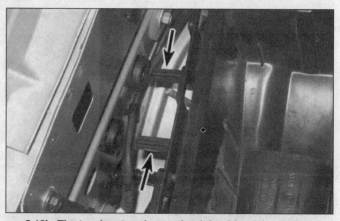

8.12b The two locator pins on the right side of the air filter housing are much longer than the pins underneath the housing, so lift the housing up first to disengage the lower pins, then pull it sideways to disengage these two pins; when installing the housing, insert these two pins first, then push down on the housing to re-engage the lower pins

9.1 To detach the throttle body cover on V6 models, remove these bolts

9.3a To disengage the accelerator cable from the cable bracket, squeeze these two locking tangs together . . .

9.3b . . . with a pair of needle nose pliers, then slip the cable out of its slot in the bracket

9.4 To disconnect the plug on the end of the accelerator cable from the throttle cam, slide the plug sideways

9.5 Trace the accelerator cable from the throttle body end back to the firewall and detach these four cable retainers

toward the engine, to free the two right side pins from their grommets **(see illustrations)**. (The two locator pins on the side are rather long, so *don't* try to pull them out first.)

13   Inspect the condition of the locator pin grommets. If they're cracked, torn or damaged, replace them.

14   Installation is the reverse of removal.

9   Accelerator cable - removal and installation

Replacement

Refer to illustrations 9.1, 9.3a, 9.3b, 9.4, 9.5, 9.6a, 9.6b, and 9.7

1   On V6 models, remove the throttle body cover **(see illustration)**. On V8 models, remove the engine cover (see Chapter 2).

2   On V8 models, remove the accelerator spring.

3   Disengage the accelerator cable from the cable bracket by squeezing the two tangs together **(see illustrations)**, then slip the cable housing out of its slot in the bracket.

4   Disconnect the end of the accelerator

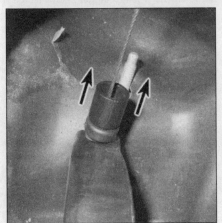

9.6a To disengage the lower end of the accelerator cable from the accelerator pedal, pull the cable end and rubber boot to the rear to detach it from the accelerator pedal . . .

cable from the throttle cam **(see illustration)**.

5   Trace the accelerator cable from the throttle body back to the firewall and detach the four cable retainers **(see illustration)**.

6   Working inside the vehicle, locate the

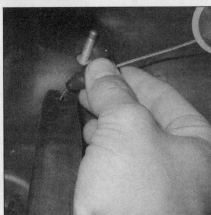

9.6b . . . then slide the cable out the slot in the top of the pedal

cable end at the top of the accelerator pedal under the dash **(see illustration)**. First, pull back on the cable end and the rubber boot to disengage the boot from the accelerator pedal, then slide the cable out the slot at the top of the pedal **(see illustration)**.

7   To remove the accelerator cable from its hole in the firewall, pull out the cable grom-

met **(see illustration)**, then pull out the cable and grommet from the engine compartment side.

8   Installation is the reverse of removal. Be sure the cable is routed correctly and the grommet seats completely in the firewall.

9   If necessary, at the engine compartment side of the firewall, apply sealant around the accelerator cable to prevent water from entering the passenger compartment.

10 Multiport Fuel Injection (MFI) system - general information

These models are equipped with a Multiport Fuel Injection (MFI) system. The MFI system consists of three basic sub-systems: the air induction system, the fuel system and the electronic control system. **Note:** *Refer to Chapter 6 for further information on the components of the electronic control system.*

Air induction system

The air induction system consists of the air filter housing, the Mass Air Flow (MAF) sensor, the air intake duct and resonator(s), the throttle body, the air intake plenum and the intake manifold. The MAF sensor is an information sensor for the Powertrain Control Module (PCM). The MAF sensor uses a heated wire system to send the PCM a constantly varying (analog) voltage signal corresponding to the volume of air passing into the engine. The Intake Air Temperature (IAT) sensor, which is an integral component of the MAF sensor, measures the temperature of the air being drawn through the MAF sensor. The PCM uses these signals to calculate the mass (density) of air entering the engine.

The throttle valve inside the throttle body is controlled by the driver, through the accelerator pedal. As the valve opens, the amount of air that can pass through the system increases. The Throttle Position (TP) sensor opens further, the MAF sensor's signal alters and the PCM opens each injector for a longer duration to increase the amount of fuel delivered to the inlet ports.

Fuel system

An electric fuel pump located inside the fuel tank supplies fuel under pressure to the fuel rail, which distributes fuel evenly to all injectors. A filter, located at the front of the fuel tank, protects the components of the MFI system. From the fuel rail, fuel is injected into the intake ports, just above the intake valves, by a fuel injector inside each intake port.

All vehicles covered by this manual are equipped with a "returnless" fuel system. The fuel pressure regulator is located on the fuel pump/fuel level sending unit module inside the fuel tank. When you replace the fuel filter, you'll note that there are two lines on the inlet side of the filter. One of these is the fuel supply line; the other line is the fuel return line, which directs excess fuel from the filter back to the fuel pump/fuel level sending unit mod-

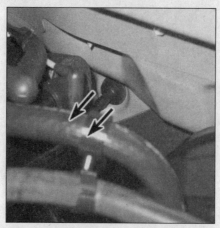

9.7 To remove the accelerator cable, pull the sealing grommet out of the firewall, then pull out the cable and grommet from the engine compartment side of the firewall

ule. If you ever have to remove or replace the fuel pump/fuel level sending unit, you'll see two fuel line couplings on top of the module, just like a conventional fuel injection system with a supply line and a return line. Both the fuel supply line and the fuel return line are pressurized. When the fuel pressure exceeds the upper threshold of the system's normal operating pressure, the fuel pressure regulator opens and fuel returns to the tank via the return line.

The amount of fuel supplied by the injectors is precisely controlled by injector "drivers" inside the PCM. The PCM uses signals from the Crankshaft Position (CKP) sensor and the Camshaft Position (CMP) sensor to determine when to trigger each injector in cylinder firing order (sequential injection), which improves fuel economy and lowers exhaust emissions.

Electronic control system

The PCM controls the MFI system and the other sub-systems of the entire engine management system. It receives signals from a number of information sensors, which monitor such variables as intake air mass and temperature, coolant temperature, engine speed and position, acceleration/deceleration, and exhaust gas oxygen content. These signals help the PCM determine the injection duration necessary for the optimum air/fuel ratio. These sensors and associated PCM-controlled relays are located throughout the engine compartment. For further information regarding the PCM and its control of the engine management system, see Chapter 6.

Idle speed and mixture adjustment

Both the idle speed and mixture are under the control of the Powertrain Control Module (PCM) and neither can be adjusted. Not only can they not be adjusted, they cannot even be checked, except with the use of

special diagnostic equipment, which makes this a task for a specialist. *Do not* attempt to "adjust" these settings in any way without such equipment. If you think that the idle speed and mixture are incorrect, take the vehicle to a dealer service department and have the system tested.

11 Fuel injection system - general check

Refer to illustrations 11.7 and 11.8
Warning: *Gasoline is extremely flammable, so take extra precautions when you work on any part of the fuel system. See the* **Warning** *in Section 2.*
Note: *The following procedure is based on the assumption that the fuel pump is working and the fuel pressure is adequate (see Section 3).*

1   Check all electrical connectors that are related to the system. Check the ground wire connections for tightness. Loose connectors and poor grounds can cause many problems that resemble more serious malfunctions.

2   Check to see that the battery is fully charged, as the control unit and sensors depend on an accurate supply voltage in order to properly meter the fuel.

3   Check the air filter element (see Chapter 1). A dirty or partially blocked filter will severely impede performance and economy.

4   Check the related fuses. If a blown fuse is found, replace it and see if it blows again. If it does, search for a wire shorted to ground in the harness.

5   Check the air intake duct to the intake manifold for leaks, which will result in an excessively lean mixture. Also check the condition of all vacuum hoses connected to the intake manifold and/or throttle body.

6   Remove the air intake duct from the throttle body and check for dirt, carbon, varnish, or other residue in the throttle body, particularly around the throttle plate. If it's dirty, clean it with carburetor cleaner spray, a toothbrush and shop towel.

7   With the engine running, place an automotive stethoscope against each injector, one at a time, and listen for a clicking sound that indicates operation **(see illustration)**. If you don't have a stethoscope, you can place the tip of a long screwdriver against the injector and listen through the handle. If you hear the injectors operating but there is a misfire condition present, the electrical circuits are functioning, but the injectors may be dirty or fouled from carbon deposits - commercial cleaning products may help, or the injectors may require replacement.

8   If you can't hear the injector operating, disconnect the injector electrical connector and measure the resistance across the terminals of each injector connector with an ohmmeter **(see illustration)**. Compare your measurement with the resistance value listed in this Chapter's Specifications. Replace any injector whose resistance value does not fall

11.7 Use a stethoscope or screwdriver to determine if the injectors are working properly - they should make a steady clicking sound that rises and falls as engine speed changes

11.8 Measure the resistance of each injector. It should be within Specifications

within the specifications.

9   If the injector is not operating, but the resistance reading is within specifications, the PCM or the circuit between the PCM and the injector might be faulty.

12 Throttle body - check, removal and installation

Check

1   Verify that the throttle linkage operates smoothly.

2   Remove the air intake duct from the throttle body (see Section 8) and look for a build-up of carbon and residue inside the mouth of the throttle body bore. Twist the throttle cam to open the throttle valve and inspect the area just downstream from the throttle valve. If the throttle bore is dirty, wipe it out with a clean shop rag. **Caution:** *Do NOT use carburetor cleaner or some other strong solvent to clean the throttle body, which is a "composite" (plastic) material that might be damaged by strong solvents. If you need to use a strong cleaning agent to clean the throttle body, check with your dealer to make sure that it's approved for use with composite materials. And make sure that it won't harm the oxygen sensors or the catalytic converters.*

Removal and installation

Refer to illustrations 12.6a, 12.6b, 12.7 and 12.8

3   Disconnect the cable from the negative battery terminal (see Chapter 5).

4   Remove the air intake duct (see Section 8).

5   Disconnect the accelerator cable from the throttle body (see Section 9).

6   If the vehicle is equipped with cruise control, disconnect the cruise control cable **(see illustrations)**.

7   Disconnect the electrical connector

12.6a To disengage the cruise control cable from this bracket, squeeze the two locking tangs together, then slide the cable out of its slot in the bracket

12.6b To disconnect the cruise control cable from the throttle cam on V6 models, pull the cable end toward the right side of the engine (1), then pull it forward (2); on V8s, disconnect the cruise control cable by pulling it forward, then to the right

12.7 Disconnect the electrical connector from the Throttle Position (TP) sensor (V6 model shown, V8 models similar)

from the Throttle Position (TP) sensor **(see illustration)**.

8   Remove the throttle body mounting bolts **(see illustration)**.

12.8 To detach the throttle body from the intake manifold, remove these four bolts (V6 model shown, V8 models similar)

4

13.3a To detach the fuel pressure relief valve from the fuel rail, remove these two mounting bolts . . .

13.3b . . . then pull off the pressure relief valve (V6 models)

13.4 Remove and discard the old O-ring; lubricate the new O-ring with a little clean engine oil (V6 models)

14.3 Disconnect the vacuum hose from the fuel pulsation damper

14.4a Remove these two bolts . . .

14.4b . . . and remove the fuel pulsation damper from the fuel rail (V6 models)

9   On V8 models, remove and discard the old throttle body gasket.

10   Installation is the reverse of removal. On V8 models, be sure to clean the gasket mating surfaces of the throttle body and the intake manifold and to use a new throttle body gasket. On all models, be sure to tighten the throttle body bolts to the torque listed in this Chapter's Specifications.

13   Fuel pressure relief valve - removal and installation

1   Relieve the fuel system pressure (see Section 2).
2   Disconnect the cable from the negative battery terminal (see Chapter 5).

V6 models

Refer to illustrations 13.3a, 13.3b and 13.4

3   Remove the fuel pressure relief valve mounting bolts **(see illustration)** and remove the fuel pressure relief valve from the fuel rail **(see illustration)**.
4   Remove the old O-ring from the fuel

pressure relief valve **(see illustration)**.
5   Lubricate the new O-ring with clean engine oil and install it on the fuel pressure relief valve.
6   Installation is the reverse of removal. Be sure to tighten the fuel pressure relief valve mounting bolts to the torque listed in this Chapter's Specifications.

V8 models

7   The fuel pressure relief valve is located on the left fuel rail.
8   Remove the cap from the fuel pressure relief valve.
9   Unscrew the fuel pressure relief valve.
10   Installation is the reverse of removal. Be sure to tighten the fuel pressure relief valve to the torque listed in this Chapter's Specifications.

14   Fuel pulsation damper - removal and installation

Refer to illustrations 14.3, 14.4a, 14.4b and 14.5

1   Relieve the fuel system pressure (see Section 2).

2   Disconnect the cable from the negative battery terminal (see Chapter 5).

V6 models

3   Disconnect the vacuum hose from the fuel pulsation damper **(see illustration)**.
4   Remove the fuel pulsation damper mounting bolts **(see illustration)** and remove the fuel pulsation damper **(see illustration)**.
5   Remove the old O-ring from the fuel pulsation damper **(see illustration)**.
6   Coat the new O-ring with a little clean engine coil and install it on the fuel pulsation damper.
7   Installation is otherwise the reverse of removal. Be sure to tighten the fuel pulsation damper mounting bolts to the torque listed in this Chapter's Specifications.

V8 models

8   The fuel pulsation damper is located on the right fuel rail.
9   Disconnect the vacuum hose from the fuel pulsation damper.
10   Remove the snap-ring.
11   Remove the fuel pressure relief valve.
12   Remove the old O-ring from the fuel

14.5 Remove the old O-ring from the fuel pulsation damper and discard it; always use a new O-ring when installing the damper (V6 models)

pressure relief valve and discard it.

13   Coat the new O-ring with a little clean engine oil and install it on the fuel pressure relief valve.

14   Installation is otherwise the reverse of removal.

15 Fuel rail and injectors - removal and installation

Warning: *Gasoline is extremely flammable, so take extra precautions when you work on any part of the fuel system. See the* **Warning** *in Section 2.*

1   Relieve the fuel system pressure (see Section 2).

2   Disconnect the cable from the negative battery terminal (see Chapter 5).

V6 models

Refer to illustrations 15.6a, 15.6b, 15.7a, 15.7b, 15.8, 15.9, 15.10, 15.11 and 15.12

3   Remove the intake manifold (see Chapter 2A). **Note:** *It's not necessary to disconnect the throttle body from the intake manifold for this procedure. Just disconnect everything from the throttle body (see Sec-*

15.6a Disconnect the electrical connectors from the fuel injectors . . .

15.7a To detach the fuel rail from the engine, remove these four bolts . . .

tion 12), *but leave it attached to the intake manifold.*

4   Disconnect the vacuum hose from the fuel pulsation damper (see Section 14).

5   Using the special spring lock coupling tool, disconnect the fuel supply line from the fuel rail (see Section 4).

6   Disconnect the electrical connectors from the fuel injectors and detach the injector

15.6b . . . then detach the fuel injector harnesses from their retaining studs by pulling each retainer straight up (V6 models)

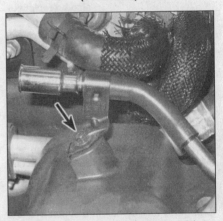

15.7b . . . and this bolt (V6 models)

harness retainers from their studs **(see illustrations)**.

7   Remove the fuel rail mounting bolts **(see illustrations)**.

8   Carefully remove the fuel rail assembly **(see illustration)**.

9   Remove the fuel injectors from the cylinder head. Try removing each injector using a rocking, side-to-side motion while pulling it

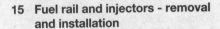

15.8 Carefully remove the fuel rail assembly from the engine (note that the injectors don't come off with the fuel rail, as they do on many fuel injection systems, but instead remain in the cylinder head)

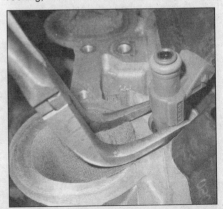

15.9 To remove each injector from the cylinder head, carefully pry it up with a pair of right-angle needle nose pliers (or some other tool that's suitable for prying)

4

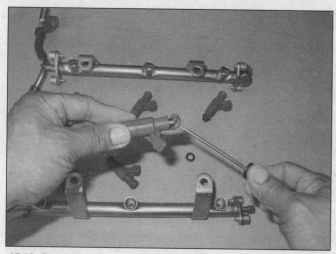

15.10 Carefully remove the old O-rings from each injector (upper O-ring shown, lower O-ring at other end of injector must also be replaced)

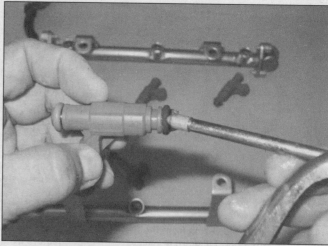

15.11 After installing the new O-rings on each injector, lubricate them with a little clean engine oil before installing the injector in the cylinder head and the fuel rail on the injectors

up. If that doesn't work, use a tool like a pair of right-angle needle nose pliers to pry it up **(see illustration)**.

10　Remove the old O-rings from each injector **(see illustration)**. (There are two O-rings, one at each end of each injector.)

11　Lubricate the new O-rings with a little clean engine oil, then install them on the injectors **(see illustration)**.

12　Install the injectors in the cylinder head **(see illustration)**. Make sure that the electrical connector side of each injector is aligned with the harness side of the connector.

13　When installing the fuel rail on the injectors, place the fuel rail in position over the injectors and carefully but firmly push the fuel rail down onto the injectors until the fuel rail is fully seated onto the upper ends of all six injectors.

14　Tighten the fuel rail mounting bolts to the torque listed in this Chapter's Specifications.

15　The remainder of installation is the reverse of removal.

V8 models

16　Disconnect the fuel supply line from the fuel rail (see Section 4).

17　Remove the air intake duct (see Section 8).

18　Disconnect the electrical connectors from the Throttle Position (TP) sensor and from the Idle Air Control (IAC) solenoid (see Chapter 6).

19　Disconnect the accelerator cable and the cruise control cable from the throttle cam and from the accelerator cable bracket (see Section 9). Disconnect the accelerator return spring.

20　Disconnect all eight fuel injector electrical connectors.

21　Remove the bolt that secures the brake booster vacuum line and set the brake booster hose and line aside.

22　Disconnect the vacuum hoses from the Exhaust Gas Recirculation (EGR) valve and from the Evaporative Emissions Control (EVAP) canister purge solenoid.

23　Disconnect the vacuum hoses from the throttle body adapter and from the fuel pulsation damper.

24　Disconnect the vapor hose from the throttle body adapter.

25　Disconnect the EGR pipe from the EGR valve (see Chapter 6).

26　Disconnect the air hose from the Idle Air

Control (IAC) valve and set it aside (see Chapter 6).

27　Disconnect the crankcase fresh air inlet hose (see Chapter 6).

28　Remove the PCV valve and crankcase ventilation hose (see Chapter 6).

29　Remove the throttle body adapter bolts and remove the throttle body adapter from the intake manifold.

30　Detach the wiring harness retainer clip from the rear of the intake manifold.

31　Disconnect the wiring harness ground.

32　Remove the EGR coolant hose from the heated EGR fitting.

33　Remove the EGR coolant hose routing clip from the fuel rail retaining stud.

34　Remove the fuel rail bolts.

35　Remove the fuel rail and the injectors as a single assembly.

36　Remove the injectors from the fuel rail.

37　Remove the old O-rings from each injector (there are two, one at each end). Install the new O-rings on each injector and lubricate them with clean engine oil.

38　Install the injectors in the fuel rail.

39　Install the fuel rail assembly and tighten the fuel rail retaining bolts to the torque listed in this Chapter's Specifications.

40　The remainder of installation is the reverse of removal.

15.12 When installing the injectors into the cylinder head, make sure that the injector side of the electrical connector is correctly aligned with the harness side of the connector, then carefully but firmly push the injector down into its bore until it's fully seated

16　Exhaust system servicing - general information

Refer to illustrations 16.1a and 16.1b

Warning: *If you're planning to inspect and/or repair exhaust system components after driving the vehicle, be sure to allow plenty of time for the the system components to cool down before touching them. Also, when working under the vehicle, make sure it is securely supported on jackstands.*

1　The exhaust system consists of the exhaust manifolds, the converter assembly, the exhaust pipe, the muffler, the tailpipe and

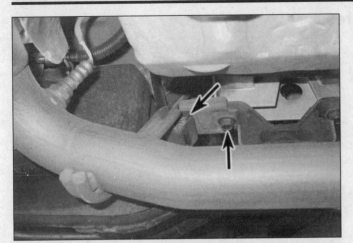

16.1a The crossover pipe between the right exhaust downpipe and the left downpipe hangs from a welded hanger that's supported by a rubber insulator inside a rigid metal bracket; to remove the bracket, remove this bolt, then slide the bracket and insulator off the hanger

16.1b A typical rubber exhaust hanger; it's a good idea to stock three or four of these rubber hangers in your garage so that you can replace torn or damaged hangers whenever you're servicing something under the vehicle

all the brackets, hangers and clamps used to suspend the exhaust underneath the vehicle. The converter assembly consists of two upstream catalysts, a downstream catalyst, and the pipes connecting them to the exhaust manifolds, to each other and to the rest of the exhaust system, all welded together into a single assembly. The exhaust system is suspended from the bottom of the vehicle pan by mounting brackets and rubber hangers **(see illustrations)**. If any of the parts are damaged or deteriorated, excessive noise and vibration will be transmitted to the body.

2   Conducting regular inspections of the exhaust system will keep it safe and quiet. Look for any damaged or bent parts, open seams, holes, loose connections, excessive corrosion or other defects which could allow exhaust fumes to enter the vehicle. Also

check the catalytic converter when you inspect the exhaust system (see Chapter 6). Deteriorated exhaust system components should not be repaired; they should be replaced with new parts.

3   If the exhaust system components are extremely corroded or rusted together, they will probably have to be cut from the exhaust system. The convenient way to accomplish this is to have a muffler repair shop remove the corroded sections with a cutting torch. If, however, you want to save money by doing it yourself (and you don't have a welding outfit with a cutting torch), simply cut off the old components with a hacksaw. If you have compressed air, special pneumatic cutting chisels can also be used. If you decide to tackle the job at home, be sure to wear safety goggles to protect your eyes from metal chips and work gloves to protect your hands.

4   Here are some simple guidelines to follow when repairing the exhaust system:

a) *Work from the back to the front when removing exhaust system components.*

b) *Apply penetrating oil to the exhaust system component fasteners to make them easier to remove.*

c) *Use new gaskets, hangers and clamps when installing exhaust systems components.*

d) *Apply anti-seize compound to the threads of all exhaust system fasteners at reassembly.*

e) *Be sure to allow sufficient clearance between newly installed parts and all points on the underbody to avoid overheating the floor pan and possibly damaging the interior carpet and insulation. Pay particularly close attention to the catalytic converter and heat shield.*

4

Notes

Chapter 5
Engine electrical systems

Contents

Specifications

Charging system

Charging voltage	13.5 to 15.0 volts
Standard amperage	
No load	30 amps or less
With load	87 amps or more

Torque specifications

	Ft-lbs	Nm
Starter motor mounting bolts	18	25

---

1 General information, precautions and battery disconnection

The engine electrical systems include all ignition, charging and starting components. Because of their engine-related functions, these components are discussed separately from body electrical devices such as the lights, the instruments, etc. (which are included in Chapter 12).

Precautions

Always observe the following precautions when working on the electrical system:

a) *Be extremely careful when servicing engine electrical components. They are easily damaged if checked, connected or handled improperly.*

b) *Never leave the ignition switched on for long periods of time when the engine is not running.*

c) *Never disconnect the battery cables while the engine is running.*

d) *Maintain correct polarity when connecting battery cables from another vehicle during jump starting - see the "Booster battery (jump) starting" section at the front of this manual.*

e) *Always disconnect the negative battery cable(s) from the battery(ies) before working on the electrical system, but read the following battery disconnection procedure first.*

It's also a good idea to review the safety-related information regarding the engine electrical systems located in the "Safety first!" section at the front of this manual, before beginning any operation included in this Chapter.

Battery disconnection

Some systems on the vehicle require battery power to be available at all times, either to maintain continuous operation (radio, alarm system, power door locks, windows, etc.), or to maintain control unit memory (Powertrain Control Module and other control units). When the battery is disconnected, the power that maintains these systems is cut. So, before you disconnect the battery, please note the following points to ensure that there are no unforeseen consequences of this action:

a) *The engine management system's Powertrain Control Module (PCM) will lose some information stored in its memory when the battery is disconnected, and will require a certain period of time to "relearn" its adaptive strategy. During this period of relearning, the vehicle might have some abnormal driveability symptoms. These symptoms will disappear once the PCM has relearned its adaptive strategy.*

b) *In some regions of the United States, the on-board diagnostics system must be tested periodically by a state-certified Inspection/Maintenance (I/M) facility. If an electrical component or system on the vehicle has just been serviced (which usually requires battery disconnection),*

3.1a Use a battery hydrometer to draw electrolyte from the battery cell - this hydrometer is equipped with a thermometer to make temperature corrections

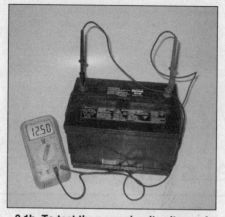

3.1b To test the open circuit voltage of the battery, connect the black probe of the voltmeter to the negative terminal and the red probe to the positive terminal of the battery - a fully charged battery should indicate approximately 12.5 volts depending on the outside air temperature

3.1c Some battery load testers are equipped with an ammeter which enables the battery load to be precisely dialed in - less expensive testers, like this one, have a load switch and a voltmeter only

or if the battery itself has just been serviced or replaced (again, requiring disconnection), the on-board diagnostics system is automatically reset to a "not ready for I/M test" status. To prepare the on-board diagnostics system for I/M testing, you'll need to drive the vehicle for at least 30 miles with the following mix of highway and city driving: First, allow the vehicle to sit for at least eight hours without starting the engine. Then start the engine, allow it to warm up to its normal operating temperature and then drive for at least 10 minutes on a freeway or highway, then drive for at least 20 minutes in stop-and-go, city-type traffic with at least four idle periods. Do NOT turn off the engine until the 30-mile drive is completed. The vehicle is now ready for an I/M test of the on-board diagnostics system.

c) *On any vehicle with power door locks, it is a wise precaution to remove the key from the ignition and to keep it with you, so that it does not get locked inside if the power door locks should engage accidentally when the battery is reconnected!*

Devices known as "memory-savers" can be used to avoid some of the above problems. Precise details vary according to the device used. The typical memory saver is plugged into the cigarette lighter and is connected to a spare battery. Then the vehicle battery can be disconnected from the electrical system. The memory saver will provide sufficient current to maintain audio unit security codes, PCM memory, etc. and will provide power to "always hot" circuits such as the clock and radio memory circuits.

Warning 1: *Some memory savers deliver a considerable amount of current in order to keep vehicle systems operational after the main battery is disconnected. If you're using a memory saver, make sure that the circuit concerned is actually open before servicing it.*

Warning 2: *If you're going to work near any of the airbag system components, the battery*

MUST *be disconnected and a memory saver must NOT be used. If a memory saver is used, power will be supplied to the airbag, which means that it could accidentally deploy and cause serious personal injury.*

To disconnect the battery for service procedures requiring power to be cut from the vehicle, peel back the insulator (if equipped), loosen the negative cable clamp nut and detach the cable from the negative battery post (see Section 3). Isolate the cable end to prevent it from coming into accidental contact with the battery post.

2 Battery - emergency jump starting

Refer to the *Booster battery (jump) starting* procedure at the front of this manual.

3 Battery - check and replacement

Warning: *Hydrogen gas is produced by the battery, so keep open flames and lighted cigarettes away from it at all times. Always wear eye protection when working around a battery. Rinse off spilled electrolyte immediately with large amounts of water.*

Check

Refer to illustrations 3.1a, 3.1b and 3.1c

1   A battery cannot be accurately tested until it is at or near a fully charged state. Disconnect the negative battery cable from the battery and perform the following tests:

a) ***Battery state of charge test*** *- Visually inspect the indicator eye (if equipped) on the top of the battery. If the indicator eye is dark in color, charge the battery as described in Chapter 1. If the battery is equipped with removable caps, check the battery electrolyte. The electrolyte level should be above the upper edge of*

the plates. If the level is low, add distilled water. DO NOT OVERFILL. The excess electrolyte may spill over during periods of heavy charging. Test the specific gravity of the electrolyte using a hydrometer **(see illustration)**. *Remove the caps and extract a sample of the electrolyte and observe the float inside the barrel of the hydrometer. Follow the instructions from the tool manufacturer and determine the specific gravity of the electrolyte for each cell. A fully charged battery will indicate approximately 1.270 (green zone) at 68-degrees F (20-degrees C). If the specific gravity of the electrolyte is low (red zone), charge the battery as described in Chapter 1.*

b) ***Open circuit voltage test*** *- Using a digital voltmeter, perform an open circuit voltage test* **(see illustration)**. *Connect the negative probe of the voltmeter to the negative battery post and the positive probe to the positive battery post. The battery voltage should be greater than 12.5 volts. If the battery is less than the specified voltage, charge the battery before proceeding to the next test. Do not proceed with the battery load test until the battery is fully charged.*

c) ***Battery load test*** *- An accurate check of the battery condition can only be performed with a load tester (available at most auto parts stores). This test evaluates the ability of the battery to operate the starter and other accessories during periods of heavy amperage draw (load). Install a special battery load-testing tool onto the battery terminals* **(see illustration)**. *Load test the battery according to the tool manufacturer's instructions. This tool utilizes a carbon pile to increase the load demand (amperage draw) on the battery. Maintain the load on the battery for 15 seconds and observe that the battery voltage does not drop below 9.6 volts. If the battery condition is weak or defective, the tool will indicate this condition immediately.*

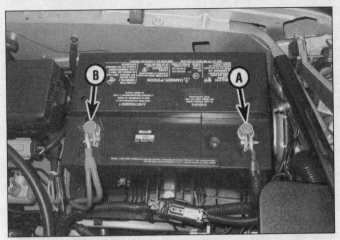

3.2 To prevent arcing at the positive battery terminal, *always* disconnect the cable(s) from the negative battery terminal (A) *first*, then disconnect the cable from the positive terminal (B)

3.3 Remove the battery heat shield

Note: *Cold temperatures will cause the minimum voltage requirements to drop slightly. Follow the chart given in the tool manufacturer's instructions to compensate for cold climates. Minimum load voltage for freezing temperatures (32 degrees F/0-degrees C) should be approximately 9.1 volts.*

d) **Battery drain test** - This test will indicate whether there's a constant drain on the vehicle's electrical system that can cause the battery to discharge. Make sure all accessories are turned Off. If the vehicle has an underhood light, verify it's working properly, then disconnect it. Connect one lead of a digital ammeter to the disconnected negative battery cable clamp and the other lead to the negative battery post. A drain of approximately 100 milliamps or less is considered normal (due to the engine control compudigital clocks, digital radios and other components which normally cause a key-off battery drain). An excessive drain (approximately 500 milliamps or more) will cause the battery to discharge. The problem circuit or component can be located by removing the fuses, one at a

time, until the excessive drain stops and normal drain is indicated on the meter.

Replacement

Refer to illustrations 3.2, 3.3, 3.4, 3.6a and 3.6b

Caution: *Always disconnect the negative cable first and hook it up last, or the tool you're using could accidentally short the battery.*

2   Disconnect the cable from the negative battery terminal. Loosen the cable clamp nut and disconnect the black battery cable(s) from the negative battery post *(see illustration)*. Isolate the cable end to prevent it from accidentally coming into contact with the battery post. Then loosen the cable clamp nut and remove the red battery cable from the positive battery post.

3   Remove the battery heat shield **(see illustration)**.

4   Remove the battery hold-down clamp bolt **(see illustration)**.

5   Lift out the battery. Be careful - it's heavy. **Note:** *Battery straps and handlers are available at most auto parts stores for a reasonable price. They make it easier to remove and carry the battery.*

3.4 To remove the battery, remove this bolt and remove the battery hold-down clamp

6   While the battery is out, inspect the battery tray for corrosion. If corrosion exists, clean the deposits with a mixture of baking soda and water to prevent further corrosion. Flush the area with plenty of clean water and dry thoroughly. If the battery tray must be replaced, or if you need to remove the battery tray to access some component(s) below it, remove the tray **(see illustrations)**.

3.6a Before removing the battery tray, disconnect these two wiring harness clips from the tray

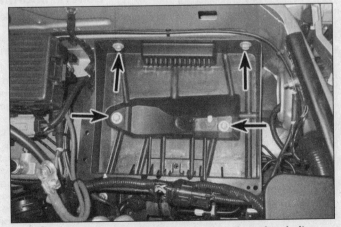

3.6b To detach the battery tray, remove these four bolts

5

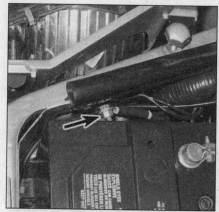

4.4a The smaller negative battery cable is grounded to the crossmember right in front of the battery by this bolt

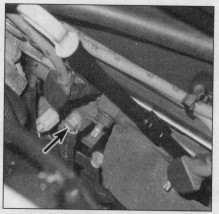

4.4b On V6 models, the larger negative battery cable is grounded to the left side of the engine block, in front of the dipstick and right below the spark plug for cylinder No. 4, by this bolt

4.4c The positive battery cable is connected to this terminal at the starter solenoid, which is located on top of the starter motor, which is located on the left rear side of the engine block, just in front of the transmission bellhousing

7   If you are replacing the battery, make sure you replace it with a battery with the identical dimensions, amperage rating, cold cranking rating, etc.

8   When installing the battery make sure it's correctly and fully seated in the battery tray. Install the hold-down clamp bolt and tighten it securely. Do not over-tighten the bolt.

9   The remainder of installation is the reverse of removal.

10   After connecting the cables to the battery apply a light coating of petroleum jelly or grease to the connections to help prevent corrosion.

4   Battery cables - check and replacement

Refer to illustrations 4.4a, 4.4b and 4.4c

1   Periodically inspect the entire length of each battery cable for damage, cracked or burned insulation and corrosion. Poor battery cable connections can cause starting problems and decreased engine performance.

2   Check the cable-to-terminal connections at the ends of the cables for cracks, loose wire strands and corrosion. The presence of white, fluffy deposits under the insulation at the cable terminal connection is a sign that the cable is corroded and should be replaced. Check the terminals for distortion, missing mounting bolts and corrosion.

3   When removing the cables always disconnect the negative cable from the negative battery post first and hook it up last or the tool used to loosen the cable clamps may short the battery. Even if you're only planning to replace the positive cable, be sure to disconnect the cable from the negative battery post first (see Chapter 1 for further information regarding battery cable maintenance).

4   Disconnect the old battery cables from the battery terminals (see Section 3), then disconnect them from the ground terminal and from the starter solenoid **(see illustrations)**. Note the routing of each cable to ensure correct installation.

5   If you are replacing either or both of the battery cables, take them with you when buying new cables. It is vitally important that you replace the cables with identical parts. Cables have characteristics that make them easy to identify: Positive cables are usually red and larger in cross-section; ground cables are usually black and smaller in cross-section.

6   Clean the threads of the starter solenoid or ground connection with a wire brush to remove rust and corrosion. Apply a light coat of battery terminal corrosion inhibitor or petroleum jelly to the threads to prevent future corrosion.

7   Attach the cable to the terminal and tighten the mounting nut/bolt securely.

8   Before connecting a new cable to the battery, make sure that it reaches the battery post without having to be stretched.

9   After installing the cables, connect the negative cable to the negative battery post.

5   Ignition system - general information and precautions

General information

1   The ignition system consists of the ignition coil(s), the spark plugs, the Crankshaft Position (CKP) sensor, the primary (low tension) and secondary (high tension) circuits, and the Powertrain Control Module (PCM). All models are equipped with a distributorless ignition system. V6 models are equipped with a six-terminal coil pack, which is located at the front of the engine. V8 models are equipped with separate coils for each cylinder; on these models, each coil is located directly above the spark plug that it fires.

2   The CKP sensor senses a missing tooth on the crankshaft damper pulse ring to generate a crankshaft position signal, which it sends to the PCM. The PCM uses this data to determine engine speed and to calculate spark timing. For more information on the CKP sensor, refer to Chapter 6.

Precautions

3   When working on the ignition system, take the following precautions:

a) *Do not keep the ignition switch on for more than 10 seconds if the engine will not start.*

b) *Always connect a tachometer in accordance with the manufacturer's instructions. Some tachometers may be incompatible with this ignition system. Consult an auto parts counterperson before buying a tachometer for use with this vehicle.*

c) *Never allow the ignition coil terminals to touch ground. Grounding the coil could result in damage to the PCM and/or the ignition coil.*

d) *Do not disconnect the battery when the engine is running.*

6   Ignition system - check

Refer to illustration 6.3

Warning: *Because of the very high voltage generated by the ignition system, extreme care should be taken whenever an operation is performed involving ignition components. This not only includes the coil and spark plugs, but related items connected to the system as well, such as the electrical connectors, tachometer and any test equipment.*

Note: *The ignition system components on these models are difficult to diagnose without a special factory scan tool. In the event of ignition system failure, if the checks do not clearly indicate the source of the ignition system problem, have the vehicle tested by a dealer service department or other qualified repair facility.*

1   If a malfunction occurs and the vehicle won't start, do not immediately assume that the ignition system is causing the problem. First, check the following items:

a) *Make sure the battery cable clamps, where they connect to the battery, are*

6.3 To use a calibrated ignition tester, simply remove a spark plug, clip the tester to a convenient ground (like this exhaust manifold bolt) and operate the starter; if there is enough power to fire the test plug, sparks will be visible between the electrode tip and the tester body

7.2 To disconnect the electrical connector from the ignition coil, release this locking tang on top of the connector with a small screwdriver and pull off the connector (V6 models)

7.3 To detach the noise suppressor (1) from the ignition coil, unplug the electrical connector (2) and remove the suppressor mounting bolt (3) (V6 models)

clean and tight.

b) *Test the condition of the battery (see Section 3). If it does not pass all the tests, replace it with a new battery.*

c) *Check the ignition coil wiring and connections.*

d) *Check the related fuses inside the fuse box (see Chapter 12). If they're burned, determine the cause and repair the circuit.*

2   If the engine turns over but won't start, make sure there is sufficient secondary ignition voltage to fire the spark plug.

3   Disconnect a spark plug wire (V6 models) or an ignition coil (V8 models) from a spark plug (see Section 7) and attach a calibrated ignition tester (available at most auto parts stores). Connect the clip on the tester to a bolt or metal bracket on the engine **(see illustration)**.

4   Relieve the fuel pressure (see Chapter 4). Keep the fuel system disabled while performing the ignition system checks.

5   Crank the engine and watch the end of the tester to see if bright blue, well-defined sparks occur (weak spark or intermittent spark is the same as no spark).

6   If sparks occur, sufficient voltage is reaching the spark plug to fire it (repeat the check at the remaining ignition coils to verify that all coils are functioning). However, the plugs themselves may be fouled, so remove and check them as described in Chapter 1 or install new ones.

7   If no sparks or intermittent sparks occur, check for battery voltage to the ignition coils. If battery voltage is not present, check the ignition fuse (see Chapter 12).

8   If all of the above checks are correct, the Crankshaft Position (CKP) sensor or the circuit between the CKP sensor and the PCM might be defective (see Chapter 6).

7   Ignition coils - replacement

1   Disconnect the cable from the negative battery terminal (see Section 1).

V6 models

Refer to illustrations 7.2, 7.3, 7.4, 7.5, 7.6 and 7.7

2   Disconnect the electrical connector from the ignition coil **(see illustration)**.

3   Detach the noise suppressor from the front of the ignition coil **(see illustration)**.

4   Note the numbering on the spark plug wires and the corresponding numbering beside each coil high-tension terminal **(see illustration)**. If either the spark plug wires or the coil high-tension terminals, or if both, are unmarked, then mark the relationship of the spark plug wires to their respective coil high-tension terminals before disconnecting the spark plug wire connectors.

5   Disconnect the spark plug wires from the ignition coil **(see illustration)**.

5

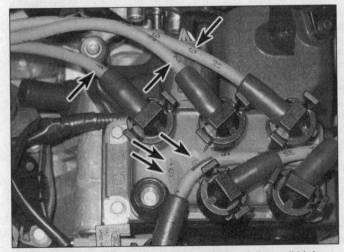

7.4 The spark plug wires and their corresponding coil high-tension terminals should be numbered, to facilitate reassembly; if either the plug wires or the coil terminals or both, are unmarked, make your own marks before disconnecting the plug wire connectors (V6 models)

7.5 To disconnect the spark plug wire connectors from the ignition coil, simply squeeze the two locking tabs on the opposite sides of each connector and pull up (V6 models)

7.6 To detach the ignition coil from the engine, remove these four bolts (V6 models)

7.7 Before reconnecting the spark plug wire connectors to the ignition coil high-tension terminals, coat the insides of the connectors with silicone dielectric compound

6   Remove the ignition coil mounting bolts **(see illustration)** and remove the ignition coil.

7   Before reconnecting the spark plug wires to the ignition coil, coat the inside of each plug wire connector with silicone dielectric compound **(see illustration)**.

8   Installation is otherwise the reverse of removal.

V8 models

Note: *There are eight separate ignition coils, one above each spark plug, on V8 models. The following procedure applies to all of them.*

9   Disconnect the electrical connector from the ignition coil. If you're going to remove more than one coil, mark each electrical connector with the correct cylinder number to prevent mix-ups during reassembly.

10   Remove the ignition coil mounting bolt, then pull the coil from the cylinder head.

11   Prior to installing the coil, coat the inside of the coil rubber boot with silicone dielectric compound.

12   Installation is otherwise the reverse of the removal.

8   Charging system - general information and precautions

The charging system supplies electrical power for the ignition system, the lights, the radio, etc. The alternator is driven by a drivebelt at the front of the engine. The charging system includes the alternator and integral voltage regulator, a charge indicator or warning light (on the instrument cluster), the battery and the wiring between all the components. Three large fusible links protect the charging system circuit. The fusible links are located in the wiring harness between the alternator and the battery junction box (which is part of the engine compartment fuse and relay box). In the event of charging system problems, check these fusible links for damage or broken contacts.

The voltage regulator limits the alternator's voltage to a preset value to prevent power surges and circuit overloads during peak voltage output. The voltage regulator is not removable or serviceable. If the regulator or the alternator is defective, the alternator/regulator assembly must be replaced as a complete unit.

The charging system doesn't ordinarily require periodic maintenance. However, the drivebelt, battery and harness connections should be inspected at the intervals outlined in Chapter 1.

Be very careful when making electrical circuit connections to a vehicle equipped with an alternator and note the following:

a)   *When reconnecting wires to the alternator from the battery, be sure to note the polarity.*

b)   *Before using arc welding equipment to repair any part of the vehicle, disconnect the wiring from the alternator and the cables from the battery.*

c)   *Never start the engine with a battery charger connected.*

d)   *Always disconnect both battery cables before using a battery charger.*

e)   *The alternator is turned by an engine drivebelt that could cause serious injury if your hands, hair or clothes become entangled in it with the engine running.*

f)   *Because the alternator is connected directly to the battery, it could arc or cause a fire if overloaded or shorted out.*

9   Charging system - check

Refer to illustration 9.2

1   If a malfunction occurs in the charging circuit, do not immediately assume that the alternator is causing the problem. First, check the following items:

a)   *Make sure the battery cable clamps, where they connect to the battery, are clean and tight.*

b)   *Test the condition of the battery (see Section 3). If it does not pass all the tests, replace it with a new battery.*

c)   *Check the external alternator wiring and connections.*

d)   *Check the drivebelt condition and tension (see Chapter 1).*

e)   *Check the alternator mounting bolts for tightness.*

f)   *Run the engine and check the alternator for abnormal noise.*

g)   *Check the fusible links in the wiring harness between the alternator and the battery junction box (which is located in the engine compartment fuse box) (see Chapter 12). If they're burned, determine the cause and repair the circuit.*

h)   *Check the charge light on the dash. It should illuminate when the ignition key is turned ON (engine not running). If it does not, check the circuit from the alternator to the charge light on the dash.*

i)   *Check all the fuses that are in series with the charging system circuit. The location of these fuses and fusible links may vary from year and model but the designations are generally the same. Refer to the wiring schematics at the end of Chapter 12 for additional information.*

2   With the ignition key turned to OFF, check the "standing" battery voltage with no accessories operating **(see illustration)**. It should be approximately 12.5 volts. It may be slightly higher if the engine had been operating within the last hour.

3   Start the engine, let it warm up and, with the engine at idle, check the battery voltage again. It should now be greater than the voltage recorded in Step 2, but not more than 14.5 volts. Then turn on all the vehicle accessories (air conditioning, blower motor, rear window defogger, sound system, etc.) and

increase the engine speed to 2,000 rpm; the voltage should not drop below the voltage recorded in Step 2.

4   If the indicated voltage is greater than the specified charging voltage, replace the voltage regulator (which, on these models, means replacing the alternator, because the voltage regulator is not serviceable separately).

5   If the indicated voltage reading is less than the specified charging voltage, the alternator is probably defective. Have the charging system checked at a dealer service department or other properly equipped repair facility. **Note:** *Some auto parts stores will bench test an alternator off the vehicle. Some of them will perform this service for free; consult your local auto parts store regarding its policy on bench testing alternators.*

9.2 To measure "standing" voltage, connect the voltmeter leads to the battery terminals and check the battery voltage with the engine off; it should be about 12.5 volts. To measure charging voltage, start the engine and check the battery voltage with the engine at idle; it should be about 13.5 to 14.5 volts

10 Alternator - removal and installation

V6 models

Refer to illustrations 10.3 and 10.4

1   Disconnect the cable from the negative terminal of the battery (see Section 1).

2   Remove the drivebelt (see Chapter 1).

3   Disconnect the electrical connectors from the alternator **(see illustration)**.

4   Remove the alternator mounting bolts **(see illustration)** and remove the alternator.

5   Installation is the reverse of removal.

V8 models

6   Disconnect the cable from the negative battery terminal (see Section 1).

7   Remove the engine cover (see Chapter 2B).

8   Position the cruise control cable and the throttle bypass hose aside.

9   Remove the drivebelt (see Chapter 1).

10   Disconnect the electrical connectors

from the alternator.

11   Remove the two upper stud bolts and the two upper alternator mounting bolts.

12   Remove the two lower alternator mounting bolts and remove the alternator.

13   Installation is the reverse of removal.

11 Starting system - general information and precautions

The starting system consists of the ignition switch, the Clutch Pedal Position (CPP) switch (manual transmission) or Digital Transmission Range (DTR) sensor (automatics), the starter relay and a 50 amp fuse (both of which are located inside the engine compartment fuse and relay box), the battery, the starter solenoid, the starter motor, and the wires that connect these components.

When the ignition key is turned to the START position, battery voltage energizes the starter relay, which closes the starting circuit and allows current to flow to the starter solenoid, which in turn closes a switch inside

the solenoid and energizes the starter motor.

The Clutch Pedal Position (CPP) switch prevents a vehicle with a manual transmission from being started unless the clutch pedal is depressed. For more information on the CPP switch, refer to Chapter 7A. The Digital Transmission Range (DTR) sensor prevents a vehicle with an automatic transmission from being started unless the shift lever is in PARK or NEUTRAL. For more information on the DTR sensor, refer to Chapter 6.

Always observe the following precautions when working on the starting system:

a)   *Excessive cranking of the starter motor can overheat it and cause serious damage. Never operate the starter motor for more than 15 seconds at a time without pausing for at least two minutes to allow it to cool.*

b)   *The starter is connected directly to the battery and could arc or cause a fire if mishandled, overloaded or short circuited.*

c)   *Always detach the battery ground cable from the negative battery terminal before working on the starting system.*

5

10.3 Disconnect the electrical connector from the alternator, then unscrew the "B+" (battery) terminal nut and disconnect the battery lead from the alternator (V6 models)

10.4 To detach the alternator from a V6 engine, remove the nut from the stud bolt (the rear bolt) and detach the coolant hose bracket, then remove all three alternator mounting bolts

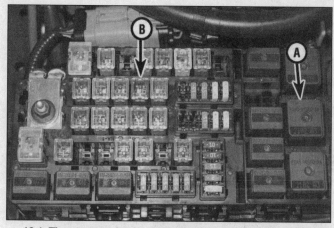

12.1 The starter relay (A) and fuse (B) are located inside the engine compartment fuse and relay box

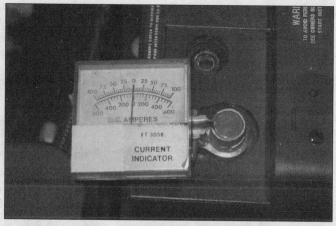

12.3 To use an inductive ammeter, simply hold the ammeter over the positive or negative battery cable (whichever cable has better clearance)

12   Starter motor and circuit - in-vehicle check

Refer to illustrations 12.1, 12.3 and 12.4

1   If a malfunction occurs in the starting circuit, do not immediately assume that the starter is causing the problem. First, check the following items:

   a)   *Make sure the battery cable clamps, where they connect to the battery, are clean and tight.*

   b)   *Check the condition of the battery cables (see Section 4). Replace any defective battery cables with new ones.*

   c)   *Test the condition of the battery (see Section 3). If it does not pass all the tests, replace it with a new battery.*

   d)   *Check the starter solenoid wiring and connections. Refer to the wiring diagrams at the end of Chapter 12.*

   e)   *Check the starter mounting bolts for tightness.*

   f)   *Check the fusible links in the starter circuit (see the wiring diagrams at the end of Chapter 12). If they're burned, determine the cause and repair the circuit. Also check the ignition switch circuit (see the wiring diagrams).*

   g)   *Check the adjustment of the Digital Transmission Range sensor (automatic transmission) or Clutch Pedal Position (CPP) switch (manual transmission). Make sure the shift lever is in PARK or NEUTRAL (automatic transmission) or the clutch pedal is pressed (manual transmission). Refer to Chapter 7B for the DTR sensor adjustment procedure. Refer to Chapter 12 wiring diagrams, if necessary, when performing circuit checks. These systems must operate correctly to provide battery voltage to the ignition switch.*

   h)   *Check the operation of the starter relay. The starter relay is located in the engine compartment fuse and relay box* **(see illustration)**. *Refer to Chapter 12 for the testing procedure.*

2   If the starter does not actuate when the ignition switch is turned to the start position, check for battery voltage to the solenoid. This will determine if the solenoid is receiving the correct voltage signal from the ignition switch. Connect a test light or voltmeter to the starter solenoid positive terminal and while an assistant turns the ignition switch to the start position. If voltage is not available, refer to the wiring diagrams in Chapter 12 and check all the fuses and relays in series with the starting system. If voltage is available but the starter motor does not operate, remove the starter (see Section 13) and bench test it (see Step 4).

3   If the starter turns over slowly, check the starter cranking voltage and the current draw from the battery. This test must be performed with the starter assembly on the engine. Crank the engine over (for 10 seconds or less) and observe the battery voltage. It should not drop below 8.0 volts on manual transmission models or 8.5 volts on auto-matic transmission models. Also, observe the current draw using an ammeter **(see illustration)**. It should not exceed 400 amps or drop below 250 amps. **Caution:** *The battery cables can become overheated by the large amount of current being drawn from the battery. If the cables get hot, discontinue this test until the starting system has cooled down. Several conditions can affect the starter's cranking potential. The battery must be in good condition and the battery cold-cranking rating must not be under-rated for the particular application. Be sure to check the battery specifications carefully. The battery terminals and cables must be clean and not corroded. Also, in extremely cold temperatures, make sure that the battery and/or engine block is warmed before performing the tests.*

4   If the starter is receiving voltage but does not activate, remove and check the starter/solenoid assembly on the bench **(see illustration)**. Most likely the solenoid is defec-

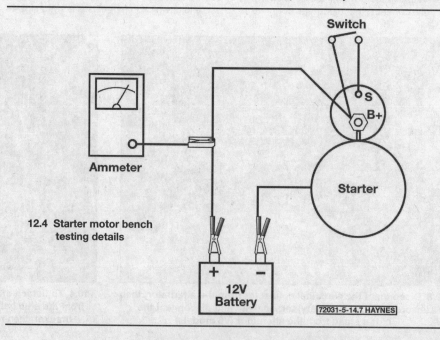

12.4 Starter motor bench testing details

72031-5-14.7 HAYNES

13.3 To remove the starter motor solenoid terminal cover, simply pull it off (V6 model shown, V8 models similar)

tive. In some rare cases, the engine may be seized so be sure to try and rotate the crankshaft pulley (see Chapter 2A or 2B) before proceeding. With the starter/solenoid assembly mounted in a vise on the bench, install one jumper cable from the negative battery terminal to the body of the starter. Install the other jumper cable from the positive battery terminal to the B+ terminal on the starter. Install a starter switch and apply battery voltage to the solenoid S terminal (for 10 seconds or less) and see if the solenoid plunger, shift lever and overrunning clutch extends and rotates the pinion drive. If the pinion drive extends but does not rotate, the solenoid is operating but the starter motor is defective. If there is no movement but the solenoid clicks, the solenoid and/or the starter motor is defective. If the solenoid plunger extends and rotates the pinion drive, the starter/solenoid assembly is working properly.

13 Starter motor - removal and installation

Refer to illustrations 13.3, 13.4, and 13.5

1   Disconnect the cable from the negative battery terminal (see Section 1).
2   Raise the vehicle and support it securely on jackstands.
3   Remove the protective cover from the starter motor solenoid terminals **(see illustration)**.
4   Disconnect the wiring from the terminals on the starter motor solenoid **(see illustration)**.
5   Remove the starter motor mounting bolts **(see illustration)** and detach the starter from the engine.
6   Installation is the reverse of removal. Be sure to tighten the starter bolts to the torque listed in this Chapter's Specifications.

13.4 Disconnect the starter circuit wiring from these two terminals on the starter solenoid (V6 model shown, V8 models similar)

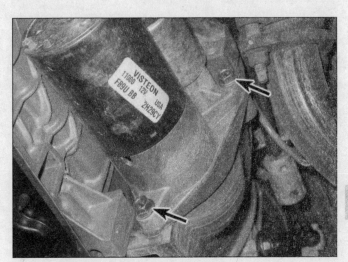

13.5 To detach the starter motor from the engine, remove these two bolts (V6 model shown, V8 models similar)

5

Notes

Chapter 6
Emissions and engine control systems

Contents

Specifications

Torque specifications

	Ft-lbs (unless otherwise indicated)	Nm
Camshaft Position (CMP) sensor retaining bolt		
V6	71 in-lbs	8
V8	89 in-lbs	10
Crankshaft Position (CKP) sensor retaining bolt	89 in-lbs	10
Cylinder Head Temperature (CHT) sensor	19	26
Digital Transmission Range (DTR) sensor bolts	89 in-lbs	10
EGR valve mounting bolts	180 in-lbs	20
Exhaust manifold-to-EGR valve pipe fittings (both ends)		
V6	25	34
V8	30	40
IAC valve mounting bolts	89 in-lbs	10
Intermediate Shaft Speed (ISS) sensor retaining bolt	89 in-lbs	10
Knock sensor retaining bolt(s)		
V6	18	25
V8		
2002	180 in-lbs	20
2003	18	25
Manual lever retaining nut	35	48
Mass Air Flow (MAF) sensor mounting bolts	89 in-lbs	10
Output Shaft Speed (OSS) sensor retaining bolt		
Automatic transmission	89 in-lbs	10
Manual transmission (2002 only)	N/A	
Transfer case (4WD models) (front or rear OSS sensor)	44 in-lbs	5
Turbine Shaft Speed (TSS) sensor retaining bolt	89 in-lbs	10

6

1   General information

Refer to illustration 1.6

To prevent pollution of the atmosphere from incompletely burned and evaporating gases, and to maintain good driveability and fuel economy, a number of emission control systems are incorporated. They include the:

Catalytic converter
Evaporative Emissions Control (EVAP) system
Exhaust Gas Recirculation (EGR) system
Multiport Fuel Injection (MFI) system
On-Board Diagnostic (OBD) II system
Positive Crankcase Ventilation (PCV) system

The Sections in this Chapter include general descriptions, checking procedures within the scope of the home mechanic and component replacement procedures (when possible) for each of the systems listed above.

Before assuming that an emissions control system is malfunctioning, check the fuel and ignition systems carefully. The diagnosis of some emission control devices requires specialized tools, equipment and training. If checking and servicing become too difficult or if a procedure is beyond your ability, consult a dealer service department or other repair shop. Remember, the most frequent cause of emissions problems is simply a loose or broken wire or vacuum hose, so always check the hose and wiring connections first.

This doesn't mean, however, that emissions control systems are particularly difficult to maintain and repair. You can quickly and easily perform many checks and do most of the regular maintenance at home with common tune-up and hand tools. **Note:** *Because of a Federally mandated warranty which covers the emissions control system components, check with your dealer about warranty coverage before working on any emissions-related systems. Once the warranty has expired, you may wish to perform some of the component checks and/or replacement procedures in this Chapter to save money.*

Pay close attention to any special pre-

1.6 The Vehicle Emission Control Information (VECI) label contains such essential information as the types of emission control systems installed on the engine, and a vacuum diagram

cautions outlined in this Chapter. It should be noted that the illustrations of the various systems might not exactly match the system installed on your vehicle because of changes made by the manufacturer during production or from year-to-year.

A Vehicle Emissions Control Information (VECI) label is attached to the underside of the hood **(see illustration)**. This label contains important emissions specifications and adjustment information. Part of this label, the Vacuum Hose Routing Diagram, provides a vacuum hose schematic with emissions components identified. When servicing the engine or emissions systems, the VECI label and the vacuum hose routing diagram in your particular vehicle should always be checked for up-to-date information.

2   On-Board Diagnostic (OBD) system and trouble codes

Scan tool information

Refer to illustrations 2.1 and 2.2

1   Hand-held scanners are the most powerful and versatile tools for analyzing engine

management systems used on later model vehicles **(see illustration)**. Early model scanners handle codes and some diagnostics for many systems. Each brand scan tool must be examined carefully to match the year, make and model of the vehicle you are working on. Often, interchangeable cartridges are available to access the particular manufacturer (Ford, GM, Chrysler, Toyota etc.). Some manufacturers will specify by continent (Asia, Europe, USA, etc.). **Note:** *An aftermarket generic scanner should work with any model covered by this manual. However, some early OBD-II models, although technically classified as OBD-II compliant by the manufacturer and by the federal government, might not be fully compliant with all SAE standards for OBD-II. Some generic scanners are unable to extract all the codes from these early OBD-II models. Before purchasing a generic scan tool, contact the manufacturer of the scanner you're planning to buy and verify that it will work properly with the OBD-II system you want to scan. If necessary, of course, you can always have the codes extracted by a dealer service department or an independent repair shop with a professional scan tool.*

2   With the arrival of the Federally mandated emission control system (OBD-II), a specially designed scanner has been developed. Several tool manufacturers have released OBD-II scan tools for the home mechanic **(see illustration)**. Ask the parts salesman at a local auto parts store for additional information concerning dates and costs.

OBD system general description

3   All models are equipped with the second generation OBD-II system. This system consists of an on-board computer known as the Powertrain Control Module (PCM), and information sensors, which monitor various functions of the engine and send data to the PCM. This system incorporates a series of

2.1 Scanners like the Actron Scantool and the AutoXray XP240 are powerful diagnostic aids - programmed with comprehensive diagnostic information, they can tell you just about anything you want to know about your engine management system

2.2 Trouble code readers like the Actron OBD-II diagnostic tester simplify the task of extracting the trouble codes

diagnostic monitors that detect and identify fuel injection and emissions control systems faults and store the information in the computer memory. This updated system also tests sensors and output actuators, diagnoses drive cycles, freezes data and clears codes.

4   This powerful diagnostic computer must be accessed using an OBD-II scan tool and 16-pin Data Link Connector (DLC) located under the driver's dash area. The PCM is mounted in the right end of the firewall on the engine compartment side. The PCM is the "brain" of the electronically controlled fuel and emissions system. It receives data from a number of sensors and other electronic components (switches, relays, etc.). Based on the information it receives, the PCM generates output signals to control various relays, solenoids (i.e. fuel injectors) and other actuators. The PCM is specifically calibrated to optimize the emissions, fuel economy and driveability of the vehicle.

5   It isn't a good idea to attempt diagnosis or replacement of the PCM or emission control components at home while the vehicle is under warranty. Because of a Federally mandated warranty which covers the emissions system components and because any owner-induced damage to the PCM, the sensors and/or the control devices may void this warranty, take the vehicle to a dealer service department if the PCM or a system component malfunctions.

Information sensors

6   **Brake Pedal Position (BPP) switch** - The BPP switch is located at the top of the brake pedal. It's a normally open switch that closes when the brake pedal is applied and sends a signal to the PCM, which interprets this signal as its cue to disengage the torque converter clutch. The BPP switch is also used to disengage the brake shift interlock.

7   **Camshaft Position (CMP) sensor** - The CMP sensor produces a signal that the PCM uses to identify the number 1 cylinder and to time the firing sequence of the fuel injectors. On V6 models, the CMP sensor is located on the left valve cover. On V8 models, the CMP sensor is located on the front of the left cylinder head, below the valve cover.

8   **Crankshaft Position (CKP) sensor** - The CKP sensor produces a signal that the PCM uses to determine the position of the crankshaft. The CKP sensor is located on the front of the engine, to the right of the crankshaft pulley.

9   **Cylinder Heat Temperature (CHT) sensor** (V8 models) - The CHT sensor is located in the front part of the valley between the cylinder heads (it's actually on the left head). The CHT sensor is a "thermistor," a type of variable resistor in which the resistance changes in accordance with the change in temperature. The CHT is known as a "negative temperature coefficient" (NTC) thermistor because as the temperature increases, the resistance decreases, and vice versa. The PCM uses the CHT sensor to monitor the operating temperature of the engine.

10   **Differential pressure feedback EGR system sensor** - The differential pressure feedback EGR system sensor, which is located between the intake manifold and the firewall, near the EGR valve, is a pressure "transducer" that monitors the pressure differential across a metering orifice located in the sensor. (A transducer is a device that receives a signal from one system and transfers that signal to another system, often in a different form.) The differential pressure feedback EGR system sensor outputs a voltage signal that's proportional to the pressure drop across its metering orifice. The PCM uses this data to calculate the EGR flow rate.

11   **Digital Transmission Range (DTR) sensor** - The DTR sensor is located at the manual lever on the left side of the automatic transmission. The DTR sensor functions like a conventional Park/Neutral Position (PNP) switch: it prevents the engine from starting in any gear other than Park or Neutral, and it closes the circuit for the back-up lights when the shift lever is moved to Reverse. The PCM also sends a voltage signal to the TR sensor, which uses a series of step-down resistors that act as a voltage divider. The PCM monitors the TR sensor's voltage output, which corresponds to the position of the manual lever. Thus the PCM is able to determine the gear selected and is able to determine the correct pressure for the electronic pressure control system of the transaxle.

12   **Engine Coolant Temperature (ECT) sensor** (V6 models) - The ECT sensor is a thermistor (temperature-sensitive variable resistor) that sends a voltage signal to the PCM, which uses this data to determine the temperature of the engine coolant. The ECT sensor helps the PCM control the air/fuel mixture ratio and ignition timing, and it also helps the PCM determine when to turn the Exhaust Gas Recirculation (EGR) system on and off. The ECT sensor is located on top of the engine, right behind the upper radiator hose.

13   **Fuel tank pressure sensor** - The fuel tank pressure sensor is located on top of the fuel tank, near the fuel pump/fuel level sending unit module. It measures the fuel tank pressure when the PCM tests the EVAP system, and it's also used to control fuel tank pressure by signaling the EVAP system to purge the tank when the pressure becomes excessive.

14   **Intake Air Temperature (IAT) sensor** - The IAT sensor, which is an integral component of the Mass Air Flow (MAF) sensor, monitors the temperature of the air entering the engine and sends a signal to the PCM. The IAT sensor cannot be replaced by itself. If it's defective, you'll have to replace the MAF sensor.

15   **Intermediate Shaft Speed (ISS) sensor** - The ISS sensor is a magnetic pick-up located on the left side of the automatic transmission. (There are *three* speed sensors on the left side of the transmission; the ISS sensor is the *middle* sensor). The ISS sensor sends data on planetary sun gear speed to the PCM, which uses this information to determine the correct operating pressure for the transmission.

16   **Knock sensor** - The knock sensor is a "piezoelectric" crystal that oscillates in proportion to engine vibration. (The term *piezoelectric* refers to the property of certain crystals that produce a voltage when subjected to a mechanical stress.) The oscillation of the piezoelectric crystal produces a voltage output that is monitored by the PCM, which retards the ignition timing when the oscillation exceeds a certain threshold. When the engine is operating normally, the knock sensor oscillates consistently and its voltage signal is steady. When detonation occurs, engine vibration increases, and the oscillation of the knock sensor exceeds a design threshold. (Detonation is an uncontrolled explosion, after the spark occurs at the spark plug, which spontaneously combusts the remaining air/fuel mixture, resulting in a "pinging" or "slapping" sound.) If allowed to continue, engine performance is diminished and damage to the pistons can result. The knock sensor is located below the intake manifold, in the valley between the cylinder heads. There is one knock sensor on V6 models and on 2002 V8 engines. On 2003 V8 engines, there are two knock sensors.

17   **Mass Air Flow (MAF) sensor** - The MAF sensor is located on the air intake duct, right at the air filter housing. The MAF sensor is the principal means by which the Powertrain Control Module (PCM) monitors intake airflow. It uses a hot-wire sensing element to measure the amount of air entering the engine. The wire is maintained at a temperature of 392 degrees F (200 degrees C) above the ambient temperature by electrical current. As intake air passes through the MAF sensor and over the hot wire, it cools the wire, and the control system immediately corrects the temperature back to its constant value. The current required to maintain the constant value is used by the PCM as an indicator of airflow. The MAF sensor also incorporates an integral Intake Air Temperature (IAT) sensor. The two components cannot be serviced separately; if either sensor is defective, replace the MAF sensor.

18   **Output Shaft Speed (OSS) sensor** - The OSS sensor is a magnetic pick-up coil. On models with an automatic transmission, it's located on the left side of the transmission. (There are *three* speed sensors on the left side of the automatic transmission; the OSS sensor is the *rear* sensor). The OSS sensor provides the Powertrain Control Module (PCM) with information about the rotational speed of the output shaft in the transmission. The PCM uses this information to control the torque converter and to calculate speed scheduling and the correct pressure for the Electronic Pressure Control system. (There

6

are also OSS sensors on 2002 models with a manual transmission and on 4WD models. On 2002 manual transmissions, the OSS sensor is located on the *right* side of the transmission. On these models, the OSS sensor functions as a vehicle speed sensor for the PCM. On 4WD models, there are *two* OSS sensors - front and rear - located on the rear part of the transfer case. On these models, the 4WD control module uses the two OSS sensors to monitor the speeds of the front and rear driveshafts. The 4WD control module uses this data to control and adjust the transfer case clutch duty cycle.)

19   **Oxygen sensors** - An oxygen sensor is a galvanic battery that generates a small variable voltage signal in proportion to the difference between the oxygen content in the exhaust stream and the oxygen content in the ambient air. The PCM uses the voltage signal from the upstream oxygen sensor to maintain a "stoichiometric" air/fuel ratio of 14.7:1 by constantly adjusting the "on-time" of the fuel injectors. There are *four* oxygen sensors, one upstream and one downstream sensor for each cylinder head. There are *three* catalysts: a smaller "fast-light-off" cat right below each exhaust manifold (the catalysts are actually an integral part of the exhaust manifolds) and another larger downstream catalyst. The oxygen sensors are located upstream and downstream in relation to the two smaller catalysts.

20   **Throttle Position (TP) sensor** - The TP sensor, which is located on the throttle body, on the end of the throttle valve shaft, is a potentiometer that produces a variable voltage signal in accordance with the opening angle of the throttle valve. This voltage signal tells the PCM when the throttle is closed, in a cruise position, or wide open, or anywhere in between. The PCM uses this information, along with data from a number of other sensors, to calculate injector on-time.

21   **Turbine Shaft Speed (TSS) sensor** (automatic transaxle models) - The TSS sensor is a magnetic pick-up coil located on the left side of the transaxle. (There are *three* speed sensors on the left side of the transmission; the TSS sensor is the *front* sensor). The TSS sensor provides the PCM with information about the rotational speed of the turbine (input) shaft. The PCM uses this information to determine control strategies for the Torque Converter Clutch (TCC) and to determine the static Electronic Pressure Control (EPC) pressure setting during shifts.

Output actuators

22   **EVAP canister purge valve** - The EVAP canister purge valve, which is located in the engine compartment, near the master cylinder, is normally closed. But when ordered to do so by the PCM, it allows fuel vapors from the EVAP canister to be drawn into the intake manifold for combustion under certain operating conditions. The PCM-controlled EVAP canister purge valve also controls this vapor flow.

23   **EVAP canister vent solenoid (2002)** or **vent valve (2003)** - The EVAP canister vent solenoid, or valve, is located underneath the vehicle, behind the fuel tank. The canister vent solenoid or valve is normally open, but it closes and seals off the EVAP system for inspection and maintenance tests and for OBD-II leak and pressure tests.

24   **Exhaust Gas Recirculation (EGR) vacuum regulator valve** - When the engine is put under a load (hard acceleration, passing, going up a steep hill, pulling a trailer, etc.), combustion chamber temperature increases. When combustion chamber temperature exceeds 2500 degrees, excessive amounts of oxides of nitrogen (NOx) are produced. NOx is a precursor of photochemical smog. When combined with hydrocarbons (HC), other "reactive organic compounds" (ROCs) and sunlight, it forms ozone, nitrogen dioxide and nitrogen nitrate and other nasty stuff. The vacuum-controlled EGR valve allows exhaust gases to be recirculated back to the intake manifold where they dilute the incoming air/fuel mixture, which lowers the combustion chamber temperature and decreases the amount of NOx produced during high-load conditions. The amount of exhaust gases recirculated to the intake is determined by the strength of the vacuum signal delivered to the EGR valve. The PCM-controlled EGR vacuum regulator valve is the electromagnetic device that regulates the supply of vacuum to the EGR valve. The EGR vacuum regulator valve is located behind the intake manifold, near the other EGR system components.

25   **Fuel injectors** - The fuel injectors, which spray a fine mist of fuel into the intake ports, where it is mixed with incoming air, are inductive coils under PCM control. For more information about the injectors, see Chapter 4.

26   **Idle Air Control (IAC) valve** - The IAC valve controls the amount of air allowed to bypass the throttle valve when the throttle valve is at its (nearly closed) idle position. The IAC valve is controlled by the PCM. When the engine is placed under an additional load at idle (low-speed maneuvers or the air conditioning compressor, for example), the engine can run roughly, stumble and even stall. To prevent this from happening, the PCM opens the IAC valve to increase the idle speed enough to overcome the extra load imposed on the engine. The IAC valve is mounted on the top of the intake manifold, near the throttle body, on V6 models. On V8 models, the IAC valve is located on the side of the intake manifold, next to the throttle body.

27   **Ignition coil(s)** - The ignition coil(s) is/are under the control of the Powertrain Control Module (PCM). There is no ignition control module. Instead, "coil drivers" inside the PCM turn the primary side of the coil(s) on and off. For more information about the ignition coil(s), see Chapter 5.

Obtaining and clearing Diagnostic Trouble Codes (DTCs)

28   All models covered by this manual are equipped with on-board diagnostics. When the PCM recognizes a malfunction in a monitored emission control system, component or circuit, it turns on the SERVICE ENGINE SOON light, also known as the Malfunction Indicator Light (MIL), on the dash. The PCM will continue to display the MIL until the problem is fixed and the Diagnostic Trouble Code (DTC) is cleared from the PCM's memory. You'll need a scan tool to access any DTCs stored in the PCM.

29   Before outputting any DTCs stored in the PCM, thoroughly inspect ALL electrical connectors and hoses. Make sure that all electrical connections are tight, clean and free of corrosion. And make sure that all hoses are correctly connected, fit tightly and are in good condition (no cracks or tears). Also, make sure that the engine is tuned up. A poorly running engine is probably one of the biggest causes of emission-related malfunctions. Often, simply giving the engine a good tune-up will correct the problem.

Accessing the DTCs

Refer to illustration 2.30

30   On these models, all of which are equipped with On-Board Diagnostic II (OBD-II) systems, the Diagnostic Trouble Codes (DTCs) can only be accessed with a scan tool. Professional scan tools are expensive, but relatively inexpensive generic scan tools **(see illustrations 2.1 and 2.2)** are available at most automotive parts stores. Simply plug the connector of the scan tool into the diagnostic connector **(see illustration)**, which is located under the left side of the dash and then follow the instructions included with the scan tool to extract the DTCs.

31   Once you have outputted all of the stored DTCs look them up on the accompanying DTC chart.

2.30 The 16-pin Data Link Connector (DLC) is located under the left part of the dash

32   After troubleshooting the source of each DTC make any necessary repairs or replace the defective component(s).

Clearing the DTCs

33   Clear the DTCs with the scan tool in accordance with the instructions provided by the scan tool's manufacturer.

Diagnostic Trouble Codes

34   The accompanying tables are a list of the Diagnostic Trouble Codes (DTCs) that can be accessed by a do-it-yourselfer working at home (there are many, many more DTCs available to dealerships with proprietary scan tools and software, but those codes cannot be accessed by a generic scan tool). If, after you have checked and repaired the connectors, wire harness and vacuum hoses (if applicable) for an emission-related system, component or circuit, the problem persists, have the vehicle checked by an automotive service technician.

OBD-II trouble codes

Note: *Not all trouble codes apply to all models.*

Code	Probable cause
P0040	Upstream oxygen sensors swapped (crossed wiring harnesses)
P0041	Downstream oxygen sensors swapped (crossed wiring harnesses)
P0068	Throttle Position (TP) sensor inconsistent with Mass Air Flow sensor
P0102	Mass Air Flow (MAF) sensor circuit, low input
P0103	Mass Air Flow (MAF) sensor circuit, high input
P0106	Barometric (BARO) pressure sensor circuit, performance problem
P0107	Barometric (BARO) pressure sensor/MAP sensor circuit, low voltage
P0108	Barometric (BARO) pressure sensor/MAP sensor circuit, high voltage
P0109	BARO/MAP sensor circuit intermittent
P0112	Intake Air Temperature (IAT) sensor circuit, low input
P0113	Intake Air Temperature (IAT) sensor circuit, high input
P0116	Engine Coolant Temperature (ECT) circuit range/performance problem
P0117	Engine Coolant Temperature (ECT) sensor circuit, low input
P0118	Engine Coolant Temperature (ECT) sensor circuit, high input
P0121	Throttle Position (TP) circuit out of range or performance problem
P0122	Throttle Position (TP) sensor circuit, low input
P0123	Throttle Position (TP) sensor circuit, high input
P0125	Insufficient coolant temperature for closed loop fuel control
P0128	Coolant temperature below thermostat regulated temperature
P0131	Upstream oxygen sensor circuit problem (right cylinder bank)
P0132	Upstream oxygen sensor circuit, high voltage (right cylinder bank)
P0133	Upstream oxygen sensor circuit, slow response (right cylinder bank)
P0135	Upstream oxygen sensor heater circuit problem (right cylinder bank)
P0136	Downstream oxygen sensor circuit problem (right cylinder bank)
P0138	Downstream oxygen sensor circuit, high voltage (right cylinder bank)
P0141	Downstream oxygen sensor heater circuit problem (right cylinder bank)
P0148	Fuel delivery error

6

OBD-II trouble codes

Note: *Not all trouble codes apply to all models.*

Code	Probable cause
P0151	Upstream oxygen sensor circuit, low voltage (left cylinder bank)
P0152	Upstream oxygen sensor circuit, high voltage (left cylinder bank)
P0153	Upstream oxygen sensor circuit, slow response (left cylinder bank)
P0155	Upstream oxygen sensor heater circuit problem (left cylinder bank)
P0156	Downstream oxygen sensor circuit problem (left cylinder bank)
P0158	Downstream oxygen sensor circuit, high voltage (left cylinder bank)
P0161	Downstream oxygen sensor heater circuit problem (left cylinder bank)
P0171	System too lean (right cylinder bank)
P0172	System too rich (right cylinder bank)
P0174	System too lean (left cylinder bank)
P0175	System too rich (left cylinder bank)
P0176	Flexible Fuel (FF) sensor circuit malfunction
P0180	Engine Fuel Temperature (EFT) sensor A circuit, low input
P0181	Engine Fuel Temperature (EFT) sensor A circuit, range/performance
P0183	Engine Fuel Temperature (EFT) sensor circuit, high input
P0190	Fuel Rail Pressure (FRP) sensor circuit malfunction
P0191	Fuel Rail Pressure (FRP) sensor circuit performance
P0192	Fuel Rail Pressure (FRP) sensor circuit, low input
P0193	Fuel Rail Pressure (FRP) sensor circuit, high input
P0196	Engine Oil Temperature sensor circuit range/performance problem
P0197	Engine Oil Temperature sensor circuit, low input
P0198	Engine Oil Temperature sensor circuit, high input
P0201	Injector no. 1 circuit malfunction
P0202	Injector no. 2 circuit malfunction
P0203	Injector no. 3 circuit malfunction
P0204	Injector no. 4 circuit malfunction
P0205	Injector no. 5 circuit malfunction
P0206	Injector no. 6 circuit malfunction
P0207	Injector no. 7 circuit malfunction
P0208	Injector no. 8 circuit malfunction
P0219	Engine over speed condition
P0221	Throttle Position (TP) sensor B circuit range/performance problem
P0222	Throttle Position (TP) sensor B circuit, low input
P0223	Throttle Position (TP) sensor B circuit, high input

Code	Probable cause
P0230	Fuel pump primary circuit malfunction
P0231	Fuel pump secondary circuit low
P0232	Fuel pump secondary circuit high
P0297	Vehicle overspeed condition
P0298	Engine oil over temperature condition
P0300	Random misfire detected
P0301	Cylinder no. 1 misfire detected
P0302	Cylinder no. 2 misfire detected
P0303	Cylinder no. 3 misfire detected
P0304	Cylinder no. 4 misfire detected
P0305	Cylinder no. 5 misfire detected
P0306	Cylinder no. 6 misfire detected
P0307	Cylinder no. 7 misfire detected
P0308	Cylinder no. 8 misfire detected
P0315	PCM unable to learn crankshaft pulse wheel tooth spacing
P0316	Misfire occurred during first 1000 engine revolutions
P0320	Ignition engine speed input circuit malfunction
P0325	Knock sensor 1 circuit malfunction (right cylinder head)
P0326	Knock sensor 1 circuit range/performance (right cylinder bank)
P0330	Knock sensor 2 circuit malfunction (left cylinder bank)
P0331	Knock sensor 2 circuit range/performance (left cylinder bank)
P0340	Camshaft Position (CMP) sensor circuit malfunction (right cylinder head)
P0345	Camshaft Position (CMP) sensor circuit malfunction (left cylinder head)
P0351	Ignition coil A primary or secondary circuit malfunction (V8 engine)
P0352	Ignition coil B primary or secondary circuit malfunction (V8 engine)
P0353	Ignition coil C primary or secondary circuit malfunction (V8 engine)
P0354	Ignition coil D primary or secondary circuit malfunction (V8 engine)
P0355	Ignition coil E primary or secondary circuit malfunction (V8 engine)
P0356	Ignition coil F primary or secondary circuit malfunction (V8 engine)
P0357	Ignition coil G primary or secondary circuit malfunction (V8 engine)
P0358	Ignition coil H primary or secondary circuit malfunction (V8 engine)
P0400	EGR flow failure (outside the minimum or maximum limits)
P0401	Exhaust Gas Recirculation (EGR) valve, insufficient flow detected
P0402	Exhaust Gas Recirculation (EGR) valve, excessive flow detected
P0403	EEGR electric motor windings or circuits to PCM shorted or open

6

OBD-II trouble codes

Note: *Not all trouble codes apply to all models.*

Code	Probable cause
P0405	DPF EGR sensor circuit, low voltage detected
P0406	DPF EGR sensor circuit, high voltage detected
P0411	Secondary Air Injection (AIR) system, upstream flow
P0412	Secondary Air Injection (AIR) system, circuit malfunction
P0420	Catalyst system efficiency below threshold (right cylinder bank)
P0430	Catalyst system efficiency below threshold (left cylinder bank)
P0442	EVAP control system, small leak detected
P0443	EVAP control system, canister purge valve circuit malfunction
P0446	EVAP control system canister vent solenoid circuit malfunction
P0451	Fuel tank pressure sensor circuit out of range or performance problem
P0452	Fuel tank pressure sensor circuit, low input
P0453	Fuel tank pressure sensor circuit, high input
P0455	EVAP control system, big leak detected
P0456	EVAP control system, very small leak detected
P0457	EVAP control system, leak detected (fuel filler neck cap loose or off)
P0460	Fuel level sensor circuit malfunction
P0462	Fuel level sensor circuit, low input
P0463	Fuel level sensor circuit, high input
P0480	Visctronic Drive Fan (VDF) primary circuit malfunction
P0481	High Fan Control (HFC) primary circuit failure
P0500	Vehicle Speed Sensor (VSS) malfunction
P0501	Vehicle Speed Sensor (VSS) range/performance problem
P0503	Vehicle Speed Sensor (VSS), intermittent malfunction
P0505	Idle Air Control (IAC) system malfunction
P0506	Idle Air Control (IAC) rpm lower than expected
P0507	Idle Air Control (IAC) rpm higher than expected
P0511	Idle Air Control (IAC) circuit malfunction
P0528	Visctronic Drive Fan (VDF) speed sensor circuit malfunction
P0534	Low air conditioning cycling period
P0537	Air conditioning evaporator temperature circuit, low input
P0538	Air conditioning evaporator temperature circuit, high input
P0552	Power Steering Pressure (PSP) sensor circuit malfunction

Code	Probable cause
P0553	Power Steering Pressure (PSP) sensor circuit malfunction
P0602	Control module programming error
P0603	Powertrain Control Module (PCM) Keep-Alive-Memory (KAM) test error
P0605	Powertrain Control Module (PCM) Read-Only-Memory (ROM) error
P0606	Powertrain Control Module (PCM) internal communication error
P0703	Brake Pedal Position (BPP) switch circuit input malfunction
P0704	Clutch pedal position switch malfunction
P0720	Insufficient input from Output Shaft Speed (OSS) sensor
P0721	Noise interference on Output Shaft Speed (OSS) sensor signal
P0722	No signal from Output Shaft Speed (OSS) sensor
P0723	Output Shaft Speed (OSS) sensor circuit, intermittent failure
P0812	Reverse Switch (RS) input circuit malfunction

3.1 The Brake Pedal Position (BPP) switch is located at the top of the brake pedal

3.4 To remove the BPP switch from the brake pedal, disconnect the electrical connector, remove the retaining clip by pulling it straight up, then slide the BPP switch to the left to disengage it from the pedal pivot pin

4.1 To remove the CMP sensor from the valve cover on a V6 model, disconnect the electrical connector and remove the retaining bolt

3   Brake Pedal Position (BPP) switch - replacement

Refer to illustrations 3.1 and 3.4

1   The BPP switch **(see illustration)** is located at the top of the brake pedal.
2   Disconnect the cable from the negative battery terminal (see Chapter 5).
3   Disconnect the electrical connector from the BPP switch **(see illustration 3.1).**
4   Remove the retaining clip from the brake pedal pivot pin **(see illustration)**, then slide off the BPP switch.
5   Installation is the reverse of removal.

4   Camshaft Position (CMP) sensor - replacement

V6 models

Refer to illustration 4.1

1   The CMP sensor **(see illustration)** is located on the left valve cover.
2   Disconnect the cable from the negative battery terminal (see Chapter 5).
3   Disconnect the electrical connector

from the CMP sensor **(see illustration 4.1).**
4   Remove the CMP sensor retaining bolt **(see illustration 4.1)** and remove the sensor.
5   Installation is the reverse of removal. Be sure to tighten the sensor retaining bolt to the torque listed in this Chapter's Specifications.

V8 models

6   The CMP sensor is located on the front of the left cylinder head, below the valve cover.
7   Disconnect the cable from the negative battery terminal (see Chapter 5).
8   On 2002 models remove the accessory drivebelt (see Chapter 1).

6

9   On 2002 models remove the power steering pump pulley (see Chapter 10).
10   On 2002 models remove the wiring harness bracket and the ground wire, which is grounded by one of the wiring harness bracket studs.
11   On 2002 models remove the upper support bracket.
12   On 2002 models remove the power steering high-pressure line.
13   On 2002 models remove the power steering pump (see Chapter 10). (Remove the bolts and set the pump aside; don't disconnect the power steering lines.)
14   On 2002 models remove the power steering reservoir mounting bracket.
15   On 2002 models detach and set aside the radio interference capacitor.
16   Disconnect the electrical connector from the CMP sensor.
17   Remove the CMP sensor retaining bolt and remove the sensor.
18   Installation is the reverse of removal.

5   Crankshaft Position (CKP) sensor - replacement

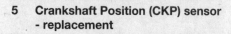

Refer to illustration 5.1

1   The CKP sensor **(see illustration)** is located on the front of the engine block, to the right of the crankshaft pulley.
2   Disconnect the cable from the negative battery terminal.
3   On V8 models remove the accessory drivebelt (see Chapter 1).
4   Raise the front of the vehicle and place it securely on jackstands.
5   On V8 models, unbolt the compressor and set it aside (see Chapter 3). (Do NOT disconnect either of the refrigerant lines!)
6   Disconnect the electrical connector from the CKP sensor **(see illustration 5.1)**.
7   Remove the CKP sensor retaining bolt **(see illustration 5.1)** and detach the sensor.

5.1   The CKP sensor is located on the front of the engine block, near the crankshaft pulley; to remove it, simply disconnect the electrical connector and remove the sensor retaining bolt

8   Installation is the reverse of removal. Be sure to tighten the sensor retaining bolt to the torque listed in this Chapter's Specifications.

6   Cylinder Head Temperature (CHT) sensor (V8 models) - replacement

1   The CHT sensor is located in the valley between the cylinder heads (it's actually mounted on the left head).
2   Remove the alternator (see Chapter 5).
3   Disconnect the electrical connector from the CHT sensor.
4   Unscrew the CHT sensor and remove it.
5   Installation is the reverse of removal. Be sure to tighten the CHT sensor to the torque listed in this Chapter's Specifications.

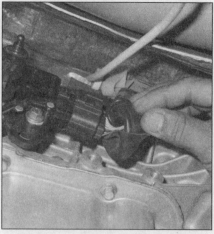

7.5a   Peel back this rubber boot from the DTR sensor electrical connector . . .

7   Digital Transmission Range (DTR) sensor - replacement and adjustment

Refer to illustrations 7.5a, 7.5b, 7.6, 7.7a, 7.7b, 7.8, 7.10, 7.11a and 7.11b
Note 1: *This procedure applies only to vehicles with an automatic transmission.*
Note 2: *The following procedure is intended for the home mechanic who does not possess or have access to the special DTR sensor alignment tool used by dealership service departments to align the DTR sensor, because it's difficult to obtain one of these special alignment tools. The method described here for aligning the DTR sensor should be adequate. If it isn't, drive the vehicle to a dealer or other repair shop after installing the DTR sensor and have it adjusted. Failure to do so might set a Diagnostic Trouble Code and cause driveability problems.*

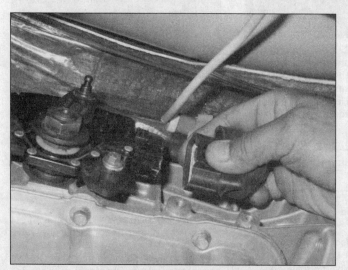

7.5b . . . then disconnect the electrical connector from the DTR sensor

7.6   To disconnect the shift cable from the manual lever, insert a trim panel removal tool (shown) or a big screwdriver between the cable end and the pin on the lever, then pry off the cable end

7.7a To detach the manual lever from the manual lever shaft, remove this big nut . . .

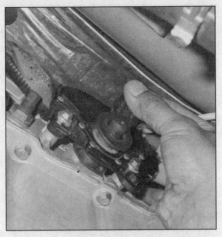

7.7b . . . then remove the manual lever from the shaft

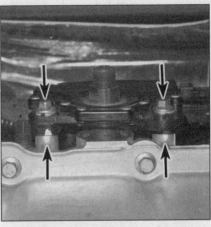

7.8 Mark the relationship of the DTR sensor to the transmission; to detach the DTR sensor from the transmission, remove these two bolts

1   Disconnect the cable from the negative battery terminal (see Chapter 5).

2   Place the shift lever inside the vehicle in the NEUTRAL ("N") position.

3   Raise the vehicle and place it securely on jackstands.

4   The DTR sensor is located at the manual lever, on the left side of the transmission.

5   Peel back the rubber boot that protects the DTR sensor electrical connector, then disconnect the electrical connector from the DTR sensor **(see illustrations)**.

6   Disconnect the shift cable from the manual control lever **(see illustration)**.

7   Remove the manual lever from the manual lever shaft **(see illustrations)**.

8   Mark the relationship of the DTR sensor to the transmission **(see illustration)**.

9   Remove the DTR sensor mounting bolts **(see illustration 7.8)** and remove the DTR sensor from the manual lever shaft.

10   Before installing the DTR sensor make sure that the transmission is still in Neutral. If you're not sure, take the manual lever and use it to rotate the manual lever shaft counterclockwise until it stops, then rotate the manual lever shaft two clicks clockwise **(see illustration)**. The transmission is now in Neutral.

11   If you look closely at the DTR sensor, you will see Neutral alignment marks on the sensor's rotating inner ring (the one that rotates with the manual lever shaft) and on the stationary ring around the periphery of the rotating ring **(see illustration)**. Align the Neutral marks on these two rings and then slide the DTR sensor onto the manual lever shaft **(see illustration)**. Note the two keyways on the manual lever shaft; the two ridges, 180-degrees apart, on the rotating ring of the DTR sensor must be aligned with these two keyways in order to install the DTR sensor on the shaft. (There are also a pair of notches, 180-degrees apart, in the circumference of the rotating ring, that are for seating the locator pins on the factory tool.) **Note:** *On a conventional Park/Neutral Position (PNP) switch, this alignment method would be sufficiently accurate to realign the PNP switch for installation (since all you're really doing is ensuring that the vehicle will start only in Park or Neutral). On a DTR sensor (which is an information sensor for the PCM), aligning the Neutral mark of the rotating ring to its corresponding Neutral mark on the stationary ring might not be sufficiently accurate, because the range of movement of the DTR sensor is very small.*

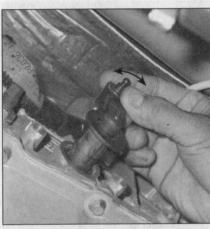

7.10 The transmission should still be in Neutral, but if it's been accidentally shifted into some other gear, put it back in Neutral by using the manual lever to turn the manual lever shaft all the way to the left (clockwise) until it stops, then turn it to the right (counterclockwise) two clicks

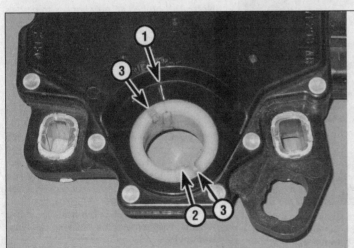

7.11a Digital Transmission Range (DTR) sensor installation details:

1   *Make sure that the Neutral alignment mark on the inner rotating ring is aligned with the Neutral alignment mark on the stationary ring*

2   *The two ridges, 180-degrees apart, on the inside of the rotating ring must be aligned with the keyways on the manual lever shaft (see next illustration)*

3   *These notches in the rotating ring are for two of the locator pins on the special factory TR sensor alignment tool*

6

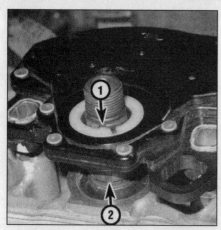

7.11b When installing the DTR sensor, make sure that the two ridges (1) on the inside of the rotating ring are aligned with the keyways (2) on the manual lever shaft (second ridge and keyway not shown)

10.5a To detach the shift cable from its bracket, use a screwdriver to pry the upper and lower locator pins on the shift cable retainer out of their slots in the bracket, then slide the cable assembly to the left, out of the bracket (upper locator pin not visible in this photo)

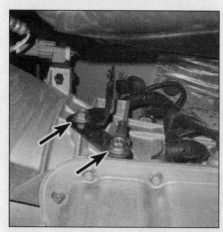

10.5b To detach the shift cable bracket from the transmission, remove these bolts

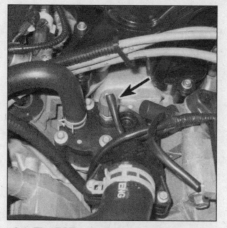

8.1 The ECT sensor is located on top of the engine, right behind the upper radiator hose

12   When everything is correctly aligned tighten the DTR sensor mounting bolts to the torque listed in this Chapter's Specifications. After you have torqued the bolts, recheck the alignment of the Neutral marks. If they're off, loosen the bolts, readjust the DTR sensor and retorque the bolts.

13   The remainder of installation is otherwise the reverse of removal.

14   If necessary, drive the vehicle to a dealer and have the DTR sensor realigned.

8   Engine Coolant Temperature (ECT) sensor (V6 models) - replacement

Refer to illustrations 8.1 and 8.5
Warning: *Wait until the engine has cooled completely before beginning this procedure.*
1   The engine coolant temperature sensor is mounted on top of the engine, right behind the upper radiator hose **(see illustration)**.
2   Disconnect the cable from the negative battery terminal (see Chapter 5).
3   Drain the cooling system level below the cylinder heads (see Chapter 1).

10.6 Disconnect the ISS sensor electrical connector; to detach the sensor from the transmission, remove this bolt

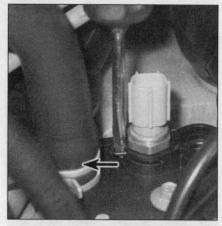

8.5 Before unscrewing the ECT sensor, pry off this retainer ring with a screwdriver in the direction of the arrow

4   Disconnect the electrical connector from the ECT sensor **(see illustration 8.1)**.
5   Remove the ECT sensor retainer **(see illustration)**.
6   Remove the ECT sensor.
7   Installation is the reverse of removal.
Caution: *Handle the ECT sensor with care. A damaged ECT sensor can affect the operation of the engine management system.*

9   Intake Air Temperature (IAT) sensor - replacement

1   The IAT sensor is located inside, and is an integral component of, the Mass Air Flow (MAF) sensor. Neither component can be serviced separately. If you need to replace the IAT sensor, you must replace the MAF sensor (see Section 12).

10   Intermediate Shaft Speed (ISS) sensor - replacement

Refer to illustrations 10.5a, 10.5b, 10.6, 10.8a and 10.8b
Note: *This procedure only applies to models with an automatic transmission.*
1   Disconnect the cable from the negative battery cable.
2   Raise the vehicle and place it securely on jackstands.
3   On 4WD models, remove the front driveshaft (see Chapter 8).
4   The ISS sensor **(see illustration)** is located on the left side of the transmission.
Note: *There are three speed sensors on the upper left side of the transmission. The ISS sensor is the middle one. Don't confuse it with the front sensor, which is the Turbine Shaft Speed (TSS) sensor, or the rear sensor, which is the Output Shaft Speed (OSS) sensor.*
5   Detach the shift cable from the cable bracket, then remove the bracket **(see illustrations)**.

10.8a Remove and discard the old ISS sensor O-ring

10.8b Before installing the new ISS sensor O-ring, be sure to lubricate it with petroleum jelly

11.4a On V6 models, note how the heat isolator pillow is packed between the intake runners of the lower intake manifold . . .

6   Disconnect the electrical connector from the ISS sensor **(see illustration)**.
7   Remove the ISS sensor retaining bolt **(see illustration 10.6)**.
8   If you're planning to reuse the old ISS sensor, remove and discard the old O-ring **(see illustration)**. Before installing the new O-ring, lubricate it with petroleum jelly **(see illustration)**. If you're installing a new ISS sensor, be sure to lubricate the new O-ring.
9   Installation is the reverse of removal. Be sure to tighten the ISS sensor bolt to the torque listed in this Chapter's Specifications.

11 Knock sensor(s) - replacement

1   The knock sensor(s) is/are located in the valley between the cylinder heads on V6 and V8 engines (2002 V8s have two knock sensors).
2   Disconnect the cable from the negative battery terminal (see Chapter 5).
3   Remove the intake manifold (V6 models, see Chapter 2A; V8 models, see Chapter 2B).

V6 models and 2002 V8 models

Refer to illustrations 11.4a, 11.4b, 11.5 and 11.6

4   On V6 models, remove the heat isolator pillow **(see illustrations)**.
5   Disconnect the knock sensor electrical connector **(see illustration)**. **Note:** *The knock sensor connector location varies with the model year and date of manufacture. On the 2003 V6 model shown here, the knock sensor connector is located on the left end of the firewall, but on some models the connector is located in the valley between the cylinder heads, closer to the knock sensor.*
6   Remove the knock sensor retaining bolt **(see illustration)** and remove the knock sensor.
7   Installation is the reverse of removal. Be sure to tighten the knock sensor retaining bolt to the torque listed in this Chapter's Specifications.

2003 V8 models

Note: *On these models, the knock sensors must be replaced as a single assembly.*

11.4b . . . then remove the pillow (V6 models)

8   Disconnect the knock sensor electrical connector.
9   Remove the knock sensor retaining bolts.
10   Installation is the reverse of removal. Be

11.5 Disconnect the knock sensor electrical connector (on some V6 models, the sensor connector is located on the firewall, as shown here; on others, and on 2002 V8s, the connector is located in the valley between the heads)

11.6 Remove the knock sensor retaining bolt (V6 model shown, 2002 V8 models similar)

6

12.3 Disconnect the electrical connector from the MAF sensor

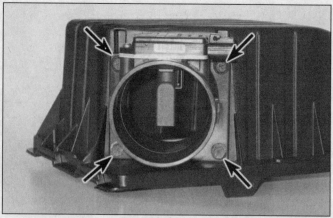

12.5 To detach the MAF sensor from the air filter housing, remove these four bolts

sure to tighten the knock sensor retaining bolts to the torque listed in this Chapter's Specifications.

12 Mass Air Flow (MAF) sensor - replacement

Refer to illustrations 12.3 and 12.5

1 The Mass Air Flow (MAF) sensor is located between the air filter housing and the air intake duct.
2 Disconnect the cable from the negative battery terminal.
3 Disconnect the electrical connector from the MAF sensor **(see illustration)**.
4 Remove the air intake duct and the air filter housing (see Chapter 4).
5 Remove the MAF sensor from the air filter housing **(see illustration)**.
6 On V8 models, remove and discard the old MAF sensor gasket.
7 When installing the MAF sensor on V8 models, be sure to use a new MAF sensor gasket.
8 Installation is otherwise the reverse of removal. Be sure to tighten the MAF sensor mounting bolts to the torque listed in this Chapter's Specifications.

13 Output Shaft Speed (OSS) sensor - replacement

Models with an automatic transmission.

1 Disconnect the cable from the negative battery cable.
2 Raise the vehicle and place it securely on jackstands.
3 On 4WD models, remove the front driveshaft (see Chapter 8).
4 The OSS sensor is located on the left side of the transmission. **Note:** *There are three speed sensors on the upper left side of the transmission. The OSS sensor is the rear one. Don't confuse it with the front sensor,*

which is the Turbine Shaft Speed (TSS) sensor, or the middle sensor, which is the Intermediate Shaft Speed (ISS) sensor.
5 Detach the shift cable from the cable bracket, then remove the bracket **(see illustrations 10.5a and 10.5b)**.
6 Disconnect the electrical connector from the OSS sensor **(see illustration 10.6)**.
7 Remove the ISS sensor retaining bolt **(see illustration 10.6)**.
8 If you're planning to reuse the old OSS sensor, remove and discard the old O-ring **(see illustration 10.8a)**. Before installing the new O-ring, lubricate it with petroleum jelly **(see illustration 10.8b)**. If you're installing a new OSS sensor, be sure to lubricate the new O-ring.
9 Installation is the reverse of removal. Be sure to tighten the OSS sensor bolt to the torque listed in this Chapter's Specifications.

2002 models with a manual transmission

10 On these models, the Output Shaft Speed (OSS) sensor is located on the right side of the transmission.
11 Disconnect the cable from the negative battery cable.
12 Raise the vehicle and place it securely on jackstands.
13 Disconnect the electrical connector from the OSS sensor.
14 Remove the OSS sensor retaining bolt and remove the sensor.
15 Installation is the reverse of removal. Be sure to tighten the OSS sensor retaining bolt securely.

4WD models

16 On these models, there are *two* Output Shaft Speed (OSS) sensors: the front OSS sensor and the rear OSS sensor. Both of them are located on the rear of the transfer case.
17 Disconnect the cable from the negative battery cable.
18 Raise the vehicle and place it securely on jackstands.

Front OSS sensor

19 Remove the transfer case shift motor (see Chapter 7C).
20 Disconnect the OSS sensor electrical connector.
21 Remove the OSS sensor retaining bolt and carefully remove the sensor.
22 Installation is the reverse of removal. Be sure to tighten the OSS sensor retaining bolt to the torque listed in this Chapter's Specifications.

Rear OSS sensor

23 Remove the heat shield from the transfer case (see Chapter 7C).
24 Detach the shift motor electrical connector from the transfer case and disconnect it.
25 Using the correct electrical connector pin removal tool, remove the wires for the OSS sensor from the shift motor electrical connector.
26 Remove the OSS sensor retaining bolt and carefully remove the sensor.
27 Installation is the reverse of removal. Be sure to tighten the OSS sensor retaining bolt to the torque listed in this Chapter's Specifications.

14 Oxygen sensors - general information and replacement

Refer to illustrations 14.1a and 14.1b

1 There are four oxygen sensors - two for each cylinder head - on all models. Each upstream oxygen sensor **(see illustration)** is located right below the exhaust manifold flanges and above the upstream catalytic converter. Each downstream oxygen sensor **(see illustration)** is located in the exhaust pipe, right behind the upstream catalyst, and ahead of the main catalyst.
2 Disconnect the cable from the negative battery cable.
3 Raise the vehicle and place it securely on jackstands.

14.1a Typical upstream oxygen sensor and electrical connector (upstream sensor for left cylinder bank on V6 model shown, left or right upstream sensors on V6 and V8 models are similar)

1   *Electrical connector*
2   *Upstream oxygen sensor (left sensor shown, right sensor similar)*

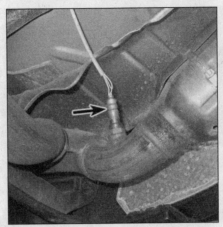

14.1b Typical downstream oxygen sensor (downstream sensor for left cylinder bank on V6 model shown, left or right downstream sensors on V6 and V8 models are similar)

14.4 Electrical connector location for right upstream oxygen sensor (V6 model shown, V8 models similar))

Upstream oxygen sensors

Refer to illustrations 14.4 and 14.5

4   Disconnect the upstream oxygen sensor electrical connector **(left upstream connector, see illustration 14.1a; right upstream connector, see illustration)**.
5   Using an oxygen sensor socket, remove the upstream oxygen sensor **(see illustration)**. If the sensor is difficult to loosen, spray some penetrant onto the sensor threads and allow it to soak in for the period of time specified by the penetrant manufacturer.
6   Apply a light coating of anti-seize compound to the threads of the new (or old) oxygen sensor to facilitate removal the next time the sensor must be replaced or removed.
7   Installation is otherwise the reverse of removal. Be sure to tighten the sensor securely.

Downstream oxygen sensors

Refer to illustrations 14.8a, 14.8b and 14.9

8   Disconnect the downstream oxygen sensor electrical connector **(see illustrations)**.
9   Using an oxygen sensor socket, remove the downstream oxygen sensor **(see illustration)**. If the sensor is difficult to loosen, spray some penetrant onto the sensor threads and allow it to soak in for the period of time specified by the penetrant manufacturer.
10   Apply a light coating of anti-seize compound to the threads of the new (or old) oxygen sensor to facilitate removal the next time the sensor must be replaced or removed.
11   Installation is otherwise the reverse of removal. Be sure to tighten the sensor securely.

14.5 Use an oxygen sensor socket to unscrew the upstream oxygen sensor; this special socket protects the sensor during removal and installation and has a slot in the socket wall for the sensor electrical lead

14.8b The electrical connector for the right downstream oxygen sensor is located on the right side of the transmission (V6 model shown, V8 models similar)

14.8a The electrical connector for the left downstream oxygen sensor is located on the upper left side of the transmission (V6 model shown, V8 models similar)

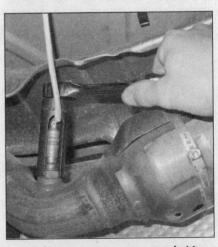

14.9 Use an oxygen sensor socket to remove the downstream oxygen sensor

6

15.1 On V6 models, the TP sensor (1) is located on the rear side of the throttle body, facing toward the firewall (on V8 models, the TP sensor is mounted on the front side of the throttle body); before detaching the TP sensor from the throttle body, disconnect the electrical connector (2)

15.3 To detach the throttle body cover on a V6 model, remove these two bolts

15 Throttle Position (TP) sensor - replacement

Refer to illustrations 15.1, 15.3, 15.5 and 15.6

1   The TP sensor **(see illustration)** is located on the throttle body.
2   Disconnect the cable from the negative battery terminal.
3   On V6 models, remove the throttle body cover **(see illustration)**. On V8 models, remove the engine cover.
4   Disconnect the electrical connector from the TP sensor.
5   Remove the TP sensor mounting screws **(see illustration)**.
6   When installing the TP sensor, make sure that one of the tangs on the backside of the sensor is above the blade on the end of the throttle valve shaft and the other tang is below the blade **(see illustration)**. To ensure that the sensor is correctly aligned, install it at an angle as shown. When it's flush against the throttle body, rotate the sensor clockwise until the mounting screw holes in the sensor are aligned with the screw holes in the throttle body
7   Installation is otherwise the reverse of removal. Be sure to align the tighten the screws securely, but don't overtighten them, or you could damage the TP sensor.

16 Turbine Shaft Speed (TSS) sensor - replacement

Note: *This procedure only applies to models with an automatic transmission.*

1   Disconnect the cable from the negative battery cable.
2   Raise the vehicle and place it securely on jackstands.
3   On 4WD models, remove the front driveshaft (see Chapter 8).
4   The TSS sensor is located on the left

15.5 To detach the TP sensor from the throttle body, remove the two mounting screws (V6 model shown, V8 models similar)

side of the transmission. **Note:** *There are three speed sensors on the upper left side of the transmission. The TSS sensor is the front one. Don't confuse it with the middle sensor, which is the Intermediate Shaft Speed (ISS) sensor, or the rear sensor, which is the Output Shaft Speed (OSS) sensor.*
5   Detach the shift cable from the cable bracket, then remove the bracket **(see illustrations 10.5a and 10.5b)**.
6   Disconnect the electrical connector from the OSS sensor **(see illustration 10.6)**.
7   Remove the ISS sensor retaining bolt **(see illustration 10.6)**.
8   If you're planning to reuse the old OSS sensor, remove and discard the old O-ring **(see illustration 10.8a)**. Before installing the new O-ring, lubricate it with petroleum jelly **(see illustration 10.8b)**. If you're installing a new OSS sensor, be sure to lubricate the new O-ring.
9   Installation is the reverse of removal. Be sure to tighten the OSS sensor bolt to the torque listed in this Chapter's Specifications.

15.6 Install the TP sensor at an angle as shown, then when it's flush against the throttle body, rotate the sensor clockwise until the mounting screw holes in the sensor are aligned with the screw holes in the throttle body (V6 model shown, V8 models similar)

17 Powertrain Control Module (PCM) - removal and installation

Refer to illustrations 17.1, 17.3, 17.4a, 17.4b and 17.6
Warning: *The models covered by this manual are equipped with Supplemental Restraint systems (SRS), more commonly known as airbags. Always disable the airbag system before working in the vicinity of any airbag system components to avoid the possibility of accidental deployment of the airbag, which could cause personal injury (see Chapter 12).*
Caution: *To avoid electrostatic discharge damage to the PCM, handle the PCM only by its case. Do not touch the electrical terminals during removal and installation. If available, ground yourself to the vehicle with an anti-static ground strap, available at computer supply stores.*

17.1 The Powertrain Control Module (PCM) is located at the right end of the firewall; before disconnecting the electrical connectors from the PCM, remove these three bolts

17.3 After removing the PCM connector retaining bolts, carefully disconnect the electrical connectors from the PCM

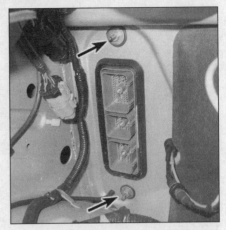

17.4a Remove these two PCM mounting nuts

17.4b The lower PCM mounting nut is difficult to access from above, so remove the wheel housing splash shield and remove the lower nut by inserting a socket and extension through this access hole in the wheel housing

1   The Powertrain Control Module (PCM) is located at the right end of the firewall **(see illustration)**.

2   Disconnect the cable from the negative battery terminal (see Chapter 5).

3   Remove the electrical connector retaining bolts **(see illustration 17.1)** and disconnect the electrical connectors **(see illustration)**.

4   Remove the upper and lower PCM mounting nuts **(see illustration)**. In order to access the lower nut, loosen the right wheel lug nuts, raise the vehicle, place it securely on jackstands and remove the right front wheel. Then remove the wheel housing splash shield (see Chapter 11). Using a ratchet and an extension, remove the lower nut **(see illustration)**.

5   Working inside the vehicle, remove the right kick panel (see Chapter 11). (You might also want to remove the glove box, but it's not absolutely necessary.)

6   Remove the PCM mounting bracket bolt **(see illustration)**.

7   Carefully remove the PCM and its mounting bracket as a single assembly. **Caution:** *Avoid any static electricity damage to the computer by grounding yourself to the body before touching the PCM and using a special anti-static pad to store the PCM on once it is removed.*

8   Separate the PCM from its mounting bracket.

9   Installation is the reverse of removal.

18 Idle Air Control (IAC) valve - replacement

V6 models

Refer to illustration 18.1 and 18.5

1   The Idle Air Control (IAC) valve **(see illustration)** is located on top of the intake manifold, right next to the throttle body.

2   Disconnect the cable from the negative battery terminal.

3   Remove the throttle body cover **(see illustration 15.3)**.

4   Disconnect the IAC valve electrical connector **(see illustration 18.1)**.

6

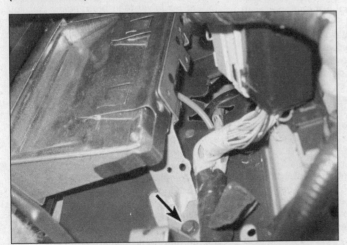

17.6 To detach the PCM mounting bracket from the vehicle body, remove this bolt

18.1 The Idle Air Control (IAC) valve is located on top of the intake manifold, next to the throttle body (V6 model shown, V8 models similar)

18.5 Before you can remove the two IAC mounting stud bolts, you must detach the wiring harness clip from the rear IAC valve mounting stud bolt and unscrew the throttle body cover spacer nut from the front IAC valve mounting stud bolt

5   Detach the wiring harness clip from the rear IAC valve mounting stud bolt **(see illustration)** and unscrew the throttle body cover spacer nut from the front IAC valve mounting stud bolt.

6   Remove the IAC valve mounting stud bolts and remove the IAC valve.

7   Installation is the reverse of removal. Be sure to tighten the IAC valve mounting bolts to the torque listed in this Chapter's Specifications.

V8 models

8   The Idle Air Control (IAC) valve is located on the side of the intake manifold, right next to the throttle body.

9   Disconnect the cable from the negative battery terminal.

10   Remove the engine cover (see Chapter 2B).

11   Disconnect the IAC valve electrical connector.

12   Disconnect the air bypass hose from the IAC valve.

13   Remove the IAC valve mounting bolts and remove the IAC valve.

14   Remove and discard the old IAC valve gasket.

15   Installation is the reverse of removal. Be sure to use a new gasket and tighten the IAC valve mounting bolts to the torque listed in this Chapter's Specifications.

---

19   Catalytic converters - general information, check and replacement

Note: *Because of a Federally mandated extended warranty which covers emissions-related components like the catalytic converter, check with a dealer service department before replacing the converter at your own expense.*

19.13a Remove the left heat shield-to-crossmember bolt . . .

General description

1   A catalytic converter (or catalyst) is an emission control device in the exhaust system that reduces certain pollutants in the exhaust gas stream. There are two types of converters: oxidation converters and reduction converters.

2   Oxidation converters contain a "monolithic substrate" (a ceramic honeycomb) coated with the semi-precious metals platinum and palladium. An oxidation catalyst reduces unburned hydrocarbons (HC) and carbon monoxide (CO) by adding oxygen to the exhaust stream as it passes through the substrate, which in the presence of high temperature and the catalyst materials converts the HC and CO to water vapor (H_2O) and carbon dioxide (CO_2).

3   Reduction converters contain a monolithic substrate coated with platinum and rhodium. A reduction catalyst reduces oxides of nitrogen (NOx) by removing oxygen, which in the presence of high temperature and the catalyst material produces nitrogen (N) and carbon dioxide (CO_2).

4   Catalytic converters that combine both types of catalysts in one assembly are known as "three-way catalysts" or TWCs. A TWC can reduce *all three pollutants*. All models covered by this manual are equipped with three-way catalysts.

5   There are three catalytic converters: one "upstream" catalyst for each exhaust manifold and a third "downstream" catalyst located in the exhaust pipe behind the junction of the outlet pipes of the upstream catalysts. None of these three catalysts are serviceable separately. If one catalyst is defective, you must replace the converters as a single assembly.

Check

6   The test equipment for a catalytic converter (a "loaded-mode" dynamometer and a 5-gas analyzer) is expensive. If you suspect that the converter on your vehicle is malfunctioning, take it to a dealer or authorized emission inspection facility for diagnosis and repair.

7   Whenever you raise the vehicle to service underbody components, inspect the

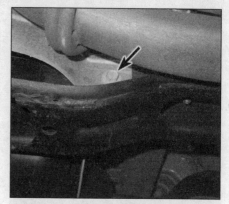

19.13b . . . and the right heat shield-to-crossmember bolt (V6 model shown, V8 models similar)

converter assembly for leaks, corrosion, dents and other damage. Carefully inspect the welds and/or flange bolts and nuts that attach the front and rear ends of the converter to the exhaust system. If you note any damage, replace the converter.

8   Although catalytic converters don't break too often, they can become clogged or even plugged up. The easiest way to check for a restricted converter is to use a vacuum gauge to diagnose the effect of a blocked exhaust on intake vacuum.

  a) *Connect a vacuum gauge to an intake manifold vacuum source (see Chapter 2).*
  b) *Warm the engine to operating temperature, place the transaxle in Park (automatic models) or Neutral (manual models) and apply the parking brake.*
  c) *Note the vacuum reading at idle and jot it down.*
  d) *Quickly open the throttle to near its wide-open position and then quickly get off the throttle and allow it to close. Note the vacuum reading and jot it down.*
  e) *Do this test three more times, recording your measurement after each test.*
  f) *If your fourth reading is more than one in-Hg lower than the reading that you noted at idle, the exhaust system might be restricted (the catalytic converter could be plugged, OR an exhaust pipe or muffler could be restricted).*

Replacement

Refer to illustrations 19.13a, 19.13b, 19.14, 19.15, 19.16, 19.17a, 19.17b, 19.18, 19.19, 19.20, 19.21a and 19.21b

9   Disconnect the cable from the negative battery terminal.

10   Raise the vehicle and place it securely on jackstands.

11   Disconnect the electrical connectors for the left and right upstream oxygen sensors **(see illustrations 14.1a and 14.4).**

12   Disconnect the electrical connectors for the left and right downstream oxygen sensors **(see illustrations 14.8a and 14.8b).**

13   Remove the left and right heat shield-to-crossmember bolts **(see illustrations).**

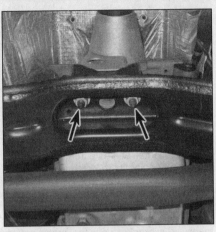

19.14 Remove the two nuts that attach the rear transmission mount to the crossmember (V6 model shown, V8 models similar)

19.15 Support the transmission with a jack; carefully position the jack head under the transmission oil pan rails (the edges) and NOT in the center of the pan, which will damage the valve body

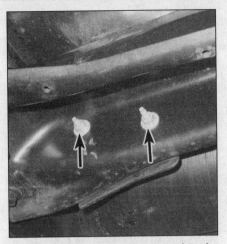

19.16 Remove these two nuts to detach the fuel tank heat shield

14   Remove the two nuts that attach the rear transmission mount to the crossmember (see illustration).

15   Support the transmission with a transmission jack or floor jack (see illustration).

16   Remove the two nuts that attach the fuel tank heat shield to the crossmember (see illustration).

17   Remove the four upper and four lower crossmember bolts (see illustrations) and remove the crossmember.

18   Remove the bolts, springs and flag nuts from the flange in front of the muffler (see illustration).

19   Using a jackstand, support the converter assembly (see illustration).

20   Unbolt the converter assembly isolator bracket from the rear transmission mount (see illustration).

21   Disconnect the converter assembly from the exhaust manifold flanges (see illustrations).

22   Carefully remove the converter assembly.

19.17a Remove the two upper left bolts (shown) and the two upper right bolts from the crossmember . . .

19.17b . . . then remove the two lower left bolts (shown) and the two lower right bolts from the crossmember and remove the crossmember

19.18 To disconnect the converter assembly from the muffler, remove these two flange bolts, springs and flag nuts (V6 model shown, V8 models similar)

19.19 Support the converter assembly with a jackstand (V6 model shown, V8 models similar)

19.20 To detach the converter assembly isolator bracket from the rear transmission mount, remove this bolt (V6 model shown, V8 models similar)

6

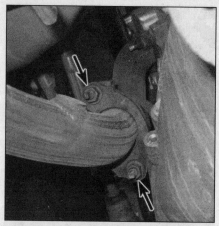

19.21a To disconnect the converter assembly from the left exhaust manifold, remove these two nuts and bolts (V6 model shown, V8 models similar)

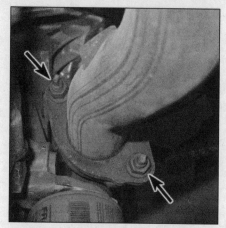

19.21b To disconnect the converter assembly from the right exhaust manifold, remove these two nuts and bolts (V6 model shown, V8 models similar)

23 Before installing the converter assembly, inspect all fasteners for damage. If any fasteners are rusty or if the threads are damaged, replace those fasteners. It's also a good idea to coat the fasteners used to mount the converter assembly with anti-seize compound to facilitate their removal next time.

24 Installation is otherwise the reverse of removal. Be sure to tighten all fasteners securely.

20 Evaporative Emissions Control (EVAP) system - general information and component replacement

General description

1 The Evaporative Emissions Control (EVAP) system prevents fuel system vapors (which contain unburned hydrocarbons) from escaping into the atmosphere. On warm days, vapors trapped inside the fuel tank expand until the pressure reaches a certain threshold. Then the fuel vapors are routed from the fuel tank through the fuel vapor vent valve and the fuel vapor control valve to the EVAP canister, where they're stored temporarily until the next time the vehicle is operated. When the conditions are right (engine warmed up, vehicle up to speed, moderate or heavy load on the engine, etc.) the Powertrain Control Module (PCM) opens the canister purge valve, which allows the fuel vapors to be drawn from the canister into the intake manifold, from which they're drawn into the engine with the air/fuel mixture. This system is complex and virtually impossible to troubleshoot without the right tools and training. However, the following description should give you a good idea of how it works:

2 The **EVAP canisters** are located under the vehicle, on top of the fuel tank. Each EVAP canister, which contains activated charcoal, is a repository for storing fuel vapors. You'll have to raise the vehicle to inspect or replace the canisters, or any other part of the EVAP system, except for the canister purge valve (which is located in the engine compartment). But the canisters are designed to be maintenance-free and should last the life of the vehicle. There are several other important components located on top of the fuel tank: the fuel tank pressure sensor and the fuel vapor vent valve (an integral part of the fuel tank on 2002 models, a separate component located behind the fuel tank on 2003 models). A couple of other components are located right behind the fuel tank: the dust separator and, on 2003 models, the fuel vapor vent valve.

3 The **fuel tank pressure sensor**, which is located near the in-tank fuel pump/fuel level sending unit module on top of the fuel tank, monitors the pressure inside the tank, and transmits its measurement to the PCM during an OBD-II leak test. It also forces the EVAP system to purge when the fuel tank pressure becomes too high.

4 The **Fuel Vapor Vent (FVV) valve** controls the flow of fuel vapors entering the EVAP system, prevents the fuel tank from overfilling during refueling and prevents liquid fuel from entering the vapor delivery system if the vehicle rolls over. The FVV valve is mounted on top of the fuel tank and is an integral component of the tank. It cannot be removed or repaired. If the FVV valve is defective, you must replace the fuel tank.

5 The **canister vent solenoid** is mounted behind the fuel tank, inline between the dust separator and the rear EVAP canister. The canister vent solenoid is normally open, but it seals off the EVAP system for inspection and maintenance (I/M 240) testing and for OBD-II leak and pressure tests.

6 The **fuel filler pipe check valve** is an integral component of either the fuel tank or the filler neck pipe. It prevents liquid fuel from escaping from the fuel tank into the fuel filler neck pipe during refueling or in the event of a vehicle rollover. The fuel filler pipe check valve is not serviceable separately. Depending on its location on your vehicle, you will have to replace either the fuel filler neck pipe or the fuel tank.

7 The **evaporative emission (EVAP) canister purge valve**, which is under the control of the Powertrain Control Module (PCM), regulates the flow of vapors being purged from the EVAP canister into the intake manifold. The canister purge valve is normally closed. It opens only when directed to do so by the PCM, which uses the availability of intake manifold vacuum and data from various information sensor inputs to determine when and how long to open the valve. The interval of time during which the purge valve is opened by the PCM is known as its "duty cycle." The purge valve is located in the engine compartment, on a bracket near the brake master cylinder.

8 The **evaporative emission (EVAP) dust separator**, which is located behind the canister vent solenoid, prevents dust and dirt particles suspended in the atmosphere from entering the EVAP system.

General system checks

9 The most common symptom of a faulty EVAP system is a strong fuel odor (particularly during hot weather). If you smell fuel while driving or (more likely) right after you park the vehicle and turn off the engine, check the fuel filler cap first. Make sure that it's screwed onto the fuel filler neck all the way. If the odor persists, inspect all EVAP hose connections, both in the engine compartment and under the vehicle. You'll have to raise the vehicle and place it securely on jackstands to inspect most of the EVAP system, since it's located under the vehicle. Be sure to inspect each hose attached to the canister for damage and leakage along its entire length. Repair or replace as necessary. Inspect the canister for damage and look for fuel leaking from the bottom. If fuel is leaking or the canister is otherwise damaged, replace it.

10 Poor idle, stalling, and poor driveability can be caused by a defective fuel vapor vent valve or canister purge valve, a damaged canister, cracked hoses, or hoses connected to the wrong tubes. Fuel loss or fuel odor can be caused by fuel leaking from fuel lines or hoses, a cracked or damaged canister, or a defective vapor valve.

11 To check for excessive fuel vapor pressure in the fuel tank, remove the gas cap and listen for the sound of pressure release. If the fuel tank emits a "whooshing" sound when you open the filler cap, fuel tank vapor pressure is excessive. Inspect the canister vapor hoses and the canister inlet port for blockage or collapsed hoses. Also inspect the vapor vent valve. A complete test can only be done with a proprietary OBD-II scan tool (see Section 2), which will run a series of checks using the fuel tank pressure sensor and other output actuators to detect excessive pressure. You'll have to take the vehicle to a dealer service department or other qualified repair shop to have the EVAP system professionally diagnosed.

20.15a To detach the front EVAP canister from the fuel tank, disconnect these two vapor hoses and remove the retaining nut

20.15b To detach the rear EVAP canister from the fuel tank, disconnect these two vapor hoses and remove the retaining nut

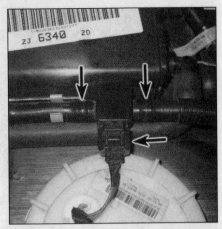

20.20 To detach the fuel tank pressure sensor from the fuel tank, disconnect the electrical connector and these two vapor hoses

Component replacement

EVAP canisters

Refer to illustrations 20.15a and 20.15b

12   Disconnect the cable from the negative battery terminal (see Chapter 5).
13   Raise the vehicle and place it securely on jackstands.
14   Remove the fuel tank (see Chapter 4).
15   Disconnect the vapor hoses from the canister and remove the canister retaining nut **(see illustrations)**, then remove the canister.
16   Installation is the reverse of removal.

Fuel tank pressure sensor

Refer to illustration 20.20

17   Disconnect the cable from the negative battery terminal (see Chapter 5).
18   Raise the vehicle and place it securely on jackstands.
19   Remove the fuel tank (see Chapter 4).
20   Disconnect the electrical connector from the fuel tank pressure sensor and disconnect the vapor hoses from the sensor **(see illustration)**. Remove the fuel tank pres-

sure sensor.
21   Installation is the reverse of removal.

EVAP canister vent solenoid

Refer to illustrations 20.24 and 20.26

22   Disconnect the cable from the negative battery terminal (see Chapter 5).
23   Raise the vehicle and place it securely on jackstands.
24   Locate the EVAP canister vent solenoid **(see illustration)** behind the fuel tank.
25   Disconnect the electrical connector and the two vapor hoses from the EVAP canister vent solenoid **(see illustration 20.24)**.
26   Using a small screwdriver, pry the EVAP canister vent solenoid from its mounting receptacle **(see illustration)** and remove the solenoid.
27   Installation is the reverse of removal.

Dust separator

Refer to illustration 20.30

28   Disconnect the cable from the negative battery terminal (see Chapter 5).
29   Raise the vehicle and place it securely on jackstands.
30   Locate the dust separator **(see illustration)** behind the EVAP canister vent solenoid.

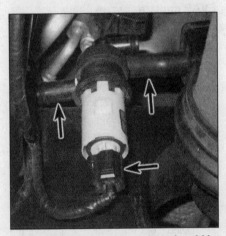

20.24 The EVAP canister vent solenoid is located behind the fuel tank; to remove it, disconnect the electrical connector and disconnect these two vapor hoses

31   Disconnect the vapor hoses from the dust separator, remove the separator retaining bolt **(see illustration 20.30)** and remove the separator.
32   Installation is the reverse of removal.

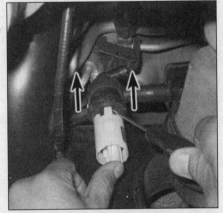

20.26 To remove the EVAP canister vent solenoid from its mounting receptacle, pry it loose from the receptacle with a small screwdriver

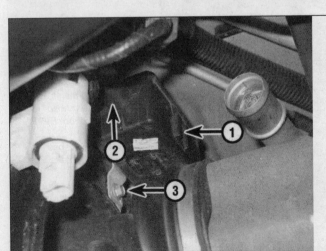

20.30 EVAP system dust separator removal details

1   *Dust separator*
2   *Vapor hose (other hose, which is connected to back end of separator, not visible)*
3   *Dust separator mounting bracket bolt*

6

20.33 The EVAP canister purge valve is located in the engine compartment, near the brake master cylinder; before removing it, disconnect the electrical connector

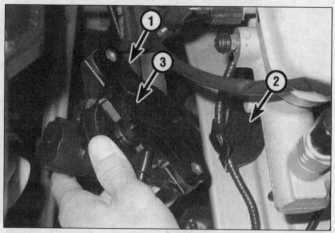

20.36 To detach the EVAP canister purge valve mounting plate (1) from its mounting bracket (2), push on the locking tab (3) and lift the EVAP canister purge valve assembly straight up

EVAP canister purge valve

Refer to illustrations 20.33, 20.36 and 20.37

33   The EVAP canister purge valve **(see illustration)** is located in the engine compartment, near the brake master cylinder.

34   Disconnect the cable from the negative battery terminal.

35   Disconnect the electrical connector from the EVAP canister purge valve **(see illustration 20.33)**.

36   The EVAP canister purge valve is attached to a mounting plate by a pair of nuts. The easiest way to disconnect everything from the purge valve is to remove the canister mounting plate from its mounting bracket **(see illustration)**, which is attached to the left inner fender.

37   Disconnect the vacuum hose from the EVAP canister purge valve **(see illustration)**.

38   Disconnect the two vapor hoses from the EVAP canister purge valve **(see illustration 20.37)**.

39   Separate the EVAP canister purge valve from its mounting plate **(see illustration 20.37)**.

40   Installation is the reverse of removal.

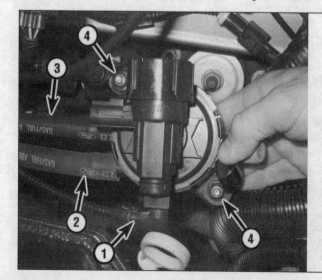

21   Exhaust Gas Recirculation (EGR) system - general information and component replacement

General description

1   Exhaust Gas Recirculation (EGR) systems on late-model vehicles have two equally important functions: they reduce oxides of nitrogen (NOx) emissions and they reduce engine detonation, or pinging. Recirculating a small amount of exhaust back to the intake system reduces combustion temperatures because exhaust is a mixture of inert gases and does not contribute to the combustion process. Because high combustion temperature is a major factor in both NOx emissions and detonation, EGR effectively reduces both.

2   When the combustion chambers reach about 2500-degrees F, they begin to produce excessive quantities of oxides of nitrogen (NOx). NOx, when combined with unburned hydrocarbons (HC), other volatile organic compounds and sunlight, forms ozone, nitrogen dioxide and nitrogen nitrate, otherwise

20.37 EVAP canister purge valve removal details

1   Vacuum hose (goes to intake manifold)

2   Fuel vapor hose (coming from EVAP canisters)

3   Fuel vapor hose (going to intake manifold)

4   Purge valve mounting nuts

known as photochemical smog. The Exhaust Gas Recirculation (EGR) system reduces (NOx) by recirculating exhaust gases from the exhaust ports through the EGR valve and back into the intake manifold, from which they're recycled back through the combustion chambers, which lowers the temperature during the combustion process.

3   The EGR system on the vehicles covered by this manual is known as a "differential pressure feedback" EGR system. The differential pressure feedback system consists of the pipe connecting the exhaust manifold to the EGR valve, the EGR valve itself, the differential pressure feedback EGR system sensor and the EGR vacuum regulator valve (or solenoid). The system is controlled by the Powertrain Control Module (PCM), which uses the Crankshaft Position (CKP) sensor, the Engine Coolant Temperature (ECT) sensor, the Intake Air Temperature (IAT) sensor, the Mass Air Flow (MAF) sensor and the Throttle Position (TP) sensor to determine when and how much EGR gas to recirculate. Before the PCM will activate the EGR system, the engine must be fully warmed up, stable and operating under a moderate load and rpm. The PCM will deactivate the EGR when the engine is at idle, during extended wide-open-throttle conditions and whenever it detects a malfunction in the EGR system or in one of its monitored components or circuits.

4   Here's how the differential pressure feedback EGR system works: The PCM determines the correct amount of EGR flow for the conditions, then it calculates the appropriate pressure drop across the metering orifice, inside the differential pressure feedback sensor, that's needed to achieve that flow rate, and then it sends a voltage signal to the EGR vacuum regulator solenoid. This signal is known as the "duty cycle." The EGR vacuum regulator solenoid receives a variable duty cycle signal that can be anywhere from 0 percent to 100 percent. The higher the duty cycle percentage, the stronger the vacuum signal diverted by the vacuum regulator solenoid to the EGR valve.

21.9 The Exhaust Gas Recirculation (EGR) valve (1) is located at the right rear corner of the intake manifold, near the firewall (V6 model shown, V8 models similar); before unbolting the EGR valve, disconnect the vacuum line (2)

21.12 Unscrew the EGR pipe fitting (1) from the EGR valve, then remove the two EGR valve mounting bolts (2) (right bolt shown, left bolt not visible)

5   Inside the EGR valve, a spring-loaded diaphragm in a vacuum chamber is connected to a pintle valve by a rod. Normally, the pintle valve is kept closed by spring pressure pushing down against the diaphragm. When the vacuum signal from the vacuum regulator solenoid becomes strong enough to overcome the pressure of the spring, the diaphragm begins to lift upward, which pulls up the rod and lifts the pintle valve off its seat, allowing exhaust gases to flow through the EGR valve and be recirculated back into the intake manifold.

6   The exhaust gases flowing through the EGR valve must first pass through the EGR metering orifice. One side of the orifice is connected to exhaust backpressure and the other side leads to the intake manifold. Whenever there is EGR flow, it creates a pressure drop across the orifice. When the EGR valve closes, EGR flow through the orifice ceases, and the pressure on both sides of the orifice is equal. The PCM tries to maintain a pressure drop across the orifice that's appropriate to the operating conditions. The differential pressure feedback sensor measures the actual pressure drop across the metering orifice and sends a voltage signal (between 0 and 5 volts) to the PCM that's proportional to the measured pressure drop. This feedback signal from the differential pressure feedback sensor is used by the PCM to make constant corrections to the EGR flow rate.

7   Typically, EGR systems are trouble-free. If the EGR valve ever fails, it will do so while it's either closed or open. If the EGR valve is closed when it fails the EGR system will no longer work, but there will be no obvious symptom, other than the fact that the engine might detonate (or "ping"), or run a little hotter, under a load on a hot day (acceleration, passing, going up a hill or pulling a trailer). And when your vehicle is subjected to a biennial "loaded-mode" (dynamometer-type) smog test, the EGR system will fail. If the

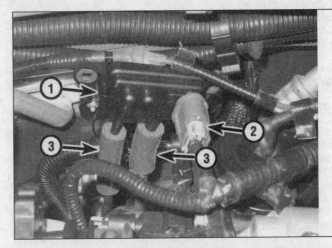

21.16 Differential pressure feedback EGR system sensor removal details

1   Differential pressure feedback EGR system sensor
2   Electrical connector
3   Rubber hoses

EGR valve is open when it fails, the symptom will be obvious. Exhaust gases metered into the combustion chambers during idle will cause the engine to run roughly and might even cause it to run so roughly that it stalls.

Component replacement

V6 models

EGR valve

Refer to illustrations 21.9 and 21.12

8   Remove the throttle body cover (**see illustration 15.3**).

9   The EGR valve (**see illustration**) is located at the right rear corner of the intake manifold.

10   Detach the cruise control cable from the air intake duct and set the cable aside.

11   Disconnect the vacuum line from the EGR valve (**see illustration 21.9**).

12   Unscrew the EGR pipe fitting from the EGR valve (**see illustration**).

13   Remove the two EGR valve mounting bolts (**see illustration 21.12**).

14   Installation is the reverse of removal. Be sure to tighten the EGR valve mounting bolts to the torque listed in this Chapter's Specifications.

Differential pressure feedback EGR system sensor

Refer to illustrations 21.16

15   Remove the throttle body cover (**see illustration 15.3**).

16   The differential pressure feedback EGR system sensor (**see illustration**) is located to the right of the EGR valve.

17   Disconnect the cable from the negative battery cable.

18   Disconnect the electrical connector from the differential pressure feedback EGR system sensor (**see illustration 21.16**).

19   The differential pressure feedback EGR system sensor is connected to the two metal pipes that connect it to the EGR pipe by a pair of rubber hoses (**see illustration 21.16**). To disconnect the two rubber hoses from the metal pipes, simply pull them straight up.

20   Disconnect the two rubber hoses from the differential pressure feedback EGR system sensor.

21   Before installing the differential pressure feedback EGR system sensor, carefully inspect the condition of the two rubber hoses. If the hoses are damaged or worn, replace them.

22   Installation is the reverse of removal.

6

Exhaust manifold-to-EGR valve pipe

Refer to illustrations 21.27

23   Remove the throttle body cover **(see illustration 15.3)**.

24   The exhaust manifold-to-EGR pipe connects the right exhaust manifold to the EGR valve.

25   Remove the differential pressure feedback EGR system sensor (see Steps 16 through 19).

26   Disconnect the exhaust manifold-to-EGR valve pipe from the EGR valve **(see illustration 21.12)**.

27   Disconnect the exhaust manifold-to-EGR valve pipe from the exhaust manifold **(see illustration)**.

28   Installation is the reverse of removal.

EGR vacuum regulator valve

Refer to illustrations 21.30, 21.33 and 21.34

29   Remove the throttle body cover **(see illustration 15.3)**.

30   The EGR vacuum regulator valve **(see illustration)** is located behind the intake manifold, near the other EGR components.

31   Disconnect the cable from the negative battery cable (see Chapter 5).

32   Disconnect the electrical connector from the EGR vacuum regulator valve **(see illustration 21.30)**.

33   Disconnect the vacuum hoses from the EGR vacuum regulator valve **(see illustration)**.

34   Remove the EGR vacuum regulator valve mounting nut or bolt **(see illustration)**.

35   Installation is the reverse of removal.

V8 models

EGR valve

36   Remove the engine cover (see Chapter 2B).

37   The EGR valve is located on the left side of the intake manifold.

38   Remove the retaining bolt that secures the brake booster vacuum hose clip and set the vacuum hose and line aside.

39   Disconnect the vacuum line from the

21.27 To disconnect the exhaust manifold-to-EGR valve pipe from the exhaust manifold, unscrew this fitting

EGR valve.

40   Disconnect the EGR pipe fitting at the EGR valve.

41   Remove the EGR mounting bolts and remove the EGR valve.

42   Remove and discard the EGR valve gasket.

43   Installation is the reverse of removal. Be sure to use a new gasket and tighten the EGR mounting bolts to the torque listed in this Chapter's Specifications.

Differential pressure feedback EGR system sensor (2002 models)

44   Disconnect the cable from the negative battery terminal (see Chapter 5).

45   Remove the engine cover (see Chapter 2B).

46   Disconnect the electrical connector from the differential pressure feedback EGR system sensor.

47   Disconnect the feedback EGR system sensor and the two rubber hoses from the EGR pipe.

48   Installation is the reverse of removal.

21.30 The EGR vacuum regulator valve (1) is located behind the intake manifold, near the other EGR components; before removing the vacuum regulator valve, disconnect the electrical connector (2)

Exhaust manifold-to-EGR valve pipe

49   Remove the engine cover (see Chapter 2B).

50   Remove the accelerator return spring, then detach the accelerator cable and the cruise control cable from their cable bracket.

51   Remove the two engine cover bracket bolts and remove the engine cover bracket.

52   Remove the differential pressure feedback sensor from the EGR pipe (see Steps 44 through 47).

53   Remove the brake booster vacuum hose retaining bolt and detach the vacuum hose and line and set them aside.

54   Disconnect the vacuum line from the EGR valve.

55   Disconnect the EGR pipe fitting at the EGR valve.

56   Disconnect the EGR pipe fitting at the exhaust manifold.

57   Installation is the reverse of removal.

EGR vacuum regulator valve

58   Remove the air filter housing (see Chapter 4).

21.33 Disconnect the vacuum hoses from the EGR vacuum regulator valve

21.34 Remove the EGR vacuum regulator valve mounting nut or bolt (earlier models use a nut, later models use a bolt), then pivot the regulator valve out and disengage it from the mounting tab on the right (intake manifold assembly removed for clarity)

22.2a On V6 models, the fresh-air inlet hose connects the air intake duct to the right valve cover

22.2b On V6 models, the PCV hose connects the left valve cover to the intake manifold (the PCV valve is located at the rear end of the valve cover, which is not visible in this photo but is accessible)

59 Disconnect the electrical connector from the EGR vacuum regulator valve.

60 Disconnect the vacuum hoses from the EGR vacuum regulator valve

61 Detach the EGR vacuum regulator valve mounting nuts.

62 Installation is the reverse of removal.

22 Positive Crankcase Ventilation (PCV) system

General description

Refer to illustrations 22.2a and 22.2b

Note: *For information on checking and replacing the PCV valve, refer to Chapter 1.*

1 The Positive Crankcase Ventilation (PCV) system reduces hydrocarbon emissions by scavenging crankcase vapors. It does this by circulating fresh air from the air cleaner through the crankcase, where it mixes with blow-by gases and is then rerouted through a PCV valve to the intake manifold. The PCV system uses intake manifold vacuum to draw crankcase vapors from the crankcase into the intake manifold. The PCV valve varies the amount of blow-by gases that can be returned to the intake manifold in proportion to the amount of intake manifold vacuum available, but in the event of a backfire it prevents the entry of combustion gases into the manifold. To maintain idle quality, the PCV valve restricts the flow when intake manifold vacuum is high.

2 The PCV system consists of a fresh-air inlet hose between the air intake duct and the crankcase, the PCV valve itself and the PCV hose (also referred to as the crankcase ventilation hose), which connects the PCV valve to the intake manifold. On V6 models, the fresh-air inlet hose connects the air intake duct to the right valve cover **(see illustration)** and the PCV hose connects the PCV valve, which is screwed into the rear end of the left valve cover, to the left rear corner of the intake manifold **(see illustration)**. On V8 models, the fresh-air inlet hose connects the air intake duct to the left valve cover and the PCV hose connects the right valve cover to the intake manifold.

3 Inspect the fresh-air inlet hose and the PCV valve hose (crankcase ventilation hose) for cracks, leaks and other damage. Disconnect the hose from the crankcase vent oil separator and the intake manifold and check the inside for obstructions. If a hose is clogged, replace it. If the PCV valve is clogged or otherwise not working properly, replace it, do not try to clean it.

6

Notes

Chapter 7 Part A
Manual transmission

Contents

Specifications

General

Transmission oil type	See Chapter 1
Transmission oil capacity	See Chapter 1

Torque specifications

	Ft-lbs	Nm
Transfer case flange nut	262	355
Crossmember mounting bolts	46	63
Transmission mount-to-crossmember	72	98
Transmission-to-mount bolts	72	98
Transmission-to-engine mounting bolts	44	60

1 General information

The vehicles covered by this manual are equipped with either a 5-speed manual or a 5-speed automatic transmission. This Part of Chapter 7 contains information on the manual transmission. Service procedures for the automatic transmission are contained in Part B. Information on the transfer case used on 4WD models can be found in Part C.

The transmission is contained in a cast-aluminum alloy casing bolted to the engine and consists of the gearbox and final drive differential - often called a transmission. The transmission unit type is stamped on a plate attached to the transmission.

Transmission overhaul

Because of the complexity of the assembly, possible unavailability of replacement parts and special tools necessary, internal repair procedures for the transmission are not recommended for the home mechanic. The bulk of the information in this Chapter is devoted to removal and replacement procedures.

2 Shift lever - removal and installation

Warning 1: *The models covered by this manual are equipped with Supplemental Restraint systems (SRS), more commonly known as airbags. Always disable the airbag system before working in the vicinity of any airbag system component to avoid the possibility of accidental deployment of the airbag, which could cause personal injury (see Chapter 12).*
Warning 2: *Do not use a memory saving device to preserve the PCM or radio memory*

when working on or near airbag system components.

1   Disconnect the cable from the negative battery terminal (see Chapter 5).
2   Remove the center console trim panel mounting screw and carefully lift the assembly approximately 2 inches.
3   Working on the left side of the center console trim panel, remove the gearshift lever mounting nut.
4   Install the nut on the front side of the gearshift lever. Tighten the nut until the eccentric stud is forced out of the gearshift lever.
5   Remove the shift lever, the dust boot, gearshift knob and console as a complete assembly.
6   Remove the nut and through-bolt securing the shift linkage rod to the shift lever.
7   Installation is the reverse of removal.

3   Extension housing oil seal - replacement

1   Oil leaks frequently occur due to wear of the extension housing seal. Replacement of this seal is relatively easy, since the repair can usually be performed without removing the transmission (2WD models) or transfer case (4WD models) from the vehicle.
2   If you suspect a leak at the extension housing seal, raise the vehicle and support it securely on jackstands. The extension housing seal is located at the rear end of the transmission, where the driveshaft is attached. If the extension housing seal is leaking, transmission lubricant will be evident on the front of the driveshaft and may be dripping from the rear of the transmission.

2WD models

Refer to illustration 3.7
3   Remove the driveshaft (see Chapter 8).
4   Using a screwdriver, prybar or seal removal tool, carefully pry out the seal. **Note:** *It may be necessary to use a special tool to remove the extension housing oil seal. These special pullers can be purchased at an automotive tool supplier.*
5   Inspect the extension housing bore for burrs. If found, remove them with emery cloth or medium grit wet-and-dry sandpaper. Use a clean cloth dipped in solvent and remove any oil or sanding residue from the bore.
6   Apply a small amount of silicone sealant to the outside diameter of the oil seal and apply multi-purpose grease to the seal lip.
7   Using a seal driver, large socket or section of pipe, install the new oil seal. Drive it into the bore squarely and make sure it's completely seated **(see illustration)**.
8   Connect the driveshaft (see Chapter 8).
9   The remainder of installation is the reverse of removal.

4WD models

10   Remove the driveshaft (see Chapter 8).
11   Using paint, index mark the rear output

3.7 Use a large socket to drive the seal into the extension housing

flange to the output shaft to insure the bolt is tightened to the original position on reassembly.
12   Remove the flange lock nut using a chain wrench to hold the flange.
13   Remove the transfer case flange; a small puller may be required for removal.
14   Using a screwdriver, prybar or seal removal tool, carefully pry out the seal. **Note:** *It may be necessary to use a special tool to remove the extension housing oil seal. These special pullers can be purchased at an automotive tool supplier.*
15   Inspect the extension housing bore for burrs. If found, remove them with emery cloth or medium grit wet-and-dry sandpaper. Use a clean cloth dipped in solvent and remove any oil or sanding residue from the bore.
16   Apply a small amount of silicone sealant to the outside diameter of the oil seal and apply multi-purpose grease to the seal lip.
17   Using a seal driver, large socket or section of pipe, install the new oil seal. Drive it into the bore squarely and make sure it's completely seated **(see illustration 3.7)**.
18   Install the flange and locknut. Tighten the locknut to the torque listed in this Chapter's Specifications.
19   Connect the driveshaft (see Chapter 8).
20   The remainder of installation is the reverse of removal.

4   Transmission mount - check and replacement

1   Insert a large screwdriver or prybar into the space between the transmission extension housing and the frame crossmember and pry up.
2   The transmission should not move significantly away from the mount. If the mount does, the mount should be replaced.
3   Place a jack under the transmission with a wood block on top of it to protect the transmission case. Apply a slight amount of jack pressure to support the weight of the transmission.

4   Remove the two nuts securing the mount to the frame crossmember and the two bolts securing the mount to the transmission extension housing.
5   Raise the transmission with the jack until the studs on the bottom of the transmission mount clear the crossmember. Remove the mount and install a new one.
6   Installation is the reverse of the removal.

5   Manual transmission - removal and installation

Removal

1   Disconnect the cable from the negative terminal of the battery (see Chapter 5).
2   Remove the radiator protective cover, the cooling fan and upper and lower fan shrouds (see Chapter 3).
3   Remove upper center console finish panel and the shift lever (see Section 2).
4   Raise the front of the vehicle and support it securely on jackstands.
5   Drain the transmission lubricant (see Chapter 1).
6   Remove the front chassis support (the crossmember-like structure under the forward part of the transmission).
7   Remove the starter (see Chapter 5).
8   Remove the driveshaft(s) (see Chapter 8).
9   On 4WD models, remove the transfer case (see Chapter 7C).
10   Disconnect the electrical connectors for the transmission range sensor and the heated oxygen sensors (see Chapter 6). Disconnect any remaining electrical connectors from the transmission. Mark each connector with tape to insure correct reassembly.
11   Disconnect the clutch hydraulic line from the transmission (see Chapter 8).
12   Place a transmission jack under the transmission and secure the transmission to the jack with safety chains or straps.
13   Remove the catalytic converters and crossmember (see Chapter 6).
14   Remove the transmission-to-engine bolts.

15 Make a final check that all wires have been disconnected from the transmission, then move the transmission and jack toward the rear of the vehicle until the bellhousing is separated from the engine and the input shaft clears the clutch assembly.

Installation

16 Lubricate the input shaft with a light coat of high-temperature grease. With the transmission secured to the jack, raise it into position behind the engine and carefully slide it forward, engaging the input shaft with the clutch. Do not use excessive force to install the transmission - if the input shaft won't slide into place, readjust the angle of the transmission or turn the input shaft so the splines engage properly with the clutch.

17 Once the transmission is flush with the engine, install the transmission-to-engine bolts. Tighten the bolts to the torque listed in this Chapter's Specifications. **Caution:** *Don't use the bolts to force the transmission and engine together.*

18 Install the catalytic converters and crossmember (see Chapter 6).

19 Install the front support and tighten the bolts securely.

20 Remove the jacks supporting the transmission and the engine.

21 Attach the clutch hydraulic line, then bleed the clutch hydraulic system (see Chapter 8).

22 Attach the shift lever to the transmission and reinstall the console (see Section 2).

23 Install the starter motor (see Chapter 5).

24 Install the transfer case (see Chapter 7C).

25 Install the driveshaft(s) (see Chapter 8).

26 Plug in the electrical connectors for the transmission.

27 Attach the negative battery cable.

28 Refill the transmission with the proper lubricant (see Chapter 1), drive the vehicle and check for leaks.

6 Manual transmission overhaul - general information

1 Overhauling a manual transmission is a difficult job for the do-it-yourselfer. It involves the disassembly and reassembly of many small parts. Numerous clearances must be precisely measured and, if necessary, changed with select-fit spacers and snap-rings. As a result, if transmission problems arise, it can be removed and installed by a competent do-it-yourselfer, but overhaul should be left to a transmission repair shop.

Rebuilt transmissions may be available - check with your dealer parts department and auto parts stores. At any rate, the time and money involved in an overhaul is almost sure to exceed the cost of a rebuilt unit.

2 Nevertheless, it's not impossible for an inexperienced mechanic to rebuild a transmission if the special tools are available and the job is done in a deliberate step-by-step manner so nothing is overlooked.

3 The tools necessary for an overhaul include internal and external snap-ring pliers, a bearing puller, a slide hammer, a set of pin punches, a dial indicator and possibly a hydraulic press. In addition, a large, sturdy workbench and a vise or transmission stand will be required.

4 During disassembly of the transmission, make careful notes of how each piece comes off, where it fits in relation to other pieces and what holds it in place.

5 Before taking the transmission apart for repair, it will help if you have some idea what area of the transmission is malfunctioning. Certain problems can be closely tied to specific areas in the transmission, which can make component examination and replacement easier. Refer to the *Troubleshooting* section at the front of this manual for information regarding possible sources of trouble.

Notes

Chapter 7 Part B
Automatic transmission

Contents

Specifications

General

Fluid type and capacity .... See Chapter 1

Torque specifications

	Ft-lbs	Nm
Crossmember mounting bolts	52	70
Cable bracket mounting bolts	30	40
Transmission mount-to-crossmember	66	90
Transmission-to-mount bolts	66	90
Torque converter nuts	28	38
Transmission line fittings	22	30
Transmission-to-engine mounting bolts	35	48

1   General information

All information on the automatic transmission is included in this Part of Chapter 7. Information for the manual transmission can be found in Part A of this Chapter.

Because of the complexity of the automatic transmission and the specialized equipment necessary to perform most service operations, this Chapter contains only those procedures related to general diagnosis, routine maintenance, adjustment and removal and installation.

The transmission is designed for low maintenance; it isn't equipped with a dipstick and the first scheduled transmission service is at 150,000 miles. However, there is a transmission fluid level check and fill procedure in Chapter 1 in the event a fluid leak has been detected and it is necessary to check the fluid level.

If the transmission requires major repair work, it should be left to a dealer service department or a transmission repair shop. Once properly diagnosed you can, however, remove and install the transmission yourself and save the expense, even if the repair work is done by a transmission shop.

2   Diagnosis - general

1   Automatic transmission malfunctions may be caused by five general conditions:

- a) Poor engine performance
- b) Improper adjustments
- c) Hydraulic malfunctions
- d) Mechanical malfunctions
- e) Malfunctions in the computer or its signal network

2   Diagnosis of these problems should always begin with a check of the easily repaired items: fluid level and condition (see

Chapter 1), shift cable adjustment and shift lever installation. Next, perform a road test to determine if the problem has been corrected or if more diagnosis is necessary. If the problem persists after the preliminary tests and corrections are completed, additional diagnosis should be performed by a dealer service department or other qualified transmission repair shop.

3   Refer to the *Troubleshooting* section at the front of this manual for information on symptoms of transmission problems.

Preliminary checks

4   Check the fluid level as described in Chapter 1:

a) *If the fluid level is unusually low, add enough fluid to bring it within the correct level, then check for external leaks (see following).*

b) *If the fluid is foaming, drain it and refill the transmission, then check for a high fluid level.*

5   Check the engine idle speed. **Note:** *If the engine is malfunctioning, do not proceed with the preliminary checks until it has been repaired and runs normally.*

6   Check and adjust the shift cable, if necessary (see Section 4).

7   If hard shifting is experienced, inspect the shift cable under the steering column and at the manual lever on the transmission (see Section 4).

Fluid leak diagnosis

8   Most fluid leaks are easy to locate visually. Repair usually consists of replacing a seal or gasket. If a leak is difficult to find, the following procedure may help.

9   Identify the fluid. Make sure it's transmission fluid and not engine oil or brake fluid (automatic transmission fluid is a deep red color).

10   Try to pinpoint the source of the leak. Drive the vehicle several miles, then park it over a large sheet of cardboard. After a minute or two, you should be able to locate the leak by determining the source of the fluid dripping onto the cardboard.

11   Make a careful visual inspection of the suspected component and the area immediately around it. Pay particular attention to gasket mating surfaces. A mirror is often helpful for finding leaks in areas that are hard to see.

12   If the leak still cannot be found, clean the suspected area thoroughly with a degreaser or solvent, then dry it thoroughly.

13   Drive the vehicle for several miles at normal operating temperature and varying speeds. After driving the vehicle, visually inspect the suspected component again.

14   Once the leak has been located, the cause must be determined before it can be properly repaired. If a gasket is replaced but the sealing flange is bent, the new gasket will not stop the leak. The bent flange must be straightened.

15   Before attempting to repair a leak,

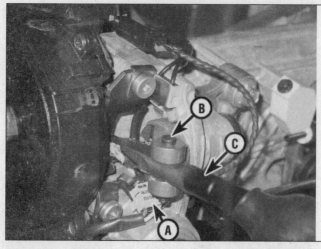

3.4 Disconnect the transmission control switch (A), drive out the gearshift lever pin (B) with a punch and remove the gear shift lever (C) from the steering column

check to make sure that the following conditions are corrected or they may cause another leak. **Note:** *Some of the following conditions cannot be fixed without highly specialized tools and expertise. Such problems must be referred to a qualified transmission shop or a dealer service department.*

Gasket leaks

16   Check the pan periodically. Make sure the bolts are tight, no bolts are missing, the gasket is in good condition and the pan is flat (dents in the pan may indicate damage to the valve body inside).

17   If the pan gasket is leaking, the fluid level or the fluid pressure may be too high, the vent may be plugged, the pan bolts may be too tight, the pan sealing flange may be warped, the sealing surface of the transmission housing may be damaged, the gasket may be damaged or the transmission casting may be cracked or porous. If sealant instead of gasket material has been used to form a seal between the pan and the transmission housing, it may be the wrong type of sealant.

Seal leaks

18   If a transmission seal is leaking, the fluid level or pressure may be too high, the vent may be plugged, the seal bore may be damaged, the seal itself may be damaged or improperly installed, the surface of the shaft protruding through the seal may be damaged or a loose bearing may be causing excessive shaft movement.

Case leaks

19   If the case itself appears to be leaking, the casting is porous and will have to be repaired or replaced.

20   Make sure the oil cooler hose fittings are tight and in good condition.

---

3   Shift lever - replacement

Refer to illustration 3.4

Warning 1: *The models covered by this manual are equipped with Supplemental Restraint systems (SRS), more commonly known as*

airbags. Always disable the airbag system before working in the vicinity of any airbag system component to avoid the possibility of accidental deployment of the airbag, which could cause personal injury (see Chapter 12).

Warning 2: *Do not use a memory saving device to preserve the PCM or radio memory when working on or near airbag system components.*

1   Disconnect the cable from the negative battery terminal (see Chapter 5).

2   Position the gearshift lever in the NEUTRAL position.

3   Remove the steering wheel/airbag module (see Chapter 10) and remove the steering column covers (see Chapter 11).

4   Disconnect the transmission control switch connector **(see illustration)**.

5   Drive out the gearshift lever pin using a punch. Be sure to discard the lever pin and use a new pin when reinstalling the lever.

6   Remove the gear shift lever from the steering column.

7   Installation is the reverse of removal.

---

4   Shift cable - replacement and adjustment

Warning 1: *The models covered by this manual are equipped with Supplemental Restraint systems (SRS), more commonly known as airbags. Always disable the airbag system before working in the vicinity of any airbag system component to avoid the possibility of accidental deployment of the airbag, which could cause personal injury (see Chapter 12).*

Warning 2: *Do not use a memory saving device to preserve the PCM or radio memory when working on or near airbag system components.*

Replacement

Refer to illustrations 4.4, 4.5, 4.9a and 4.9b

1   Disconnect the cable from the negative battery terminal (see Chapter 5).

2   Place the transmission in Neutral.

3   Remove the steering column covers (see Chapter 11).

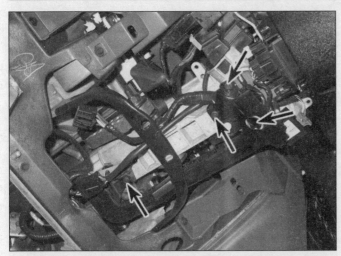

4.4 Remove the mounting screws for the wire shield and lower the shield from the steering column (arrows)

4.5 Disconnect the shift cable from the column by first releasing the pressure tabs on the column flange (A) and then removing the cable end from the lever pin (B) by carefully prying it off

4 Working under the steering column, remove the mounting screws and position the wire shield to the side (see illustration).

5 Disconnect the shift cable from the shift lever and steering column bracket (see illustration).

6 Disconnect the shift cable retainer from the bracket. Squeeze the two lock tabs and pull the retainer down.

7 Push the rubber grommet through the firewall.

8 Raise the vehicle and secure it on jackstands.

9 Working under the vehicle, disconnect the shift cable from the shift lever (see illustration) and transmission mounting bracket (see illustration), then remove the cable from the vehicle.

10 Installation is the reverse of removal.

11 Install the shift cable onto the shift lever ballstud on the transmission and lock it into place.

a) New shift cables are equipped with a

locking band that sets the lock tab in the UNLOCK position. Install the cable end onto the shift lever on the transmission and cut the band to allow the lock tab to release into the lock position.

b) If the original shift cable is to be installed, use a small screwdriver tip and lift the lock tab and push the lock tab out into the UNLOCK position. Install the cable end onto the shift lever on the transmission and push the lock tab into the cable housing to lock it into position.

12 Before installing the steering column shrouds and connecting the battery, be sure to adjust the cable as specified.

Adjustment

13 Rotate the gearshift lever clockwise until it stops (first gear) and rotate it counterclockwise three clicks into DRIVE, then have an assistant hold the lever firmly in position.

14 Raise the vehicle and support it securely on jackstands.

15 Disconnect the shift cable from the shift lever ballstud (see illustration 4.5).

16 Position the lock tab in the UNLOCK position (see Step 11).

17 Install the shift cable end onto the shift lever ballstud and push the lock tab down to the lock position.

18 Make sure the engine starts in PARK and NEUTRAL positions and the reverse lights activate when REVERSE is selected. If necessary, adjust the transmission range sensor (see Chapter 6).

19 Replace the steering column covers.

5 Shift indicator cable - replacement and adjustment

Refer to illustration 5.4

1 Remove the upper steering column covers (see Chapter 11).

2 Move the shift lever clockwise until it stops (all the way to the 1st gear position),

7B

4.9a Disconnect the shift cable from the shift lever using a flat-bladed screwdriver to release the lock and . . .

4.9b . . . release the transmission bracket retainer by prying the lock tab out of the recess with a screwdriver tip

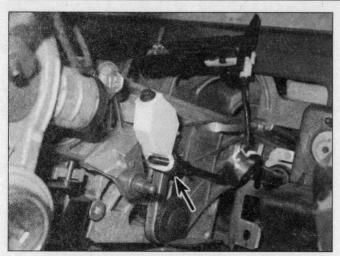

5.4 Rotate the thumbwheel to center the indicator needle in the drive position

6.2a Pry out the cover using a pick or small screwdriver . . .

then move it back three detent positions to the Drive position.

3   Hold the shift lever and apply slight pressure to hold it in place.

4   Rotate the thumbwheel on the bottom of the steering column to center the indicator needle in the drive position (see illustration).

5   Have an assistant move the shift lever through all gear positions and verify that the indicated positions correspond with the actual gear positions at the manual lever. If necessary, readjust the cable until these conditions are met.

6   Install the upper steering column cover.

6   Transmission control switch - check and replacement

Refer to illustrations 6.2a and 6.2b

1   The Transmission Control Switch located on the shift lever allows the driver to turn the Overdrive capability On or Off. In normal driving the Overdrive is always turned On.

2   Pry off the cover on the end of the shift lever (see illustration) and pull out the trans-

mission control switch (see illustration).

3   Make sure the ignition key is in the Off position. Position the leads of an ohmmeter on the exposed terminals at the bottom of the switch (it isn't necessary to remove the wires from the switch) and check for continuity when the switch is depressed. If continuity is not indicated when the switch is depressed, replace the switch.

4   To replace the switch, unclip the connector lock and swing it open, then pull the wires out of the switch. Insert the wire terminals into the new switch and swing the connector lock shut.

5   Guide the new switch into the lever, making sure the four small grooves on the switch align with the projections in the lever. Press the cover back into place.

7   Transmission fluid cooler - removal and installation

Refer to illustration 7.2

1   To gain access to the transmission fluid cooler, remove the radiator (see Chapter 3).

2   Disconnect the cooler lines and the

bolts securing the cooler (see illustration).

3   Remove the cooler from the vehicle.

4   Installation is the reverse of removal. Be sure to install new clamps onto the cooler lines and tighten all fasteners securely.

5   Check the transmission fluid level (see Chapter 1), adding fluid as necessary.

8   Automatic transmission - removal and installation

Refer to illustrations 8.12, 8.13, 8.15a and 8.15b

Removal

1   Disconnect the cable from the negative terminal of the battery (see Chapter 5).

2   Remove the air filter housing (see Chapter 4).

3   Remove the radiator protective cover, the cooling fan and upper and lower fan shrouds (see Chapter 3).

4   On V6 engines, remove the EGR pipe (see Chapter 6).

5   On V8 engines, remove the battery

6.2b . . . then pull out the transmission control switch (you might need to use a pair of needle-nose pliers to do this)

7.2 Use cutting pliers to remove the clamps from the transmission fluid cooler lines

8.12 Location of the transmission fluid cooler lines at the transmission (V6 model shown)

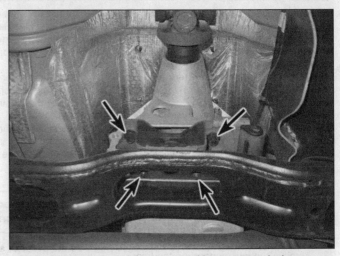

8.13 Location of the upper and lower transmission mount bolts and nuts (V6 model shown)

ground cable and position the harness off to the side.

6   Attach an engine support fixture to the lifting hook located on the cylinder heads. If no hook is provided, use a bolt of the proper size and thread pitch to attach the support fixture chain to a hole at the end of the cylinder head (see Chapter 2C). **Note:** *Engine support fixtures can be obtained at most equipment rental yards and some auto parts stores.*

7   Raise the front of the vehicle and support it securely on jackstands.

8   Remove the driveshaft(s) (see Chapter 8).

9   Disconnect the electrical connectors for the transmission range sensor and the heated oxygen sensors (see Chapter 6). Disconnect any remaining electrical connectors from the transmission and transfer case (4WD models). Mark each connector with tape to insure correct reassembly.

10   Disconnect the shift cable from the transmission shift lever (see Section 4).

11   If the transmission will be repaired or overhauled, drain the fluid before removing it from the vehicle.

12   Disconnect the transmission oil cooler lines from the transmission **(see illustration)**.

13   Remove the transmission mount bolts **(see illustration)**.

14   Place a transmission jack under the transmission and transfer case (4WD models) and secure the transmission to the jack with safety chains or straps.

15   Raise the transmission slightly to take the weight off the crossmember, then remove the crossmember bolts and remove the crossmember **(see illustrations)**.

16   Remove the catalytic converters (see Chapter 6).

17   Remove the exhaust heat shields.

18   Remove the starter (see Chapter 5) and the bellhousing inspection cover.

19   Working through the starter hole, mark the relationship of the torque converter to the driveplate, then remove the torque converter retaining nuts. Rotate the crankshaft to bring

each nut within reach through the inspection cover hole.

20   Remove the transmission-to-engine bolts.

21   Make a final check that all wires have been disconnected from the transmission and transfer case (4WD models), then move the transmission and jack toward the rear of the vehicle until the bellhousing is separated from the engine. Secure the torque converter to the transmission so it won't fall out during removal.

Installation

22   Prior to installation, make sure the torque converter is fully engaged in the transmission. To do this, rotate the converter while pushing it towards the transaxle. If it wasn't already fully in place, you'll feel it "clunk" into position as it engages with the input shaft and front pump. It may even "clunk" more than once. Lubricate the torque converter hub with multi-purpose grease.

7B

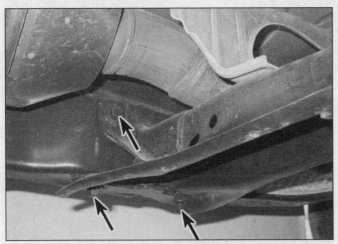

8.15a Location of three of the crossmember mounting bolts (one hidden from view) on the left side and . . .

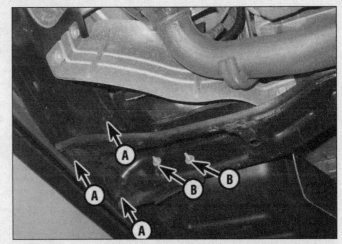

8.15b . . . the right side (A) of the vehicle (V6 model shown) - the fuel tank shield mounting nuts (B) and shield must be removed to access the rear mounting crossmember bolt that is hidden from view

23   With the transmission and transfer case (4WD models) secured to the jack, raise it into position. Be sure to keep it level so the torque converter doesn't fall out and disengage itself from the pump gear.

24   Turn the torque converter until the marks on the converter and driveplate are aligned.

25   Move the transmission forward carefully until the dowel pins engage with the holes in the bellhousing.

26   Install the transmission-to-engine bolts and tighten them to the torque listed in this Chapter's Specifications.

27   Install the catalytic converters (see Chapter 6).

28   Install the transmission mount and crossmember and tighten all nuts and bolts securely.

29   Remove the jack supporting the transmission. Also remove the engine support fixture.

30   Attach the two transmission oil cooler lines.

31   Attach the shift cable to the transmission shift lever (see Section 4).

32   Install new torque converter nuts and tighten them to the torque listed in this Chapter's Specifications.

33   Install the starter motor (see Chapter 5).

34   Install the driveshaft(s) (see Chapter 8).

35   Plug in the electrical connectors for the transmission.

36   Attach the negative battery cable.

37   Check the transmission fluid level (see Chapter 1), drive the vehicle and check for fluid leaks.

9   Automatic transmission overhaul - general information

In the event of a problem occurring, it will be necessary to establish whether the fault is electrical, mechanical or hydraulic in nature, before repair work can be contemplated. Diagnosis requires detailed knowledge of the transmission's operation and construction, as well as access to specialized test equipment, and so is deemed to be beyond the scope of this manual. It is therefore essential that problems with the automatic transmission are referred to a dealer service department or other qualified repair facility for assessment.

Note that a faulty transmission should not be removed before the vehicle has been diagnosed by a knowledgeable technician equipped with the proper tools, as troubleshooting must be performed with the transmission installed in the vehicle.

Chapter 7 Part C
Transfer case

Contents

Specifications

Transfer case fluid type	See Chapter 1	
Torque specifications	**Ft-lbs**	**Nm**
Electronic shift motor mounting bolts	89 in-lbs	10
Crossmember mounting bolts		
Automatic transmission models	52	70
Manual transmission models	46	63
Transmission mount-to-crossmember		
Automatic transmission models	66	90
Manual transmission models	72	98
Transmission-to-mount bolts		
Automatic transmission models	66	90
Manual transmission models	72	98
Transfer case-to-transmission nuts	30	41

7C

1 General information

These models are equipped with two different types of transfer cases; All Wheel Drive (AWD) or Automatic 4 Wheel Drive (A4WD). Both transfer cases mount to the transmission in a similar design.

All Wheel Drive (AWD) systems

AWD models are equipped with a chain drive with viscous coupling to transfer torque to the front and rear wheels. There are no external controls mounted inside the passenger compartment. AWD systems are constantly activated.

Automatic 4 Wheel Drive (A4WD) systems

A4WD models are equipped with a control module, mode select switch on the dash, electronic shift motor and gearmotor encoder inside the transfer case. The electronic mode select switch allows the operator to select between 4X4 AUTO, 4X4 HIGH and 4X4 LOW. In AUTO mode, the 4X4 electronic module activates the transfer case clutch to a minimal level. Slight differences between the front and rear driveshafts are detected by speed sensors and the information is sent to the control module. Torque is then applied by the transfer case clutch thereby controlling slip at the wheels.

Due to the complexity of the transfer cases installed in these vehicles and the need for specialized equipment to perform most service operations, this chapter contains only routine maintenance and removal and installation procedures.

If the transfer case requires major repair work, it should be taken to a dealer service department or an automotive or transmission repair shop. You can, however, remove and install the transfer case yourself and save the expense of that labor, even if the repair work is done by a transmission shop. Keep in mind, however, that diagnosis must be performed with the transfer case in the vehicle.

2   Electronic shift control module (A4WD models) - removal and installation

Warning: *The models covered by this manual are equipped with Supplemental Restraint systems (SRS), more commonly known as airbags. Always disable the airbag system before working in the vicinity of any airbag system component to avoid the possibility of accidental deployment of the airbag, which could cause personal injury (see Chapter 12).*

1   Disconnect the cable from the negative battery terminal (see Chapter 5).
2   Lower the glovebox door and remove the lower trim panel (see Chapter 11). The module is mounted on the evaporator housing in front of the blower motor resistor (see Chapter 3).
3   Disconnect the electrical connector from the electronic shift control module.
4   Remove the module mounting screws and remove it from the evaporator housing.
5   Installation is the reverse of removal.

3   Electronic shift motor - replacement

Note: *The electronic shift motor must be replaced as an assembly.*

1   Raise the vehicle and support it securely on jackstands.
2   Position the gear select lever in the NEUTRAL position.
3   Remove the three bolts from the heat shield. Remove the heat shield.
4   Disconnect the shift motor connector.
5   Use a pin removal tool and separate the magnetic clutch coil wire (pin 11), the front speed sensor (pin 7) and the rear output shaft speed sensor (pin 3). Be sure to mark each wire to insure correct reassembly.
6   Remove the bolts and separate the shift motor from the transfer case.
7   Installation is the reverse of removal. Torque the bolts to the Specifications listed in this Chapter.

4   Transfer case front driveshaft oil seal - removal and installation

The transfer case front driveshaft oil seal requires complete transfer case disassembly. Have the transfer case front oil seal installed by a qualified automotive repair facility.

5   Mode select switch (A4WD models) - replacement

Warning: *The models covered by this manual are equipped with Supplemental Restraint systems (SRS), more commonly known as airbags. Always disable the airbag system before working in the vicinity of any airbag system component to avoid the possibility of accidental deployment of the airbag, which could cause personal injury (see Chapter 12).*

1   Disconnect the cable from the negative battery terminal (see Chapter 5).
2   Remove the instrument center trim panel (see Chapter 11).
3   Disconnect the switch electrical connector.
4   Press the locking tabs then remove the switch.
5   Installation is the reverse of removal.

6   Transfer case - removal and installation

1   Raise the vehicle and support it securely on jackstands.
2   Remove the front driveshaft and the rear driveshaft from the transfer case (see Chapter 8). Always remove the driveshaft from the transfer case first to prevent the boot from tearing in the event the driveshaft drops to a lower angle.
3   Drain the transfer case fluid if the transfer case will be repaired (see Chapter 1).
4   On A4WD models, disconnect the electronic shift motor connector (see Section 3).
5   Disconnect the vent hose.
6   Place a floor jack under the transmission. Place a wood block between the jack head and the transmission to protect the case.
7   Place a transmission jack under the transfer case and secure the transfer case to the jack with safety chains or straps.
8   Remove the bolts securing the crossmember and remove the crossmember. Lower the transmission slightly.
9   Remove the upper mounting nuts and the fuel line bracket. Remove the lower mounting nuts. Remove the transfer case from the transmission.
10   Installation is the reverse of removal, noting the following points:
   a)   *Install a new transfer case gasket to the transmission case.*
   b)   *Tighten the driveshaft fasteners to the torque listed in the Chapter 8 Specifications.*
   c)   *Tighten all other fasteners to the torque listed in this Chapter's Specifications.*
   d)   *If necessary, refill the transfer case with the proper type and amount of fluid (see Chapter 1).*

Chapter 8
Clutch and driveline

Contents

Specifications

Clutch
Clutch fluid type.. See Chapter 1

Driveaxles
Driveaxle length
  Front driveaxle
    Right side... 24.22 inches (615.3 mm)
    Left side.. 26.98 inches (685.3 mm)
  Rear driveaxle
    Right side... 33.94 inches (862.1 mm)
    Left side.. 32.82 inches (833.7 mm)

Torque specifications

	Ft-lbs (unless otherwise indicated)	Nm
Clutch		
Clutch master cylinder mounting nuts	84 in-lbs	10
Clutch pressure plate-to-flywheel bolts	21	28
Clutch release cylinder mounting bolts	108 in-lbs	12
Differential		
Front differential mounting bolts	67	90
Rear differential upper mounting bolts	111	150
Rear differential lower housing bolt	66	90
Driveaxles		
Driveaxle/hub nut		
Front	184	250
Rear	203	275
Driveshafts		
Front driveshaft-to-transfer case flange bolts	22	30
Front driveshaft universal joint bolts	156 in-lbs	18
Rear driveshaft-to-differential bolts	83	112

1   General information

The information in this Chapter deals with the components from the rear of the engine to the front wheels, except for the transmission and transfer case, which are dealt with in Chapter 7. For the purposes of this Chapter, these components are grouped into three categories - clutch, driveshaft(s) and axle(s).

Since nearly all the procedures covered in this Chapter involve working under the vehicle, make sure it's securely supported on sturdy jackstands or on a hoist where the vehicle can be easily raised and lowered.

2   Clutch - description and check

1   All vehicles with a manual transmission have a single dry plate, diaphragm spring-type clutch. The clutch disc has a splined hub which allows it to slide along the splines of the transmission input shaft. The clutch and pressure plate are held in contact by spring pressure exerted by the diaphragm in the pressure plate.

2   The clutch release system is operated by hydraulic pressure. The hydraulic release system consists of the clutch pedal, a master cylinder and a shared common reservoir with the brake master cylinder, a release (or slave) cylinder and the hydraulic line connecting the two components.

3   When the clutch pedal is depressed, a pushrod pushes against brake fluid inside the master cylinder, applying hydraulic pressure to the release cylinder, which pushes the release bearing against the diaphragm fingers of the clutch pressure plate.

4   Terminology can be a problem when discussing the clutch components because common names are in some cases different from those used by the manufacturer. For example, the driven plate is also called the clutch plate or disc, the clutch release bearing is sometimes called a throwout bearing, the release cylinder is sometimes called the slave cylinder.

5   Unless you're replacing components with obvious damage, do these preliminary checks to diagnose clutch problems:

a)   *The first check should be of the fluid level in the master cylinder. If the fluid level is low, add fluid as necessary and inspect the hydraulic system for leaks. If the master cylinder reservoir is dry, bleed the system as described in Section 8 and recheck the clutch operation.*

b)   *To check "clutch spin-down time," run the engine at normal idle speed with the transmission in Neutral (clutch pedal up - engaged). Disengage the clutch (pedal down), wait several seconds and shift the transmission into Reverse. No grinding noise should be heard. A grinding*

noise would most likely indicate a bad pressure plate or clutch disc.

c)   *To check for complete clutch release, run the engine (with the parking brake applied to prevent vehicle movement) and hold the clutch pedal approximately 1/2-inch from the floor. Shift the transmission between 1st gear and Reverse several times. If the shift is rough, component failure is indicated.*

d)   *Visually inspect the pivot bushing at the top of the clutch pedal to make sure there's no binding or excessive play.*

3   Clutch master cylinder - removal and installation

Removal

1   Clamp a pair of locking pliers onto the clutch fluid feed hose, a couple of inches downstream of the brake fluid reservoir (the clutch master cylinder is supplied with fluid from the brake fluid reservoir). The pliers should be just tight enough to prevent fluid flow when the hose is disconnected. Disconnect the reservoir hose from the clutch master cylinder.

2   Working under the dashboard, disconnect the clutch master cylinder pushrod from the pedal by removing the clip and the washer from the clutch pedal pin.

3   Working under the dash, remove the mounting bolts and detach the cylinder from the clutch pedal bracket.

4   Pull the clutch master cylinder forward and release the line clip at the hydraulic line fitting. Separate the hydraulic line from the cylinder. Also detach the reservoir feed hose from the master cylinder. Have rags handy, as some fluid will be lost as the line is removed. Cap or plug the ends of the lines to prevent fluid leakage and the entry of contaminants. **Caution:** *Don't allow brake fluid to come into contact with the paint, as it will damage the finish.*

Installation

5   Connect the hydraulic line fitting to the clutch master cylinder and install the retaining clip at the fitting (junction).

6   Attach the fluid feed hose from the reservoir to the clutch master cylinder and tighten the hose clamp. Remove the locking pliers.

7   Place the master cylinder in position on the clutch pedal bracket and install the pushrod, mounting bolts finger tight. Install pushrod, the washer and the clip onto the clutch pedal pin.

8   Tighten the mounting bolts to the torque listed in this Chapter's Specifications.

9   Fill the reservoir with brake fluid conforming to DOT 3 specifications and bleed the clutch system as outlined in Section 5.

4   Clutch release cylinder - removal and installation

Removal

1   Remove the clip and disconnect the hydraulic line at the transmission. Have a small can and rags handy, as some fluid will be spilled as the line is removed. Plug the line to prevent excessive fluid loss and contamination.

2   Remove the transmission (see Chapter 7, Part A).

3   Remove the release cylinder mounting bolts.

4   Remove the release cylinder.

Installation

5   Install the release cylinder into the transmission. Tighten the bolts to the torque listed in this Chapter's Specifications.

6   Install the transmission (see Chapter 7, Part A).

7   Connect the hydraulic line fitting to the transmission and install the clip.

8   Check the fluid level in the brake fluid reservoir, adding brake fluid conforming to DOT 3 specifications until the level is correct.

9   Bleed the system as described in Section 5, then recheck the brake fluid level.

5   Clutch hydraulic system - bleeding

1   Bleed the hydraulic system whenever any part of the system has been removed or the fluid level has fallen so low that air has been drawn into the master cylinder. The bleeding procedure is very similar to bleeding a brake system.

2   Fill the brake master cylinder reservoir with new brake fluid conforming to DOT 3 specifications. **Caution:** *Do not re-use any of the fluid coming from the system during the bleeding operation or use fluid which has been inside an open container for an extended period of time.*

3   Remove the cap from the bleeder valve and attach a length of clear hose to the valve. Place the other end of the hose into a container partially filled with clean brake fluid.

4   Have an assistant depress the clutch pedal and hold it. Open the bleeder valve on the hydraulic line, allowing fluid and any air to escape. Close the bleeder valve when the flow of fluid (and bubbles) ceases. Once closed, have your assistant release the pedal.

5   Continue this process until all air is evacuated from the system, indicated by a solid stream of fluid being ejected from the bleeder valve each time with no air bubbles. Keep a close watch on the fluid level inside the brake master cylinder reservoir - if the level drops too far, air will get into the system and you'll have to start all over again.

Note: *Wash the area with water to remove any excess brake fluid.*

6   Check the brake fluid level again, and add some, if necessary, to bring it to the appropriate level. Check carefully for proper operation before placing the vehicle into normal service.

6   Clutch release bearing - removal, inspection and installation

The clutch release bearing and bearing hub are integral component of the clutch release cylinder. Replace the release cylinder as a single assembly (see Section 4).

7   Clutch components - removal, inspection and installation

Warning: *Dust produced by clutch wear is hazardous to your health. DO NOT blow it out with compressed air and DO NOT inhale it. DO NOT use gasoline or petroleum-based solvents to remove the dust. Brake system cleaner should be used to flush the dust into a drain pan. After the clutch components are wiped clean with a rag, dispose of the contaminated rags and cleaner in a covered, marked container.*

Removal

Refer to illustration 7.5

1   Access to the clutch components is normally accomplished by removing the transmission, leaving the engine in the vehicle. If the engine is being removed for major overhaul, check the clutch for wear and replace worn components as necessary. However, the relatively low cost of the clutch components compared to the time and trouble spent gaining access to them warrants their replacement anytime the engine or transmission is removed, unless they are new or in near-perfect condition. The following procedures are based on the assumption the engine will stay in place.

2   Remove the transmission from the vehicle (see Chapter 7, Part A). Support the engine while the transmission is out. Prefer-

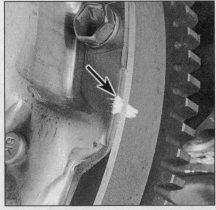

7.5 Mark the relationship of the pressure plate to the flywheel (if you're planning to re-use the old pressure plate)

ably, an engine support fixture or a hoist should be used to support it from above.

3   The release bearing can remain attached to the transmission housing for the time being.

4   To support the clutch disc during removal, install a clutch alignment tool through the clutch disc hub.

5   Carefully inspect the flywheel and pressure plate for indexing marks. The marks are usually an X, an O or a black mark. If they cannot be found, scribe or paint marks yourself so the pressure plate and the flywheel will be in the same alignment during installation **(see illustration)**.

6   Turning each bolt a little at a time, loosen the pressure plate-to-flywheel bolts. Work in a criss-cross pattern until all spring pressure is relieved. Then hold the pressure plate securely and completely remove the bolts, followed by the pressure plate and clutch disc.

Inspection

Refer to illustrations 7.9, 7.11a, 7.11b and 7.13

7   Ordinarily, when a problem occurs in the clutch, it can be attributed to wear of the clutch driven plate assembly (clutch disc). However, all components should be inspected at this time.

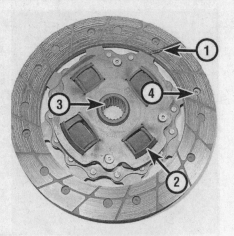

7.9 The clutch disc

1   *Lining* - this will wear down in use
2   *Springs or dampers* - check for cracking and deformation
3   *Splined hub* - the splines must not be worn and should slide smoothly on the transmission input shaft splines
4   *Rivets* - these secure the lining and will damage the flywheel or pressure plate if allowed to contact the surfaces

8   Inspect the flywheel for cracks, heat checking, grooves and other obvious defects. If the imperfections are slight, a machine shop can machine the surface flat and smooth, which is highly recommended regardless of the surface appearance. Refer to Chapter 2 for the flywheel removal and installation procedure.

9   Inspect the lining on the clutch disc. There should be at least 1/16-inch of lining above the rivet heads. Check for loose rivets, distortion, cracks, broken springs and other obvious damage **(see illustration)**. As mentioned above, ordinarily the clutch disc is routinely replaced, so if in doubt about the condition, replace it with a new one.

10   The release bearing and release cylinder should also be replaced along with the clutch disc (see Section 4).

11   Check the machined surfaces and the diaphragm spring fingers of the pressure plate **(see illustrations)**. If the surface is

8

NORMAL FINGER WEAR

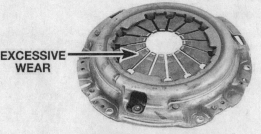

EXCESSIVE WEAR

EXCESSIVE FINGER WEAR

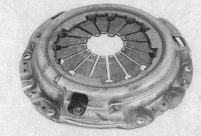

BROKEN OR BENT FINGERS

7.11a Replace the pressure plate if excessive wear or damage are noted

7.11b   Inspect the pressure plate surface for excessive score marks, cracks and signs of overheating

7.13   A slide hammer with an internal puller attachment is handy for removing a pilot bearing

grooved or otherwise damaged, replace the pressure plate. Also check for obvious damage, distortion, cracking, etc. Light glazing can be removed with emery cloth or sandpaper. If a new pressure plate is required, new and re-manufactured units are available.

12   Check the pilot bearing in the end of the crankshaft for excessive wear, scoring, dryness, roughness and any other obvious damage. If any of these conditions are noted, replace the bearing.

13   Removal can be accomplished with a slide hammer and puller attachment **(see illustration)**, which are available at most auto parts stores or tool rental yards.

Installation
Refer to illustrations 7.14 and 7.17

14   To install a new pilot bearing, lightly lubricate the outside surface with grease, then drive it into the recess with a bearing driver or a socket **(see illustration)**. **Note:** *The seal end of the bearing must be facing toward the transmission*

15   Before installation, clean the flywheel and pressure plate machined surfaces with brake cleaner, lacquer thinner or acetone. It's important that no oil or grease is on these surfaces or the lining of the clutch disc. Handle the parts only with clean hands.

16   Adjust the clutch pressure plate before installing it onto the flywheel. Position the pressure plate in a hydraulic press. Apply pressure to the pressure plate until the adjusting ring is loose. Rotate the ring counterclockwise until it stops. This will place the pressure plate in the reset position.

17   Position the clutch disc and pressure plate against the flywheel with the clutch held in place with an alignment tool **(see illustration)**. Make sure the disc is installed properly (most replacement clutch discs will be marked "flywheel side" or something similar - if not marked, install the clutch disc with the damper springs toward the transmission).

18   Tighten the pressure plate-to-flywheel bolts only finger tight, working around the pressure plate.

19   Center the clutch disc by ensuring the alignment tool extends through the splined hub and into the pilot bearing in the crankshaft. Wiggle the tool up, down or side-to-side as needed to center the disc. Tighten the pressure plate-to-flywheel bolts a little at a time, working in a criss-cross pattern to prevent distorting the cover. After all of the bolts are snug, tighten them to the torque listed in this Chapter's Specifications. Remove the alignment tool.

20   Install the clutch release bearing and release cylinder (see Section 4).

21   Install the transmission and all components removed previously.

8   Driveaxles - removal and installation

Front driveaxles (4WD models)
Removal
Refer to illustrations 8.1, 8.5 and 8.7

1   Remove the wheel cover or hub cap. Break the driveaxle/hub nut loose with a

7.14   Tap the bearing into place with a bearing driver or a socket that is slightly smaller than the outside diameter of the bearing

7.17   Center the clutch disc in the pressure plate with a clutch alignment tool

socket and large breaker bar **(see illustration)**.

2   Loosen the wheel lug nuts, raise the vehicle and support it securely on jackstands. Remove the wheel.

3   Separate the upper control arm and tie-rod end from the steering knuckle (see Chapter 10).

4   Remove the stabilizer bar link (see Chapter 10).

5   Remove the driveaxle/hub nut from the axle and discard it. Use a puller tool to push the driveaxle out of the hub **(see illustration)**.

6   Swing the knuckle/hub assembly out (away from the vehicle) until the end of the driveaxle is free of the hub. Support the outer end of the driveaxle with a piece of wire to avoid unnecessary strain on the inner CV joint.

7   Carefully pry the inner CV joint off the front differential (left side) or axle tube (right side) using a large screwdriver or prybar positioned between the CV joint housing and the front differential **(see illustration)** or axle tube. Be careful not to damage the seal.

8   Support the CV joints and carefully remove the driveaxle from the vehicle.

Installation

9   Pry the old spring clip from the inner end of the driveaxle and install a new one. Lubricate the differential or axle tube shaft seal with multi-purpose grease and raise the driveaxle into position while supporting the CV joints. **Note:** *Position the spring clip with the opening facing up; this will ease insertion of the driveaxle and prevent damage to the clip.*

10   Push the splined end of the inner CV joint into the differential side gear (left side) or into the axle tube (right side) and make sure the spring clip locks in its groove.

11   Apply a light coat of multi-purpose grease to the outer CV joint splines, pull out on the steering knuckle assembly and install the stub axle into the hub.

12   Reconnect the tie-rod end and upper

8.1 With the weight of the vehicle on the tires, loosen (but do not remove) the driveaxle/hub nut with a long breaker bar

control arm to the steering knuckle (see Chapter 10).

13   Install the stabilizer bar link (see Chapter 10).

14   Install a *new* driveaxle/hub nut. Tighten the hub nut securely, but don't try to tighten it to the actual torque specification until you've lowered the vehicle to the ground.

15   Grasp the inner CV joint housing (not the driveaxle) and pull out to make sure the driveaxle has seated securely in the front differential or the axle tube shaft.

16   Install the wheel and lug nuts, then lower the vehicle. Tighten the lug nuts to the torque listed in the Chapter 1 Specifications.

17   Tighten the driveaxle/hub nut to the torque listed in this Chapter's Specifications. Install the hub cap or wheel cover.

Rear driveaxles

Removal

Refer to illustration 8.25

18   Block the front wheels to prevent the vehicle from rolling. Loosen the wheel lug nuts, raise the rear of the vehicle and support it securely on jackstands. Remove the wheel.

8.5 Use a puller like this to push the driveaxle shaft from the knuckle/hub assembly

19   Have an assistant depress the brake pedal while you unscrew the driveaxle/hub nut.

20   Remove the brake disc (see Chapter 9). Be sure to use mechanics wire to suspend the brake caliper.

21   Remove the bolt that retains the parking brake cable to the control arm.

22   Cover the stabilizer bar link stud threads with a piece of rubber hose to prevent the CV boots from tearing.

23   Detach the upper control arm and the toe link from the rear knuckle (see Chapter 10). **Caution:** *Don't let the driveaxle hang by the inner CV joint.*

24   Use a puller tool to push the driveaxle out of the hub **(see illustration 8.5)**.

25   Drive the inner end of the driveaxle out of the differential **(see illustration)** and remove it from the vehicle.

Installation

26   Pry the old spring clip from the inner end of the driveaxle and install a new one.

27   Apply a light film of grease to the area on the inner CV joint stub shaft where the seal rides, then insert the splined end of the

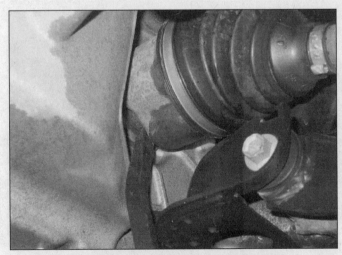

8.7 Carefully pry the inner end of the driveaxle from the transmission

8.25 Drive the inner driveaxle housing from the differential using a large punch and hammer

8

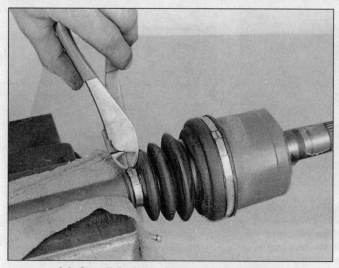

9.3 Cut off the boot clamps and discard them

9.4 Mark the relationship of the tri-pod assembly to the outer race

inner CV joint into the differential. Make sure the spring clip locks in its groove.

28   Apply a light film of grease to the outer CV joint splines, pull the knuckle assembly outward and insert the outer end of the driveaxle into the hub.

29   Connect the upper control arm and toe link to the knuckle (see Chapter 10). Tighten the fasteners to the torque listed in the Chapter 10 Specifications.

30   Install a new driveaxle/hub nut. Tighten the hub nut securely, but don't try to tighten it to the actual torque specification yet.

31   Install the parking brake cable to the lower control arm (see Chapter 9).

32   Install the brake disc and caliper (see Chapter 9).

33   Have an assistant push on the brake pedal, then tighten the driveaxle/hub nut to the torque listed in this Chapter's Specifications. Install the wheel cover or hub cap.

34   Install the wheel and lug nuts, then lower the vehicle. Tighten the lug nuts to the torque listed in the Chapter 1 Specifications.

9   Driveaxle boot - replacement

Note 1: *If the CV joints are worn, indicating the need for an overhaul (usually due to torn boots), explore all options before beginning the job. Complete rebuilt driveaxles are available on an exchange basis, which eliminates much time and work.*

Note 2: *Some auto parts stores carry "split" type replacement boots, which can be installed without removing the driveaxle from the vehicle. This is a convenient alternative; however, the driveaxle should be removed and the CV joint disassembled and cleaned to ensure the joint is free from contaminants such as moisture and dirt which will accelerate CV joint wear.*

1   Remove the driveaxle from the vehicle (see Section 8).

2   Mount the driveaxle in a vise. The jaws of the vise should be lined with wood or rags to prevent damage to the driveaxle.

Inner CV joint and boot

Refer to illustrations 9.3, 9.4, 9.5, 9.6a, 9.6b, 9.7, 9.11, 9.14, 9.16a, 9.16b, 9.17a, 9.17b, 9.17c, 9.17d and 9.17e

Removal

3   Remove the boot clamps **(see illustration)**.

4   Pull the boot back from the inner CV joint and slide the joint housing off. Be sure to mark the relationship of the tripod to the outer race **(see illustration)**.

5   Use a center punch to mark the tri-pod and axleshaft to ensure that they are reassembled properly **(see illustration)**.

6   Remove the bearing retainer clip from the end of the axleshaft **(see illustrations)**.

7   Use a hammer and a brass punch to drive the tri-pod joint from the driveaxle **(see illustration)**.

8   Remove the ring from the axleshaft. Discard it if it isn't a tight fit.

9.5 Use a center punch to place marks on the tri-pod and the driveaxle to ensure that they are properly reassembled

9.6a Move the stop-ring down the axleshaft (this only applies to front driveaxles) . . .

9.6b . . . slide the tri-pod back and remove the circlip

9.7 Drive the tri-pod joint from the axleshaft with a brass punch and hammer - make sure you don't damage the bearing surfaces or the splines on the shaft

9.11 Wrap the splined area of the axleshaft with tape to prevent damage to the boot(s) when installing it

Inspection

9   Clean the old grease from the outer race and the tripod bearing assembly. Carefully disassemble each section of the tripod assembly, one at a time so as not to mix up the parts, and clean the needle bearings with solvent.

10   Inspect the rollers, tri-pod, bearings and outer race for scoring, pitting or other signs of abnormal wear, which will warrant the replacement of the inner CV joint.

Reassembly

11   Slide the clamps and boot onto the axleshaft. It's a good idea to wrap the axleshaft splines with tape to prevent damaging the boot **(see illustration)**.

12   Install a new stop-ring (front driveaxles only).

13   Place the tri-pod on the shaft (making sure the marks are aligned) and install a new circlip. Slide the tri-pod out to the end of the shaft, then install the stop-ring into its groove.

14   Apply grease to the tri-pod assembly, the inside of the joint housing and the inside of the boot **(see illustration)**.

15   Slide the boot into place.

16   Adjust the length of the driveaxle **(see illustration)**, then equalize the pressure in the boot **(see illustration)**.

17   Tighten the boot clamps **(see illustrations)**.

18   Install the driveaxle assembly (see Section 8).

9.14 Pack the outer race with grease and slide it over the tri-pod assembly - make sure the match marks on the CV joint housing and tri-pod line up

9.16b Equalize the pressure inside the boot by inserting a small, dull screwdriver between the boot and the outer race

9.16a Before tightening the boot clamps, adjust the length of the driveaxle to the dimension listed in this Chapter's Specifications

9.17a To install new fold-over type clamps, bend the tang down . . .

9.17b . . . and flatten the tabs to hold it in place

8

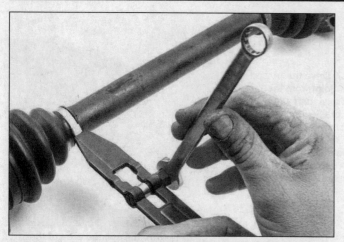

9.17c To install band-type clamps you'll need a special tool; install the band with its end pointing in the direction of axle rotation and tighten it securely, then pivot the tool up 90-degrees and tap the center of the clip with a center punch . . .

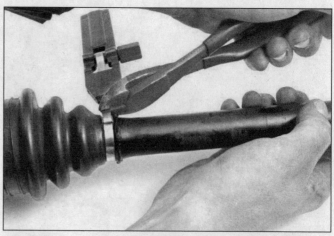

9.17d . . . then bend the end of the clamp back over the clip and cut off the excess

Outer CV joint

Disassembly

19   Remove the driveaxle (see Section 8).

20   Mount the driveaxle in a vise with wood-lined jaws to prevent damage to the axle-shaft. Check the outer CV joint for excessive play in the radial direction, which indicates worn parts. Check for smooth operation throughout the full range of motion for each CV joint. If a boot is torn, the recommended procedure is to disassemble the joint, clean the components and inspect for damage due to loss of lubrication and possible contamination by foreign matter. If the CV joint is in good condition, lubricate it with CV joint grease and install a new boot.

21   Remove the inner CV joint and boot as described previously.

22   Cut the outer CV joint boot clamps with side-cutters, then remove and discard them.

23   Slide the outer boot off the shaft.

Inspection

Refer to illustration 9.24

24   Rotate the outer CV joint housing at an angle to the driveaxle to expose the bearings, inner race and cage **(see illustration)**. Inspect the bearing surfaces for signs of wear. If the CV joint is worn, replace the driveaxle.

Reassembly

25   Slide the new outer boot onto the axle-shaft. It's a good idea to wrap tape around the splines of the shaft to prevent damage to the boot **(see illustration 9.11)**. When the boot is in position, fill the outer joint with CV joint grease (pack the joint with as much grease as it will hold and put the rest into the boot). Slide the boot on the rest of the way and install the new clamps **(see illustrations 9.17a through 9.17e)**. **Note:** *The length of the outer joint isn't adjustable; just make sure that each end of the boot is seated properly and that there are no dimples in the folds in the boot.*

26   Clean and reassemble the inner CV joint by following Steps 9 through 17, then install the driveaxle as outlined in Section 8.

---

10 Driveshaft - removal and installation

Front driveshaft (4WD models)

Removal

Note: *The manufacturer recommends replacing driveshaft fasteners with new ones when installing the driveshaft.*

1   Raise the vehicle and support it securely on jackstands, place the selector lever in Neutral.

2   Use chalk or a scribe to "index" the relationship of the driveshaft to the front differential pinion yoke. This ensures correct alignment when the driveshaft is reinstalled.

3   Use chalk or a scribe to "index" the relationship of the driveshaft to the transfer case flange. This ensures correct alignment when the driveshaft is reinstalled.

4   Remove the bolts securing the universal joint to the differential pinion yoke and the bolts on the transfer case flange.

5   Remove the driveshaft flange from the front differential first to prevent any damage to the boot. **Note:** *At the time of writing, the front driveshaft boot was not repairable. The entire front driveshaft must be replaced as a complete assembly. Consult an automotive parts retailer or a driveline specialist.*

6   Remove the driveshaft from the vehicle.

Installation

7   Installation is the reverse of removal. Tighten the fasteners in a criss-cross pattern to the torque listed in this Chapter's Specifications. **Note:** *Make sure the metal flange retainer is seated inside the CV joint housing correctly. Install a new driveshaft if this flange retainer cannot seat properly.*

9.17e If you're installing crimp-type boot clamps, you'll need a pair of special crimping pliers (available at most auto parts stores)

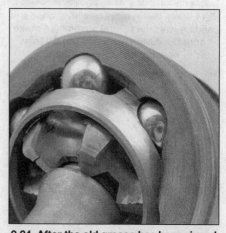

9.24 After the old grease has been rinsed away, move the inner race through its full range of motion and inspect the bearing surfaces for wear or damage - if any of the balls, the race or the cage look damaged, replace the outer joint and axleshaft as an assembly

10.10 Mark the relationship of the driveshaft to the differential pinion yoke

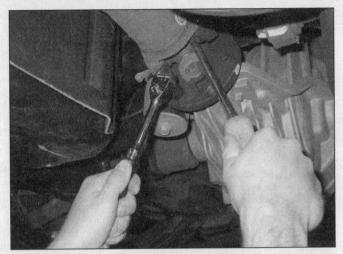

10.11 Immobilize the driveshaft by placing a screwdriver into the universal joint while loosening the bolts

Rear driveshaft

Removal

Refer to illustrations 10.10 and 10.11

Note: *The manufacturer recommends replacing driveshaft fasteners with new ones when installing the driveshaft.*

8   Raise the vehicle and support it securely on jackstands, place the selector lever in Neutral.

9   Remove the skidplate (4WD models).

10   Use chalk or a scribe to "index" the relationship of the driveshaft to the differential flange. This ensures correct alignment when the driveshaft is reinstalled **(see illustration)**. **Note:** *On 4WD models, mark the position of the driveshaft at each side of the boot if you plan on replacing the boot. Replace the boot if it is damaged.*

11   Remove the bolts securing the driveshaft flange from the differential flange **(see illustration)**. If you're working on a 4WD model, also remove the bolts securing the front of the driveshaft to the transfer case flange.

12   Separate the driveshaft from the differ-ential flange. On 2WD models, pull the slip yoke out of the transmission extension hous-ing. On 4WD models, detach the driveshaft from the transfer case.

13   Remove the driveshaft from the vehicle.

Installation

14   Installation is the reverse of removal. Tighten the bolts in a crossing pattern to the torque listed in this Chapter's Specifications.

11 Differential oil seals - replacement

1   Oil leaks frequently occur due to wear of the differential oil seals. Replacement of these seals is relatively easy, since the repair can usually be performed without removing the transmission from the vehicle.

2   Driveaxle oil seals are located at the sides of the differential, where the driveaxles are attached. The driveshaft seal is located behind the differential flange. If leakage at the seal is suspected, raise the vehicle and sup-port it securely on jackstands. If the seal is leaking, lubricant will be found below the seals.

Driveaxle seals

Refer to illustrations 11.4 and 11.6

3   Refer to Section 8 and remove the driveaxles.

4   Use a screwdriver or prybar to carefully pry the oil seal out of the differential bore **(see illustration)**.

5   If the oil seal cannot be removed with a screwdriver or prybar, a special oil seal removal tool (available at auto parts stores) will be required. **Note:** *On front differentials, the axle tube seal will require a special puller to reach inside the tube to extract the seal.*

6   Using a seal installation tool, large sec-tion of pipe or a large deep socket (slightly smaller than the outside diameter of the seal) as a drift, install the new oil seal **(see illustra-tion)**. Drive it into the bore squarely and make sure it's completely seated. Coat the seal lip with transmission lubricant.

7   Install the driveaxle(s). Be careful not to damage the lip of the new seal.

11.4 Use a large screwdriver to remove the seal

11.6 Install a new seal, preferably using a seal driver

8

Pinion seal

Refer to illustrations 11.10, 11.12, 11.13a, 11.13b, 11.14, 11.15 and 11.17

8   Refer to Section 10 and remove the driveshaft. **Caution:** *This procedure disturbs the pinion bearing preload adjustment. Follow the procedure very carefully to reset the pinion bearing preload during reassembly.*

9   Depending on which differential pinion seal is being replaced. Remove the rear or front wheels and brake calipers. **Note:** *The removal of the wheels and brake calipers is advisable to eliminate the added pinion shaft rotation resistance that otherwise might contribute to a false pinion shaft rotation preload torque value.*

10   Using an inch-pound torque wrench (scale from approximately 0 to 40 inch-pounds) on the drive pinion nut, measure and record the torque necessary to rotate the drive pinion in a load-free state **(see illustration)**.

11   Count the number of threads visible between the end of the nut and the end of the pinion shaft and record it for use later.

12   Mark the drive pinion-to-companion flange orientation for proper location of flange to pinion upon reassembly **(see illustration)**. Also count the number of threads

exposed from the top of the nut to the end of the shaft (write this number down).

13   Using a flange holding tool (available at most auto parts stores), or a chain wrench to prevent the flange from turning while removing the nut, unscrew the pinion flange locknut **(see illustrations)**. Discard the nut - a new one must be used when reassembling.

14   Using a two-jaw puller, remove the companion flange from the drive pinion shaft **(see illustration)**. **Note:** *Some fluid loss may occur.*

15   Avoiding contact with the pinion shaft/threads, remove the seal using a special seal removal tool **(see illustration)**.

16   Prior to installing the new seal, clean the seal mating surfaces.

17   Lubricate the lips of the new seal with high-temperature grease and tap it evenly into position with a seal installation tool or a large socket. Make sure it enters the housing squarely and is tapped in to its full depth **(see illustration)**.

18   Align the mating marks made before disassembly and install the companion flange and a new nut. If necessary, tighten the pinion nut to draw the flange into place. Do not try to hammer the flange into position.

11.10 Use an inch-pound torque wrench to check the torque necessary to rotate the pinion shaft

19   Using a suitable holding tool, secure the companion flange while tightening the nut carefully until the original number of threads are exposed on the shaft.

20   Measure the torque required to rotate the pinion and tighten the nut in small increments until it matches the figure recorded in

11.12 Mark the relative positions of the pinion and flange before removing the nut

11.13a A chain wrench or . . .

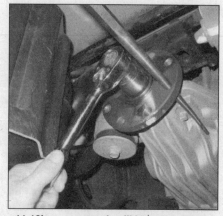

11.13b . . . a punch will keep the flange stationary while removing the pinion nut

11.14 Use a two-jaw puller to pull the flange from the differential

11.15 Use a seal removal tool to extract the pinion seal

11.17 Use a large socket to drive the seal into the differential

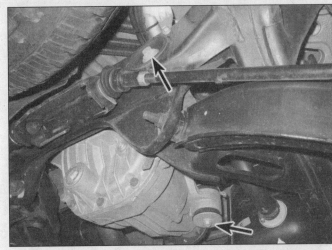

12.16 Location of the differential upper mounting bolts (one upper mounting bolt hidden from view) and lower mounting bolt

Step 4. In order to compensate for the drag of the new oil seal, the nut should be tightened more until the rotational torque of the pinion exceeds earlier recording by no more than 5 in-lbs.

21   The remainder of installation is the reverse of removal. Be sure to check the differential lubricant level and add if required (see Chapter 1).

12   Differential - removal and installation

Front differential (4WD models)

Removal

1   Loosen the driveaxle/hub nut and the wheel lug nuts. Raise the front of the vehicle and support it securely on jackstands. Block the rear wheels to prevent the vehicle from rolling.

2   Drain the differential lubricant (see Chapter 1).

3   Remove the driveshaft (see Section 10) and the driveaxles (see Section 8)

4   Use a shop rag to plug the axle tube.

5   Remove the front stabilizer bar (see Chapter 10).

6   Disconnect the differential vent hose.

7   Support the differential with a floor jack. Remove the bolts securing the differential to the mounting brackets.

8   Carefully lower the differential.

Installation

9   Installation is the reverse of removal, noting the following points:

a) *Install new mounting bolts for the front differential.*

b) *Tighten all fasteners to the torque listed in this Chapter's specifications.*

c) *Tighten the wheel lug nuts to the torque listed in the Chapter 1 Specifications.*

Rear differential

Removal

Refer to illustration 12.16

10   Loosen the wheel lug nuts. Raise the rear of the vehicle and support it securely on jackstands. Block the front wheels to prevent the vehicle from rolling.

11   Remove the driveshaft (see Section 10).

12   Remove the driveaxles (see Section 8)

13   Remove the spare tire.

14   Remove the differential vent hose.

15   At the top of the differential, disconnect the electrical connector from the vehicle speed sensor.

16   Support the differential with a floor jack. Remove the bolts securing the differential to the mounting brackets **(see illustration).**

17   Remove the lower mounting bolt and carefully lower the differential.

Installation

18   Installation is the reverse of removal, noting the following points:

a) *Install the upper and the lower axle housing bolts.*

b) *Tighten all fasteners to the torque listed in this Chapter's specifications.*

13   Universal joints - general information and check

1   Universal joints are mechanical couplings which connect two rotating components that meet each other at different angles.

2   These joints are composed of a yoke on each side connected by a crosspiece called a trunnion. Cups at each end of the trunnion contain needle bearings which provide smooth transfer of the torque load. Snap-rings, either inside or outside of the bearing cups, hold the assembly together.

3   Wear in the needle roller bearings is characterized by vibration in the driveline,

noise during acceleration, and in extreme cases of lack of lubrication, metallic squeaking and ultimately grating and shrieking sounds as the bearings disintegrate.

4   It is easy to check if the needle bearings are worn with the driveshaft in position, by trying to turn the shaft with one hand, the other hand holding the rear axle flange when the rear universal joint is being checked, and the front half coupling when the front universal joint is being checked. Any movement between the driveshaft and the front half couplings, and around the rear half couplings, is indicative of considerable wear. Another method of checking for universal joint wear is to use a prybar inserted into the gap between the universal joint and the driveshaft or flange. Leave the vehicle in gear and try to pry the joint both radially and axially. Any looseness should be apparent with this method. A final test for wear is to attempt to lift the shaft and note any movement between the yokes of the joints.

5   If any of the above conditions exist, replace the universal joints with new ones.

14   Universal joints - replacement

Refer to illustrations 14.2, 14.4 and 14.9

Note 1: *This procedure does not apply to the front driveshaft on a 4WD model. The front driveshaft is retained to the yoke by a clamp instead a casting which requires the bearing pressed into the U-joint assembly.*

Note 2: *A press or large vise will be required for this procedure. It may be advisable to take the driveshaft to a local dealer service department, service station or machine shop where the universal joints can be replaced for you, normally at a reasonable charge.*

1   Remove the driveshaft as outlined in Section 10.

2   On U-joints with external snap-rings, use a small pair of pliers to remove the snap-rings from the spider **(see illustration).**

8

14.2 A pair of needle nose pliers can be used to remove the universal joint snap-rings

14.4 To press the universal joint out of the driveshaft yoke, set it up in the vise with the small socket pushing the joint and bearing cap into the large socket

3   Supporting the driveshaft, place it in position on a workbench equipped with a vise.

4   Place a piece of pipe or a large socket, having an inside diameter slightly larger than the outside diameter of the bearing caps, over one of the bearing caps. Position a socket with an outside diameter slightly smaller than that of the opposite bearing cap against the cap **(see illustration)** and use the vise or press to force the bearing cap out (inside the pipe or large socket). Use the vise or large pliers to work the bearing cap the rest of the way out.

5   Transfer the sockets to the other side and press the opposite bearing cap out in the same manner.

6   Pack the new universal joint bearings with grease. Ordinarily, specific instructions for lubrication will be included with the uni-

versal joint servicing kit and should be followed carefully.

7   Position the spider in the yoke and partially install one bearing cap in the yoke.

8   Start the spider into the bearing cap and then partially install the other cap. Align the spider and press the bearing caps into position, being careful not to damage the dust seals.

9   Install the snap-rings. If difficulty is encountered in seating the snap-rings, strike the driveshaft yoke sharply with a hammer. This will spring the yoke ears slightly and allow the snap-rings to seat in the groove **(see illustration)**.

10   Install the grease fitting and fill the joint with grease. Be careful not to overfill the joint, as this could blow out the grease seals.

11   Install the driveshaft (see Section 10).

14.9 If the snap-ring will not seat in the groove, strike the yoke with a brass hammer - this will relieve the tension that has set up in the yoke and slightly spring the yoke ears (this should also be done if the joint feels tight when assembled)

Chapter 9 Brakes

Contents

Specifications

General
Brake fluid type .... See Chapter 1

Disc brakes
Brake pad minimum thickness	See Chapter 1
Disc minimum thickness	Cast into disc
Minimum Pad lining thickness	See Chapter 1
Disc lateral runout limit	0.001 inch (0.025 mm)
Disc thickness variation limit (parallelism)	0.0004 inch (0.009 mm)

Parking brakes
Shoe lining minimum thickness .... See Chapter 1

Torque specifications
	Ft-lbs (unless otherwise indicated)	Nm
Brake hose inlet fitting bolt	29	40
Caliper mounting bracket bolts	83	112
Caliper (front)-to-mounting bracket bolts	24	32
Caliper (rear)-to-knuckle bolts	24	32
Master cylinder mounting nuts	16	22
Power brake booster mounting nuts	16	22
Wheel speed sensor mounting bolt		
Front	71 in-lbs	8
Rear	20	27
Wheel lug nuts	See Chapter 1	

9

1 General information

The vehicles covered by this manual are equipped with hydraulically operated front and rear brake systems. The front and rear brakes are disc type. Both the front and rear brakes are self adjusting. The disc brakes automatically compensate for pad wear.

Hydraulic system

The hydraulic system consists of two separate circuits. The master cylinder has separate reservoirs for the two circuits, and, in the event of a leak or failure in one hydraulic circuit, the other circuit will remain operative.

Power brake booster

The power brake booster, utilizing engine manifold vacuum and atmospheric pressure to provide assistance to the hydraulically operated brakes, is mounted on the firewall in the engine compartment.

Parking brake

The parking brake mechanically operates the rear brakes only. The parking brake cables actuate a pair of parking brake shoes mounted inside the drum (hub) portion of each rear brake disc.

Service

After completing any operation involving disassembly of any part of the brake system, always test drive the vehicle to check for proper braking performance before resuming normal driving. When testing the brakes, perform the tests on a clean, dry, flat surface. Conditions other than these can lead to inaccurate test results.

Test the brakes at various speeds with both light and heavy pedal pressure. The vehicle should stop evenly without pulling to one side or the other.

Tires, vehicle load and wheel alignment are factors which also affect braking performance.

Precautions

There are some general cautions and warnings involving the brake system on this vehicle:

a) *Use only brake fluid conforming to DOT 3 specifications.*

b) *The brake pads and linings may contain asbestos fibers which are hazardous to your health if inhaled. Whenever you work on brake system components, clean all parts with brake system cleaner. Do not allow the fine dust to become airborne. Also, wear an approved filtering mask.*

c) *Safety should be paramount whenever any servicing of the brake components is performed. Do not use parts or fasteners which are not in perfect condition, and be sure that all clearances and*

torque specifications are adhered to. If you are at all unsure about a certain procedure, seek professional advice. Upon completion of any brake system work, test the brakes carefully in a controlled area before putting the vehicle into normal service. If a problem is suspected in the brake system, don't drive the vehicle until it's fixed.

2 Anti-lock Brake System (ABS) - general information

General information

Refer to illustration 2.2

1   The anti-lock brake system is designed to maintain vehicle steerability, directional stability and optimum deceleration under severe braking conditions on most road surfaces. It does so by monitoring the rotational speed of each wheel and controlling the brake line pressure to each wheel during braking. This prevents the wheels from locking up.

2   The ABS system has three main components - the wheel speed sensors, the anti-lock brake control module and the hydraulic control unit **(see illustration)**. Wheel speed sensors - one at each front wheel and another located on the rear differential - send a variable voltage signal to the control unit, which monitors these signals, compares them to its program and determines whether a wheel is about to lock up. When a wheel is about to lock up, the control unit signals the hydraulic unit to reduce hydraulic pressure (or not increase it further) at that wheel's brake caliper. Pressure modulation is handled by electrically-operated solenoid valves. The ABS system is equipped with either a 3 channel system (four-wheel ABS) or 4 channel system (four-wheel ABS with Advanced Trac traction control).

3   If a problem develops within the system, an "ABS" warning light will glow on the dashboard. Sometimes, a visual inspection of the

2.2 Location of the hydraulic control unit on a four wheel Anti Lock Brake system

ABS system can help you locate the problem. Carefully inspect the ABS wiring harness. Pay particularly close attention to the harness and connections near each wheel. Look for signs of chafing and other damage caused by incorrectly routed wires. If a wheel sensor harness is damaged, the sensor must be replaced. **Warning:** *Do NOT try to repair an ABS wiring harness. The ABS system is sensitive to even the smallest changes in resistance. Repairing the harness could alter resistance values and cause the system to malfunction. If the ABS wiring harness is damaged in any way, it must be replaced.* **Caution:** *Make sure the ignition is turned off before unplugging or reattaching any electrical connections.*

ABS with Traction Control and Stability Assist

4   Some models are equipped with a stability control system. The stability assist/traction control switch allows the driver to activate the stability assist system while the ABS continues to operate. This activation will illuminate a stability assist/traction control light on the switch. If the ABS system does not activate because of damage, the yellow ABS light will illuminate.

5   The stability assist/traction control system along with the ABS can monitor and compare rotational speed of the wheels, yaw rate (side-to-side motion above the center of gravity), lateral acceleration (force of the vehicle sliding sideways), longitudinal acceleration (4WD models) (forward and back shifting motion), steering wheel position and brake booster control. The sophisticated module can process all this information and correct vehicle instability using the hydraulic actuator and the braking system of the ABS.

Diagnosis and repair

6   If a dashboard warning light comes on and stays on while the vehicle is in operation, the ABS system requires attention. Although special electronic ABS diagnostic testing tools are necessary to properly diagnose the system, you can perform a few preliminary checks before taking the vehicle to a dealer service department.

a) *Check the brake fluid level in the reservoir.*

b) *Verify that the computer electrical connectors are securely connected.*

c) *Check the electrical connectors at the hydraulic control unit.*

d) *Check the fuses.*

e) *Follow the wiring harness to each wheel and verify that all connections are secure and that the wiring is undamaged.*

7   If the above preliminary checks do not rectify the problem, the vehicle should be diagnosed by a dealer service department or other qualified repair shop. Due to the complex nature of this system, all actual repair work must be done by a qualified automotive technician.

2.12 Location of the retaining bolt for the front wheel speed sensor

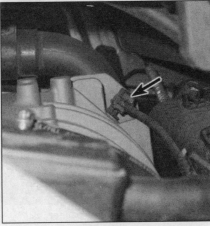

2.18 The rear wheel speed sensor on models with three-channel ABS is located on the differential

3 Disc brake pads - replacement

Warning: *Disc brake pads must be replaced on both wheels at the same time - never replace the pads on only one wheel. Also, the dust created by the brake system is harmful to your health. Never blow it out with compressed air and don't inhale any of it. An approved filtering mask should be worn when working on the brakes. Do not, under any circumstances, use petroleum-based solvents to clean brake parts. Use brake system cleaner only!*

1   Remove the cap from the brake fluid reservoir.

Wheel speed sensor - removal and installation

Front wheel speed sensors

Refer to illustration 2.12

8   Loosen the wheel lug nuts, raise the vehicle and support it securely on jackstands. Remove the wheel.

9   Remove the brake disc (see Section 5).

10   Make sure the ignition key is turned to the Off position.

11   Trace the wiring back from the sensor, detaching all brackets and clips while noting its correct routing, then disconnect the electrical connector.

12   Remove the mounting bolt **(see illustration)** and carefully pull the sensor out from the knuckle or brake backing plate.

13   Installation is the reverse of the removal procedure. Tighten the mounting bolt securely.

14   Install the wheel and lug nuts, tightening them securely. Lower the vehicle and tighten the lug nuts to the torque listed in the Chapter 1 Specifications.

Rear wheel speed sensor

Refer to illustration 2.18

Note: *The following procedure is for the three-channel ABS system. If your vehicle is equipped with the four-channel system (with traction control), use the front wheel speed sensor procedure.*

15   The rear wheel speed sensor on models with the three-channel ABS is located on the differential. Raise the rear of the vehicle and support it securely on jackstands.

16   Make sure the ignition key is turned to the Off position.

17   Trace the wiring back from the sensor, detaching all brackets and clips while noting its correct routing, then disconnect the electrical connector.

18   Remove the mounting bolt **(see illustration)** and carefully pull the sensor out from the differential.

19   Installation is the reverse of the removal procedure. Tighten the mounting bolt securely.

Front disc brake pads

Refer to illustrations 3.5 and 3.6a through 3.6o.

Caution: *Install new caliper slippers onto the knuckle assembly with new brake pad installation. Do not re-use old slippers!*

2   Loosen the wheel lug nuts, raise the front of the vehicle and support it securely on jackstands. Block the wheels at the opposite end.

3   Remove the wheels. Work on one brake assembly at a time, using the assembled brake for reference if necessary.

4   Inspect the brake disc carefully as outlined in Section 5. If machining is necessary, follow the information in that Section to remove the disc, at which time the pads can be removed as well.

5   Push the piston back into its bore to provide room for the new brake pads. A C-clamp can be used to accomplish this **(see illustration)**. As the piston is depressed to the bottom of the caliper bore, the fluid in the master cylinder will rise. Make sure that it doesn't overflow. If necessary, siphon off some of the fluid.

6   Follow the accompanying photos **(illustrations 3.6a through 3.6o)**, for the actual pad replacement procedure. Be sure to stay in order and read the caption under each illustration.

3.5 Before removing the caliper, be sure to depress the piston into the bottom of its bore in the caliper with a large C-clamp to make room for the new pads

3.6a Always wash the brakes with brake cleaner before disassembling anything

9

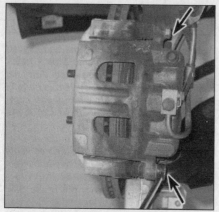

3.6b Remove the caliper mounting bolts . . .

3.6c . . . remove the caliper . . .

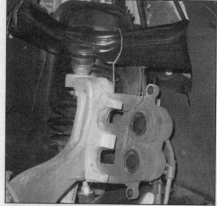

3.6d . . . and use a piece of wire to tie it to the coil spring. Never let the caliper hang by the brake hose

3.6e Separate the inner pad from the caliper mounting bracket . . .

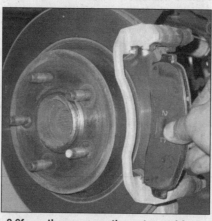

3.6f . . . then remove the outer pad from the caliper mounting bracket

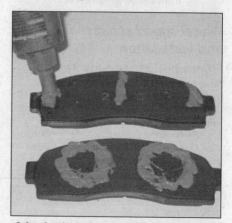

3.6g Apply anti-squeal compound to the back of the pads

7   When reinstalling the caliper, be sure to tighten the mounting bolts to the torque listed in this Chapter's Specifications. After the job has been completed, firmly depress the brake pedal a few times to bring the pads into contact with the disc. Check the level of the brake fluid, adding some if necessary. Check the operation of the brakes carefully before placing the vehicle into normal service.

Rear disc brake pads

Refer to illustrations 3.11 and 3.12a through 3.12n
Caution: *Do not remove the guide pins or the guide pin boots from the caliper. The guide pins are not serviceable - they are designed to last for the life of the vehicle.*
Caution: *Install new caliper slippers onto the*

knuckle assembly with new brake pad installation. Do not re-use old slippers!
8   Loosen the wheel lug nuts, raise the rear of the vehicle and support it securely on jackstands. Block the wheels at the opposite end.
9   Remove the wheels. Work on one brake assembly at a time, using the assembled brake for reference if necessary.
10   Inspect the brake disc carefully as out-

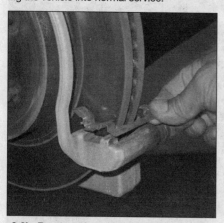

3.6h Remove the stainless steel slippers from the upper and lower parts of the caliper mounting bracket

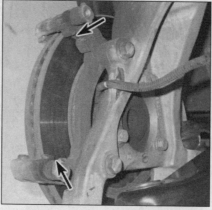

3.6i Inspect the caliper mounting bracket for burrs, deposits or other damage that may interfere with the brake pads moving properly during normal braking

3.6j Pull out the sliding pins and clean them off, then apply a coat of high temperature grease to the pins

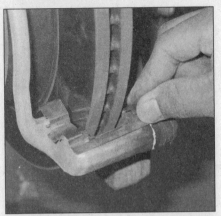

3.6k Install the stainless steel slippers on the mounting bracket

3.6l Install the inner pad

3.6m Install the outer pad

3.6n Install the caliper . . .

3.6o . . . and the caliper mounting bolts, then tighten the bolts to the torque listed in this Chapter's Specifications

3.11 Before removing the rear caliper, be sure to depress the piston into the bottom of its bore in the caliper with a large C-clamp to make room for the new pads

lined in Section 5. If machining is necessary, follow the information in that Section to remove the disc, at which time the pads can be removed as well.

11   Push the piston back into its bore to provide room for the new brake pads. A C-clamp can be used to accomplish this **(see illustration)**. As the piston is depressed to the bottom of the caliper bore, the fluid in the master cylinder will rise. Make sure that it doesn't overflow. If necessary, siphon off some of the fluid.

12   Follow the accompanying photos **(illustrations 3.12a through 3.12n)**, for the actual pad replacement procedure. Be sure to stay in order and read the caption under each illustration. Also, refer to illustration 3.6g for the application of the anti-squeal compound.

13   When reinstalling the caliper, be sure to tighten the mounting bolts to the torque listed in this Chapter's Specifications. After the job has been completed, firmly depress the brake pedal a few times to bring the pads into contact with the disc. Check the level of the brake fluid, adding some if necessary. Check the operation of the brakes carefully before placing the vehicle into normal service.

9

3.12a Always wash the brakes with brake cleaner before disassembling anything

3.12b Loosen and remove the caliper bolts

3.12c Remove the caliper

3.12d Unclip the outboard brake pad

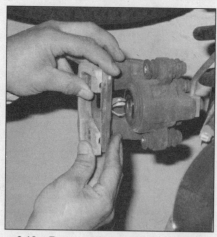

3.12e Remove the inboard brake pad

3.12f Never let the caliper hang by the brake hose - use a piece of wire to tie it to the coil spring

3.12g Remove the stainless steel slippers from the caliper mounting bosses of the rear knuckle

3.12h Install new slippers onto the knuckle and make sure they are snug against the outboard end of the anchor plate rail

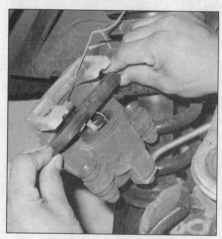

3.12i Install the inner pad

3.12j Use a caliper piston tool to force the piston in until it is fully retracted (a C-clamp could also be used)

3.12k Install the outer pad, making sure the projections on the pad backing plate and the spring arms engage properly with the caliper frame

3.12l Install the caliper . . .

3.12m . . . making sure the notches in the brake pads are aligned properly onto the slippers

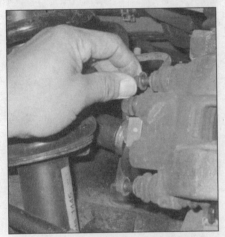

3.12n Install the caliper mounting bolts and tighten them to the torque listed in this Chapter's Specifications

4   Disc brake caliper - removal and installation

Warning: *Dust created by the brake system is harmful to your health. Never blow it out with compressed air and don't inhale any of it. An approved filtering mask should be worn when working on the brakes. Do not, under any circumstances, use petroleum-based solvents to clean brake parts. Use brake system cleaner only.*

Note: *If replacement is indicated (usually because of fluid leakage), it is recommended that the calipers be replaced, not overhauled. New and factory rebuilt units are available on an exchange basis, which makes this job quite easy. Always replace the calipers in pairs - never replace just one of them.*

Removal

Refer to illustrations 4.2a and 4.2b

1   Loosen the wheel lug nuts, raise the vehicle (front or rear) and place it securely on jackstands. Remove the wheel.

2   Remove the inlet fitting bolt and disconnect the brake hose from the caliper **(see illustrations)**. Plug the brake hose to keep contaminants out of the brake system and to prevent losing any more brake fluid than is necessary. **Note:** *If the caliper is being removed for access to another component, don't disconnect the hose.*

3   Refer to Section 3 for the caliper removal procedure. If the caliper is being removed for access to another component, hang it from the coil spring with a piece of wire **(see illustration 3.6d)**.

Installation

4   Install the caliper by reversing the removal procedure.

5   Bleed the brake circuit according to the procedure in Section 9. Make sure there are no leaks from the hose connections. Test the brakes carefully before returning the vehicle to normal service.

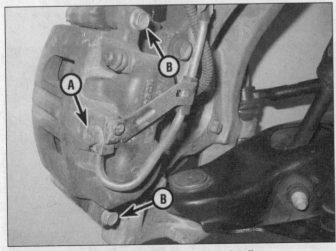

4.2a Front caliper mounting details

A   Inlet fitting bolt   B   Caliper mounting bolts

4.2b Rear caliper mounting details

A   Inlet fitting bolt   B   Caliper mounting bolts

9

5.2 The front caliper mounting bracket is retained by two bolts

5.3 The brake pads on this vehicle were obviously neglected, as they wore down completely and cut deep grooves into the disc - wear this severe means the disc must be replaced

5.4a To check disc runout, mount a dial indicator as shown and rotate the disc

5.4b Using a swirling motion, remove the glaze from the disc surface with sandpaper or emery cloth

5 Brake disc - inspection, removal and installation

Inspection

Refer to illustrations 5.2, 5.3, 5.4a, 5.4b, 5.5a, 5.5b and 5.5c

1 Loosen the wheel lug nuts, raise the vehicle and support it securely on jackstands. Remove the wheel and install the lug nuts to hold the disc in place against the hub flange. **Note:** *If the lug nuts don't contact the disc when screwed on all the way, install washers under them.*

2 Remove the brake caliper as outlined in Section 4. It isn't necessary to disconnect the brake hose. After removing the caliper bolts, suspend the caliper out of the way with a piece of wire **(see illustration 3.6d or 3.12f)**. On front disc brakes, remove the two caliper mounting bracket-to-steering knuckle bolts **(see illustration)** and detach the mounting bracket. On rear disc brakes, the disc can be removed after the caliper has been removed.

3 Visually inspect the disc surface for score marks and other damage. Light scratches and shallow grooves are normal after use and may not always be detrimental to brake operation, but deep scoring requires

disc removal and refinishing by an automotive machine shop. Be sure to check both sides of the disc **(see illustration)**. If pulsating has been noticed during application of the brakes, suspect disc runout.

4 To check disc runout, place a dial indicator at a point about 1/2-inch from the outer edge of the disc **(see illustration)**. Set the indicator to zero and turn the disc. The indicator reading should not exceed the specified allowable runout limit. If it does, the disc should be refinished by an automotive machine shop. **Note:** *The discs should be resurfaced regardless of the dial indicator reading, as this will impart a smooth finish and ensure a perfectly flat surface, eliminating any brake pedal pulsation or other undesirable symptoms related to questionable discs. At the very least, if you elect not to have the discs resurfaced, remove the glaze from the surface with emery cloth or sandpaper, using a swirling motion* **(see illustration)**.

5 It's absolutely critical that the disc not be machined to a thickness under the specified minimum thickness. The minimum (or discard) thickness is cast or stamped into the inside of the disc **(see illustration)**. The disc

thickness can be checked with a micrometer **(see illustration)**.

Removal

Refer to illustration 5.6

6 Remove the lug nuts which were installed to hold the disc in place and remove the disc from the hub **(see illustration)**.

5.5a The minimum thickness dimension is cast into the front side of the disc on front wheel discs

5.5b Location of the minimum thickness dimension on rear discs

5.5c Use a micrometer to measure disc thickness

5.6 Use cutting pliers to remove the metal retaining washers from the wheel studs

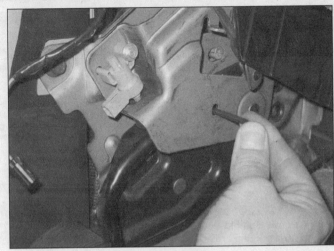

6.3 Insert a 5/32 inch drill bit into the control actuator to lock it into position

6.8 Use locking pliers to remove the brake shoe retracting spring

Installation

7   Place the disc in position over the threaded studs.

8   On front disc brakes, install the caliper mounting bracket, tightening the bolts to the torque value listed in this Chapter's Specifications.

9   Install the caliper and tighten the bolts to the torque listed in this Chapter's Specifications.

10   Install the wheel, then lower the vehicle to the ground. Tighten the lug nuts to the torque listed in the Chapter 1 Specifications. Depress the brake pedal a few times to bring the brake pads into contact with the disc. Bleeding won't be necessary unless the brake hose was disconnected from the caliper. Check the operation of the brakes carefully before driving the vehicle.

6   Parking brake shoes - replacement

Refer to illustrations 6.3, 6.8, 6.9a, 6.9b, 6.10 and 6.11

1   Release the parking brake.
2   Remove the cowl trim panel from the left side of the driver's compartment for access to the parking brake pedal.
3   Pull back on the parking brake cable toward the control assembly (parking brake) and insert a 5/32 inch drill bit into the control actuator to lock the assembly into position **(see illustration)**. **Note:** *It's actually easier to pull on the parking brake cable from under the vehicle, but you'll need an assistant to help you do this.*
4   Loosen the rear wheel lug nuts. Raise the vehicle and support it securely on jackstands. Remove the wheels. Be sure to block the front tires.
5   Remove the brake calipers (see Section 4) and the brake discs (see Section 5).
6   Detach the parking brake cable from the actuator arm.
7   Clean the parking brake assembly with brake system cleaner before beginning work.
8   Remove the brake shoe retracting spring **(see illustration)**.
9   Remove the adjusting screw spring **(see illustration)**. Remove the adjusting screw **(see illustration)**.

6.9a Remove the adjusting screw spring . . .

6.9b . . . and remove the adjusting screw

9

6.10 Remove the hold-down springs from the parking brake shoes

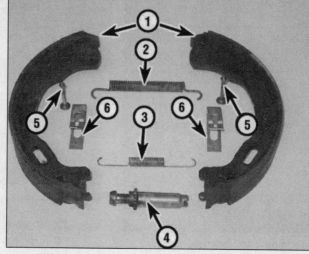

6.11 Parking brake shoes and component details

1   Parking brake shoes
2   Retracting spring
3   Adjusting screw spring
4   Adjusting screw assembly
5   Hold-down spring retainers
6   Hold-down springs

10   Remove the hold-down springs from the shoes **(see illustration)**.
11   Remove the parking brake shoes from the actuator **(see illustration)**.
12   Clean the brake disc/parking brake drum and check it for score marks, deep grooves, hard spots (which will appear as small discolored areas) and cracks. If the disc/drum is worn, scored or out-of-round, it can be resurfaced by an automotive machine shop.
13   Install the shoes by reversing the removal procedure. Turn the adjusting screw so the disc just fits over the new shoes. When the disc is installed, the shoes should not rub as the disc is turned. If you have a brake shoe adjusting gauge, adjust the diameter of the shoes to 0.042-inch less than that of the drum surface of the rear brake disc.
14   Repeat this procedure for the other parking brake assembly.
15   Install the brake discs (see Section 5) and the brake calipers (see Section 4). Reconnect the parking brake cable to the actuator arm.
16   Remove the rubber plug from the brake backing plate and, using a screwdriver or brake adjusting tool, turn the adjusting screw star wheel until the parking brake shoes start to drag as the disc is turned, then back off

the start wheel until the shoes don't drag.
17   Install the rear wheels and lug nuts, lower the vehicle and tighten the lug nuts to the torque listed in the Chapter 1 Specifications.

7   Master cylinder - removal and installation

Caution: *Bleeding the master cylinder on a vehicle equipped with a four wheel ABS system requires a scan tool. Follow the instructions on the scan tool or have the hydraulic control unit and master cylinder bled by a dealer service department or other qualified auto repair facility.*

Removal

Refer to illustrations 7.6 and 7.8
1   The master cylinder is located in the engine compartment, mounted to the power brake booster.
2   On models with Traction Control and Stability Assist systems, disconnect the speed control deactivation switch.
3   Disconnect the brake fluid level warning switch connector.

7.6 Master cylinder mounting details

A   Fluid level warning switch connector
B   Speed control deactivation switch connector
C   Brake line fitting
D   Mounting nuts

4   Remove as much fluid as you can from the reservoir using a syringe, such as an old turkey baster. **Warning:** *If a baster is used, never again use it for the preparation of food.*
5   Place rags under the fluid fittings and prepare caps or plastic bags to cover the ends of the lines once they are disconnected. **Caution:** *Brake fluid will damage paint. Cover all body parts and be careful not to spill fluid during this procedure.*
6   Loosen the fittings at the ends of the brake lines where they enter the master cylinder **(see illustration)**. To prevent rounding off the corners on these nuts, the use of a flare-nut wrench, which wraps around the nut, is preferred. Pull the brake lines slightly away from the master cylinder and plug the ends to prevent contamination.
7   Disconnect the electrical connector at the brake fluid level switch on the master cylinder reservoir, then remove the nuts attaching the master cylinder to the power booster. Pull the master cylinder off the studs and out of the engine compartment. Again, be careful not to spill the fluid as this is done.
8   If a new master cylinder is being installed, remove the reservoir from the master cylinder and transfer it to the new master cylinder. **Note:** *Be sure to install new seals when transferring the reservoir* **(see illustration)**.

Installation

Refer to illustrations 7.10 and 7.15
9   Bench bleed the new master cylinder before installing it. Mount the master cylinder in a vise, with the jaws of the vise clamping on the mounting flange.
10   Attach a pair of master cylinder bleeder tubes to the outlet ports of the master cylinder **(see illustration)**.
11   Fill the reservoir with brake fluid of the recommended type (see Chapter 1).
12   Slowly push the pistons into the master cylinder (a large Phillips screwdriver can be used for this) - air will be expelled from the pressure chambers and into the reservoir. Because the tubes are submerged in fluid, air can't be drawn back into the master cylinder

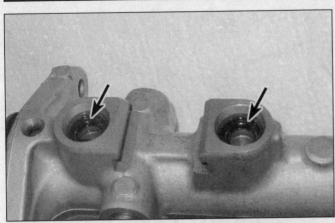

7.8 After the reservoir has been removed, replace the O-rings with new ones

7.10 The best way to bleed air from the master cylinder before installing it on the vehicle is with a pair of bleeder tubes that direct brake fluid into the reservoir during bleeding

when you release the pistons.

13   Repeat the procedure until no more air bubbles are present.

14   Remove the bleed tubes, one at a time, and install plugs in the open ports to prevent fluid leakage and air from entering. Install the reservoir cap.

15   Install the master cylinder over the studs on the power brake booster and tighten the attaching nuts only finger tight at this time. **Note:** *Be sure to install a new O-ring into the sleeve of the master cylinder* **(see illustration).**

16   Thread the brake line fittings into the master cylinder. Since the master cylinder is still a bit loose, it can be moved slightly in order for the fittings to thread in easily. Do not strip the threads as the fittings are tightened.

17   Fully tighten the mounting nuts, then the brake line fittings. Tighten the nuts to the torque listed in this Chapter's Specifications.

18   Fill the master cylinder reservoir with fluid, then bleed the master cylinder and the brake system as described in Section 9. To bleed the cylinder on the vehicle, have an assistant depress the brake pedal and hold the pedal to the floor. Loosen the fitting to allow air and fluid to escape. Repeat this pro-

cedure on both fittings until the fluid is clear of air bubbles. **Caution:** *Have plenty of rags on hand to catch the fluid - brake fluid will ruin painted surfaces. After the bleeding procedure is completed, rinse the area under the master cylinder with clean water.*

19   Test the operation of the brake system carefully before placing the vehicle into normal service. **Warning:** *Do not operate the vehicle if you are in doubt about the effectiveness of the brake system. It is possible for air to become trapped in the anti-lock brake system hydraulic control unit, so, if the pedal continues to feel spongy after repeated bleedings or the BRAKE or ANTI-LOCK light stays on, have the vehicle towed to a dealer service department or other qualified shop to be bled with the aid of a scan tool.*

8   Brake hoses and lines - inspection and replacement

Warning: *If air has found its way into the hydraulic control unit, the system must be bled with the use of a scan tool. If the brake pedal feels "spongy" even after bleeding the brakes, or the ABS light on the instrument panel does not go off, or if you have any*

doubts whatsoever about the effectiveness of the brake system, have the vehicle towed to a dealer service department or other repair shop equipped with the necessary tools for bleeding the system.

1   About every six months, with the vehicle raised and placed securely on jackstands, the flexible hoses which connect the steel brake lines with the front and rear brake assemblies should be inspected for cracks, chafing of the outer cover, leaks, blisters and other damage. These are important and vulnerable parts of the brake system and inspection should be complete. A light and mirror will be needed for a thorough check. If a hose exhibits any of the above defects, replace it with a new one.

Flexible hoses

Refer to illustrations 8.3, 8.4a and 8.4b

2   Clean all dirt away from the ends of the hose.

3   To disconnect a front brake hose from the metal line, unscrew the metal fitting with a flare-nut wrench, then remove the hose-to-frame bolt **(see illustration)**.

4   Disconnect the hose from the caliper, discarding the sealing washers **(see illustrations)**.

9

7.15 Be sure to install a new rubber O-ring on the master cylinder

8.3 Location of the flexible hose-to-frame mounting bolt

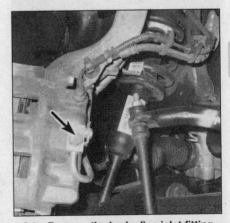

8.4a Remove the brake line inlet fitting bolt at the front brake caliper

8.4b Location of the rear brake line inlet fitting bolt

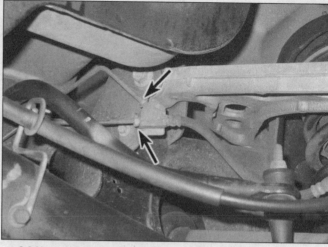

8.9 Unscrew the brake line threaded fittings with a flare-nut wrench to protect the fitting corners from being rounded off

5   Using new sealing washers, attach the new brake hose to the caliper.

6   To reattach a brake hose to the junction, route the line to its original position. Make sure the hose isn't twisted, then attach it to the caliper by tightening the bolt securely. **Note:** *The weight of the vehicle must be on the suspension, so the vehicle should not be raised while positioning the hose.*

7   Carefully check to make sure the suspension or steering components don't make contact with the hose. Have an assistant push down on the vehicle and also turn the steering wheel lock-to-lock during inspection.

8   Bleed the brake system (see Section 9).

Metal brake lines

Refer to illustration 8.9

9   To disconnect a metal brake line from the junction, unscrew the metal tube nut with a flare nut wrench and remove the brake line end from the junction **(see illustration)**.

10   When replacing brake lines, be sure to

9.8 When bleeding the brakes, a hose is connected to the bleed screw at the caliper and submerged in brake fluid - air will be seen as bubbles in the tube and container (all air must be expelled before moving to the next wheel)

use the correct parts. Don't use copper tubing for any brake system components. Purchase steel brake lines from a dealer parts department or auto parts store.

11   Prefabricated brake line, with the tube ends already flared and fittings installed, is available at auto parts stores and dealer parts departments. These lines can be bent to the proper shapes using a tubing bender.

12   When installing the new line make sure it's well supported in the brackets and has plenty of clearance between moving or hot components.

13   After installation, check the master cylinder fluid level and add fluid as necessary. Bleed the brake system as outlined in Section 9 and test the brakes carefully before placing the vehicle into normal operation.

9   Brake hydraulic system - bleeding

Refer to illustration 9.8

Warning: *Wear eye protection when bleeding the brake system. If the fluid comes in contact with your eyes, immediately rinse them with water and seek medical attention.*

Note: *Bleeding the brake system is necessary to remove any air that's trapped in the system when it's opened during removal and installation of a hose, line, caliper, wheel cylinder or master cylinder.*

1   It will probably be necessary to bleed the system at all four brakes if air has entered the system due to low fluid level, or if the brake lines have been disconnected at the master cylinder.

2   If a brake line was disconnected only at a wheel, then only that caliper must be bled.

3   If a brake line is disconnected at a fitting located between the master cylinder and any of the brakes, that part of the system served by the disconnected line must be bled.

4   Remove any residual vacuum from the brake power booster by applying the brake several times with the engine off.

5   Remove the master cylinder reservoir cap and fill the reservoir with brake fluid. Reinstall the cap. **Note:** *Check the fluid level often during the bleeding operation and add fluid as necessary to prevent the fluid level from falling low enough to allow air bubbles into the master cylinder.*

6   Have an assistant on hand, as well as a supply of new brake fluid, an empty clear plastic container, a length of plastic, rubber or vinyl tubing to fit over the bleeder valve and a wrench to open and close the bleeder valve.

7   Beginning at the right rear wheel, loosen the bleeder screw slightly, then tighten it to a point where it's snug but can still be loosened quickly and easily.

8   Place one end of the tubing over the bleeder screw fitting and submerge the other end in brake fluid in the container **(see illustration)**.

9   Have the assistant slowly depress the brake pedal and hold it in the depressed position.

10   While the pedal is held depressed, open the bleeder screw just enough to allow a flow of fluid to leave the valve. Watch for air bubbles to exit the submerged end of the tube. When the fluid flow slows after a couple of seconds, tighten the screw and have your assistant release the pedal.

11   Repeat Steps 9 and 10 until no more air is seen leaving the tube, then tighten the bleeder screw and proceed to the left rear wheel, the right front wheel and the left front wheel, in that order, and perform the same procedure. Be sure to check the fluid in the master cylinder reservoir frequently.

12   Never use old brake fluid. It contains moisture which can boil, rendering the brake system inoperative.

13   Refill the master cylinder with fluid at the end of the operation.

14   Check the operation of the brakes. The pedal should feel solid when depressed, with no sponginess. If necessary, repeat the entire process. **Warning:** *Do not operate the vehicle*

if you are in doubt about the effectiveness of the brake system. It is possible for air to become trapped in the anti-lock brake system hydraulic control unit, so, if the pedal continues to feel spongy after repeated bleedings or the BRAKE or ANTI-LOCK light stays on, have the vehicle towed to a dealer service department or other qualified shop to be bled with the aid of a scan tool.

10 Power brake booster - check, removal and installation

Operating check

1   Depress the brake pedal several times with the engine off and make sure that there is no change in the pedal reserve distance.
2   Depress the pedal and start the engine. If the pedal goes down slightly, operation is normal.

Airtightness check

3   Start the engine and turn it off after one or two minutes. Depress the brake pedal several times slowly. If the pedal goes down farther the first time but gradually rises after the second or third depression, the booster is airtight.
4   Depress the brake pedal while the engine is running, then stop the engine with the pedal depressed. If there is no change in the pedal reserve travel after holding the pedal for 30 seconds, the booster is airtight.

Removal and installation

Refer to illustrations 10.7 and 10.10

5   Disassembly of the power unit requires special tools and is not ordinarily performed by the home mechanic. If a problem develops, it's recommended that a new or factory rebuilt unit be installed.
6   In the engine compartment, remove the nuts attaching the master cylinder to the booster and carefully pull the master cylinder

10.7 Location of the power brake booster vacuum connection - disconnect the hose from the check valve (don't pull the check valve out of the booster)

forward until it clears the mounting studs. Be careful not to bend or kink the brake lines.
7   Disconnect the vacuum hose from the check valve on the power brake booster **(see illustration)**.
8   On models equipped with Traction Control and Stability Assist systems, disconnect the solenoid connectors from the booster.
9   In the passenger compartment, remove the retaining pin and washer, then disconnect the pushrod from the top of the brake pedal.
10   Remove the nuts attaching the booster to the firewall **(see illustration)**.
11   Carefully lift the booster unit away from the firewall and out of the engine compartment.
12   To install the booster, place it into position and tighten the retaining nuts. Connect the pushrod to the brake pedal.
13   Install the master cylinder. Reconnect the vacuum hose.
14   Carefully test the operation of the brakes before placing the vehicle in normal service.

11 Parking brake cable - adjustment

1   The parking brake pedal, when properly adjusted, should travel three to five clicks, when a moderate stepping force is applied with the left foot. If it travels less than the specified minimum number of clicks, there's a chance the parking brake might not be releasing completely and might be dragging on the disc. If the pedal can be depressed more than the specified maximum number of clicks, the parking brake may not hold adequately on an incline, allowing the car to roll.
2   To gain access to the parking brake cable adjuster, raise the rear of the vehicle and secure it on jackstands.
3   Remove the rubber plug from the brake backing plate and, using a screwdriver or brake adjusting tool, turn the adjusting screw star wheel until the parking brake shoes start to drag as the disc is turned, then back off the star wheel until the shoes don't drag.
4   Install the rubber plug(s) and lower the vehicle.

12 Brake light switch - replacement

Refer to illustration 12.2

1   Disconnect the electrical connector at the switch.
2   Remove the retaining pin to release the switch from the brake pedal arm **(see illustration)**.
3   Slide the bushing out and remove the brake light switch and the pushrod from the brake pedal. **Note:** *Once the pushrod is removed, the brake pedal return spring will force the brake pedal up.*
4   To install the brake light switch, install the pushrod, the switch, the bushing and retaining pin onto the brake pedal.
5   Connect the switch electrical connector.

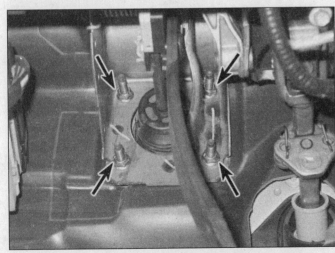

10.10 To detach the power brake booster from the firewall, remove these four nuts

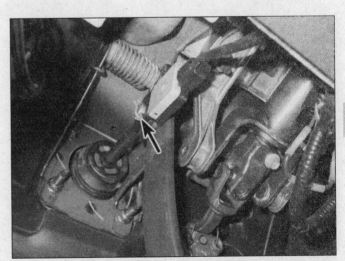

12.2 Remove the retaining pin and slide the brake light switch off the stud on the brake pedal arm

9

Notes

Chapter 10
Suspension and steering systems

Contents

Specifications

General

Power steering fluid type .... See Chapter 1

Torque specifications

	Ft-lbs (unless otherwise indicated)	Nm

Front suspension

Shock absorber-to-lower control arm bolt/nut	258	350
Shock absorber upper mounting nuts	22	30
Shock absorber damper rod-to-insulator nut	41	55
Stabilizer bar-to-link nut	18	25
Stabilizer bar bracket-to-frame bolt	52	70
Upper control arm-to-frame nuts	111	150
Upper control arm balljoint-to-steering knuckle nut	41	55
Lower control arm-to-frame bolt/nuts		
Forward bolt/nut	295	400
Rear nuts	111	150
Lower control arm balljoint-to-steering knuckle nut	129	175

Rear suspension

Shock absorber-to-lower control arm bolt/nut	184	250
Shock absorber upper mounting nuts	22	30
Shock absorber damper rod-to-insulator nut	52	70
Stabilizer bar-to-link nut	18	25
Stabilizer bar bracket-to-frame nut	41	55
Upper control arm-to-frame nuts (forward)	98	133
Upper control arm-to-bushing assembly bolts (rear)	59	80
Upper control arm balljoint-to-knuckle nut	66	90
Lower control arm-to-frame nuts	129	175
Lower control arm-to-knuckle nut/bolt	111	150
Toe link-to-knuckle nut	66	90
Toe link-to-frame nut	59	80

10

Torque specifications (continued)

	Ft-lbs (unless otherwise indicated)	Nm
Steering		
Airbag module mounting screws	80 in-lbs	9
Power steering fluid cooler bolts	96 in-lbs	11
Power steering pressure and return line clamp nut	18	25
Power steering pressure line fitting	48	65
Power steering pump pulley bolts	18	25
Power steering pump mounting fasteners		
V6 models	18	25
V8 models	132 in-lbs	15
Steering wheel bolt	30	40
Steering gear mounting bolts	148	200
Steering column mounting nuts	132 in-lbs	15
Intermediate shaft pinch bolt	22	30
Power steering gear-to-intermediate shaft bolt	35	48
Steering gear mounting bracket-to-crossmember bolts	52	70

1   General information

Front suspension

Refer to illustrations 1.1a and 1.1b

The front suspension system is fully independent **(see illustrations)**. The steering knuckles are connected to the upper and lower control arms by balljoints. The control arms are bolted to the frame. The shock absorbers and coil springs are integral assemblies (coil over shock); the upper ends are bolted to brackets on the frame and the lower ends are bolted to the lower control arms. All models use a front stabilizer bar to reduce vehicle roll during cornering.

Rear suspension

Refer to illustration 1.2

The rear suspension system is also fully independent **(see illustration)**. The steering knuckles are connected to the upper control arms by balljoints and the lower control arms by bushings. The control arms are bolted to the frame. The shock absorbers and coil springs are integral assemblies (coil over shock); the upper ends are bolted to brackets on the frame and the lower ends are bolted to the rear side of the lower control arms. A rear stabilizer bar reduces vehicle roll during cornering. The rear suspension includes toe links for toe in/out adjustments.

1.1a Front suspension and steering components (2WD models)

1	*Shock absorber/coil spring assembly*	*4*	*Lower control arm*	*7*	*Tie-rod end*
2	*Steering knuckle*	*5*	*Steering gear*	*8*	*Stabilizer bar*
3	*Balljoint*	*6*	*Suspension crossmember*	*9*	*Upper control arm*

1.1b Additional view of front suspension components (2WD models)

1 Upper control arm
2 Upper balljoint
3 Shock absorber/coil spring assembly
4 Steering knuckle
5 Lower balljoint
6 Stabilizer bar
7 Lower control arm

Steering

All models are equipped with power-assisted rack-and-pinion steering systems. The steering gear is bolted to the crossmember and is connected to the steering knuckles by a pair of tie-rods.

Precautions

Frequently, when working on the suspension or steering system components, you may come across fasteners which seem impossible to loosen. These fasteners on the underside of the vehicle are continually subjected to water, road grime, mud, etc., and can become rusted or "frozen," making them extremely difficult to remove. In order to unscrew these stubborn fasteners without damaging them (or other components), be sure to use lots of penetrating oil and allow it to soak in for a while. Using a wire brush to clean exposed threads will also ease removal of the nut or bolt and prevent damage to the threads. Sometimes a sharp blow with a hammer and punch is effective in breaking the bond between a nut and bolt threads, but care must be taken to prevent the punch from slipping off the fastener and ruining the threads. Heating the stuck fastener and surrounding area with a torch sometimes helps too, but isn't recommended because of the obvious dangers associated with fire. Long breaker bars and extension, or "cheater," pipes will increase leverage, but never use an extension pipe on a ratchet - the ratcheting mechanism could be damaged. Sometimes, turning the nut or bolt in the tightening (clockwise) direction first will help to break it loose. Fasteners that require drastic measures to unscrew should always be replaced with new ones.

Since most of the procedures that are dealt with in this Chapter involve jacking up

1.2 Rear suspension components (2WD models)

1 Upper control arm
2 Stabilizer bar
3 Knuckle
4 Toe link
5 Lower control arm

10

2.2 To detach the upper end of the shock absorber/coil spring assembly from the vehicle frame, remove these three nuts (NOT the nut in the middle, which is the damper rod nut; it must never be removed unless the spring is compressed with a spring compressor)

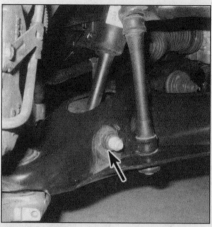

2.4 To detach the lower end of the shock absorber from the lower control arm, remove this bolt and nut - turn the bolt, NOT the nut (the nut has an anti-rotation "flag" attached to it)

2.8 Install the spring compressor(s) in accordance with the tool manufacturer's instructions; compress the spring until you can wiggle it before removing the damper rod nut

the vehicle and working underneath it, a good pair of jackstands will be needed. A hydraulic floor jack is the preferred type of jack to lift the vehicle, and it can also be used to support certain components during various operations. **Warning:** *Never, under any circumstances, rely on a jack to support the vehicle while working on it. Also, whenever any of the suspension or steering fasteners are loosened or removed they must be inspected and, if necessary, replaced with new ones of the same part number or of original equipment quality and design. Torque specifications must be followed for proper reassembly and component retention. Never attempt to heat or straighten suspension or steering components. Instead, replace bent or damaged parts with new ones.*

2   Shock absorber/coil spring (front) - removal, component replacement and installation

Refer to illustrations 2.2, 2.4, 2.8, 2.9, 2.11, 2.12 and 2.14

Warning: *Before undertaking the following procedure, be aware that disassembling the shock absorber/coil spring assemblies is a potentially dangerous job. Careless or unsafe work can cause serious injury. Use only a high-quality spring compressor and be sure to follow the spring compressor manufacturer's instructions. After removing the compressed spring, set it aside in a safe, isolated place.*

Note: *If the shock absorber/coil spring assemblies must be replaced, you can save time by simply installing new complete shock/coil assemblies. Or, you can replace just the shocks or just the springs. But, to do so, you will have to disassemble the shock absorber/coil spring assemblies. Therefore, before deciding which way you want to go,*

find out the cost of each option. You may find that the cost for two assembled complete shock/coil assemblies is only slightly higher than the cost for two new shock absorbers or coil springs.

Removal

1   Loosen the front wheel lug nuts. Raise the vehicle and support it securely on jackstands. Remove the front wheels.
2   Remove the three nuts that attach the upper end of the shock to the frame **(see illustration)**.
3   Remove the stabilizer bar link (see Section 3).
4   Remove the bolt attaching the lower end of the shock absorber to the lower control arm **(see illustration)**. **Warning:** *The manufacturer states that a new nut should be installed on the lower mounting bolt during reassembly.*
5   Remove the shock absorber/coil spring assembly.
6   Inspect the shock absorber for leaking fluid, dents, cracks and other damage. Inspect the coil spring for chips and cracks which could cause premature failure. Inspect

the spring seats for hardness and general deterioration. If either the shock or the spring is worn or damaged, replace it. If you're installing new complete units, proceed to Step 15; if you're going to install new shocks or coil springs, proceed to the next Step.

Component replacement

7   Secure the shock/coil assembly in a bench vise. If you're planning to reuse the old shock absorbers, line the jaws of the vise with wood or shop rags to protect the shock bodies. And don't tighten the jaws any more than necessary; overtightening the vise will crush the shock body.
8   Install a spring compressor in accordance with the tool manufacturer's instructions **(see illustration)**. (You can buy a spring compressor at most auto parts stores or rent one from most equipment yards on a daily basis.) Compress the spring far enough to relieve all pressure from the spring seat; when you can wiggle the spring, it's compressed enough to disassemble the shock/spring assembly. **Warning:** *Don't compress the spring any more than necessary.*
9   Hold the damper rod with a socket and

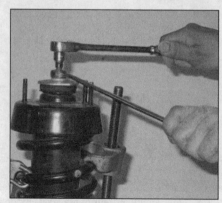

2.9 Unscrew the damper rod nut while preventing the damper rod from turning by holding it with a wrench or socket

2.11 Lift the dust shield from the shock absorber/coil spring assembly

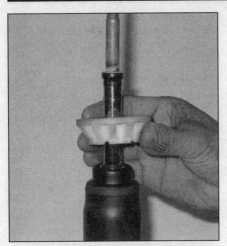

2.12 Lift the lower insulator from the shock absorber

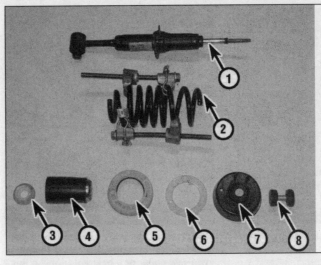

2.14 An exploded view of the shock absorber/coil spring assembly

1 Shock absorber
2 Coil spring with compressing tools installed
3 Washer
4 Dust shield
5 Upper insulator
6 Friction bearing
7 Mount
8 Bushings

remove the damper rod nut **(see illustration)**. **Warning:** *The manufacturer states that a new nut should be installed during reassembly.*

10 Remove the upper washer, the bushing and the mount.

11 Remove the insulator, compressed spring and dust shield **(see illustration)**. Set the spring in a safe place.

12 Remove the lower insulator **(see illustration)**.

13 Inspect the insulators for cracks and tears and general deterioration. Replace them if they're damaged. Make sure the bushings and washers are in good condition too. If they're distorted or otherwise damaged, replace them.

14 Reassembly is the reverse of disassembly **(see illustration)**. Make sure the lower end of the coil spring is correctly seated in the low spot in the lower spring seat. Tighten the damper rod nut to the torque listed in this Chapter's Specifications before releasing tension on the spring.

Installation

15 Installation is the reverse of removal. Be sure to tighten the upper and lower fasteners to the torque listed in this Chapter's Specifications. Tighten the wheel lug nuts to the torque listed in the Chapter 1 Specifications. **Warning:** *The manufacturer states that a new nut should be installed on the lower mounting bolt during reassembly.* **Note:** *The shock absorber lower mounting bolt should be tightened with the vehicle at normal ride height. This can be done after the vehicle has been lowered to the ground (on vehicles with adequate clearance), or can be simulated by raising the lower control arm with a floor jack.*

3   Stabilizer bar and bushings (front) - removal and installation

Refer to illustrations 3.2 and 3.3

1 Loosen the front wheel lug nuts. Raise the vehicle and support it securely on jackstands. Remove the front wheels.

2 Remove the nuts from the stabilizer bar links and detach the links from the bar **(see illustration)**. Note how the bushings are arranged on the ends of the links. **Warning:** *The manufacturer states that new nuts should be installed on the stabilizer bar links during reassembly.*

3 Remove the stabilizer bar bushing bracket bolts and/or nuts **(see illustration)**. **Warning:** *The manufacturer states that new bolts should be installed during reassembly.*

4 Remove the stabilizer bar.

5 Remove the rubber bushings from the stabilizer bar.

6 Inspect the rubber bushings for cracks, tears and deterioration. If they're worn or damaged, replace them.

7 Check each stabilizer link for signs of excessive wear.

8 Installation is the reverse of removal. Be sure to tighten all fasteners to the torque listed in this Chapter's Specifications.

4   Steering knuckle (front) - removal and installation

Refer to illustration 4.7

1 Apply the parking brake. Loosen the wheel lug nuts. Raise the front of the vehicle and support it securely on jackstands. Remove the wheel.

2 Detach the brake hose bracket from the steering knuckle. Detach the wheel speed sensor from the steering knuckle (see Chapter 9).

3 Remove the brake caliper and brake disc (see Chapter 9). Hang the caliper with a length of wire - don't let it hang by the brake hose.

4 Disconnect the tie-rod end from the steering knuckle (see Section 18).

5 On 4WD models, remove the driveaxle/hub nut (see Chapter 8).

6 Disconnect the upper and lower control arms from the steering knuckle (see Sections 5 and 6), then remove the steering knuckle.

7 On 4WD models, guide the driveaxle out of the hub, being careful to not overextend the inner CV joint. If the driveaxle is stuck in the hub splines, it will be necessary to use a puller to push the driveaxle out of the hub

3.2 Stabilizer bar link nut location

3.3 To separate the stabilizer bar from the frame, remove the bolts from both bushing brackets

10

4.7 **If the driveaxle is stuck in the hub, use a puller to push it out**

5.4 **The best way to separate the upper control arm from the balljoint is to use a two-jaw puller or a balljoint tool like this**

5.5 **The upper control arm is attached to the frame with two nuts (forward mounting nut shown); remove the nuts and shims and lift the upper arm off the frame**

(see illustration). Support the driveaxle with a length of wire - don't let it hang by the inner CV joint.

8   Remove the hub and bearing assembly (see Section 7).

9   Installation is the reverse of removal. Tighten all suspension fasteners to the torque values listed in this Chapter's Specifications.

10 On 4WD models, tighten the driveaxle/hub nut to the torque listed in the Chapter 8 Specifications.

11 On all models, tighten the wheel lug nuts to the torque listed in the Chapter 1 Specifications.

---

5 Upper control arm (front) - removal and installation

Refer to illustrations 5.4 and 5.5

1   Loosen the wheel lug nuts, raise the front of the vehicle and support it securely on jackstands. Apply the parking brake. Remove the wheel.

2   Disconnect the wheel speed sensor wiring harness from the upper control arm and steering knuckle.

3   Remove the rear inner fender apron seal.

4   Loosen the upper balljoint nut a few turns. Using a two-jaw puller to separate the balljoint from the upper control arm **(see illustration)**. Remove the nut and separate the upper control arm and balljoint from the steering knuckle. **Caution:** *Don't allow the steering knuckle to fall outward, as the brake hose may be damaged. It's a good idea to wire the steering knuckle to the coil spring so this doesn't happen.* **Warning:** *The manufacturer states that a new nut should be installed during reassembly.*

5   Remove the two nuts and shims and detach the upper control arm from the frame **(see illustration)**. **Warning:** *The manufacturer states that new nuts should be installed on the upper control arm-to-frame bolts during reassembly.*

6   Inspect the bushings for wear and deterioration. If they're cracked or damaged, take the arm to an automotive machine shop and have new bushings installed.

7   Installation is the reverse of removal. Be sure to tighten all suspension fasteners to the torque listed in this Chapter's Specifications.

8   It's a good idea to have the wheel alignment checked and, if necessary, adjusted.

---

6 Lower control arm (front) - removal and installation

Refer to illustrations 6.4 and 6.6

1   Loosen the wheel lug nuts, raise the front of the vehicle and support it securely on jackstands. Apply the parking brake. Remove the wheel.

2   Remove the shock absorber/coil spring assembly (see Section 2).

3   Remove the cotter pin, then loosen the lower balljoint nut a few turns.

4   Using a C-clamp type balljoint separator, separate the balljoint from the steering knuckle **(see illustration)**.

5   On 4WD models, rotate the front axle so that the crimped area of the CV joint boot clamp is not facing down, or it will interfere with the lower control arm removal.

6   Remove the nut and pivot bolt from the

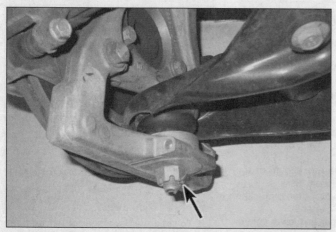

6.4 **Remove the cotter pin from the lower balljoint nut, unscrew the nut a few turns, then separate the balljoint from the steering knuckle**

6.6 **Location of the forward pivot bolt/nut and the rear mounting nuts securing the lower control arm**

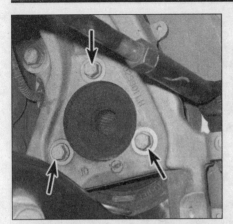

7.2 Working on the backside of the steering knuckle, remove the bolts and separate the hub from the knuckle

8.2 Remove the three upper mounting nuts from the shock absorber/coil spring assembly - one nut hidden from view

8.4 Location of the shock absorber/coil spring assembly lower mounting nut/bolt

front of the control arm, and the two nuts from the rear bushing bracket **(see illustration)**, then remove the control arm from the frame. **Warning:** *The manufacturer states that new nuts should be installed during reassembly.*

7   Inspect the bushings for wear and deterioration. If they're cracked or damaged, take the control arm to an automotive machine shop and have new bushings installed.

8   Installation is the reverse of removal. Be sure to tighten all suspension fasteners to the torque listed in this Chapter's Specifications, and use a new cotter pin on the lower control arm balljoint nut. If necessary, tighten the balljoint nut a little more to align the hole in the ballstud with the slots in the nut - don't loosen the nut to achieve this alignment. **Note:** *The pivot bolt nut should be tightened with the vehicle at normal ride height. This can be done after the vehicle has been lowered to the ground (on vehicles with adequate clearance), or can be simulated by raising the lower control arm with a floor jack.*

10   Have the wheel alignment checked and, if necessary, adjusted.

7   Hub and bearing assembly (front) - replacement

Refer to illustration 7.2

1   If you are working on a 4WD model, loosen the driveaxle/hub nut **(see illustration 13.1).**

2   Loosen the wheel lug nuts, raise the front of the vehicle and support it securely on jackstands, then remove the wheel.

3   Remove the brake caliper and brake disc. Also remove the wheel speed sensor from the steering knuckle (see Chapter 9).

4   Working on the backside of the steering knuckle, remove the hub mounting bolts **(see illustration)**. If you're working on a 2WD model, remove the hub and bearing assembly from the steering knuckle. If it's stuck, you can tap on it with a hammer to work it out of the knuckle bore.

5   If you're working on a 4WD model, remove the driveaxle/hub nut and push the driveaxle through the hub splines as the hub and bearing assembly is removed. If the driveaxle sticks in the hub, you'll have to push it out with a puller **(see illustration 4.7)**. **Caution:** *Be careful not to overextend the inner CV joint.* Once the hub has been removed, support the outer end of the driveaxle with a length of wire or rope.

6   Installation is the reverse of removal, noting the following points:

a) *Tighten the hub mounting bolts to the torque listed in this Chapter's Specifications.*

b) *Tighten the brake caliper mounting bracket bolts, caliper mounting bolts and the wheel speed sensor bolt to the torque listed in the Chapter 9 Specifications.*

c) *Tighten the wheel lug nuts to the torque listed in the Chapter 1 Specifications.*

8   Shock absorber/coil spring (rear) - removal, component replacement and installation

Refer to illustrations 8.2, 8.4 and 8.6

Warning: *Before undertaking the following procedure, be aware that disassembling the shock absorber/coil spring assemblies is a potentially dangerous job. Careless or unsafe work can cause serious injury. Use only a high-quality spring compressor and be sure to follow the spring compressor manufacturer's instructions. After removing the compressed spring, set it aside in a safe, isolated place.*

Note: *If the shock absorber/coil spring assemblies must be replaced, you can save time by simply installing new complete shock/coil assemblies. Or, you can replace just the shocks or just the springs. But, to do so, you will have to disassemble the shock absorber/coil spring assemblies. Therefore, before deciding which way you want to go, find out the cost of each option. You may find*

that the cost for two assembled complete shock/coil assemblies is only slightly higher than the cost for two new shock absorbers or coil springs.

Removal

1   Loosen the rear wheel lug nuts. Raise the vehicle and support it securely on jackstands. Remove the rear wheels.

2   Remove the three nuts that attach the upper end of the shock to the frame bracket **(see illustration)**. **Warning:** *The manufacturer states that new nuts should be installed during reassembly.*

3   Remove the nut from the stabilizer link (see Section 9). **Warning:** *The manufacturer states that new nuts should be installed on the stabilizer bar links during reassembly.*

4   Remove the nut and bolt attaching the lower end of the shock absorber to the lower control arm **(see illustration)**. **Warning:** *The manufacturer states that a new nut should be installed during reassembly.*

5   Separate the lower control arm from the knuckle (see Section 11). Also detach the toe link from the rear knuckle (see Section 12).

6   Remove the shock absorber/coil spring assembly **(see illustration)**.

8.6 Use a long screwdriver or prybar to pry the lower control arm down far enough to allow shock absorber removal

10

9.2 Location of the stabilizer bar link nut

9.3 Remove the stabilizer bar bracket mounting nuts and guide the stabilizer bar out from the right side of vehicle

7   Inspect the shock absorber for leaking fluid, dents, cracks and other damage. Inspect the coil spring for chips and cracks which could cause premature failure. Inspect the spring seats for hardness and general deterioration. If either the shock or the spring is worn or damaged, replace it. If you're installing new complete units, proceed to Step 16; if you're going to install new shocks or coil springs, proceed to the next Step.

Component replacement

8   Secure the shock/coil assembly in a bench vise. If you're planning to reuse the old shock absorbers, line the jaws of the vise with wood or shop rags to protect the shock bodies. And don't tighten the jaws any more than necessary; overtightening the vise may crush the shock body.

9   Install a spring compressor in accordance with the tool manufacturer's instructions **(see illustration 2.8)**. (You can buy a spring compressor at most auto parts stores or rent one from most equipment yards on a daily basis.) Compress the spring far enough to relieve all pressure from the spring seat; when you can wiggle the spring, it's compressed enough to disassemble the shock/spring assembly. **Warning:** *Don't compress the spring any more than necessary.*

10 Hold the damper rod with a wrench and remove the damper rod nut **(see illustration 2.9)**. **Warning:** *The manufacturer states that a new nut should be installed during reassembly.*

11 Remove the upper washer, the bushing and the mount.

12 Remove the compressed spring assembly and set it safely aside.

13 Remove the dust shield and the rubber insulator.

14 Inspect the insulator for cracks and tears and general deterioration. Replace them if they're damaged. Make sure the bushings are in good condition too. If they're distorted or otherwise damaged, replace them.

15 Reassembly is the reverse of disassem-

bly. Make sure the lower end of the coil spring is correctly seated in the low spot in the lower spring seat. Tighten the damper rod nut to the torque listed in this Chapter's Specifications before releasing tension on the spring.

Installation

16 Installation is the reverse of removal. Be sure to tighten all fasteners to the torque listed in this Chapter's Specifications. **Note:** *The lower control arm/shock absorber bolt/nut should be tightened with the vehicle at normal ride height. This can be done after the vehicle has been lowered to the ground (on vehicles with adequate clearance), or can be simulated by raising the lower control arm with a floor jack.*

9   Stabilizer bar and bushings (rear) - removal and installation

Refer to illustrations 9.2 and 9.3

1   Loosen the rear wheel lug nuts. Raise the vehicle and support it securely on jackstands. Remove the rear wheels.

2   Remove the nuts from the stabilizer bar links and detach the links from the bar **(see illustration)**. Note how the bushings are arranged on the ends of the links. **Warning:** *The manufacturer states that new nuts should be installed on the stabilizer bar links during reassembly.*

3   Remove the stabilizer bar bushing bracket bolts **(see illustration)**.

4   Remove the rear caliper (see Chapter 9).

5   Separate the upper balljoints from the knuckles (see Section 10).

6   Disconnect the fuel line from the fuel tank retaining clip.

7   Remove the stabilizer bar out from the right side of the vehicle. It will be necessary to angle the stabilizer bar to clear the fuel tank.

8   Remove the rubber bushings from the stabilizer bar.

9   Inspect the rubber bushings for cracks, tears and deterioration. If they're worn or damaged, replace them.

10 Check each stabilizer link for signs of excessive wear.

11 Installation is otherwise the reverse of removal. Be sure to tighten all fasteners to the torque listed in this Chapter's Specifications.

10 Upper control arm (rear) - removal and installation

Refer to illustrations 10.3, 10.5a and 10.5b

1   Block the front tires. Loosen the wheel lug nuts, raise the rear of the vehicle and support it securely on jackstands. Remove the wheel.

2   Disconnect the wheel speed sensor wiring harness from the upper control arm and steering knuckle.

3   Unscrew the nut, remove the pinch bolt and separate the upper balljoint from the steering knuckle **(see illustration)**. **Warning:** *The manufacturer states that a new nut should be installed during reassembly.*

10.3 Location of the upper balljoint pinch bolt nut

10.5a Remove the forward pivot bolt/nut . . .

10.5b . . . and the rear mounting bolts to remove the upper control arm from the frame

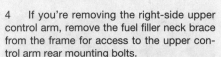

11.4 Location of the lower control arm pivot bolt/nut at the knuckle

4   If you're removing the right-side upper control arm, remove the fuel filler neck brace from the frame for access to the upper control arm rear mounting bolts.

5   Remove the rear mounting bolts and flag nuts and the forward mounting nut, washer and pivot bolt and detach the upper control arm from the frame **(see illustrations)**. **Warning:** *The manufacturer states that new nuts should be installed during reassembly.* Remove the arm.

6   Inspect the bushings for wear and deterioration. If they're cracked or damaged, take the arm to an automotive machine shop and have new bushings installed.

7   Installation is the reverse of removal. Be sure to tighten all suspension fasteners to the torque listed in this Chapter's Specifications. **Note:** *The pivot bolt/nut should be tightened with the vehicle at normal ride height. This can be done after the vehicle has been lowered to the ground (on vehicles with adequate clearance), or can be simulated by raising the lower control arm with a floor jack.*

8   It's a good idea to have the wheel alignment checked and, if necessary, adjusted.

11   Lower control arm (rear) - removal and installation

Refer to illustrations 11.4, 11.5a and 11.5b

1   Loosen the wheel lug nuts, raise the front of the vehicle and support it securely on jackstands. Block the front tires. Remove the wheel.

2   Remove the parking brake cable bracket mounting bolt from the lower control arm.

3   Detach the stabilizer bar link from the lower control arm (see Section 9). Also remove the shock absorber lower mounting nut and bolt (see Section 8).

4   Remove the lower control arm-to-knuckle nut/bolt **(see illustration)**. Separate the knuckle from the lower control arm. **Warning:** *The manufacturer states that a new nut should be installed during reassembly.*

5   Mark the position of the shim in relation to the frame under the rear pivot bolt-to-frame nut, then unscrew the pivot bolt nuts **(see illustrations)**. Remove the bolts and detach the control arm from the frame. **Warning:** *The manufacturer states that new*

nuts should be installed during reassembly.

6   Inspect the bushings for wear and deterioration. If they're cracked or damaged, take the arm to an automotive machine shop and have new bushings installed.

7   Installation is the reverse of removal. Make sure that the shims are installed correctly (original position). Be sure to tighten all suspension fasteners to the torque listed in this Chapter's Specifications. **Note:** *The pivot bolt nuts should be tightened with the vehicle at normal ride height. This can be done after the vehicle has been lowered to the ground (on vehicles with adequate clearance), or can be simulated by raising the lower control arm with a floor jack.*

8   Have the wheel alignment checked and, if necessary, adjusted.

12   Toe link - removal and installation

Refer to illustration 12.2 and 12.3

1   Block the front tires. Loosen the wheel

11.5a Remove the forward nut and pivot bolt . . .

11.5b . . . and the rear nut and pivot bolt to separate the lower control arm from the frame

12.2 Location of the toe link pinch bolt/nut at the knuckle

12.3 Location of the toe link mounting nut at the frame

13.1 Use a breaker bar and socket to loosen the driveaxle/hub nut while the tires are on the shop floor - do not remove the nut from the axle yet

lug nuts. Raise the rear of the vehicle and support it securely on jackstands. Remove the wheel.

2   Remove the nut and bolt and separate the toe link from the rear knuckle (**see illustration**).

3   Remove the nut from the toe link at the frame (**see illustration**) and remove the toe link from the vehicle. **Warning:** *The manufacturer states that a new nut should be installed during reassembly.*

4   Installation is the reverse of the removal procedure. Tighten the fasteners to the torque listed in this Chapter's Specifications.

5   Have the wheel alignment checked and, if necessary, adjusted.

13   Knuckle (rear) - removal and installation

Refer to illustration 13.1

1   Use a breaker bar and socket to loosen the rear driveaxle/hub nut (**see illustration**). Do not remove the nut from the driveaxle at this time. Loosen the nut just enough to be able to remove it later, when the vehicle is positioned on jackstands.

2   Block the front tires. Loosen the wheel lug nuts. Raise the rear of the vehicle and support it securely on jackstands. Remove the wheel.

3   If the vehicle is equipped with four-channel ABS, detach the ABS wheel speed sensor from the knuckle (see Chapter 9).

4   Remove the brake caliper and brake disc (see Chapter 9). Hang the caliper with a length of wire - don't let it hang by the brake hose.

5   Remove the parking brake shoes (see Chapter 9).

6   Disconnect the toe link from the rear knuckle (see Section 12).

7   Remove the driveaxle/hub nut (see Chapter 8).

8   Disconnect the upper and lower control arms from the rear knuckle (see Sections 10 and 11).

9   Guide the driveaxle out of the hub, being careful to not overextend the inner CV joint. If the driveaxle sticks in the hub, you'll have to push it out with a puller (**see illustration 4.7**). Support the driveaxle with a length of wire - don't let it hang by the inner CV joint.

10   Remove the knuckle.

11   Installation is the reverse of removal. Tighten all suspension fasteners to the torque values listed in this Chapter's Specifications.

12   Tighten the brake caliper mounting bolts and wheel speed sensor (if equipped with four-channel ABS) to the torque listed in the Chapter 9 Specifications. Tighten the driveaxle/hub nut to the torque listed in the Chapter 10 Specifications, and the wheel lug nuts to the torque listed in the Chapter 1 Specifications.

14   Hub and bearing assembly (rear) - replacement

Due to the special tools and expertise required to press the hub and bearing from the rear knuckle, this job should be left to a professional mechanic. However, the knuckle may be removed and taken to an automotive machine shop or other qualified repair facility equipped with the necessary tools. See Section 13 for the knuckle removal procedure.

15   Balljoints - check and replacement

Check

Refer to illustration 15.4

1   Inspect the upper and lower balljoints for looseness whenever the vehicle is raised for any reason. You can check the balljoints with the suspension assembled as follows.

2   Loosen the wheel lug nuts. Raise vehicle and support it securely on jackstands. Remove the wheels.

3   Wipe the balljoints clean and inspect the seals for cuts and tears. If a balljoint seal is damaged, replace the balljoint.

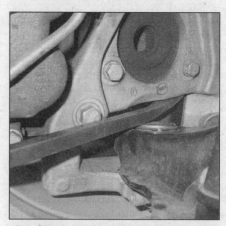

15.4 Check for play in the balljoints with a large screwdriver or breaker bar positioned between the control arm and the steering knuckle; try to pry the control arm up-and-down and observe the balljoints for excessive movement

4   Check the balljoints for wear by trying to move each control arm up and down with a pry bar (**see illustration**) to ensure that the balljoint has no play. If any balljoint does have play, replace it.

Replacement

5   The balljoints on these models are not serviceable. If the balljoint must be replaced, the control arm and balljoint must be replaced as a single assembly.

16   Steering wheel - removal and installation

Refer to illustrations 16.3a, 16.3b, 16.4, 16.5, 16.6 and 16.8

Warning: *The models covered by this manual are equipped with Supplemental Restraint systems (SRS), more commonly known as airbags. Always disable the airbag system before working in the vicinity of any airbag*

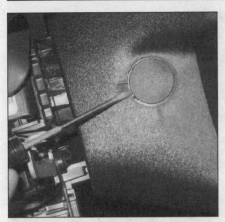

16.3a Pry off the covers on the sides of the steering wheel . . .

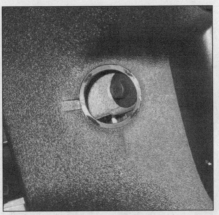

16.3b . . . then unscrew the bolts that retain the airbag module

16.4 To unplug the electrical connectors from the airbag module, squeeze the locking tabs on the sides of each connector, then pull the connectors out

system component to avoid the possibility of accidental deployment of the airbag, which could cause personal injury (see Chapter 12).

1   Park the vehicle with the front wheels pointed straight ahead and the steering wheel centered. Disconnect the cable from the negative terminal of the battery (see Chapter 5).

2   Refer to Chapter 12 and disable the airbag system.

3   Pry out the two small covers, one on each side of the steering wheel, and unscrew the two bolts that retain the airbag module (see illustrations).

4   Lift the airbag module off the steering wheel and disconnect the airbag electrical connectors (see illustration). Warning: When handling the airbag module, hold it with the trim side facing away from you. Set the airbag module down in a safe location with the trim side facing up.

5   Unplug any other electrical connectors, such as the one for the horn (see illustration).

6   Remove the steering wheel retaining bolt and mark the position of the steering wheel to the shaft, if marks don't already exist or don't line up (see illustration).

7   Lift the steering wheel off the shaft. If it's

stuck and won't come off, reinstall the bolt finger-tight, then loosen it a few turns. Now use a two-jaw puller to break the bond between the steering wheel and the shaft (the puller screw must bear down on the steering wheel bolt so as not to damage the threads in the steering shaft). Finally, remove the bolt and take the wheel off the shaft. Caution: Don't hammer on the shaft or the steering wheel in an attempt to dislodge the wheel! Warning: While the steering wheel is removed, do NOT turn the steering shaft. If the steering shaft is turned, the clockspring will be uncentered and the harness will break, rendering the airbag inoperative. If the clockspring is accidentally uncentered, it must be centered before installing the steering wheel.

8   Make sure the clockspring is centered, as follows: Verify that the front wheels are pointing straight ahead. Turn the clockspring housing counterclockwise by hand until it becomes hard to turn (don't apply too much force, though, because the cable could break). Turn the clockspring clockwise about 3 turns and align the marks (see illustration).

9   If it's necessary to remove the clockspring from the steering column, apply two pieces of tape across the hub of the clockspring to the housing to prevent it from rotat-

ing. Remove the screws, follow the wiring harness down the steering column and disconnect the electrical connector, then remove the clockspring. Reverse the removal procedure to install the clockspring, but be sure to center it as described in the previous Step.

10   To install the wheel, align the mark on the steering wheel hub with the mark on the shaft and slide the wheel onto the shaft. Install the nut and tighten it to the torque listed in this Chapter's Specifications.

11   Installation is otherwise the reverse of removal. Be sure the electrical connectors are securely plugged into the airbag module, and tighten the airbag module retaining bolts to the torque listed in this Chapter's Specifications.

17   Steering column - removal and installation

Warning: The models covered by this manual are equipped with Supplemental Restraint

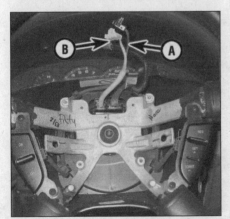

16.5 Unplug the horn (A) and airbag (B) connectors and any other electrical connectors that would interfere with steering wheel removal

16.6 Remove the steering wheel bolt, then mark the relationship of the steering wheel to the steering shaft

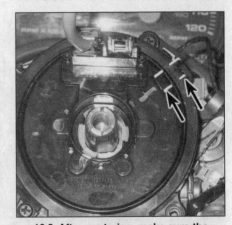

16.8 After centering, make sure the alignment marks on the clockspring align with the marks on the housing

10

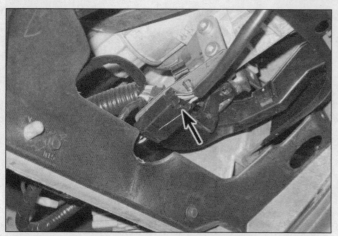

17.5a Depress the locking tab and release the harness connector

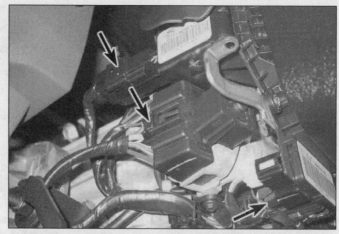

17.5b Disconnect the turn signal switch, the ignition switch and airbag electrical connectors

17.6 Disconnect the shift cable from the column by first releasing the pressure tabs on the column flange (A) and then carefully prying the cable end from the lever pin (B)

17.7 Release the transmission range indicator from the instrument cluster

systems (SRS), more commonly known as airbags. Always disable the airbag system before working in the vicinity of any airbag system component to avoid the possibility of accidental deployment of the airbag, which could cause personal injury (see Chapter 12).

Removal

Refer to illustrations 17.5a, 17.5b, 17.6, 17.7, 17.8, 17.9, 17.10 and 17.11

1 Park the vehicle with the wheels pointing straight ahead. Disconnect the cable from the negative terminal of the battery (see

Chapter 5).

2 Remove the steering wheel (see Section 16), then turn the ignition key to the LOCK position to prevent the steering shaft from turning. **Caution:** *If this is not done, the airbag clockspring could be damaged.*

17.8 Remove the cable conduit mounting screws and separate the conduit from the steering column

17.9 Mark the U-joint to the steering shaft, then remove the pinch bolt

17.10 Location of the steering column brace mounting bolts

17.11 Location of the steering column fasteners

3   Remove the lower finish panel under the steering column (see Chapter 11).
4   Remove the steering column covers (see Chapter 11).
5   Disconnect the electrical connectors for the steering column harness **(see illustrations)**.
6   On models with an automatic transmission, detach the shift cable **(see illustration)** and shift interlock cable (see Chapter 7B).
7   Disconnect the transmission range indicator from the instrument cluster **(see illustration)**.
8   Remove the mounting screws from the cable conduit **(see illustration)**. Separate the cable conduit from the steering column.
9   Mark the relationship of the intermediate shaft U-joint to the steering shaft. Remove the intermediate shaft pinch bolt **(see illustration)**. **Warning:** *The manufacturer states that a new bolt should be installed during reassembly.*
10   Remove the steering column brace **(see illustration)**.
11   Remove the steering column mounting nuts **(see illustration)**. Lower the column and pull it to the rear, making sure nothing is still

connected. Separate the intermediate shaft from the steering shaft and remove the column.

Installation

12   Guide the steering column into position, connect the intermediate shaft, then install the mounting fasteners, but don't tighten them yet.
13   Install the pinch bolt, tightening it to the torque listed in this Chapter's Specifications.
14   Tighten the column mounting fasteners to the torque listed in this Chapter's Specifications.
15   The remainder of installation is the reverse of removal.

18   Tie-rod ends - removal and installation

Refer to illustrations 18.2, 18.3a and 18.3b

1   Loosen the wheel lug nuts, raise the vehicle and place it securely on jackstands. Remove the wheel.
2   Loosen the tie-rod end locknut and

mark the position of the tie-rod end on the threaded portion of the tie-rod **(see illustration)**.
3   Remove the cotter pin and loosen the castle nut from the tie-rod end balljoint stud, then install a puller and separate the tie-rod end from the steering knuckle **(see illustrations)**. Remove the nut and detach the tie-rod end from the steering knuckle arm.
4   Unscrew the old tie-rod end and install the new one. Make sure the new tie-rod end is aligned with the mark you made on the threads of the tie-rod.
5   Installation is the reverse of removal. Be sure to tighten the tie-rod end balljoint nut to the torque listed in this Chapter's Specifications. Tighten the locknut securely.

19   Steering gear boots - replacement

Refer to illustration 19.4

1   If a steering gear boot is torn, dirt and moisture can damage the steering gear. Replace it.

18.2 Loosen the tie-rod end locknut and mark the position of the tie-rod end on the threaded portion of the tie-rod

18.3a Remove the cotter pin . . .

18.3b . . . and loosen (don't remove) the castle nut from the tie-rod end balljoint stud, then install a puller and separate the tie-rod end from the steering knuckle

10

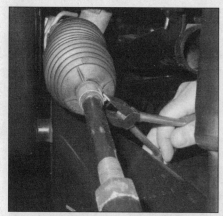

19.4 The outer clamp on the steering gear boot can be removed with a pair of pliers - the inner clamp must be cut off

20.8 Mark the relationship of the intermediate shaft U-joint coupler to the steering gear and intermediate shaft, then remove the coupler pinch bolt and detach it from the steering gear

20.9 Remove this nut and clamp, then detach the pressure and return lines from the steering gear

2   Loosen the wheel lug nuts, raise the vehicle and place it securely on jackstands. Remove the front wheels.

3   Remove the tie-rod end and locknut (see Section 18).

4   Remove the boot clamps **(see illustration)** and slide the boot off the tie-rod.

5   Installation is the reverse of removal. Be sure to use new clamps on the boot.

20 Steering gear - removal and installation

Warning 1: *The models covered by this manual are equipped with Supplemental Restraint systems (SRS), more commonly known as airbags. Always disable the airbag system before working in the vicinity of any airbag system component to avoid the possibility of accidental deployment of the airbag, which could cause personal injury (see Chapter 12).*

Warning 2: *Make sure the steering column shaft is not turned while the steering gear is removed or you could damage the airbag system clockspring. To prevent the shaft from turning, turn the ignition key to the lock posi-*

tion before beginning work, and run the seat belt through the steering wheel and clip it into its latch.

1   Park the vehicle with the front wheels pointing straight ahead.

2   Loosen the wheel lug nuts. Raise the front of the vehicle and support it securely on jackstands. Apply the parking brake. Remove the wheels. Remove the under-vehicle splash shield. On V8 models, remove the protective shield from the left side of the suspension crossmember.

3   Remove the power steering fluid cooler (see Section 23).

4   Disconnect the tie-rod ends from the steering knuckles (see Section 18).

4WD models

5   Remove the stabilizer bar nut from the left link (see Section 3).

6   Remove the left lower shock absorber/coil spring assembly mounting bolt and nut (see Section 2).

7   Detach the left lower control arm from the frame (see Section 6). Move the control arm away from the power steering gear.

All models

Refer to illustrations 20.8, 20.9 and 20.10

8   Mark the relationship of the U-joint to the intermediate shaft and the steering gear **(see illustration)**, remove the U-joint pinch bolts, then slide the U-joint up and off the steering gear input shaft.

9   Disconnect the pressure and return lines from the steering gear **(see illustration)**.

10   Remove the steering gear mounting fasteners **(see illustration)**. **Warning:** *The manufacturer states that new nuts should be installed during reassembly.*

11   Remove the steering gear mounting bracket-to-crossmember. Separate the mounting bracket from the crossmember.

12   Remove the steering gear assembly.

13   Installation is the reverse of removal. Be sure to align the matchmarks made in Step 8 and tighten all suspension and steering gear fasteners to the torque listed in this Chapter's Specifications. Tighten the wheel lug nuts to the torque listed in the Chapter 1 Specifications.

14   Bleed the power steering system when you're done (see Section 22).

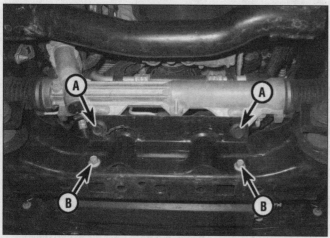

20.10 Location of the steering gear mounting bolts (A) and mounting bracket bolts (B)

21.3 Use a pin spanner to lock the pulley in position while removing the mounting bolts

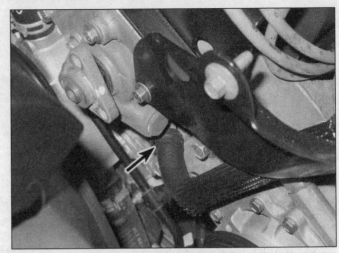

21.4a Remove the pressure line . . .

21.4b . . . and the reservoir hose at the power steering pump

21 Power steering pump - removal and installation

1   Disconnect the cable from the negative terminal of the battery (see Chapter 5).
2   Remove the drivebelt (see Chapter 1).

V6 models

Refer to illustrations 21.3, 21.4a, 21.4b and 21.6

3   Remove the power steering pump pulley mounting bolts **(see illustration)**. Remove the pulley.
4   Position a drain pan under the power steering pump. Disconnect the pressure and return hoses from the pump **(see illustrations)**. Plug the hoses to prevent contaminants from entering. Discard the O-ring from the pressure line - a new one should be used during installation.
5   Remove the pressure and return line mounting brackets and move the lines away from the pump.
6   Remove the pump mounting fasteners **(see illustration)** and lift the pump from the

engine compartment, taking care not to spill fluid on the painted surfaces.
7   Installation is the reverse of removal. Tighten the pressure line and the pump mounting bolts and nuts to the torque listed in this Chapter's Specifications.

V8 models

Refer to illustrations 21.8 and 21.13

8   Remove the power steering pump pulley. A special pulley removal tool, available at most auto parts stores, will be required for this **(see illustration)**.
9   Loosen the wheel lug nuts on the front left wheel. Raise the front of the vehicle and support it securely on jackstands. Apply the parking brake. Remove the wheel.
10   Working through the left wheelwell, disconnect the pressure line bracket from the pressure line and return line.
11   Position a drain pan under the power steering pump. Disconnect the pressure and return hoses from the pump. Plug the hoses to prevent contaminants from entering. Discard the O-ring from the pressure line - a new one should be used during installation.

12   Remove the pump mounting bolts and guide the pump out, taking care not to spill fluid. **Warning:** *The manufacturer states that new bolts should be installed during reassembly.*
13   Installation is the reverse of removal. Use a new O-ring on the pressure line fitting. Tighten the pressure line fitting and the pump mounting bolts to the torque listed in this Chapter's Specifications. A special pulley installation tool, available at most auto parts stores, will be needed to press the pulley onto the pump shaft **(see illustration)**.

All models

14   Fill the power steering reservoir with the recommended fluid (see Chapter 1) and bleed the system following the procedure described in the next Section.

22 Power steering system - bleeding

1   Following any operation in which the power steering fluid lines have been disconnected, the power steering system must be

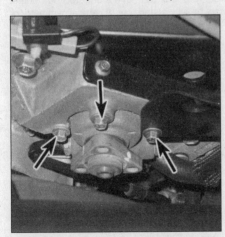

21.6 Remove the power steering pump mounting bolts (V6 engine)

21.8 Remove the pulley from the power steering pump with a pulley removal tool (typical)

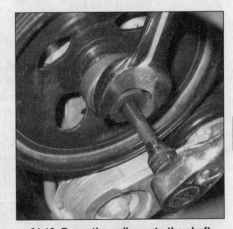

21.13 Press the pulley onto the shaft using a pulley installation tool - don't attempt to drive it on with a hammer or push it on with a traditional press! (typical)

10

bled to remove all air and obtain proper steering performance.

2   With the front wheels in the straight ahead position, check the power steering fluid level and, if low, add fluid until it reaches the MIN mark on the reservoir.

3   Start the engine and allow it to run at fast idle. Recheck the fluid level and add more if necessary to reach the MIN mark on the reservoir.

4   Bleed the system by turning the wheels from side-to-side, without hitting the stops. This will work the air out of the system. Keep the reservoir full of fluid as this is done.

5   When the air is worked out of the system, return the wheels to the straight ahead position and leave the vehicle running for several more minutes before shutting it off.

6   Road test the vehicle to be sure the steering system is functioning normally and noise free.

7   Recheck the fluid level to be sure it's up near the MAX mark on the reservoir while the engine is at normal operating temperature. Add fluid if necessary (see Chapter 1).

23 Power steering fluid cooler - removal and installation

Refer to illustration 23.3

1   Raise the vehicle and place it securely on jackstands.

2   Place a drain pan below the power

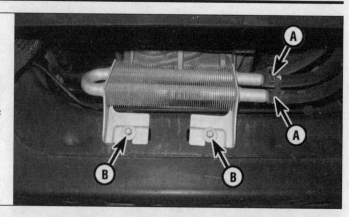

23.3 Power steering fluid cooler mounting details

A   Hose clamps
B   Mounting bolts

steering fluid cooler to collect excess fluid.

3   Loosen the clamps and detach the hoses from the power steering fluid cooler **(see illustration)**. Mark these hoses to insure correct reassembly.

4   Remove the mounting bolts and detach the cooler from the crossmember.

5   Installation is the reverse of the removal.

6   Add power steering fluid as necessary (see Chapter 1), then bleed the power steering system (see Section 22).

24 Wheels and tires - general information

Refer to illustration 24.1

All vehicles covered by this manual are equipped with metric-size fiberglass or steel belted radial tires **(see illustration)**. These models require the specific tire size, speed rating, load range and construction type to insure the correct ride, handling, speedometer/odometer calibration, tire/body clearance, wheel bearing tolerance and brake cooling characteristics. Use of other size or type of tires may affect all/one of these conditions. Don't mix different types of tires, such as radials and bias belted, on the same vehicle as handling may be seriously affected. It's recommended that tires be replaced in pairs on the same axle, but if only one tire is being replaced, be sure it's the same size, structure and tread design as the other.

Some models are equipped with the Tire Pressure Monitoring System (TPMS). A module receives signals from the antennae on the valve stems of the tires and constantly monitors the tire pressure. The module can calculate high or low tire pressure(s), communicate with the SCP network on the vehicle message center and set a warning light on the dash.

Because tire pressure has a substantial effect on handling and wear, the pressure on all tires should be checked at least once a month or before any extended trips (see Chapter 1).

Wheels must be replaced if they're bent, dented, leak air, have elongated bolt holes, are heavily rusted, out of vertical symmetry or if the lug nuts won't stay tight. Wheel repairs that use welding or peening are not recommended.

Tire and wheel balance is important to the overall handling, braking and performance of the vehicle. Unbalanced wheels can adversely affect handling and ride characteristics as well as tire life. Whenever a tire is installed on a wheel, the tire and wheel should be balanced by a shop with the proper equipment.

25 Wheel alignment - general information

Refer to illustration 25.1

A wheel alignment refers to the adjustments made to the front and rear wheels so they're in proper angular relationship to the

METRIC TIRE SIZES

P 185 / 80 R 13

TIRE TYPE
P-PASSENGER
T-TEMPORARY
C-COMMERCIAL

ASPECT RATIO
(SECTION HEIGHT)
_____
(SECTION WIDTH)
70
75
80

RIM DIAMETER
(INCHES)
13
14
15

SECTION WIDTH
(MILLIMETERS)
185
195
205
ETC

CONSTRUCTION TYPE
R-RADIAL
B-BIAS - BELTED
D-DIAGONAL (BIAS)

24.1 Metric tire size code

SECTION WIDTH

SECTION HEIGHT

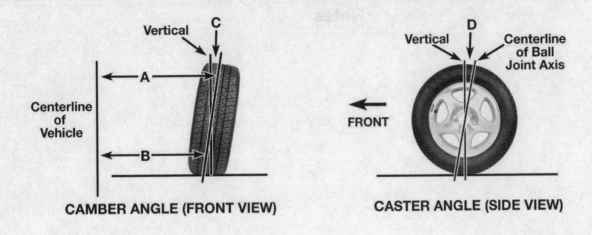

CAMBER ANGLE (FRONT VIEW)

CASTER ANGLE (SIDE VIEW)

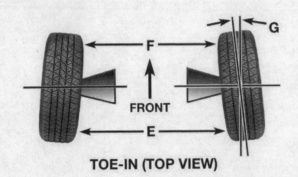

TOE-IN (TOP VIEW)

25.1 Front end alignment details

A minus B = C (degrees camber)
D = degrees caster
E minus F = toe-in (measured in inches)
G = toe-in (expressed in degrees)

suspension and the ground **(see illustration)**. Wheels that are out of proper alignment not only affect steering control, but also increase tire wear.

Getting the proper front and rear wheel alignment is a very exacting process, one in which complicated and expensive machines are necessary to perform the job properly. Because of this, you should have a technician with the proper equipment perform these tasks. We will, however, use this space to give you a basic idea of what is involved with front end alignment so you can better understand the process and deal intelligently with the shop that does the work.

Toe-in is the turning in of the front wheels. The purpose of a toe specification is to ensure parallel rolling of the front wheels.

In a vehicle with zero toe-in, the distance between the front edges of the wheels will be the same as the distance between the rear edges of the wheels. The actual amount of toe-in is normally only a fraction of an inch. At the front end, toe-in adjustment is controlled by the tie-rod length. At the rear end, toe-in is adjusted by altering the toe link length. Incorrect toe-in will cause the tires to wear improperly by making them scrub against the road surface.

Camber is the tilting of the front wheels from vertical when viewed from the front of the vehicle. When the wheels tilt out at the top, the camber is said to be positive (+). When the wheels tilt in at the top the camber is negative (-). The amount of tilt is measured in degrees from the vertical and this mea-

surement is called the camber angle. This angle affects the amount of tire tread which contacts the road and compensates for changes in the suspension geometry when the vehicle is cornering or traveling over an undulating surface. Camber is adjusted by loosening the upper control arm-to-frame bolts and moving the arm in (to decrease camber) or out (to increase camber).

Caster is the tilting of the top of the front steering axis from the vertical. A tilt toward the rear is positive caster and a tilt toward the front is negative caster. Caster is also adjusted by loosening the upper control arm-to-frame bolts, but instead of moving the arm in or out, the outer end of the arm is moved toward the front (to decrease caster) or toward the rear (to increase caster).

10

Notes

Chapter 11 Body

Contents

1 General information

These models feature a traditional body-on-frame construction. The body incorporates the cab, backseat area and cargo compartment in one unitized structure.

Certain components are particularly vulnerable to accident damage and can be unbolted and repaired or replaced. Among these parts are the body moldings, bumpers, hood, fenders, doors, liftgate and all glass.

Only general body maintenance practices and body panel repair procedures within the scope of the do-it-yourselfer are included in this Chapter.

2 Body - maintenance

1 The condition of your vehicle's body is very important, because the resale value depends a great deal on it. It's much more difficult to repair a neglected or damaged body than it is to repair mechanical components. The hidden areas of the body, such as the wheel wells, the frame and the engine compartment, are equally important, although they don't require as frequent attention as the rest of the body.

2 Once a year, or every 12,000 miles, it's a good idea to have the underside of the body steam cleaned. All traces of dirt and oil will be removed and the area can then be inspected carefully for rust, damaged brake lines, frayed electrical wires, damaged cables and other problems.

3 At the same time, clean the engine and the engine compartment with a steam cleaner or water soluble degreaser.

4 The wheel wells should be given close attention, since undercoating can peel away and stones and dirt thrown up by the tires can cause the paint to chip and flake, allowing rust to set in. If rust is found, clean down to the bare metal and apply an anti-rust paint.

5 The body should be washed about once a week. Wet the vehicle thoroughly to soften the dirt, then wash it down with a soft sponge

11

and plenty of clean soapy water. If the surplus dirt is not washed off very carefully, it can wear down the paint.

6   Spots of tar or asphalt thrown up from the road should be removed with a cloth soaked in solvent.

7   Once every six months, wax the body and chrome trim. If a chrome cleaner is used to remove rust from any of the vehicle's plated parts, remember that the cleaner also removes part of the chrome, so use it sparingly.

3   Vinyl trim - maintenance

Don't clean vinyl trim with detergents, caustic soap or petroleum-based cleaners. Plain soap and water works just fine, with a soft brush to clean dirt that may be ingrained. Wash the vinyl as frequently as the rest of the vehicle.

After cleaning, application of a high quality rubber and vinyl protectant will help prevent oxidation and cracks. The protectant can also be applied to weatherstripping, vacuum lines and rubber hoses (which often fail as a result of chemical degradation) and to the tires.

4   Upholstery and carpets - maintenance

1   Every three months remove the carpets or mats and clean the interior of the vehicle (more frequently if necessary). Vacuum the upholstery and carpets to remove loose dirt and dust.

2   Leather upholstery requires special care. Stains should be removed with warm water and a very mild soap solution. Use a clean, damp cloth to remove the soap, then wipe again with a dry cloth. Never use alcohol, gasoline, nail polish remover or thinner to clean leather upholstery.

3   After cleaning, regularly treat leather upholstery with a leather wax. Never use car wax on leather upholstery.

4   In areas where the interior of the vehicle is subject to bright sunlight, cover leather seats with a sheet if the vehicle is to be left out for any length of time.

5   Body repair - minor damage

See photo sequence

Repair of minor scratches

1   If the scratch is superficial and does not penetrate to the metal of the body, repair is very simple. Lightly rub the scratched area with a fine rubbing compound to remove loose paint and built-up wax. Rinse the area with clean water.

2   Apply touch-up paint to the scratch, using a small brush. Continue to apply thin layers of paint until the surface of the paint in the scratch is level with the surrounding

paint. Allow the new paint at least two weeks to harden, then blend it into the surrounding paint by rubbing with a very fine rubbing compound. Finally, apply a coat of wax to the scratch area.

3   If the scratch has penetrated the paint and exposed the metal of the body, causing the metal to rust, and a different repair technique is required. Remove all loose rust from the bottom of the scratch with a pocket knife, then apply rust inhibiting paint to prevent the formation of rust in the future. Using a rubber or nylon applicator, coat the scratched area with glaze-type filler. If required, the filler can be mixed with thinner to provide a very thin paste, which is ideal for filling narrow scratches. Before the glaze filler in the scratch hardens, wrap a piece of smooth cotton cloth around the tip of a finger. Dip the cloth in thinner and then quickly wipe it along the surface of the scratch. This will ensure that the surface of the filler is slightly hollow. The scratch can now be painted over as described earlier in this Section.

Repair of dents

4   When repairing dents, the first job is to pull the dent out until the affected area is as close as possible to its original shape. There is no point in trying to restore the original shape completely as the metal in the damaged area will have stretched on impact and cannot be restored to its original contours. It is better to bring the level of the dent up to a point which is about 1/8-inch below the level of the surrounding metal. In cases where the dent is very shallow, it is not worth trying to pull it out at all.

5   If the back side of the dent is accessible, it can be hammered out gently from behind using a soft-face hammer. While doing this, hold a block of wood firmly against the opposite side of the metal to absorb the hammer blows and prevent the metal from being stretched.

6   If the dent is in a section of the body which has double layers, or some other factor makes it inaccessible from behind, a different technique is required. Drill several small holes through the metal inside the damaged area, particularly in the deeper sections. Screw long, self-tapping screws into the holes just enough for them to get a good grip in the metal. Now pulling on the protruding heads of the screws with locking pliers can pull out the dent.

7   The next stage of repair is the removal of paint from the damaged area and from an inch or so of the surrounding metal. This is done with a wire brush or sanding disk in a drill motor, although it can be done just as effectively by hand with sandpaper. To complete the preparation for filling, score the surface of the bare metal with a screwdriver or the tang of a file, or drill small holes in the affected area. This will provide a good grip for the filler material. To complete the repair, see the subsection on filling and painting later in this Section.

Repair of rust holes or gashes

8   Remove all paint from the affected area and from an inch or so of the surrounding metal using a sanding disk or wire brush mounted in a drill motor. If these are not available, a few sheets of sandpaper will do the job just as effectively.

9   With the paint removed, you will be able to determine the severity of the corrosion and decide whether to replace the whole panel, if possible, or repair the affected area. New body panels are not as expensive as most people think and it is often quicker to install a new panel than to repair large areas of rust.

10   Remove all trim pieces from the affected area except those which will act as a guide to the original shape of the damaged body, such as headlight shells, etc. Using metal snips or a hacksaw blade, remove all loose metal and any other metal that is badly affected by rust. Hammer the edges of the hole in to create a slight depression for the filler material.

11   Wire brush the affected area to remove the powdery rust from the surface of the metal. If the back of the rusted area is accessible, treat it with rust inhibiting paint.

12   Before filling is done, block the hole in some way. This can be done with sheet metal riveted or screwed into place, or by stuffing the hole with wire mesh.

13   Once the hole is blocked off, the affected area can be filled and painted. See the following subsection on filling and painting.

Filling and painting

14   Many types of body fillers are available, but generally speaking, body repair kits which contain filler paste and a tube of resin hardener are best for this type of repair work. A wide, flexible plastic or nylon applicator will be necessary for imparting a smooth and contoured finish to the surface of the filler material. Mix up a small amount of filler on a clean piece of wood or cardboard (use the hardener sparingly). Follow the manufacturer's instructions on the package, otherwise the filler will set incorrectly.

15   Using the applicator, apply the filler paste to the prepared area. Draw the applicator across the surface of the filler to achieve the desired contour and to level the filler surface. As soon as a contour that approximates the original one is achieved, stop working the paste. If you continue, the paste will begin to stick to the applicator. Continue to add thin layers of paste at 20-minute intervals until the level of the filler is just above the surrounding metal.

16   Once the filler has hardened, the excess can be removed with a body file. From then on, progressively finer grades of sandpaper should be used, starting with a 180-grit paper and finishing with a 600-grit wet-or-dry paper. Always wrap the sandpaper around a flat rubber or wooden block, otherwise the surface of the filler will not be completely flat. During the sanding of the filler surface, the wet-or-

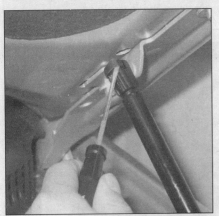

9.2 Use a small screwdriver to pry the clip out of its locking groove, then detach the end of the strut from the locating stud

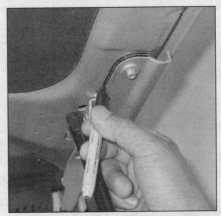

10.2 Before removing the hood, draw a mark around the hinge plate . . .

10.3 . . . and be sure to detach the windshield washer hose

dry paper should be periodically rinsed in water. This will ensure that a very smooth finish is produced in the final stage.

17   At this point, the repair area should be surrounded by a ring of bare metal, which in turn should be encircled by the finely feathered edge of good paint. Rinse the repair area with clean water until all of the dust produced by the sanding operation is gone.

18   Spray the entire area with a light coat of primer. This will reveal any imperfections in the surface of the filler. Repair the imperfections with fresh filler paste or glaze filler and once more smooth the surface with sandpaper. Repeat this spray-and-repair procedure until you are satisfied that the surface of the filler and the feathered edge of the paint are perfect. Rinse the area with clean water and allow it to dry completely.

19   The repair area is now ready for painting. Spray painting must be carried out in a warm, dry, windless and dust free atmosphere. These conditions can be created if you have access to a large indoor work area, but if you are forced to work in the open, you will have to pick the day very carefully. If you are working indoors, dousing the floor in the work area with water will help settle the dust, which would otherwise be in the air. If the repair area is confined to one body panel, mask off the surrounding panels. This will help minimize the effects of a slight mismatch in paint color. Trim pieces such as chrome strips, door handles, etc., will also need to be masked off or removed. Use masking tape and several thickness of newspaper for the masking operations.

20   Before spraying, shake the paint can thoroughly, then spray a test area until the spray painting technique is mastered. Cover the repair area with a thick coat of primer. The thickness should be built up using several thin layers of primer rather than one thick one. Using 600-grit wet-or-dry sandpaper, rub down the surface of the primer until it is very smooth. While doing this, the work area should be thoroughly rinsed with water and the wet-or-dry sandpaper periodically rinsed as well. Allow the primer to dry before spray-

ing additional coats.
21   Spray on the top coat, again building up the thickness by using several thin layers of paint. Begin spraying in the center of the repair area and then, using a circular motion, work out until the whole repair area and about two inches of the surrounding original paint is covered. Remove all masking material 10 to 15 minutes after spraying on the final coat of paint. Allow the new paint at least two weeks to harden, then use a very fine rubbing compound to blend the edges of the new paint into the existing paint. Finally, apply a coat of wax.

6   Body repair - major damage

1   Major damage must be repaired by an auto body shop specifically equipped to perform these repairs. Most shops have the specialized equipment required to do the job properly.

2   If the damage is extensive, the frame must be checked for proper alignment or the vehicle's handling characteristics may be adversely affected and other components may wear at an accelerated rate.

3   Due to the fact that all of the major body components (hood, fenders, etc.) are separate and replaceable units, any seriously damaged components should be replaced rather than repaired. Sometimes the components can be found in a wrecking yard that specializes in used vehicle components, often at considerable savings over the cost of new parts.

7   Hinges and locks - maintenance

Once every 3000 miles, or every three months, the hinges and latch assemblies on the doors, hood and trunk should be given a few drops of light oil or lock lubricant. The door latch strikers should also be lubricated with a thin coat of grease to reduce wear and ensure free movement. Lubricate the door and trunk locks with spray-on graphite lubricant.

8   Windshield and fixed glass - replacement

Replacement of the windshield and fixed glass requires the use of special fast-setting adhesive/caulk materials and some specialized tools. It is recommended that these operations be left to a dealer or a shop specializing in glass work.

9   Hood and rear liftgate support struts - removal and installation

Refer to illustration 9.2
Note: *The hood and rear liftgate are heavy and somewhat awkward to hold - at least two people should perform this procedure.*
1   Open the hood or rear liftgate and support it securely.
2   Using a small screwdriver, detach the retaining clips at both ends of the support strut. Then pry or pull sharply to detach it from the post **(see illustration)**.
3   Installation is the reverse of removal.

10   Hood - removal, installation and adjustment

Note: *The hood is heavy and somewhat awkward to remove and install - at least two people should perform this procedure.*

Removal and installation
Refer to illustrations 10.2 and 10.3
1   Use blankets or pads to cover the cowl area of the body and fenders. This will protect the body and paint as the hood is lifted off.
2   Make marks or scribe a line around the hood hinge to ensure proper alignment during installation **(see illustration)**.
3   Disconnect any cables or wires that will interfere with removal **(see illustration)**.
4   Have an assistant support one side of the hood while you support the other. Simultaneously remove the hinge-to-hood bolts.
5   Lift off the hood.
6   Installation is the reverse of removal.

These photos illustrate a method of repairing simple dents. They are intended to supplement *Body repair - minor damage* in this Chapter and should not be used as the sole instructions for body repair on these vehicles.

1 If you can't access the backside of the body panel to hammer out the dent, pull it out with a slide-hammer-type dent puller. In the deepest portion of the dent or along the crease line, drill or punch hole(s) at least one inch apart . . .

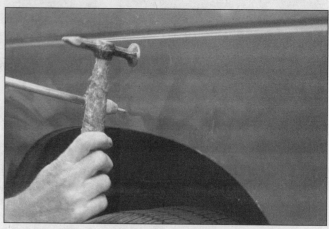

2 . . . then screw the slide-hammer into the hole and operate it. Tap with a hammer near the edge of the dent to help 'pop' the metal back to its original shape. When you're finished, the dent area should be close to its original contour and about 1/8-inch below the surface of the surrounding metal

3 Using coarse-grit sandpaper, remove the paint down to the bare metal. Hand sanding works fine, but the disc sander shown here makes the job faster. Use finer (about 320-grit) sandpaper to feather-edge the paint at least one inch around the dent area

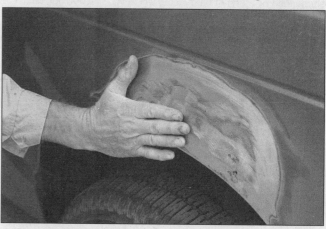

4 When the paint is removed, touch will probably be more helpful than sight for telling if the metal is straight. Hammer down the high spots or raise the low spots as necessary. Clean the repair area with wax/silicone remover

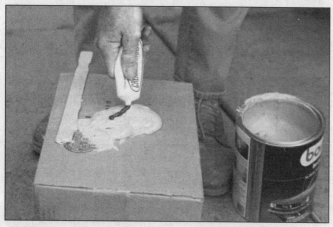

5 Following label instructions, mix up a batch of plastic filler and hardener. The ratio of filler to hardener is critical, and, if you mix it incorrectly, it will either not cure properly or cure too quickly (you won't have time to file and sand it into shape)

6 Working quickly so the filler doesn't harden, use a plastic applicator to press the body filler firmly into the metal, assuring it bonds completely. Work the filler until it matches the original contour and is slightly above the surrounding metal

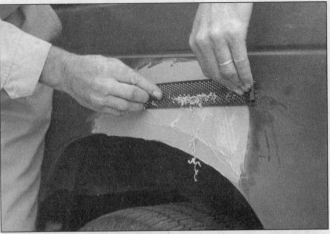

7 Let the filler harden until you can just dent it with your fingernail. Use a body file or Surform tool (shown here) to rough-shape the filler

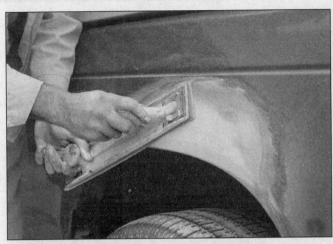

8 Use coarse-grit sandpaper and a sanding board or block to work the filler down until it's smooth and even. Work down to finer grits of sandpaper - always using a board or block - ending up with 360 or 400 grit

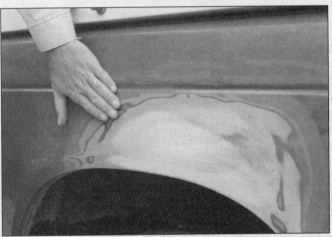

9 You shouldn't be able to feel any ridge at the transition from the filler to the bare metal or from the bare metal to the old paint. As soon as the repair is flat and uniform, remove the dust and mask off the adjacent panels or trim pieces

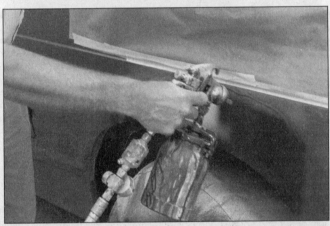

10 Apply several layers of primer to the area. Don't spray the primer on too heavy, so it sags or runs, and make sure each coat is dry before you spray on the next one. A professional-type spray gun is being used here, but aerosol spray primer is available inexpensively from auto parts stores

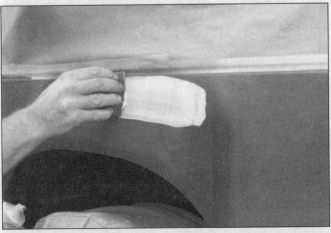

11 The primer will help reveal imperfections or scratches. Fill these with glazing compound. Follow the label instructions and sand it with 360 or 400-grit sandpaper until it's smooth. Repeat the glazing, sanding and respraying until the primer reveals a perfectly smooth surface

12 Finish sand the primer with very fine sandpaper (400 or 600-grit) to remove the primer overspray. Clean the area with water and allow it to dry. Use a tack rag to remove any dust, then apply the finish coat. Don't attempt to rub out or wax the repair area until the paint has dried completely (at least two weeks)

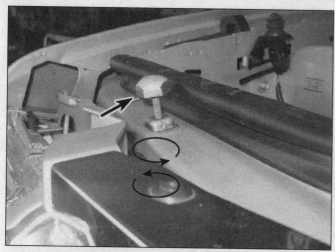

10.11 Adjust the height of the hood when closed by turning the hood bumpers in or out

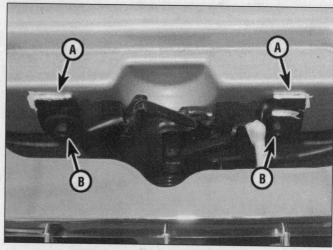

11.2 Mark the hood latch location (A), then remove the latch bolts (B)

Adjustment

Refer to illustration 10.11

7   Fore-and-aft and side-to-side adjustment of the hood is done by moving the hinge plate slot after loosening the bolts.

8   Scribe a line around the entire hinge plate so you can determine the amount of movement **(see illustration 10.2)**.

9   Loosen the bolts or nuts and move the hood into correct alignment. Move it only a little at a time. Tighten the hinge bolts and carefully lower the hood to check the position.

10   If necessary after installation, the entire hood latch assembly can be adjusted up-and-down as well as from side-to-side on the radiator support so the hood closes securely and flush with the fenders. To make the adjustment, scribe a line or mark around the hood latch mounting bolts to provide a reference point, then loosen them and reposition the latch assembly, as necessary. Following adjustment, retighten the mounting bolts.

11   Finally, adjust the hood bumpers on the radiator support so the hood, when closed, is flush with the fenders **(see illustration)**.

12   The hood latch assembly, as well as the hinges, should be periodically lubricated with white, lithium-base grease to prevent binding and wear.

11   Hood latch and release cable - removal and installation

Latch

Refer to illustrations 11.2, 11.4a and 11.4b

1   Remove the grille and the radiator opening panel (see Section 12).

2   Mark the location of the latch to aid alignment when reinstalling the latch assembly **(see illustration)**.

3   Remove the bolts securing the latch to the radiator support and remove the latch.

4   Disconnect the hood release cable by disengaging the cable casing from the latch, then unhooking the cable end from the lever **(see illustrations)**.

5   Installation is the reverse of the removal procedure. **Note:** *Adjust the latch so the*

hood engages securely when closed and the hood bumpers are slightly compressed.

Cable

Refer to illustrations 11.7a, 11.7b, 11.7c, 11.7d, 11.7e and 11.7f

6   Remove the hood latch as described earlier in this Section, then detach the cable from the latch.

7   Working inside the vehicle, remove the retaining screw and detach the hood release lever, remove the sill panel and kick panel, then detach the cable end and housing from the actuator **(see illustrations)**.

8   Attach a length of wire to the end of the cable (in the passenger compartment). This will be used to pull the new cable back into the vehicle.

9   Working in the engine compartment, detach the cable from all of its retaining clips. It may be necessary to remove the battery and the radiator upper cover for access to some of the clips. Now pull the cable and grommet into the engine compartment, detach the wire from the old cable, and then attach it to the lever end of the new cable.

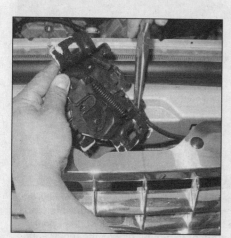

11.4a Use needle-nose pliers to squeeze the retaining tangs on the cable casing . . .

11.4b . . . then detach the cable from the latch and lever

11.7a Remove the screw and detach the hood release lever

11.7b Detach the sill trim piece

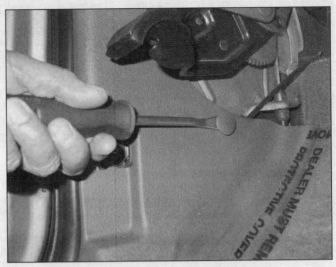

11.7c Remove the trim panel retainer

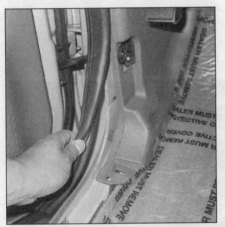

11.7d Peel back the weatherstripping . . .

11.7e . . . then remove the kick panel

Note: *Make sure the new cable is equipped with a grommet.*

10 Working inside the vehicle, pull the new cable through the firewall. Move to the engine compartment and seat the grommet in the firewall.

11 The remainder of installation is the reverse of removal.

12 Radiator grille and opening panel - removal and installation

Grille

Refer to illustrations 12.1a, 12.1b and 12.1c

1 Open the hood and remove the plastic trim fasteners along the top, then detach the grille assembly by pulling it upward **(see illustrations)**.

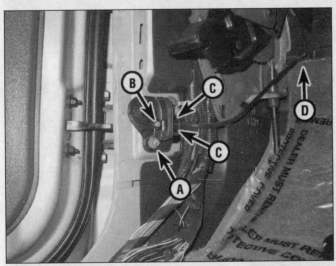

11.7f Unscrew this bolt (A) and remove the actuator, detach the cable end (B), then squeeze the tangs (C) and detach the cable casing from the actuator. Peel back the carpet and insulator at the firewall (D) for access to the cable grommet

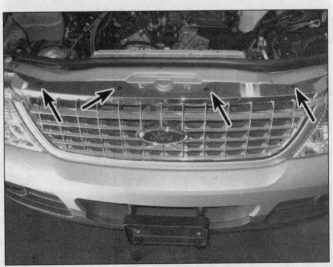

12.1a Grille retainer locations

11

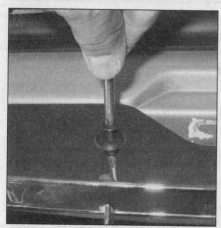

12.1b To remove the plastic retainers, unscrew the center a few turns, then pull the entire retainer out

12.1c Once all the retainers are out, remove the grille by lifting it straight up

2   To install, place the grille in position and press the fasteners into place.

Radiator opening panel

Refer to illustrations 12.4a and 12.4b
3   Remove the grille.

4   Remove the fasteners and detach the panel **(see illustrations)**.
5   Installation is the reverse of removal.

13   Bumpers - removal and installation

1   Apply the parking brake, raise the vehicle and support it securely on jackstands.

Front bumper

Refer to illustrations 13.3a, 13.3b, 13.3c, 13.3d, 13.3e, 14.4a and 14.4b
2   Working under the vehicle, disconnect the fog light electrical connections.
3   Remove the front bumper cover retaining bolts and screws and detach the cover **(see illustrations)**.
4   Working from the backside of the bumper, remove the retaining nuts securing

12.4a Remove the radiator opening panel fasteners

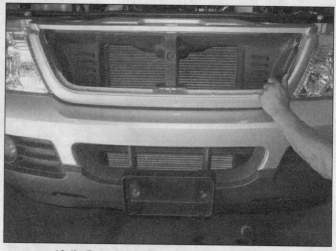

12.4b Detach the panel by pulling straight out

13.3a Remove the front bumper cover bolts from the inner fender . . .

13.3b . . . and lower fender splash shield push pins, then . . .

13.3c . . . remove the upper inner bolts on each side . . .

13.3d . . . and the retaining bolts along the bottom

13.3e Remove the front bumper cover by rotating the lower edge up while pushing on the top to release the four tabs

the bumper brackets to each frame rail and remove the bumper from the vehicle (see illustrations).

5   Installation is the reverse of removal.

Rear bumper

Refer to illustration 13.8

6   Unplug any electrical connectors, which would interfere with bumper removal and remove the spare tire.

7   Remove the screws or clips and detach the bumper cover.

8   Working from the backside of the bumper, remove the retaining bracket bolts securing the bumper brackets to each frame rail (see illustration). Then remove the bumper from the vehicle.

9   Installation is the reverse of removal.

14   Front fender - removal and installation

Refer to illustrations 14.2, 14.4, 14.5, 14.6 and 14.7

1   Loosen the wheel lug nuts. Raise the front of the vehicle, support it securely on jackstands and remove the front wheel.

2   Remove the retainers and pull the moulding back, then remove the inner fender splash shield (see illustration).

3   Remove the parking and turn signal light housings (see Chapter 12).

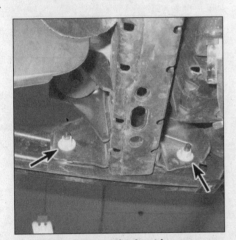

13.4a Remove the front bumper retaining nuts . . .

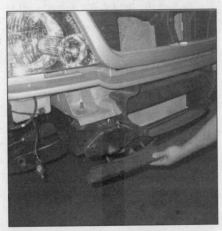

13.4b . . . and detach the front bumper from the vehicle

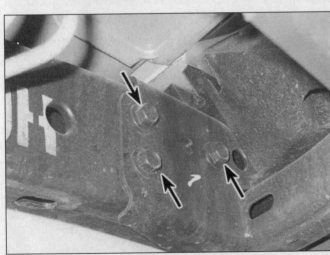

13.8 Remove the bolts and lower the rear bumper from the vehicle

14.2 Locations of the moulding and inner fender splash shield fasteners

11

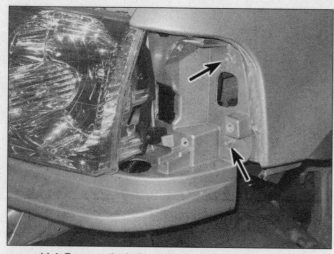

14.4 Remove the bolts at the front edge of the fender

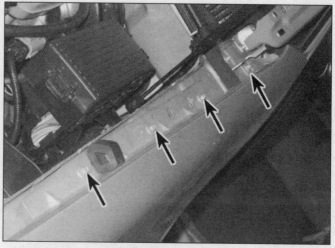

14.5 Remove the bolts along the top edge of the fender

4   Remove the fender retaining bolts in the parking and turn signal light opening (see illustration).
5   Remove the mounting bolts along the top of the fender (see illustration).
6   Remove the fender-to-A pillar bolts (see illustration). If you're removing the right-side

fender, also remove the bolt securing the antenna mast, and disconnect the antenna cable (see Chapter 12).
7   Remove the two bolts securing the lower part of the fender to the bottom of the A-pillar (see illustration).
8   Detach the fender. It's a good idea to

have an assistant support the fender while it's being moved away from the vehicle to prevent damage to the surrounding body panels.
9   Installation is the reverse of removal.

15   Door trim panels - removal and installation

Refer to illustrations 15.2, 15.3a, 15.3b, 15.3c, 15.4, 15.5 and 15.6
1   Disconnect the cable from the negative battery terminal (see Chapter 5).
2   Carefully detach the door handle bezel (see illustration).
3   Pry out the front edge of the armrest switch control plate and disconnect the electrical connections, then remove the retaining screw from the opening (see illustrations).
4   Remove the lower trim panel retaining screws (see illustration).
5   Once all of the screws are removed, grasp the trim panel at the switch opening and pull it up and out (see illustration). Dis-

14.6 Remove the two fender-to-A-pillar bolts . . .

14.7 . . . and the two lower mounting bolts at the rear of the wheel opening

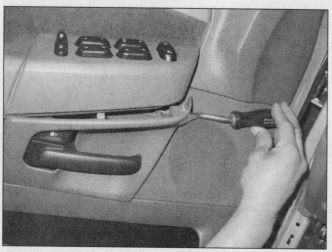

15.2 Carefully pry the door handle bezel off

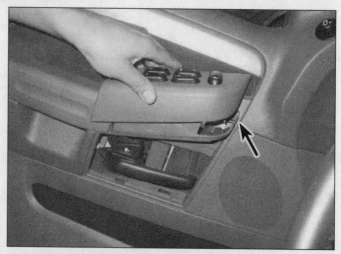

15.3a Pry up on the front edge of the armrest switch control plate to detach it

connect the power mirror electrical connector.

6   For access to the inner door components, remove the speaker and any screws that would interfere with watershield removal then carefully peel the watershield from the door **(see illustration)**.

7   Installation is the reverse of removal.

16   Door - removal, installation and adjustment

Note: *The door is heavy and somewhat awkward to remove and install - at least two people should perform this procedure.*

Removal and installation

Refer to illustrations 16.6a and 16.6b

1   Raise the window completely in the door and disconnect the cable from the negative battery terminal (see Chapter 5).

2   Open the door all the way and support it on jacks covered with rags to prevent damaging the paint.

3   Remove the door trim panel and watershield as described in Section 15.

4   Unplug all electrical connections,

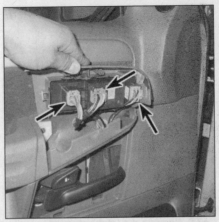

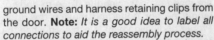

15.3b After detaching the front edge, lift the switch panel out and disconnect the electrical connectors

ground wires and harness retaining clips from the door. **Note:** *It is a good idea to label all connections to aid the reassembly process.*

5   Working through the door opening, detach the rubber conduit between the body and the door. Then pull wiring harness through the conduit hole.

15.3c Remove the trim panel retaining screw in the switch opening

6   Mark around the door hinges with a marking pen or scribe to facilitate alignment during reassembly, then remove the bolts securing the doorstop **(see illustration)**. With an assistant supporting the door, remove the hinge-to-door bolts and remove the door **(see illustration)**.

7   Installation is the reverse of the removal.

15.4 Remove the screws from the lower edge of the trim panel

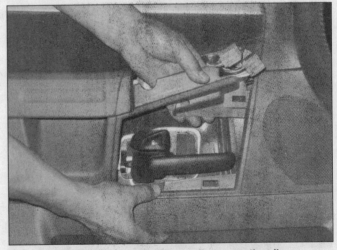

15.5 Lift the trim panel up to disengage the clips

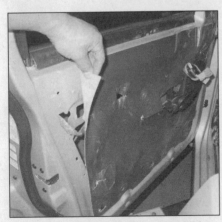

15.6 Carefully peel the watershield from the door

16.6a Remove the doorstop retaining bolts

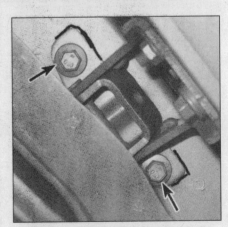

16.6b Remove the hinge-to-door bolts

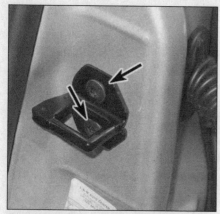

16.11 Adjust the door lock striker by loosening the mounting screws and gently tapping the striker in the desired direction

17.2 Remove the latch retaining screws from the end of the door

hinge-to-door bolts, body alignment shims may have to be purchased and inserted behind the hinges to achieve correct alignment.

10   To adjust the door-closed position, first check that the door latch is contacting the center of the latch striker. If not, remove the striker and add or subtract shims to achieve correct alignment.

11   Finally adjust the latch striker as necessary to provide positive engagement with the latch mechanism **(see illustration)** and so the door panel is flush with the body.

Adjustment

Refer to illustration 16.11

8   Having proper door-to-body alignment is a critical part of a well functioning door assembly. First check the door hinge pins for excessive play. Fully open the door and lift up and down on the door without lifting the body. If a door has 1/16-inch or more exces-

sive play, the hinges should be replaced.

9   Door-to-body alignment adjustments are made by loosening the hinge-to-body or hinge-to-door bolts and moving the door. Proper body alignment is achieved when the top of the door is aligned with the top of the front fender and rear door or quarter panel and the bottom of the door is aligned with the lower rocker panel. If these goals can't be reached by adjusting the hinge-to-body or

17   Door latch, lock cylinder and handles - removal and installation

Door latch

Refer to illustrations 17.2 and 17.3

1   Raise the window then remove the door trim panel and watershield as described in Section 15.

2   Remove the screws securing the latch to the door **(see illustration)**.

3   Working through the large access hole, position the latch as necessary to disconnect

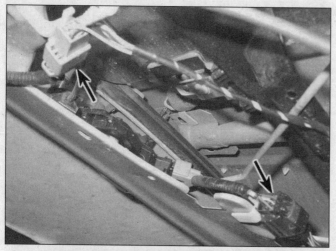

17.3 Disconnect the door latch electrical connectors

17.7a Detach the door handle . . .

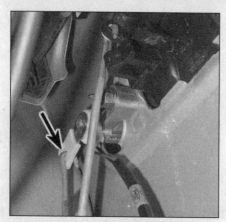

17.7b . . . and lock cylinder control rod clips

17.10 Remove the outer door handle retaining nuts

17.12 Remove the screw and detach the interior handle

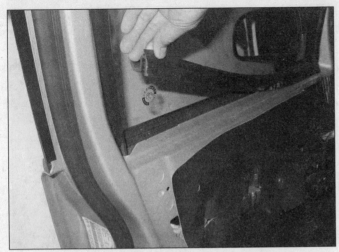

18.1 Detach the weatherstrip from the top of the door

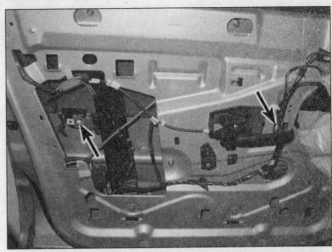

18.3 Lower the window just enough to access the glass retaining bolts through the holes in the door frame - remove the bolts securing the glass to the regulator

the electrical connectors **(see illustration).** Disengage the outside door handle and out-side lock cylinder-to-latch rods.

4   Detach the locking rods by unsnapping the portion of the plastic clip engaging the connecting rod, then pulling the rod out of its locating hole. Remove the latch assembly from the door.

5   Installation is the reverse of removal.

Door lock cylinder and outside handle

Refer to illustrations 17.7a, 17.7b and 17.10

6   To remove the outside handle and door lock cylinder assembly, raise the window and remove the door trim panel and watershield as described in Section 15.

7   Working through the access hole, detach the door handle and the lock cylinder actuating rods **(see illustrations).**

8   Disconnect any electrical connectors which would interfere with removal.

9   Remove the nuts and remove the door handle and lock cylinder from the door **(see illustration).**

10   Installation is the reverse of removal.

Inside handle and cable

Refer to illustration 17.12

11   remove the door trim panel and water-shield as described in Section 15.

12   Remove the securing screw, disengage the inside handle from the cable and remove it from the inner door panel **(see illustration).**

13   Installation is the reverse of removal.

18   Door window glass - removal and installation

Refer to illustrations 18.1, 18.3 and 18.4

1   Carefully pry the inner weatherstrips out of the door window opening **(see illustration).**

2   Remove the door trim panel and the watershield (see Section 15).

3   Lower the window glass for access to the bolts retaining the glass to the regulator and remove them **(see illustration).**

4   Remove the glass by tilting it forward, then lifting it out of the door **(see illustration).**

5   Installation is the reverse of removal.

19   Door window glass regulator - removal and installation

Refer to illustration 19.4, 19.5 and 19.6

1   Raise the glass halfway up the window opening.

2   Remove the inner glass weatherstrip, the door trim panel and the plastic water-shield (see Section 15).

3   Detach the door lock rod from the han-dle and move it out of the way.

4   Detach the window glass from the regu-lator (see Section 18). Push the glass up all the way and tape it to the top of the door frame **(see illustration).**

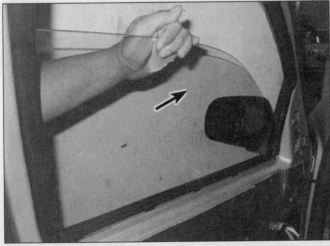

18.4 Lift the glass up and out of the door

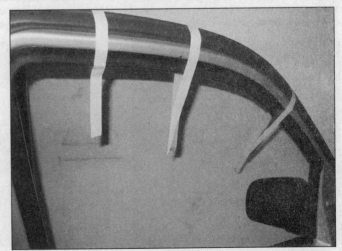

19.4 Tape the glass to the door frame in the full up position

11

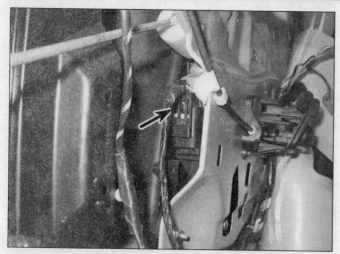

19.5 Disconnect the window regulator electrical connector

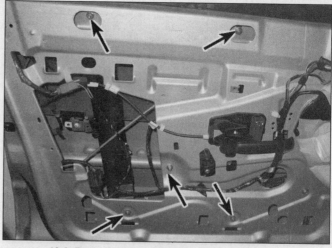

19.6 Remove the regulator/motor-to-door bolts

5   Disconnect the electrical connector from the window regulator motor **(see illustration)**.
6   Remove the regulator retaining bolts/rivets **(see illustration)**.
7   Pull the regulator assembly through the service hole in the door frame to remove.
8   Installation is the reverse of removal.

20 Sideview mirrors - removal and installation

Refer to illustration 20.2
1   Remove the door trim panel and the watershield (see Section 15). Disconnect the electrical connector from the mirror.
2   Remove the retaining nuts and detach the mirror from the vehicle **(see illustration)**.
3   Installation is the reverse of removal.

21 Liftgate - removal, installation and adjustment

Note: *The liftgate is heavy and somewhat awkward to hold - at least two people should perform this procedure.*

Removal and installation
Refer to illustration 21.2a, 21.2b, 21.2c, 21.2d, 21.3 and 21.6
1   Open the liftgate and support it securely.
2   Remove the liftgate trim panel **(see illustrations)**.
3   Disconnect the washer hose and all wiring harness connectors leading to the lift-

gate **(see illustration)**
4   Pull the harness through the liftgate.
5   While an assistant supports the liftgate, remove the support struts (see Section 9).
6   Mark the location of the hinge, then remove the hinge-to-liftgate bolts and detach the liftgate from the vehicle **(see illustration)**.
7   Installation is the reverse of removal.

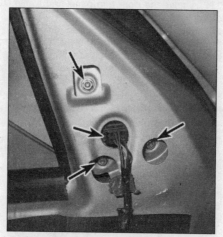

20.2 Detach the electrical connector and remove the mirror retaining nuts

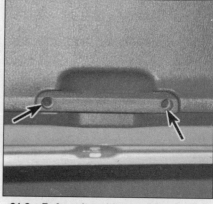

21.2a Before detaching the liftgate trim panel, remove the screws, including these two retaining the pull handle . . .

21.2b . . . and the two plastic screws

21.2c Use a screwdriver or similar tool to detach the retaining clips . . .

21.2d . . . and remove the trim panel from the liftgate

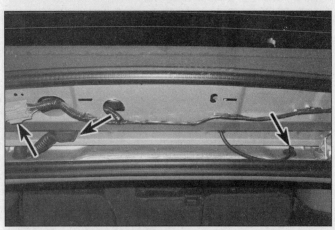

21.3 Disconnect the liftgate electrical connectors and the washer hose

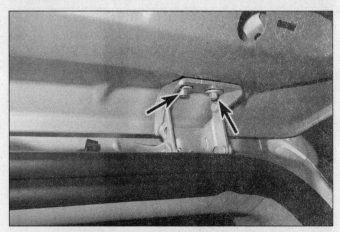

21.6 After marking their locations, remove the liftgate hinge retaining bolts

Adjustment

8   Adjustments are made by loosening the hinge-to-liftgate bolts and moving the liftgate. Proper alignment is achieved when the edges of the liftgate are parallel with the rear quarter panels and the top of the vehicle.

9   Finally, adjust the latch striker assembly as necessary (up and down) to provide positive engagement with the latch mechanism.

22   Liftgate latch assembly - removal and installation

Refer to illustrations 22.2, 22.3 and 22.4

1   Raise the liftgate and remove the liftgate trim cover and watershield (see Section 21).
2   Remove the latch mounting screws (see illustration).
3   Disconnect the liftgate latch electrical connector (see illustration).
4   Disconnect the control cable and remove the latch from the door (see illustration).
5   Installation is the reverse of removal. The manufacturer recommends using new screws when reinstalling the latch.

23   Center console - removal and installation

Refer to illustrations 23.2, 23.4a, 23.4b, 23.5a, 23.5b, 23.6a and 23.6b

Warning 1: *These models are equipped with airbags. Always disable the airbag system before working in the vicinity of any airbag system component to avoid the possibility of accidental deployment of the airbag(s), which could cause personal injury (see Chapter 12).*

Warning 2: *Do not use a memory saving device to preserve the ECM's memory when working on or near airbag system components.*

1   Disconnect the cable from the negative battery terminal (see Chapter 5).
2   Detach the front of the console side covers from the instrument panel support (see illustration).

22.2 Remove the liftgate latch retaining screws

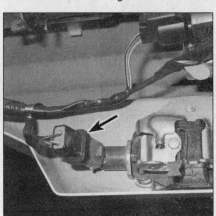

22.3 Disconnect the electrical connector

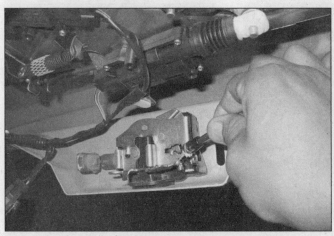

22.4 Disconnect the release cable from the latch

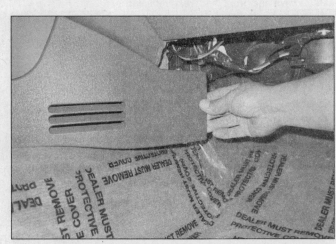

23.2 Detach the front of the console from the instrument panel

11

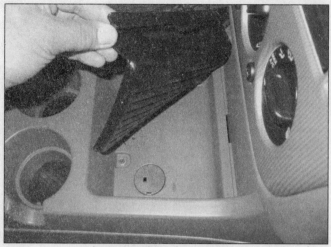

23.4a Remove the trim mat . . .

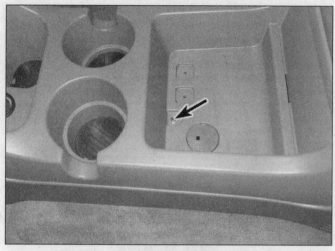

23.4b . . . and the console retaining screw

23.5a Detach the console cover for access . . .

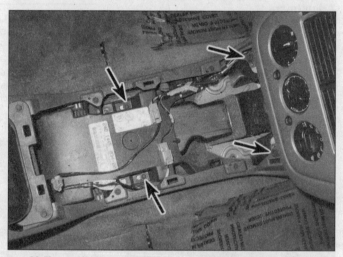

23.5b . . . then remove the front and rear retaining screws

3   Remove the shift lever (manual transmission models) or ashtray assembly (automatic transmission).

4   Remove the console trim mat and the screw underneath **(see illustrations)**.

5   Remove the console cover for access and remove the front and rear retaining screws **(see illustrations)**.

6   Detach the rear access covers and remove the bolts **(see illustrations)**.

7   Disconnect any electrical connections and remove the console from the vehicle.

8   Installation is the reverse of removal.

24 Instrument cluster bezel - removal and installation

Refer to illustrations 24.3a and 24.3b

Warning 1: *These models are equipped with airbags. Always disable the airbag system before working in the vicinity of any airbag system component to avoid the possibility of accidental deployment of the airbag(s), which could cause personal injury (see Chapter 12).*

Warning 2: *Do not use a memory saving device to preserve the ECM's memory when working on or near airbag system components.*

1   Disconnect the cable from the negative battery terminal (see Chapter 5).

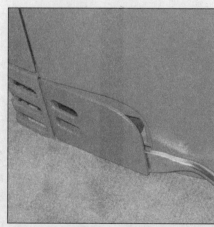

23.6a Carefully pry off the console rear side covers . . .

2   Remove the instrument panel end cap, driver's side under dash panel and knee bolster, the steering column covers and the center bezel (see Sections 25 and 26).

3   Remove the screws and pull the bezel back, then disconnect the electrical connec-

23.6b . . . for access to the retaining bolts

24.3a Remove the four retaining screws on the left side of the cluster bezel . . .

24.3b . . . and one retaining screw from the right side

25.2 Use a screwdriver or trim panel tool to remove the dashboard end caps

tors and remove the bezel from the vehicle **(see illustrations)**.

4   Installation is the reverse of removal.

25   Dashboard trim panels - removal and installation

Warning 1: *These models are equipped with airbags. Always disable the airbag system before working in the vicinity of any airbag system component to avoid the possibility of accidental deployment of the airbag(s), which could cause personal injury (see Chapter 12).*
Warning 2: *Do not use a memory saving device to preserve the ECM's memory when working on or near airbag system components.*

1   Disconnect the cable from the negative battery terminal (see Chapter 5).

Dashboard end caps

Refer to illustration 25.2

2   Carefully pry the end caps from the dashboard **(see illustration)**.
3   Install by pushing the end cap into place until the retainers lock.

Center bezel

Refer to illustration 25.4

4   Use a screwdriver or trim panel tool to carefully detach the clips, then pull the center bezel out **(see illustration)**.
5   Disconnect the electrical connectors and remove the bezel from the dashboard.
6   Installation is the reverse of removal.

Knee bolster

Refer to illustration 25.7

7   Remove the steering column covers (see Section 26). Remove the two screws at the bottom, detach the retainers and lower the knee bolster from the dashboard **(see illustration)**.
8   Installation is the reverse of removal.

Glove box

Refer to illustrations 25.9 and 25.10

9   Open the glove box door. Press inward on the doorstops to release the upper half of

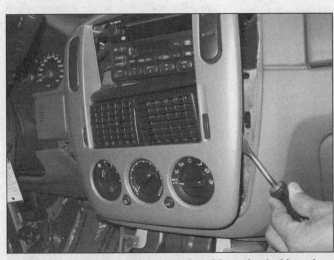

25.4 Carefully detach the center bezel from the dashboard

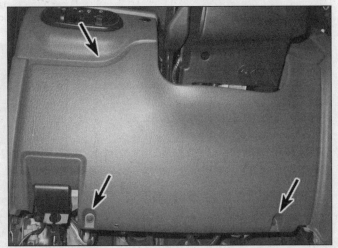

25.7 Remove the two screws at the lower edge, then use a screwdriver or trim panel tool to detach the upper edge of the knee bolster

11

25.9 Squeeze in the sides of the glove box and lower it . . .

25.10 . . . then remove the hinge retaining screws

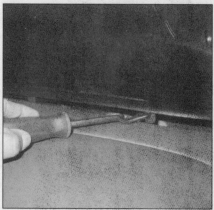

25.12 Detach the clips along the rear edge of the dashboard cover

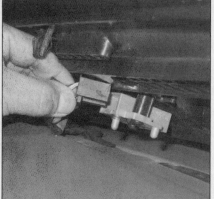

25.13 Disconnect the electrical connector and remove the dashboard cover

26.2a Remove the screws from the lower column cover . . .

the glove box and rotate it out of the dashboard **(see illustration)**.
10   Remove the hinge screws and detach the glove box **(see illustration)**.
11   Installation is the reverse of removal.

Dashboard cover

Refer to illustrations 25.12 and 25.13
12   Working along the rear edge, use a screwdriver or similar tool to detach the rear edge of the cover **(see illustration)**.
13   Disconnect the electrical connector and withdraw the cover from the dashboard **(see illustration)**.
14   Installation is the reverse of removal.

26   Steering column covers - removal and installation

Refer to illustrations 26.2a and 26.2b
1   Remove the knee bolster (see Section 25).
2   Remove the screws, detach the lower half from the steering column for access to the hidden screw retaining the upper cover, then remove the screw and lift off the upper cover **(see illustrations)**.
3   Installation is the reverse of removal.

27   Cowl cover - removal and installation

Refer to illustrations 27.2a and 27.2b
1   Remove the windshield wiper arms (see Chapter 12).
2   Detach the clips and remove the cowl covers **(see illustrations)**.
3   Installation is the reverse of removal.

26.2b . . . then remove the screw retaining the upper column cover

28   Seats - removal and installation

Warning 1: *Some models are equipped with seat belt pre-tensioners, which are pyrotechnic (explosive) devices that tighten the seat belts during an impact of sufficient force. Always disable the airbag system before working in the vicinity of any restraint system component to avoid the possibility of acci-*

27.2a Detach the cowl retaining clips . . .

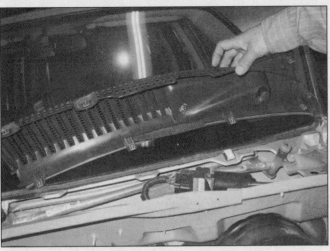

27.2b . . . and rotate the cowl pieces up and out of the opening

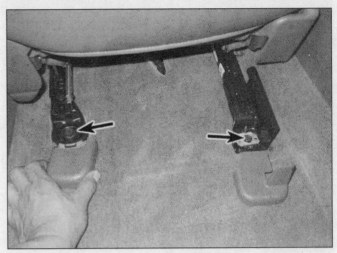

28.3 Detach the trim covers and remove the seat retaining bolts

dental deployment of the airbag(s) and seat belt pre-tensioners, who could cause personal injury (see Chapter 12).

Warning 2: *Do not use a memory saving device to preserve the ECM's memory when working on or near restraint system components.*

Front seat

Refer to illustrations 28.3 and 28.4

1 Position the seat so the retaining bolts are accessible.

2 Disconnect the cable from the negative battery terminal (see Chapter 5).

3 Detach any bolt trim covers and remove the retaining bolts **(see illustrations)**.

4 Disconnect any electrical connectors and lift the seat from the vehicle **(see illustration)**.

5 Installation is the reverse of removal.

Rear seat

Refer to illustrations 28.6 and 28.7

6 Release the seat and rotate it forward

28.4 Disconnect the electrical connectors

for access to the retaining bolts **(see illustration)**.

7 Remove the seat-to-floor mounting bolts and nuts, then lift the seat out of the vehicle **(see illustration)**.

8 Installation is the reverse of removal.

29 Instrument panel - removal and installation

Refer to illustrations 29.5 through 29.18

Warning 1: *These models are equipped with airbags. Always disable the airbag system before working in the vicinity of any airbag system component to avoid the possibility of accidental deployment of the airbag(s), which could cause personal injury (see Chapter 12).*

Warning 2: *Do not use a memory saving device to preserve the ECM's memory when working on or near airbag system components.*

1 Disconnect the cable from the negative battery terminal (see Chapter 5).

2 Remove the knee bolster, dashboard end caps, center bezel, cover and glove box (see Section 25).

3 Remove the passenger side airbag (see Chapter 12).

4 Remove the steering column cover (see Section 26) and center console (see Section 23).

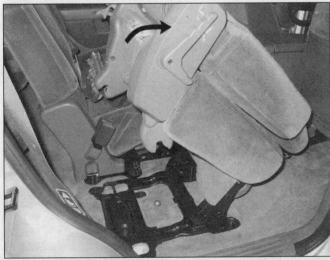

28.6 Release the rear seat and rotate it forward

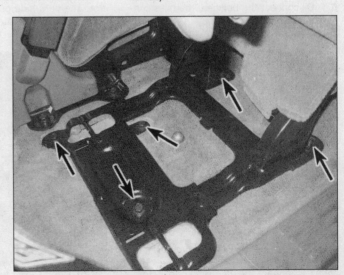

28.7 Remove the rear seat retaining bolts and nuts

11

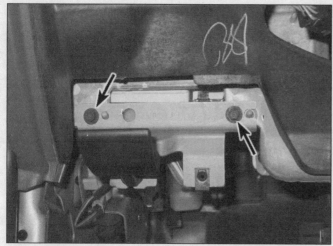

29.5 Remove the parking brake release handle bracket bolts

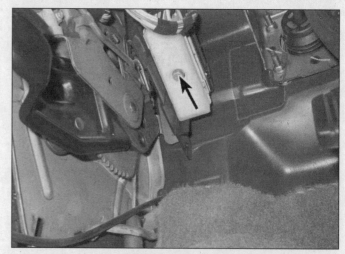

29.6 Loosen the bolt and disconnect the bulkhead electrical connector

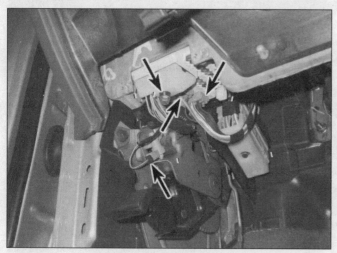

29.7 Also disconnect the electrical connectors from the fuse panel and parking brake switch

29.8 Disconnect the electrical connectors from the right side of the instrument panel support

5   Remove the bolts and detach the parking brake release handle bracket **(see illustration)**.

6   Disconnect the bulkhead harness connector **(see illustration)**.

7   Disconnect the electrical connectors from the fuse panel and the parking brake switch **(see illustration)**.

8   Disconnect the electrical connectors from the right side of the instrument panel support **(see illustration)**.

9   Disconnect the electrical connectors from under the center console **(see illustration)**.

10   Disconnect the bolt retaining the ground wire from where the console was **(see illustration)**.

11   Disconnect the bulkhead electrical con-

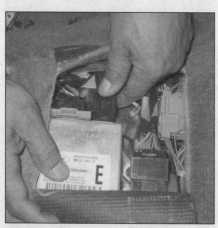

29.9 Disconnect the electrical connectors from under the center console

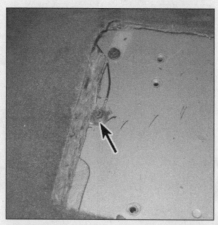

29.10 Don't forget to detach the console ground wire connections

29.11 Disconnect the bulkhead connectors

29.12 Instrument panel upper bolt locations

29.13 The cowl bolts are located below the wiper motor

29.14 Steering shaft U-joint pinch bolt location

29.15 Disconnect the shift cable

nector **(see illustration)**.
12   Remove the bolts along the top of the instrument panel **(see illustration)**.
13   Remove the cowl bolts **(see illustration)**.
14   Remove the pinch bolt and disconnect

the steering column shaft **(see illustration)**.
15   On automatic transmission models, disconnect the shift cable **(see illustration)**.
16   Remove the bolts and nuts and detach the center instrument panel brackets **(see illustration)**.

17   Remove the bolts from each end of the instrument panel.
18   Detach the instrument panel and steering column assembly and lift it out of the vehicle **(see illustration)**.
19   Installation is the reverse of removal.

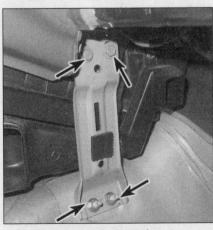

29.16 Instrument panel center bracket nuts and bolts

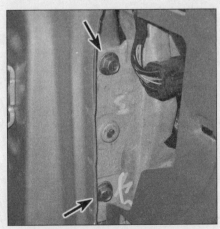

29.17 Remove the bolts from each end of the instrument panel

29.18 Lift the assembly from the vehicle

11

Notes

Chapter 12
Chassis electrical system

Contents

1   General information

The electrical system is a 12-volt, negative ground type. Power for the lights and all electrical accessories is supplied by a lead/acid-type battery, which is charged by the alternator.

This Chapter covers repair and service procedures for the various electrical components not associated with the engine. Information on the battery, alternator, distributor and starter motor can be found in Chapter 5.

It should be noted that when portions of the electrical system are serviced, the negative battery cable should be disconnected from the battery to prevent electrical shorts and/or fires.

2   Electrical troubleshooting - general information

Refer to illustrations 2.5a, 2.5b, 2.6 and 2.9

A typical electrical circuit consists of an electrical component, any switches, relays, motors, fuses, fusible links or circuit breakers related to that component and the wiring and connectors that link the component to both the battery and the chassis. To help you pinpoint an electrical circuit problem, wiring diagrams are included at the end of this Chapter.

Before tackling any troublesome electrical circuit, first study the appropriate wiring diagrams to get a complete understanding of what makes up that individual circuit. Noting if other components related to the circuit are operating properly, for instance, can often narrow trouble spots, down. If several components or circuits fail at one time, chances are the problem is in a fuse or ground connection, because several circuits are often routed through the same fuse and ground connections.

Electrical problems usually stem from simple causes, such as loose or corroded connections, a blown fuse, a melted fusible link or a failed relay. Visually inspect the condition of all fuses, wires and connections in a problem circuit before troubleshooting the circuit.

If test equipment and instruments are going to be utilized, use the diagrams to plan ahead of time where you will make the necessary connections in order to accurately pinpoint the trouble spot.

12

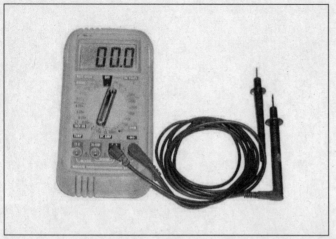

2.5a The most useful tool for electrical troubleshooting is a digital multimeter that can check volts, amps, and test continuity

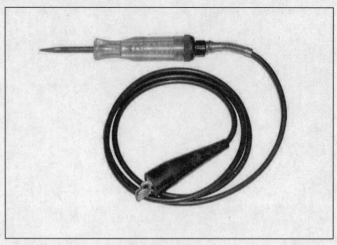

2.5b A simple test light is a very handy tool for testing voltage

The basic tools needed for electrical troubleshooting include a circuit tester or voltmeter (a 12-volt bulb with a set of test leads can also be used), a continuity tester, which includes a bulb, battery and set of test leads, and a jumper wire, preferably with a circuit breaker incorporated, which can be used to bypass electrical components **(see illustrations)**. Before attempting to locate a problem with test instruments, use the wiring diagram(s) to decide where to make the connections.

Voltage checks

Voltage checks should be performed if a circuit is not functioning properly. Connect one lead of a circuit tester to either the negative battery terminal or a known good ground. Connect the other lead to a connector in the circuit being tested, preferably nearest to the battery or fuse **(see illustration)**. If the bulb of the tester lights, voltage is present, which means that the part of the circuit between the connector and the battery is problem free.

Continue checking the rest of the circuit in the same fashion. When you reach a point at which no voltage is present, the problem lies between that point and the last test point with voltage. Most of the time the problem can be traced to a loose connection. **Note:** *Keep in mind that some circuits receive voltage only when the ignition key is in the Accessory or Run position.*

Finding a short

One method of finding shorts in a live circuit is to remove the fuse and connect a test light in place of the fuse terminals (fabricate two jumper wires with small spade terminals, plug the jumper wires into the fuse box and connect the test light). There should be voltage present in the circuit. Move the suspected wiring harness from side-to-side while watching the test light. If the bulb goes off, there is a short to ground somewhere in that area, probably where the insulation has rubbed through.

Ground check

Perform a ground test to check whether a component is properly grounded. Disconnect the battery and connect one lead of a continuity tester or multimeter (set to the ohm scale), to a known good ground. Connect the other lead to the wire or ground connection being tested. If the resistance is low (less than 5 ohms), the ground is good. If the bulb on a self-powered test light does not go on, the ground is not good.

Continuity check

A continuity check is done to determine if there are any breaks in a circuit - if it is passing electricity properly. With the circuit off (no power in the circuit), a self-powered continuity tester or multimeter can be used to check the circuit. Connect the test leads to both ends of the circuit (or to the "power" end and a good ground), and if the test light comes on the circuit is passing current properly **(see illustration)**. If the resistance is low

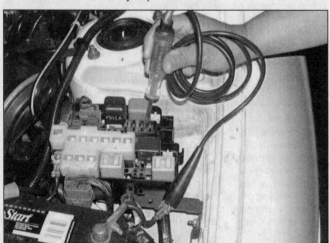

2.6 In use, a basic test light's lead is clipped to a known good ground, then the pointed probe can test connectors, wires or electrical sockets - if the bulb lights, the circuit being tested has battery voltage

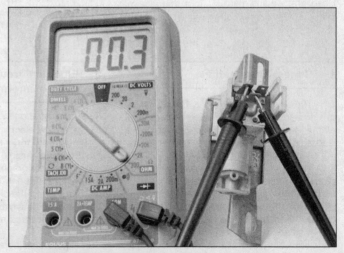

2.9 With a multimeter set to the ohms scale, resistance can be checked across two terminals - when checking for continuity, a low reading indicates continuity, a high reading or infinity indicates high resistance or lack of continuity

3.1a The main fuse/relay box is mounted to the left inner fenderwell in the engine compartment behind the battery - it contains miniaturized fuses, cartridge-type fusible links, relays and circuit breakers

3.1b The auxiliary fuse/relay block is located under the driver's side of the instrument panel, behind the fuse panel cover

(less than 5 ohms), there is continuity; if the reading is 10,000 ohms or higher, there is a break somewhere in the circuit. The same procedure can be used to test a switch, by connecting the continuity tester to the switch terminals. With the switch turned On, the test light should come on (or low resistance should be indicated on a meter).

Finding an open circuit

When diagnosing for possible open circuits, it is often difficult to locate them by sight because the connectors hide oxidation or terminal misalignment. Merely wiggling a connector on a sensor or in the wiring harness may correct the open circuit condition. Remember this when an open circuit is indicated when troubleshooting a circuit. Intermittent problems may also be caused by oxidized or loose connections.

Electrical troubleshooting is simple if you keep in mind that all electrical circuits are basically electricity running from the battery, through the wires, switches, relays, fuses and fusible links to each electrical component (light bulb, motor, etc.) and to ground, from which it is passed back to the battery. Any electrical problem is an interruption in the flow of electricity to and from the battery.

Connectors

Most electrical connections on these vehicles are made with multiwire plastic connectors. The mating halves of many connectors are secured with locking clips molded into the plastic connector shells. The mating halves of large connectors, such as some of those under the instrument panel, are held together by a bolt through the center of the connector.

To separate a connector with locking clips, use a small screwdriver to pry the clips apart carefully, then separate the connector halves. Pull only on the shell, never pull on the wiring harness as you may damage the

individual wires and terminals inside the connectors. Look at the connector closely before trying to separate the halves. Often the locking clips are engaged in a way that is not immediately clear. Additionally, many connectors have more than one set of clips.

Each pair of connector terminals has a male half and a female half. When you look at the end view of a connector in a diagram, be sure to understand whether the view shows the harness side or the component side of the connector. Connector halves are mirror images of each other, and a terminal shown on the right side end-view of one half will be on the left side end view of the other half.

3   Fuses and fusible links - general information

Fuses

Refer to illustrations 3.1a, 3.1b and 3.3

The electrical circuits of the vehicle are protected by a combination of fuses, circuit breakers and fusible links. Fuse/relay blocks are located behind the battery in the engine

compartment, under the driver's side instrument panel and in the auxiliary block on the right rear side of the luggage compartment **(see illustrations)**.

Each of the fuses is designed to protect a specific circuit, and the various circuits are identified on the fuse panel cover.

Miniaturized fuses are employed in the fuse blocks. These compact fuses, with blade terminal design, allow fingertip removal and replacement. If an electrical component fails, always check the fuse first. The best way to check a fuse is with a test light. Check for power at the exposed terminal tips of each fuse. If power is present on one side of the fuse but not the other, the fuse is blown. A blown fuse can also be confirmed by visually inspecting it **(see illustration)**.

Be sure to replace blown fuses with the correct type. Fuses of different ratings are physically interchangeable, but only fuses of the proper rating should be used. Replacing a fuse with one of a higher or lower value than specified is not recommended. Each electrical circuit needs a specific amount of protection. The amperage value of each fuse is molded into the fuse body.

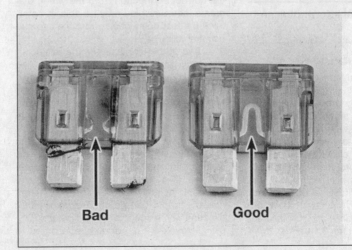

3.3 When a fuse blows, the element between the terminals melts - the fuse on the left is blown, the fuse on the right is good

Bad   **Good**

12

If the replacement fuse immediately fails, don't replace it again until the cause of the problem is isolated and corrected. In most cases, this will be a short circuit in the wiring caused by a broken or deteriorated wire.

Fusible links

Some circuits are protected by fusible links. The links are used in circuits which are not ordinarily fused, or which carry high current.

Cartridge type fusible links are located in the engine compartment fusible link box and are similar to a large fuse. After disconnecting the negative battery cable, simply unplug and replace a fusible link with one of the same amperage.

4   Circuit breakers - general information

Circuit breakers protect certain circuits, such as the power windows or heated seats. Depending on the vehicle's accessories, there may be one or two circuit breakers, located in the fuse/relay box in the engine compartment **(see illustration 3.1a)**.

Because the circuit breakers reset automatically, an electrical overload in a circuit-breaker-protected system will cause the circuit to fail momentarily, then come back on. If the circuit does not come back on, check it immediately.

For a basic check, pull the circuit breaker up out of its socket on the fuse panel, but just far enough to probe with a voltmeter. The breaker should still contact the sockets.

With the voltmeter negative lead on a good chassis ground, touch each end prong of the circuit breaker with the positive meter probe. There should be battery voltage at each end. If there is battery voltage only at one end, the circuit breaker must be replaced.

Some circuit breakers must be reset manually.

5   Relays - general information and testing

General information

1   Several electrical accessories in the vehicle, such as the fuel injection system, horns, starter, and fog lamps use relays to transmit the electrical signal to the component. Relays use a low-current circuit (the control circuit) to open and close a high-current circuit (the power circuit). If the relay is defective, that component will not operate properly. Most relays are mounted in the engine compartment fuse/relay box, with some specialized relays located above the interior fuse box in the dash and rear auxiliary relay box **(see illustrations 3.1a and 3.1b)**. If

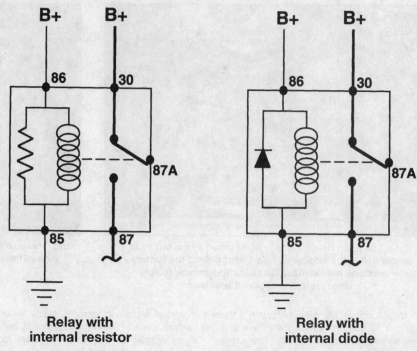

Relay with internal resistor   **Relay with internal diode**

24053-12-5.2a HAYNES

5.2a Typical ISO relay designs, terminal numbering and circuit connections

a faulty relay is suspected, it can be removed and tested using the procedure below or by a dealer service department or a repair shop. Defective relays must be replaced as a unit.

Testing

Refer to illustrations 5.2a and 5.2b

2   Most of the relays used in these vehicles are of a type often called "ISO" relays, which refers to the International Standards Organization. The terminals of ISO relays are numbered to indicate their usual circuit connections and functions. There are two basic layouts of terminals on the relays used in these vehicles **(see illustrations)**.

3   Refer to the wiring diagrams for the circuit to determine the proper connections for the relay you're testing. If you can't determine the correct connection from the wiring diagrams, however, you may be able to determine the test connections from the information that follows.

4   Two of the terminals are the relay control circuit and connect to the relay coil. The other relay terminals are the power circuit. When the relay is energized, the coil creates a magnetic field that closes the larger contacts of the power circuit to provide power to the circuit loads.

5   Terminals 85 and 86 are normally the control circuit. If the relay contains a diode, terminal 86 must be connected to battery positive (B+) voltage and terminal 85 to ground. If the relay contains a resistor, terminals 85 and 86 can be connected in either direction with respect to B+ and ground.

6   Terminal 30 is normally connected to

the battery voltage (B+) source for the circuit loads. Terminal 87 is connected to the ground side of the circuit, either directly or through a load. If the relay has several alternate terminals for load or ground connections, they usually are numbered 87A, 87B, 87C, and so on.

7   Use an ohmmeter to check continuity through the relay control coil.

a)   Connect the meter according to the polarity shown in the illustration for one check; then reverse the ohmmeter leads and check continuity in the other direction.

b)   If the relay contains a resistor, resistance will be indicated on the meter, and should be the same value with the ohmmeter in either direction.

Control circuits   Power circuits

963221B U.S.A.

5.2b Most relays are marked on the outside to easily identify the control circuits and the power circuits - four terminal type shown

7.3a Remove the retaining screw and push on the release lever . . .

7.3b . . . then unplug the electrical connectors and remove the multi-function switch

c) If the relay contains a diode, resistance should be higher with the ohmmeter in the forward polarity direction than with the meter leads reversed.

d) If the ohmmeter shows infinite resistance in both directions, replace the relay.

8   Remove the relay from the vehicle and use the ohmmeter to check for continuity between the relay power circuit terminals. There should be no continuity between terminal 30 and 87 with the relay de-energized.

9   Connect a fused jumper wire to terminal 86 and the positive battery terminal. Connect another jumper wire between terminal 85 and ground. When the connections are made, the relay should click.

10   With the jumper wires connected, check for continuity between the power circuit terminals. Now, there should be continuity between terminals 30 and 87.

11   If the relay fails any of the above tests, replace it.

6   Turn signal and hazard flasher - check and replacement

Warning: *The models covered by this manual are equipped with Supplemental Restraint systems (SRS), more commonly known as airbags. Always disable the airbag system before working in the vicinity of any airbag system component to avoid the possibility of accidental deployment of the airbag, which could cause personal injury (see Section 25).*

1   The turn signal and hazard flashers are controlled from a single electronic flasher unit, which is, mounted in the relay box behind the left end of the dash.

2   When the flasher unit is functioning properly, an audible click can be heard during its operation. If the turn signal indicator (on the instrument panel) on one side of the vehicle flashes much more rapidly than normal, a faulty turn signal bulb is indicated.

3   If both turn signals fail to blink, the problem may be due to a blown fuse, a faulty flasher unit, a broken switch or a loose or open connection. If a quick check of the fuse box indicates that the turn signal fuse has blown, check the wiring for a short before installing a new fuse.

4   To replace the flasher, simply the flasher unit from the block.

5   Make sure that the replacement unit is identical to the original. Compare the old one to the new one before installing it.

6   Installation is the reverse of removal.

7   Steering column switches - replacement

Warning: *The models covered by this manual are equipped with Supplemental Restraint systems (SRS), more commonly known as airbags. Always disable the airbag system before working in the vicinity of any airbag system component to avoid the possibility of accidental deployment of the airbag, which could cause personal injury (see Section 25).*

Multi-function switch

Refer to illustrations 7.3a and 7.3b

1   Disconnect the cable from the negative battery terminal (see Chapter 5).

2   Remove the steering column covers (see Chapter 11).

3   Remove the retaining screw, push on the release lever then detach the switch from the steering column. Use a small screwdriver to disconnect the electrical connectors so the switch assembly can be removed from the vehicle **(see illustrations)**.

4   Installation is the reverse of removal.

Cruise control switches

Refer to illustration 7.7

5   Disconnect the cable from the negative battery terminal (see Chapter 5).

6   Remove the driver's side airbag from the steering wheel (see Chapter 10).

7   Remove the retaining screws, disconnect the electrical connectors and detach cruise control switches from the steering wheel **(see illustration)**.

7.7 Remove the cruise control switch screws and disconnect the electrical connectors

12

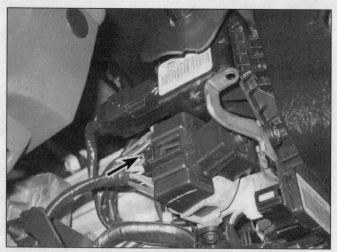

8.5 Unplug the ignition switch electrical connector

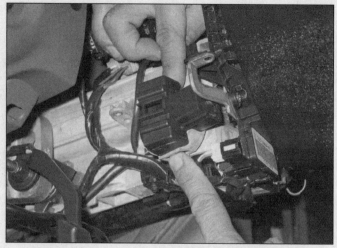

8.6 Press in on the clips to release the ignition switch

Audio control switch

8   Disconnect the cable from the negative battery terminal (see Chapter 5).
9   Remove the driver's side airbag from the steering wheel (see Chapter 10).
10   Remove the audio control switch retaining screws, disconnect the electrical connectors and detach the switch from the steering wheel.
11   Installation is the reverse of removal.

8   Ignition switch and key lock cylinder - replacement

Warning: *The models covered by this manual are equipped with Supplemental Restraint systems (SRS), more commonly known as airbags. Always disable the airbag system before working in the vicinity of any airbag system component to avoid the possibility of accidental deployment of the airbag, which could cause personal injury (see Section 25).*

Ignition switch

Refer to illustrations 8.5 and 8.6

1   Disconnect the cable from the negative battery terminal (see Chapter 5).

2   Remove the steering column covers (see Chapter 11).
4   Remove the multi-function switch (see Section 7).
5   Disconnect the electrical connector from the ignition switch **(see illustration)**.
6   Release the two tabs and detach the ignition switch **(see illustration)**.
7   Installation is the reverse of removal, making sure the spring located under the switch is in position on the column locking rod.
8   Check for proper operation of the ignition switch in the lock, start and accessory positions.

Lock cylinder

Refer to illustration 8.12

9   Disconnect the cable from the negative battery terminal (see Chapter 5).
10   Remove the steering column covers (see Chapter 11).
11   Remove the Passive Anti-Theft System (PATS) transceiver, if equipped.
12   Turn the ignition key lock cylinder to the ACC position. Insert a 1/8-inch punch into the hole at the bottom of the lock cylinder. Depress the punch while pulling out on the lock cylinder to remove it from the steering column housing **(see illustration)**. **Note:** *If*

the lock cylinder is jammed and won't turn, or if you can't insert the ignition key into it, the retaining pin will have to be drilled out with a 3/16-inch drill bit. If you have to resort to this method, be sure to remove all metal shavings from the housing before installing the new lock cylinder.
13   To install the lock cylinder, depress the retaining pin on the side of the lock cylinder and rotate the ignition key/lock cylinder to the On position.
14   Install the lock cylinder into the steering column housing, making sure it's fully seated and aligned in the interlocking washer.
15   Rotate the key back to the Off position. This will allow the retaining pin to extend itself back into the locating hole in the steering column housing.
16   Turn the lock to ensure that operation is correct in all positions.
17   The remainder of installation is the reverse of removal.

9   Instrument panel switches - replacement

Warning: *The models covered by this manual are equipped with Supplemental Restraint systems (SRS), more commonly known as airbags. Always disable the airbag system before working in the vicinity of any airbag system component to avoid the possibility of accidental deployment of the airbag, which could cause personal injury (see Section 25).*

Headlight, panel dimmer and parking aid switch assembly

Refer to illustrations 9.2a and 9.2b

1   Disconnect the cable from the negative battery terminal (see Chapter 5).
2   Carefully pry the switch housing from the instrument panel, then unplug the electrical connectors from the switches **(see illustrations)**.
3   Installation is the reverse of the removal procedure.

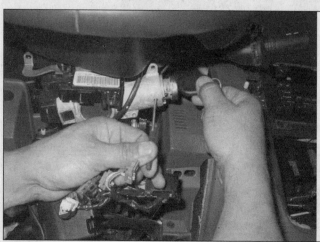

8.12 To remove the ignition lock cylinder, place the key in the "ACC" position, push in on the release pin with a small punch and pull the cylinder straight out

9.2a Pry the switch housing out of the instrument panel . . .

9.2b . . . then pull the switch assembly out and disconnect the electrical connectors

10.3 Location of the instrument cluster screws

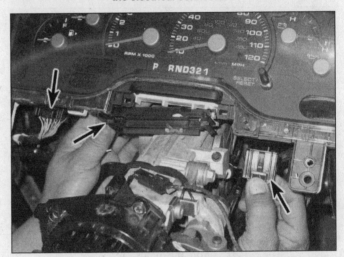

10.4 Disconnect the cluster electrical connectors and the shift indicator

Message center and 4WD switches

4   Disconnect the cable from the negative battery terminal (see Chapter 5).
5   Remove center dash panel bezel (see Chapter 11).
6   Disconnect the electrical connectors, squeeze the retaining tabs and detach the switches from the bezel.
7   Installation is the reverse of the removal procedure.

10 Instrument cluster - removal and installation

Refer to illustrations 10.3 and 10.4
Warning: *The models covered by this manual are equipped with Supplemental Restraint systems (SRS), more commonly known as airbags. Always disable the airbag system before working in the vicinity of any airbag system component to avoid the possibility of accidental deployment of the airbag, which could cause personal injury (see Section 25).*

1   Disconnect the cable from the negative battery terminal (see Chapter 5).
2   Tilt the steering wheel to its lowest position and remove the instrument cluster bezel (see Chapter 11).
3   Remove the instrument cluster retaining screws **(see illustration)**.
4   Pull the instrument cluster out, unplug the electrical connectors from the backside and the shift indicator from the bottom (automatic transmission models), then remove the cluster from the instrument panel **(see illustration)**.
5   Installation is the reverse of removal.

11 Wiper motor - replacement

1   Disconnect the cable from the negative battery terminal (see Chapter 5).

Front wiper motor

Refer to illustrations 11.2a, 11.2b, 11.4 and 11.11
2   Mark the positions of the wiper blades on the windshield, then remove the wiper

11.2a Release the wiper locking tab using a small screwdriver or pick . . .

arms **(see illustration)**.
3   Remove the windshield cowl cover (see Chapter 11).

12

11.2b . . . then pull the wiper arm off the shaft

11.4 Remove the windshield wiper assembly mounting bolts and disconnect the electrical connector

11.6a Remove the nut and separate the wiper crank from the motor

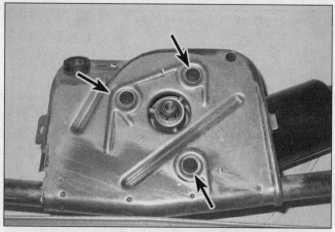

11.6b Remove the wiper motor mounting bolts

4   Disconnect the wiper motor harness connector and remove the windshield wiper motor/linkage assembly mounting bolts **(see illustration)**.
5   Lift the windshield wiper motor assembly from the cowl area.
6   Remove the nut and detach the wiper crank from the shaft, then remove the wiper motor mounting nuts and separate the motor

from the assembly **(see illustrations)**.
7   Installation is the reverse of removal.
Note: *Before installing the wiper arms, make sure the wiper motor is in the park position. It will be necessary to pull the locking tab on the wiper arm to its full open position while assembling the wiper arms onto their shafts. Also, align the wiper blades with the marks you made on the windshield.*

Rear wiper motor
Refer to illustrations 11.9a, 11.9b, 11.9c and 11.11
8   Remove the liftgate trim panel (see Chapter 11).
9   Remove the wiper arm pivot cover, mark the position of the wiper arm to the shaft so it can be reinstalled in the same position **(see illustration)**. Remove the nut and detach the

11.9a Mark the alignment of the rear wiper arm to the wiper motor shaft

11.9b Remove the nut and the wiper arm

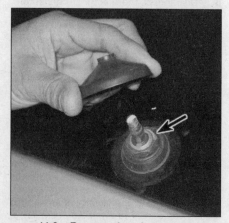

11.9c Remove the wiper motor retaining nut

11.11 Remove the rear wiper motor nuts and disconnect the electrical connector

12.3a Remove the retaining bolts, pull the radio out . . .

wiper arm **(see illustrations)**.

10   Remove the pivot nut and rubber grommet.

11   Disconnect the wiper motor harness connector and remove the windshield wiper motor mounting nuts **(see illustration)**.

12   Lower the wiper motor assembly from the liftgate.

13   Installation is the reverse of removal, taking care when installing the wiper arm to align the marks on the arm and shaft before installing the nut and cover.

12   Radio and speakers - removal and installation

Warning: *The models covered by this manual are equipped with Supplemental Restraint systems (SRS), more commonly known as airbags. Always disable the airbag system before working in the vicinity of any airbag system component to avoid the possibility of accidental deployment of the airbag, which could cause personal injury (see Section 25).*

1   Disconnect the cable from the negative battery terminal (see Chapter 5).

Radio

Refer to illustration 12.3a and 12.3b

2   Remove the dash center bezel (see Chapter 11).

3   Remove the radio retaining bolts and pull the assembly out of the instrument panel, disconnect the antenna and electrical connectors and remove the unit from the vehicle **(see illustrations)**.

4   Install by connecting the electrical connectors and antenna cable, sliding the radio into position and installing bolts and tightening them securely.

Speakers

Refer to illustration 12.6

5   Remove the door trim panel (see Chapter 11).

6   Remove the mounting screws, withdraw the speaker, unplug the electrical connector and remove the speaker from the vehicle **(see illustration)**.

7   Installation is the reverse of removal.

12.3b . . . then disconnect the electrical connector and antenna cable

13   Antenna and cable - removal and installation

Refer to illustrations 13.1, 13.2 and 13.3

1   Lower the glove box (see Chapter 11) and disconnect the antenna cable connection **(see illustration)**.

12.6 Remove the speaker retaining screws, separate the speaker from the door and disconnect the electrical connector

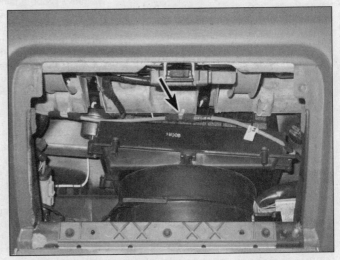

13.1 Disconnect the antenna cable connector

12

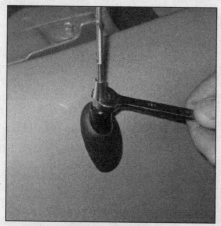

13.2 Use a wrench to remove the antenna from its base

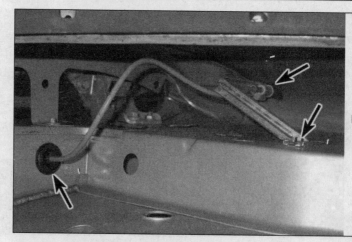

13.3 Remove the antenna base bracket mounting bolt and detach the cable grommets

2   Remove the antenna mast **(see illustration)**.
3   Loosen the right front wheel lug nuts. Raise the vehicle and secure it on jackstands.
4   Remove the right front wheel and the inner fender splash shield (see Chapter 11).
5   Remove the antenna base mounting bolt and detach the grommet and cable from the body, then lower the assembly from the wheel opening **(see illustration)**.
6   Installation is the reverse of removal.

14   Rear window defogger - check and repair

1   The rear window defogger consists of a number of horizontal elements baked onto the glass surface.
2   Small breaks in the element can be repaired without removing the rear window.

Check

Refer to illustrations 14.4, 14.5 and 14.7
3   Turn the ignition switch and defogger system switches to the ON position. Using a voltmeter, place the positive probe against the defogger grid positive terminal and the negative probe against the ground terminal. If battery voltage is not indicated, check the fuse, defogger switch and related wiring. If voltage is indicated, but all or part of the defogger doesn't heat, proceed with the following tests.
4   When measuring voltage during the next two tests, wrap a piece of aluminum foil around the tip of the voltmeter positive probe and press the foil against the heating element with your finger **(see illustration)**. Place the negative probe on the defogger grid ground terminal.
5   Check the voltage at the center of each heating element **(see illustration)**. If the voltage is 5 or 6-volts, the element is okay (there is no break). If the voltage is 0-volts, the element is broken between the center of the element and the positive end. If the voltage is 10 to 12-volts the element is broken between the center of the element and ground. Check

14.4 When measuring the voltage at the rear window defogger grid, wrap a piece of aluminum foil around the positive probe of the voltmeter and press the foil against the wire with your finger

each heating element.
6   Connect the negative lead to a good body ground. The reading should stay the same. If it doesn't, the ground connection is bad.
7   To find the break, place the voltmeter negative probe against the defogger ground terminal. Place the voltmeter positive probe with the foil strip against the heating element at the positive terminal end and slide it toward the negative terminal end. The point at which the voltmeter deflects from several volts to zero is the point at which the heating element is broken **(see illustration)**.

Repair

Refer to illustration 14.13
8   Repair the break in the element using a repair kit specifically recommended for this purpose, available at most auto parts stores. Included in this kit is plastic conductive epoxy.
9   Prior to repairing a break, turn off the system and allow it to cool off for a few minutes.
10   Lightly buff the element area with fine steel wool, then clean it thoroughly with rubbing alcohol.

14.5 To determine if a heating element has broken, check the voltage at the center of each element - if the voltage is 5 or 6-volts, the element is unbroken - if the voltage is 10 or 12-volts, the element is broken between the center and the ground side - if there is no voltage, the element is broken between the center and the positive side

14.7 To find the break, place the voltmeter negative lead against the defogger ground terminal, place the voltmeter positive lead with the foil strip against the heating element at the positive terminal end and slide it toward the negative terminal end - the point at which the voltmeter reading changes abruptly is the point at which the element is broken

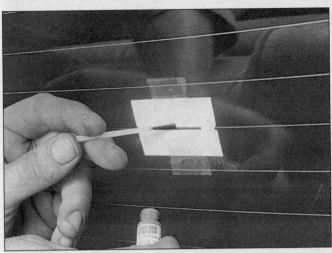

14.13 To use a defogger repair kit, apply masking tape to the inside of the window at the damaged area, then brush on the special conductive coating

15.2 Disconnect the headlight bulb electrical connector

11   Use masking tape to mask off the area being repaired.

12   Thoroughly mix the epoxy, following the instructions provided with the repair kit.

13   Apply the epoxy material to the slit in the masking tape, overlapping the undamaged area about 3/4-inch on either end **(see illustration)**.

14   Allow the repair to cure for 24 hours before removing the tape and using the system.

15   Headlight bulb - replacement

Refer to illustrations 15.2 and 15.3

Warning: *Halogen gas filled bulbs are under pressure and may shatter if the surface is scratched or the bulb is dropped. Wear eye protection and handle the bulbs carefully, grasping only the base whenever possible. Do not touch the surface of the bulb with your fingers because the oil from your skin could* cause it to overheat and fail prematurely. If you do touch the bulb surface, clean it with rubbing alcohol.

Note: *Always replace a headlight bulb with another one immediately. Damage to the headlight assembly could result if it is left without a bulb for a length of time.*

1   Remove the headlight housing (see Section 17).

2   Disconnect the electrical connector from the bulb holder **(see illustration)**. If you're working on a Mountaineer, remove the bulb access cover from the back of the headlight housing.

3   Rotate the headlight bulb assembly counterclockwise and withdraw the bulb assembly from the headlight housing **(see illustration)**.

4   Without touching the glass with your bare fingers, insert the new bulb assembly into the headlight housing and install by turning it clockwise.

5   Plug in the electrical connector, then install the headlight housing (see Section 17).

16   Headlights - adjustment

Refer to illustrations 16.1 and 16.3

Note: *The headlights must be aimed correctly. If adjusted incorrectly they could blind the driver of an oncoming vehicle and cause a serious accident or seriously reduce your ability to see the road. The headlights should be checked for proper aim every 12 months and any time a new headlight housing is installed or front end body work is performed. It should be emphasized that the following procedure is only an interim step, which will provide temporary adjustment until a properly equipped shop can adjust the headlights.*

1   The vertical adjustment screws are located behind each headlight housing **(see illustration)**. (There are no horizontal adjustment screws.)

2   There are several methods of adjusting the headlights. The simplest method requires masking tape, a blank wall and a level floor.

3   Position masking tape vertically on the

15.3 Rotate the headlight bulb assembly counterclockwise and pull it out of the housing - when installing the new bulb, don't touch the surface; clean it with rubbing alcohol if you do

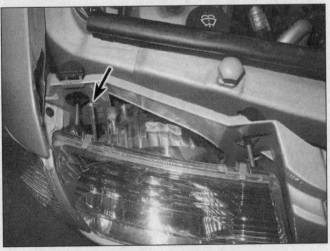

16.1 Location of the headlight adjustment screw

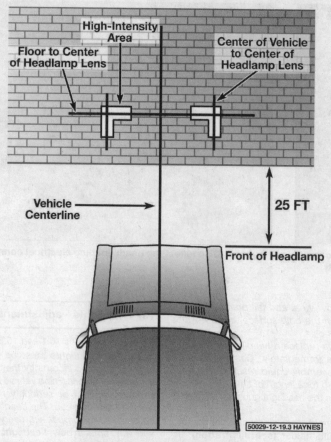

16.3 Headlight adjustment details

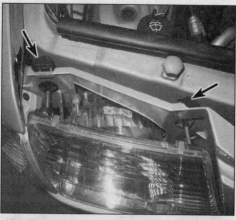

17.1 The headlight housing is retained by two slide locks (Explorer shown, Mountaineer slightly different) - pull the slide locks up . . .

wall in reference to the vehicle centerline and the centerlines of both headlights **(see illustration)**.

4   Position a horizontal tape line in reference to the centerline of all the headlights. **Note:** *It may be easier to position the tape on the wall with the vehicle parked only a few inches away.*

5   Adjustment should be made with the vehicle parked 25 feet from the wall, sitting level, the gas tank half-full and no heavy load in the vehicle.

6   Starting with the low beam adjustment,

position the high intensity zone so it is two inches below the horizontal line and two inches to the side of the headlight vertical line, away from oncoming traffic. Adjustment is made by turning the top (sealed beam) or inner adjusting screw clockwise to raise the beam and counterclockwise to lower the beam. The adjusting screw on the side should be used in the same manner to move the beam left or right.

7   With the high beams on, the high intensity zone should be vertically centered with the exact center just below the horizontal

line. **Note:** *It may not be possible to position the headlight aim exactly for both high and low beams. If a compromise must be made, keep in mind that the low beams are the most used and have the greatest effect on safety.*

8   Have the headlights adjusted by a dealer service department or service station at the earliest opportunity.

17   Headlight housing - replacement

Refer to illustrations 17.1 and 17.2

1   Open the hood, then pull up on the two slide locks that retain the headlight **(see illustration)**.

2   Pull the headlight housing forward and disconnect the electrical connector(s) **(see illustration)**.

3   Installation is the reverse of removal.

18   Horn - replacement

Refer to illustration 18.4

1   Loosen the left front wheel lug nuts. Raise the vehicle and secure it on jackstands.

2   Remove the front wheel.

17.2 . . . to free the headlight. When reinstalling, make sure the mounting posts seat properly in their holes

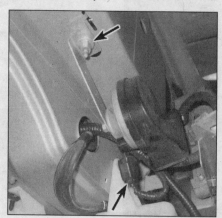

18.4 Disconnect the horn electrical connector and remove the retaining nut

19.1 Location of the front turn signal housing mounting screw

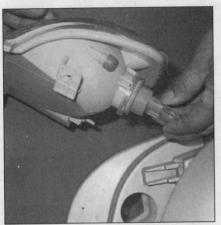

19.2a Disconnect the electrical connector

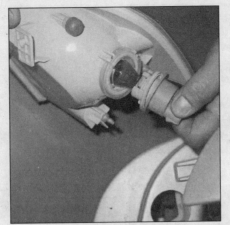

19.2b Remove the bulb and
the bulb holder

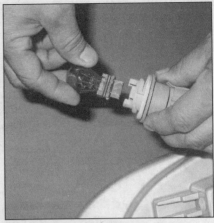

19.3 Pull the bulb straight out
of the holder

3   Remove the inner fender splash shield (see Chapter 11).
4   Disconnect the horn electrical connector and mounting nut then separate the horn from the body (see illustration).
6   Installation is the reverse of removal.

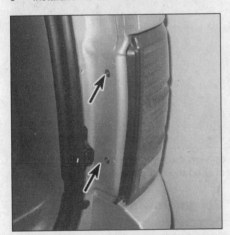

19.6a Remove the rear tail light housing
mounting screws

19   Bulb replacement

Front turn signal

Refer to illustrations 19.1, 19.2a, 19.2b and 19.3

1   Remove the front turn signal housing mounting screw and pull the assembly forward, out of the vehicle body (see illustration).
2   Disconnect the electrical connector and turn the socket counterclockwise to remove it (see illustrations).
3   Remove the bulb from the holder (see illustration).
4   Installation is the reverse of removal.

Rear turn signal, brake, tail and back-up lights

Refer to illustrations 19.6a and 19.6b

5   Open the liftgate.
6   Remove the retaining screws securing the rear tail light housing, then pull the tail light assembly outward to access the tail light bulbs (see illustrations).

7   Twist the bulb holder counterclockwise, then remove the holder from the housing.
8   The defective bulb can then be pulled straight out of the holder from the socket and replaced.
9   Installation is the reverse of removal.

License plate light

10   Remove the license plate light screws and detach the housing from the liftgate.
11   Remove the bulb holder and replace the bulb(s).
12   Installation is the reverse of removal.

High-mounted brake light

Refer to illustrations 19.13, 19.14a and 19.14a

13   Remove the lens retaining screws and pull the lamp assembly outward to access the bulbs (see illustration).
14   Press on the tabs to rotate the light housing out and remove the bulbs (see illustrations).
15   The defective bulb can then be pulled straight out of the socket and replaced.

12

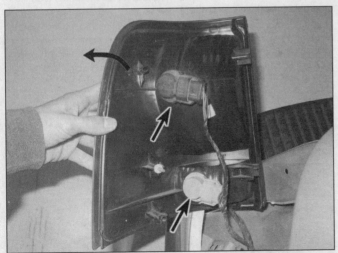

19.6b Rotate the tail light housing outward for access to the bulb
holders - turn the bulb holders counterclockwise to
unlock them from the housing

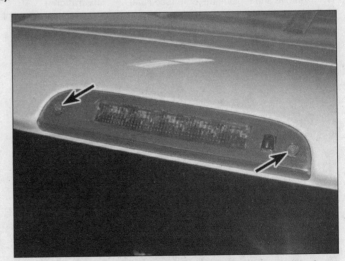

19.13 Remove these screws to detach the high-mounted
brake light housing

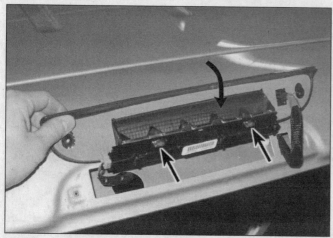

19.14a Press the two release tabs and rotate
the bulb carrier out of the housing

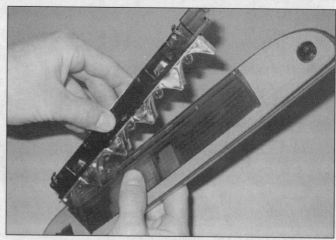

19.14b Pull the bulb carrier away from the housing
for access to the bulbs

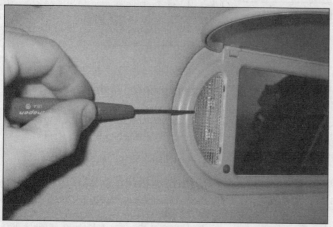

19.16 Use a small screwdriver to carefully remove
the vanity light lens

19.17 Remove the bulb from the terminals - if it's necessary to
pry it out, pry only on the ends, not on the glass

Vanity light

Refer to illustrations 19.16 and 19.17

16   Use a small screwdriver to detach the
light lens **(see illustration)**

17   Remove and replace the bulb **(see illustration)**.

Front row dome light

Refer to illustrations 19.18a, 18b and 19.19

18   Open the overhead console, remove the
screw and detach the console housing **(see
illustrations)**.

19   Remove and replace the bulb **(see illustration)**.

Second row dome light

Refer to illustrations 19.20 and 19.21

20   Carefully pry off the lens **(see illustration)**.

21   Remove and replace the bulb **(see illustration)**.

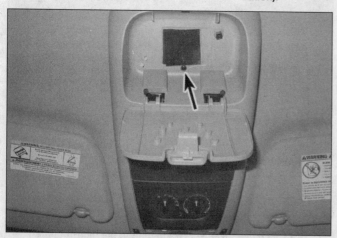

19.18a Remove the overhead console retaining screw

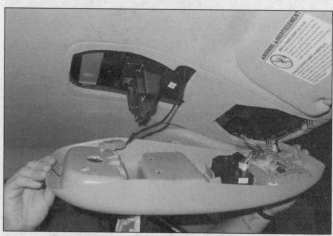

19.18b Lower the overhead console housing

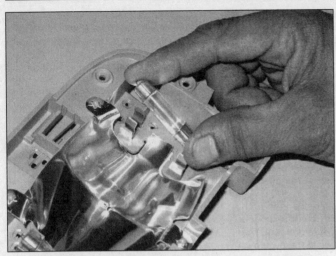

19.19 Detach the bulb from the terminals at each end

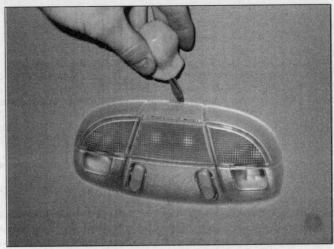

19.20 Detach the dome light lens with a screwdriver

Rear dome light

Refer to illustrations 19.22 and 19.23

22   Detach the light lens **(see illustration)**
23   Remove and replace the bulb **(see illustration)**.

Instrument cluster illumination

24   To gain access to the instrument cluster illumination lights, the instrument cluster will

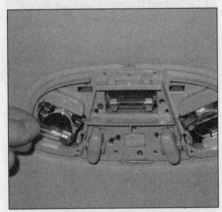

19.21 Remove the bulb from the terminals

have to be removed (see Section 10). The bulbs can then be removed and replaced from the rear of the cluster.

20   Electric side view mirrors - description

1   Most electric rear view mirrors use two motors to move the glass; one for up and down adjustments and one for left-right adjustments.
2   The control switch has a selector portion, which sends voltage to the left or right side, mirror. With the ignition ON but the engine OFF, roll down the windows and operate the mirror control switch through all functions (left-right and up-down) for both the left and right side mirrors.
3   Listen carefully for the sound of the electric motors running in the mirrors.
4   If the motors can be heard but the mirror glass doesn't move, there's a problem with the drive mechanism inside the mirror.
5   If the mirrors do not operate and no sound comes from the mirrors, check the fuse (see Chapter 1).

6   If the fuse is OK, remove the mirror control switch. Have the switch continuity checked by a dealership service department or other qualified automobile repair facility.
7   Test the ground connections. If the mirror still doesn't work, remove the mirror and check the wires at the mirror for voltage.
8   If there's not voltage in each switch position, check the circuit between the mirror and control switch for opens and shorts.
9   If there's voltage, remove the mirror and test it off the vehicle with jumper wires. Replace the mirror if it fails this test.

21   Cruise control system - description

Refer to illustration 21.1

1   The cruise control system maintains vehicle speed with an electrically-operated motor located in the engine compartment, which is connected to the accelerator pedal by a cable. The system consists of the cruise control module **(see illustration)**, the brake switch, control switches and vehicle speed sensor. Some features of the system require

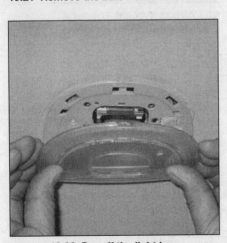

19.22 Pry off the light lens

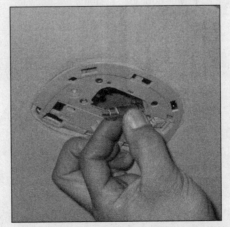

19.23 Detach the bulb from the terminals

21.1 Location of the cruise control module

12

special testers and diagnostic procedures, which are beyond the scope of this manual. Listed below are some general procedures that may be used to locate common problems.

2   Check the fuses (see Section 3).

3   Have an assistant operate the brake lights while you check their operation (voltage from the brake light switch deactivates the cruise control).

4   If the brake lights don't come on or if they stay on all the time, correct the problem and retest the cruise control.

5   Visually inspect the control cable between the cruise control motor and the throttle linkage for free movement. Replace it if necessary.

6   The cruise control system uses inputs from the Vehicle Speed Sensor (VSS). Refer to Chapter 6 for more information on the VSS.

7   Test drive the vehicle to determine if the cruise control is now working. If it isn't, take it to a dealer service department or an automotive electrical specialist for further diagnosis.

22 Power window system - description

1   The power window system operates electric motors, mounted in the doors, which lower and raise the windows. The system consists of the control switches, the motors, regulators, glass mechanisms and associated wiring.

2   The power windows can be lowered and raised from the master control switch by the driver or by remote switches located at the individual windows. Each window has a separate motor, which is reversible. The position of the control switch determines the polarity and therefore the direction of operation.

3   The circuit is protected by a fuse and a circuit breaker. Each motor is also equipped with an internal circuit breaker; this prevents one stuck window from disabling the whole system.

4   The power window system will only operate when the ignition switch is ON. In addition, many models have a window lockout switch at the master control switch which, when activated, disables the switches at the rear windows and, sometimes, the switch at the passenger's window also. Always check these items before troubleshooting a window problem.

5   These procedures are general in nature, so if you can't find the problem using them, take the vehicle to a dealer service department or other properly equipped repair facility.

6   If the power windows won't operate, always check the fuse and circuit breaker first.

7   If only the rear windows are inoperative, or if the windows only operate from the master control switch, check the rear window lockout switch for continuity in the unlocked

position. Replace it if it doesn't have continuity.

8   Check the wiring between the switches and fuse panel for continuity. Repair the wiring, if necessary.

9   If only one window is inoperative from the master control switch, try the other control switch at the window. **Note:** *This doesn't apply to the driver's door window.*

10   If the same window works from one switch, but not the other, check the switch for continuity.

11   If the switch tests OK, check for a short or open in the circuit between the affected switch and the window motor.

12   If one window is inoperative from both switches, remove the trim panel from the affected door and check for voltage at the switch and at the motor while the switch is operated.

13   If voltage is reaching the motor, disconnect the glass from the regulator (see Chapter 11). Move the window up and down by hand while checking for binding and damage. Also check for binding and damage to the regulator. If the regulator is not damaged and the window moves up and down smoothly, replace the motor. If there's binding or damage, lubricate, repair or replace parts, as necessary.

14   If voltage isn't reaching the motor, check the wiring in the circuit for continuity between the switches and motors. You'll need to consult the wiring diagram for the vehicle. If the circuit is equipped with a relay, check that the relay is grounded properly and receiving voltage.

23 Power door lock system - description

1   A power door lock system operates the door lock actuators mounted in each door. The system consists of the switches, actuators, a control unit and associated wiring. Diagnosis can usually be limited to simple checks of the wiring connections and actuators for minor faults that can be easily repaired.

2   Power door lock systems are operated by bi-directional solenoids located in the doors. The lock switches have two operating positions: Lock and Unlock. When activated, the switch sends a ground signal to the door lock control unit to lock or unlock the doors. Depending on which way the switch is activated, the control unit reverses polarity to the solenoids, allowing the two sides of the circuit to be used alternately as the feed (positive) and ground side.

3   Some vehicles may have an anti-theft system incorporated into the power locks. If you are unable to locate the trouble using the following general Steps, consult a dealer service department or other qualified repair shop.

4   Always check the circuit protection first. Some vehicles use a combination of circuit breakers and fuses.

5   Operate the door lock switches in both directions (Lock and Unlock) with the engine off. Listen for the click of the solenoids operating.

6   Test the switches for continuity. Remove the switches and have them checked by a dealer service department or other qualified automobile repair facility.

7   Check the wiring between the switches, control unit and solenoids for continuity. Repair the wiring if there's no continuity.

8   Check for a bad ground at the switches or the control unit.

9   If all but one lock solenoids operate, remove the trim panel from the affected door (see Chapter 11) and check for voltage at the solenoid while the lock switch is operated. One of the wires should have voltage in the Lock position; the other should have voltage in the Unlock position.

10   If the inoperative solenoid is receiving voltage, replace the solenoid.

11   If the inoperative solenoid isn't receiving voltage, check the relay for an open or short in the wire between the lock solenoid and the control unit. **Note:** *It's common for wires to break in the portion of the harness between the body and door (opening and closing the door fatigues and eventually breaks the wires).*

24 Daytime Running Lights (DRL) - general information

The Daytime Running Lights (DRL) system illuminates the headlights whenever the engine is running and the headlight switch is in the OFF or parking lights position. The only exception is with the engine running and the parking brake engaged. Once the parking brake is released, the lights will remain on as long as the ignition switch is on, even if the parking brake is later applied.

The DRL system supplies reduced power to the headlights so they won't be too bright for daytime use, while prolonging headlight life.

25 Airbag system - general information

General information

1   All models are equipped with a Supplemental Restraint System (SRS), more commonly known as an airbag. This system is designed to protect the driver, and the front seat passenger, from serious injury in the event of a head-on or frontal collision. It uses the Restraints Control Module (RCM) mounted on the center tunnel behind the instrument panel and, on models built after 3/02, a front impact severity sensor, which is mounted on the front of the lower radiator support. The airbag assemblies are mounted on the steering wheel and the right side of the passenger's side dash. The seat belts are equipped with pre-tensioners.

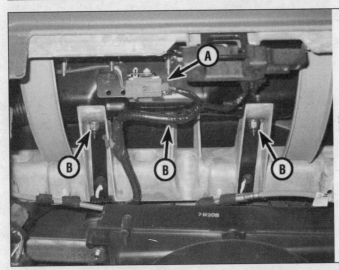

25.14 Location of the passenger's side airbag connector (A) and airbag module mounting nuts (B)

These are pyrotechnic devices controlled by the Restraints Control Module (RCM) that reduce the slack in the seat belts during an impact of sufficient force to trigger the airbags.

Some later models are optionally equipped with a safety canopy system mounted along both sides of the headliner that deploys in the event of side impact or rollover. On models equipped with this system, side impact sensors are mounted on the B and C-pillars.

Airbag module

Driver's side

2   The airbag inflator module contains a housing incorporating the cushion (airbag) and inflator unit, mounted in the center of the steering wheel. The inflator assembly is mounted on the back of the housing over a hole through which gas is expelled, inflating the bag almost instantaneously when an electrical signal is sent from the system. A "clockspring" on the steering column under the steering wheel carries this signal to the module.

3   This clockspring assembly can transmit an electrical signal regardless of steering wheel position. The igniter in the airbag converts the electrical signal to heat and ignites the powder, which inflates the bag.

Passenger's side

4   The airbag is mounted above the glove compartment. It consists of an inflator containing an igniter, a reaction housing/airbag assembly and a trim cover.

5   The airbag is considerably larger than the steering wheel-mounted unit and is supported by the steel reaction housing. The trim cover is textured and painted to match the instrument panel and has a molded seam, which splits when the bag inflates.

Restraints Control Module (RCM) diagnostic unit

6   This unit supplies the current to the airbag system (and seat belt pre-tensioners, on models so equipped) in the event of the collision, even if battery power is cut off. It checks this system every time the vehicle is started, causing the "SRS" light to go on then off, if the system is operating properly. If there is a fault in the system, the light will go on and stay on, flash, or the dash will make a beeping sound. If this happens, the vehicle should be taken to your dealer immediately for service.

Disarming the system and other precautions

Warning: *Failure to follow these precautions could result in accidental deployment of the airbag and personal injury.*

7   Whenever working in the vicinity of the steering wheel, instrument panel or any of the other SRS system components, the system must be disarmed. To disarm the system:

a) *Point the wheels straight ahead and turn the key to the Lock position.*

b) *Disconnect the cable from the negative battery terminal.*

c) *Wait at least two minutes for the back-up power supply to be depleted.*

8   Whenever handling an airbag module, always keep the airbag opening (the trim side) pointed away from your body. Never place the airbag module on a bench or other surface with the airbag opening facing the surface. Always place the airbag module in a safe location with the airbag opening facing up.

9   Never measure the resistance of any SRS component or use any electrical test equipment on any of the wiring or components. An ohmmeter has a built-in battery supply that could accidentally deploy the airbag.

10   Never use electrical welding equipment on a vehicle equipped with an airbag without first disconnecting the airbag electrical connectors. On models with seat belt pre-tensioners, the pre-tensioner electrical connectors are located behind the B-pillar trim panels and/or under the seats, depending on the model.

11   Never dispose of a live airbag module or seat belt pre-tensioner. Return it to a dealer service department or other qualified repair shop for safe deployment and disposal.

Airbag module removal and installation

Driver's side airbag module and clockspring

12   Refer to Chapter 10, *Steering wheel - removal and installation*, for the driver's side airbag module and clockspring removal and installation procedures.

Passenger's side airbag module

Refer to illustration 25.14

13   Disarm the airbag system as described previously in this Section.

14   Lower the glovebox door fully to gain access to the airbag by pressing the glovebox door tabs and pushing down, then unplug the electrical connector **(see illustration)**. Remove the airbag module mounting nuts and bolts. Be sure to heed the precautions outlined previously in this Section.

15   Reach up behind the airbag module and push it out of the instrument panel.

16   Installation is the reverse of the removal procedure. Tighten the airbag module mounting nuts securely.

Safety canopy system

17   Any work on the safety canopy system should be left to a dealer service department.

---

26   Wiring diagrams - general information

Since it isn't possible to include all wiring diagrams for every year covered by this manual, the following diagrams are those that are typical and most commonly needed.

Prior to troubleshooting any circuits, check the fuse and circuit breakers (if equipped) to make sure they're in good condition. Make sure the battery is properly charged and check the cable connections (see Chapter 1).

When checking a circuit, make sure that all connectors are clean, with no broken or loose terminals. When unplugging a connector, do not pull on the wires. Pull only on the connector housings themselves.

Notes

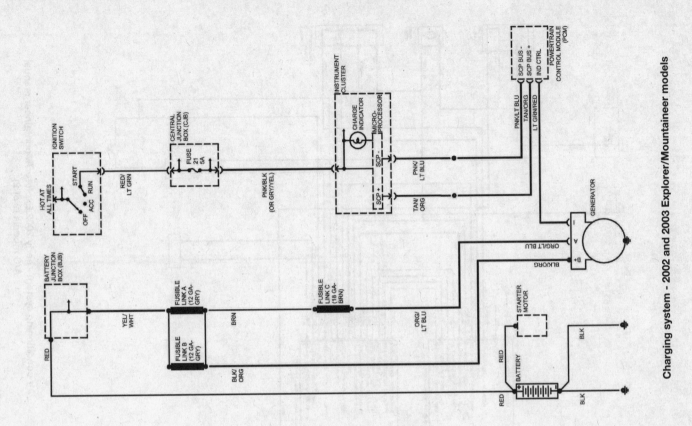

Charging system - 2002 and 2003 Explorer/Mountaineer models

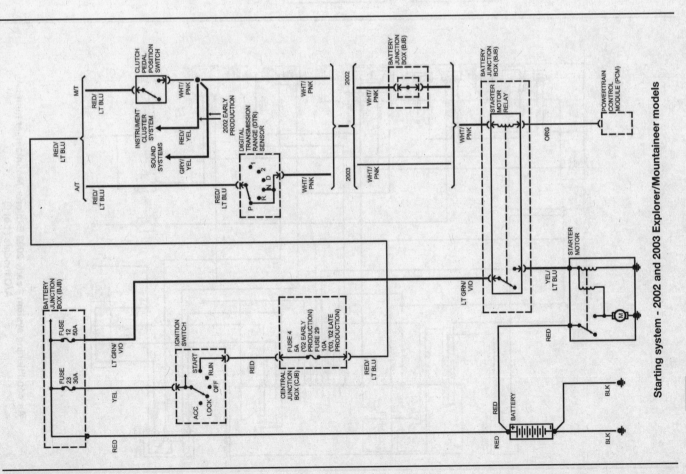

Starting system - 2002 and 2003 Explorer/Mountaineer models

12

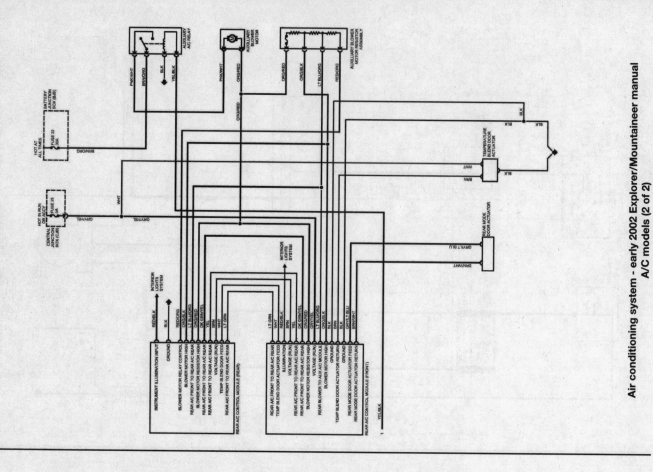

Air conditioning system - early 2002 Explorer/Mountaineer manual A/C models (2 of 2)

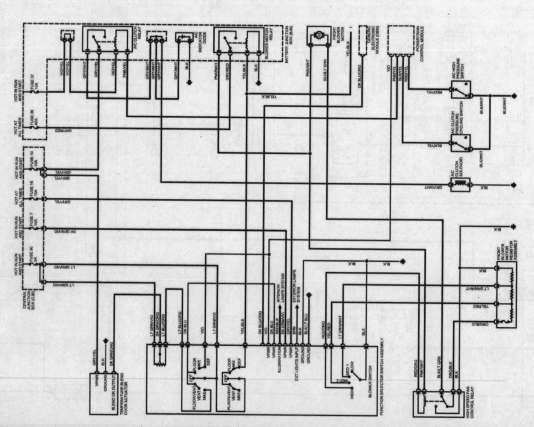

Air conditioning system - early 2002 Explorer/Mountaineer manual A/C models (1 of 2)

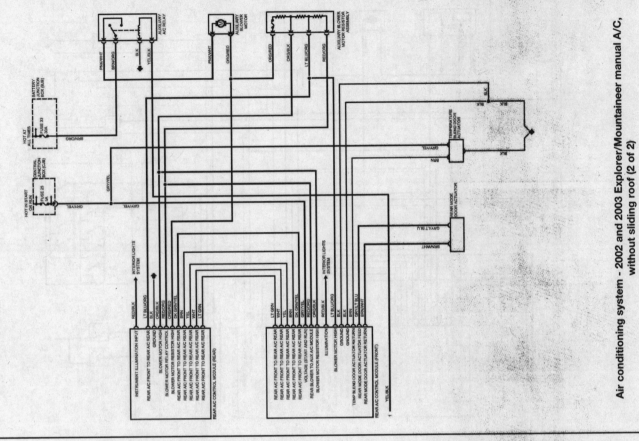

Air conditioning system - 2002 and 2003 Explorer/Mountaineer manual A/C, without sliding roof (2 of 2)

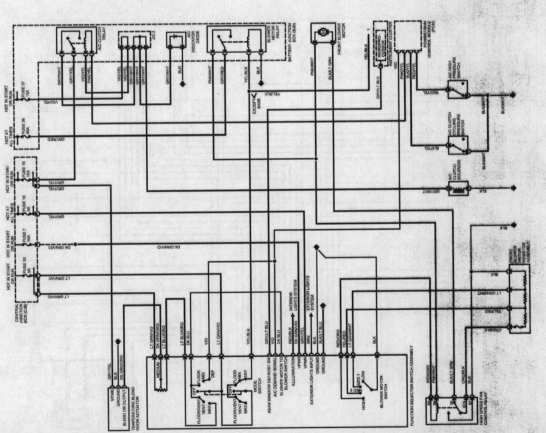

Air conditioning system - 2002 and 2003 Explorer/Mountaineer manual A/C, without sliding roof (1 of 2)

12

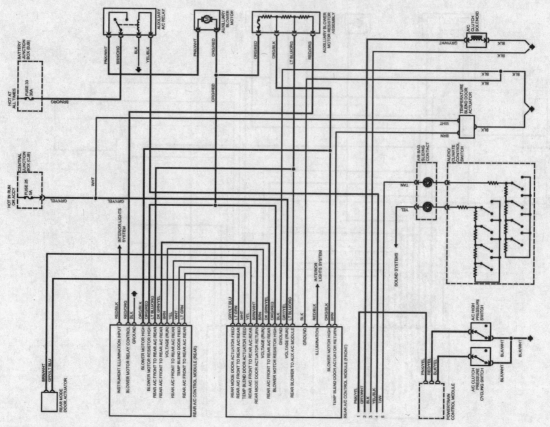

Air conditioning system - early 2002 Explorer/Mountaineer automatic A/C models (2 of 2)

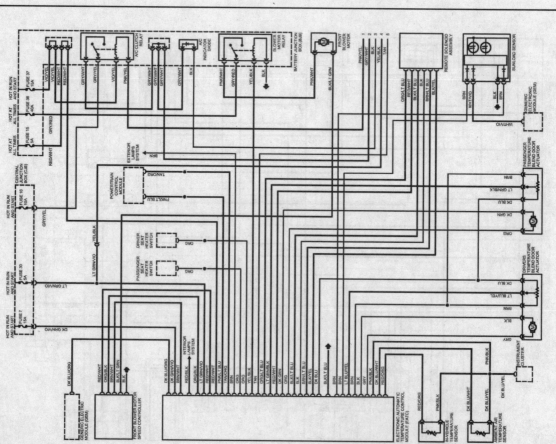

Air conditioning system - early 2002 Explorer/Mountaineer automatic A/C models (1 of 2)

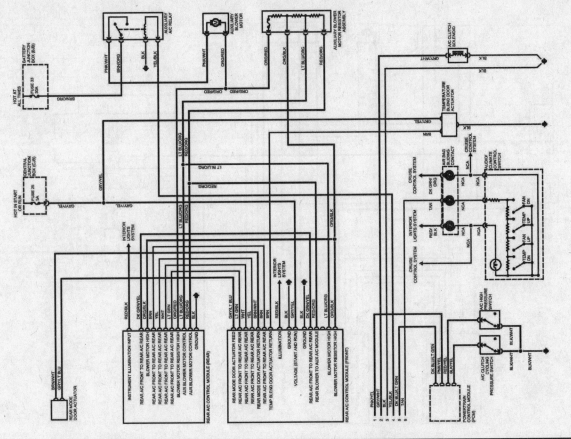

Air conditioning system - late 2002 and 2003 Explorer/Mountaineer automatic A/C models (2 of 2)

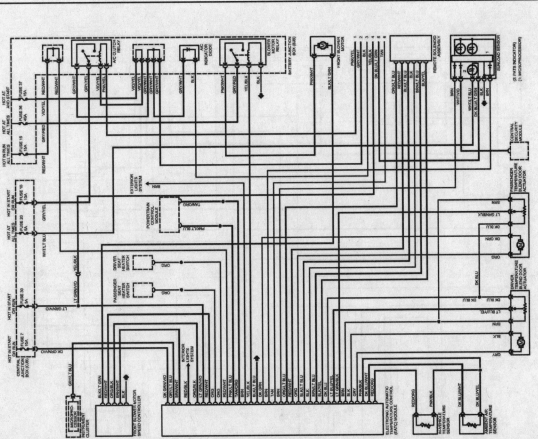

Air conditioning system - late 2002 and 2003 Explorer/Mountaineer automatic A/C models (1 of 2)

12

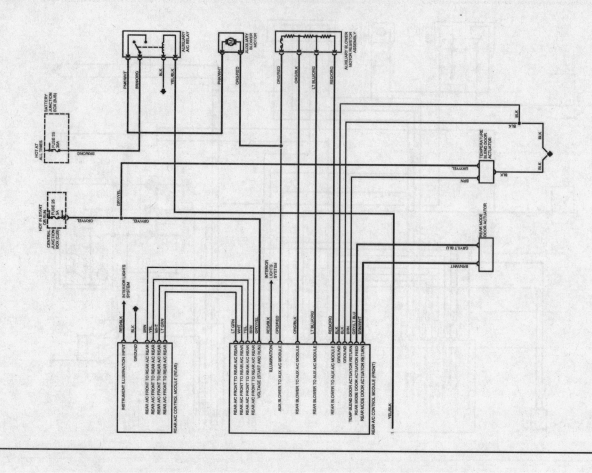

Air conditioning system - 2003 Explorer/Mountaineer manual A/C, with sliding roof (2 of 2)

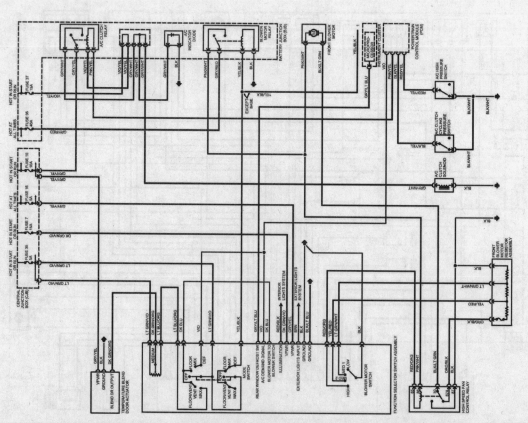

Air conditioning system - 2003 Explorer/Mountaineer manual A/C, with sliding roof (1 of 2)

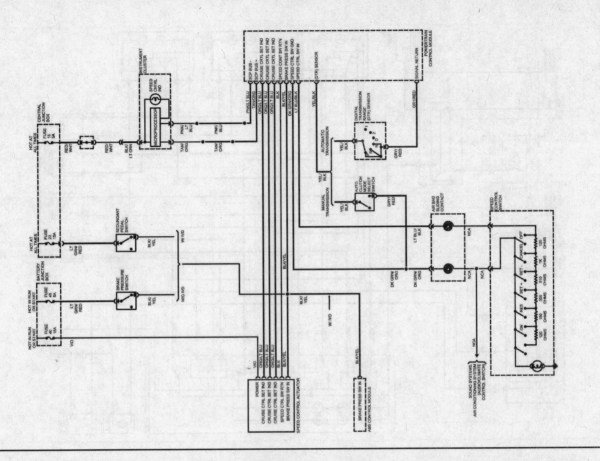

Cruise control system – late 2002 Explorer/Mountaineer models

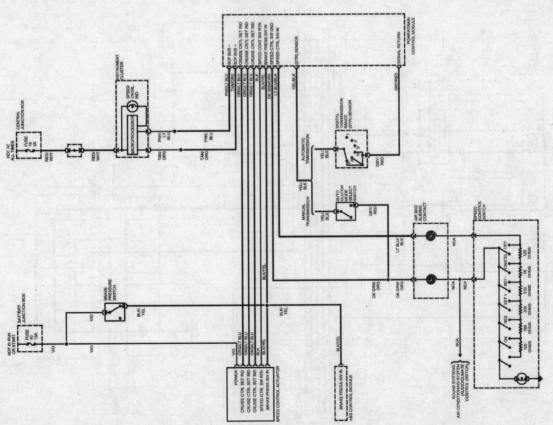

Cruise control system – early 2002 Explorer/Mountaineer models

Power window control system - 2002 and 2003 Explorer/Mountaineer models

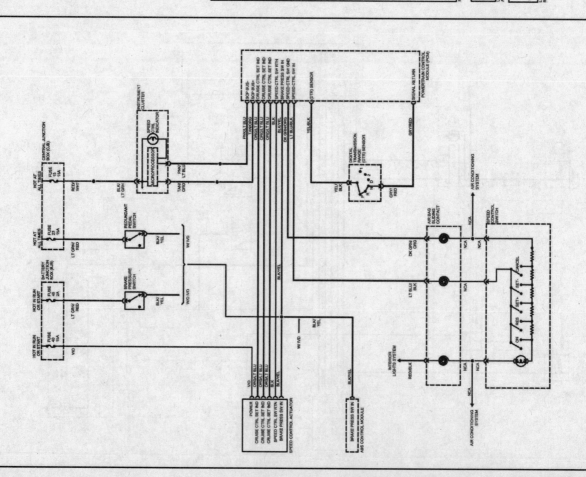

Cruise control system - 2003 Explorer/Mountaineer models

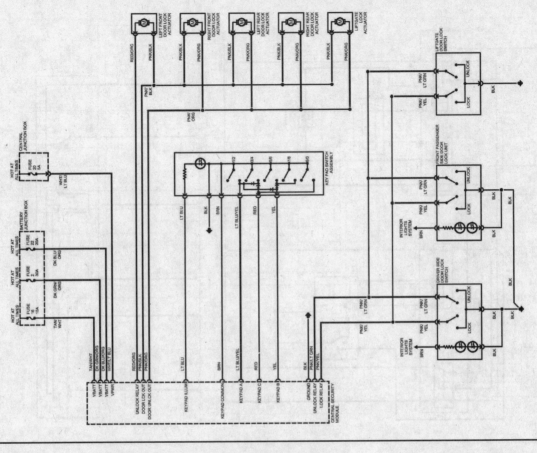

Door lock system - late 2002 Explorer/Mountaineer models

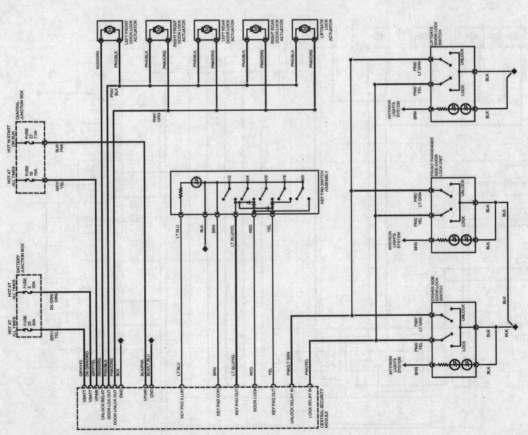

Door lock system - early 2002 Explorer/Mountaineer models

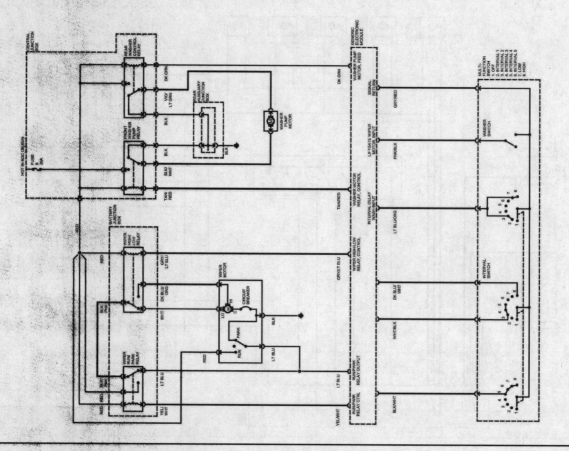

Windshield wiper/washer system - early 2002 Explorer/Mountaineer models

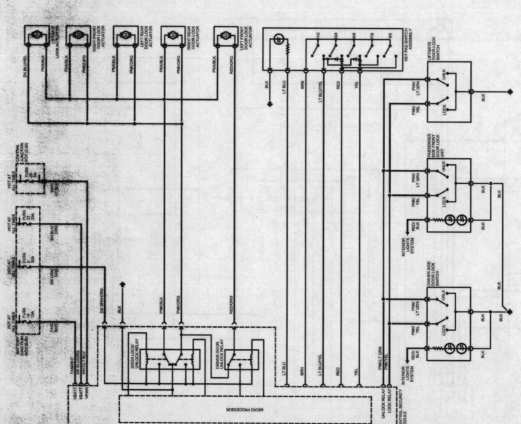

Door lock system - 2003 Explorer/Mountaineer models

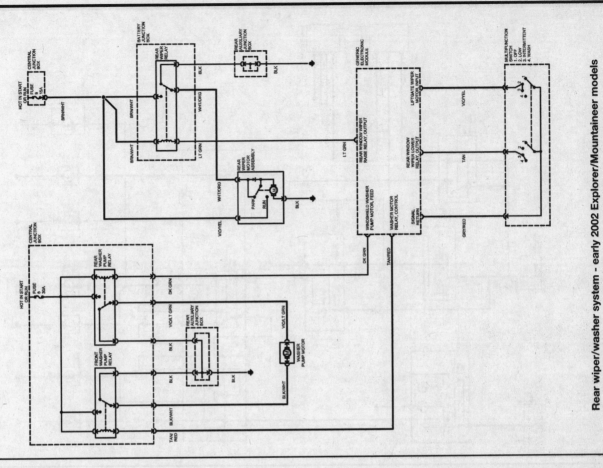

Rear wiper/washer system - early 2002 Explorer/Mountaineer models

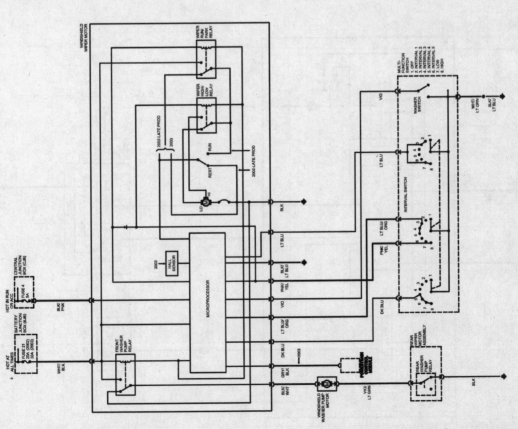

Windshield wiper/washer system - late 2002 and 2003 Explorer/Mountaineer models

12

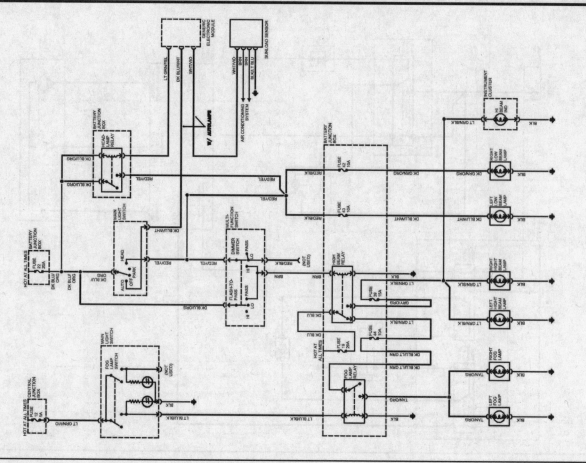

Headlight system - early 2002 Explorer models without Daytime Running Lights

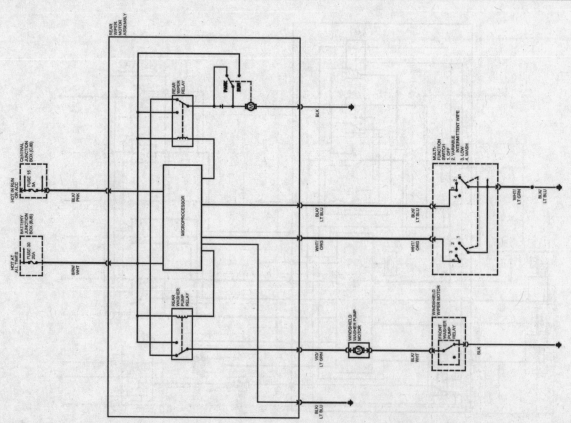

Rear wiper/washer system - late 2002 and 2003 Explorer/Mountaineer models

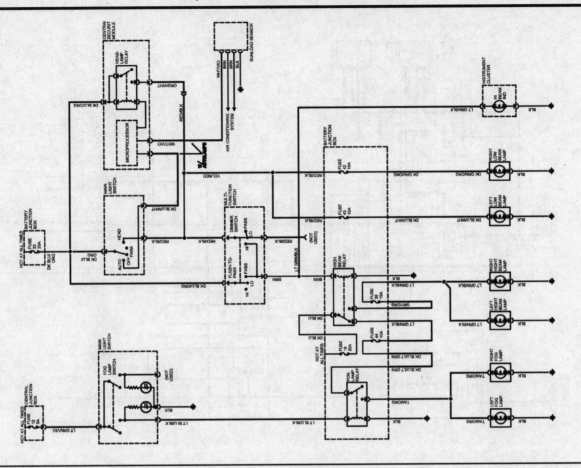

Headlight system - late 2002 Explorer models without Daytime Running Lights

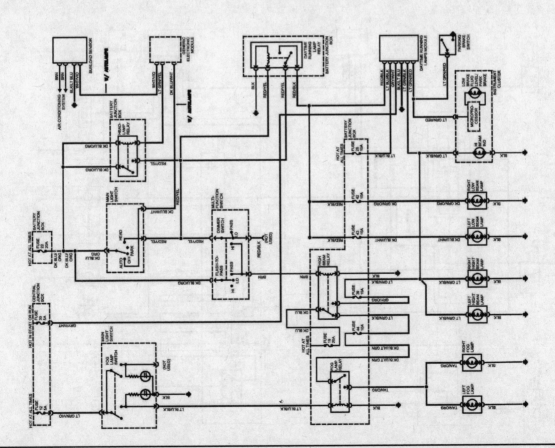

Headlight system - early 2002 Explorer models with Daytime Running Lights

12

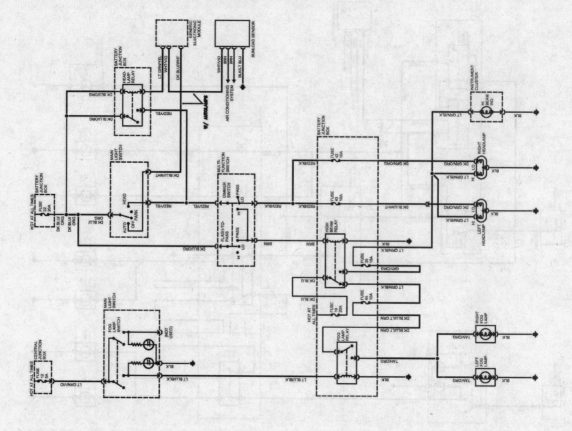

Headlight system - early 2002 Mountaineer models

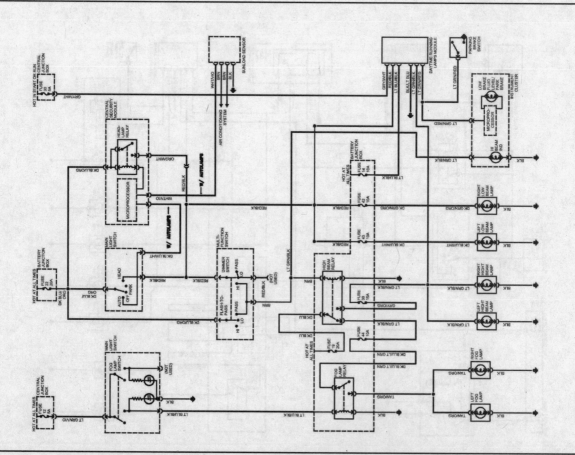

Headlight system - late 2002 Explorer models with Daytime Running Lights

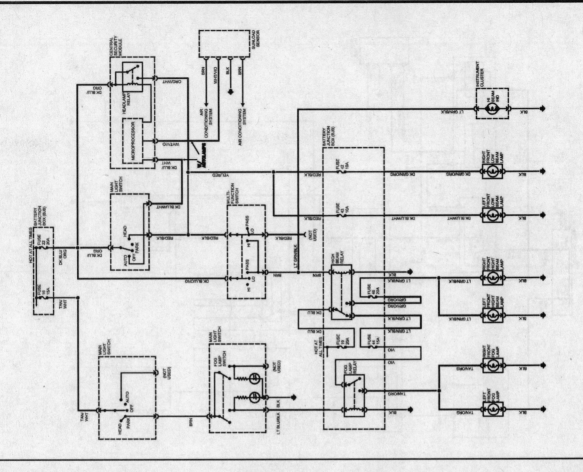

Headlight system - 2003 Explorer models without Daytime Running Lights

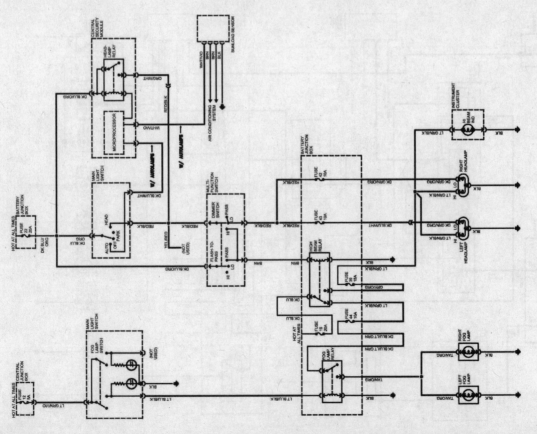

Headlight system - late 2002 Mountaineer models

12

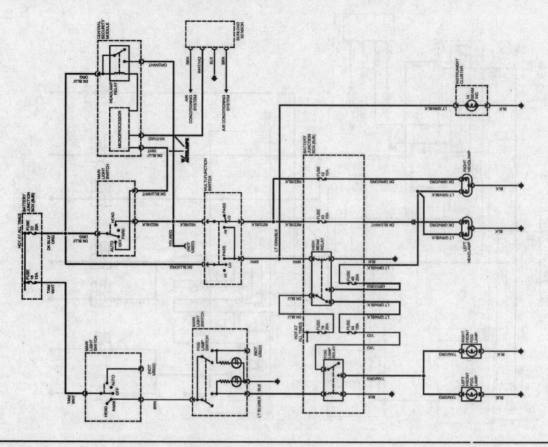

Headlight system – 2003 Mountaineer models

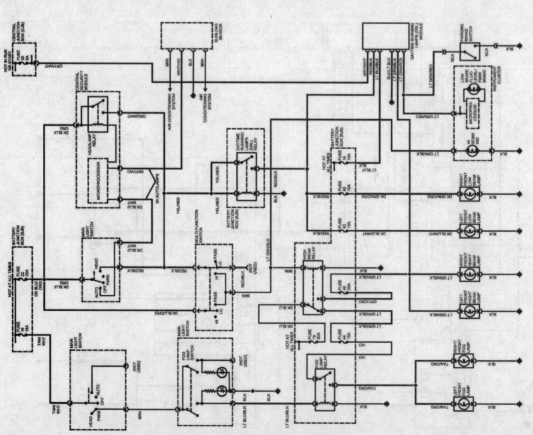

Headlight system – 2003 Explorer models with Daytime Running Lights

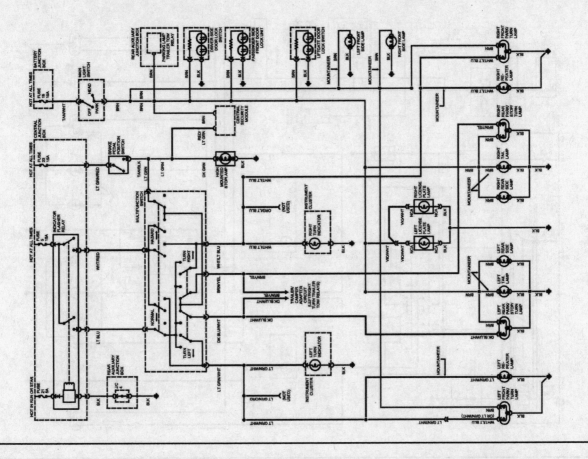

Exterior lighting system - early 2002 Explorer/Mountaineer models

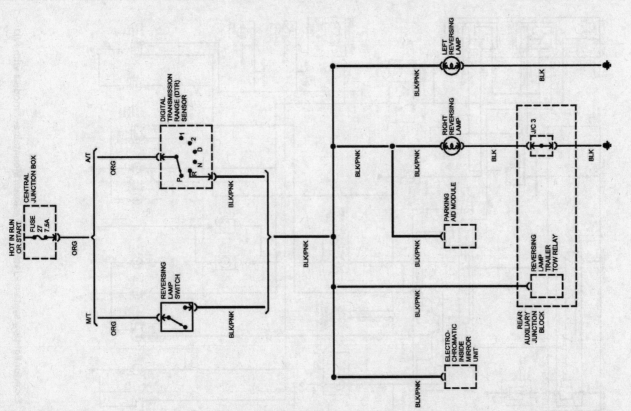

Back-up light system - 2002 and 2003 Explorer/Mountaineer models

12

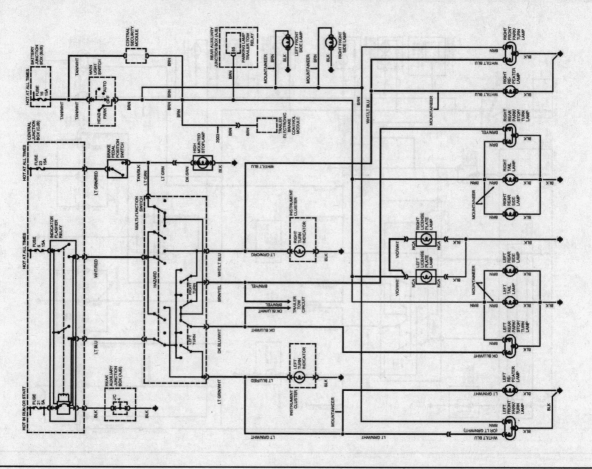

Exterior lighting system – late 2002 and 2003 Explorer/Mountaineer models without IVD

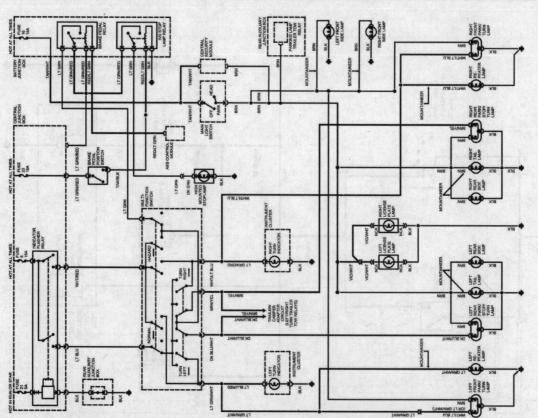

Exterior lighting system – late 2002 Explorer/Mountaineer models with IVD

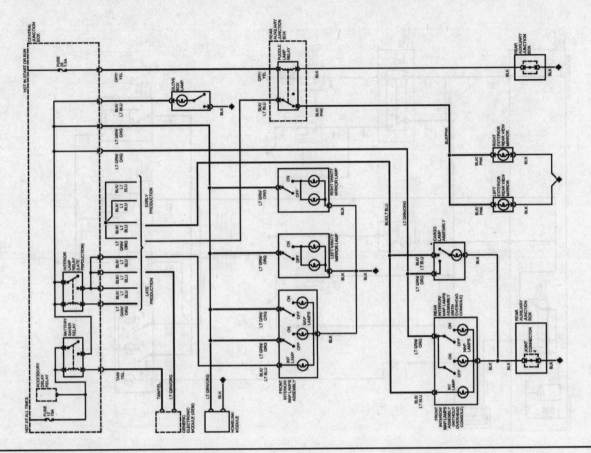

Courtesy lighting system - 2002 Explorer/Mountaineer models

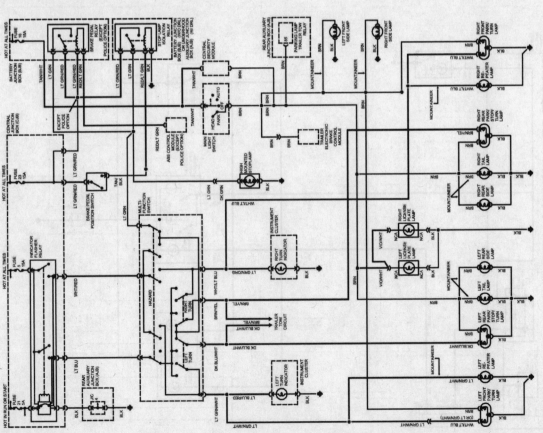

Exterior lighting system - 2003 Explorer/Mountaineer models with IVD

12

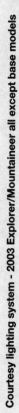

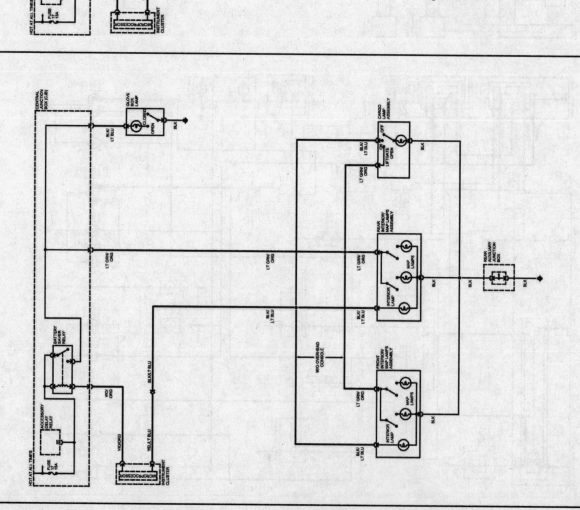

Courtesy lighting system - 2003 Explorer/Mountaineer all except base models

Courtesy lighting system - 2003 Explorer/Mountaineer base models

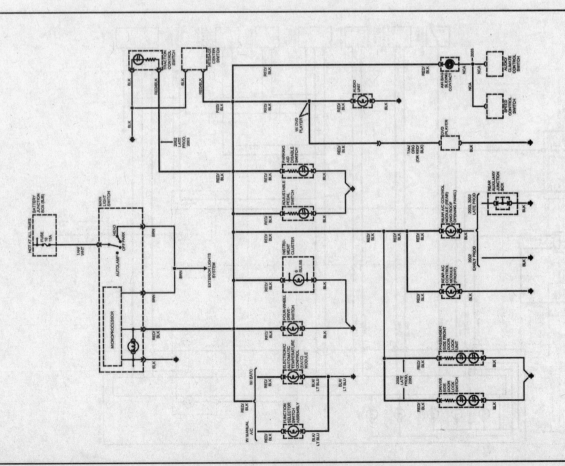

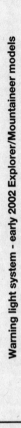

Warning light system - early 2002 Explorer/Mountaineer models

Interior lighting system - 2002 and 2003 Explorer/Mountaineer models

12

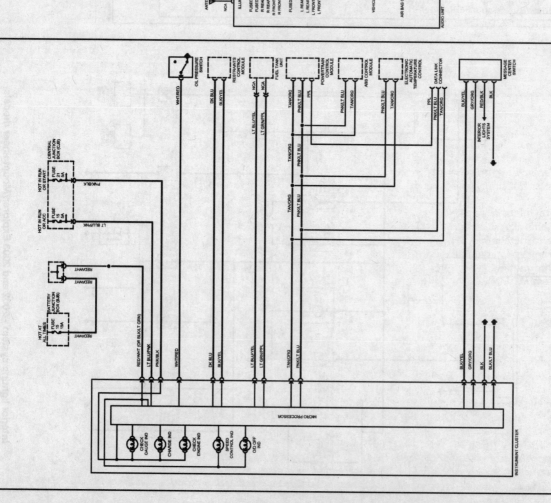

Radio system - 2002 and 2003 Explorer/Mountaineer base models

Warning light system - late 2002 and 2003 Explorer/Mountaineer models

Index

Haynes Automotive Manuals

NOTE: New manuals are added to this list on a periodic basis. If you do not see a listing for your vehicle, consult your local Haynes dealer for the latest product information.

ACURA
12020 **Integra** '86 thru '89 & **Legend** '86 thru '90
12021 **Integra** '90 thru '93 & **Legend** '91 thru '95

AMC
Jeep CJ - see JEEP (50020)
14020 **Mid-size models** '70 thru '83
14025 **(Renault) Alliance & Encore** '83 thru '87

AUDI
15020 **4000** all models '80 thru '87
15025 **5000** all models '77 thru '83
15026 **5000** all models '84 thru '88

AUSTIN-HEALEY
Sprite - see MG Midget (66015)

BMW
*18020 **3/5 Series** not including diesel or all-wheel drive models '82 thru '92
18021 **3-Series** incl. Z3 models '92 thru '98
18025 **320i** all 4 cyl models '75 thru '83
18050 **1500 thru 2002** except Turbo '59 thru '77

BUICK
*19010 **Buick Century** '97 thru '02
Century (front-wheel drive) - see GM (38005)
*19020 **Buick, Oldsmobile & Pontiac Full-size** (Front-wheel drive) '85 thru '02
Buick Electra, LeSabre and Park Avenue; **Oldsmobile** Delta 88 Royale, Ninety Eight and Regency; **Pontiac** Bonneville
19025 **Buick Oldsmobile & Pontiac Full-size** (Rear wheel drive)
Buick Estate '70 thru '90, Electra'70 thru '84, LeSabre '70 thru '85, Limited '74 thru '79
Oldsmobile Custom Cruiser '70 thru '90, Delta 88 '70 thru '85, Ninety-eight '70 thru '84
Pontiac Bonneville '70 thru '81, Catalina '70 thru '81, Grandville '70 thru '75, Parisienne '83 thru '86
19030 **Mid-size Regal & Century** all rear-drive models with V6, V8 and Turbo '74 thru '87
Regal - see GENERAL MOTORS (38010)
Riviera - see GENERAL MOTORS (38030)
Roadmaster - see CHEVROLET (24046)
Skyhawk - see GENERAL MOTORS (38015)
Skylark - see GM (38020, 38025)
Somerset - see GENERAL MOTORS (38025)

CADILLAC
21030 **Cadillac Rear Wheel Drive** all gasoline models '70 thru '93
Cimarron - see GENERAL MOTORS (38015)
DeVille - see GM (38031 & 38032)
Eldorado - see GM (38030 & 38031)
Fleetwood - see GM (38031)
Seville - see GM (38030, 38031 & 38032)

CHEVROLET
*24010 **Astro & GMC Safari Mini-vans** '85 thru '03
24015 **Camaro V8** all models '70 thru '81
24016 **Camaro** all models '82 thru '92
24017 **Camaro & Firebird** '93 thru '02
Cavalier - see GENERAL MOTORS (38016)
Celebrity - see GENERAL MOTORS (38005)
24020 **Chevelle, Malibu & El Camino** '69 thru '87
24024 **Chevette & Pontiac T1000** '76 thru '87
Citation - see GENERAL MOTORS (38020)
24032 **Corsica/Beretta** all models '87 thru '96
24040 **Corvette** all V8 models '68 thru '82
24041 **Corvette** all models '84 thru '96
10305 **Chevrolet Engine Overhaul Manual**
24045 **Full-size Sedans** Caprice, Impala, Biscayne, Bel Air & Wagons '69 thru '90
24046 **Impala SS & Caprice and Buick Roadmaster** '91 thru '96
Impala - see LUMINA (24048)
Lumina '90 thru '94 - see GM (38010)
*24048 **Lumina & Monte Carlo** '95 thru '03
Lumina APV - see GM (38035)
24050 **Luv Pick-up** all 2WD & 4WD '72 thru '82
Malibu '97 thru '00 - see GM (38026)
24055 **Monte Carlo** all models '70 thru '88
Monte Carlo '95 thru '01 - see LUMINA (24048)

24059 **Nova** all V8 models '69 thru '79
24060 **Nova and Geo Prizm** '85 thru '92
24064 **Pick-ups '67 thru '87** - Chevrolet & GMC, all V8 & in-line 6 cyl, 2WD & 4WD '67 thru '87; Suburbans, Blazers & Jimmys '67 thru '91
24065 **Pick-ups '88 thru '98** - Chevrolet & GMC, full-size pick-ups '88 thru '98, C/K Classic '99 & '00, Blazer & Jimmy '92 thru '94; Suburban '92 thru '99; Tahoe & Yukon '95 thru '99
*24066 **Pick-ups '99 thru '03** - Chevrolet Silverado & GMC Sierra full-size pick-ups '99 thru '02, Suburban/Tahoe/Yukon/Yukon XL '00 thru '02
24070 **S-10 & S-15 Pick-ups** '82 thru '93, Blazer & Jimmy '83 thru '94,
*24071 **S-10 & S-15 Pick-ups** '94 thru '01, Blazer & Jimmy '95 thru '01, Hombre '96 thru '01
*24072 **Chevrolet TrailBlazer & TrailBlazer EXT, GMC Envoy & Envoy XL, Oldsmobile Bravada** '02 and '03
24075 **Sprint** '85 thru '88 & Geo Metro '89 thru '01
24080 **Vans - Chevrolet & GMC** '68 thru '96

CHRYSLER
25015 **Chrysler Cirrus, Dodge Stratus, Plymouth Breeze** '95 thru '00
10310 **Chrysler Engine Overhaul Manual**
25020 **Full-size Front-Wheel Drive** '88 thru '93
K-Cars - see DODGE Aries (30008)
Laser - see DODGE Daytona (30030)
25025 **Chrysler LHS, Concorde, New Yorker, Dodge Intrepid, Eagle Vision**, '93 thru '97
*25026 **Chrysler LHS, Concorde, 300M, Dodge Intrepid**, '98 thru '03
25030 **Chrysler & Plymouth Mid-size** front wheel drive '82 thru '95
Rear-wheel Drive - see Dodge (30050)
*25035 **PT Cruiser** all models '01 thru '03
*25040 **Chrysler** Sebring, **Dodge** Avenger '95 thru '02

DATSUN
28005 **200SX** all models '80 thru '83
28007 **B-210** all models '73 thru '78
28009 **210** all models '79 thru '82
28012 **240Z, 260Z & 280Z** Coupe '70 thru '78
28014 **280ZX** Coupe & 2+2 '79 thru '83
300ZX - see NISSAN (72010)
28016 **310** all models '78 thru '82
28018 **510 & PL521 Pick-up** '68 thru '73
28020 **510** all models '78 thru '81
28022 **620 Series Pick-up** all models '73 thru '79
720 Series Pick-up - see NISSAN (72030)
28025 **810/Maxima** all gasoline models, '77 thru '84

DODGE
400 & 600 - see CHRYSLER (25030)
30008 **Aries & Plymouth Reliant** '81 thru '89
30010 **Caravan & Plymouth Voyager** '84 thru '95
*30011 **Caravan & Plymouth Voyager** '96 thru '02
30012 **Challenger/Plymouth Saporro** '78 thru '83
30016 **Colt & Plymouth Champ** '78 thru '87
30020 **Dakota Pick-ups** all models '87 thru '96
*30021 **Durango** '98 & '99, **Dakota** '97 thru '99
30025 **Dart, Demon, Plymouth Barracuda, Duster & Valiant** 6 cyl models '67 thru '76
30030 **Daytona & Chrysler Laser** '84 thru '89
Intrepid - see CHRYSLER (25025, 25026)
*30034 **Neon** all models '95 thru '99
30035 **Omni & Plymouth Horizon** '78 thru '90
30040 **Pick-ups** all full-size models '74 thru '93
*30041 **Pick-ups** all full-size models '94 thru '01
30045 **Ram 50/D50 Pick-ups & Raider and Plymouth Arrow Pick-ups** '79 thru '93
30050 **Dodge/Plymouth/Chrysler** RWD '71 thru '89
30055 **Shadow & Plymouth Sundance** '87 thru '94
30060 **Spirit & Plymouth Acclaim** '89 thru '95
*30065 **Vans - Dodge & Plymouth** '71 thru '03

EAGLE
Talon - see MITSUBISHI (68030, 68031)
Vision - see CHRYSLER (25025)

FIAT
34010 **124 Sport Coupe & Spider** '68 thru '78
34025 **X1/9** all models '74 thru '80

FORD
10355 **Ford Automatic Transmission Overhaul**
36004 **Aerostar Mini-vans** all models '86 thru '97
36006 **Contour & Mercury Mystique** '95 thru '00
36008 **Courier Pick-up** all models '72 thru '82
*36012 **Crown Victoria & Mercury Grand Marquis** '88 thru '00
10320 **Ford Engine Overhaul Manual**
36016 **Escort/Mercury Lynx** all models '81 thru '90
36020 **Escort/Mercury Tracer** '91 thru '00
36022 **Ford Escape & Mazda Tribute** '01 thru '03
36024 **Explorer & Mazda Navajo** '91 thru '01
36025 **Ford Explorer & Mercury Mountaineer** '02 and '03
36028 **Fairmont & Mercury Zephyr** '78 thru '83
36030 **Festiva & Aspire** '88 thru '97
36032 **Fiesta** all models '77 thru '80
*36034 **Focus** all models '00 and '01
36036 **Ford & Mercury Full-size** '75 thru '87
36044 **Ford & Mercury Mid-size** '75 thru '86
36048 **Mustang V8** all models '64-1/2 thru '73
36049 **Mustang II** 4 cyl, V6 & V8 models '74 thru '78
36050 **Mustang & Mercury Capri** all models Mustang, '79 thru '93; Capri, '79 thru '86
*36051 **Mustang** all models '94 thru '03
36054 **Pick-ups & Bronco** '73 thru '79
36058 **Pick-ups & Bronco** '80 thru '96
*36059 **F-150 & Expedition** '97 thru '02, F-250 '97 thru '99 & Lincoln Navigator '98 thru '02
*36060 **Super Duty Pick-ups, Excursion** '97 thru '02
36062 **Pinto & Mercury Bobcat** '75 thru '80
36066 **Probe** all models '89 thru '92
36070 **Ranger/Bronco II** gasoline models '83 thru '92
*36071 **Ranger** '93 thru '00 & Mazda Pick-ups '94 thru '00
36074 **Taurus & Mercury Sable** '86 thru '95
*36075 **Taurus & Mercury Sable** '96 thru '01
36078 **Tempo & Mercury Topaz** '84 thru '94
36082 **Thunderbird/Mercury Cougar** '83 thru '88
36086 **Thunderbird/Mercury Cougar** '89 and '97
36090 **Vans** all V8 Econoline models '69 thru '91
*36094 **Vans** full size '92 thru '01
*36097 **Windstar Mini-van** '95 thru '03

GENERAL MOTORS
10360 **GM Automatic Transmission Overhaul**
38005 **Buick Century, Chevrolet Celebrity, Oldsmobile Cutlass Ciera & Pontiac 6000** all models '82 thru '96
*38010 **Buick Regal, Chevrolet Lumina, Oldsmobile Cutlass Supreme & Pontiac Grand Prix** (FWD) '88 thru '02
38015 **Buick Skyhawk, Cadillac Cimarron, Chevrolet Cavalier, Oldsmobile Firenza & Pontiac J-2000 & Sunbird** '82 thru '94
*38016 **Chevrolet Cavalier & Pontiac Sunfire** '95 thru '04
38020 **Buick Skylark, Chevrolet Citation, Olds Omega, Pontiac Phoenix** '80 thru '85
38025 **Buick Skylark & Somerset, Oldsmobile Achieva & Calais and Pontiac Grand Am** all models '85 thru '98
*38026 **Chevrolet Malibu, Olds Alero & Cutlass, Pontiac Grand Am** '97 thru '00
38030 **Cadillac Eldorado** '71 thru '85, **Seville** '80 thru '85, **Oldsmobile Toronado** '71 thru '85, **Buick Riviera** '79 thru '85
*38031 **Cadillac Eldorado & Seville** '86 thru '91, **DeVille** '86 thru '93, **Fleetwood & Olds Toronado** '86 thru '92, **Buick Riviera** '86 thru '93
38032 **Cadillac DeVille** '94 thru '02 & **Seville** - '92 thru '02
38035 **Chevrolet Lumina APV, Olds Silhouette & Pontiac Trans Sport** all models '90 thru '96
*38036 **Chevrolet Venture, Olds Silhouette, Pontiac Trans Sport & Montana** '97 thru '01
General Motors Full-size Rear-wheel Drive - see BUICK (19025)

GEO
Metro - see CHEVROLET Sprint (24075)
Prizm - '85 thru '92 see CHEVY (24060), '93 thru '02 see TOYOTA Corolla (92036)

(Continued on other side)

---

* Listings shown with an asterisk (*) indicate model coverage as of this printing. These titles will be periodically updated to include later model years - consult your Haynes dealer for more information.

Haynes North America, Inc., 861 Lawrence Drive, Newbury Park, CA 91320-1514 • (805) 498-6703

Haynes Automotive Manuals (continued)

NOTE: New manuals are added to this list on a periodic basis. If you do not see a listing for your vehicle, consult your local Haynes dealer for the latest product information.

40030 Storm all models '90 thru '93
Tracker - *see SUZUKI Samurai (90010)*

GMC
Vans & Pick-ups - *see CHEVROLET*

HONDA
42010 Accord CVCC all models '76 thru '83
42011 Accord all models '84 thru '89
42012 Accord all models '90 thru '93
42013 Accord all models '94 thru '97
*****42014** Accord all models '98 thru '02
42020 Civic 1200 all models '73 thru '79
42021 Civic 1300 & 1500 CVCC '80 thru '83
42022 Civic 1500 CVCC all models '75 thru '79
42023 Civic all models '84 thru '91
42024 Civic & del Sol '92 thru '95
*****42025** Civic '96 thru '00, CR-V '97 thru '00, Acura Integra '94 thru '00
42026 Civic '01 thru '04, CR-V '02 thru '04
42040 Prelude CVCC all models '79 thru '89

HYUNDAI
*****43010** Elantra all models '96 thru '01
43015 Excel & Accent all models '86 thru '98

ISUZU
Hombre - *see CHEVROLET S-10 (24071)*
*****47017** Rodeo '91 thru '02; Amigo '89 thru '94 and '98 thru '02; Honda Passport '95 thru '02
47020 Trooper & Pick-up '81 thru '93

JAGUAR
49010 XJ6 all 6 cyl models '68 thru '86
49011 XJ6 all models '88 thru '94
49015 XJ12 & XJS all 12 cyl models '72 thru '85

JEEP
50010 Cherokee, Comanche & Wagoneer Limited all models '84 thru '01
50020 CJ all models '49 thru '86
*****50025** Grand Cherokee all models '93 thru '04
50029 Grand Wagoneer & Pick-up '72 thru '91 Grand Wagoneer '84 thru '91, Cherokee & Wagoneer '72 thru '83, Pick-up '72 thru '88
*****50030** Wrangler all models '87 thru '00
50035 Liberty '02 thru '04

LEXUS
ES 300 - *see TOYOTA Camry (92007)*

LINCOLN
Navigator - *see FORD Pick-up (36059)*
*****59010** Rear-Wheel Drive all models '70 thru '01

MAZDA
61010 GLC Hatchback (rear-wheel drive) '77 thru '83
61011 GLC (front-wheel drive) '81 thru '85
61015 323 & Protogé '90 thru '00
*****61016** MX-5 Miata '90 thru '97
61020 MPV all models '89 thru '94
Navajo - *see Ford Explorer (36024)*
61030 Pick-ups '72 thru '93 Pick-ups '94 thru '00 - *see Ford Ranger (36071)*
61035 RX-7 all models '79 thru '85
61036 RX-7 all models '86 thru '91
61040 626 (rear-wheel drive) all models '79 thru '82
61041 626/MX-6 (front-wheel drive) '83 thru '91
61042 626 '93 thru '01, MX-6/Ford Probe '93 thru '97

MERCEDES-BENZ
63012 123 Series Diesel '76 thru '85
63015 190 Series four-cyl gas models, '84 thru '88
63020 230/250/280 6 cyl sohc models '68 thru '72
63025 280 123 Series gasoline models '77 thru '81
63030 350 & 450 all models '71 thru '80

MERCURY
64200 Villager & Nissan Quest '93 thru '01
All other titles, see FORD Listing.

MG
66010 MGB Roadster & GT Coupe '62 thru '80
66015 MG Midget, Austin Healey Sprite '58 thru '80

MITSUBISHI
68020 Cordia, Tredia, Galant, Precis & Mirage '83 thru '93
68030 Eclipse, Eagle Talon & Ply. Laser '90 thru '94
*****68031** Eclipse '95 thru '01, Eagle Talon '95 thru '98
68035 Mitsubishi Galant '94 thru '03
68040 Pick-up '83 thru '96 & Montero '83 thru '93

NISSAN
72010 300ZX all models including Turbo '84 thru '89
72015 Altima all models '93 thru '04
72020 Maxima all models '85 thru '92
*****72021** Maxima all models '93 thru '01
72030 Pick-ups '80 thru '97 Pathfinder '87 thru '95
*****72031** Frontier Pick-up '98 thru '01, Xterra '00 & '01, Pathfinder '96 thru '01
72040 Pulsar all models '83 thru '86
Quest - *see MERCURY Villager (64200)*
72050 Sentra all models '82 thru '94
72051 Sentra & 200SX all models '95 thru '99
72060 Stanza all models '82 thru '90

OLDSMOBILE
73015 Cutlass V6 & V8 gas models '74 thru '88
For other OLDSMOBILE titles, see BUICK, CHEVROLET or GENERAL MOTORS listing.

PLYMOUTH
For PLYMOUTH titles, see DODGE listing.

PONTIAC
79008 Fiero all models '84 thru '88
79018 Firebird V8 models except Turbo '70 thru '81
79019 Firebird all models '82 thru '92
79040 Mid-size Rear-wheel Drive '70 thru '87
For other PONTIAC titles, see BUICK, CHEVROLET or GENERAL MOTORS listing.

PORSCHE
80020 911 except Turbo & Carrera 4 '65 thru '89
80025 914 all 4 cyl models '69 thru '76
80030 924 all models including Turbo '76 thru '82
80035 944 all models including Turbo '83 thru '89

RENAULT
Alliance & Encore - *see AMC (14020)*

SAAB
*****84010** 900 all models including Turbo '79 thru '88

SATURN
*****87010** Saturn all models '91 thru '02
87020 Saturn all L-series models '00 thru '04

SUBARU
89002 1100, 1300, 1400 & 1600 '71 thru '79
89003 1600 & 1800 2WD & 4WD '80 thru '94

SUZUKI
90010 Samurai/Sidekick & Geo Tracker '86 thru '01

TOYOTA
92005 Camry all models '83 thru '91
92006 Camry all models '92 thru '96
*****92007** Camry, Avalon, Solara, Lexus ES 300 '97 thru '01
92015 Celica Rear Wheel Drive '71 thru '85
92020 Celica Front Wheel Drive '86 thru '99
92025 Celica Supra all models '79 thru '92
92030 Corolla all models '75 thru '79
92032 Corolla all rear wheel drive models '80 thru '87
92035 Corolla all front wheel drive models '84 thru '92
92036 Corolla & Geo Prizm '93 thru '02
92040 Corolla Tercel all models '80 thru '82
92045 Corona all models '74 thru '82
92050 Cressida all models '78 thru '82
92055 Land Cruiser FJ40, 43, 45, 55 '68 thru '82
92056 Land Cruiser FJ60, 62, 80, FZJ80 '80 thru '96
92065 MR2 all models '85 thru '87
92070 Pick-up all models '69 thru '78
92075 Pick-up all models '79 thru '95
*****92076** Tacoma '95 thru '00, 4Runner '96 thru '00, & T100 '93 thru '98
*****92078** Tundra '00 thru '02 & Sequoia '01 thru '02
92080 Previa all models '91 thru '95

*****92082** RAV4 all models '96 thru '02
92085 Tercel all models '87 thru '94

TRIUMPH
94007 Spitfire all models '62 thru '81
94010 TR7 all models '75 thru '81

VW
96008 Beetle & Karmann Ghia '54 thru '79
*****96009** New Beetle '98 thru '00
96016 Rabbit, Jetta, Scirocco & Pick-up gas models '74 thru '91 & Convertible '80 thru '92
96017 Golf, GTI & Jetta '93 thru '98 & Cabrio '95 thru '98
*****96018** Golf, GTI, Jetta & Cabrio '99 thru '02
96020 Rabbit, Jetta & Pick-up diesel '77 thru '84
96023 Passat '98 thru '01, Audi A4 '96 thru '01
96030 Transporter 1600 all models '68 thru '79
96035 Transporter 1700, 1800 & 2000 '72 thru '79
96040 Type 3 1500 & 1600 all models '63 thru '73
96045 Vanagon all air-cooled models '80 thru '83

VOLVO
97010 120, 130 Series & 1800 Sports '61 thru '73
97015 140 Series all models '66 thru '74
97020 240 Series all models '76 thru '93
97040 740 & 760 Series all models '82 thru '88
97050 850 Series all models '93 thru '97

TECHBOOK MANUALS
10205 Automotive Computer Codes
10210 Automotive Emissions Control Manual
10215 Fuel Injection Manual, 1978 thru 1985
10220 Fuel Injection Manual, 1986 thru 1999
10225 Holley Carburetor Manual
10230 Rochester Carburetor Manual
10240 Weber/Zenith/Stromberg/SU Carburetors
10305 Chevrolet Engine Overhaul Manual
10310 Chrysler Engine Overhaul Manual
10320 Ford Engine Overhaul Manual
10330 GM and Ford Diesel Engine Repair Manual
10340 Small Engine Repair Manual, 5 HP & Less
10341 Small Engine Repair Manual, 5.5 - 20 HP
10345 Suspension, Steering & Driveline Manual
10355 Ford Automatic Transmission Overhaul
10360 GM Automatic Transmission Overhaul
10405 Automotive Body Repair & Painting
10410 Automotive Brake Manual
10411 Automotive Anti-lock Brake (ABS) Systems
10415 Automotive Detailing Manual
10420 Automotive Eelectrical Manual
10425 Automotive Heating & Air Conditioning
10430 Automotive Reference Manual & Dictionary
10435 Automotive Tools Manual
10440 Used Car Buying Guide
10445 Welding Manual
10450 ATV Basics

SPANISH MANUALS
98903 Reparación de Carrocería & Pintura
98905 Códigos Automotrices de la Computadora
98910 Frenos Automotriz
98915 Inyección de Combustible 1986 al 1999
99040 Chevrolet & GMC Camionetas '67 al '87 Incluye Suburban, Blazer & Jimmy '67 al '91
99041 Chevrolet & GMC Camionetas '88 al '98 Incluye Suburban '92 al '98, Blazer & Jimmy '92 al '94, Tahoe y Yukon '95 al '98
99042 Chevrolet & GMC Camionetas Cerradas '68 al '95
99055 Dodge Caravan & Plymouth Voyager '84 al '95
99075 Ford Camionetas y Bronco '80 al '94
99077 Ford Camionetas Cerradas '69 al '91
99088 Ford Modelos de Tamaño Mediano '75 al '86
99091 Ford Taurus & Mercury Sable '86 al '95
99095 GM Modelos de Tamaño Grande '70 al '90
99100 GM Modelos de Tamaño Mediano '70 al '88
99110 Nissan Camioneta '80 al '96, Pathfinder '87 al '95
99118 Nissan Sentra '82 al '94
99125 Toyota Camionetas y 4Runner '79 al '95

Over 100 Haynes
motorcycle manuals
also available

* Listings shown with an asterisk (*) indicate model coverage as of this printing. These titles will be periodically updated to include later model years - consult your Haynes dealer for more information.

2-05

Haynes North America, Inc., 861 Lawrence Drive, Newbury Park, CA 91320-1514 • (805) 498-6703